From the Wilderness to Appomattox

CIVIL WAR SOLDIERS AND STRATEGIES
Brian S. Wills, Series Editor

Richmond Must Fall: The Richmond-Petersburg Campaign, October 1864
    HAMPTON NEWSOME
Work for Giants: The Campaign and Battle of Tupelo/Harrisburg, Mississippi, June–July 1864
    THOMAS E. PARSON
"My Greatest Quarrel with Fortune": Major General Lew Wallace in the West, 1861–1862
    CHARLES G. BEEMER
Phantoms of the South Fork: Captain McNeill and His Rangers
    STEVE FRENCH
At the Forefront of Lee's Invasion: Retribution, Plunder, and Clashing Cultures on Richard S. Ewell's Road to Gettysburg
    ROBERT J. WYNSTRA
Meade: The Price of Command, 1863–1865
    JOHN G. SELBY
James Riley Weaver's Civil War: The Diary of a Union Cavalry Officer and Prisoner of War, 1863–1865
    EDITED BY JOHN T. SCHLOTTERBECK, WESLEY W. WILSON,
    MIDORI KAWAUE, AND HAROLD A. KLINGENSMITH
Blue-Blooded Cavalryman: Captain William Brooke Rawle in the Army of the Potomac, May 1863–August 1865
    EDITED BY J. GREGORY ACKEN
No Place for Glory: Major General Robert E. Rodes and the Confederate Defeat at Gettysburg
    ROBERT J. WYNSTRA
From the Wilderness to Appomattox: The Fifteenth New York Heavy Artillery in the Civil War
    EDWARD A. ALTEMOS

From the Wilderness to Appomattox

The Fifteenth New York Heavy Artillery in the Civil War

Edward A. Altemos

THE KENT STATE UNIVERSITY PRESS
Kent, Ohio

© 2023 by The Kent State University Press, Kent, Ohio 44242
All rights reserved
ISBN 978-1-60635-464-3
Published in the United States of America

No part of this book may be used or reproduced, in any manner whatsoever, without written permission from the Publisher, except in the case of short quotations in critical reviews or articles.

Cataloging information for this title is available at the Library of Congress.

To:
Jacob Altemos, Private, Company C, Fifteenth New York Heavy Artillery, my great-grandfather.

And to my children and their children, that they may know of him, of the men with whom he served, and of the struggles and sacrifices of all soldiers—whether wearing blue or gray—in the great American conflict.

But men and officers—for discipline presses as hardly on the officers as on the men—must obey, no matter at what cost to their feelings, for obedience to orders, instant and unhesitating, is not only the life-blood of armies but the security of States; and the doctrine that under any conditions whatever deliberate disobedience can be justified is treason to the commonwealth.
—Lt. Col. G. F. R. Henderson, C.B., *Stonewall Jackson and the American Civil War*

Contents

List of Maps and Map Key · xi
Foreword by Christian B. Keller · xiii
Prologue · xv
Introduction · xxvii
1 The Fifteenth New York Heavy · 1
2 Into the Wilderness · 19
3 To Spotsylvania Court House · 39
4 To the Harris Farm · 57
5 To the North Anna · 76
6 To the Totopotomoy and Bethesda Church · 96
7 Across the James · 117
8 In the Trenches before Petersburg · 137
9 Cutting the Weldon Railroad and the Battle of Globe Tavern · 156
10 The Battle of Peebles's Farm · 177
11 The Raid on the Weldon Railroad and the Battle of Hatcher's Run · 196
12 To the White Oak Road and Five Forks · 219
13 To Appomattox Court House · 243
14 To the Defenses of Washington—and Home · 262
Conclusion: The Fifteenth New York Heavy Considered · 274
Acknowledgments · 278
Appendix 1 · 281
Appendix 2 · 295
Notes · 297
Bibliography · 353
Index · 363

Maps and Key

Map Key

Union Army — Confederate Army
Infantry Corps ☒ ☒ Cavalry Corps   Infantry Corps ☒ ☒ Cavalry Corps
Infantry Division ☒ ☒ Cavalry Division   Infantry Division ☒ ☒ Cavalry Division
Infantry Brigade ☒ ☒ Cavalry Brigade   Infantry Brigade ☒ ☒ Cavalry Brigade

Eastern Theater, May 1864 · 26
Into the Wilderness, May 4–5, 1864 · 28
Widow Tapp Field, May 6, 1864, 7–8 A.M. · 35
Spotsylvania Court House, May 8–21, 1864 · 47
Bloody Angle, May 12, 1864 · 53
Harris Farm, May 19, 1864 · 71
To the North Anna, May 21–22, 1864 · 80
Jericho Mills, May 23, 1864 · 87
To the Pamunkey, May 27–28, 1864 · 99
Bethesda Church, May 30, 1864 · 107
Cold Harbor, June 3, 1864 · 115
Across the James, June 12–17, 1864 · 123
Petersburg, June 18, 1864 · 133
Siege of Petersburg, August 1864 · 158
Globe Tavern, August 18, 1864 · 163
Globe Tavern, August 19, 1864 · 167
Globe Tavern, August 21, 1864 · 174
Chappell Farm, October 1, 1864 · 188

Hicksford Raid, December 7–12, 1864 · 204
Hatcher's Run, February 6, 1865 · 214
White Oak Road, March 31, 1865 · 229
Five Forks, April 1, 1865 · 238
Appomattox Campaign, April 3–8, 1865 · 246
Appomattox Court House, April 9, 1865 · 254

Foreword

The history of ethnic soldiers in the American Civil War is still being written. It is one of those subgenres within the field that, until the last thirty years or so, remained relatively unexplored and misunderstood. Ella Lonn's landmark works, *Foreigners in the Union Army and Navy* (1950) and *Foreigners in the Confederacy* (1940), offered all subsequent scholars a starting point. But for the remainder of the twentieth century, there were very few who followed. Earl Hess, William Burton, Walter Kamphoefner, Joseph Reinhart, James Pula, Susannah Ural, and I, among others, have since attempted to fill the veritable historiographical gap, but much remains to be done. It is important work, as new estimates of the sheer numbers of German, Irish, and other ethnic troops in the Federal armies are now approaching 30–40 percent, depending on the author and the study. Those percentages alone should merit increased research into the motivations, experiences, and contributions to final victory of immigrant Americans. But beyond that, these men all had unique voices of their own, some of which offer us valuable and diverse insights into the timeless issue of the life of the Civil War soldier.

Edward Altemos offers us exactly such insight in this important book. Much of the extant scholarship on German Americans in the war has focused on the lives and deeds of members of the highly ethnic infantry regiments that marched in the Army of the Potomac's Eleventh Corps, a good deal of which dwells on their service from the beginning of the conflict through the climactic Battle of Gettysburg. Precious little has been either researched or written on what happened to such men after the summer of 1863, with very little indeed on the experiences of ethnic artillery regiments. This new history of the Fifteenth New York Heavy Artillery proves that German immigrant artillerists-turned-infantrymen played key roles in Lt. Gen. Ulysses S. Grant's Overland Campaign, the Siege of Petersburg, and the final chapters of the war in the East. It reveals that these soldiers retained certain aspects of their ethnic identity and shed others while sharing some characteristics with their Anglo-American comrades in blue. Moreover, the Fifteenth, as a heavy artillery unit converted into infantry, exemplified in many ways the service and fate of other such regiments in the Union army.

As the following pages will explain, the experiences of the "heavies" (as they were colloquially called) was different from that of the regular foot soldiers. Trained to operate artillery in the defenses of Washington, these men found themselves suddenly thrust into active campaigning in the field in arguably the bloodiest and toughest period of the war, carrying muskets and charging entrenchments rather than defending them. It was vicious and soul-numbing work, but as Altemos relates in vivid prose based on scrupulous research, it transformed them into solid and seasoned veterans, earning them the respect of friend and foe alike. By the end of the war, the soldiers of the Fifteenth had undergone more than their fair share of combat and belied the nativist adage that the "damn Dutch" could not fight. Indeed, they had disproven that prejudicial canard through perseverance, toil, and blood.

Christian B. Keller
Professor of History, US Army War College

PROLOGUE

The Defenses of Washington and the Third Battalion New York Heavy Artillery

Tuesday, June 9, 1863, began as usual for the men of the Third Battalion New York Artillery (Heavy) garrisoning Fort Lyon. Having reported for duty in the defenses surrounding Washington City some eighteen months prior, they were used to the day-to-day routine of garrison life. On this day the sun had risen before 5 A.M., and by 7 A.M., the temperature was a refreshing fifty-seven degrees. Some fifty miles to the southwest, the Battle of Brandy Station, the largest cavalry engagement ever fought in North America, was unfolding. In sharp contrast to the distant actions of the dashing cavaliers, the artillerists at Fort Lyon, most of whom were German immigrants, performed the routine tasks that defined service in the camps and fortifications defending Washington. Sentries made rounds on the parapets, stood at their posts, or were out on the picket line in advance of the fort. Other men of the battalion engaged in mundane and interminable drills or fatigue duties. One detail set to work near the fort's north magazine inspecting ammunition and filling shells with black powder.[1]

As the day wore on, the sun ascended high into the clear June sky, and by midafternoon the temperature had climbed above eighty degrees. Then at approximately 2 P.M., a devastating explosion ripped through Fort Lyon's north magazine, shattering the day's calmness and demolishing the northwest bastion. The force of the blast sent dirt, logs, ammunition, and men hurling through the air. It upended a private standing guard on the parapet—he landed in a clump of bushes a hundred yards from the fort while still holding his musket. Stunned but uninjured, within ten minutes he had resumed his rounds, with his musket again on his shoulder. The blast threw another sentinel fifty yards out of the fort, where he landed in a ditch, also with musket still in hand. Seeing several officers about to pass, the man gathered himself up, face and hands begrimed with powder and clothing in shreds, and, with soldierly habit, presented arms. Lewis Bissell, a private in the Nineteenth Connecticut Infantry who was assigned to one of Fort Lyon's redoubts, was walking nearly a half mile to the southeast when he heard "a popping of shells" that he later wrote "sounded like fire crackers only a great deal louder." This was followed by "a stunning crash" and immediately by "shells . . . flying over our heads and all around us," compelling Bissell to retreat to the protection afforded by nearby stumps and logs. Other men, however, were not so fortunate. Twenty-one men of the Third Battalion were killed instantly, while two others died within days.[2]

When the dust cleared, Bissell made his way back to Fort Lyon. In a letter to his father, he described the damage. Where the magazine should have been there "was a hole as large as [a] barn cellar," and around the hole lay the mangled bodies of men. "The first I saw," recounted Bissell, "lay with a hole as large as your fist in the top of his head. His body was cut and mangled, his legs were broken and nearly torn off, both arms were gone and the skin nearly all torn away from what remained." One body was without a head or legs; the dead man's head was later located some distance outside the fort. Another body, Bissell reported, "was found down by Hunting Creek Bridge a distance of half a mile" and torn into four pieces. The lieutenant who had been in charge of the detail "was so badly mangled that the only way he could be identified was by part of his shoulder strap which was about all of his clothing left."[3]

That afternoon both Brig. Gen. John Slough, the military governor of Alexandria, and Brig. Gen. Gustavus De Russy, commanding the defenses south of the Potomac, visited the fort to assess the damage. Slough reported that some of the men had been engaged "at the open door of the north magazine, when, from some cause, one shell exploded; immediately a few others and then the magazine," adding "everything in the vicinity is a wreck." De Russy estimated the casualties at twenty dead and fourteen wounded, further observing that "the rubbish" would be cleared from the work by afternoon of the following day. He concluded his report: "Destruction complete."[4]

Bissell explained to his father the circumstances surrounding the explosion. He noted that that the work party was detailed to remove powder that had become damp and caked in some of the artillery shells. The men were provided with wooden spoons for this delicate task in order to avoid creating sparks. But when the work did not proceed as quickly as the lieutenant in charge desired, the officer "sent one of the men for some priming wires" as are used "to prick the cartridge after it is rammed down." They then used the stiff metal wires instead of wooden spoons to loosen the powder in the iron shells. Bissell surmised, "It is supposed that some of the powder was ignited and exploded the shell and as there was loose powder lying around and shells with their plugs out they caught." This initial blast "blew in the magazine door and the whole magazine went up."[5]

At approximately 4 P.M. a procession of seventeen ambulances carried coffins containing the remains of those killed from Fort Lyon to the Soldiers' Cemetery in Alexandria's western outskirts. Marching to mournful music played by the First Connecticut Artillery's band, the men and officers of the Third Battalion escorted their fallen comrades to their final resting places. Although June 9, 1863, had begun like any routine day in the Washington defenses, it had ended in disaster. Yet given the intensity of the blast, the consequences could have been much worse. The Third would carry on.[6]

The Fort Lyon explosion had indeed been very powerful. More than a year after the blast, the army's chief engineer, Brig. Gen. Richard Delafield, issued a report assessing the effects of several large explosions. With regard to the Fort Lyon incident, it documented: "The earth over and on top of the magazine was scattered in every direction, principally upwards . . . , [falling] in considerable quantities at a distance of 400 to 500 yards. . . . The logs on top of the powder room were thrown in every direction . . . , in one case 600 yards. The breadth of the cavity in the earth formed by the explosion was about forty-five [feet] on top. . . . The loaded shells in the magazine were thrown to various distances; in one case as far as 2,500 yards."[7]

Two years prior to the great explosion, neither the Third Battalion nor Fort Lyon or the other forts composing the Washington defenses even existed. When on April 15, 1861, Pres. Abraham Lincoln called on the states to supply 75,000 volunteer troops to suppress the rising rebellion, regiments formed throughout the North. In addition, work began on the construction of a ring of forts to protect the Federal capital. One of the first of these, across the Potomac River in Alexandria, Virginia, was named Fort Ellsworth after Col. Elmer Ephraim Ellsworth of the Eleventh New York "Fire" Zouave Regiment. Ellsworth had been shot dead by a secessionist in Alexandria when the town was first occupied by Federal troops on May 24, thereby earning him the dubious distinction of being the first Union officer killed in the war.[8]

Situated nearly two miles to the southwest of Alexandria and south of Hunting Creek, Fort Lyon was completed near the end of September. It was named for Brig. Gen. Nathaniel Lyon, the first Union general to die in combat in the war, who was killed at Wilson's Creek in Missouri a month earlier. Fort Lyon was the second largest of the fortifications defending the capital city. Its primary purpose was to guard the southern and southwestern approaches to Alexandria. As a major port on the tidal Potomac as well as the eastern terminus of the Orange and Alexandria Railroad, the town was a transportation hub of great strategic and operational importance. Moreover, Alexandria and its surrounding heights commanded both the river approach to Washington and the city itself. Owing to the large size of the fort—its 937-yard perimeter enclosed nine acres—its bombproof was approximately 420 feet long and 14 feet wide. Lyon accommodated two magazines and emplacements for forty guns.[9]

Approximately three miles upriver from Georgetown, the Chain Bridge spanned the Potomac. Security of this link to the Washington side of the river was also of paramount importance. To protect this approach, in late September 1861 two forts were constructed on the heights above the Virginia side of the bridge. The larger of these, named Fort Ethan Allen, was located south of its terminus and had emplacements for thirty-six guns. The smaller one, situated north of the bridge, could mount eighteen guns and was named Fort Marcy after Maj. Gen. George B. McClellan's father-in-law and chief of staff, Brig. Gen. Randolph Barnes Marcy.[10]

Brig. Gen. John G. Barnard, chief engineer of the Washington defenses, quickly recognized that a serious defect existed in the position of Fort Lyon. The problem was that "over the readiest approach of an enemy the ground is not seen beyond 200 or 300 yards." To rectify this deficiency, he ordered lunettes constructed in advance of the fort. These

Facing page: Fort Lyon—Engineer Drawing. The magazine that exploded is shown in the bastion at top right of center. (NIAD: 117886747, Fortifications Map File Plans of Military Forts, 1818–1941, RG 77, National Archives)

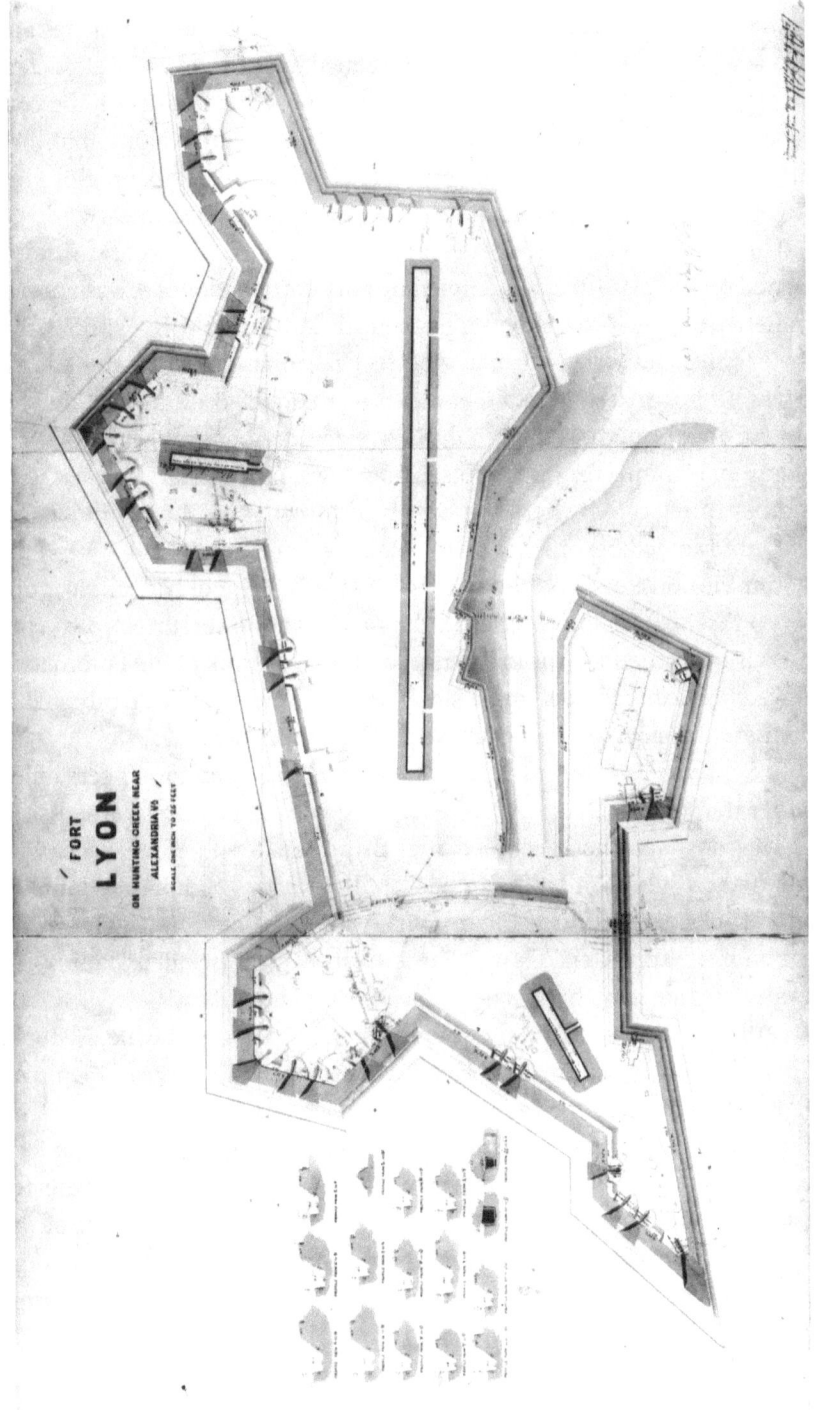

would command the field of fire necessary to protect the approaches and also serve to generally strengthen the left flank of the line of defenses. Except at one point, at a large ravine, these outer works were to be connected by a rifle trench or rifle pits, and at three points along that line, auxiliary positions for field artillery were constructed. Work on these improvements commenced in late 1862 and was completed in early 1863.[11]

The first two of these lunettes, identified as Redoubts A and B, were located on the plateau also occupied by Fort Lyon. Redoubt A was approximately 1,000 feet to the south of the fort and Redoubt B a similar distance to the southeast and about 500 feet east of its companion. Redoubt C was approximately 1,200 feet south of Redoubt B on a spur above a wide ravine through which ran the Gravel Road. About midway along the rifle trench connecting Redoubts B and C was an auxiliary battery, with another one located where the trench terminated on the ravine's edge. Redoubt D stood beyond the ravine on a spur of the heights between the Mount Vernon Road and the Accotink Turnpike. Not only could its guns sweep the western approaches to the ravine and to the three roads, but they also commanded the broad flats on the west bank of the Potomac. A rifle trench extended down the slope from Redoubt D and terminated at another auxiliary battery just above the Accotink Turnpike.[12]

In September 1863 these redoubts were named to honor officers killed earlier that year at Gettysburg. Redoubt A, which had emplacements for twelve guns, became Fort Weed after Brig. Gen. Stephen H. Weed, who had died on July 2 on Little Round Top. Its nearby neighbor, Redoubt B, with emplacements for thirteen guns, was designated Fort Farnsworth in honor of Brig. Gen. Elon J. Farnsworth, who was killed leading his cavalry brigade in a charge late in the afternoon of July 3.[13]

Farther down the hill on the spur overlooking the large ravine, Redoubt C became Fort O'Rourke, honoring Col. Patrick H. O'Rourke of the 140th New York Infantry, a regiment in Weed's Brigade. O'Rourke, like his brigadier, was killed on Little Round Top on July 2. The smallest of the four redoubts in terms of perimeter, it nevertheless featured emplacements for sixteen guns. Finally, anchoring the far left of the defenses south of the Potomac, Fort Willard, formerly Redoubt D, was named after Col. George L. Willard, who fell near sunset on July 2 while leading his Second Corps

Facing page: Sector Map from Fort Willard to Fort Lyon (NIAD: 122207481, Fortifications Map File Plans of Military Forts, 1818–1941, RG 77, National Archives)

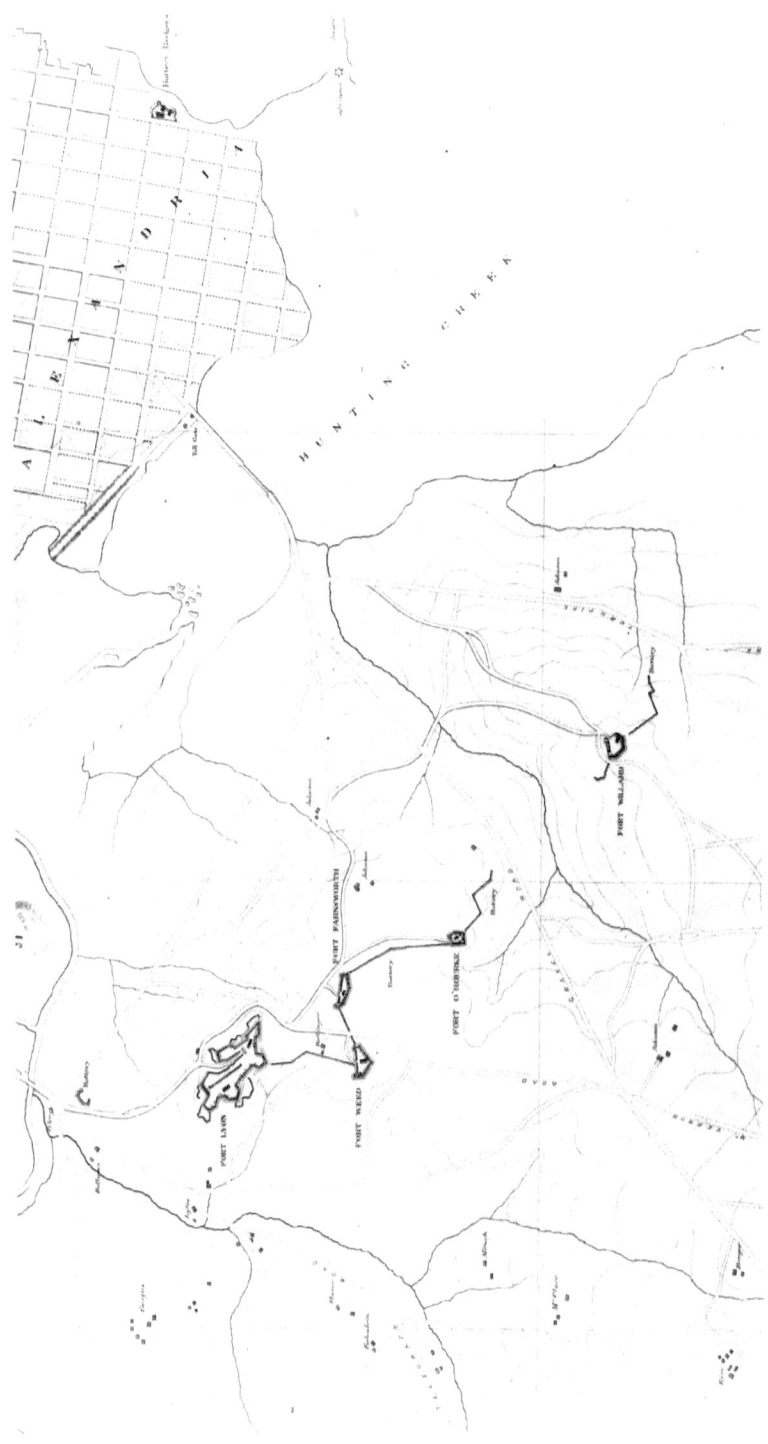

brigade of New Yorkers in a desperate counterthrust to protect the center of the Union line. Fort Willard had emplacements for fourteen guns. Adjacent to it, three large barracks, officers' quarters, a guardhouse, a cookhouse, and ordnance sergeant's quarters were eventually constructed.[14]

Meanwhile, as the defenses of Washington were taking shape, men throughout the United States were responding to Lincoln's call to enlist. Those who did so often originally hailed from other nations—and cities and counties with large immigrant populations gladly enlisted these recent arrivals. Prominent among enlistees were the large numbers of German immigrants throughout the North who rallied promptly to support the Union. In New York City alone, thousands of Germans offered their services shortly after the Confederates fired on Fort Sumter. By the war's end, more than 200,000 men of German birth or extraction had served in the US military. Many of these had been associated with the German revolutionary movement of the late 1840s, while they and others could claim prior military experience in armies of the various German states and principalities. These men brought with them valuable experience in the combat arms, including artillery. Indeed, a report written in July 1861 by Maj. Henry Hunt—he served most of the war as the Army of the Potomac's chief of artillery—noted that among the regiments in the works near the capital, several predominantly German regiments had in their ranks many artillerists. He postulated that these "instructed" men could be put to good use in the forts defending Washington.[15]

Among the immigrants volunteering to serve were the men composing the five companies of New York's Third Battalion Heavy Artillery. They had been recruited in New York City and mustered into Federal service between October 14 and December 19, 1861, for a three-year period. Thirty-eight-year-old Lt. Col. Adam Senges commanded the battalion. After the companies organized, they traveled to Washington, with orders to report to Brig. Gen. Louis Blenker's division. Once assembled, the battalion garrisoned Forts Ethan Allen and Marcy, where it remained through July 1862, with little break in the monotony of normal camp routine.[16]

That Senges's battalion was initially assigned to Blenker's outfit was probably not coincidence. Like most of the enlistees in that division, the men of the Third Battalion were German speakers and the vast majority German born. Sprinkled among them were a handful of Danes, Austrians, Swiss, and other Europeans as well as some American-born men of German extraction. Indeed, German was the working language within the

Third. Battalion and company administrative records were for the most part maintained in German until mid-1863, when many non–German speakers joined the unit. A soldier in the defenses of Washington who came to know the men of the Third Battalion before these later additions observed: "They are all 'Dutchman.' Officers and men can speak but little English."[17]

In the middle of August 1862, General Barnard assumed command of the troops manning the fortifications around Washington. On August 21 Brig. Gen. A. W. Whipple, commanding the defenses south of the Potomac, directed that the Fourth New York Heavy Artillery Regiment relieve the Third Battalion at Forts Ethan Allen and Marcy. This change was accomplished the following day, and the roughly 300-man battalion was distributed among a number of forts in the defensive sector south and west of Alexandria. One company was sent to Fort Barnard, another company to Fort Ward, and one platoon to each of Forts Richardson, Scott, Worth, Blenker, and Ellsworth. Barnard noted that new troops, although "raw, uninstructed, and unreliable," had been brought in to be drilled at the guns and to guard the lines. With only about 1,000 "experienced" troops, including the Third Battalion, to man the guns these had been so spread out "as to barely afford a relief for each gun."[18]

By August 27 McClellan had withdrawn from his base at Harrison's Landing on the James River and reached Alexandria by water with much of his army. Two days later an order from headquarters directed the Third Battalion, with the exception of the contingent then at Fort Ellsworth, to proceed to Fort Lyon. This originated from McClellan, who had long before been relieved of his collateral authority as general in chief, and frustrated Whipple. In response, on the afternoon of August 28, McClellan's assistant adjutant general attempted to soothe him, explaining that his boss "had no intention of interfering with your command." Only because McClellan wanted the forts well garrisoned, "and it was exceedingly difficult for him to ascertain who was in command of the forts and what the functions of each of the commanders are," had he issued the directive. In any event, McClellan's order stood, and Fort Lyon became the new home of the Third Battalion. The contingent that had remained in Fort Ellsworth likely rejoined the battalion by mid-September.[19]

Regardless of the particular fort to which the men of the Third Battalion were assigned, garrison duty was more or less the same. Drill, parade, fatigue details, guard duty, and picket duty were the staples of life.

To provide ample warning of any enemy advance, picket lines south and west of Alexandria stretched from the Potomac on either end in a wide semicircle approximately three miles in advance of the forts. Sentries were typically instructed that they should issue a challenge if approached and should fire if the proper response was not given. Private Bissell of the Nineteenth Connecticut described one such incident involving pickets of the Third Battalion. "One of the Dutchmen saw a lantern going through the bushes. 'Who come dar' he challenged. No one answered so the Dutchman let drive. Then a nigger who carried the lantern sung out, 'It's me massa. Don't shoot.'" The terrified man continued his journey, though undoubtedly somewhat worse for the wear.[20]

Periodically, the garrisons conducted artillery target practice. On these occasions local residents were well advised to seek shelter as far from the forts as possible. Bissell described some of his outfit's efforts to be "of a poor pattern," with rounds from rifled guns often going "end over end." One shot, fired at a target half a mile away, struck within two feet of the target "then glanced and struck in a hollow, glanced again and struck in a meadow, went over a house, came down, went through a picket fence, hit a half cord of wood and knocked it into all manner of shapes, next struck an oak log as large as the crown of your hat and split it through the middle." He mentioned that his neighbors at Fort Lyon had a similar experience: "The Dutchmen . . . shot a shell at a target and when it was a few rods beyond a house it exploded scattering fragments all around the country," fortunately, injuring no one.[21]

Nevertheless, all was not work, and the men of the Third Battalion found diversions to liven the dull routine of camp life. One pastime was music and singing—the latter in German, of course. Bissell reported to his father: "The music sounds very pleasant but we cannot understand a single word of it. It sounds like so many blackbirds chattering." Another of the Germans' leisure activities was drinking, which frequently went hand in hand with the singing. Of this Bissell observed—clearly with a hint of sour grapes—that the "'Dutchmen' drink a good deal of lager beer. Our men are not allowed in the fort so they do not get any beer. This they do not like. The officers go in and get all they want, which of course, makes the men mad." His Fort Lyon neighbors apparently also had an affinity for dogs. Bissell reported that the Germans "have quite a drove of little whelps who keep up a continual barking a long time after honest dogs ought to be in bed." On another occasion he observed, "If you wish any dogs to hunt rats, there are plenty of them in Fort Lyon as the Dutchmen have three dogs to every man and a peck of fleas in the bargain."[22]

Meanwhile, by the spring of 1863, Senges's tenue as commander of the Third Battalion drew to a close when he resigned due to health issues. Lt. Col. Louis Schirmer took command of the battalion on May 20, officially mustering in on June 9—coincidentally, the day of the great explosion in Fort Lyon's north magazine. Schirmer was born in Prussia in 1832 and entered military service there at an early age. He later emigrated to the United States and by 1860 was living in Memphis, Tennessee, with his New York–born wife and their two young children. With a personal estate valued at $300, his business as a produce dealer provided a comfortable, though far from extravagant, living. When the war broke out, unwilling to cast his lot with the South, Schirmer moved with his family to New York, where he very soon joined the army.[23]

By September more changes were in the offing. Bissell wrote to his brother from Redoubt A on September 15, "We are to turn over Redoubts C & D to the 15th New York Heavy Artillery." His unit would, toward the end of that month, "finish up what little there is to do around here and then the Dutchmen will take possession." In early October, safely ensconced in his new station some distance from Fort Lyon, Bissell leveled a parting shot at the old Third Battalion: "We are now out from under the Dutchmen so if they want to blow up any more magazines we are so far off they will not hurt us."[24]

Schirmer's arrival at Fort Lyon was to herald even more significant changes. The Third Battalion was soon to be grown into a full heavy artillery regiment—a very large one, in fact.

Introduction

Not long after sunrise on Friday, May 6, 1864, the officers and men of the Fifteenth New York Heavy Artillery Regiment slogged through woods and dense undergrowth in a region known as the Wilderness, located about ten miles west of Fredericksburg, Virginia, toward the thunder of a raging battle. Most of these men had joined the regiment during the second half of 1863, having enlisted and trained to serve as heavy artillerymen. As such their primary duties were to crew large-caliber artillery guns and mortars in fixed fortifications. In fact, the men in the regiment began their service as would be expected—garrisoning several of the forts in the extensive ring of defenses protecting Washington, DC. Like those in most outfits assigned that duty, they had not yet experienced combat. As they approached the sounds of combat that bright May morning, many of the men likely questioned how they found themselves preparing to engage their Confederate enemies not as artillerymen, but as infantrymen. Like all soldiers heading into battle—especially for the first time—they certainly must have wondered what would become of them.

    This book recounts the story of the Fifteenth New York Heavy Artillery Regiment. My interest in the Fifteenth Heavy began some fifteen years ago, when I discovered that my great-grandfather—a nineteen-year-old German-born immigrant living with his parents in Buffalo, New York—had served in that regiment. I soon learned that it had seen considerable combat, although further investigation disclosed that books on the Civil War and other resources made only passing reference to the Fifteenth, if it was mentioned at all. Aware for some time that Union army commanders employed some heavy artillery regiments as infantry in the later years of the war, I was intrigued to discover that my ancestor had been one such soldier who had undergone this unusual "conversion." Since it appeared that little had been written by modern historians (at least in book format) concentrating on heavy artillerymen called upon to serve in the role of infantrymen in the Army of the Potomac—moreover, virtually nothing had been written about the Fifteenth Heavy—I concluded that a regimental history would disclose a missing perspective on the American Civil War. It would shed additional light not only on the experiences of German American soldiers but also on the experiences of the many heavy artillery regiments pressed into service as infantry. At the same time, from the purely military point of view, a history of the Fifteenth could add a further perspective to some of the most important campaigns in Virginia.

To that end, *From the Wilderness to Appomattox: The Fifteenth New York Heavy Artillery in the Civil War* chronicles the last two years of the Civil War in the eastern theater as seen through the eyes of the officers and men in the Fifteenth New York Heavy Artillery as well as through those of other soldiers in the brigades, divisions, and corps in which the regiment served. But this is not a regimental history of these "heavies" in the traditional sense. Instead, it is an amalgam of a traditional unit history with a campaign history. It examines the metamorphosis of the members of the Fifteenth from artillerymen to infantrymen in the context of the operations and battles in which the regiment and its parent commands engaged. This book draws heavily on primary sources, including reports and communications in the *Official Records*, regimental records, compiled service records, and letters written by men in the regiment. It also makes use of letters, diaries, journals, reports, and recollections written by men and officers outside of the Fifteenth who observed and campaigned with the heavies.

The "underexplored" story of the Fifteenth New York Heavy Artillery Regiment is not only noteworthy in terms of the unit's service but also for what it reveals about the demographics of the volunteer units that fought for the United States as well as those that fought for the Confederacy. Recent German immigrants composed the bulk of the regiment. Although many ethnic units served during the war and many other heavy artillery regiments ultimately served in the Army of the Potomac as infantry, the Fifteenth was unique in becoming the only heavy artillery regiment comprised mainly of German immigrants to do so. When the unit joined the army in the field in March 1864, neither German immigrants nor heavy artillerymen were held in high regard by much of its rank and file. As a result, the men of the Fifteenth did not find themselves in an enviable position. Their identity as both German immigrants and heavy artillerymen would color their experiences as they settled into their new role as infantrymen.[1]

While this book is, and indeed was intended to be, principally a campaign, or military, history of the Fifteenth, these dual aspects of the regiment's identity should not—cannot—be ignored. Consequently, the negative perceptions within the army of not only Germans but also heavy artillerymen are explored in some depth both here and in the conclusion. The military history of the regiment, on which the balance of this book primarily focuses, should be viewed through the lens of the overarching prejudices against both heavies and Germans that permeated the army when the Fifteenth joined the Army of the Potomac in the spring of 1864. As if the challenges facing all neophyte infantry outfits were not great enough, these men had also to overcome these biases before being accepted by their army peers as both solid infantrymen and worthy inheritors of the American dream.

The officers of the Fifteenth raised the regiment principally in New York City and its environs, although it boasted men from all corners of the state. In addition to German immigrants, the outfit, initially numbering over 2,000 strong, also included men from virtually every other European country, native-born Americans, and even a few Canadians. German enlistees found the promise of serving in a unit with men of similar backgrounds, language, and culture appealing. With nearly 70 percent of its members born in one of the European states collectively referred to at the time as "Germany" and a number of other German-speakers hailing from Switzerland, Austria, and neighboring countries, the regiment displayed a decidedly German character. To outsiders, however, they were all simply "Dutch"—a corruption of the German word *Deutsch*—or even worse, "damn Dutch." Over the next two years, this "Dutch" regiment would participate in all the key military engagements in the Overland, Petersburg, and Appomattox Campaigns.[2]

Although the unit was viewed as and considered itself German, that generic term hides the ethnic diversity within it. In 1860 more than 1,275,000 German-born immigrants resided in the United States, representing nearly one-third of the foreign-born population of the country. Contrary to how they were likely viewed by Anglo-Americans or even by the immigrant Irish, these Germans hardly constituted a monolithic group. Upon arrival in America, immigrants from the various German states set aside their often quite significant Old World rivalries and identities to form German communities and ultimately, when war broke out, German regiments. Although often harboring very different views concerning such fundamental matters as religion, American politics, and even slavery, Prussians, Bavarians, Hessians, Badeners, and those from the other German states strived to find common ground wherever possible. Importantly, and unlike most Americans, many of these immigrant enlistees had prior military experience from their homelands. By the end of the Civil War, more than 200,000 men of German birth or descent—around 16 percent of the German American population—had served in the Federal army. This constituted nearly 10 percent of the men who fought for the Union, and of these, the vast majority volunteered—only about one in six had been drafted.[3]

Those Germans who had immigrated to the United States in large numbers during the mid-nineteenth century faced anti-immigrant prejudices before and during their time in the army. When the Fifteenth departed the Washington defenses to join the Army of the Potomac at Brandy Station near Culpepper, Virginia, in March 1864, the men faced criticism from other soldiers whose nativist assumptions led them to assert that Germans lacked the qualities of good soldiers. This bias existed throughout the army. In fact, many Americans had made the Union Eleventh Corps, composed of many, but certainly not entirely, German regiments, the scapegoat for the Federal defeat at Chancellorsville (May 1863). Anglo-American soldiers, the Northern public, and the English-language press placed that defeat squarely on the shoulders of the "cowardly" Germans of the Eleventh Corps. They conveniently ignored the facts that the corps contained many Anglo-American regiments and that Lt. Gen. Thomas "Stonewall" Jackson's force, which outnumbered the Eleventh Corps three to one, swept the Eleventh from the field in a powerful flank attack that could have defeated troops of any national origin. The commander of a New Jersey regiment, in an example of this biased blame, reported that the Germans "were panic-stricken and perfectly worthless" and were treated "with perfect contempt" by the "brave boys" in his regiment. One soldier commented, "every Dutchman was making for the river . . . trying to save his own cowardly body." The Germans soon came to be derided as "flying Dutchmen." Interestingly, these prejudices went both ways. Some Germans considered Americans as generally inferior culturally, intellectually, and militarily, even going so far as to attribute the American derision of German soldiers to "jealousy."[4]

By the time the Fifteenth arrived at Brandy Station, the Eleventh Corps had been detached from the Army of the Potomac. As a result, the regiment was one of a very few predominantly German outfits remaining in that army and became a target of the nativist sentiments previously directed toward the corps. Several weeks into the Overland Campaign, after the Federal army crossed the Pamunkey River to take positon less than fourteen miles northeast of the Confederate capital of Richmond, Maj. Gen. George G. Meade's aide-de-camp, Lt. Col. Theodore Lyman, described an encounter with men of the Fifteenth near Fifth Corps headquarters. As he rode in search of Meade, Lyman "got among a lot of German artillery men, who could not tell whether they were on their heads or heels, much less whether they had seen the Staff go that way." He found it "surprising how poorly the Germans show, out of their own country, where they are honest and clever, though rather slow people." Instead, "*here* they seem almost idiotic, and, what is worse, they will plunder and they won't fight. Really, as soldiers they are miserable. . . . [A] Yankee regiment would drive a brigade of them. They have no grit as a rule." Lyman's dismissal of the military abilities of the Germans, as well as his assumptions that they lacked both discipline and courage, clearly revealed his nativist bias and highlights the attitudes of others in the army.[5]

But Lyman's attitude is not surprising. His and many other Anglo-Americans' negative perceptions of German immigrants did not begin with the Chancellorsville debacle. In the early 1850s, the American, or "Know Nothing," Party drew upon and fomented fear and distrust of immigrants among the population. It targeted the Germans and the Irish in particular, pointing to their dedication to their religion in the case of Roman Catholics, their affinity for beer and liquor, their strange native tongues when non-English, and other aspects of their cultures that were at odds with the mores of mid-nineteenth century Anglo-American culture. Many immigrants, including those from Germany, saw the Civil War as an opportunity to dispel these nativist sentiments and prove their value to their adopted homeland. To make their case, Germans enlisted in both German and nonethnic regiments in numbers well exceeding their share of the population as compared to, for example, Irish and white, native-born Americans. Yet their perceived opportunity at redemption seemed lost after the Chancellorsville defeat. Nativist perceptions persisting after that battle ultimately resulted in many Germans turning inward toward their own communities, which, according to several prominent historians, in turn had the effect of slowing their full assimilation into American society and culture.[6]

The Fifteenth's ethnic character provided one basis for bias against the unit when it reported to the Army of the Potomac, but its existence as a heavy artillery unit provided another. To some soldiers, merely having enlisted in such a regiment—any heavy artillery regiment—was a strike against the men in the unit. A natural and generally good-natured rivalry existed between the infantry and field artillery; infantrymen and field artillerymen often stood shoulder to shoulder and faced the specter of death together in combat, reliant on one another for mutual self-preservation. In contrast, both viewed the heavy artillerymen, who for the first few years of the war had remained relatively safe and sound in forts in rear areas, as a breed apart. They often mocked heavy artillerymen as "band box soldiers," in reference to their clean, neat uniforms, sometimes with white gloves, and their lack of combat experience. Col. Charles Wainwright, commanding the Fifth Corps Artillery Brigade, likely reflected the thinking of many in the army when in late August 1864 he accused those who had joined heavy artillery regiments as "look[ing] for comfort and safety on enlisting." He observed, however, that the actions at "Cold Harbor and Petersburg" had by that time changed everything and caused potential enlistees to rethink joining such units.[7]

In early 1864, prior to the spring offensives, the new general in chief of the Union armies, Lt. Gen. Ulysses S. Grant, determined that heavy artillerymen would better serve the Union cause by fighting in the field than by garrisoning fixed fortifications, including the Washington defenses, in the North. In implementing this policy, one of the first heavy artillery regiments ordered to reinforce the Army of the Potomac in Virginia was the Fifteenth. When asked by Maj. Gen. Henry W. Halleck if they should first reorganize the regiment as light artillery, Grant quickly responded to the US Army's chief of staff that he should send them "as they are"—a clear indication of his intent to employ the heavies as infantry.[8]

Ironically, many of the men who enlisted in the Fifteenth in middle to late 1863 likely did so specifically to avoid infantry service. In early March 1863, to provide fresh manpower for the army, Congress enacted the Enrollment

Act of 1863, establishing a draft. The law made every able-bodied male citizen between the ages of twenty and forty-five, as well as able-bodied males of that age "of foreign birth who shall have declared on oath their intention to become citizens," subject to enrollment. Under the circumstances, many Northern men, native or immigrant, who had not already served viewed joining a heavy artillery regiment preferable to being conscripted into the infantry, in which the probability of serious injury, dismemberment, or death seemed greater. For Germans, the opportunity to serve in the Fifteenth with men of similar backgrounds, language, and culture offered an added incentive to volunteer for the regiment as a means of fulfilling their service obligation rather than risk the vagaries of the draft.[9]

The Fifteenth, however, was not made entirely of raw recruits. The regiment counted among its ranks many veteran soldiers, with approximately one-third of the men and officers having seen prior service or already in the army when the unit was formed. While most of these veterans were heavy artilleryman, many others had served in combat in the field artillery or another service arm. Yet as heavies, all were painted with the same broad brush. Only time and their actions would dispel the notion that, as Wainwright opined, their aim was simply to serve in leisurely security.

The Fifteenth first saw combat at the Wilderness and Spotsylvania Court House. The regiment went on to fight at, sometimes playing a pivotal role, the Harris farm, North Anna River, Bethesda Church, the initial assaults on the Petersburg defenses, Globe Tavern, Peebles's and Chappell's farms, Hatcher's Run, White Oak Road, and Five Forks as well as during the Appomattox Campaign. From a decidedly inauspicious beginning in the Wilderness, where they engaged the battle-hardened Fifteenth Alabama Infantry, the men's confidence and skill grew with each day and with each battle. By the war's end, many considered the Fifteenth the equal of any infantry regiment in the Army of the Potomac.

Despite its service and sacrifice on many fields of battle in the final year of the war, the regiment has received little scholarly attention. It appears, for the most part, only in the orders of battle in appendices of battle histories. This book aims to fill the void and chronicle the experiences and contributions of the Fifteenth New York Heavy Artillery Regiment. To reconstruct the story of the Fifteenth, this narrative relies heavily on sources from other units, especially from the regiments with which it served in various brigades, divisions, and corps. Their observations illuminate the experiences of the men in the Fifteenth as both an ethnic German unit and a heavy artillery regiment employed in the role of infantry.

The Fifteenth's wartime service also highlights what other units in similar situations experienced. As noted, it was one of just over a dozen heavy artillery regiments that fought as infantry in the Army of the Potomac beginning in May 1864. Although contemporary works on the campaigns and battles describe the important part these heavies played in combat as well as the substantial casualty rates they incurred, few discuss these soldiers' previous lives as heavy artillerymen. This volume's inclusion of that earlier experience helps us understand the stark contrasts the artillerymen experienced when sent to the field and the difficult evolution required of them in performing in their new role as infantrymen. The daily life of the German American soldiers of the Fifteenth, first in the forts protecting Washington and then in the field, reflects that of heavy artillerymen in nonethnic regiments. The heavies of all regiments inhabited similar forts and camps, conducted the same drills, performed the same fatigue duties, and, once in the field, spent their days in the same wretched trenches; endured the same long, difficult marches; and slept on the same hard ground through rain, snow, and ice. As a result, this account of the Fifteenth provides insight into what all heavy artillery regiments experienced as they transitioned to and served as infantrymen.

The story of the Fifteenth New York Heavy contributes to the military history of the Civil War by recounting the experiences of a regiment that has been largely ignored as well as its contribution to the US victory, with the consequent preservation of the Union and all that it entailed. It is also the story of a group of men who, like the other repurposed heavy artillerymen, the army called upon to serve in combat in a role for which most had neither volunteered nor been appropriately trained or equipped. Despite that handicap and in true American military tradition, they did so to the utmost of their abilities and with ultimate success. Finally, this story of a unit composed largely of immigrants highlights how men who endured nativist sentiments overcame them through hard work and sacrifice. In contributing to a US victory, these men helped preserve their adopted homeland as a beacon for others who might leave their home countries in search of security and a better life.[10]

After fifteen years of researching and writing about the Fifteenth New York Heavy, my one regret has been my failure to uncover more primary sources penned, either in English or German, by its rank-and-file German members. Thus, the common soldiers' perspectives offered are mainly those of the minority, Anglo component of the regiment. While likely this is sufficient to tell the military history of the Fifteenth as well as what the men collectively experienced, it undoubtedly leaves a void in terms of describing what the German members were thinking and feeling and how they perceived events—at least to the extent those thoughts, feelings, and perceptions differed from those of their Anglo comrades.

At the same time, this dearth of information is not entirely unusual or unexpected. Prominent historians who have devoted much of their careers to studying the ethnic German experience in the Civil War appear to agree that suitable source material is not always easy to find, especially in the United States. In the epilogue to *A German Hurrah!*, Joseph Reinhart bemoans the paucity of German Civil War soldiers' writings, noting that archival institutions in the United States tend to concentrate on preserving documents written in English. Christian Keller similarly acknowledges the scarcity of such materials. The collection of 956 letters written by 258 German immigrants that Walter Kamphoefner and Wolfgang Helbich employed in their work, *Germans in the Civil War*, are letters written in German that, during the period under consideration, were mailed or carried from the United States to Germany, where they remain to this day.[11]

This being the case, it is not necessarily surprising that in my years-long investigation, by zooming in from the broader German war experience considered by these historians to that of a single regiment, little material generated by the German soldiers of the Fifteenth turned up. This is not to say nothing exists. But if items such as soldiers' letters have survived, they likely reside in private collections and not in public archives—at least not in public repositories in the United States. Perhaps if the task of recounting the history of the Fifteenth had fallen to an abler researcher and writer, this void could have been filled. But be that as it may, the story of the Fifteenth New York Heavy Artillery deserves to finally be told, examining and recognizing the significant contributions made by the men and officers of the regiment to the Union war effort.

CHAPTER ONE

The Fifteenth New York Heavy

With the war entering its third year, the Fifteenth New York Heavy Artillery Regiment was to be fashioned of human assets derived from a variety sources. At its core would be the Third Battalion New York Heavy Artillery. Augmenting this veteran group were to be not only newly enlisted officers and men but also many others—particularly in leadership roles—who had seen prior service in disparate New York volunteer outfits. Nevertheless, throughout this formative process, the regiment would mostly continue to maintain the German character of its core battalion.

One volunteer regiment that included Germans with prior experience in the artillery arm, and which was specifically identified by Brig. Gen. Henry Hunt in his July 1861 report, was Col. Adolf von Steinwehr's "German Regiment," the Twenty-Ninth New York Infantry. Louis Schirmer, who would go on to command the Third Battalion at Fort Lyon, enlisted in von Steinwehr's regiment for two years, mustering in on June 4, 1861, as a first lieutenant in Company H.[1]

Throughout the war, it was not uncommon for commanders to group German regiments together to form cohesive units. During the First Bull Run Campaign, von Steinwehr's Twenty-Ninth New York was assigned to Col. Louis Blenker's predominantly German brigade, which also included the German Eighth New York Infantry and its artillery company, Varian's Battery. The day before the battle, July 20, 1861, the ninety-day term of service of the artillerymen expired, and many of them, including Capt. Joshua M. Varian, elected to retire from the field, leaving the guns behind.

To counter this loss, Blenker proposed to Col. Dixon S. Miles, his division commander, that they organize "a company of experienced European artillerists" from within his brigade to crew the guns. The resulting makeshift battery, served by a detachment consisting mainly of men from Company H, Twenty-Ninth New York under Capt. Charles Bookwood, was brought forward late the next day to cover the fleeing Federals and hamper their pursuit by Confederate forces. In the face of the precipitous Union retreat, Bookwood's hastily contrived battery successfully covered the withdrawing infantry and brought the guns and one caisson off of the field.[2]

Bull Run marked the beginning of a new life for the improvised unit. After its noteworthy performance on July 21, the battery returned to the Washington defenses, reorganized, and incorporated additional men from Blenker's command. Then, on August 16, 1861, it became an independent battery, with Schirmer as its commander. He was promoted to captain on November 25. Then, in early December, New York's military authorities designated it the Second Independent Battery, Light Artillery.[3]

Assigned to Blenker's division of Maj. Gen. John C. Frémont's small army, the Second Independent Battery served in the Shenandoah Valley in the spring of 1862. Later that year, during the Second Bull Run Campaign, it served in Maj. Gen. Franz Sigel's First Corps of the Army of Virginia, with Schirmer temporarily taking charge of the corps's Reserve Artillery when its commander was killed. At Chancellorsville in May 1863, Schirmer commanded the Eleventh Corps Reserve Artillery, which included the Second Independent Battery. As the end of the battery's two-year term of service neared—it would be released from Federal service and disbanded in mid-June—and upon his promotion to lieutenant colonel at the end of March, Schirmer left the unit. On May 20 he assumed command of the Third Battalion New York Heavy Artillery, with a directive from the New York State Adjutant General's Office to recruit additional companies to form a new regiment "to be known and designated as the 15th Regiment of Artillery, New York State Volunteers." He was given sixty days to complete the assignment.[4]

Schirmer faced a daunting task in forming his new regiment in the time allotted. He needed to enlist enough men to fill seven additional companies, each with a complement of approximately 150 artillerists. In addition, he required men to replenish the ranks of the Third Battalion, depleted through disease, desertion, and expiration of enlistments. As directed, Schirmer established his headquarters in New York City, which necessitated he remotely command the five companies already serving at Fort Lyon in Virginia. Although most of the new enlistees joined in the city, Schirmer also sent detachments seeking volunteers throughout the state, establishing recruiting stations in Buffalo and Troy. He spent much of that summer in New York City looking to fill his new regiment.[5]

The New York state adjutant general appointed William Bundy adjutant of the new regiment and ordered him to the New York City headquarters, where he played a major role in raising the regiment. Other members of the battalion assisted Schirmer, while an officer from Brooklyn not yet attached to Schirmer's command, Capt. Julius Dieckmann, also contributed to the effort.[6]

Dieckmann had previously served with Schirmer, and the two knew each other well. In 1861 thirty-four-year-old Dieckmann enlisted in the Twenty-Ninth New York Infantry as second lieutenant in Company H under 1st Lieutenant Schirmer. When Company H became the Second Independent Battery, Dieckmann remained with it as its first lieutenant, continuing with the unit throughout the early part of the 1862 Valley Campaign. After a promotion to captain on May 15, Dieckmann joined the New York Thirteenth Independent Battery, another unit attached to Blenker's division.[7]

During the Second Bull Run Campaign, Dieckmann's Thirteenth Independent Battery served in the Reserve Artillery under Schirmer's command in Sigel's First Corps. The battery saw action on both August 29 and 30, 1862.[8]

The Battle of Chancellorsville found the Thirteenth in Maj. Gen. Oliver O. Howard's Eleventh Corps, with Lieutenant Colonel Schirmer commanding the corps artillery. A section of Dieckmann's battery anchored the far right flank of Howard's line, which hung "in the air," with the two guns facing west down the Orange Turnpike. This section absorbed the initial shock when Lt. Gen. Thomas J. "Stonewall" Jackson's powerful flank attack shattered Howard's right and rolled up much of the Eleventh Corps's line. During this attack, Dieckmann's gunners only managed to fire twice—an already loaded round and a quickly readied second one. The aggressive Confederate assault forced the gunners to abandon their pieces as they ran for their lives. Amid the panicky Union retreat, the four remaining guns of the battery limbered up and withdrew. Howard later reported, "Dieckmann's guns and caissons, with the battery men scattered, rolled and tumbled like runaway wagons and carts in a thronged city."[9]

Shortly after this harrowing experience, Dieckmann tendered his resignation as captain of the Thirteenth, noting that he "had no expectation or intention of serving for a longer period" than his initial two-year term. He justified his departure by citing "very urgent family circumstances [that] demand my presence in Brooklyn, N.Y.," noting that his battery, "consisting at present of only four guns," had enough officers without him. Officials accepted his resignation the following day. But the state adjutant general subsequently issued an order authorizing Dieckmann to enlist men for the Fifteenth Heavy Artillery, and he spent the late spring and summer of 1863 recruiting for the regiment. After promotion to major and despite earlier protests about his desire not to serve beyond two years, he mustered into the Fifteenth on September 9.[10]

Throughout the enlistment drive, Dieckmann and others in the same role used recruiting cards printed in German. These announced a need to raise 1,800 men for Schirmer's new heavy artillery regiment, directed candidates to apply to the headquarters at 91 Bowery Street, and offered generous bounties—$677 for new recruits, $852 to reenlisting veterans. Although many of the recruits were not born in Germany, a large majority were. Consequently, the new regiment retained the "Dutch" identity of the Third Battalion. In addition to those who volunteered to serve in the Fifteenth, the regiment also included men who had enlisted for two light batteries that were never completed—Schirmer's old Second Independent Battery, which had been authorized to reorganize, and the new Thirty-Fourth Independent Battery. Also transferred into the Fifteenth was a full company comprising men who had enlisted in the never completed Twelfth Heavy Artillery Regiment as well as a handful of others from that outfit.[11]

The newly enrolled men headed to Fort Lyon with their companies. Recruitment efforts in different parts of the state led to a diverse, although predominantly German, composition. Company F, the unit acquired from the Twelfth Heavy, mustered in at Staten Island on June 19, 1863, and reached Fort Lyon later that month. Recruited mainly in New York City, it also included men from cities and towns all across the state. Composed of about equal numbers of German- and American-born soldiers, it also included men from various other European countries and several Canadians.[12]

Companies G and H arrived at Fort Lyon in early August, with Company I coming in several days later. Also recruited mainly in New York City, these three units still drew from other parts of the state. For example, Company G included a large contingent from Buffalo, while Company I had a handful of men from Buffalo and Troy. Native-born Germans comprised most of Company G, but that outfit also contained enlistees born in the United States and immigrants from other countries. German natives filled the bulk of the ranks of Companies H and I. Each, however, also featured more than a dozen Americans and about the same number from other countries. Of its enlistees claiming birth in countries other than Germany or the United States, Company I fielded about ten Irishmen. The large numbers of Germans in these units did not preclude men from other nations—Ireland, England, Scotland, Switzerland, Austria, Denmark, Sweden, Holland, France, Italy, Canada, and others—from serving in them.[13]

Company K, composed mostly of men recruited in New York City, with a small group from Buffalo and Troy, reached Alexandria about a month later. Despite the recruits' geographical similarities to those in the other companies, German-born men made up only about half of this unit. Recruits born in the United States formed approximately one-quarter of the company, with the balance born in Ireland and other countries.

The regiment's dramatic increase in size led to the appointment of a second field-grade officer. On September 9, 1863, thirty-nine-year-old Leander Schamberger mustered in as the regiment's newly promoted major. Prior to this, Schamberger served in Company A, first as a lieutenant in 1861 and later as its captain.[14]

On September 30, 1863, the old Third Battalion officially transferred into the Fifteenth New York Heavy Artillery Regiment, its companies retaining their former designations A through E. Ten days later Schirmer, having been promoted, mustered in as the regiment's colonel.[15]

The Fifteenth's final companies, L and M, mustered in during December 1863 at Fort Lyon and January 1864 at Goshen, New York, respectively. As with the other companies, most of the men of Company L enlisted in New York City, with several from Troy and other towns across the state. Similar to the makeup of the Fifteenth's other companies, German immigrants comprised the bulk of Company L. Men born in America as well as some Irishmen formed the next largest contingents, with several Swiss and those of a handful of other nationalities completing the ranks.[16]

Company M's recruitment took place largely in Orange County, upstate from New York City. Unlike the enlistees in other companies in the regiment, the men in Company M primarily spoke English as their first language, having been born in the United States. Approximately twenty claimed German birth, and an equal number had Irish roots. A handful of English, Scots, and Canadians rounded out the company.[17]

Pvt. Amherst Belcher highlighted the adventure of traveling with other members of Company M from Orange County to join the regiment. "There were perhaps as many as 75 men waiting . . . some of whom were anxious to begin killing rebels as soon as possible," he recalled. They did not have to wait long; the men left for New York City two or three days later on what Belcher called "a special train." He noted that "almost every man had a silver-plated revolver and a bowie knife, and at every considerable collection of houses they would thrust their arms out of the car windows, flourish their weapons, and scream like maniacs." Belcher abstained from his comrades' boisterous behavior. "Having neither revolver nor knife, I kept silent."[18]

Upon arriving in the city, Belcher and his comrades marched across to board the steamer *Thomas P. Way*. The vessel took them to Fort Schuyler, at the confluence of the East River and Long Island Sound, where the men trained for about two weeks. At the end of this period, the same vessel transported them back to lower New York harbor, where they next boarded the *Cahawha*, "a rotten old side-wheel ship." After four days at sea, the *Cahawha* docked on the Virginia Peninsula at Fortress Monroe, where the men "stocked up with boiled pork and bread" before continuing by ship up the Chesapeake Bay and the Potomac River to Alexandria. Landing there, Belcher and his comrades "marched out back of the city to the next chain of hills, where we joined our regiment." He recalled that at Fort Lyon the men "found good quarters awaiting us," including "Sibley tents, with board floors, straw beds, and stoves." Upon arrival they "got to work at once on the smooth-bore guns in these forts and learned as fast, I suppose, as greenhorns usually do."[19]

As the enlistees settled in and learned their roles, the regiment's command structure continued to grow. In early March 1864 a third officer joined the Fifteenth as a major. A former artillery officer in the regular army of the German state of Hesse-Cassel, thirty-four-year-old Emil Duysing began the war as lieutenant colonel of Col. Leopold von Gilsa's "De Kalb Regiment," the Forty-First New York Infantry. But in August 1861 he felt "constrained" to offer his resignation "in consequence of the wish expressed by officers of [the] regiment." Von Gilsa, unmoved by Duysing's predicament, forwarded the resignation to his commander,

Brig. Gen. William T. Sherman, with the endorsement: "I personally and the whole Officer Corps will consider it a very great favor, if the General will approve this and recommend a speedy discharge." In November Duysing joined the old Third Battalion as captain of Company D but resigned in July 1862, citing health issues. With Duysing's health apparently restored, in September 1863 the New York state adjutant general authorized him to enroll volunteers for the Fifteenth. On Christmas Day 1863, he mustered in as captain of Company L, then gained promotion to major on March 6, 1864.[20]

But the Fifteenth New York Heavy Artillery still needed one key element in its command structure—an executive officer. On November 18, 1863, Colonel Schirmer recommended Adam Senges for the job, assuring Gov. Horatio Seymour of Senges's good health. Seymour, however, did not take the colonel's recommendation. Instead, on March 6, 1864, he appointed Lt. Col. Michael Wiedrich as second in command of the Fifteenth. Prior to joining the regiment and since October 1, 1861, Wiedrich served as captain of Battery I, First New York Light Artillery, a battery raised in and around Buffalo and composed exclusively of Germans.[21]

Wiedrich got off to a rocky start soon after his battery arrived in Washington when he faced charges of drunkenness on duty. His commander, Colonel von Steinwehr, reported the captain as "drunk, lying under one of his cannons," when "an attack from the enemy was suspected." On December 19 Steinwehr's division commander, Blenker, forwarded the charges to Maj. Gen. George McClellan, general in chief, requesting approval for a trial by general court-martial; twice in early January 1862 Blenker requested a decision so the court-martial could convene. Finally, on January 16 McClellan instead approved the recommendation of his staff "that Genl. Blenker be ordered to restore Capt. Wiedrich to duty without trial—he has now been a long time in arrest." With the charges withdrawn, the captain returned to his command. Despite his inauspicious beginning with the army, Wiedrich proved himself an energetic, capable, and courageous officer.[22]

Wiedrich's later experiences in Battery I for a time paralleled those of other officers who later joined the Fifteenth; many of them fought in the same battles under the same commanders. In the 1862 Valley Campaign, Battery I, like the Second and Thirteenth Independent Batteries under Schirmer and Dieckmann, respectively, served in Blenker's division of Frémont's command. Battery I saw more hard service later that year with Maj. Gen. John Pope's Army of Virginia, culminating at the Second Battle of Bull Run. Like the Second and Thirteenth Independent Batteries, it served in Sigel's First Corps—for a time under Schirmer in the Reserve Artillery. Battery I was nearly overrun by swarms of Maj. Gen. James Longstreet's infantry attacking up Chinn Ridge on the third day of the battle, but after holding as long as possible, it successfully withdrew. Wiedrich's battery served in Howard's Eleventh Corps at the Battle of Chancellorsville along with Dieckmann's Thirteenth Battery, with Schirmer commanding the corps's Reserve Artillery.[23]

Yet unlike Schirmer and Dieckmann, Wiedrich and his unit remained with the Eleventh Corps after Chancellorsville. On the evening of the second day of the fight at Gettysburg, Battery I found itself directly in the path of a Confederate assault across open ground south and east of the town and up onto Cemetery Hill. The attackers charged the battery and swarmed into its lunettes, but Wiedrich's gunners "rallied with the infantry, and, seizing upon any weapons they could reach, threw themselves upon the enemy, and assisted to drive them back." A persisting story of this event has it that a Rebel officer placed himself across the muzzle of one of Battery I's guns, shouting, "I take command of this gun!" To this claim, the gunner replied, "Du sollst sie haben!"—and tugging the lanyard blew the Confederate to pieces.[24]

November 1863 saw Battery I engaged in the battles for Chattanooga. It supported the Federal infantry attack along the western slopes of Lookout Mountain in the famous "Battle above the Clouds." Of Battery I's work and that of other batteries under Wiedrich's overall command that day, the Eleventh Corps chief of artillery remembered: "In the attack on the mountain they are reported to have done good service. Generals Hooker, Butterfield and Osterhaus have spoken of their practice as excellent." Wiedrich mustered out of Battery I at Lookout Valley, Tennessee, on February 29, 1864, in order to accept promotion to lieutenant colonel in the Fifteenth New York Heavy Artillery.[25]

By the time Wiedrich reported for duty at Fort Lyon in March 1864, Schirmer had pulled together over sixty officers and more than 2,000 men to fill the ranks of the regiment. But long before—since the day he took command of the old Third—he had begun the task of honing the men's skills and converting his growing command into a tight fighting unit.[26]

Immediately upon assuming command of the Third Battalion, on June 5, 1863, Schirmer established a strict daily routine to both train the men and keep them ready for action. Each morning at 8 A.M. they participated in a one hour of infantry drill, then at 5 P.M. reported for an hour-long artillery drill. They performed fatigue duty—cleaning, gathering supplies, maintenance, and other labors—between 5 A.M. and 8 A.M. Soldiers also had to deal with restrictions on their movements. Orders warned that men "straying" from Fort Lyon "beyond a mile or Bugle sound" without permission would be punished "severely." To prevent them from slipping across Hunting Creek and into nearby Alexandria on the pretext of going down to the creek to wash, Schirmer directed that men could only visit the stream under a sergeant's watchful eye.[27]

As the newly enrolled companies of the Fifteenth began arriving in Alexandria, they relieved the men manning Fort Lyon's four redoubts. Schirmer sent Company G to Redoubt C (soon Fort O'Rourke) and Companies A, D, and H to Redoubt D (soon Fort Willard) on September 14, 1863. He assigned Companies E, F, and I to Fort Lyon, where they joined Companies B and C already in that garrison. Yet the companies shuffled between the forts for several weeks. Company D garrisoned Fort Weed from middle to late September through the end of November, when Company L relieved the men so they could return to Fort Lyon. Companies F and H manned Fort Willard beginning in September, and Company E joined them there in November. Finally, Company K relieved the garrison of Fort Farnsworth in October. Schirmer assigned Companies A, B, C, D, and I to Fort Lyon. The companies would remain in these garrisons until the end of March 1864.[28]

Regardless of the fort, life for the soldiers of the Fifteenth in the defenses south of the Potomac continued in much the same manner as it had for those in its precursor Third Battalion. Days and weeks melded together against the backdrop of drills, fatigue duties, inspections, reviews, picket and guard duties, and occasionally target practice. But in a change of pace, in mid-September 1863, two of the Fifteenth's companies joined three companies of the Nineteenth Connecticut Infantry and, with five days' rations, proceeded south from the defenses toward Occoquan Creek to, according to Private Bissell of the Nineteenth, "look after guerrillas and bushwackers" thought to be operating in the region. Having slogged many miles—Bissel reported slightly over 100—the weary soldiers trudged back to their quarters near Fort Lyon five days later. During the expedition, "they went south until they met some of Meade's army out on the same business. They fetched in one grey-back and some stragglers and deserters from Lee's army." Despite the initial excitement of leaving the defenses, by the time they returned, the march had taken its toll on the bluecoats, who to Bissel "looked pretty well used up."[29]

In October 1863 Schirmer established battalions within the regiment based not on the alphabetical designation of companies, but rather on the geographical proximity of their now widely dispersed camps. Initially, three battalions were organized, but in November the order establishing the Third Battalion was revoked. This two-battalion organization remained in effect until around the time of Duysing's promotion to major. Then, in February 1864, the garrisons of Forts Weed, Farnsworth, and O'Rourke became a new Third Battalion, placed under Duysing's command. On March 12 Schirmer made one final change to the then existing command structure—he reversed Dieckmann's and Schamberger's roles, with Dieckmann assuming command of the First Battalion at Fort Lyon and Schamberger moving to Fort Willard to command the Second Battalion.[30]

Throughout their time at Fort Lyon and its redoubts, the New York soldiers faced disciplinary actions for a variety of possible infractions. Entertainments of many kinds in Alexandria frequently proved irresistible to certain of Schirmer's men. Consequently, absence without leave became a common problem. Men also faced consequences for disobedience to orders, insubordination, striking a superior officer, drunkenness, gambling, conduct unbecoming a soldier or noncommissioned officer, and myriad other offenses common to soldiers. Courts-martial addressed the more egregious offenses, but for the most part, the commanding officer dealt with the alleged infractions, meting out penalties when necessary.[31]

Punishments for violations varied. Less serious offenses often resulted in extra guard duty, performed either with or without a knapsack. Remedies for more serious infractions included forfeiture of pay and, for noncommissioned and even some commissioned officers, reduction in rank or reduction to the ranks. The penalty for egregious offenses or repeat offenders was frequently "hard labor with chain and ball" for ten days or longer. Those found guilty sometimes faced a punishment of drawing only bread and water for a week or more; others had their "hair cut short." On occasion commanders imposed more inventive sentences. For example, for disobedience to orders Schirmer directed a private in Company K to stand three extra guards with knapsack and also "to be tied to one of the guns of Fort Farnsworth for six (6) hours, namely for two (2) hours at a time, & 2 hours between each time."[32]

During the summer of 1863, Schirmer devoted considerable effort to bringing the regiment up to his military expectations in appearance. For example, before an August 2 morning inspection, company commanders were directed to ensure their commands were "employed in cleaning and preparing themselves for tomorrow's inspection, in washing—They will also see that their men bathe" before the 9 A.M. inspection. That inspection was followed at 6 P.M. by a dress parade. Later that month Schirmer instructed his company commanders that their men should not wear their uniform coat or cap "except when specially ordered," as these must "be kept clean and in proper order for parade purposes & etc." Further, he wanted each man issued a pair of white cotton gloves; company commanders could determine whether company funds or the men themselves paid for them. As a jab at the attire of the heavy artillerymen manning the Washington defenses, troops in the field often referred to them as "band box soldiers."[33]

Not only did Schirmer and other officers at Fort Lyon inspect the men, but other officials also visited to perform inspections and to view the regiment's dress parades. The brigade inspection staff visited periodically; high-ranking officers also conducted reviews occasionally. For example, on Saturday, November 14, 1863, Maj. Gen. Christopher C. Auger, commander of the Twenty-Second Corps, Department of Washington, visited the forts manned by the Fifteenth. Schirmer directed the garrisons of the various posts to be ready at 11 A.M. "with dress uniform, without knapsacks, & unfixed bayonets," and to stand at command when gunners fired a salute from Fort Lyon.[34]

The soldiers again donned their dressy white gloves on Tuesday, December 15, when they marched "to the drill ground in front of Fort Weed" to be reviewed by Brig. Gen. Gustavus De Russy, commander of the defenses south of the Potomac. Again, company commanders had "to see to it that every man turns out clean and in good dress uniform with white gloves." All personnel had to attend, even "Company Clerks, Tailors, Shoemakers & Quartermasters Department." Similar inspections, reviews, and dress parades continued more or less unabated throughout the winter.[35]

Well dressed did not necessarily mean well fed. Soldiers often found military rations lacking in taste and variety. Some ventured to the nearby countryside to pick their own blackberries and mulberries. Others depended on locally sold produce. In late summer and into early fall, food from the harvest offered soldiers limited relief from the daily diet of army rations.

Local farmers and peddlers brought produce, including lettuce, potatoes, cucumbers, corn, apples, and cherries, to the camps to sell, often at inflated prices. A soldier serving in one of Fort Lyon's redoubts commented, "All kinds of vegetables fetch a high price in the Alexandria market because not enough is raised to supply the city." He enjoyed green apples but not their wartime price. "If they did not taste so strong of money we would like them much better." But during the war, most items had inflated prices. In addition to produce, soldiers could often purchase milk at ten cents per quart or occasionally a pie for the same ten cents.[36]

The drudgery of army rations formed but one part of the soldiers' daily life and struggles. Living conditions in the forts around Washington similarly left much to be desired. Although the men often used the forts' bombproofs as barracks, these structures were typically damp and rat infested. The soldiers viewed wooden barracks buildings as superior to the bombproofs or tents, at least until the barracks became lice infested. Nevertheless, in October, with winter rapidly approaching, Schirmer directed company commanders to "turn out every man that understands anything at all about wood-working so as to be of use in erecting the barracks." Barracks constructed for the garrisons of the Washington forts during this period shared a standardized design. They were made of wood and usually consisted of a single story, measuring approximately 20 feet wide by 100 feet long, with bunk beds in varying arrangements and doors at either end. Some also incorporated a veranda, with additional doors opening onto it. The buildings included small cupolas on the roof to assist with ventilation. For a garrison the size of Fort Lyon's five companies, up to five such structures may have been necessary, although it remains unclear how many were actually built there. Work proceeded steadily. Nevertheless, even with so many men dedicated to the task, the barracks remained incomplete at the end of November. On the twenty-sixth Schirmer ordered, "The work on the Barracks and around the different works will be pushed forward as much as possible."[37]

As the soldiers constructed barracks and drilled regularly, Schirmer also worked to enhance the professional knowledge of the commissioned and noncommissioned officers under his command. In November he issued an order directing all first and second lieutenants not on duty to assemble at the officer's mess each weekday at 8 P.M. for one hour of "theoretical instruction." Any officer missing this discussion, led by Capt. Otto Christl of Company B, was reported to regimental headquarters.

Similarly, all noncommissioned officers were to report at 2 P.M. daily, weekends excepted, for their own lectures on military theory, administered by a sergeant. The captain then "examined" each of the noncommissioned officers every week. Christl oversaw all theoretical instruction and each Sunday reported to Schirmer on the previous week's classes.[38]

Being part of the Fifteenth Heavy also offered enlistees other types of professional training. On December 11 Schirmer ordered his company commanders to "send in the names of such men as are fit to be instructed as Buglers," requiring at least two per company. These men then received military musical training. The candidates had to "assemble every day in front of Fort Farnsworth at 10 AM and 2 PM for instruction by Band Leader Stein for one hour at each time." Conditions in the area during December 1863 and January 1864 did not allow for a pleasant outdoor experience, certainly offering a difficult introduction to the art, but the practice undoubtedly helped the men become better buglers.[39]

During more-structured time, companies participated in regularly scheduled artillery target practice. Before having his men begin firing, the commander of each fort prepared and placed the targets. They also had to "caution residents in the vicinity of the ranges & use every precaution to avoid accidents." In addition to honing marksmanship and gunnery skills, the exercise helped generate important range and targeting data that could be applied to successfully direct fire at an enemy during periods of poor visibility or in darkness. To achieve this larger goal, commanders had to continually make sure that the "different ranges of the obstructions, points of approaches such as the mouth of ravines etc. [were] noted and a record kept for each gun." They also had to keep track of the "trim and elevation . . . & pieces trailed for night firing, so as to cover the roads in front and flank of each work."[40]

On infrequent occasions garrison life offered more than drilling and artillery practice. Perhaps to mark the approaching end of a long winter, on Sunday, February 21, 1864, instead of their usual military routine, the soldiers were treated to a regimental picnic. The festivities began at 1:30 P.M., when the men were to "turn out equipped in Dress uniform with Caps"—not necessarily the most appropriate dress for outdoor dining in February. Once formed, the regiment marched to the picnic ground, Mason's farm, just over a quarter mile south of Fort O'Rourke. The artillerists undoubtedly welcomed the opportunity to escape their daily drudgery, if only for a few hours. In the end, the men spent a pleasant afternoon, fortuitously experiencing unseasonably warm temperatures approaching fifty degrees.[41]

Despite the rare break from the monotony of drilling, building, and other military tasks they participated in each day at Fort Lyon, the men of the Fifteenth looked for other escapes from the hard work and tedium. As with the Third Battalion artillerists before them, many of the men of the Fifteenth enjoyed the occasional hard beverage. Drinking became such a problem among the soldiers that in early January 1864 Schirmer had to take action. "Hereafter no intoxicating liquor will be allowed to be brought in to any of the Forts in this command without a special order from the commanding officer of the post." Moreover, he ordered that the men extinguish all lights and be in their beds by five minutes after taps. Fort commanders strictly enforced this policy. But their efforts did not always succeed. On March 24 Duysing had to issue an order to his Third Battalion reiterating that "no intoxicating drinks, Lagerbeer, etc. will be allowed to be brought into the barracks or guard house of any company." He made the noncommissioned officers in charge of barracks or guardhouses responsible for the "strict execution" of the prohibition, warning that failure to do so would result in being brought before a general court-martial.[42]

One source of the illicit "intoxicating liquor" enjoyed by the men was a civilian entrepreneur named Adolphus Becker. In late February Becker filed a complaint with Schirmer's division commander, General De Russy, alleging that men of the Fifteenth had destroyed some of his property. De Russy invited the colonel to provide his account of the events giving rise to the accusation. In response, Schirmer explained that Becker had been "for some months past around the camps of this command, selling sausages and such other articles." But after a while Becker "emerged in the Whiskey Business, having sold it to the men by the canteen." After learning about the alcohol sales, Schirmer directed the salesman "to be driven out of the camps and instructed him not to reappear." Yet Becker refused to sacrifice his lucrative liquor business. Instead of disappearing, a few days after being ordered to leave, he "put up a shanty near Hunting Creek and it was again reported to me that he was selling Whiskey." In response, Schirmer dispatched the officer of the day, 1st Lt. Gottlieb Jungk of Company B, to go down to the banks of the creek and escort Becker to regimental headquarters, where he would be warned "to move before Sundown" or be arrested.[43]

Yet when Jungk and his patrol arrived at Becker's shanty, the man "refused to move . . . and refused admittance to Lieut. Jungk." In response,

Jungk "forced down the door, after which some articles of an inflammable nature appear to have come in contact with the stove which fired the place." Although the blaze may not have been accidental, Schirmer stood by his officer, asserting, "It does not appear that the Lieut. made use of the expressions as stated by Becker neither that he encouraged the men under his command." Having convened a three-officer panel to investigate the event, the colonel concluded that Becker was "a notorious Whiskey Smuggler and not worthy [of] the protection or sympathy of the Authorities." Schirmer's report satisfied De Russy; the general took no disciplinary action against the colonel, Jungk, or any of the men of the Fifteenth in connection with the incident.[44]

Becker's presence around the camp resulted, at least in part, from the men's constant desire for alternate food. Although in the summer and early fall, soldiers could buy fresh produce from local farmers, they could not do so during the long winter months. In March Pvt. Martin Cole of Company M described that for breakfast on most days, they were issued "Dry Brad and Coffee," then for dinner and supper, "Bains Sup and Coffee and Dry Brad." Cole assured his family and friends that although "enbodey hu reads this Letter ma think I Lie [but] it is true." The meager diet and the cold and damp winter months, combined with having so many people living in such close quarters, led to serious health consequences. Cole reported, "The men is Dying every Day and is twenty of our men Sick now and two Ded and more reddy to Dy." Even though "it is a vary Bad plase . . . I like it vary well." Perhaps despite the meager rations, his army life offered some improvement, greater interest, or even adventure in comparison to his civilian circumstances.[45]

As winter turned to spring, Schirmer had those under his command performing duties with an increased focus on readiness, discipline, and infantry drill. On March 3 he directed his company commanders to "immediately make requisition upon the Quartermaster for everything necessary to fully equipp [sic] every man in their commands." Further, he instructed them to inspect their companies to ensure that "everything is in good and proper condition" before the colonel inspected the regiment the following Sunday. He also directed battalion commanders to "drill their commands twice each week in Infantry and . . . see that the manual of arms is thoroughly practiced and understood." To do so, they issued each man ten rounds of blank ammunition "in order to learn firing by file, rank and Company."[46]

Beginning in mid-March, men not on fatigue drilled daily in both infantry and artillery routines. In addition, Schirmer told his company commanders to make sure the enlisted men "have the necessary implements for taking apart or setting up the small arms (rifles)." If they did not, the officers should "make immediate requisitions for deficiencies in the same." At the same time, a board began to review men who might be candidates for the Invalid Corps. Beginning with Companies A through D, captains had to send for review those men "as may come under that class." A little more than a week later, they had consulted with the regimental surgeon to determine who would be transferred to the Invalid Corps and how many men needed to be discharged for disability. In addition, they dropped from the rolls as deserters all men absent without leave for over six days. Once the commanders counted up how many men could no longer serve due to injury, illness, or desertion, they reported to regimental headquarters the number who were fit for service in each company. Schirmer transferred any men in excess of 150 to another company.[47]

To further tighten up the ranks, on March 21 commanders informed all enlisted men that any absence without leave for over twenty-four hours constituted desertion and would result in forfeiture of thirty dollars from their pay. Three days later they warned that, although each company would still be allowed ten passes a day, any man "over staying his pass will have his head shaved." Schirmer also threatened those not following these rules to further punishment of "be[ing] transferred to an Infantry Regiment," a threat the men took very seriously. It is quite likely that in the wake of the early 1863 conscription law, some if not many of the enlistees in the Fifteenth had joined the regiment specifically to avoid serving as foot soldiers. Although service in the heavy artillery certainly had risks, many considered it a relatively less dangerous position. Furthermore, the men felt that their positions in what they considered the more technically sophisticated artillery arm had more glamour than infantry service. In addition, they knew that duty in the forts offered a better quality of life than living in the field. As a result, Schirmer's threats of transfer to an infantry command were not taken lightly.[48]

As all of these drills, preparations, and orders shaped the lives of the soldiers in the Fifteenth, Schirmer also instructed his commanders to read an order, once in English and once in German so that all would understand, that revealed some problems in the regiment. The colonel announced that "unprincipled and evil disposed persons" had made false charges against him claiming that he was "selling his men to other states." On the basis of these accusations, the Relief Committee of New York had "stopped the Payment to many families of soldiers serving in the regiment." In order to defend his honor and regain support for the men in his regiment, Schirmer asserted the "absurdity and injustice" of the false reports. His protests met with success, and the Relief Committee resumed its disbursements. Even so, some payments, including of bounties, were delayed, and he asked his men for patience. After dealing with the problem, Schirmer assured his soldiers, "The inconvenience & injustice caused by the reports is not to be attributed to any Officers of the Regiment, but to unprincipled men who seek to injure both Officers and men of this Regiment." For most of the members of the Fifteenth, this announcement was likely the first official acknowledgement of a developing problem that would haunt Schirmer for the remainder of his time in the army.[49]

Meanwhile, as the Fifteenth spent the winter months drilling, working, and training in the Washington defenses, the field armies had generally ceased operations after the long and bloody campaigns of 1863. In the eastern theater of the war, Maj. Gen. George Gordon Meade's Army of the Potomac had by early December settled into winter quarters near Brandy Station, on the Orange and Alexandria Railroad, in the wide angle formed by the Rappahannock and Rapidan Rivers and generally east of Culpepper Court House. Across the Rapidan lay the winter camps of the bulk of two corps of Gen. Robert E. Lee's Army of Northern Virginia.[50]

Throughout the winter, the opposing commanders eyed each other's positions warily. Each observed the other's movements for any sign of an offensive thrust or for any defensive lapse that might allow a long-sought-after knockout punch. Pickets on each side guarded the river fords while cavalry and infantry protected the armies' flanks. During this period, the Orange and Alexandria Railroad, which stretched northeastward from its camps for some fifty miles to Alexandria, served as the Army of the Potomac's lifeline, carrying supplies and mail.[51]

When on February 26, 1864, a new law restored the permanent rank of lieutenant general, Lincoln nominated Maj. Gen. Ulysses S. Grant for promotion to the position. Later that month the president granted Maj. Gen. Henry W. Halleck's request for relief from his position as general in chief of the army, and Grant replaced him in that post. Halleck then became the US Army chief of staff, serving under the direction of Secretary of War Edwin M. Stanton and the newly minted general in chief.[52]

As he prepared for the upcoming spring campaigns, Grant suggested to Halleck, almost as an afterthought, "If practicable to spare them from their present stations, three regiments of heavy artillery, one commanded by Colonel Tidball to be one of them, could be advantageously used with the Army of the Potomac." The next day Halleck replied that an estimated 1,800 men could be sent from the defenses of Washington to aid operations in Virginia. After the chief of staff asked if the men should be organized into field batteries or sent to the field as heavy artillery, Grant fired back, "Send the heavy artillery as they are; there is light artillery sufficient with the army." Halleck then ordered two regiments of heavy artillery, numbering about 3,000 men total, to march and join the Army of the Potomac. They would leave for the field as soon as replacements from other forts arrived to take over their garrison duties.[53]

On March 25, 1864, the Second Pennsylvania Heavy Artillery and the Tenth New York Heavy Artillery transferred from their defensive posts north of the Potomac to relieve the Fourth New York Heavy Artillery, Col. John C. Tidball commanding, and the Fifteenth New York Heavy Artillery, respectively. The Fourth and Fifteenth, as ordered, would "proceed without delay by rail to the Army of the Potomac" and report to Meade.[54]

Consequently, Schirmer directed battalion commanders to have their commands in readiness "to march at a moment's notice." They supplied each man with three days' cooked rations and forty rounds of ammunition. The men turned in unnecessary military-issued clothing and other effects to the quartermaster's depot. In addition, Schirmer directed any men with "any surplus things, which they do not desire to take with them," to pack them with their names on the packages along with either the address to which they were to be sent or an indication that they should be stored by the Quartermaster's Department. The following morning Headquarters, Fifteenth New York Heavy Artillery issued Special Orders No. 62, informing the soldiers, "To-morrow morning at half past seven o'clock the Regiment will assemble in front of these headquarters in full dress uniform, fully equipped, with sack and pack for departure."[55]

On March 27, a cool and damp Easter Sunday, the officers and men of the Fifteenth assembled at the appointed hour. The regiment marched down the hill from Fort Lyon, crossed the Hunting Creek Bridge, and continued on to the nearby Orange and Alexandria Railroad depot. There they boarded the trains that would take them to Brandy Station and duty in the field with the Army of the Potomac. For most of these New Yorkers, life was about to change in ways they could scarcely imagine.[56]

CHAPTER TWO

Into the Wilderness

Amherst Belcher of Company M, Fifteenth New York Heavy Artillery recalled his regiment's journey that gloomy Easter Sunday. "We marched to Alexandria, were loaded on flat cars, many with legs hanging over the edge." After what seemed a long journey, "near dusk [the men] got off the train at Brandy Station." The events of the day stood out to Belcher not only because of the change in location but also due to the weather conditions. "It was cold and rainy, we were wet and chilled from riding all day in the open air, and as may readily be imagined, we were a pretty forlorn lot that night with plain Virginia mud for a bed and practically no shelter."[1]

Although the fifty-mile rail journey from Alexandria to Brandy Station took only a few hours, to the men of the Fifteenth, it seemed as though they had been transported to a new world. Upon arrival the regiment immediately began to transition from life in a garrison to life in the field. A first order of business was to establish a "proper guard" over its camps. Schirmer also ordered the men to participate in a dress parade each day at 5 P.M. and the company commanders to drill their outfits "a few hours daily." The weather, however, did not cooperate. Lt. Col. Theodore Lyman recorded that rain fell in a "deluge" three days after the Fifteenth arrived, causing the Rappahannock River to swell at a rate of two feet an hour. This downpour presaged the precipitation, sometimes in the form of snow and sleet, that fell almost every day over the next week.[2]

When it joined the army in Virginia, the Fifteenth came under the overall command of its chief of artillery, Brig. Gen. Henry J. Hunt. After he allocated batteries to the infantry and cavalry corps, the Fifteenth and the balance of Hunt's other men, including the Fourth New York Heavy, also dispatched from the Washington defenses, joined the Reserve Artillery, under Col. Henry S. Burton's command. Hunt now considered options for how best to employ the two recently assigned regiments of "foot artillery."[3]

Meanwhile, the members of the regiment continued to settle into their new role and their new daily routine, which included frequent drill, guard and fatigue duties, and even serenades by the Fifteenth's band at several times throughout the day. Arrival at the Brandy Station camp also brought about a reorganization of the battalions. Although in the Washington defenses companies were grouped into battalions based on the fort in which each served, Colonel Schirmer reorganized the companies into battalions based on the traditional alphabetical progression. As a result, Companies A, B, C, and D now constituted the First Battalion, under the command of Major Schamberger, and Companies E, F, G, and H formed Major Dieckmann's Second Battalion. Companies I, K, L, and M comprised the Third Battalion, commanded by Major Duysing.[4]

During his regiment's transition from Washington to the field, Schirmer absented himself twice to fulfill other obligations. Soon after arriving at Brandy Station, he applied to Burton and Hunt for four days' leave of absence so that he could travel to Fort Lyon, his "presence there [being] absolutely necessary in order to have the Ordnance and Q. M. Stores left behind in Fort Lyon and in the other Forts under [his] Command, properly turned over to the respective authorities." His leave request granted, Schirmer left the regiment on April 2. He resumed his duties in the field six days later.[5]

On April 16 Schirmer again applied for leave—this time for ten days so he could travel to New York City with Lt. William Bundy, whom the colonel described in his application as a former adjutant of the regiment. This time the purpose was, he said, "to settle up and arrange old matters connected with recruiting my Regiment which cannot possibly be achieved without my personal presence, and to arrange a difficulty that imperils my honor." Although Burton recommended approval, Hunt denied the request because "the exigencies of the service will not permit of such leaves." Schirmer persisted and eventually received approval for four days' leave. The colonel departed on April 21 and resumed command six days later.[6]

Even in the absence of their commander, the men of the Fifteenth continued to drill and prepare for battle. Although they had devoted many hours to performing the manual of arms and drilling with their rifles, like many other soldiers they had little experience in firing them. Indeed, Meade observed, "It is believed there are men in this army who have been in numerous actions without ever firing their guns, and it is known that muskets taken on the battle-fields have been found filled nearly to the muzzle with cartridges." Consequently, in preparation for the approaching campaign, the general allocated ammunition for training the troops in the use of their weapons. The men of the Fifteenth began their "target practice" on April 14, with such training subsequently held for two hours a day, three days a week. One officer recorded that with the entire army engaged in this practice, "between 10 & 12 on firing days, the echoes respond with popping."[7]

Apparently some of the infantrymen at Brandy Station derived a certain malevolent pleasure in the heavy artillerymen's fate in having been turned out of the forts and sent to the field. Meade's aide-de-camp Lyman, in a letter to his wife, described the "joke" of the "heavy sell that has been practiced" on them. "Now these gentry, having always been in fortifications, took it for granted there they should continue." This resulted, according to Lyman, in a "patriotic rush of recruits (getting a big bounty)" that was "most gratifying." The heavies then "returned to the forts round Washington, with the slight difference that the cars kept on, till they got to Brandy Station; and now these mammoth legions are enjoying the best of air under shelter-tents!" He teased that a "favorite salutation now is, 'How are you, Heavy Artillery.'"[8]

On April 7 Meade ordered his troops to prepare for active operations and limited what they could carry with them during the upcoming campaign. Officers could bring a moderate allowance of bedding and mess articles as well as a valise or carpetbag for extra clothes and blankets. Further, at Schirmer's direction, on the march each battalion of the Fifteenth could bring one mess chest with the necessary cooking utensils and rations for the officers. In addition, each battalion commander could carry two wall tents, while company officers were allotted one shelter tent each.[9]

Regular soldiers had to travel more lightly than officers. Orders required the troops to turn in their overcoats, surplus blankets, and other items superfluous to summer operations. Each man could carry with him only one half of a shelter tent, a rubber blanket, one cap, one blouse or dress coat, one pair of trousers, one undershirt, one pair of drawers, two pairs of stockings, one blanket, and sewing and cleaning materials. Before they departed, commanders inspected their companies to ensure that the men obeyed the restrictions on equipment and personal effects.[10]

As the preparations for the campaign continued, Hunt decided to distribute the heavy artillerymen of the Fourth New York Heavy Artillery equally among the infantry corps by battalions; one battalion from the Fourth was assigned to the artillery brigade in the Second, Fifth, and Sixth Corps. The Fifteenth, on the other hand, remained intact, brigaded with the Sixth New York Heavy Artillery, which had served in the Army of the Potomac following the Battle of Gettysburg; since August 1863 it had been guarding the army's ammunition train. On April 15 Hunt designated this new unit as the First Brigade, Reserve Artillery. Col. J. Howard Kitching, commanding officer of the Sixth, assumed command of the new brigade.[11]

Born in New York City in July 1838, John Howard Kitching was only twenty-five years old when he assumed command of the First Brigade. As a youth he had spent many summers with his family near West Point, where he observed with great interest the training of the cadets. He considered a career in the military, but his mother was against it, and he eventually joined in his father's mercantile business. But the outbreak of the Civil War gave him the opportunity to pursue the career he had once desired. After his commissioning as a captain in the Second New York Artillery, Kitching served in the Washington defenses. In early April 1862, anxious to participate in the upcoming campaign of the Army of the Potomac, he joined Battery D, Second US Artillery, commanded by Lt. Emory Upton, and served under the lieutenant throughout the Peninsula Campaign in command of a section. Upton recorded that at Gaines's Mill Kitching's section "was exposed to the full view of the enemy, and received much more than its proportion of fire." Despite the danger and being wounded by a shell fragment, Kitching remained at his post throughout the action. During the entire battle, he "served his guns with great coolness, and was a brilliant example to the men."[12]

After the Peninsula Campaign, Kitching transferred to the newly raised 135th New York Infantry and became its colonel. The men of the regiment came from areas just upstate from New York City, largely from the counties of Putnam, Rockland, and Westchester. It mustered into Federal service at Yonkers in September 1862, soon converted to an artillery regiment, and was redesignated the Sixth New York Heavy Artillery on October 6, 1862. Shortly thereafter, two newly recruited companies joined the regiment, giving it the full complement for artillery regiments of twelve companies, or "batteries." Before it joined the Army of the Potomac in July 1863, the regiment served at Harpers Ferry, the defenses of the upper Potomac, and in Baltimore.[13]

Within days of taking charge of the brigade, Kitching reported that he now commanded about 4,000 men, "two thousand being Dutchmen" of the Fifteenth. He explained to his mother that he was "organizing it to suit his own ideas; and changing many things." He bragged, "After I get the machine running regularly I shall not have as much to do, as when commanding officer of my regiment, there being fewer details." Two weeks later he wrote to his father about how the men of the Fifteenth "say that I am 'ter duyvil,' because I gives 'em so much drill, and so little lager."[14]

After Grant's review of the Reserve Artillery on April 18, 1864, the general "complimented [Kitching] very highly upon [his brigade's] appearance, their perfect drill, and splendid marching." Meade's aide Lyman, who had accompanied Grant that day, was similarly impressed. He observed that the two heavy artillery regiments were "both very large and both marching with great steadiness." He also noted the Fifteenth's ethnic makeup: "Schirmer's is composed chiefly of Germans, and many an old Prussian soldier might one recognize, as they marched in review."[15]

Rumors that the Fifteenth would become an infantry unit had circulated since shortly after the outfit's arrival in the field. Consequently, Schirmer considered it "necessary to stop the different rumors now prevailing in the Regiment." Read aloud twice to the unit, presumably in both English and German, his April 10 circular assured the men that their unit "is a Heavy, or Foot Artillery Regiment and it is not the intention of the Government or the General Commanding to make it anything else." Furthermore, the colonel made sure the message came across clearly as he declared that, in accordance with army regulations, "the duties of the Regiment will be . . . to take charge of siege guns and trains & hold permanent positions against the enemy, and to guard and protect Batteries." He further urged "all good soldiers should not . . . show fear to meet the enemy in the field; there they can only gain honor and respect." In closing, Schirmer assured his men, "I will make it my utmost duty to take care of my soldiers as I always have done, as well as I have worked for the benefit of the service of our country."[16]

Another regimental circular issued on April 21, however, seemingly contradicted these assurances. The newer circular ordered the regiment to assemble that afternoon for brigade drill, where it would execute a number of evolutions described in the third volume of *Casey's Tactics*. These infantry movements included breaking to the front or left into columns, breaking to the rear by the right or the left into columns, being in column by company to form division, deploying by battalion in mass faced to the right, breaking the lines formed by battalions in mass into columns, and passing from column at full distance into line of battle. Only the day before, perhaps in a last-ditch attempt to maintain the regiment's identity as artillerymen, company commanders had ordered each man to properly display the company letter and the number of the regiment "with crossed cannons" on his cap. Yet these drills convinced the troops that, while it may in name remain a heavy artillery regiment, in the upcoming campaign the Fifteenth would be employed as infantry.[17]

The armament of the Reserve Artillery included a battery of eight 24-pounder brass Coehorn mortars. The tube of these pieces looked much like a short section of pipe and weighed approximately 164 pounds; when mounted on a wooden base, the complete weapon weighed slightly less than 300 pounds. Handles affixed to the base allowed four soldiers to move the mortar with relative ease, although two could do it with more effort. Employing a fixed angle of fire of forty-five degrees, with range adjusted by varying the propellant charge, Coehorns could lob their shells in a high arc for distances of up to 1,000 yards. As a result, the mortar could wreak havoc on an entrenched enemy otherwise protected by breastworks, an impossible feat for regular field guns. Troops could transport four of these mortars, with their beds, in a standard wagon. As the spring campaign commenced, the heavies in the Fifteenth's Company E manned the reserve's eight Coehorns, which they employed "whenever circumstances would permit their use, and always with good results."[18]

After an inspection of the First Brigade by Hunt and Burton at the end of April, Kitching congratulated his men, informing them that the two officers "spoke in warmest terms of their soldierly appearance and the precision of their movements. A continuance to the close attention to duty & drill shown by this Brigade since its organization, must render any [sic] command second to none in the Army." As a result, Kitching "[felt] justly proud of a Command, which although composed exclusively of Artillerists has shown the ability to equal our Infantry Comrades in their own arm of service."[19]

With its integration into the army at Brandy Station, the Fifteenth was but a small cog in a great machine assembled to execute the general in chief's overall battle plan for the 1864 campaigns. Grant believed that "active and continuous operation by all troops that could be brought into the field, regardless of season and weather, was essential to a speedy termination of the war." To accomplish this goal, he would employ the greatest number of troops practicable to simultaneously engage the enemy in all theaters of war. This tactic, Grant asserted, would prevent the Confederates "from using the same force at different seasons against first one and then another of our armies." He also planned "to hammer continuously against the armed force of the enemy and his resources until by mere attrition, if in no other way, there will be nothing left to him." The Union's overwhelming superiority in resources such as men and materiel, coupled with its ability to sustain this superiority, allowed his latter element to remain a viable operational concept.[20]

To execute his ambitious battle plans, Grant contemplated a virtually simultaneous movement of all Federal armies against their Confederate counterparts. In the eastern theater three principal commands would assume the offensive. Major General Sigel, with a force of approximately 7,000 men, would advance up (southwestward) the Shenandoah Valley so as to threaten the enemy in that region, while a combined infantry and cavalry force, also under his command, would operate farther to the west against the East Tennessee and Virginia Railroad. Next, Maj. Gen. Benjamin Butler and his Army of the James, with an aggregate strength of approximately 33,000 men, would operate from his base at Fortress Monroe on the south side of the James River as he worked to threaten, if not capture, the Confederacy's capital city, Richmond.[21]

The third major component of this plan in the East was Meade's Army of the Potomac. Unlike commanders before him, Grant's objective was not solely the capture of enemy territory and the destruction of Rebel infrastructure but also the destruction of the Confederacy's legendary Army of Northern Virginia, led by General Lee. He understood that Lee and his army not only had won successes on the field of battle but also were revered by, and a source of pride and inspiration to, the citizens of the South. In April Grant stressed to Meade, "Lee's army will be your objective." He wanted the Army of the Potomac, with an aggregate strength of just under 100,000 men, to focus on defeating the Army of Northern Virginia. "Wherever Lee goes, there you will go also." The approximately 25,000 men of Maj. Gen. Ambrose E. Burnside's Ninth Army Corps would support, but not be incorporated into, Meade's army. Instead, Grant would coordinate Burnside's movements in the field. This awkward arrangement was necessitated because Burnside, himself a former commander of the Army of the Potomac, outranked Meade.[22]

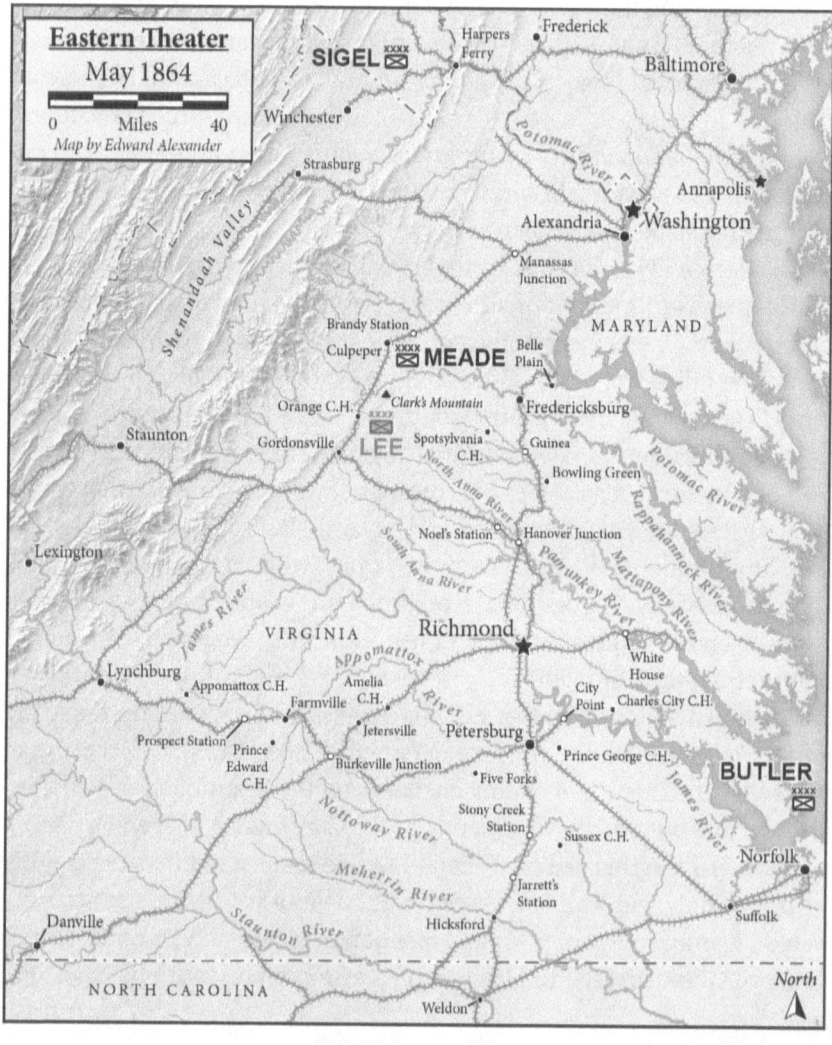

The Fifteenth would participate in the operations designed to take Lee's army out of the war. As the heavies drilled and prepared at Brandy Station, the Confederates were in camp nearby. Across the Rapidan River beyond Lee's right flank, a little more than ten miles to the southeast of the Brandy Station camps, lay the Wilderness, an area consisting of a nearly impenetrable thicket of second-growth forest and underbrush. The prior May, when the Army of the Potomac's spring campaign culminated in the Battle of Chancellorsville, heavy fighting and horrible carnage filled parts of the Wilderness. The topography of that region meant that very few people lived or farmed there, so clearings were uncommon. Instead, the forest and undergrowth made the movement of even small bodies of troops extremely difficult and severely limited the effective employment of artillery. Nevertheless, the Union high command hoped that a swift movement to launch its campaign would allow the Federals to pass through the Wilderness before the Confederates could confront them. Consequently, Meade's chief of staff, Brig. Gen. Andrew A. Humphreys, who planned the operation, directed the army to move through the Wilderness after crossing the Rapidan, thereby turning Lee's right.[23]

On May 1, with the roads finally passable after the long winter, Grant ordered a general movement of all armies not later than the fourth. Plans for the Army of the Potomac on the first day of the offensive called for a two-pronged movement. The Fifth Corps, followed by the Sixth Corps, would march through Stevensburg and cross the Rapidan at Germanna Ford. From its camps above Stevensburg, the Second Corps would enter the Stevensburg–Richardsville Road at Madden's Tavern, pass through Richardsville, and cross the Rapidan at Ely's Ford. After departing Brandy Station, the Reserve Artillery would cross Mountain Run at Hamilton's place, proceed southward to Madden's to join the road to Richardsville, and follow the Second Corps's route to cross the Rapidan at Ely's Ford.[24]

Meanwhile, south of the river, Confederates throughout the winter had monitored activities in the Federal camps from an observation post atop Clark's Mountain. There, on May 2, Lee and several of his senior commanders surveyed the positions of the Federal army across the Rapidan, searching for any sign of the beginning of the Yankees' spring campaign. While the bustle of enemy troops indicated preparations for a move were under way, Lee had no alternative but to maintain his army in its current position until Meade tipped his hand on where he would strike. At the time, the three divisions of Lt. Gen. Richard S. Ewell's Second Corps were

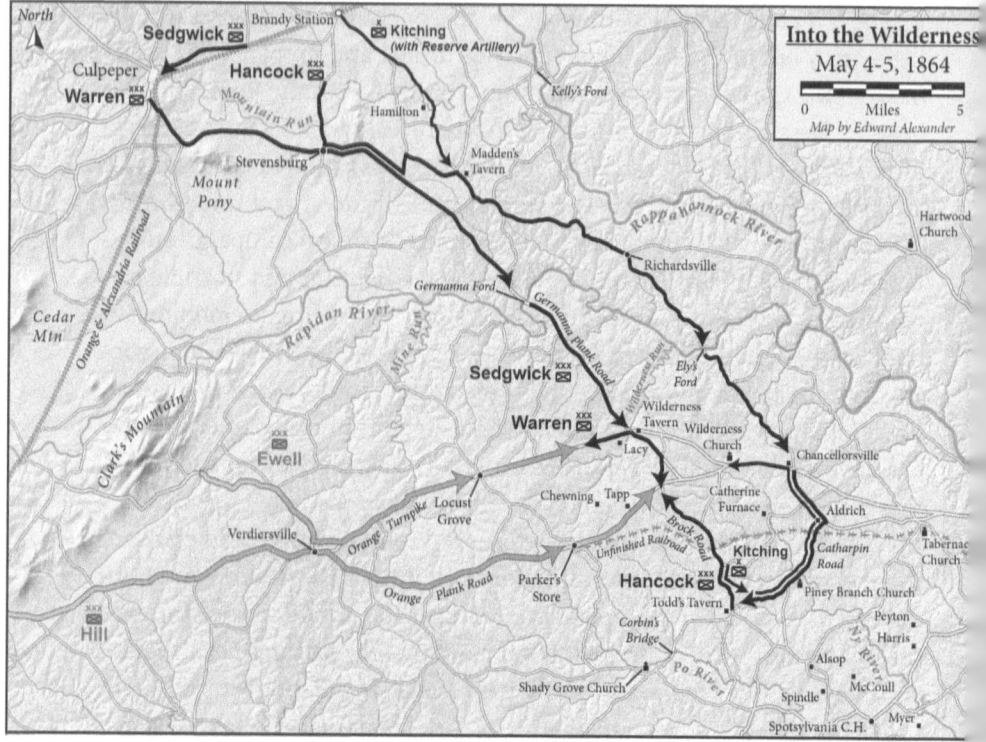

camped from the vicinity of Mine Run southwest along the Rapidan to near Clark's Mountain. Lt. Gen. Ambrose P. Hill's Third Corps, also three divisions in size, continued the line to the southwest higher up the Rapidan. In addition, two of the three divisions of the army's First Corps, commanded by Lt. Gen. James Longstreet, camped in the vicinity of Gordonsville and Mechanicsville, nearly ten miles south of Orange Court House.[25]

In the Federal camps, few of the soldiers had a sense of the impending movements planned for them in Grant's grand offensive. As they enjoyed the pleasant spring weather on May 3, Kitching's heavies spent their morning much as they had on previous days. "We came in at noon for soup and lay down, tired as dogs," a member of the Fifteenth later recalled. Rumors of a campaign began to circulate, but the troops gave them little credence. "The men began to prospect on the possibility of a move, but decided it was an impossibility, as the commissary stores were in piles yet." When "someone passed along and said, jokingly, 'Boy, we are ordered to move by one o'clock,'" the soldiers "pooh-poohed." Much to their surprise, however, they very soon found out, "*We were going by 12:15!*"[26]

Early in the afternoon of May 3, the Fifteenth New York Heavy Artillery broke camp north of Brandy Station and moved several miles south to just across the railroad, where it camped. Although the bulk of the regiment departed the next morning, Company B remained at Brandy Station to serve as provost guard. The Army of the Potomac began moving shortly after midnight on a warm, starlit May 4. As dawn broke on a "fine morning," everything went smoothly and according to plan. Kitching's brigade and the rest of the Reserve Artillery got under way at 2 A.M., crossed Mountain Run, and, passing Madden's Tavern, swung into its line of march behind the Second Corps. A private in the brigade reflected upon the "great splender" created by the sight of troops and trains stretching before him as they moved toward the Rapidan. The Second Corps, under Maj. Gen. Winfield Scott Hancock, crossed at Ely's Ford and pressed on toward Chancellorsville. The head of the column arrived at the crossroads between 9 and 10 A.M., and the entire corps soon bivouacked on part of the previous May's battlefield. The Reserve Artillery crossed the Rapidan that afternoon, eventually halting for the night near the site of the Chancellor house.[27]

Meanwhile, the Fifth Corps, commanded by Maj. Gen. Gouverneur Kemble Warren, had marched through Stevensburg, crossed the Rapidan at Germanna Ford, and reached the Wilderness Tavern, near the intersection of the Germanna Plank Road and the Orange Turnpike, where it bivouacked. Behind the Fifth, Maj. Gen. John Sedgwick's Sixth Corps was camped just south of the Rapidan. Reflecting on the day's accomplishments, Grant breathed a sigh of relief. Slightly over a year later, he admitted that he had held "the most serious apprehensions" that the crossing of the army, with its supply train of about 4,000 wagons, would have been opposed by the "active, large, well-appointed, and ably commanded army" that occupied the country south of the river. Instead, all had gone smoothly, according to plan, and without serious opposition.[28]

After confirming the general direction of the Federal movement at daybreak on May 4, Lee began to slide his army to its right to meet the Union thrust. Ewell's Corps advanced by the Orange Turnpike and Hill's Corps by the Orange Plank Road, which ran south of and generally parallel to the turnpike. Longstreet, meanwhile, hurried to support Hill. The First Corps departed its camps at about 4 P.M. that afternoon and that night rested near Brock's Bridge at the crossing of the North Anna River.[29]

Following Meade's plans, Hancock's corps marched from Chancellorsville at 5 A.M. on May 5, moving first south and then west on the Catharpin

Road through Todd's Tavern. The Fifth Corps set out about an hour later, moving southwest along the road to Parker's Store on the Orange Plank Road. At about 7 A.M., with the vanguard of Warren's column approaching Parker's Store, Meade received word that the enemy had been sighted on the Orange Turnpike about two miles west of Wilderness Tavern. He directed Warren to halt his column, concentrate his command on the Orange Turnpike, and strike the Confederates to his front when he had sufficient forces assembled.[30]

When Ewell's Corps began its eastward advance along the Orange Turnpike earlier that morning, lookouts spotted a Federal column crossing the road ahead. As his troops formed a line of battle across the turnpike, Ewell informed Lee of the development. Lee instructed him not to bring on a general engagement until Longstreet's Corps arrived. Yet when Warren attacked around noon, Ewell had few options; the two armies faced off in a furious contest astride the turnpike.[31]

Skirmishes loomed farther south on the Orange Plank Road, too. Upon learning of Confederate forces in the area, Meade directed Hancock to move from Todd's Tavern up the Brock Road to its intersection with the Plank Road, where Brig. Gen. George W. Getty's Sixth Corps division awaited. As Hancock's troops began to arrive around 2 P.M., he formed the men into a line of battle on the Brock Road, where they set to work building entrenchments. At approximately 4:15 P.M. Getty advanced and almost immediately encountered the enemy in force. Hancock went forward in support, and before long all four of the Second Corps's divisions were engaged.[32]

Elements of Hill's Corps reversed the initial Union success, and a bloody struggle ensued. Between 4 and 5 P.M., Brig. Gen. James S. Wadsworth's large Fifth Corps division proceeded between the two wings of the army to strike the left and rear of the Confederate force opposing Hancock and Getty. But Wadsworth's troops arrived late in the day, so they could only push in the enemy's skirmishers. Fortunately for Hill, whose troops were shattered, confused, and disorganized, the firing subsided around 8 P.M. Nearly all semblance of command and control had vanished in the chaos of the Wilderness. Both sides suffered heavily in dead, wounded, and captured.[33]

Grant intended to seize the initiative and resume the attack at dawn on May 6, ordering Meade's three corps to attack promptly at 5 A.M. and two divisions of the Ninth Corps to move between the two wings of the Army of the Potomac. If successful, this maneuver would place Burnside's troops between Warren on the Orange Turnpike and Wadsworth's division, just beyond Hancock's right and nearly perpendicular to it, on the Plank Road. The plan called for Burnside to attack as soon as he had his troops in position, presumably in conjunction with the Army of the Potomac's three corps. Meanwhile, as Hancock's corps and Getty's division attacked to their front, Wadsworth's men would drive forward from their position, directly into Hill's left flank. If all went according to plan, they would crush what remained of Hill's Corps.[34]

In preparation for the attack the next morning, Meade ordered that "every man who can shoulder a musket must be in the ranks" and directed Hunt to "order all the regiments and detachments of heavy artillery" to report at Meade's headquarters near the Lacy house "before daylight to-morrow morning for service at the front." Later that evening Meade informed Warren that the heavy artillery serving with the Artillery Reserve would reinforce his position.[35]

The Fifteenth New York Heavy Artillery had left its Chancellorsville bivouac with the rest of the Reserve Artillery early on May 5, following the Second Corps as it moved toward Todd's Tavern. After several miles of marching, the column halted at news of Confederate activity. At 10 A.M. Hunt directed the reserve to follow the Second Corps and move up the Brock Road to its intersection with the Orange Plank Road. But he amended the orders shortly after noon to have the reserve retrace its route back to the Chancellorsville crossroads, proceed west, and halt at Wilderness Church at the junction of the Orange Turnpike and Orange Plank Road. This new route placed them about two miles west of Chancellorsville and approximately the same distance from Wilderness Tavern. The column reached the designated place at 3:30 P.M. The bulk of the Reserve Artillery remained in this location throughout the battle. But that evening Kitching's heavies discovered that they would be employed as infantry for the next day's fighting.[36]

Schirmer, Wiedrich, Dieckmann, and others in the Fifteenth knew the ground around Wilderness Church well. They now bivouacked in almost the same place they had a year earlier, practically to the day, as part of Howard's Eleventh Corps. Some paid tribute to comrades who had fallen on the field at that time. Belcher of Company M reported: "Sergeant Riemann (as good a soldier as ever lived) took me a few rods to show me where his battery stood the year before at the Battle of Chancellorsville. The lunettes were still there." Many of the fallen from 1863 lay in shallow graves around where the men now camped. Rains had eroded the mounds, in many cases exposing skeletal remains that still had bits of clothing clinging to them. Those of the Fifteenth who had fought at that battle knew that their former comrades from other batteries rested among the hastily interred of the Eleventh Corps.[37]

Throughout the day Kitching's heavies heard the roar of cannon and the rattle of musketry from the current battlefield nearby. As midnight approached, some of them held a small prayer meeting among the graves. The bright moon lit the strange, almost macabre scene. Kitching later described the moment, recalling the earnest, simple prayers of the soldiers; "prayers as are only offered at such times."[38]

The Fifteenth broke camp around 2 A.M. on Friday, May 6, and marched along the Orange Turnpike toward army headquarters near the turnpike's intersection with the Germanna Plank Road, headed for its baptism under fire. The sun rose near 5 A.M. on that fine spring day. After reaching headquarters around 5:30 A.M., the men rested while Kitching reported to Warren at Fifth Corps headquarters at the Lacy house, a short distance away. The colonel received orders to take his brigade forward in support of Wadsworth's division.[39]

According to plan, at 5 A.M. Hancock advanced two of his divisions along the Plank Road simultaneously with Getty's troops. The bluecoats struck the disorganized rebels "with great vigor." Soon after the assault began, Hancock gleefully told Meade's aide Lyman, "we are driving them most beautifully." But the general's unbridled joy evaporated when Lyman informed him that Burnside's divisions, which were to attack on his right, were not yet in position. Nevertheless, Hancock's and Getty's outfits, joined by Wadsworth's division, continued to advance. They broke the Confederate line at all points and drove the enemy "in confusion through the forest for about 1½ miles, suffering severe losses in killed, wounded and prisoners." Despite this success, fighting through the thick woods and scrub underbrush had disordered the Federal ranks. Commanders halted to reorganize their lines before continuing the push forward.[40]

On the north side of the Plank Road, the Federal advance neared Lee's headquarters in the clearing at the Tapp farm. As bullets whizzed around him, Lee attempted to stem the tide of Hill's fleeing men while also directing the fire of Lt. Col. William T. Poague's artillery in the field nearby. At that moment Longstreet's Corps suddenly appeared, "swinging down the Orange Plank Road at a trot." In perfect order and with ranks well closed, they pushed onward impervious to the chaos "like 'a river in the sea' of confused and troubled human waves around them." Longstreet's arrival ameliorated the desperate situation facing Lee's army.[41]

To the right of the Plank Road, Brig. Gen. Joseph B. Kershaw's butternuts formed a line of battle under heavy fire and sprang forward to strike the Federal left. They drove back the still-disorganized Yankees. Maj. Gen. Charles W. Field's division moved to the left of the Plank Road, with Brig. Gen. John Gregg's Texas Brigade leading, followed by Brig. Gen. Henry G. "Rock" Benning's Georgians and Law's Alabama Brigade, under Col. William F. Perry's command. From atop his horse in the Tapp field, Lee watched Field's men forming for battle. Although spurring his horse forward to lead Gregg's men in their charge, he abandoned that effort at the insistence of the Texans and instead went to confer with Longstreet.[42]

Gregg's Texans surged forward through the field, with their right guiding on the Plank Road. Scattered pines fringed the far end of the opening before yielding to the thicker woods and underbrush more characteristic of the Wilderness. As the Federals advanced through the pines, Gregg's 800 men struck them with "a terrible crash, mingled with wild yells, which settled down into a steady roar of musketry." In less than twenty minutes, half of Gregg's outfit lay dead or wounded, but the Texans had broken the momentum of the Union advance.[43]

At the western end of the Tapp field, two more of Field's brigades—Benning's and Perry's—prepared to attack. Benning's brigade followed Gregg's general line of advance along the Plank Road and plowed into the Federals, who were still reeling from the Texans' attack. But pushing back this enemy line exposed Benning's right to a deadly fire from Yankees south of the road, which checked his brigade's progress and inflicted heavy losses. With the Georgians' stalled, Perry's veteran brigade, consisting of the Fourth, Fifteenth, Forty-Fourth, Forty-Seventh, and Forty-Eighth Alabama, would be the next to enter the fray. The brigade formed line of battle, with the crack Fifteenth on the left of the line. The open ground in front of the Alabamians sloped gradually downward for several hundred yards before abruptly descending into a morass running nearly perpendicular to the line of advance. Beyond the swampy area, the ground rose in a moderately steep ascent for several hundred yards; while covered with trees, it had only sparse undergrowth.[44]

Meanwhile, about two hours earlier at around 5:30 A.M., the head of Burnside's column finally advanced past Fifth Corps headquarters, marching on the road to the Chewning farm and Parker's Store beyond. Warren reported to Meade's chief of staff that, "in consequence of [Burnside] not being in position, I have sent the heavy artillery, under Colonel Kitching, 2,400, to support General Wadsworth." The narrow, little-used wood road between the Lacy house and the Chewning farm had been expanded to a width of twenty feet by the Fifth Corps, which had also constructed three bridges over the western branches of Wilderness Run. Kitching's men followed the leading Ninth Corps division down the Parker's Store road for about three quarters of a mile, where another road branched off in a southerly direction leading to the Tapp farm and eventually the Plank Road. Here Kitching turned off the Parker's Store road and proceeded toward Wadsworth's last known position north of the Plank Road, about two miles distant. With every step the heavies took, the roar of musketry grew louder.[45]

From near the Lacy house, Capt. Augustus C. Brown, a western New Yorker and the commander of a company in the Second Battalion, Fourth New York Heavy, now assigned to the Fifth Corps Artillery Brigade, saw "the Sixth New York and other regiments of Heavy Artillery" pass him going forward "to fill a gap in the line through which the enemy is momentarily expected to pour its charging columns." As the day had dawned, "the pattering of the skirmishers" was soon "lost in the terrible roll of musketry of the main lines." He reflected that he had never heard anything more thrilling than that morning's engagement. "The loudest and longest peals of thunder," he recalled, "were no more to be compared to it in depth and volume, than the rippling of a trout brook to the roaring of Niagara." As he contemplated the battle, to Brown's "mortification," a staff officer asked him what battery he commanded. After the captain gestured toward his company of "foot soldiers," the officer replied almost apologetically, "Ah, you are one of the Heavies." Brown fumed in his diary: "I shall never cease to condemn in the strongest terms the action of the government in enlisting us for one branch of the service and then, without our consent, transferring us to another."[46]

When Kitching's heavies neared the front, they encountered men of Wadsworth's division, now near its breaking point, streaming to the rear. Allowing them to pass, the brigade filed to the left off the road and, marching through woods in which Cpl. William Daily could see "lots laying dead," began to form line of battle facing toward the open ground of the Tapp field. The Fifteenth took position on the brigade's right, with the

Sixth to its left. It formed with the First Battalion on the left, the Second in the center, and the Third on the right flank. The thick undergrowth in their position had nothing in common with the parade grounds on which they had prepared for battle. Despite all of their drilling, the men had never experienced anything like the conditions of this maneuver.[47]

As Perry's Alabamians commenced their advance down the descending ground toward the morass, they began to take fire from their left. The colonel observed that this came from "a force of the enemy"—Kitching's brigade—that had crossed the morass and ascended the heights beyond to occupy the woods at the fringe of the open ground and about 200 yards to Perry's left. He ordered Col. William C. Oates to wheel his Fifteenth Alabama, the largest regiment in the brigade, to the left while advancing "and to attack furiously" to suppress the enemy fire. Oates executed the change of direction despite the din of the battle; his regiment crossed

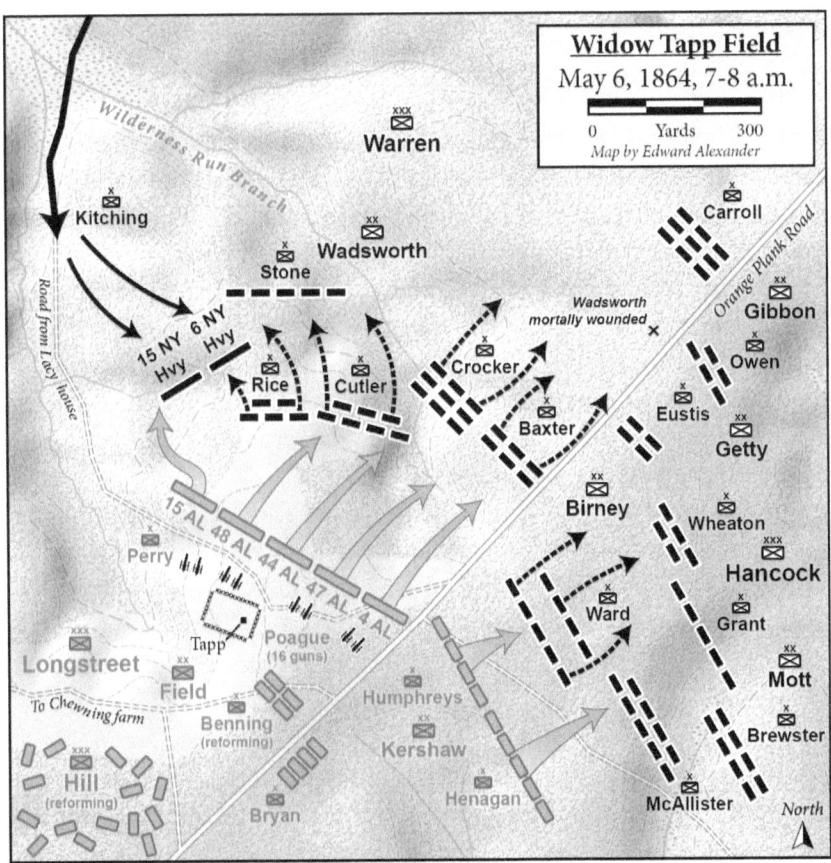

the open ground and charged headlong into the woods. Meanwhile, Perry's other four regiments stormed down the slope, where they confronted "dense masses" of the enemy. After the front rank fired a volley, the whole line "bounded forward with their characteristic yell." The movement had the intended effect. Perry reported, "the suddenness of our appearance on the crest, the volley, the yell, and the impetuous advance caused them to forget their guns." In response, the Yankees returned only a scattering of fire and began to give way. Capt. John Gedney of the Sixth Heavy reported, "we had just got in line when the enemy made a charge on the 5th Corps and drove them back on us."[48]

About this time the Fifteenth Alabama struck the right of the Fifteenth New York before the heavies' had fully established their line of battle. Forced to deploy "under a lively fire," the New Yorkers still repulsed an initial thrust. Some of the heavies even pursued fleeing Confederates nearly 200 yards toward the Tapp field. But the main force of the Fifteenth Alabama drove the Fifteenth New York back through the woods behind their initial position. This maneuver exposed the right of the Sixth, compelling it, too, to fall back. According to Perry, who had gone to his left to check on the state of affairs there, Oates's men drove an enemy force of more than twice their number "in the wildest confusion before them." Although Lieutenant Colonel Wiedrich held that the men of the Fifteenth fell back "in good order," Kitching's interpretation differed: "at first fire my right regiment broke and ran away, leaving the right of my line unprotected, and the best I could do was to fall back fighting." Kitching asserted, "my own regiment did splendidly, maneuvering as coolly as if on drill." The brigade reformed to retake its first position, the Fifteenth again on the right. But, Wiedrich reported, "an order from higher authority did not allow this to be carried out."[49]

After the war Oates recalled that he "learned from prisoners taken that the force I encountered was the Fifteenth New York Regiment, which had been stationed in Washington City, and used as heavy siege artillerymen during the greater part of the war." Although the New Yorkers had numbered between 1,000 and 1,200 men, Oates had taken into the engagement not more than 450 officers and men, only 2 of whom were killed, with 11 others wounded. He attributed his success to two things: "First, that the troops of the enemy were not veterans—they were unused to battle; and secondly, the rapidity and boldness of my movement, and the accuracy of the fire of my men." In a sense Wiedrich agreed. He defended his regiment and asserted that it "was not armed according to the duties it had to perform, carrying old Remington rifles with sword bayonets; and also that it had never been sufficiently drilled as infantry, this having been considered but a secondary part of its duty during its stay in fortifications around Washington, D.C."[50]

Kitching's condemnation of the performance of the Fifteenth as opposed to that of "his own" regiment does not take into account that Oates's attack fell squarely on the right of the Fifteenth and did not initially strike the brigade's left regiment. The casualties the Fifteenth suffered, as compared to those of the Sixth, confirmed that it bore the brunt of the attack. In his report Wiedrich counted one officer and seven men killed, with thirty-five men wounded, "the largest part of this loss falling on the Third Battalion, which had to sustain the most of the enemy's attack." Another eight men were reported missing, four of whom would ultimately perish in the infamous Confederate prison camp at Andersonville, Georgia. The Sixth, on the other hand, lost no officers and suffered only four men killed or mortally wounded, another wounded, and ten others missing.[51]

The battle continued raging along the Orange Plank Road. Not long after the Confederates repulsed Kitching's brigade, Longstreet exploited the bed of an unfinished railroad to move to the left of Hancock's line. Late that morning he launched an attack in the direction of the Plank Road. The thrust fell on the left and rear of the Union line and caught the weary and disorganized Federals by surprise. Trapped in dense undergrowth and under heavy fire, Hancock could not successfully reorganize his lines. North of the Plank Road, Wadsworth continued to rally his troops until he was mortally wounded. But both sides had to deal with the effects of significant casualties that morning. Friendly fire struck Longstreet in the throat; members of his staff lowered Lee's grievously wounded right-hand man from his horse to the ground. After a long, chaotic morning, unable to counter the irresistible force of the latest Rebel onslaught, Hancock withdrew his troops to the relative safety of their works along the Brock Road.[52]

That afternoon around 2 P.M., Burnside attacked W. F. Perry's Alabamians and Brig. Gen. Edward A. Perry's Floridians with two divisions north of the Tapp field. But reinforcements rushed in to help the Confederates hold their ground. Meade remarked that Burnside was "unable to produce any impression." That evening the Ninth Corps withdrew and took position between the Second and Fifth Corps.[53]

Along the Orange Turnpike to the north, opposing forces sparred throughout the day. The Federals attempted to turn Ewell's left and made heavy assaults on the Rebel line. Yet the entrenched Confederate positions made any significant progress impossible, dangerous, and untenable. Nevertheless, late in the day Ewell seized an opportunity to execute a flanking movement against the Union extreme right held by Sedgwick's Sixth Corps, the attack driving the Yankees from a large portion of their works. But as the momentum of the Confederate attack faded, the Federals rallied and eventually preserved the integrity of their line. The action ebbed as darkness fell, ending the Battle of the Wilderness. Both sides suffered heavily in the tactical draw. While estimates vary, Union casualties from the two days' fighting amounted to over 17,000, while the Confederates suffered around 11,000 killed, wounded, and missing.[54]

After their encounter with the veteran Fifteenth Alabama, the men of Kitching's brigade retraced their steps toward the Lacy house. During the withdrawal, they could see "the desperate fighting of our troops, who in some parts of the line were engaged in an awful hand to hand fight." As the heavies continued along the road, bullets whistled through the woods, "sometimes with a 'Zip' or a prolonged wail or a spat against a tree or other obstruction," until eventually "the woods seemed alive with the death dealing missiles." Arriving at the Parker's Store road junction, the brigade took position about three-quarters of a mile in front of the Lacy house in a line of earthworks constructed perpendicular to the Orange Turnpike. The Sixth took position on the left of the road and the Fifteenth on the right. At about 10 P.M. the enemy launched an assault on their position. After a short engagement, the Fifteenth "handsomely repulsed" the attacking Confederates. Maj. Washington Roebling, Warren's aide-de-camp, reported that the rebels established their line within about 100 yards of one advanced Fifth Corps regiment and spent most of the night hunting for water "and congratulating themselves upon the way in which they had made the Yankees run."[55]

The Fifteenth's metamorphosis from a garrison outfit in the Washington defenses to a combat regiment in the field had been culminated in the Wilderness. Although they wished things had gone better, the heavies had engaged the enemy as infantrymen for the first time. They, like other soldiers, would learn from the mistakes made in their first battle and apply those lessons on other battlefields. The heavies would have many opportunities to redeem themselves for their lackluster first performance and to prove their mettle as infantrymen.

CHAPTER THREE

To Spotsylvania Court House

The Fifteenth New York Heavy Artillery "layed . . . all night under fire" in the works near the road to Parker's Store. As dawn broke, Ewell's butternuts probed for weaknesses or gaps in the Union defenses. To Kitching's front, Rebels crept through the underbrush. Then, announced by "blood curdling yells," a long gray line, barely visible in the early morning light, lunged toward the Yankee works. Immediately, a battery to the right opened on them, cutting great swaths in the Rebel line. The Confederates staggered, halted, closed ranks, and with even fiercer yells resumed their advance. Sgt. Stephen Burger of the Sixth New York Heavy Artillery recalled that "the air was cut with canister and spherical case shell," which stopped the advancing infantry. "No longer able to withstand the terrible storm of iron which crashed in among them," Burger remembered, "they suddenly turned and made for Dixie as fast as their legs would carry them." Although most of the graycoats returned to their lines, Capt. Calvin Shaffer, commanding Company F of the Fifteenth, reported that "others appeared to suddenly grow very tired and lay down to rest, silent as the grave." After reaching the safety of their own works, "that terrible yell" again broke forth "from a thousand [Rebel] throats, as if to show us Yanks that, although repulsed, they were not subdued, that, though beaten back, they were not whipped."[1]

By early on May 7, Warren had decided to fill his defenses only with Fifth Corps units. He proposed to Humphreys the development of "a provisional line . . . on the other side of Wilderness Run facing west, near the edge of the wood." This position would be behind the one currently occupied and nearer to the Lacy house. "Batteries of Reserve Artillery might do this, and the heavy artillery move with them that I do not want (Colonel Kitching's I mean)." Thus, once relieved by men of the Fifth Corps, the Fifteenth heavies set to work building a second line of breastworks running "a short distance behind the first." Upon completion, the men rested until the afternoon.[2]

Meanwhile, Grant concluded that the two days' fighting in the Wilderness had forced Lee to recognize "his inability to further maintain the contest in the open field . . . and that he would await an attack behind his works." Early on the seventh, unwilling to accommodate his adversary's wishes, Grant decided that the Federals would try to draw the Confederates out of their defenses and into a general engagement in more open country, where the Union's superiority in men and artillery could be exploited. To lure Lee from his position, Grant set the small crossroads hamlet of Spotsylvania Court House, some ten miles to the southeast, as the Army of the Potomac's next objective. The movement would commence after dark.[3]

At 4 P.M. Fifth Corps troops relieved Kitching's brigade, which was "wanted with the Reserve Artillery." The heavies departed their newly constructed breastworks and rejoined the reserve in the vicinity of Wilderness Church. Burton's reunited command then marched toward Chancellorsville. Halting for a short rest as the twilight faded, many of the exhausted heavies quickly drifted off to sleep.[4]

Suddenly, the clattering of horses' hooves and the roaring of wheels from down the road, as if "a squadron of cavalry was upon us," awakened them. Every man sprang from the road "to escape he knew not what." Six runaway horses drawing a caisson or limber tore madly down the road toward Fredericksburg. "It flew by us like the wind," one soldier remembered, "and disappeared into darkness. The brigade resumed its march, following the Plank Road from Chancellorsville, swinging to the right into the Catharpin Road at Aldrich's and continuing south to Piney Branch Church just beyond the Ny River crossing. The heavies halted there around 4 A.M. after a twelve-hour march.[5]

The Fifth Corps began marching along the Brock Road toward Spotsylvania Court House at 9 P.M. As its vanguard approached Hancock's Second Corps headquarters, Grant and his staff with Meade and his wheeled into the road to lead the column. Grant later recalled that as they proceeded south down the Brock Road, "the greatest enthusiasm was manifested by Hancock's men." The soldiers, accustomed to retiring to regroup after major engagements with Lee's army, were "inspired by the fact that the movement was south. It indicated to them that they had passed through the 'beginning of the end' in the battle just fought."[6]

When he heard the distinctive sound of infantry moving along the Brock Road, Lee knew his adversary was heading south. He directed his new First Corps commander, Maj. Gen. Richard Heron Anderson, to march his troops south on a parallel road. The corps set out at 11 P.M., four hours earlier than ordered to commence the movement. These four hours were to prove of incalculable value to the Confederates as both sides raced toward Spotsylvania Court House.[7]

Soldiers encountered some of the trappings of antebellum life as they marched along the Brock Road. A little less than halfway between the Plank Road and Spotsylvania, at the intersection of the Brock and Catharpin Roads, sat Todd's Tavern. With a large porch, dirt floor, a fireplace at each end, and several outbuildings, its dilapidated wooden structure had seen better days. A residence as well as a tavern, it also had served the surrounding community as a store and post office. To the east from Todd's, the Catharpin Road ran past Piney Branch Church and over the Ny River toward Fredericksburg. To the west it crossed the Po River at Corbin's Bridge.[8]

When Grant and Meade arrived at Todd's Tavern shortly after midnight, they discovered Brig. Gen. David McMurtrie Gregg's and Brig. Gen. Wesley Merritt's cavalry divisions already there awaiting orders. Meade fumed, directing Merritt to immediately open the road heading south to Spotsylvania, "as an infantry corps is now on its way to occupy that place." The irascible army commander then issued a dispatch rebuking his cavalry commander, informing Maj. Gen. Philip Sheridan that he had taken matters into his own hands because the cavalry were "in the way of the infantry. . . . [T]here is no time to refer to you."[9]

The Fifth Corps's slow nighttime march along the dark and narrow Brock Road proved exceedingly difficult. Riding ahead of his column around 3 A.M., and despite Meade's instructions to Merritt, Warren discovered the road below Todd's Tavern still blocked by elements of Maj. Gen. Fitzhugh Lee's Rebel cavalry. Two hours lapsed without significant progress; Lee's cavalry had barricaded the road with felled trees and disputed every foot of ground. As he lost time to the roadblock, Warren grew increasingly impatient. Still unable to dislodge the Confederate defenders, about 6 A.M. the Federal cavalry, according to Warren, "gave it up . . . and got out of our way." He then pushed two divisions forward, instructing the lead division "to spare no effort to clear the road." At 8 A.M. Warren reported, "The opposition to us amounts to nothing as yet; we are advancing steadily."[10]

At about 8:30 A.M. the lead element of the Fifth Corps, Brig. Gen. John C. Robinson's division, emerged from the woods into the open ground of the Alsop farm, where the road split into two lanes for about a mile. Robinson advanced his command along the left fork, while behind him Brig. Gen. Charles Griffin's division moved out on the right fork. Where the roads reunited, Robinson reformed his line and advanced to a gradual slope within 200–300 yards of a tree line into which the road disappeared. Suddenly, Confederates unleashed intense artillery and musketry fire from an entrenched line just inside the woods. Staggered by the sudden blow, Robinson's men fell back in disarray, their division commander seriously wounded by a musket ball to his knee. As they advanced along the right fork, Griffin and his men also faced enemy fire. At 10:15 A.M. Warren informed Humphreys of the situation and that Rebel infantry now opposed his advance. Sheridan's failure to clear the way had allowed Rebel infantry to win the race to Grant's immediate objective, Spotsylvania Court House.[11]

More Confederates arrived on the field. Col. John W. Henagan had his brigade of South Carolinians entrench west of the Old Courthouse Road just inside the wood line along a low-lying ridge called Laurel Hill. This position overlooked the broad, gently rising fields of the Spindle farm as well as the road passing Alsop's farm. Confederate brigadier general Benjamin F. Humphreys formed his line in a wooded area east of the Old Courthouse Road, his left resting near the point where that road intersected the Brock Road. W. F. Perry's brigade of Field's Division soon joined Henagan, extending the line along the crest of Laurel Hill to his left. Before noon these units would repulse, "with great slaughter," uncoordinated assaults made by all four divisions of the Fifth Corps. With these repulses, Warren's bluecoats began throwing up breastworks at the northern end of the Spindle field opposite the Rebel line.[12]

Near noon, Sheridan approached Meade and his staff. Meade again scolded him for the cavalry's failure to clear the Brock Road. A member of Meade's staff reported that Sheridan "was plainly full of suppressed anger." Sheridan complained that "he could see nothing to oppose the advance of the 5th Corps" and that "the behavior of the infantry was disgraceful." Lyman would later speculate, "Maybe this [incident] was the beginning of [Sheridan's] dislike of Warren and ill-feeling against Meade."[13]

Hancock's corps waited for daylight on May 8 to begin its southward trek; lead elements of the Second Corps arrived at Todd's Tavern around 9 A.M. The general arrayed his outfit in a broad, west-facing arc centered on Todd's Tavern. Near 11 A.M., he sent Col. Nelson A. Miles's brigade and a brigade of Gregg's cavalry west out the Catharpin Road toward Corbin's Bridge on a reconnaissance mission. The expedition encountered Confederates about a half mile from the bridge on the high ground south of the Po River. At approximately 5:30 P.M. Brig. Gen. William "Little Billy" Mahone's brigade attacked Miles's outfit as it was withdrawing to Todd's Tavern. Hancock advanced a brigade in support and held the troops remaining at the tavern in readiness to march in that direction if Miles needed further assistance.[14]

Hunt, meanwhile, had directed Kitching's men, then resting at Piney Branch Church after their all-night march, to "be ready to move at a moments warning." At about the time Rebels attacked Miles's troops, Meade ordered Kitching's heavies to report to Hancock at Todd's Tavern. The brigade immediately set off on the two-and-one-half-mile trek, arriving at approximately 6:30 P.M. Hancock ordered the heavies to take position behind his line. Miles skillfully executed a fighting withdrawal, his troops repulsing Mahone while inflicting "severe loss upon him." With the immediate crisis averted, Hancock pondered what to do with the heavies. "I don't know the condition of the Artillery Reserve," he informed Humphreys at 7:30 P.M., "and I don't know whether to send back the heavy artillery if there is no assault tonight." After further thought he directed it to return, explaining, "I have two brigades in reserve and some little reserve elsewhere." Kitching's heavies trudged back up the Catharpin Road to the Piney Branch camps.[15]

The following morning Hancock again detected signs of a possible enemy advance along the Catharpin Road toward Todd's Tavern. Consequently, the First Brigade, Reserve Artillery once more traipsed to support the Second Corps. On the march at 7 A.M., Kitching's heavies retraced their steps to the tavern. Upon arrival, Hancock sent the brigade, supported by two guns detached from Capt. Edwin B. Dow's Sixth Maine Battery, about 800 yards out the Catharpin Road to picket the approaches to the tavern crossroads. Once there, the heavies busied themselves constructing breastworks.[16]

Around noon, with the perceived threat subsided and leaving behind Brig. Gen. Gersham Mott's division, the Second Corps moved southward toward Spotsylvania Court House. While informing Humphreys of leaving Mott in charge at Todd's Tavern, Hancock expressed uncertainty regarding whether to leave the heavies there or take them along as a reserve for his other three divisions. Meade advised him to "leave the heavy artillery with Mott, as they will be nearer to Piney Branch Church." Chief of Artillery Hunt subsequently notified Reserve Artillery commander Colonel Burton that Kitching's brigade was "not to be moved except in case of absolute necessity or by orders."[17]

Since leaving Brandy Station, Kitching's heavies had spent an inordinate time marching. Hunt noted, "From this time this brigade was marched to and fro from one corps to another, always being either in action or on the march until it was finally, on the breaking up of the [Artillery] Reserve, attached to the Fifth Corps, Major General Warren." Furthermore, he declared that the First Brigade had "done more marching than any infantry troops in the army so far." He recounted the movement across the Rapidan continuing beyond Chancellorsville to near Catherine Furnace, the immediate return to Chancellorsville, and the movement to Wilderness Church. They followed this march with another one to the front the next morning to support Wadsworth in the Wilderness, then withdrew to Warren's front that night. The subsequent move to Piney Branch Church, Hunt observed, required "14 hours on the march at night with trains." Then, upon finally arriving in camp early on May 8, the brigade "cleaned arms, got ready for service, pitched tents, and were at once ordered to strike them and be ready to move at a moment's warning," which they did as they moved to and from Todd's Tavern. "Their constant marching—their own duty as guard to the Res. Art.—their detail first to Genl. Warren then to Genl. Hancock and the constant alert on which they have been kept have deprived the men entirely of sleep. They are worn out and will continue so if thus fooled with." But Hunt's observations would not bring about an end to the heavies' constant marching and exhaustion.[18]

The continuous movement, of course, did not go unnoticed by the soldiers engaged in it. Amherst Belcher shared Hunt's view. After the war he complained, "we were used principally to patch up weak spots in the line, no matter where; that accounts for us being rushed the length of the line so frequently." In fact, Belcher remembered, before the fighting at Spotsylvania would be concluded, "our brigade . . . went from the right to the left, from the left to the right, and back to the left again." Of this period, Pvt. Carl Matteson of the Fifteenth similarly recalled "hard, hard marches. . . . [T]he clay was ankle deep on our last two night marches."[19]

That afternoon Meade instructed Hancock to transfer Mott's division to the left of the Sixth Corps, which had moved up on the Fifth Corps's left. Meade chose this position to prevent the enemy from interposing between the Sixth Corps and Burnside's Ninth Corps, now in position across the Fredericksburg Road to the east of and somewhat more than a mile from Spotsylvania Court House. He directed Hancock to "order [Mott] to leave at 3 A.M. tomorrow," adding that the heavy artillery brigade should then return to the Artillery Reserve. Mott informed Kitching that his division would depart "at 3 A.M. tomorrow" and that, as soon as he left, "you will call in your pickets and return again to Piney Branch Church." First, however, Kitching's heavies would spend a long night in the breastworks in front of Todd's Tavern.[20]

The night did not remain quiet. Captain Shaffer, commander of Company F, remembered that night as "dark and gloomy," with "the heavy timber and thick, dense undergrowth serv[ing] to intensify the gloom." He arranged with his second in command to stand the later watch, then drifted off to sleep. But the lieutenant soon awoke him inquiring whether the captain had heard "that yell." Sound asleep, Shaffer had heard nothing. The officer informed him of "an unearthly yell away off to the left" followed by what sounded like a pistol shot and then complete silence. Another man in the brigade described the noise as "the most frightful sound that ever penetrated human ears." As Shaffer shook himself awake, and absent any enemy activity, firing commenced in his own brigade, which progressed along the line from his left and seemed certain to reach his company soon. The captain hurried to the left of his outfit, reminded his men that they had pickets out front, and ordered them not to fire unless told to do so. He posted his lieutenant there to enforce the directive and worked his way to the right of the company, repeating the order as he passed along the line. When the firing reached the left of Company F, it ceased.[21]

To Shaffer's surprise, however, the shooting recommenced at the brigade's far right, held by the Sixth New York Heavies, and again progressed down the line from the opposite direction. He went through the same drill as he had initially, and at Company F the firing again halted.

Yet one soldier, who Shaffer characterized as "one of those men who never can learn to speak or fully understand our language," positioned near the center of the company commenced firing. The captain seized the man by the collar, yanked him out of the line, and snatched his musket from his hands, turning it over to the orderly sergeant. The sergeant, who spoke German, explained that the man had not understood the order, "and hearing so much firing thought he should have a hand in it" but now knew better. The soldier, in turn, pleaded for the return of his musket. Shaffer acceded to the request and received the man's "profuse thanks." The next morning Kitching delivered a "mild lecture" to his officers "on the evils and the demoralizing effects of night alarms and fusillades in the presence of the enemy." Although within hearing of all of the officers of the brigade, Shaffer opined that the colonel "addressed his remarks more particularly to his own officers." As ordered, early on the morning of May 10, the brigade pulled out and again retraced its steps to Piney Branch Church.[22]

By that afternoon the Confederate defensive line around Spotsylvania Court House stretched approximately seven miles, with virtually all of it entrenched except where it crossed water courses or main roads. Beginning about four miles west of the village, the line angled across and then paralleled the Shady Grove Church Road, crossed the Po River, and then followed the crest of Laurel Hill in the Fifth Corps's front. It traversed the Brock Road near its intersection with the Old Court House Road and continued in a generally northeasterly direction through the Sixth Corps's front for more than a mile. The line then turned abruptly to the southeast, crossing the Fredericksburg Road a quarter mile east of Spotsylvania. The line's abrupt change from a northeasterly to a southeasterly direction created a bulge that the men referred to as the salient or, owing to its odd shape, the "Mule Shoe."[23]

From late in the afternoon through the early evening of the tenth, Warren's corps, supported by two Second Corps divisions, launched attacks against the nearly impregnable Laurel Hill position. Rebel musketry and canister-spewing artillery swept the open ground to the Yankees' front. In some areas advancing Federals had to struggle through dense woods filled with a low growth of now dead cedar trees, whose sharply pointed branches stuck out in all directions. The disorganized Union ranks emerged from the woods into an open field raked by murderous Rebel fire. Although some of the attackers ultimately reached the Confederate positions, in the end, every assault that day failed, with the Yankees incurring heavy losses.[24]

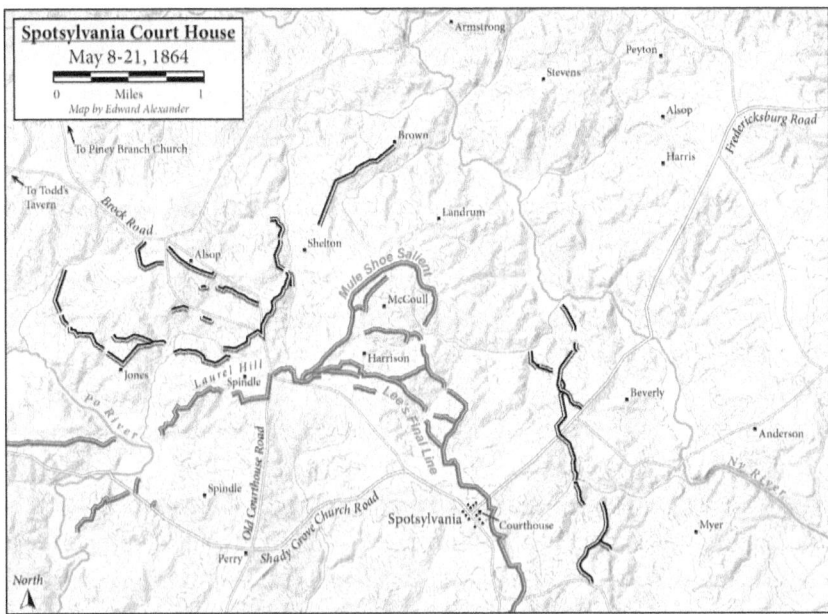

Kitching's heavies early that morning had returned to Piney Branch Church, where they brewed coffee and rested. Meanwhile, Hunt ordered Burton to dispatch an officer to the army's supply trains at Aldrich's to find out if they could exchange the Remington rifles that many of the foot artillery, including the men of the Fifteenth, carried for newer Springfield rifles. He directed the colonel "to take every opportunity to effect exchange, destroying the Remington rifles and accoutrements if necessary." Later that afternoon Hunt ordered two of the Coehorns to the extreme right of the Sixth Corps line near the point where a Confederate sharpshooter had killed Maj. Gen. John Sedgwick the day before. Despite this activity, most of Kitching's men got a chance to rest even as they heard the violent struggle along the lines.[25]

Just before 6:30 P.M. on May 10, as the rattle of musketry and the roar of artillery finally began to subside, Hunt again ordered Kitching's brigade forward, instructing the colonel to employ a strong advance guard and flankers on the right. After advancing two and a half miles down the road from Piney Branch Church to Alsop's, the heavies took position in open ground on the right of the Second Corps. Here, the line faced west, overlooking a small tributary of the Po River. The Coehorn wagons, carrying the six remaining mortars, were parked to their right in a field south of the Brock Road near the intersection. Although Meade had directed Hunt to send these Coehorns from the reserve late that morning so they could shell Confederate positions across the Po, the mortars still sat unused.[26]

Kitching's dispatch to the front stemmed from a desire to counter a perceived enemy flanking movement from the west and to protect army headquarters. Meade had established his command post across the Brock Road and about a half mile east from Kitching's new position. Earlier, Meade's staff had feared that Confederate forces threatened their position. Reports, which turned out to be inaccurate, that an enemy column had crossed the Po and was advancing around the army's right flank, held by the Second Corps, caused panic at headquarters. The staff hastily loaded the wagons and prepared for a rapid exit. Meade even ordered Hancock, in the process of preparing for a joint assault with the Fifth Corps, to defer his advance of any troops not already in motion so he could send a force to intercept any enemy interlopers. Grant, meanwhile, puzzled over the chaos, reportedly commenting, "I don't see any of these Greybacks." Calm returned when everyone realized the reports of the enemy advance were erroneous.[27]

A week of nearly constant marching and fighting had exhausted the men of the Army of the Potomac, so they welcomed a short respite on Wednesday, May 11. This gave them the opportunity to replenish their supplies—each man would receive two days' rations and fifty rounds of ammunition—as well as to rest as they prepared for the next phase in the campaign. The men could see and hear the wagons that traveled to the supply base at Belle Plain to the east of Fredericksburg and returned loaded with supplies. Other vehicles moved the thousands of wounded to Fredericksburg for treatment. Heavy rain fell that afternoon, the first rainfall since they had crossed the Rapidan. An officer in the Fourth New York Heavy Artillery recalled that at first "this rain was hailed as a relief from the dust and heat." But after it thoroughly soaked all the men and then became a nightlong drizzle, "our delight was somewhat modified."[28]

That morning Hunt had once more directed Kitching's brigade to report to Warren. Unlike the earlier assignment to the Fifth Corps, this would mark the beginning of a long relationship. Although the First Brigade had thus far served as infantry during the campaign, its primary responsibility remained guarding the Reserve Artillery and the army's ammunition train, for which Hunt ordered a battalion of Kitching's heavies to Aldrich's. Dieckmann's Second Battalion of the Fifteenth—Companies E, F, G, and H—drew the assignment, with Companies F, G, and H guarding the train and artillery and Company E remaining in charge of the Coehorn battery. Company B still remained at Brandy Station as provost guard, leaving only seven companies of the Fifteenth serving under Warren at the front. When Hunt ordered the mortars, still near the front, to rejoin the reserve at Aldrich's, the men of the Fifteenth's First and Third Battalions bade farewell to their comrades in the Second Battalion.[29]

As the troops rested and replenished, Grant made plans to launch an assault on the salient at the right-center of Lee's line. He ordered Meade to transfer, under cover of night, Hancock's three divisions from the far right of the Federal line to the left of the Sixth Corps. Once in position and reunited with Mott's division, the Second Corps would join Burnside's corps in a "vigorous" assault on the enemy at 4:00 A.M. the next morning, May 12. Hancock's men would form in the fields surrounding the Brown house, where open ground extended due south and over which the troops would attack the apex of the salient. Grant directed the Fifth and Sixth Corps commanders to "hold their corps as close to the enemy as possible to take advantage of any diversion" created by the attacks on the Confederate center and right and to "push in if the opportunity presents itself."[30]

After dark and in heavy rain, Hancock's three divisions began moving north. Navigating the narrow and difficult road in such conditions "rendered the marching extremely fatiguing for the men." As Hancock's men withdrew, Fifth Corps outfits replaced them by stretching to their right, significantly thinning the Union line in this sector. To help reinforce the position, at 3:00 A.M. Major Roebling brought Kitching's heavies farther forward, placing them on the right of the Fifth Corps in an area vacated by the Second Corps. In south-facing earthworks on the Jones farm overlooking the Po River, the brigade again took position near the extreme right of a much-shortened Federal line. Before daylight, Kitching sent a picket line down the slope to the Po, across the river, and up the hill on the south bank. They engaged with their Confederate counterparts and, although "the enemy opposed us stubbornly," as one of Kitching's men recalled, they "were forced to give way." After several hours the Union pickets returned to the north side of the river and discovered that the remainder of their brigade had vanished.[31]

The vanguard of Hancock's column reached the fields surrounding the Brown house shortly after midnight and formed grimly for the attack. From this position, some 1,200 yards from the Rebel entrenchments, the ground first descended and then ascended to the Confederate works.

With the exception of the open ground between the Brown house and the enemy's line, much of the advance would be through thick woods until the attackers got to the Landrum farm fields abutting the salient. The men "took position quietly and promptly, although it was an unusually dark and stormy night." An artillerist in the Second Corps observed that the formation created "almost a solid, rectangular mass of nearly twenty thousand men to hurl upon the enemy's works."[32]

Thursday, May 12, dawned foggy and rainy. The rain would persist throughout the day and into the night with varying intensity. The clouds, fog, and mist that blanketed the area at 4 A.M. made it too dark for an effective and coordinated advance, so Hancock postponed the attack until there was enough light to see. At 4:35 A.M. he ordered his division commanders to commence the assault.[33]

Grant and Meade anxiously awaited news from Hancock. At a quarter past five, Brig. Gen. Seth Williams, Meade's assistant adjutant general, approached his commander from the telegraph tent with a broad smile on his face and good news. Hancock's men had carried the first Confederate line at the salient. A half hour later they heard that a second line within the salient had also been taken. In the attack the Federals captured two Confederate generals, approximately 4,000 prisoners, twenty artillery pieces with horses and caissons, and more than thirty stand of enemy colors. Grant's chief of staff exulted: "By God! They are done! Hancock will just drive them to Hell." Shortly after 6 A.M. they received a report that Brig. Gen. Robert B. Potter's Second Division of Burnside's Ninth Corps had established a junction with Hancock's men at the east-facing Confederate fortifications at the Mule Shoe's base. Despite this initial success, Rebel enforcements soon began to pour into the salient.[34]

With his now disorganized outfit having lost momentum and the Rebels threatening to counterattack, Hancock called up two Sixth Corps divisions from their positions in the rear. Brig. Gen. Horatio G. Wright, commanding the corps following Sedgwick's death, sent his men into the west angle of the salient, which had become a writhing, tangled mess of bodies. In the constant rain men clung like leeches to the mud in the works. Dead lay everywhere, many torn to pieces by musketry and by canister fire from the few Federal guns near the works. As soldiers churned the muddy soil, they effectively buried the fallen at their feet. In this close space soldiers engaged in hand-to-hand combat using bayonets, clubbed muskets, and virtually anything else they could employ as a weapon. Often separated only by the parapets, opponents rose briefly to thrust their bayonets or fire directly into the faces of their antagonists. Throughout the battle, men covered in gore and blood trailed to the rear. The dead lay in hideous heaps, sometimes with wounded trapped beneath them and suffocating in the blood-saturated mud.[35]

Meanwhile, hunkered down against the rain in their breastworks overlooking the Po, Kitching's men at daybreak had heard to their left "a crash of musketry—quick, short and decisive." Soon after, they received news that their Union comrades had taken the Rebel line and captured numerous enemy soldiers and artillery pieces. Then "a cheer—a real Yankee cheer—broke from a thousand throats." This celebration "was taken up and carried along by each successive Brigade until it reached us." After the cheering ceased the firing recommenced, the volume of musketry increasing as command after command became engaged. Soon "the roar of artillery, the crashing of small arms, all the fearful adjuncts of a terrible battle made the woods ring, echo and reverberate with a noise such as Pandemonium itself could only equal, never surpass."[36]

As the first of Wright's divisions went forward, Meade directed Warren to "keep up as threatening an attitude as possible to keep the enemy in your front." Although the high command could not confirm that the enemy had left their entrenchments in the Fifth Corps's front, clearly large numbers of Confederate reinforcements were rushing into the salient. Further, Burnside's simultaneous attack on the Mule Shoe's east face seemed to pin down the enemy in that sector. Consequently, both Meade and Grant concluded that the enemy in Warren's front could not be strong. This belief was heightened when, by 7:30 A.M., Wright encountered heavy resistance. They decided to attack the Confederate left to hold enemy troops there and prevent further reinforcement of the salient. Meade informed Warren, "your attack will in a measure relieve [Wright], but you must also support him with some of your troops." At 8 A.M. he ordered Warren to "attack immediately, with all the force you can, and be prepared to follow up any success with the rest of your force."[37]

Despite his orders, Warren did not attack immediately. Knowing the strength of the entrenched position held by the enemy on the Laurel Hill front, he asked the army commander to consider the untenable position created for his troops by an advance. Meade refused to budge: "The order of the Major General commanding is peremptory that you attack at once at all hazards with your whole force, if necessary." Left with no alternative,

Warren ordered his divisions forward. Then, in an about-face at 10 A.M., Humphreys told Warren: "The major-general commanding infers from the tenor of your dispatches that, in your judgment, your attack will not be successful." If the attack failed, the missive continued, Warren should withdraw and immediately send his troops to support Wright and Hancock. Before long, reports from division and brigade commanders revealed what Warren had known all along. He suspended the failing attack and withdrew, but not before the Fifth Corps sustained heavy casualties.[38]

Meanwhile, shortly before Warren had attacked, around 9 A.M. an aide dashed up to the Kitching's headquarters. The colonel was directed to move his brigade to the left to reinforce Wright's line near the salient. The heavies left so quickly that their still forward-deployed picket line remained in place beyond the Po River.[39]

As Kitching's outfit neared the salient, bullets whistled through the ranks, over the heavies' heads, and under their feet. From time to time a man cried out in pain, signaling "a ticket for a furlough" for that soldier. One injured soldier in the Sixth New York Heavy dropped his musket, clutched his right arm with his left hand, and moved to the rear. As the troops got closer to the action, they encountered a steady stream of wounded heading in the opposite direction. Sergeant Burger remembered that "ghastly wounds, blood marking footsteps through the leafy ground, groans and cries of anguish attested but too well the fearful tragedy that was being enacted at the Slaughter Pen on that dismal, rainy May morning." As the brigade rushed ahead, the wounded flooding to the rear warned them, "it's a hot place in there. Give them H . . . , boys!" The heavies arrived in rear of the Sixth Corps's position at the salient near 10:30 A.M. Kitching, wearing "a very tall felt [hat], the brim turned down to shed the rain," formed his brigade in two lines in open space on the edge of the woods just to the right of Wright's command post. Despite the fearful situation, he "rode in a cheery manner" and, once he had organized his men, reported to Wright.[40]

Kitching then led his men into the battle. He sent forward a squad of his heavies to man two artillery pieces advanced earlier toward the enemy lines. Probably the section commanded by Lt. Richard Metcalf, Fifth US Artillery, the guns had delivered a devastating fire of double canister until, as Lyman reported, the crews "were shot off."[41]

Shortly after noon Kitching advanced his brigade into a sheltered dip in the woods to the right of Col. Emory Upton's brigade. He ordered the heavies to lie down and cover themselves as best they could, and if the line in front of them broke, they were to let the remnants pass over them before they moved forward. The brigade lay there all day without "a moment's cessation of that death-dealing storm of lead and iron" or rain and with "the air . . . thick with the flying messengers of death." Shells crashed through the trees above them, lopping of huge limbs and bursting everywhere. Bullets struck trees "with a spiteful splat, or some poor unfortunate comrade with a horrible thud." Even with the flying projectiles and the fierce fighting in front of them, some of the men fell asleep, thoroughly exhausted from the previous eight days. In one case, Burger recalled, "a bullet crashed through the brains" of a comrade "who, having fallen asleep, was awakened by it in another world."[42]

That afternoon the Fifteenth's Company E brought up their battery of Coehorn mortars. Moving in on the left-rear of Col. Henry W. Brown's

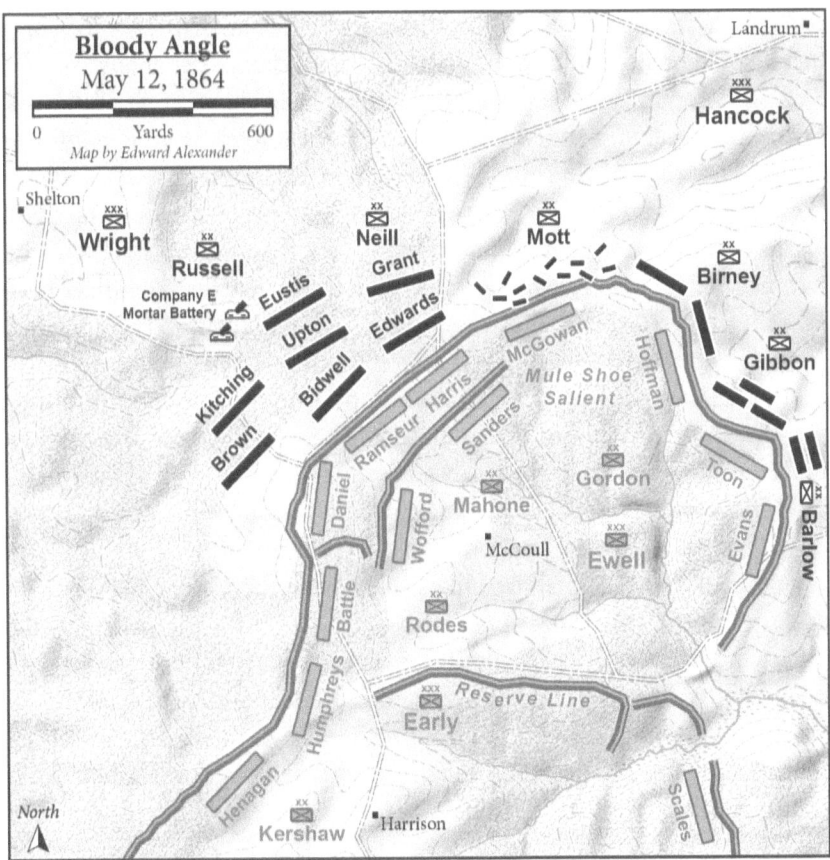

"Jersey Brigade" of Brig. Gen. David A. Russell's Sixth Corps division, and with Upton's brigade to their front, the heavies prepared their pieces for action. "A plucky, but rather green Dutch officer" commanded the battery, observed one of Upton's men. Although they took position at what the infantrymen considered a relatively safe distance from the front, several bullets sang through the air near the officer, who "jumped up in the air, and, clasped his hands to his ears." He cried, "'Oh my-my-that just skipped mine ear,'" eliciting "merry peals of laughter" from the infantrymen.[43]

The bullets continued to fly, and the heavies soon opened with the mortars. One man in Upton's brigade recalled, "Having obtained perfect range, the motor shells were dropped into that angle with fearful effect, completely silencing, at that point, the heretofore troublesome customers . . . , a result devoutly to be desired." Another of Upton's men recalled that the mortars "sent their shells with admirable precision gracefully curving over us." The men in the Jersey Brigade also witnessed the bombardment, and "bets [were] being made whether an arm or a foot or a head would be thrown into the air" upon explosion of the shells.[44]

Brig. Gen. Nathanial Harris's Mississippi Brigade was one of the outfits on the receiving end of this mortar barrage. Rushed in as reinforcements, and wished "God speed" by Lee when passing the McCoull house, the brigade spent the day in the west angle of the salient on the Sixth Corps's front, the area later called the "Bloody Angle." Throughout the day, piles of corpses accumulated so frequently there that an officer periodically ordered "clear the ditch." Soldiers leapt to their feet and pitched from the earthworks the bodies of both the Rebel and Yankee dead. Although Confederate private David Holt thought that the mortar rounds mostly either overshot or undershot their targets and fell harmlessly to his rear or among Yankees hunkered to the ground in front of the works, the growing numbers of corpses showed that not all went astray. At one point a perfectly aimed Coehorn shell burst between two men of Holt's regiment sitting to the right of their colors with their backs to the works and their feet in the ditch. The explosion blew one of the men into the ditch "in fragments" and took off the other's head without moving the body. Holt watched in horror as a severed artery in the headless body "spurted a fountain of blood, high at first, but lower with each succeeding pulsation of the heart." When the officer ordered "clear the ditch," Holt sprang to his feet to cast out the corpses.[45]

Meanwhile, as the fighting raged at the salient, after the morning's unsuccessful attack against Lee's left, Humphreys, now overseeing the Army of the Potomac's right, had directed Warren to send Brig. Gen. Lysander Cutler's division to Wright and be ready to follow with his entire corps. Cutler's troops supported Wright's corps in the early afternoon, with Griffin's division close behind. Left alone to hold not only the Fifth Corps line but also a portion of the Sixth Corps's entrenchments vacated by Ricketts's division, Brig. Gen. Samuel W. Crawford extended his division's ever-thinning line to the left. But before the Fifth Corps mounted yet another attack, late in the afternoon the Federal high command abandoned further assaults on the salient, realizing their futility. Burnside's attacks from the east were also unsuccessful. Meade later reported the Ninth Corps efforts as "without any other decisive results than keeping occupied a large force of the enemy." Eventually, night ended the carnage and temporarily cloaked the fearful scene. The next morning the Federals discovered that Lee had abandoned the Mule Shoe.[46]

When Holt and his fellow Mississippians left their position at the Bloody Angle early on May 13, he paused to cast a final glance over the ghastly picture. As it continued to drizzle, a mist hung over everything. Holt saw an oak tree, twenty-two inches in diameter, severed completely by the volume of small-arms fire that had filled the air the previous day. He also saw the bloody ditch filled with dead and wounded. "One wounded man was cursing, another praying to the Blessed Virgin"; others cried for water and some begged to have the dead moved off of them. "I don't expect to go to hell," Holt later reflected, "but if I do, I am sure that Hell can't beat that terrible scene."[47]

Curiosity about the previous day's battle brought other soldiers to visit the site, too. In the morning some of the New Jersey men went over the breastworks to examine the results; they returned sickened. Rain had half-filled the trenches, turning them, as one of the men recalled, into "a narrow canal of blood" and covering many of the dead. Some of the wounded lay partially submerged; witnesses observed every conceivable type of wound. Although many of the wounded lay helpless, the New Jersey boys assisted those who could walk and carried the helpless ones to a more sheltered spot. An officer in Kitching's brigade described the sight in the Rebel rifle pits as "horrible and sickening." The dead and wounded, "in some places four and five tiers deep," filled the trenches. "One Rebel

Lieutenant lay a short distance to the rear of the rifle pit," he reported, "with 21 bullet holes in his body and an iron ramrod through his neck." Another soldier described how "one poor rebel soldier" had been killed when a tree limb, "which had been cut off by bullets, fell, passing through the soldier's head, as he lay upon the ground, pinning him to the earth." A man from the Fifth Maine observed: "The shells of the mortar had been terribly effective. It was sight from which the hardest heart recoiled."[48]

After the war Amherst Belcher of the Fifteenth described the dreadful scene he encountered. "The only place I ever saw dead soldiers piled up was at the close of this battle," he remembered. "The enemy fought from behind breastworks, and all their dead were close behind them where they had been thrown back out of the way, while our dead covered a space equivalent to the range of a rifle."[49]

Although the struggle for the salient was over, the battles in and around Spotsylvania Court House continued. Grant had gained some advantage, but he had not broken the stalemate. Kitching's heavies witnessed the most brutal fighting of the war so far and were adapting to their new role as infantry. They would be put to the test again before the armies rolled on, leaving the Spotsylvania battlefield behind them.

CHAPTER FOUR

To the Harris Farm

Early in the morning on May 13, and still in positon near the salient, J. Howard Kitching reassured his wife, "I thank God, I am still alive, and able to write you a line, for I know that you must be terribly anxious." He described himself as "sitting in the mud and rain, the very dirtiest object you ever beheld." It had been a mere nine days since his brigade and the Army of the Potomac had crossed the Rapidan, and of this brief period he reflected: "We have all been going through the most terrible experiences for the past week, reaching the climax yesterday and last night. The world never saw such fighting. Both sides feel this to be the last struggle and contend with a fierceness that is awful." The colonel had made it through, but "our losses have been fearful." He confided, "I am not well, darling, and after the excitement is over will probably feel worse." The recent events haunting him, Kitching mused, "Would that this were the last of this terrible struggle!"[1]

After spending the night awake because of the relentless rain, the men in Griffin's and Cutler's Fifth Corps divisions retuned to Warren on the morning of May 13. At 7:45 A.M. Sixth Corps commander Wright reminded Meade's chief of staff, Brigadier General Humphreys, that Kitching's command was still with him and inquired, "What shall I do with them?" Kitching also noted, "General Wright . . . does not require me any longer," so he asked Meade's assistant adjutant general, Seth Williams, if he and his men could rejoin the Artillery Reserve. Later that morning, at Williams's direction, Wright "order[ed] Colonel Kitching, Sixth New

York Artillery, commanding brigade of heavy artillery, to send a battalion of his command to report to the commander of the Artillery Reserve near Tabernacle Church, and with the remainder of his troops to report to Major-General Warren, commanding Fifth Corps." Williams quickly informed Warren of the changes.[2]

New orders in hand and the brigade relieved, Kitching's heavies headed back to Warren's front on the right. As the men trudged through the mud, wet and tired, they approached an approximately mile-wide opening in the woods. While the heavies moved through this clearing, a Confederate battery spotted them, and as an officer in the brigade remembered, "the Rebs commenced to shell us quite hard and kept it up until we had got out of reach." The many shells that rained down on them had little effect on the exhausted troops. After reaching the Fifth Corps's sector, the brigade again took position on the extreme right. Later that afternoon the two regiments took up a new line to the west and north of the Alsop house to guard against an enemy movement toward the Union rear. The men then set about their now familiar task of felling trees and building log breastworks.[3]

Meanwhile, Grant's main concern remained the Army of Northern Virginia, which, with the salient eliminated, was now hunkered behind a contracted and inherently stronger line along the base of the old Mule Shoe. He concluded, "We must get by the right flank of the enemy for the next fight." Accordingly, Meade directed Warren to move the Fifth Corps immediately after dark, by way of Shelton's and Landrum's houses, then via a narrow, muddy farm road through dense woods, to a ford across the Ny River about one-half mile east of the Landrum place. Swinging southward, the corps would march cross-country to the Fredericksburg Road, then southwest along that road toward Spotsylvania Court House. Recrossing the Ny, Warren would form his command on the left of the Ninth Corps and attack the Confederate position at 4 A.M. the following morning, May 14. The Sixth Corps would follow the Fifth and mass on Warren's left to simultaneously strike along the Massaponax Church Road. As a distraction, Hancock's and Burnside's corps would assume "a threatening attitude."[4]

Grant's ambitious plan depended upon rapid movement, undetected by the enemy, followed by a vigorous and decisive attack. But as Warren's aide Major Roebling saw it, "we were expected to march all night, get into position on the left of Burnside's in an unknown country, in the midst of an Egyptian darkness, up to our knees in the mud, and assault the enemy's position which we had never seen, at 4 o'clock in the morning, in conjunction with the 9th Corps who had been whipped the day before, and felt in fine spirits for such work." At 8:10 P.M. Warren ordered his corps to move at once. Griffin's division led, followed by Cutler's and Crawford's commands. Next came Col. Richard Bowerman's Maryland Brigade and then Kitching's heavies. Warren directed his officers "to make every exertion to keep their men closed up regardless of the mud" because "success depends on it, and [so does] the saving of many lives."[5]

Under normal conditions, even large bodies of troops could execute a seven-mile march in as many hours. But conditions this night were far from normal. It was rainy and so intensely dark that, according to Humphreys, "literally you could not see your hand before your face." To contend with the darkness, Warren had fires built along the line of march, but these were of little or no avail as the heavy rain and mist obscured and extinguished them. The soldiers struggled through deep mud for much of the route. "The fatigue of floundering along in such a sea of mud but few can apprehend," Humphreys observed. Grant recalled the roads were so bad that the troops had to cut trees and corduroy them a part of the way just to get through.[6]

The exhaustion of the men in the Fifth Corps further slowed their progress. Many of them had spent the previous night awake in the mud and rain near the salient, and large numbers fell asleep along the route. Kitching's heavies, marching at the rear of the long column, would have to maneuver through mud churned into a deep, gooey paste by the shoes of the thousands before them. They did not get started until around 11 P.M. and then marched, as one officer remembered, "all night through the mud knee deep." Another man similarly described the difficult and exhausting march: "Night dark, roads muddy, we moved drearily along until daylight."[7]

Although Grant planned the attack to start at 4 A.M., the troops were not yet in place at that hour. At Warren's Beverly house headquarters, the vanguard of the Fifth Corps was only then trickling in. The nightlong mud march had taken a severe toll. Most of the men fell out of ranks from sheer exhaustion, and part of the column lost its way. The general realized, "I have nothing to go forward, for those who have come up are excessively weary." Indeed, initially only about 1,000 men, a number he considered "not more than would make a good skirmish line for the corps," had made it through. At 6:30 A.M., as fatigued men not "in condition to fight to advantage" continued to straggle in, Warren asked Humphreys for "any further directions." He was told that Meade still wanted him to "make your dispositions to attack and report as soon as you are ready."[8]

Exhausted stragglers continued to arrive at Beverly's and form in the fields surrounding the house. Finally, at 8 A.M. Warren informed Humphreys, "My men are nearly all in the position I wish them." His assembled 5,000 men included about 1,000 of Kitching's troops. The weary, wet, and muddy heavies, with their Fifth Corps comrades, waited for the command to move forward. To their surprise, at 9 A.M. they received word that their commanders had suspended the attack. Instead of advancing en masse, the bulk of the troops concealed themselves as best they could while skirmishers probed to ascertain the enemy's strength and position.[9]

Kitching's brigade remained near the Beverly house, a neat, L-shaped structure surrounded by broad fields extending from it down to the river. Perched on high ground known as Whig Hill west of the Ny and a quarter mile southeast from the Fredericksburg Road, it afforded an excellent view of the Confederate positions near the crossroads village. On a hill—Bleak or Myer's Hill—a mile southeast of the Beverly house stood the two-story Myer house. At the time the residence was occupied by Mrs. Myer and her three children, along with a caretaker named Jett; Mr. Myer was but a few miles away serving in Lee's army. Warren, peering through his field glasses, viewed Myer's Hill from the upper story of the Beverly house and discovered it occupied by Rebel cavalry and artillery. He realized that the enemy's presence there made the Union position around the Beverly house untenable. Grant and Meade, viewing from the Anderson house, also noted the threat. At Meade's behest, Warren ordered Lt. Col. Elwell S. Otis to take his 140th New York Infantry Regiment and the Ninety-First Pennsylvania of Brig. Gen. Romeyn B. Ayres's First Division brigade and capture the position.[10]

Around 8:00 A.M. Otis charged the Confederates on Myer's Hill. Watching from near the Beverly house, Sgt. Stephen Burger, one of Kitching's heavies, "could see our boys as they made a dash across an open field." As a Union battery to his left sent shells into a wooded area, which "seemed full of greybacks," Rebel guns "returned the compliments of the season in the shape of Rail Road iron." Burger remembered one of the missiles "striking the ground a few rods in our front, [and it] hurtled with a terrifying noise over our heads and fell into the woods behind us." The

Confederate rounds continued to pass over and around the heavies, sometimes landing uncomfortably close, creating "an evident desire on the part of those in the immediate vicinity to evade a too close acquaintanceship with these uncaring visitors." The fight for Myer's Hill escalated as additional troops from both sides rushed in. The Federals eventually secured the position after a seesaw struggle lasting much of the day.[11]

The transfer of the Fifth and Sixth Corps to the east of Spotsylvania Court House had shifted the axis of the Federal army farther to Lee's right. For this reason, on the afternoon of May 12, Hunt ordered the Reserve Artillery eastward toward Fredericksburg to the vicinity of Tabernacle Church. Then, on the fifteenth, Meade's adjutant general Williams directed Major Dieckmann's battalion of the Fifteenth, guarding the reserve, to immediately move to the intersection of the Telegraph Road with the Spotsylvania and Fredericksburg Road and "extend its pickets well on both roads" to provide warning of any enemy movement in the rear toward the reserve and its trains.[12]

Despite its valuable service, the Army of the Potomac's Reserve Artillery had now became superfluous. Grant realized that the army had more artillery than it needed. The reserve "occupied much of the road in marching, and taxed the trains in bringing up forage." Although it proved "very useful when it can be brought into action," he considered it "a very burdensome luxury when it cannot be used." Consequently, on May 16, according to Hunt, "superior orders" directed that the Reserve Artillery be "broken up." Lt. Col. Freeman McGilvery remained in command of the army's ammunition train, with Dieckmann's Second Battalion still serving as train guard.[13]

A day prior to the reserve's dissolution, Kitching protested the increasingly "awkward" position in which he and his command found themselves as they moved between corps. Not foreseeing what the reserve's future held, he hoped "that either my Command be placed in a different position or that I may be relieved from command of it." The colonel complained that since ordered to report to Warren on May 6, "I have reported to and been engaged with every Corps of this Army." He emphasized the problems arising from these constant details. "This continual changing of position of my Command through out [sic] the entire lines of the Army has rendered it utterly impossible to get at my wagons or rations for my men." As a result, "I have twice been in action without either Ambulances or Stretchers. . . . Being so far from my proper Corps (The

Artillery Reserve) I have no regular medical supplies or transportation for my sick." He also stressed the lack of food resulting from these constant changes. "From same Cause my Officers as well as my self [sic] have had nothing to eat other than rations obtained from the men." Although Kitching understood the reason for these shortages, "the cause of all this . . . is not so apparent to the officers and men of my Brigade and . . . I consider it impossible to properly provide for them so long as I am not definitely assigned to some Command." As a result, he concluded, as a commander, "I am placed under the circumstances in the most trying position . . . and I earnestly beg that these facts may be considered, and that I be in some way relieved from the awkwardness of my position."[14]

Williams agreed with Kitching's grievances and transmitted the letter to Hunt, who referred it to Colonel Burton, the Artillery Reserve's commander. When he forwarded the letter, Williams stressed that the brigade of heavies "should have been accompanied by its proper proportion of ambulances and authorized supplies" when it went to the front. He tried to rectify this oversight, directing that "these will now be sent forward with as little delay as practicable." In the end, the brigade's permanent assignment to the Fifth Corps resolved Kitching's "awkward" position. The Fifteenth New York Heavy Artillery would now serve in the independent Heavy Artillery Brigade within the Fifth Corps, Kitching reporting directly to Warren.[15]

On May 15 Kitching's brigade—fifty-seven officers and 1,966 men—enjoyed a welcome respite from the almost constant hard marching and fighting that had filled the days since departing Brandy Station. Although late that afternoon both the Fifth and Sixth Corps received orders to prepare to attack the enemy to their front, after the men spent several hours in line of battle, their commanders again rescinded the order. The troops finally had the opportunity to relax. One sergeant described Sunday, May 15, as "remarkably quiet" and the next day as "another calm, restful day." Others agreed. When writing about the sixteenth, Cpl. William Daily observed: "Day fine. Quiet all day."[16]

Pvt. Carl Matteson seized the opportunity to write to a friend about his experiences. "We have been marching and fighting for eight consecutive days and hard hard marches to, the clay was ankle deep on our last two nights march." He also reported the loss of close friends in Company M: "My Chum was killed beside me at Mine Run two other fellow tentors of mine are wounded." In addition to the mud and the casualties, the "quartermaster burned our hard tack, so we were a little short of grub." Matteson opined that these problems did not discourage the soldiers, who would do "anything to put the rebellion down, the boys all feel tip top and go in strong for Old Abe and Grant." He hopefully predicted, "We are bound to clean out the Johneys this time."[17]

As a result of the heavy losses during the campaign, Grant needed additional men to replenish the ranks of the Army of the Potomac. Chief of Staff Halleck identified thousands of troops to send forward as replacements. Soon on its way to the front was a division of heavy artillery, which included the First Maine and the First Massachusetts as well as the Second, Seventh, and Eighth New York. Commanded by Brig. Gen. Robert O. Tyler, an experienced and well-respected officer, the division reached the Army of the Potomac late on May 17 and joined the Second Corps as infantry. Designated the Fourth Division, it infused the corps's depleted ranks with thousands of fresh, but untried, troops.[18]

Grant and Meade elected to launch a simultaneous attack by both the Second and Sixth Corps against the new Confederate line across the base of the Mule Shoe at 4:00 A.M. on May 18. The shift of Hancock's and Wright's outfits to the right in preparation for the attack left the Fifth Corps holding the left flank of the Union line. Col. Charles S. Wainwright, commander of the Fifth Corps's artillery, positioned four of his batteries on the Andersen house plateau, located across the Ny and about a mile east of the Beverly house. From there his gunners not only could provide fire support for the attack but also, as Wainwright noted, "had a beautiful position completely protecting our left rear, where the country was all open." Kitching's brigade, augmented by the temporary assignment to it of Companies D, H, and K of the Second Battalion, Fourth New York Heavy Artillery, which had been serving in Wainwright's Artillery Brigade, left its position near the Fredericksburg Road to support these batteries. The Heavy Artillery Brigade reached the vicinity of the Anderson house shortly before the attack began. Kitching then deployed detachments along the Ny below the guns and extending down the river to the left, including about 100 men of the Fifteenth under the command of Lt. Gustave Schimmel of Company I.[19]

One of these detachments was to locate and connect with the cavalry supposed to be picketing along the Ny on the army's extreme left. At 8:00 A.M. Kitching reported that after having proceeded down the river a distance of two miles, the patrol had not encountered the enemy or any

Federal cavalry. "I have sent out another party to advance still further," he assured Warren, and would report again upon their return. Kitching's men eventually did locate the cavalrymen. Later in the morning the troopers reported that the Confederates had thrown out a strong line of skirmishers, advancing "with heavy support" toward their front. At 11:15 A.M. Kitching transmitted this intelligence to Warren. The general, however, correctly concluded that no concerted push was under way, and the Rebels were only responding to the Federals' shift to the right, which was "plainly visible" to them.[20]

Having arrived near Landrum's before daylight that morning, Hancock deployed Barlow's and Gibbon's divisions in front. Tyler's recently arrived heavies and Birney's division remained in reserve. With the Sixth Corps on Hancock's right, the assault began at 4 A.M. as planned. As the blue-clad battle line advanced, the stench of rotting flesh from those who had fallen within the Mule Shoe six days earlier was sickening. "The appearance of the dead who had been exposed to the sun so long, was horrible to the extreme," Hancock reported, "a sight never to be forgotten by those who witnessed it." Although the attackers persisted in the face of a withering fire, they could not breach the formidable Confederate entrenchments. By 9 A.M. they abandoned the attack. Wright's corps returned to its former position on the Fifth Corps's left. The Second Corps, with the exception of Tyler's division, withdrew and occupied a line of entrenchments in front of the Landrum house. Tyler's heavies recrossed the Ny ahead of Wright's corps.[21]

Kitching's brigade headed back to its camp near the Fredericksburg Road around 3 P.M. The site lay west of the road and north of where it crossed the Ny River, not far from the Clement Harris house and farm. Later that day Tyler's heavy artillery division took position along the Fredericksburg Road in rear of the Fifth Corps, not far from the Heavy Artillery Brigade. When Kitching's men withdrew from around the Anderson house earlier that afternoon, Schimmel's detachment remained in position along the Ny. They did not rejoin the regiment until the evening of May 19.[22]

Although the Army of Northern Virginia emerged from the more than ten days of fighting in and around Spotsylvania Court House severely mauled, on May 18 that army held a strongly entrenched interior position and remained a very dangerous opponent. Understanding his enemy's resilience and hoping to break the stalemate, Grant conceived of an alternative to merely bludgeoning Lee's line. He surmised that if he sent one corps some twenty miles south toward Richmond, he could trick his opponent into attacking the isolated corps. If Lee took the bait, Grant would then rapidly dispatch the remainder of the Federal army to engage the Confederates before they could entrench. If he did not pursue the isolated corps and once this became apparent, then the balance of Grant's forces would pull out and move south toward the North Anna River, thereby converting the operation into simply another turning movement to which Lee would be forced to respond. That afternoon Grant ordered Meade to implement the plan by dispatching Hancock's Second Corps toward Bowling Green.[23]

The plan called for Hancock's and Burnside's corps to withdraw before daylight on the nineteenth. While the Ninth Corps slipped to the left of the Sixth to occupy the left of the Union line, the Second would take up a position as if to support the Sixth and Ninth. At midnight or shortly thereafter on May 20, Hancock's corps would move quickly toward the Confederate capital along the Richmond, Fredericksburg, and Potomac Railroad. Lee's response would then dictate the Federals' next move.[24]

Hancock's and Burnside's withdrawals would leave only the Fifth Corps to protect the right of the Federal position. As Meade forewarned Warren, during this operation, "There will be nothing to your right or rear." As a result, he advised, "you had better send a brigade to the Harris house or vicinity to keep a watch." Warren resolved to "send Colonel Kitching to the point you have indicated." He also informed Meade that his own right flank, held by Cutler's division, remained entrenched in the southwestern quadrant of the intersection between the Fredericksburg Road and the Ny River.[25]

Warren directed Kitching to shift his brigade to the vicinity of the Harris house at daybreak and to "picket very strong our right flank from General Cutler's right flank on the Ny River outside the country north as far as you can, covering the pike to Fredericksburg." He further cautioned the colonel, "All our troops are going to be moved to the left of our corps." Thus, he gave the Heavy Artillery Brigade primary responsibility for protecting the army's right flank, the supply trains parked along the Fredericksburg Road, and the main line of supply and communication back to Fredericksburg. The heavies would also shield the headquarters of the Army of the Potomac and the general in chief, situated just across the Fredericksburg Road from Kitching's assigned position.[26]

As directed, Kitching deployed his brigade early on May 19. He placed the Fifteenth New York in choppy, wooded ground about 400 yards southwest of the Harris house and the Sixth New York on its left, nearer the Ny. The line rested about 800 yards northwest of and roughly parallel to the Fredericksburg Road. Both outfits threw out pickets, and by 9:00 A.M. those of the Sixth, with some difficulty, successfully located and connected with Cutler's picket line across the Ny to their left and south. The three companies of the Fourth New York Heavy Artillery now serving in Kitching's outfit took a detached positon farther to the right. Their left flank was situated about 300 yards west of the Harris house, which at the time was occupied by Harris, his wife, and their three children. This left a several-hundred-yard-gap between the Fourth's left and the right of the Fifteenth. From that point the Fourth's line extended to the north beyond the neighboring Susan Alsop house—the twenty-five-year-old widow and her four-year-old child were inside—and then curved back to intersect the Fredericksburg Road near the Peyton house. One company and about half of another of the Fourth formed the picket, while the rest of the men remained near the Alsop house. Kitching later reflected, "I made my dispositions as well as I could, but from the length of the line which I was required to hold, I had to scatter my brigade too much." At 9:00 A.M. General Humphreys informed Warren that a detachment of 500 cavalry, with which Kitching was to communicate, covered the right flank. He also advised the corps commander that Tyler's newly arrived "infantry" division resting near army headquarters was being "held ready for any service required of it."[27]

Thursday, May 19, had dawned clear and sunny. As Kitching's men settled in, they continued with their everyday tasks. In the morning some of the heavies prepared to butcher an ox they had driven around with them for many days. To some, the animal now seemed almost a pet, and one of the men remarked that it seemed a pity to slaughter the old fellow. "Gettin' tender-hearted, eh?" replied the butcher, quipping, quite prophetically, "I shouldn't wonder if you fellers would be a-killin' men afore night."[28]

Meanwhile, the Confederates had little firm intelligence concerning their opponents' latest movements. From the evidence they had gathered for him, Lee suspected that Grant had abandoned his positions opposite the Confederate left to shift his forces south to the Federal left. Alarmed that this movement might place the enemy in a position to interpose his force between his army and Richmond, Lee decided to definitively establish the location of the Union right. To this end, he directed Ewell, whose Second Corps held the Confederate left, to "demonstrate" against the Union line to his front.[29]

Fearing a costly encounter with a strongly entrenched enemy, Ewell sought and received permission to instead take his entire corps—by now of greatly diminished manpower—on a sweeping reconnaissance in force around the Union flank. That afternoon the Second Corps slipped out of its works along the base of the old Mule Shoe and marched up the Brock Road, swinging right onto the Gordon Road. After crossing the Ny near the Armstrong house, Ewell again turned the column to the right and proceeded southeast on farm roads to the charred ruins of the Stevens house, where his troops paused. Ahead, another farm road led directly to the Harris house, beyond which was the Union rear along the Fredericksburg Road. Not quite midway between the Stevens and Harris houses, the farm road crossed a tributary of the Ny running generally parallel to the Fredericksburg road and was, at its head near the Peyton farm, quite marshy.[30]

Union forces detected troubling indications of Ewell's movement. In command of the cavalry detachment guarding the army's flank, Maj. George A. Forsyth reported at 12:30 P.M. that the enemy had "made quite a demonstration toward" his horsemen and had sent sharpshooters down along the banks of the Ny. In response, Kitching formed his regiments nearest the river into line of battle, which quickly prompted the probing Confederates to withdraw. Still concerned, the colonel advanced his picket line across the tributary and up to the crest of the hill beyond. He also suggested that Forsyth throw his vedettes down the hill and along the Ny to better detect any enemy advance by that route. The major demurred, insisting that the position on the crest afforded a "fine view" of the river. Kitching reported to Warren that he had observed enemy troops crossing a point in the woods northwest of Cutler's right flank but soon after noted that the activity had ceased and he and his troops were "all right." He complained to the corps commander, "The cavalry with me are all new and are not at all useful as scouts."[31]

Nevertheless, Meade took precautionary measures to bolster his right. Shortly after 2:00 P.M. the First Massachusetts Heavy Artillery from Tyler's division moved up the Fredericksburg Road and took position on the west side of a knoll several hundred yards west of the Harris house, plugging the gap between the right of the Fifteenth and the left of the battalion of the Fourth. Two companies of Bay Staters advanced into the woods to the First's left-front as pickets. The Second New York Heavy Artillery followed the First Massachusetts, halting to the left and rear of the First and nearer the Fredericksburg Road. By this hour, the day that had begun so beautifully had turned gray; soon thunder rolled and rain fell in torrents.[32]

Meanwhile, Ewell's column resumed its advance from the Stevens house ruins. Brig. Gen. John B. Gordon, in temporary command of Early's Division, moved his men past Brig. Gen. Stephen D. Ramseur's brigade of Tar Heels and continued east through the woods in the direction of the Alsop and Peyton houses. Ramseur's outfit, followed by the remainder of Maj. Gen. Robert E. Rodes's division, then resumed the march, proceeding in a more southerly direction along the road to the Harris house.[33]

At about 4:30 P.M. Ramseur's advance struck the picket line of the Fourth New York, which was formed in the shape of a fishhook. As he adjusted the right of his line, Capt. Augustus Brown, commander of the Fourth's Company H, which manned the right of the picket line, heard a scattering of shots to his left. Brown raced across the fishhook toward the left flank only to discover a Confederate skirmish line advancing across the open field to his front. To make matters worse, he saw two gray-clad lines of battle emerging from the woods at the far end of the field with their battle flags flying. "It was a magnificent sight," Brown remembered, "for the lines moved as steadily as if on parade, and if ever I longed for a battery of artillery with guns shotted with grape and canister, and my own men behind those guns, it was then and there." He estimated that the enemy line was only 200 or 300 yards away, but he knew the swampy ground in his front would slow them and break their formation. Brown ordered a gradual, fighting withdrawal and ran to the right of the line, where he discovered that his subordinates had already directed the men to commence firing. Returning to the open field on the left, Brown saw "the enemy struggling through the swamp and our boys peppering them as fast as they could load and fire." As the action developed on his far right, Kitching saw his pickets retiring and informed Warren, "Do not know the force, but it must be quite large as our picket was strong." The men of the Fourth's Companies D, H, and K continued to resist and delayed the Confederate advance for almost an hour.[34]

To the left of the Fourth, Ramseur's advance had struck the First Massachusetts's skirmishers. Maj. Frank A. Rolfe advanced his battalion of heavies down from the knoll as if on parade, crossed the field, and continued into the woods beyond. About fifty yards into the woods, they "met with a perfect hail of lead from a body of men who seemed to rise from the earth," as one of the heavies recalled. The attack "was like a stroke of lightening from clear skies." Rolfe fell from his horse, his body pierced by eleven bullets. In what seemed like an instant, the enemy killed or wounded half of the battalion's 350 men. Then "with the most terrific yells," Ramseur's line of battle surged toward the hapless Yankees, firing as they advanced "and not pausing to take prisoners." The Confederates forced the remnants of the battalion back to the top of the knoll.[35]

As Ramseur's men pursued the fleeing bluecoats, the two other battalions of the First poured a hot fire into the left flank of the North Carolinians. In addition, from the knoll two guns of Paddy Hart's Fifteenth New York Independent Battery belched round after round of canister into the faces of the Rebels, with terrifying results. The Second New York Heavy Artillery advanced to the sound of the firing and delivered a devastating volley into Ramseur's right flank, forcing the butternuts to fall back about 200 yards into the woods. His line reformed, and now with Brig. Gen. Bryan Grimes's brigade on the left and Brig. Gen. Cullen Battle's on the right, Ramseur again charged. This thrust was met, a Bay Stater recalled, "with a withering fire from our men, who, although sorely pressed, [held] their ground and finally by a counter charge [sent] them back into the woods again." The heavies pressed their counterattack. Pegram's Brigade of Gordon's division, under Col. John Hoffman's command, rushed forward to counter the threat and avert near-disaster as the Federals almost turned the left of the Confederate line. The desperate struggle in this sector continued for several hours, but ultimately the Yankees held the ground.[36]

Meanwhile, the Confederate attackers sought an easier path around the stiff resistance encountered at the initial point of contact. Working toward the Ny and seeking an advantage near the Union left, the graycoats struck the pickets of the Fifteenth and Sixth New York. Overpowered, the heavies fell back on their main line. As one of Kitching's officers described it, "our pickets were driven in and the Rebs came upon us in Two lines of Battle." The graycoats hit the Fifteenth, which fielded only six companies at the time, hard. Lieutenant Colonel Wiedrich reported that "several attacks made with all the energy of desperation were repulsed." To their left, a soldier in the Sixth described the scene. As the battle heated up, Kitching encouraged the men of the brigade "with a cheerful remark for all, and a word of consolation for the wounded." Even during the heat of battle, "with the shells flying over us, and the bullets whizzing past us," the colonel "walk[ed] leisurely up and down the line, and if any of the boys should dodge, he [would] say with a smile, 'No ducking,—stand up!'" The man admired Kitching's "demeanor and example in battle," as it "made heroes of the meanest cowards." Despite their repeated attempts, the Confederates could not make an inroad against the heavies defending the left that day.[37]

Back on the Union right, graycoats began to slip past the thin, overextended line at the fishhook curving back toward the Fredericksburg Road. Those who reached the supply trains on the road east of the Alsop house began plundering them. Chaos ensued. One of Warren's staff noted that as he approached the area, "a small body of our cavalry came running down the pike in great confusion, likewise wagons at the top of their speed, many without drivers." Several musket shots from the southeast side of the road convinced the officer that enemy skirmishers had now actually crossed the Fredericksburg Road, making the Federals' situation even more desperate.[38]

When the fighting first erupted, the First Maine Heavy Artillery had begun moving up the Fredericksburg Road. Approaching at the double-quick, the heavies drove the Rebel interlopers from the trains. Swinging left off the road, they then advanced through the fields between the Alsop and Peyton houses until they struck Gordon's main line and entered the fight. The First Maryland Veteran Volunteer Regiment, on their way to rejoin the Maryland Brigade after a veteran furlough, heard the battle as they happened to be marching down the road from Fredericksburg. As they neared the Peyton house, regimental commander Col. Nathan T. Dushane prepared his outfit to join the fray.[39]

Dushane advanced his Marylanders west toward the Peyton house, coming in upon the extreme left of Gordon's division. They quickly engaged the enemy, with the First Maine Heavy now on their left. Then the arrival of Col. Richard Bowerman's Maryland Brigade helped fill in the gap between the First Maryland and the First Maine. The combined pressure exerted by these fresh troops bent back and eventually turned Gordon's left. Disorganized after the attack and unable to regain the initiative, his division fell back, exposing Ramseur's left. It was at that moment that Hoffman's brigade had rushed forward to stem the blue tide, arresting the domino effect that would likely have resulted in Rodes's Division suffering the same fate as Gordon's. During the mayhem, a bullet struck Ewell's horse, and the general was pitched to the ground, the wounded animal falling upon him. The resulting injury would plague Ewell in the weeks to come.⁴⁰

As the fighting raged, the heavies of the Seventh and Eighth New York, along with Crawford's and Birney's divisions, hastened to the aid of the

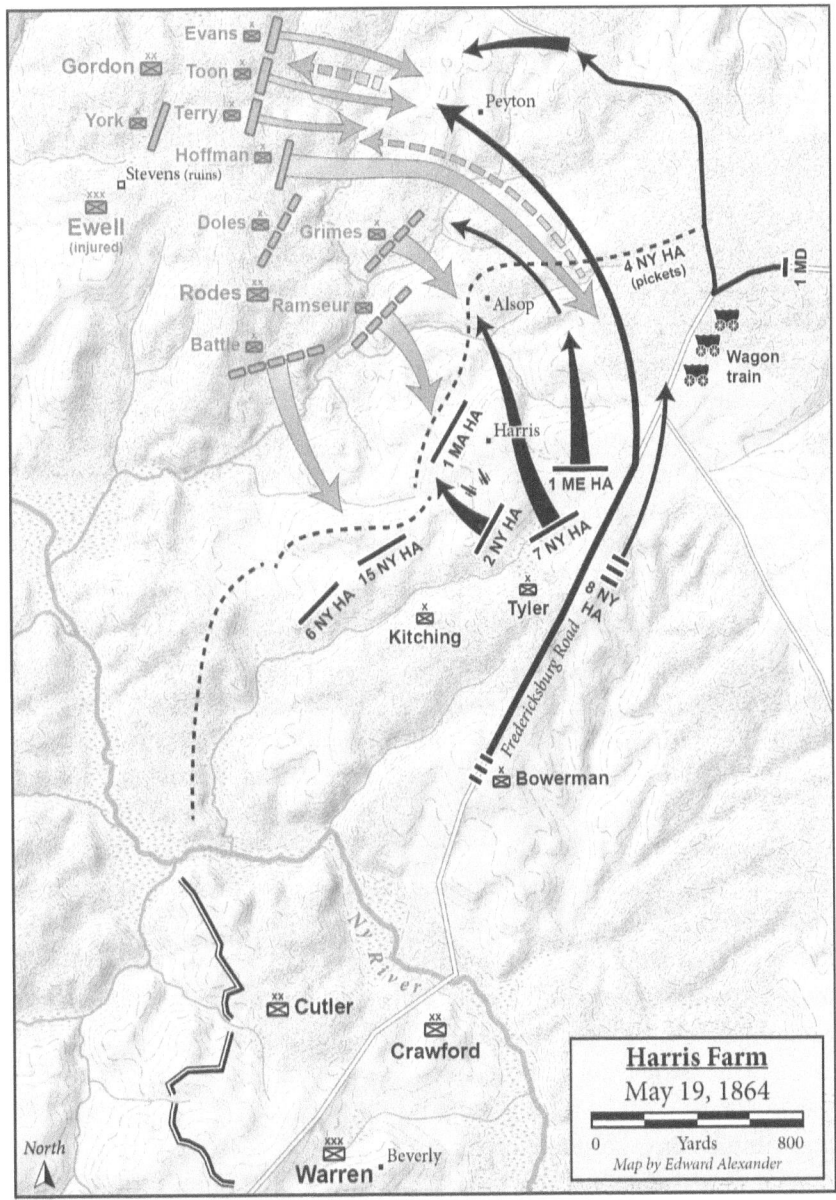

troops already engaged. By the time they arrived, however, it was clear that the Federals had prevailed. Shortly after 7:00 P.M., as darkness approached, Warren reported to Meade, "it has all quieted down with the repulse of the enemy." An hour later he received orders to leave Crawford's division in position to support Kitching's heavies for the night. The lateness of the hour, the current disposition of the commands, and the nagging concern that the Confederates had not fully abandoned their thrust against the Union right had consequences well beyond the immediate effects of the day's fight. The action at the Harris farm, which at its end found both Birney's and Tyler's Second Corps divisions on the battlefield, made it necessary for Grant to temporarily postpone his plan to send Hancock's corps beyond Lee's right flank early the following morning.[41]

After the battle many of those engaged mused over Union casualties sustained from friendly fire. One man recorded that while Company D, First Massachusetts Heavy tried to repel one of Ramseur's attacks, a battery on the hill to the rear opened on the enemy. Two of the rounds landed instead amid his company, killing one man and taking a leg off of another. Then, he claimed, the Second New York Heavy arrived and fired a volley into the Bay Staters instead of at the enemy. Lyman recalled that the newly arrived heavies "behaved well, but from their greenness, lost heavily"; they "had no idea of covering themselves and even shot each other in the excitement of battle." Roebling of Warren's staff remembered, "A thick cloud of powder smoke hung over everything, especially in the ravine between the two lines and I am sure that many of our men were killed by our own fire." He reported his personal experience with friendly fire, noting that "Gen. Hunt and myself were fired at in that way."[42]

Trying to explain the friendly fire, Fifth Corps artillery chief Wainwright opined that since it was the first time in battle for many, they "went in very much jumbled up, and doubtless did fire at our own men in some few cases, but not nearly to the extent talked of." Trying to make light of the situation, he recounted an interpretation of the battle offered by a quartermaster who summed up the complex action: "First there was Kitching's men firing at the enemy; then Tyler's men fired into his; up came Birney's division and fired into Tyler's; while the artillery fired into the whole d—d lot." An exaggeration to be sure, but undoubtedly it was not without some kernel of accuracy.[43]

At daybreak the next morning, Crawford pushed out a skirmish line to locate the enemy while the men of the Fifteenth, who had remained in positon, began to construct breastworks to protect against a renewed attack. Crawford's men only encountered stragglers, taking them prisoner. During the night Ewell had withdrawn across the Ny. With the enemy gone, the soldiers turned to the grim task of dealing with the battle's casualties. After tending to the wounded, work details from the heavy artillery regiments began to bury both Union and Confederate dead.[44]

Burying the dead required quick work and strong stomachs. The soldiers who drew the unwelcome assignment dug trenches about six feet wide, two or three feet deep, and as long as several hundred feet. They then laid the bodies in the trench side by side. Often, overcoats or blankets covered the bodies, and the men took care to protect the fallen soldiers' faces. The process made a strong impression on those who had survived the fighting. Captain Brown of the Fourth New York recalled a young Confederate soldier he helped bury. The teen wore the dirty butternut uniform of a private but "showed every indication of a gentle birth and refined home surroundings." Brown further observed, "His hands and feet were small and delicately moulded; his skin white and soft as a woman's, and his hair, where not matted by the blood from a cruel wound in the forehead, was fair and wavy as silk." The thought "of the desolate home somewhere in the South, thus robbed of its pride and joy, and of the loving mother who would never know where her darling was laid" affected Brown greatly, and he admitted, "tears actually came to my eyes." Distraught, he turned away, "leaving the poor boy to find a resting place at the hands of a burial party of a not ungenerous foe."[45]

All across the Confederacy and the Union, families worried about and mourned their loved ones on the battlefield. Fast-moving and continuous campaigns like this one left the men little time to write home, leaving their families and friends to wonder at their whereabouts and fates. Those on the home front depended on newspaper accounts of the horrific battles of 1864 for any glimmer of information on their loved ones. They wanted more dependable information and did whatever they could to get it. For example, on the day of the fight at the Harris farm, Pvt. David Mills's wife wrote to his commander in Company M of the Fifteenth. She asked Capt. William Dickey "if God has spared any of your company." Mrs. Mills was terribly worried: "I have not got a letter from my Husband in two weeks and i have written to him and not received any answer. if God has spared him will you please write to me and let me know." She entrusted her questions to him, "as David has wrote to me so much about his kind Captain." Mills survived the battle and eventually got back in touch with his wife.[46]

Gradually, the widely scattered troops who had survived the Battle of the Harris Farm returned to their camps. Kitching's men joyously welcomed a missing captain from the brigade with the announcement that he was not "kilted after all." Many others, however, never returned, as both sides had suffered heavily. Officials estimated Confederate losses at 900 killed, wounded, or missing; more than 400, excluding wounded, were taken prisoner. The Union casualties, as reported to Washington late on May 20, were 196 killed, 1,090 wounded, and 249 missing.[47]

The Fifteenth New York Heavy Artillery did not emerge from the battle unscathed. The six companies engaged that day suffered 18 men killed, one officer and 75 men wounded, and one officer and 4 men taken prisoner. The wounded officer, First Battalion commander Major Schamberger, succumbed to his wounds eight days later in Washington; thirteen of the wounded men also subsequently died. The Sixth, closer to the Ny but fielding twice as many companies as the Fifteenth, reported 15 men killed and two officers and 18 men mortally wounded. Those killed outright in the Fifteenth amounted to over 9 percent of the 196 total reported Union deaths on the day of the battle. When combined with those in the Sixth, Kitching's brigade, minus the battalion of the Fourth, accounted for nearly 17 percent of the Federals killed. Although many postwar narratives concentrate mainly on the right of the Union line during this battle, scarcely acknowledging that any action occurred farther to the left, the casualties sustained by the Fifteenth and Sixth at the Harris farm confirm a deadly contest was waged on that flank as well.[48]

Although Kitching's men had already learned the importance of cover and concealment during combat, the newly arrived heavies had no such knowledge. Instead, Roebling noted, "the fighting was done as if on parade, and the loss correspondingly heavy; the idea of fighting under cover seemed to be unknown." When the previously untried heavies took to the field, "the whole line, perfectly dressed stood unprotected in an open field, and fired as if on drill, scores of men falling all the time." They did not recognize that "ten yards in their rear was a fence in a little raised bank which would have given them very good cover and enabled them to do the same execution." Nevertheless, the newcomers still achieved a victory. Despite their greenness in battle, "this unbroken front of Heavys, with new muskets and uniforms, taking the rebel fire without flinching scared back the rebels as much as the musketry."[49]

The heavies' actions on the battlefield that day impressed Meade, who quite obviously was thankful for the successful defense of his flank and rear. Early on May 20 he issued a congratulatory order to "express his satisfaction with the good conduct of Tyler's division and Kitching's brigade of heavy artillery in the affair of yesterday evening." Meade stressed, "The gallant manner in which these commands (the greater portion being for the first time under fire) met and checked the persistent attack of a corps of the enemy led by one of its ablest generals, justifies the commanding general in his special commendation of troops who henceforth will be relied upon as were the tried veterans of the Second and Fifth Corps at the same time engaged." The heavies had proved their mettle, and the infantry would now think twice before deriding them as "band box soldiers."[50]

The battle-weary troops resumed reporting home to their families. That afternoon Philemon Heath of the Sixth sent a letter to his sister Amelia, in far upstate New York, who he had promised to write after every fight, "iff I dont get put out of business." Recounting the action of the previous afternoon in which four men in his company had been killed "& a good many wounded I don't know how many," he explained how his company had been on picket in the woods when they were surprised by the enemy. "The rebs got within five rods of us before we saw them & they holerd Surrender Yanks & we gave them a round for an answer." Responding to an earlier question about how many Confederates he had killed, Heath replied, "I dont know as I have killed any but have had some pretty good shots at them, but one thing I would rather be shooting ducks on the old St. Lawrence." Heath would have many more opportunities for good shots at his enemies. The Army of the Potomac now readied itself to execute Grant's next, bold thrust deep into enemy territory.[51]

CHAPTER FIVE

To the North Anna

Determined to immediately renew the campaign and seize the initiative, Meade instructed Hancock on May 20, "The orders given you yesterday will be repeated to-night." With the repulse of Ewell's attack the evening before and the Army of the Potomac's right flank secured, the general renewed his orders to Hancock to begin pushing his corps south the next morning toward Bowling Green and Milford Station, about twenty miles away. He wanted the troops to move quickly to cover as much ground as possible before the Rebels detected the movement. A cavalry brigade commanded by Brig. Gen. Alfred T. A. Torbert would support Hancock's infantry.[1]

Late that afternoon Meade directed Warren to hold his Fifth Corps ready to withdraw at 10 A.M. the next morning. Warren's subsequent movements would be dictated by Lee's actions. If he took the bait and pursued Hancock, Warren should pursue Lee. If not, the Fifth Corps would march to link up with the Second Corps, initiating a general movement to turn the Confederates' right. As the Federals remained focused on Lee's reaction to Hancock's withdrawal, that evening Chief of Staff Humphreys ordered Warren to immediately report "any movement or stir on the part of the enemy."[2]

Meanwhile, Major Dieckmann's heavies still picketed along the intersection of the Telegraph Road and Fredericksburg Road. In preparation for the swing south, Chief of Artillery Hunt ordered ammunition-train commander McGilvery to move with the army's general trains that night and on the way "pick up" Dieckmann and his men to resume their duty as guard for the ammunition train. Hunt also directed Capt. Casper Wolf of the Fifteenth's Company E to withdraw the Coehorn mortars still at the front and join the Fifth Corps ammunition train for the upcoming march.³

Throughout the day on May 20, Lee contemplated not only his next move but also his opponent's intentions. He had detected the movement of the two Union corps shifting closer to the Massaponax Church Road on the Federal left the day before. Having received no reports from Ewell of enemy activity in his front on the Confederate far left, Lee decided that evening to transfer the Second Corps to the extreme right of the line to counter the Federal slide in that direction. He directed Ewell to march at daybreak. When early on May 21 Lee's scouts and signal stations reported a Federal advance toward Bowling Green, the general chose to extend his line to the east all the way to the Telegraph Road. Fortuitously, the force to accomplish this was already in motion.⁴

When Federal reconnaissances early on May 21 revealed that the Army of Northern Virginia remained entrenched around Spotsylvania Court House, Grant and Meade decided to execute the effort to turn Lee out of his lines and draw his army into the open. At 7:30 A.M. Meade instructed Warren that, if not attacked by 10 A.M., he should withdraw the Fifth Corps from its position near the Fredericksburg Road, cross over to the Massaponax Church Road, and proceed east to the Telegraph Road, where Lt. Col. Edmund M. Pope with his detachment from the Eighth New York Cavalry would report to him to support the operation.⁵

At 9:45 A.M. Humphreys informed Warren that rather than following the Telegraph Road south, just below Massaponax Church he should turn east and proceed to Guinea Station. Crawford's division stepped out at about 10:30 A.M., followed closely by Kitching's Heavy Artillery Brigade, the Maryland Brigade, and then the corps's artillery. An hour later the column had safely cleared the open ground of the Anderson farm. About noon Griffin's and Cutler's divisions withdrew and took up the line of march. Free of the entrenchments they had occupied for nearly two weeks, the men of the Fifth Corps now moved rapidly to the east toward Guinea Station. As usual, those in the ranks had no idea where they were going or why. One of Kitching's heavies pondered, "The whole army changes position, for what purpose yet to be known."⁶

After passing Massaponax Church, the Fifth Corps column turned right and proceeded less than a mile down the Telegraph Road before swinging left onto the road to Guinea Station. Although the rapid march was hot and the road dusty, they preferred this relatively open country over the Spotsylvania Wilderness. Meade's aide-de-camp, Lieutenant Colonel Lyman, commented that this march revealed "not a few decent houses, and many fields, . . . where the corn was now miles high. . . . [T]he contrast to the Wilderness tract [was] most pleasant." By 6 P.M., after nearly eight hours of marching, the leading elements of the Fifth Corps, including Kitching's heavies, approached Guinea Station. Around this time, after cautiously withdrawing from near Spotsylvania, the Ninth Corps began heading toward Guinea Station to join them, with the Sixth Corps close on its heels.[7]

Lee worried about the large Federal force (Hancock's corps) well to the south of his army as well as the movement of the Fifth Corps in the same general direction, and he acted to counter the threat. Around midday on May 21, he ordered Ewell's Corps to march south on the Telegraph Road toward Hanover Junction and the strong defensive position on the south bank of the North Anna River. By late in the afternoon, when Federal intentions had become clearer, Lee ordered Anderson's First Corps to withdraw and follow Ewell down the Telegraph Road toward the junction. The Third Corps would march south after dark on roads to the west of and parallel to the Telegraph Road, passing through Chilesburg. The race to Hanover Junction and the North Anna now was on, and Lee's Army of Northern Virginia once again seized the inside track.[8]

West of Guinea Station, the road taken by the Fifth Corps forked at Hugh Catlett's farm. The right fork led west to the Telegraph Road, intersecting it some three miles distant at the site of Mud Tavern. The left fork headed south across the Matta River. At Madison's Ordinary a mile and a half beyond the Matta crossing, the fork struck another road running in a generally east–west direction. To the west, beyond Lebanon Church and approximately two miles from Madison's, it intersected the Telegraph Road at Nancy Wright's Corner. As the lead element of the Fifth Corps approached the Catlett house, the bluecoats were welcomed by the slaves there as the owner and his wife cowered in the cellar. Halting at the fork, Warren established his headquarters there. Meade then directed him to move beyond Catlett's on the left fork toward Madison's Ordinary to seize and hold the Matta River crossing. As Warren digested the orders, and with darkness approaching, rain began falling heavily.[9]

Warren dispatched Crawford's division out the right fork, where it soon halted about one and one-half miles from the intersection. Griffin's division moved out the left fork, but only about one-third of a mile beyond Catlett's, it went into bivouac near the Schooler house. Cutler's division remained at Catlett's. Warren directed Kitching's heavies and two companies of Pope's cavalry to advance to seize and hold the Matta crossing, then, if possible, to continue as far as Madison's Ordinary. Preceded by the horsemen, the heavies trudged wearily down the road toward Madison's. The cavalry scattered a few enemy troopers, and Kitching's brigade advanced to its objective with little opposition. Arriving around 9 P.M., the day's march had taken a toll on the troops. Only about 500 of the 1,500 men who had started that morning initially came up, and they were completely worn out. Warren's aide Washington Roebling, who accompanied the brigade on the march to Madison's, recalled, "so much Dutch cursing will never be heard again in the valley of the Ta."[10]

Madison's Ordinary was a wooden building situated at the small crossroads. Lyman explained in a letter home, "An 'Ordinary' in Virginia seems to be what we should call a fancy variety store, back in the country." The building, he observed, "was all shut, barred, and deserted; and, strange to say, had not been broken open." The grass was strewn with old shopping orders, "which people sent by their negroes, to get—well, to get every conceivable thing." Lyman examined a sampling of the documents, which included orders for "quarts of molasses, hymn-books, blue cotton, and Jaynes's pills!" Typically, ordinaries also served as a local tavern and offered regular meals.[11]

Arriving at Madison's, Kitching deployed his brigade. The exhausted men, positioned in an arc with its center resting on the road from Madison's to Nancy Wright's Corner at the Telegraph Road, began throwing up a defensive rail barricade despite their lack of tools. The Sixth straddled the road, with the battalion of the Fourth to their right facing obliquely back toward the Matta crossing. Kitching placed the Fifteenth to the left of the Sixth, angling back to the east. After arranging his troops, the colonel transmitted a dispatch to Warren with a sketch showing his brigade's deployment.[12]

Kitching reported that he would remain at the intersection as long as possible but that his force was "quite insufficient to hold the position against a determined attack" in the relatively open country. He requested "that when it can be done with propriety, my command be allowed some time to rest, as we have been doing picket duty so constantly that officers and men are completely exhausted." The colonel also hoped to find rations for his men: "If I can find any cattle here I will appropriate them as you suggest." An officer in the brigade similarly noted in his diary, "The men were thoroughly tired out and hungry as bears, having had nothing to eat on the long march of twenty-five miles." Lyman, without sympathy for the

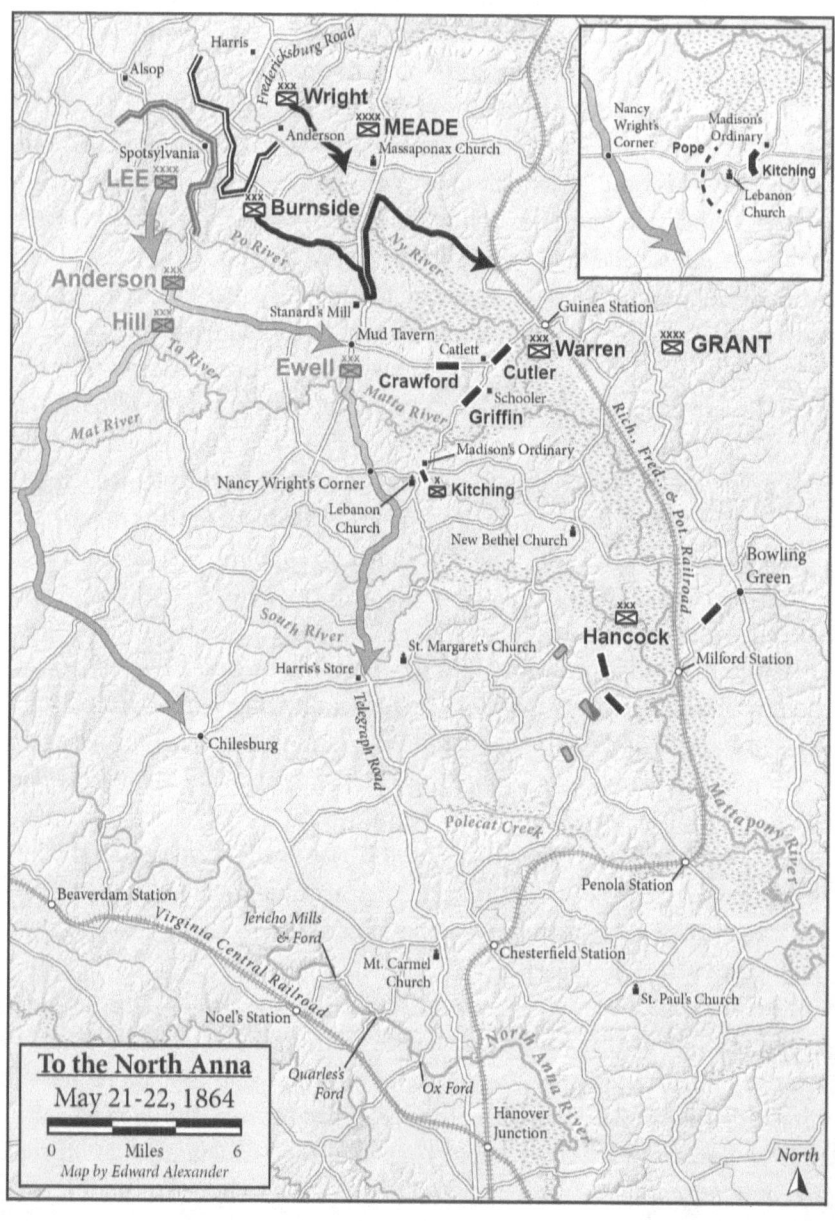

To the North Anna
May 21–22, 1864
Map by Edward Alexander

exhausted heavies, recorded several days later: "They [the infantrymen] are still joking the Heavy Artillery and now affirm that, near Madison's Ordinary, they called for volunteers to go on picket."[13]

Pope, meanwhile, dispatched a detachment of his cavalry toward Nancy Wright's Corner as far as Lebanon Church to screen to the west. While Kitching's position at Madison's Ordinary afforded a valuable foothold on the plateau across which ran the all-important Telegraph Road, it was at the same time precarious—advanced and isolated without close infantry support. With the potential for disaster in mind, at 11:15 P.M. the Federal high command directed Warren to withdraw Kitching's brigade and concentrate his whole corps around Catlett's, with Pope's cavalry pulling back to cover the rickety truss bridge over the Matta River. Warren issued the withdrawal order but later countermanded it. Upon inspection of his lines, he informed Meade of his confidence that their strength was such that "no enemy knowing it would attack." Given the late hour, Warren must have also considered an attack unlikely. Leaving the tired heavies to rest where they were, he elected to send a brigade to relieve them early in the morning.[14]

Warren might also have logically assumed that Pope's troopers would give warning of any significant enemy activity to their west. But Roebling later reported that, quite remarkably, "no one went out to the Telegraph Road that night and, we did not know what was going on out there." Unfortunately for the Federals, the lack of such reconnaissance allowed the entire Confederate First Corps and its trains to evade detection while passing down the road barely a mile beyond Pope's cavalry and considerably less than two miles from Kitching's advanced position.[15]

Despite the large Confederate force slipping by, the Heavy Artillery Brigade passed the night relatively unmolested. A squadron of Rebel cavalry attempting to rejoin its command approached within sight of the heavies' campfires, but in the dark the riders could not determine whether the encampment belonged to friend or foe. Two scouts advanced toward several soldiers standing in the road to find out. When they learned from hailing the heavies that the camp belonged to the "Fourth New York," the graycoats scurried away to search out an alternate route. Well before daylight on May 22, Col. William W. Robinson's Iron Brigade set out from near the Catlett farm to relieve Kitching's command. Upon their arrival, and with the relief effected, Robinson's men began throwing up breastworks. The tired and hungry heavies retraced their steps to Guinea

Station and the corps supply trains, where they at last drew rations and got several hours of well-deserved rest.[16]

Meanwhile, Roebling, who had accompanied Robinson to Madison's, galloped out to the cavalry vedettes at Lebanon Church. From a point 200 yards west of it, he observed a wagon train and ambulances moving rapidly off to the south on the Telegraph Road. He saw no infantry escort nor any enemy troops between his position and the train. The cavalrymen informed the major that they had heard wagons rumbling down the Telegraph Road all night, although for some unexplained reason, they had not passed that information up the line to corps headquarters.[17]

For a half hour, until about 5:30 A.M., Roebling watched as the wagons moved continuously along. He suggested to Pope that he should order his cavalry after the train. Pope declined. A half hour later Roebling reported the situation directly to Humphreys, opining that the cavalry on hand could capture the train if they only tried. The chief of staff, similarly, took no action. Roebling decried the inaction: "Never was the want of cavalry more painfully felt. Such opportunities are presented only once in a campaign and should not be lost." After learning of the failure to harvest the Confederate wagons and stragglers, Fifth Corps Artillery Brigade commander Colonel Wainwright placed the blame squarely on the absent Sheridan's shoulders. The general and the majority of the army's cavalry had been cut loose on May 8 for a raid toward Richmond against the enemy's cavalry. Consequently, Wainwright recorded, "had Sheridan been here, instead of no one knows where, we should have been sure of the junction."[18]

Discovering from scouting reports that the Army of Northern Virginia had slipped away toward the North Anna, Grant laid plans to pursue. Meade directed the Fifth Corps to advance via Madison's Ordinary to Nancy Wright's Corner, then south on the Telegraph Road for slightly less than five miles to Harris's Store; the Sixth Corps would follow. He instructed Hancock to maintain his position near Milford, where Warren would open communications with him upon reaching Harris's Store. Meanwhile, Burnside's corps would head south to New Bethel Church.[19]

The farther Warren's men advanced down the Telegraph Road, the more Confederate stragglers they captured, most from Andersen's corps. Warren reported taking about fifty. Yet Wainwright believed the actual number to be over three hundred, reflecting in his journal that "a brigade of cavalry ahead of us would have secured five times as many." Roebling estimated that the rear of the Army of Northern Virginia was only about three hours march ahead of the Fifth Corps vanguard but ruminated, "as we had no cavalry we had no expectation of catching up."[20]

As the head of the Fifth Corps column neared Harris's Store, the rear only just began to move. After resting most of the day in camp near the corps's train at Guinea Station, Kitching's heavies now had to trail the wagons as corps rear guard, with the Sixth Corps marching behind them. Departing about 4 P.M., the brigade fell into line behind the train and proceeded slowly down the narrow road. At one point the head of Wright's column caught and passed the heavies. But the narrow road and adjacent dense woods would not allow the two columns to proceed side by side. Consequently, shortly after 5 P.M. Wright halted his corps to permit the rear of Warren's column to pass. The heavies plodded along for another four or five hours and then bivouacked for the night. One of Kitching's officers quipped that the slow but difficult day's march left everyone confused: "why we were kept moving about in this way no one seemed to know."[21]

As the heavies slept, Warren issued orders for the Fifth Corps to begin its march to the North Anna at 5 A.M. the following morning, May 23. From its camp near Saint Margaret's Church about a mile and a half east of Harris's Store, Cutler's division would head west to the Telegraph Road, turn south, and take the lead in the march. Next would come Crawford's division, then Griffin's, and then the engineers, with their equipment and pontoon trains. The wagon train, with Kitching's heavies as its flank guard, would follow, with the Maryland Brigade now bringing up the rear.[22]

The movement began as planned, with the Fifth Corps commencing its march at 5 A.M. Leading the procession, Cutler's division passed Mount Carmel Church and continued south until eventually striking the North Anna about a mile upstream from the railroad bridge spanning the river. No sooner had Warren established his whereabouts when he encountered Torbert's cavalry, heralding the approach of Hancock's corps. Now about a mile and a half from Mount Carmel Church, the Second Corps infantry angled in from the northeast toward the Fifth Corps's position. One of Hancock's staff officers informed the corps commander that his column occupied the road that the Second Corps intended to take toward what was thought to be Chesterfield Ford. Warren, exasperated by a map "so erroneous that it is difficult to tell which way to go by anything named on it," turned the road over to the Second Corps. He ordered Griffin's division, still near Mount Carmel Church, to clear the way by taking the road leading west from the church while staff officers searched for a suitable crossing upriver. Warren also directed Crawford and Cutler to countermarch their divisions to the church and turn left to follow Griffin. It was by now around 1 P.M.[23]

"An old negro who had not been on the road for 53 years," Roebling recalled, guided the Fifth Corps as they marched west from Mount Carmel Church. After about two and a half miles, Griffin's vanguard turned left on an old road that their guide assured them had, at least at one time, led to a ford. About a mile down they found Jericho Mills on the banks of the North Anna, where they discovered above the milldam what Roebling described as "a row boat ferry" rather than a true ford. The Jericho Bridge identified on the erroneous maps did not exist. The river here was approximately 150 feet wide and 4 feet deep, making it impossible for wagons to cross. To complicate matters, the banks were nearly 100 feet high and quite precipitous, while the road on both sides was very rough, consisting in some places of a series of rocky steps.[24]

Despite these impediments, with no significant enemy force visible on the opposite bank, Warren decided to cross immediately. Col. Jacob B. Sweitzer's brigade of Griffin's division splashed across the river. Scrambling up the heights on the far side and advancing across a broad plain, blueclad skirmishers soon encountered a few of their enemy counterparts. So close now were the Yankees to the Virginia Central Railroad that they could hear locomotives. After learning of this progress, Meade ordered Warren to get his entire corps across the river at once. As the engineers began laying the pontoon bridge, the rest of Griffin's division waded through the water, followed by Crawford's. The bridge was completed shortly after 4:15 P.M., and Cutler's division crossed on it. Meanwhile, a Rebel prisoner informed the Fifth Corps commander that Maj. Gen. Cadmus Wilcox's division of Hill's Third Corps waited beyond the railroad.[25]

Once across the river, the Fifth Corps formed on a broad plain, with open space to the right and woods beyond a field to their front. Sweitzer advanced his brigade along a country road, forming line of battle facing generally south across the road and just inside the northern edge of the woods. Ayres's brigade formed on his left, and Griffin's final brigade, that of Brig. Gen. Joseph J. Bartlett, remained to the rear in reserve. Crawford's division connected with Ayres's left and extended the Union line along the high ground to near the river. Wainwright paused on the heights to watch the spectacle unfolding across the river on the plain below. "The deployment of the troops on the opposite bank," he recalled later, "was a beautiful sight as we watched it from the north side." Returning to his work, the colonel positioned three batteries of rifled guns along these heights, where they could sweep the plain. He then led the 12-pounder smoothbore batteries across the 160-foot-long pontoon bridge and posted Capt. Patrick Hart's Fifteenth New York Independent Battery and Lt. James Stewart's Battery B, Fourth US close to a barn in rear of Crawford's right. Wainwright then positioned Capt. Charles E. Mink's Battery H, First New York to the far right of the line in rear of where Cutler's division would extend the line. The other three batteries waited in reserve near a small barn on the heights above the bridge. Meanwhile, Cutler's division continued from the bridge to extend the line from Sweitzer's right. The men already in position began settling in for the night and cooking dinner. It was now nearing 6 P.M.[26]

Earlier that day, just before noon, the Fifth Corps train reached Mount Carmel Church and parked. Kitching's heavies, their duty as train guard during the march completed, had earned a brief rest. While they boiled their coffee, the men watched the Second Corps pass to their left down the Telegraph Road toward the North Anna while the Fifth Corps passed to their right. At the end of their short respite, the brigade fell into line and followed the Fifth Corps toward Jericho Mills, arriving around 5 P.M. Cpl. William Dailey, who had not been feeling well and thought the day "very warm," decided to seize the opportunity to make some tea. He later recalled that he did "not get it drank for a battle commences in front." Similarly, one of Kitching's officers noted that the brigade "halted at 5 P. M.," and the men "had just got down when the Ball opened."[27]

At 6 P.M. Cutler's division prepared to extend the line from Griffin's right. His First Brigade, the famed Iron Brigade commanded by Robinson, had just taken position on Sweitzer's right, and Col. Edward S. Bragg's brigade of Pennsylvanians readied to form next in line. Col. J. William Hoffman's brigade advanced along the road from the river crossing to support them, while Col. Peter Lyle's brigade remained in reserve on the heights south of the pontoon bridge. Cutler rode forward with Mink to select a suitable position for the captain's battery. Suddenly, an unnerving rebel yell rent the air as grayclad infantry surged forward, slamming into the Union position. On the Federal left, Brig. Gen. James H. Lane's Tar Heels struck the blue skirmish line and drove on toward Ayres's position and the gap between it and Crawford's extreme right. McGowan's Brigade of South Carolinians, commanded by Col. Joseph N. Brown, rushed headlong into Switzer's brigade on the right of Griffin's line.[28]

The situation on the Union right quickly became desperate. Brig. Gen. Edward L. Thomas's brigade of Georgians rushed out of the tree line and into the open field, where Cutler's division was still forming. On his left came Scales's Brigade of North Carolinians, led that day by Col. William L. Lowrance. With their lines not fully formed and their flanks exposed, both Bragg's Pennsylvanians and the Iron Brigade broke immediately; most of the men fled back toward the river, and some even across it. As Thomas's and Lowrance's graycoats pursued, Sweitzer's fully exposed right flank wavered. Without waiting for orders, at the first sound of fire, Mink's battery rushed toward a slight prominence in rear of what would have been Cutler's line. Observing the guns race forward, Wainwright "could not help [but feel] a glow of pleasure and pride as I watched the four little guns moving straight through the fugitive infantry and forming on the very ground a whole brigade had abandoned." The artillerymen wheeled into battery and, as soon as the fleeing infantrymen cleared from their front, opened a devastating fire of canister that cut broad swaths into the advancing Confederate lines. Lt. Angell Matthewson's Battery E, First New York and Lt. Aaron Walcott's Third Massachusetts Battery (C) advanced from reserve. Wainwright placed them on Mink's right at intervals of about fifty yards. "All three batteries opened within canister range," he reported, "and did not spare ammunition." The Rebel line staggered.[29]

Across the North Anna above Jericho Mills, Kitching's heavies could hear the rifled batteries on the high ground as they opened fire on the long gray lines that had suddenly appeared. Ordered forward to support the crumbling Fifth Corps right flank, the brigade crossed the pontoon bridge at the double-quick. Forming line of battle on the other side, the heavies charged up and over the rising ground to their front, where they encountered Warren and his aides. The general was sitting on his horse "calmly" watching the fight. As the brigade passed, Sgt. Stephen Burger heard Warren remark, "loud enough for some of us to hear, 'There goes a fine lot of men.'" The troops now "felt we were under his eye," Burger remembered, "and the thought seemed to nerve every heart in that Brigade and each man fought as if the salvation of the Army depended wholly on his individual effort." Moving forward under heavy fire and posted near the river to form a right flank for Cutler's remaining two brigades, the heavies had unleashed several volleys when ordered to cease fire. Despite their relatively brief encounter, Roebling reported that Kitching's brigade had "held its ground" against the Confederate assault.[30]

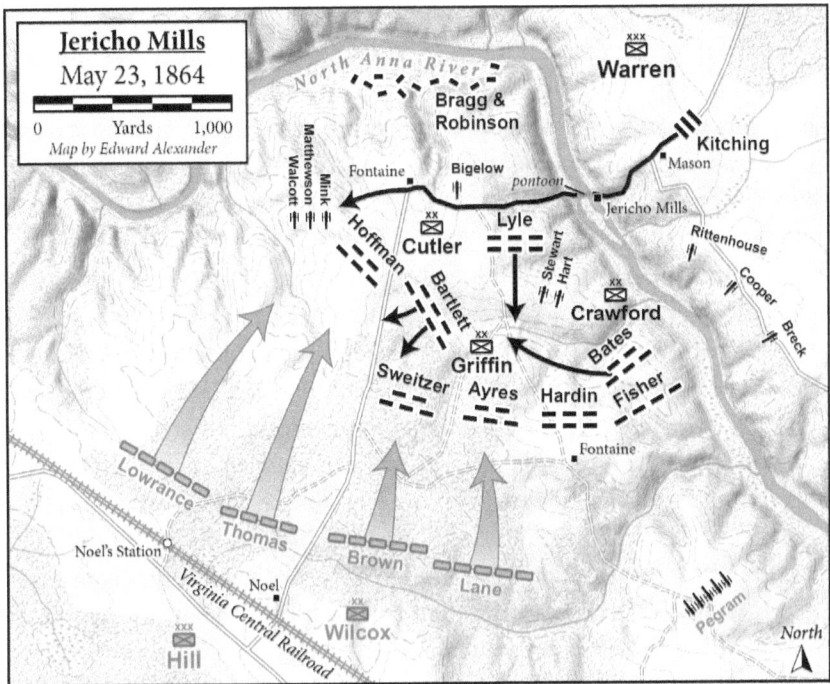

As the heavies took position, the tide of battle was beginning to turn. Hoffman's brigade rushed forward to support Mink's battery and to partially fill the gap between it and Griffin's right. Bartlett's First Division brigade helped bolster Hoffman's left and Sweitzer's right. Elements of Robinson's and Bragg's shattered brigades began to rally around Mink's battery. To the left, Griffin's division held despite being severely pressed, and Crawford's division remained unengaged. In the face of a withering fire of canister and musketry, Lowrance's and Thomas's brigades fell back. As they did, Union artillerists switched to case shot and then to solid shot, firing into the retreating graycoats until they had driven them back across the railroad. Heth's Division, which had come up to support Wilcox, did not exploit the tenuous condition of the Union right flank. Instead it shifted to the opposite flank when Wilcox discovered how far Crawford overlapped the Confederate line in that sector. By then, however, darkness precluded any further advance. The fight had lasted nearly two hours.[31]

Kitching described his brigade's action as a "brisk fight." He wrote to his father: "A sharpshooter succeeded in breaking the skin of my neck, but it did not hurt me much. We afterward wounded and captured him, and he said that 'he had fired seven times at that little colonel and would die happy if he could have hit him.'" Kitching surmised that now that the Federals had crossed the North Anna and gotten so close to Richmond, Lee would not try to make another stand outside of the capital's defenses. "If we can pen him up there we shall wind up this arrangement very soon," he postulated. "I should be quite content to retire now, if the campaign were ended."[32]

The Fifth Corps had endured a long and exceedingly difficult day but managed to hang on and, in the end, turn near-defeat into victory of a kind. Nevertheless, some of its most vaunted and battle-tested outfits had fled the field after barely firing a shot. That night Wainwright wrote that although no brigade in the entire army had enjoyed a higher reputation than the famed Iron Brigade, whose "pre-eminence in the old First Corps was very generally acknowledged," the day's battle had showed its weaknesses. "Yet one-half of it ran clear across the river without firing a shot, and two thirds of the other half were brought back with difficulty by their officers to support the batteries, a service in which they have always taken especial pride." The colonel considered this behavior a prime example of how panic could seize a whole command.[33]

With the dust settled, Meade sent a message to Warren commending the Fifth Corps on its success that day. "I congratulate you and your gallant corps for the handsome manner in which you repulsed the enemy's attack." This statement of praise, however, did not impress Wainwright. "I presume he includes the batteries in the corps, but I think that they ought to have had special mention, particularly Mink's," he complained in his journal. Adding to his frustration, "General Warren has not given me one word of commendation for myself or my batteries," although considering the disproportionately high loses sustained within the artillery as compared to the infantry, "he might have said something that I could transmit to the men."[34]

The repulse of the Confederate attack infuriated Lee. The discomfort of a severe case of dysentery served only to heighten his irritation with Hill. "Why," the commanding general demanded, "did you not do as Jackson would have done—thrown your whole force upon those people and driven them back?" Hill had no answer. Indeed, the Army of Northern Virginia could ill afford the heavy losses incurred that day, especially with nothing to show for them. Wilcox's Division, the outfit that had borne the brunt of the fight, suffered 642 casualties, while the whole of Hill's Corps was represented among the prisoners taken.[35]

In the wake of Hill's repulse and the consequent establishment of a secure Federal lodgment south of the river, that evening the ailing Lee called together his senior commanders to solicit opinions on the Army of Northern Virginia's next move. They knew protection of Hanover Junction, where the Richmond, Fredericksburg, and Potomac and the Virginia Central Railroads met, was critical. The question remained how best to achieve that aim and keep the junction out of enemy hands. Lee ultimately fixed on a plan that not only could effectively protect Hanover Junction but also might afford an opportunity to strike a decisive blow.[36]

Lee determined to construct a strong line in the shape of an inverted V, the apex resting on the high banks of the North Anna above Ox Ford. One leg would run southwest across the Virginia Central and terminate at the Little River, facing the plain then occupied by the Fifth Corps. The other would parallel the riverbank a short distance and continue southeasterly along the cord of a bend in the river until reaching Hanover Junction. There the line would make a right angle to the south and terminate in a swampy area. The masterful design not only would give Lee the advantages of interior lines but also split the Federal army into three segments, each separated by the river and rendering communication between them tenuous. Furthermore, if his men could lure either wing of the Union force into an isolated position, Lee could exploit the advantages of his interior lines and strongly fortified position to strike the enemy a disabling blow.[37]

Meanwhile, after the long day of marching and fighting, Kitching's heavies constructed a line of breastworks and lay behind them all night. Pvt. Amherst Belcher recalled that the Fifteenth "had been practically without rations for two days and were promised a fresh supply that night." But to his dismay, Belcher drew picket duty that evening. Alone, hungry, and in his advanced position, he remembered, "all night long I listened to the Confederate cattle herders whooping up a drive of beef cattle that were evidently too tired to be driven, though they had to go or die; in fact, that had to go *and* die." Returning to the Fifteenth's camp in the morning, Belcher reported being sent back across the river, "this time to buy rations from the officers' sales wagons."[38]

Both Grant and Meade transferred their headquarters to Mount Carmel Church early on May 24. Meade's staffer Lyman described the new headquarters as a "mean little church" on a "barren corner." "If you want a horrible hole for a halt," he opined, "just pick out a Virginia Church, at a Virginia cross-roads, after the bulk of the army has passed, on a hot, dusty Virginia day!" Boards laid to span the broad aisle, their ends resting on the pews, formed a makeshift table upon which the generals and their staffs set to work. Meade lamented to his wife: "I am writing this letter from a House of God, used for general headquarters. What a scene and commentary on the times!"[39]

As Kitching's men rested near the North Anna, some of their compatriots made their way toward them. Four days earlier, late on May 20, Dieckmann's battalion had joined the army's ammunition train as it passed the junction of the Telegraph and Spotsylvania Roads and resumed its duty as train guard. The ammunition wagons moved slowly with the army's main trains by a more circuitous route through Bowling Green. The march took its toll on Dieckmann's men, who finally, with the wagons, reached Mount Carmel Church on May 24. Seeing the condition of the men, Hunt warned McGilvery, the ammunition-train commander, "against the straggling of his guard—to keep his train closed up on the march and in park, and well guarded." The general reminded him of the importance of the trains, stressing "that the result of the next battle might depend upon his keeping the Ammunition train—infantry and artillery—in readiness to move up at a moments warning." With this rebuke instead of a welcome, Dieckmann's exhausted men settled in to rest near the church.[40]

Before 6:15 A.M. two divisions of the Sixth Corps had crossed the pontoon bridges at Jericho Ford and moved up to support the Fifth, the remaining division soon to follow. The Second Corps crossed down river, leaving Burnside's command, in the center of the Union line, as the only corps north of the river. On the densely wooded opposite bank, Burnside observed an enemy battery, protected in flank and in front by rifle pits, on high ground to the rear. He began preparations to force a crossing.[41]

Around 9:30 A.M. Warren ordered Crawford's division to advance down the south bank of the North Anna in an effort to connect with the Second Corps's right. Reaching Quarles's Mill and ford by 1 P.M., having driven Confederate skirmishers while advancing, Crawford's outfit established communication with Burnside across the river. Informing his corps commander of his current position, Crawford described the ford as "a sort of falls," albeit one that infantry could easily cross. He added that

Burnside had ordered Maj. Gen. Thomas L. Crittenden's First Division, Ninth Corps to cross there.[42]

By now nearly all of Hancock's corps was across the river but began to encounter increased fire from Confederate skirmishers in rifle pits. Meanwhile, after clearing Quarles's Ford for use by the Ninth Corps, Warren informed Crawford that he need not advance further and should extend his skirmishers out to the right toward the Virginia Central, with a view to developing the enemy's position. As the division commander extended his right along the road running south from the ford toward the railroad, his men encountered Confederate skirmishers. Behind them, breastworks were visible extending all the way from the North Anna to the Little River, south of the railroad. Crawford now became concerned that his communication with the rest of the Fifth Corps might get cut off. Crittenden, meanwhile, continued to cross and deployed his division to face the enemy force that opposed Brig. Gen. Orlando Willcox's Ninth Corps division at Ox Ford.[43]

At 3 P.M. Crittenden received instructions to advance Brig. Gen. James H. Ledlie's brigade along the river toward the Confederate strongpoint. Ledlie, his courage fortified by whiskey, ordered his troops forward into the thick woods along the riverbank. Upon emerging from the woods, skirmishers observed a heavily defended line of strong and freshly constructed earthworks on a high ridge about a half mile away. As a severe thunderstorm storm broke and sporadic lightning lit the field, Ledlie's men marched forward resolutely against the nearly impregnable Confederate position. Before 7 P.M. the tattered remnants of Ledlie's brigade streamed back toward Quarles's Ford. The ill-advised attack had cost about 450 casualties. As night approached, Confederates continued to make inroads, as skirmishers slipped around the Union right flank, cutting Crawford off from all communication. He drew his right back to form an arc, the flanks of his division resting on the river, the Federals' backs against it. Isolated from outside support and trapped by the now rising North Anna, Crawford's division and Crittenden's men hastily threw up defensive works and hunkered down for the night.[44]

Nearer Jericho Ford, Kitching's heavies had remained in their works, with pickets thrown out as far as the railroad. All afternoon they heard heavy fighting off to their left in the vicinity of Quarles's Ford. But without orders to go to the front, most of the men made the best of the opportunity to rest and to "police" themselves by bathing in the nearby North Anna. They picked up Confederate stragglers and deserters all day. Once safe within the Union lines, the prisoners offered divergent opinions on the state of the Confederate army. A captain in the brigade recalled that some enemy troops claimed they had nothing to eat, that all Lee's men were tired of the war, and that whole brigades would come over but for the fact they had been told they would have to take the oath of allegiance and serve for three years in the Union army. But other captured Confederates emphasized that they had more than enough to eat and the army was prepared to fight forever. Kitching's men could not get a clear picture of the state of affairs from them. In any case, late that afternoon the Heavy Artillery Brigade slowly advanced until darkness prevented any further movement.[45]

The strong resistance to the Union probes above, below, and at Ox Ford dispelled any thought that the Confederates were withdrawing and confirmed to the Federal high command that Lee's army remained in force at the North Anna. They had blundered into the trap Lee laid with his inverted-V line, and the Confederates now had the opportunity to crush Hancock's corps, isolated and with the river behind it. But Lee's severe illness prevented him from personally directing the operation, and he had no proven lieutenant he could rely upon to spring the trap. Instead, the general lay nearly delirious in his cot repeating, "We must strike them a blow—we must never let them pass us again—we must strike them a blow." The golden opportunity to do so would soon slip away.[46]

That night, after constructing their own works, the Federals laid bridges to mitigate the precarious position they now occupied. There were some positive developments. Word arrived that Sheridan's cavalry would rejoin the army the next day, so the Federals would no longer have to stumble blindly through unknown and hostile territory. Moreover, Grant had tired of the fictive notion of treating Burnside's Ninth Corps as a command unto itself and ordained that it be folded into the Army of the Potomac. Burnside would now report to Meade, his junior.[47]

Early the next morning, May 25, the men of Company E, Fifteenth New York Heavy struggled in the darkness to manhandle their Coehorn mortars into position on the high banks above Ox Ford. Col. John C. Tidball, commanding the Second Corps Artillery Brigade, had grown increasingly frustrated with the Rebel battery in the earthworks at the apex of the inverted V. The enemy guns had not only harried the Second Corps as the men crossed the river the day before but also continued to do so in the

Union troops' current position south of the river. To silence them, Tidball requested the use of six of Hunt's mortars. The men positioned them under cover of darkness; as dawn broke the Coehorns sat about 600 yards from the enemy's works. Shortly after daylight the heavies opened fire on the Confederates in the apex of the inverted V. They successfully lobed the shells in high arcs directly into the enemy works. "The effect was magical," Tidball recalled, "even the fire of the sharp-shooters was stopped, and the enemy sought new ways of covering himself from this strange fire."[48]

Kitching's brigade had spent the night a little over a mile in front of the pontoon bridge at Jericho Mills and in the rear of most other Fifth Corps outfits. In the morning, as an effort to develop the enemy position unfolded, commanders hurried the men of the Sixth and Fifteenth New York Heavies off by their left flank toward the Fifth Corps line as they sent the Second Battalion, Fourth New York Heavy to the right. The men of the Sixth and Fifteenth halted about two miles nearer the main line and could distinctly hear the sharp musketry to their front as Fifth Corps skirmishers probed the Rebel defenses. In the afternoon they also heard Union artillery to their right laying an enfilading fire on the enemy position. Yet at about 5 P.M., without having engaging the enemy, they retraced their steps to where they had spent the past night and remained in line of battle throughout this night.[49]

With the Army of the Potomac drawn close upon its strongly entrenched enemy, its wings widely separated and straddling the North Anna, the stalemate created by Lee became all too abundantly clear. On the evening of May 25, Grant called together his chief lieutenants to figure out how to break the deadlock. Opinions varied. Turning Lee's left would require them to cross three rivers—the Little, New Found, and South Anna. On the other hand, Grant reasoned that turning Lee's right and moving southeast to cross the Pamunkey at or near Hanovertown meant that all three of these rivers, which merged to form the Pamunkey, would in effect be crossed at once while still allowing him to maintain his existing lines of communication and supply from the east. The general in chief elected to again move to the left. "Lee's army is really whipped. The prisoners we now take show it, and the action of his army shows it unmistakably," Grant confidently informed Chief of Staff Halleck in Washington. "I may be mistaken, but I feel our success over Lee's army is already assured."[50]

Not everyone agreed with Grant's plan. Fifth Corps artillery chief Wainwright saw the situation differently. Never at a loss for an opinion, he wondered: "Can it be that this is the sum of our lieutenant-general's abilities? Has he no other resource in tactics? Or is it sheer obstinacy?" The colonel pointed to the previous failures. "Three times he has tried this move, around Lee's right, and three times been foiled." As a result "officers and men are getting a [bit] tired of it," Wainwright declared, "and would like a little variety on night marches and indiscriminant attacks on earthworks in the daytime."[51]

Late on May 25, Grant ordered Meade to carry out the latest planned sweep around the right flank of the Army of Northern Virginia. The following day, he directed, "Wright's best division, or division under its ablest commander," should carefully withdraw from the line and recross the North Anna. In the afternoon he planned for cavalry to strike off down the Pamunkey to screen and protect critical fords until the infantry and artillery passed to their rear. Simultaneously, cavalry remaining behind would make a heavy demonstration on Lee's left to cover the withdrawal and feign a sweep around that flank of the Army of Northern Virginia. At dark on the evening of May 26, the Sixth Corps division selected to lead would begin marching to Hanovertown. The Fifth and the remainder of the Sixth Corps would withdraw under cover of darkness, cross the North Anna, and follow the lead division. The Second and Ninth Corps would take to the road once the two proceeding corps cleared.[52]

The Fifteenth had not escaped its early encounter at the North Anna unscathed. William Dickey, commanding Company M, soon received another letter from the wife of one of his men seeking news on her husband's condition. "As you are a stranger to me i wish you wood in form me about My Husben i hante herde from him since the 30 of April i feale very uneasy A bout him his name is John H Hamilton," wrote young Phebe Hamilton from her home in the Catskill Mountains. She implored, "i Donte know whether he is well or sick i wish you would please write to Me and let Me know how he is wether he is alive or not." She enclosed a letter addressed to her "Dearest Husben John Hamilton," informing him she was well and expressing hope he was the same. Dickey did not have good news for her; Hamilton never saw her letter. He had been wounded and captured in the fight at Jericho Mills on May 23, four days before Phebe wrote. He would die a month later of typhoid fever while a prisoner of war at Richmond.[53]

Grant's latest attempt to draw Lee's army into the open for a decisive engagement had failed, finding the Confederate commander in as strong, if not stronger, entrenched positon than that he had abandoned at

Spotsylvania Court House. Yet as Lee countered each of Grant's turning maneuvers, the armies crept closer and closer to Richmond. As planned, Grant's next move would place the Army of the Potomac virtually on the Rebel capital's doorsteps. When Kitching's heavies settled in on the evening of May 26, they like the rest of the army's rank and file could only speculate as to what the future held in store for them. They would soon discover it would begin with yet another long, hard march, followed by another desperate and bloody battle.

CHAPTER SIX

To the Totopotomoy and Bethesda Church

Although, according to one of Kitching's officers, "the morning [of May 26] was rainy and disagreeable," at 10 A.M. Meade ordered his Army of the Potomac to begin disentangling itself from its position in the immediate front of a still very powerful foe in order to sweep around the flank. He selected Brig. Gen. David A. Russell's Sixth Corps division to lead the infantry in its dash alongside the Pamunkey River toward Hanovertown, some thirty-two miles to the southeast. Russell's outfit would take the road closest to the river and be followed by the rest of the Sixth Corps. After dark the Fifth Corps would recross the North Anna and march southeast toward Hanovertown. Once these corps cleared the roads around Mount Carmel Church, the Second and Ninth Corps would follow. The army's supply and other main trains, including the ammunition train guarded by Major Dieckmann's battalion, would move that night through Bowling Green and then along the north bank of the Mattapony River to the vicinity of Dunkirk. Turning south, the column would cross that river and continue toward Hanovertown.[1]

The Fifth Corps began withdrawing at dark, using the bridge at Quarles's Mill. Warren's aide Major Roebling recalled the "night intensely dark" and the "roads very muddy." Col. John Tidball, commander of the Second Corps Artillery Brigade, agreed that "the night was as dark as Erebus" and the roads "softened by the water and cut up by the wagons and artillery," with mud "so deep and liquid that the course was rather a stream than a road." The heavies of Colonel Kitching's brigade trudged along in the darkness "in mud knee deep," as one company commander remembered, eventually halting at Mount Carmel Church about 1 A.M. In the difficult conditions "it was utterly impossible to keep the men in line," the officer lamented, "and I had but *sixteen* of my company with me when we halted." After reaching the church the men built fires to warm themselves and collected their rations. Gradually, the stragglers trickled into camp. It took most of the night for the rear of the Fifth Corps column to get across river, but the Confederates did not pursue. Meade's chief of staff Humphreys concluded that "the withdrawal was effected apparently without the knowledge of the enemy." As the heavies dried out and tried to rest, rumors of another impending long march circulated.[2]

As daylight broke on May 27, the members of the Fifteenth awoke in the center of a beehive of activity. Men and wagons clogged the roads around Mount Carmel Church. The Sixth Corps had not yet cleared the area and now blocked Warren's intended route of march. Colonel Wainwright, commanding the Fifth Corps Artillery Brigade, described the scene. With his own corps halted as its men received rations, the Sixth Corps "closed up alongside us, and the Second came up the other road." The confluence of troops made it "so that with the hundreds of waggons, and the three corps, it seemed . . . inextricable confusion. There was a large open plain here that was completely covered with carriages of one kind and another." The Heavy Artillery Brigade finally began moving around 9 A.M. As they had in the march to the North Anna, the heavies remained near the rear of the column guarding the corps's trains.[3]

Crossing the Richmond, Fredericksburg, and Potomac Railroad on a high bridge near Old Chesterfield, Kitching's heavies and their Fifth Corps comrades rolled along a road generally parallel to, but several miles north of, the Sixth Corps's route. They marched through a warm morning and a hot afternoon, with scant supplies of good drinking water. After an hour's halt at Saint Paul's Church, the march resumed. The landscape they crossed impressed Wainwright. "This country is better than any we have come across yet," he recorded, "with some really fine plantations and comfortable homes." That afternoon, with army headquarters now established at Mangohick Church, Humphreys directed Warren to take the Fifth Corps across the Pamunkey several miles downriver from the church at Hanovertown. By 7 P.M. his two lead divisions had halted and set up camp on Dowell's Creek, with the third division coming up and the artillery and trains following. Warren established his headquarters at a Mrs. Tuck's house about two miles north of the church. The men of Kitching's brigade, at the very rear of the column, did not arrive to bivouac until after midnight. An officer estimated that they had marched twenty-five miles that day, "losing from the ranks more than two-thirds of the men." The stragglers, he recalled, "fell out from sheer exhaustion but joined us later."[4]

The Fifth Corps resumed its march by first light, which occurred soon after 4 A.M. on May 28, in the same order as the previous day. As a result, following behind the trains as rear guard for the long column, Kitching's heavies did not begin to move until about three hours later. At around 6:30 A.M. the lead elements of the corps passed Mangohick Church, a structure, according to Meade's aide-de-camp Lieutenant Colonel Lyman, "built of old bricks brought from England, and laid 'header and stretcher' fashion." He recorded that the church had served as "a great rendezvous for rebel volunteers at the beginning of the war," which the Fifth Corps now marched past "with bands playing and men in good spirits cheering." A short distance beyond the column turned right, heading southeast through Enfield and on toward Dabney Ferry and Hanovertown. As the day wore on, straggling became a problem again. Exhausted soldiers fell out to rest in such numbers that Warren eventually directed that any "men found straggling away from the column be brought back by shooting at them." After trudging along at the rear of the column as the long day grew progressively hotter, one of the heavies described the affair as "very hard marching." Still, one of Kitching's officers recalled "passing many attractive looking places." At one point along the route, he remembered the column came upon a commissary, where "those of us who could afford the luxury supplemented our usual and limited rations of hard-tack, brown sugar and coffee, with something equally bad but different in kind."[5]

The vanguard of the Fifth Corps column reached the Pamunkey River about 9 A.M. and crossed on pontoon bridges. About a mile past the small hamlet of Hanovertown, Warren's men encountered Russell and his Sixth Corps division camped in the river bottom. The arrival of these reinforcements allayed Russell's anxiety about holding the Hanovertown crossing without additional infantry support. Warren established headquarters at the Newton house, near where the road along the river intersected the road to Haw's Shop. The owner of the residence, Capt. William Newton of the Fourth Virginia Cavalry, had been killed at Kelly's Ford in 1863, but his widow and their three children still lived there. Bringing up the rear of the Fifth Corps column, Kitching's exhausted heavies finally tramped across the pontoon bridges around 5 P.M. and encamped near Warren's headquarters slightly over a mile from the river. As the men settled in, word spread that a large enemy force in front of them had been detected earlier in the day by Sheridan's troopers.[6]

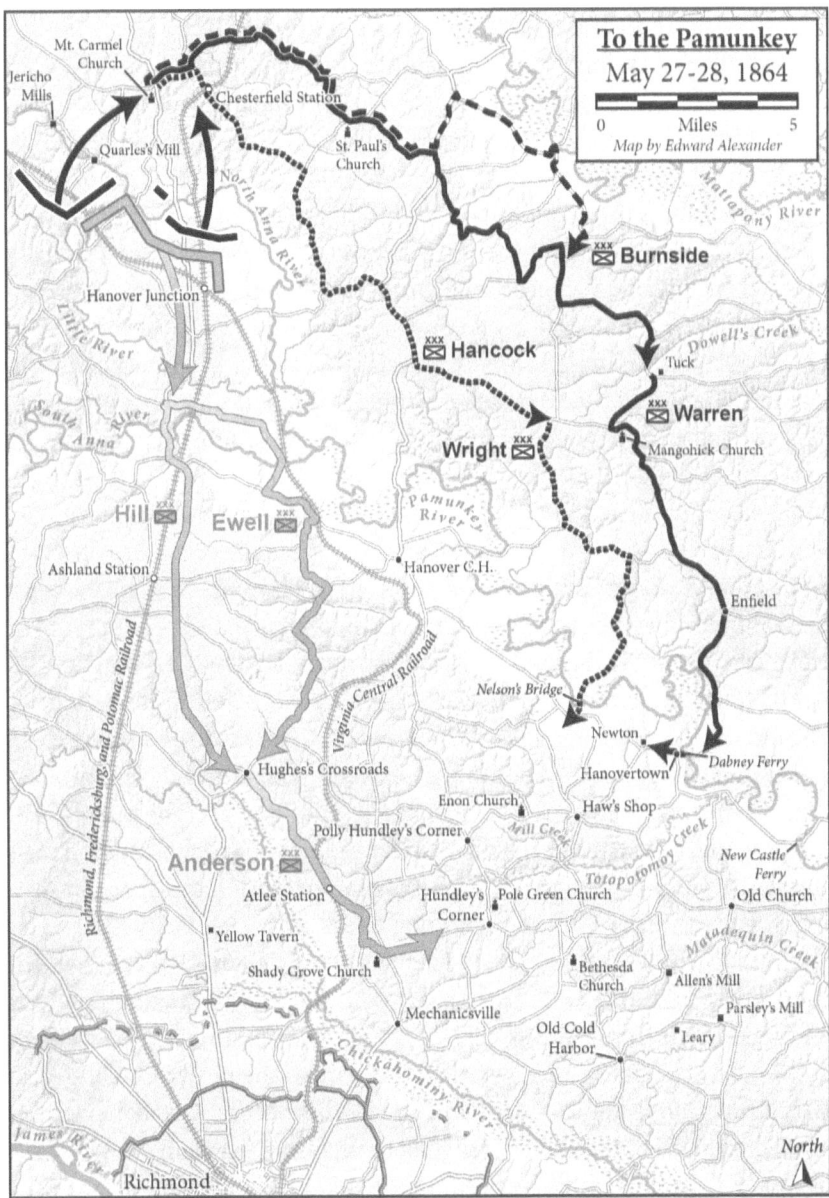

The Union cavalry had that morning reconnoitered along the road between Haw's Shop, situated about two miles southwest of the Newton house, and Atlee's Station. At approximately 10 A.M., after proceeding west from Haw's Shop about three-quarters of a mile and near Enon Church, Sheridan's horsemen struck Confederate cavalry dismounted and posted behind temporary breastworks of rails. The Federals eventually broke the position and sent the graycoats scurrying back along the road toward Atlee's, leaving their dead behind. Confederate prisoners reported that Ewell's and Longstreet's Corps were only four miles to the west and marching to keep pace with, or even head off, the Federal advance.[7]

Although the withdrawal of Union forces from the North Anna went undetected for a time, on May 27 Lee confirmed that the Federals were retiring. When reports filtered in of enemy cavalry and infantry activity down the Pamunkey, the general immediately began to move his own army south. By that evening Lee's vanguard was well below Ashland; by the next afternoon all three Confederate corps were in a positon to counter Grant and Meade's well-executed and rapid turning movement. The two old adversaries prepared to face off once more, this time on the outskirts of the Confederate capital, Richmond.[8]

After falling ill as the critical march to counter the Federal sweep began, Ewell delegated temporary command of the Second Corps to Maj. Gen. Jubal A. Early. With Ewell still too ill to leave his tent, on May 29 Lee relieved him, placing Early in permanent command of the Army of Northern Virginia's Second Corps. Brig. Gen. Stephen D. Ramseur, a North Carolinian commanding a brigade in Maj. Gen. Robert Rodes's Second Corps division, assumed command of Early's former division.[9]

Meanwhile, Sunday, May 29, had dawned a beautiful day. Midmorning, Warren received orders to advance to Haw's Shop. There, the Fifth Corps would connect with Hancock's left and extend south along the road running from the shop across the Totopotomoy, with the corps's left resting at the confluence of Totopotomoy Creek with Mill Creek. By 1 P.M. the Fifth Corps was in position, with the right of Cutler's Fourth Division connecting to the Second Corps's left, and the left of Crawford's Third Division on the Totopotomoy at Mill Creek. Warren directed the artillery and Kitching's brigade of heavies to "move up to the position assigned to Generals Crawford and Cutler." Griffin took his Second Division over the Totopotomoy with instructions to make a reconnaissance in the direction of Shady Grove. Griffin advanced his troops up the hill and into the fifteen-acre open field surrounded by woods at Mrs. Via's large, eighteenth-century, Georgian-style house, where they engaged Confederate skirmishers. After driving the butternuts west down the Shady Grove Road, Griffin withdrew and halted for the night with his division in line across the Via property.[10]

Several organizational changes to the Army of the Potomac occurred that day. The Fourth New York Heavy Artillery reorganized as a full regiment in the Second Corps, so the battalion then serving in Kitching's brigade rejoined its parent command. In addition, Tyler's division of heavy artillery was disbanded, and the regiments distributed among the various divisions in the Second Corps. The Fifth Corps underwent even more far-sweeping changes. Under Meade's orders, newly arrived Brig. Gen. Henry H. Lockwood organized a new Fifth Corps division, which became the Second Division, comprising veteran regiments that arrived with him as well as the Maryland regiments already serving with the Fifth Corps "and any other troops that the corps commander can assign to the division." Kitching's Heavy Artillery Brigade, however, was not included in the revamped Second Division. Instead, it would become part of Crawford's Third Division.[11]

Approximately two miles west of the Fifth Corps's position, the morning of May 30 saw the Union Second Corps in positon on the heights east of Totopotomoy Creek. Hancock had directed his artillery chief, Colonel Tidball, to "put in as many batteries as practicable" on the crest above the creek near the Shelton house, known as Rural Plains. Tidball toiled throughout the morning to bring up the guns and develop the line. By noon the task was nearly completed, with one battery placed to the left of the house, one to the right, and the Coehorn mortar battery of the Fifteenth's Company E just moving into position in the middle, directly in front of the house. The heavies could not have failed to be impressed by the building. Rural Plains had been constructed in the early eighteenth century of glazed bricks, originally carried from England as ships' ballast, laid in the Flemish-bond pattern. In 1754 it was the venue of the great American patriot Patrick Henry's marriage to Sarah Shelton. The current owner, a Colonel Shelton, was away at the time. The arriving Yankees found his wife, their five daughters—one of whom was pregnant—a son, an infant grandchild, and several servants huddled in the basement. Although urged by Union officers to flee and offered safe conduct, the family chose to stay in their home. When fighting commenced, they would seek refuge in the cellar. Concerned officers carried beds down and barricaded the windows with logs to provide some comfort and protection to the distraught civilians.[12]

With the Coehorns finally in position, Tidball, without authority, abruptly relieved Capt. Casper Wolf and Company E from their duties serving them, replacing them with Company D from his former command, the Fourth New York Heavy. General Hunt, who had assigned Company E to the Coehorn mortars, remained unaware of Tidball's action for some time. Indeed, on May 31 he directed that Wolf "Comdg. Mortar Battery," be issued 150 rounds of ammunition for the battery. Tidball waited until June 6 to inform the general of his actions, explaining that he made the change because in Company E, "There is scarcely a man . . . who can speak or understand English and it is impossible therefore to do any good with them." Despite the language barrier, and in contradiction to his assertion, Tidball also observed, "these pieces have performed most excellent service." He then detailed for Hunt the changes he had already made. "I placed Company D, 4th N. Y. Arty. in charge of the mortars and this company is doing so well with them I would respectfully recommend that the Company of the 15th N. Y. Arty be sent back to the regiment."[13]

Hunt did not intervene, and Company E returned to Dieckmann's battalion. Despite their shortened service with the Coehorns, Company E's heavies had proved themselves and the mortars valuable assets throughout the campaign, employed, as Hunt later reported, "wherever circumstances would permit of their use, and always with good results." In fact, with the likelihood of siege operations becoming greater with each passing day, on June 6 Hunt urged Meade to request delivery of more Coehorn mortars and permanently assign six to each infantry corps. The army commander immediately granted this request.[14]

Meanwhile, in the Fifth Corps's sector, at 4 A.M. on May 30, Kitching reported as ordered to his new division commander. In addition to the newly assigned brigade of heavies, Crawford's division now consisted of two other brigades made up of regiments of the Pennsylvania Reserves. Col. Martin D. Hardin commanded the First Brigade, comprising the First, Second, Sixth, Seventh, Eleventh, and Thirteenth Regiments, the latter renowned as the "Bucktails" because most of the men wore a deer's tail on their caps. The Fifth, Tenth, and Twelfth Pennsylvania Reserve Regiments composed Col. Joseph W. Fisher's Third Brigade. The Pennsylvania Reserves had previously fought in Virginia with the Army of the Potomac during the 1862

Peninsular Campaign. But after performing long and valuable service earlier with the army, on this morning most of the men were not thinking of battle. Many of the Pennsylvanians' three-year enlistments expired the next day, and they planned to depart for home.[15]

By 9 A.M. Warren had ordered the balance of the Fifth Corps to join Griffin south of the Totopotomoy. He planned to move south to the Old Church Road, which ran northeast from Mechanicsville to Old Church and roughly parallel to and less than a mile south of the Shady Grove Road. Warren assured Humphreys that it was "easy to come over from one to the other" of these parallel roads by means of a narrow north–south connecting road running between them, so the separation of his corps should not pose a problem. This connecter intersected the Old Church Road near a grove where, as described by a newspaper correspondent, "an old, unpainted, dilapidated building"—Bethesda Church—stood.[16]

Earlier that day Lee saw an opportunity to administer the severe blow to the Federals he had intended with his unsprung trap at the North Anna. The Fifth Corps's current isolated position south of Totopotomoy Creek presented an inviting target. Lee interpreted Warren's movements to be but a "repetition of their former movements" in attempting to turn the Confederate right, so he decided "to strike at once that part of their force that has crossed the Totopotomoy in General Early's front." He directed the Second Corps to lead this attack, with Anderson's First Corps supporting it.[17]

By noon Early's men had cut a road from their position near Pole Green Church to the Old Church–Mechanicsville Road, striking the latter about a mile west of Bethesda Church. The general informed Lee that he wanted to withdraw Rodes's Division from the right of his line and send it out the Old Church Road toward Bethesda . If an opportunity presented itself to attack the Federals, Early's other divisions, including his former unit now under Ramseur's command, would support Rodes. The First Corps should then fill the vacated positions in the line and advance east along the Shady Grove Road supporting the Second Corps's left. Lee approved Early's plan and communicated it to Anderson.[18]

When at midafternoon Hardin's First Brigade of Crawford's Third Division started south down the narrow connecting road toward Old Church Road, Fisher's Third Brigade remained along the Shady Grove Road near the Bowles farm at the head of the connecter. The farm, one Federal officer observed, was inhabited by "a man, his wife, and a large brood of young rebels." About midway between the Shady Grove Road and Bethesda Church, Hardin's men encountered Confederate skirmishers in a strip of woods to the right of and extending slightly across their path. The advance stalled, and eventually the Bucktails deployed in a skirmish line to drive out the graycoats. Armed with Sharps breech-loading rifles, the Pennsylvanians continued their advance while delivering three to five shots as the butternuts reloaded after one round. Pushing the enemy skirmishers through the wooded strip, across an old cornfield, and into the forest beyond, the Bucktails pressed ahead, as Hardin remembered, "in a manner to excite the admiration of friend and foe." The Sharps rifles "told with deadly effect upon the dense masses of grey, which were plainly discernable not forty yards distant," one Bucktail recounted. Hardin's brigade continued to the Old Church Road. They then turned right and advanced several hundred yards to the west of the Bethesda Church intersection before halting near the Tinsley house. There the men began to hastily throw up works across the road that, as one Pennsylvanian observed, were "of a pour Contriving." To connect Hardin's isolated brigade and Fisher's, Kitching's heavies moved down the connecting road to the strip of woods near its halfway point and formed a line facing west toward the Confederate position.[19]

Hardin's men had been at their labors, Hardin remembered, only long enough to "pile up some fence rails and lay behind them" when Rodes's Division, with Brig. Gen. Bryan Grimes's brigade of Tar Heels in the vanguard, swept at a run down the Old Church Road from the west. Plowing into the hapless Pennsylvanians, the Confederates soon ran over and around the "poorly contrived" defensive line. With the Union position breeched, "the volley or two delivered by our feeble force made no impression on the enemy," Hardin recalled. The sheer momentum of the division-strength attack was so great that the graycoats rolled over and beyond Hardin's position and down the Old Church Road past Bethesda Church. Swept along in the flood of their dramatic success, Rodes's men did not stop to secure their Yankee prisoners. Seizing the opportunity, the remnants of Hardin's brigade fled back to safety toward the Bowles farm.[20]

When the enemy struck the First Brigade, Kitching and his men moved immediately to its support. As the order "Forward, double quick! March!" rang out, the brigade of heavies raced down the road toward Bethesda Church. After moving a short distance, however, as one man recalled, they encountered "a murderous fire of musketry from a Rebel line of battle, which, screened by the underbrush, we had stumbled upon." The attack "was so sudden . . . that the entire brigade was thrown into the greatest confusion." Four of Kitching's staff fell at the first volley, leaving the colonel later to ponder his luck at being "so miraculously spared." Having swept over and beyond Hardin's original position, Rodes's men now poured an intense, enfilading fire into the heavies. "This terrible fire right into the head of the column broke the men, many of whom had fallen killed or wounded," Kitching wrote to his wife the next day. In fact, he continued, "in less time than I have been telling you," his brigade "was sailing across the plain." A man in the Sixth New York Heavy concurred: "We were handled pretty rough. Came all very near being captured."[21]

Observing from a position on the high ground near the Shady Grove Road, Colonel Wainwright watched as the Confederates struck Hardin's brigade. He did not have to wait long "to see how much of an attack it was. . . . In five minutes Hardin's brigade was running." After "finding the enemy quite on their flank," the Union troops "were rather indiscriminately hurrying back to the Shady Grove Road." Wainwright galloped off to bring up his artillery, realizing that "things [were] looking very squally for a complete turning of our left."[22]

As the momentum of Rodes's thrust ebbed, the attack ground to a halt. Officers began restoring order to the disorganized outfits along the Old Church Road. Realizing that the axis of the attack paralleled the main Federal line, Rodes's units changed front to face the Yankees to their north and sent a line of skirmishers forward. Meanwhile, what could be mustered from the brigades of Pennsylvania Reserves and the heavies reformed along the crest of the hill above the Old Church Road. The heavies took position to the left of the connecting road across from the strip of trees. On the Fifteenth's front the First Battalion formed on the right and the Third Battalion on the left in the open field. Here they faced a "heavy fire," Lieutenant Colonel Wiedrich remembered, "both from front and flank." One of Kitching's heavies recalled the Rebels came at them "like swarms of bees and their Yi, Yi, Yi always made the blood curdle in my veins."[23]

Observing Rodes's men changing front to resume the offensive, Hardin and his men began falling back to the main line along the road. As he prepared to withdraw, Hardin saw Kitching's heavies still standing on the crest of the hill firing as rapidly as possible at the Confederates below them. He "tried his best to get the men to lie down, as the skirmish line (the only fire of the enemy) was dealing destruction amongst them," but discovered that "no amount of persuasion nor orders could make the men" do so. Hardin suggested that Kitching order his heavies back to the main line as well. Kitching agreed, and as one of his officers recalled, "we fell back under a heavy fire and halted and commenced to build a line of Breast Works." The delaying action had lasted approximately thirty minutes. While Crawford's division reformed, Griffin rode up and questioned Hardin about the need to so feverously pursue preparations to receive an attack. In response, the colonel invited the division commander to ride with him to the crest of the hill near the strip of trees where Kitching's men had been, overlooking the Confederate force. "I'm satisfied," Griffin called to Hardin, galloping off to prepare his own division to meet the forthcoming attack.[24]

The Federal line along the Shady Grove Road soon began to take shape. With Griffin fully aware of the Confederate threat, he rushed two batteries operating with his division to Crawford's support. Capt. Charles E. Mink's Battery H, First New York Light rolled into position on the north side of the road immediately in front of the Bowles house, and Lt. Lester I. Richardson's Battery D, also of the First New York, came into battery south of the road at its junction with the connecter from Bethesda Church. Richardson immediately opened with solid shot on a Rebel column. An enemy battery near Bethesda Church responded, killing four of the battery's horses. Unable to dislodge the Confederate guns, Richardson held his fire and ordered his men to cover themselves as best as possible, having never seen "the enemy's artillery used to better advantage than here."[25]

Meanwhile, other units prepared for the impending attack. Crawford's infantry began to file into place as Fisher's Third Brigade took position on the right of the line to the west of the road junction. Hardin took the center at the intersection itself in between the two batteries. Kitching's heavies slipped into line across the road from the field surrounding the Bowles house, with Mink's battery on its right. Fisher's and Kitching's men formed slightly in front of and oblique to Hardin's center brigade so that they could lay a crossfire on the ground immediately in front of the formation. Griffin fell back to take up position on Crawford's right, Lockwood's Second Division advanced to Crawford's left, and Cutler waited in reserve to the rear of Crawford. Wainwright pushed Rittenhouse's, Walcott's, and Bigelow's batteries forward near the Armstrong house at the far left of the Fifth Corps line, while Breck's battery wheeled into position about 100 yards to Richardson's left. The men hunkered down and prepared for the now inevitable fight.[26]

The Confederates prepared, too. Around 6 P.M. Early's old division, now commanded by the twenty-six-year-old Ramseur, approached Bethesda Church from the west. The division consisted of Pegram's Brigade of the Thirteenth, Thirty-First, Forty-Ninth, Fifty-Second, and Fifty-Eighth Virginia, commanded that day by twenty-three-year-old Georgian and former West Point cadet Col. Edward Willis, and Col. Thomas F. Toon's North Carolina brigade. According to Col. William Allan, a Second Corps ordnance officer, "Willis was in the highest spirits & was determined to win his spurs or die in the attempt."[27]

The Forty-Ninth Virginia had lost nine color-bearers since the start of the campaign. When regimental commander Col. Charles B. Christian, a Virginia Military Institute graduate, strode down the line to select another, he paused in front of a tall, lanky, beardless boy wearing a red cap

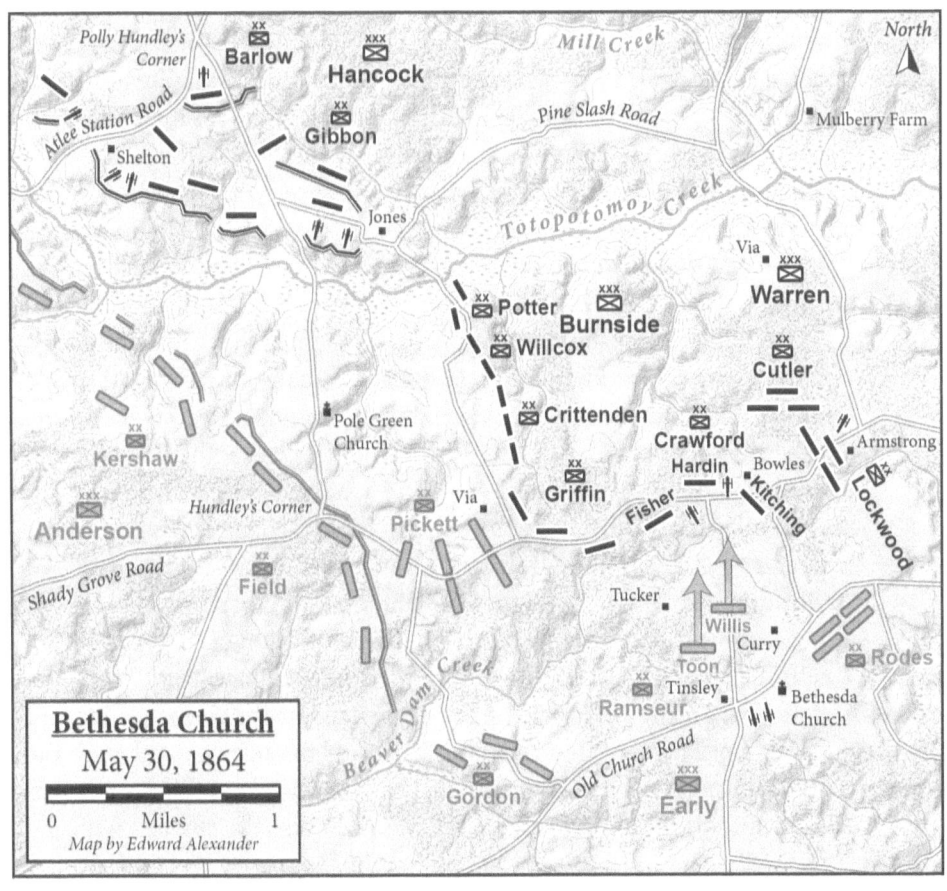

Bethesda Church
May 30, 1864

0   Miles   1
Map by Edward Alexander

and asked, "Orendorf, will you carry the colors?" The soldier replied: "Yes, Colonel, I will carry them. They killed my brother the other day; now damn them let them kill me too." Orendorf took the colors, and, with the Forty-Ninth in the vanguard, the brigade marched down the Old Church Road. As it approached Bethesda Church, Ramseur's Division came under the fire of Richardson's guns. Christian, at the head of the column, heard Ramseur urge Early to "let me take that gun out of the wet." He recalled that "Early vigorously advised and protested against it," but the North Carolina general insisted, so Early finally consented. Willis's brigade fronted to the left, and the advance commenced, with the Forty-Ninth Virginia on the line's extreme right. The Federal guns fell silent as the Yankee gunners conserved their ammunition until the Rebels had closed. In the wood line at the opposite end of the field leading to the Shady Grove Road, Christian could see the heavy concentration of Union artillery as well as "bayonets bristling as thick as the 'leaves of Vallambrosa,' [sic]" arrayed in three distinct lines of battle. Even so, he and his comrades pressed ahead.[28]

The Federal artillery resumed firing when the Confederates were about 200 yards from Crawford's line. The infantry held their fire until the enemy had advanced to within 50 yards of their breastworks and then opened on them with a crushing blast of musketry. "Volley after volley is poured into them," recalled a veteran of the Eleventh Pennsylvania Reserves, "and their ranks melt before the terrible fire." Canister and the zipping bullets of musketry tore great gaps in the advancing line, "a blast as if from the pit, crashing, tearing, grinding, enfilading their lines, leaving in its track a swath of dead and dying." A man in Kitching's brigade reported the companies firing alternately in volleys. "Ready! Aim! Fire! Load!" the orders rang out. "On they came," he remembered, although now "without their accustomed yell." The batteries opened on them "with terrific effect, . . . fairly raking the field in front of us, the shells screaming and crashing through the trees and strewing the ground with the killed and wounded of the beaten foe, who, finding more than they had looked for, were slowly and sullenly retiring to the protection of their works."[29]

On the right of Willis's line and moving in Kitching's front, Christian ordered his Forty-Ninth Virginia to "right-shoulder shift arms" to prevent the men from firing and breaking ranks during the advance. Although the Confederates "pushed at a run through this maelstrom of death and carnage," the colonel remembered, "the men who usually charged with the 'rebel yell' rushed on in silence." As the Virginians neared the Union breastworks, they met with two volleys in rapid succession. "Our line already decimated was now almost annihilated," Christian reported; it "melted away as if by magic." The color-bearer Orendorf "stood erect within twenty feet of the muzzles of the enemy guns and waved his flag defiantly in their faces." The colonel mused that the enemy "must have hesitated to kill him in admiration of his bravery." But any hesitation was brief. A gunner yanked a lanyard, and a charge of canister spewed from the muzzle of a gun trained directly on Orendorf. "His little red cap flew up ten feet, one arm went up one way, the other another—fragments of his flesh were dashed in our faces," lamented Christian. Orendorf had joined his brother in death, surely bringing more heartbreak to his mother near Amherst, Virginia.[30]

A canister ball mortally wounded Willis, tearing into his bowels and driving his pocket knife out his back. The engagement also cost the Thirteenth Virginia's Colonel Terrill his life. Indeed, as Christian later recalled, "every brigade, staff and field officer was cut down, (mostly killed outright) in an incredibly short time." As the Forty-Ninth Virginia struggled to hold its advanced position, one of his officers urged, "Colonel, in five minutes you won't have a man left, let them surrender!" With only three officers and eighteen men still standing, Christian reluctantly agreed. "Captain," he called out, "that is so, let them surrender, but I'll be hanged if I will." Hearing this, one of his wounded men raised a blood-and-black-powder-stained white flag. The Federals ceased their fire, and the remnants of the Forty-Ninth Virginia stood. Seizing this opportunity, Christian bolted for the rear. After only about fifty yards, Yankee fire struck him three times. He slumped to the ground, falling into a furrow that protected him from being riddled with more rounds. When a Union skirmish line moved through soon afterward, a sandy-haired soldier leveled his gun at the colonel as he ordered him to stand up. When Christian reported his injury and his fear of bleeding to death, the soldier replied: "What a likely fellow! What a pity! What a pity!" Moving on but a few feet, a shot rang out from the woods, wounding the Federal. As he staggered back, the young soldier cried, "Johnny Reb, please kill me," as he fell crying in pain. After struggling to his feet and staggering a few more yards, he "fell and all was hushed in death." After dark Union soldiers took him and the other wounded to the Union lines, where, Christian recalled, "the enemy treated me with great consideration and kindness."[31]

As daylight faded, the firing gradually tapered off. The outfits in Crawford's division began to assess their losses. Hardin's brigade reported 7 killed, 46 wounded, and 81 missing, for a total of 134 casualties. Fisher lost 22 men—18 wounded and the balance missing. Kitching's brigade suffered the heaviest loss in the division—16 men killed, 3 officers and 141 men wounded, and 101 men missing, 261 casualties in all. From the seven companies of the Fifteenth engaged at Bethesda Church, Wiedrich reported 5 men killed and 2 officers and 57 men wounded. Nevertheless, as Cpl. William Daily of the Sixth New York recorded in his diary, the hard-fighting Pennsylvanians and New York heavy artillerymen had managed to "whip the rebels well." Crawford reported "over 300 dead rebels in our front"; up to 70 prisoners, 6 of them officers; and about 31 wounded Confederates at Union hospitals.[32]

In a message to Lee that night, Early blamed Anderson for the defeat. The Second Corps commander complained of having requested that the First Corps advance a division, "and when I supposed he was advancing I sent forward two brigades with the intention of supporting them by other troops." Yet when Early found the enemy in heavy force and intrenched, "and hearing nothing from Anderson I desisted from the effort to break the enemy's line, as it was evident it would be attended with considerable loss." At 4:30 A.M. the following morning, Early again defended his actions to Lee, this time declaring, "If Anderson had moved down the road from Hundley's Corner, I think we could have struck the enemy a severe blow." But as it was, he opined, "all we have to regret is the loss of valuable officers and men in Pegram's brigade, which is one I much deplore." Indeed, on visiting the dying Willis on May 31, Colonel Allan could not bring himself to wake the sleeping man. He later wrote, "after taking a last look at a noble soul I turned away," feeling "low down at the bloody sacrifice of men Early had made the day before."[33]

After an intense day of battle, the exhausted heavies slept on their arms in the rifle pits. At daybreak they and others from Crawford's division moved out into the previous day's killing field to bury the dead. They found a horrific scene. A sergeant in the Sixth described the discovery of a comrade: "Flandrian when found was stripped of everything but drawers & blouse. Corporal Gerhardt sketched the spot where he & Butterfield lay buried." A Pennsylvania Bucktail found a dead Confederate "struck with a charge of grape, or by a bursting shell, and his body from his knees to his neck was crushed and torn into an indistinguishable mass." A man from Hardin's brigade remembered how "we buried our fallen comrades, and those of the enemy on the field of honor, and left them to 'sleep their last sleep,' peacefully side by side." The soldiers continued the grim task throughout the morning.³⁴

Early on May 31, a Federal reconnaissance revealed that a general assault held little, if any, likelihood of success. The Confederates were in a strong position and well entrenched on the Sixth, Ninth, and Second Corps fronts. On the army's left flank, they were posted in strength in Griffin's front. But scouts also discovered that the enemy had withdrawn from Bethesda Church during the night. By 9:45 A.M. Warren decided to exploit this opening and slide the left of his corps toward the church, with the Ninth Corps to take up the slack and occupy the vacated positions. He directed Griffin to extend to his division's left and replace Cutler's troops. "Do not take any account of Kitching's detachment," he added, "for I shall move them." Cutler placed his division across the Old Church Road west of the church, with Griffin's division connecting to his right and Lockwood's to his left, angling sharply to the east. Kitching's heavies advanced south about a mile to the vicinity of Bethesda Church and took position in rifle pits. Around 7 P.M. they advanced again a short distance and piled behind what Wiedrich later described as "very strong breast-works."³⁵

By midmorning on June 1, Warren sighted enemy columns and trains moving to his left. Fifth Corps skirmishers advanced beyond the woods to about a half mile below Bethesda Church, while its main line began sliding farther to the left. Warren directed Griffin to extend to his left so as to relieve as much of Cutler's division as possible. He told Cutler to maintain his command "in the neighborhood of Bethesda Church" and kept Kitching's heavies in reserve near Fifth Corps headquarters, soon established at the church. At 11:30 A.M. Warren reported that his skirmish line "everywhere comes up in sight of intrenchments." He paused to organize his lines, with the Fifth Corps's left resting "on an impassable swamp, about a half mile southeast of the church."³⁶

Just as Warren had slid his corps to the south, so now was much of the Federal army moving in that direction—and along with it the epicenter of fighting. The prior afternoon, May 31, Sheridan's troopers overpowered Rebel cavalry and infantry to occupy the strategically important Old Cold Harbor crossroads. That night the Sixth Corps went to their support, arriving throughout the day on June 1. Also approaching the vicinity was Maj. Gen. William F. "Baldy" Smith's Eighteenth Corps, detached from Butler's Army of the James and ferried to White House on the Pamunkey River on transports. At 6 P.M. Wright's and Smith's corps attacked the enemy position in the vicinity of Old Cold Harbor. Although unable to rout the defenders, they made limited gains but suffered heavy losses. The Federals then began to entrench where their advance stalled.[37]

To prevent the Confederates from interposing between the now widely separated wings of Meade's army, Warren had earlier in the day dispatched Roebling, with part of the former Maryland Brigade (now the Third Brigade, Second Division), to locate and establish a connection with the forces near Cold Harbor. That evening, after successfully completing that assignment, the major witnessed two brigades rushing to the east through the woods. He pursued the column and discovered it was Lockwood with two of his Second Division brigades. "They were lost," Roebling later recorded, "and had no definite idea where they were going—except in the direction of the firing." He halted them and placed them in line, establishing, he reported, "a pretty fair connection with the Md. Brig. and the main body of our troops around the [church] with a gap of perhaps a half a mile to the latter."[38]

Warren was livid when he leaned what had transpired and "earnestly beg[ged]" Meade "that [Lockwood] may be at once relieved from duty with this army." The response was swift, Grant ordering Lockwood be relieved that night. When Meade informed Warren of this, he proposed that without Lockwood "you can now make a good division for Crawford." Early on the morning of June 2, Crawford was named commander of the Second Division, Fifth Army Corps. Furthermore, "the troops of the old Third Division since the mustering out of the organization of the Pennsylvania Reserve Corps" would also join the Second Division, including Kitching and his two regiments of heavies.[39]

During the night of June 1, the Second Corps had transferred to the far left of the line to support the Sixth and Eighteenth Corps. Hancock's withdrawal left the Ninth Corps on the extreme right of the nearly six-mile-long Federal line, with the Fifth Corps on its left in the vicinity of Bethesda Church. This arrangement stretched Warren's command to the limit, especially as he had still not established a sound connection with Smith's Eighteenth Corps. Reporting to Meade early on June 2, he informed the army commander that by entrenching and through his use of artillery, "I believe we can hold against any probable efforts of the enemy, but it is too weak to attack from the connection, and is not very secure on my right." Grant and Meade decided to shorten the line on the army's right. They ordered Burnside to withdraw "as soon as he can do so securely" and mass in rear of the Fifth Corps's right, where the Ninth Corps should prepare to resist an attack to turn the flank and also to support Warren's men.[40]

About 10 A.M. Crawford proceeded to the left of the Fifth Corps line to position his new command. Swampy areas surrounding the headwaters of Matadequin Creek interrupted the line, forming natural obstacles that effectively shortened the line and reducing the number of men required to defend it. Wainwright's artillery remained in position to further protect the position and have "more equal footing" with the Confederate artillery and sharpshooters that kept the Fifth Corps under constant fire, inflicting numerous casualties. Dushane's Marylanders were on the far left, the brigade's left resting about a mile northwest of the home of David Woody, which stood a little over a mile from Cold Harbor on the road running north toward Bethesda Church. Between the right of the Maryland Brigade and the left of Col. Peter Lyle's First Brigade, Crawford positioned the remnants of the Pennsylvania Reserves. Col. James Bates's Second Brigade connected to Lyle's right, and between Bates's outfit and the left of Cutler's division Crawford placed Kitching's Heavy Artillery Brigade.[41]

Late in the day, as Burnside was executing his withdrawal, elements of Rodes's Division struck him. At the same time, Gordon's Division hit Griffin's front from the west, as Heth's Third Corps division swung around above the Shady Grove Road and veered south past the Via house and into the rear of the Federal right flank. Wiedrich, with his heavies in line well south of Bethesda Church, observed, "[Burnside's] fight took place nearly in our rear, and we had very good luck not to suffer losses from shells exploding in and near our works." The Confederate attack seemed unending. Another of Kitching's officers recalled, "the enemy commenced to shell us . . . with 20 lb. Parrotts" and "kept it up until . . . they were silenced by our batteries." After about two hours, as darkness approached, the fighting ebbed, and both sides dug in where they stood. The opposing forces now found themselves in the opposite positions from those they had occupied after the May 30 fight at Bethesda Church. Warren reported to Meade, "The enemy now have the breast-works we built when we had our fight night before last and we hold their position."[42]

With the Second Corps now in position on the Federal left, at 2:30 P.M. Meade ordered an attack all along the line beginning at 4:30 A.M. on June 3. On the far right, the night of June 2 found the Fifth and Ninth Corps still recovering from the evening's line-contracting debacle. Furthermore, the length of the line the Fifth Corps now covered as well as its tenuous connection to Smith's corps via a line of division skirmishers made Warren wary about the ordered early morning attack. Despite his protests and explanations, that night Chief of Staff Humphreys emphasized, "the major-general commanding expects you to attack in the morning at the hour appointed." Warren dispatched Roebling to army headquarters to plead his case, urging Meade to personally evaluate the situation on the right flank. "He refused at once," Roebling remembered. Instead, the general told him "that at 3 AM he had ordered his coffee, at 4 he was going to mount with his staff, and at 6 he would smash the rebel army at Coal [sic] Harbor."[43]

At dawn on Friday, June 3, the Confederates remained in force along the Shady Grove Road, now behind the high breastworks they had thrown up overnight. Neither Warren nor Burnside attacked at 4:30 A.M. Instead, the Fifth Corps waited for much-needed ammunition to be brought forward over the muddy roads while the Ninth Corps scrambled to get in position. Nevertheless, at approximately 6 A.M., the advance, which involved a swinging around of the Federal right, began. Pivoting on Bartlett's and Ayres's brigades, the Ninth Corps commenced to push the Confederate left flank in an attempt to extend the line across and beyond Shady Grove Road. Despite meeting strong resistance, Burnside's men successfully took the first line of the Confederate works. To the left of the Ninth Corps, Sweitzer's brigade pushed forward despite heavy enemy fire but soon ground to a halt in the face of their strong fieldworks. Elements of Gordon's Division concurrently launched what Wainwright described as a "savage charge" along the Old Church Road and through the woods north of it into the right-center of Griffin's division. After the butternuts advanced to within canister range of the Union line, Ayres's brigade along with Hart's and Rittenhouse's batteries repulsed the attack.[44]

On the Fifth Corps's left, Kitching's heavies and the other units posted in that sector faced somewhat different circumstances. There, Roebling recalled, "our corps was strung out in such a thin line that we would do well if we would hold our own." Humphreys acknowledged that despite the orders to attack all along the line, particularly the Fifth Corps pushing forward its left to relieve the pressure on Smith's corps, "no effective attack could be made upon the enemy." His own and Crawford's men "were constantly under a galling fire from the enemy's batteries," Cutler reported, and "suffered severely from their sharpshooters." Although dangerous and deadly work, Warren pushed his skirmish lines forward to press the Confederates into their entrenchments. One of Kitching's heavies recalled how "their sharpshooters were hidden in trees and buildings and from there picked off many a good Union soldier." Furthermore, "the Johnnies had a battery which enfiladed our line and sent us tokens of their regard in the shape of spherical shell and other missiles of destruction."[45]

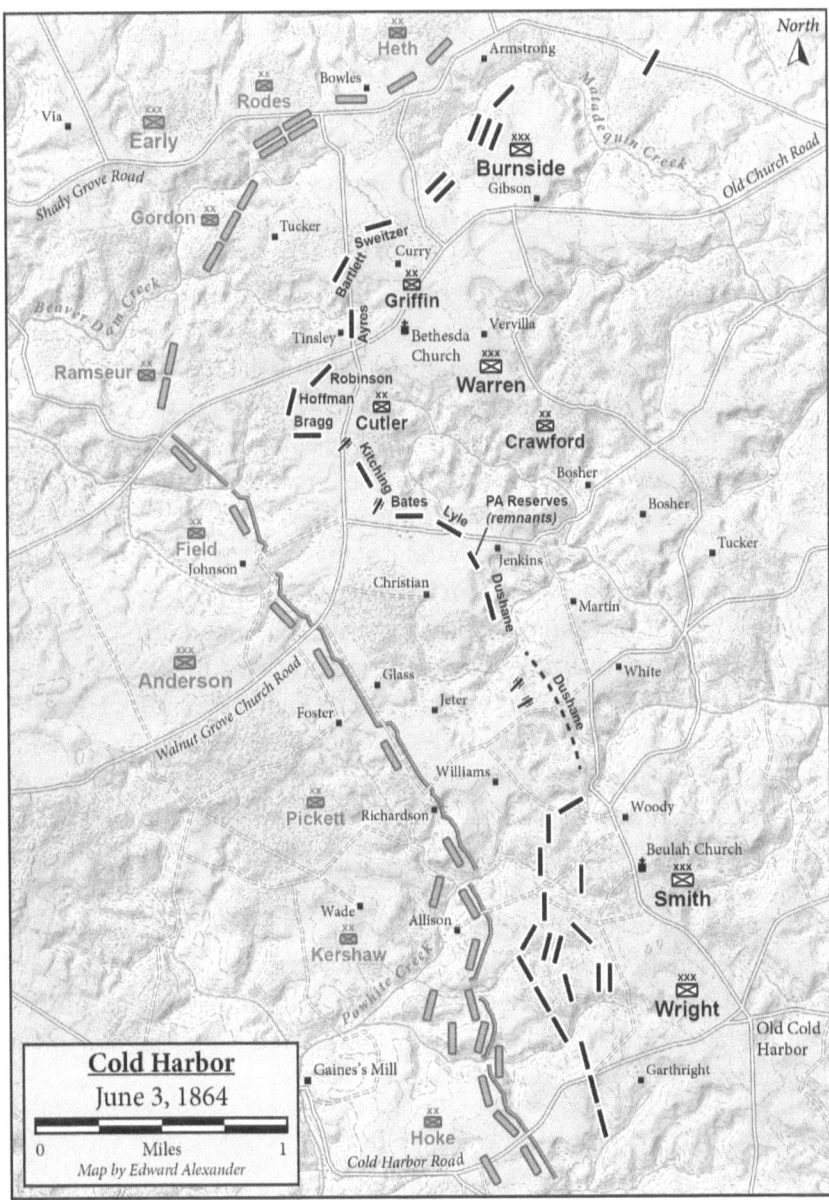

Cold Harbor
June 3, 1864

0 — Miles — 1
Map by Edward Alexander

Meanwhile, the Federal left wing struck the heaviest blow to Lee's line that morning near the Old Cold Harbor crossroads, where each army had concentrated the bulk of its forces. The attack by the Union's Second, Sixth, and Eighteenth Corps went forward at 4:30 A.M. as ordered. The bluecoats captured some of the enemy's forward positions, and in some cases even gained the main line of works, before the advance ground to a halt. As one brigade commander reported, the fire from front and flank became "too murderous for any troops to long sustain. The ground was swept with canister and rifle bullets until it was literally covered by the slain." The Confederates repulsed all further attempts to press forward and take their main line. Men began digging in with whatever utensils they could lay their hands on where their advance stalled, sometimes only thirty to forty yards from the Rebel line.[46]

Meade continued to press his corps commanders, but the inability to properly coordinate their actions combined with the commanders' reluctance to continue the seemingly hopeless assault doomed the operation. The attack's momentum sapped and the participating forces horribly bloodied, the assault could not resume. "The opinion of corps commanders not being sanguine of success in case an assault is ordered," Grant informed Meade, "you may direct a suspension of a farther advance for the present." Meade subsequently did just that at 12:30 P.M., directing his corps commanders to entrench in the positions they held.[47]

The Army of the Potomac lost in the neighborhood of 6,000 men that morning. Heavy artillery regiments spearheaded the Second Corps assaults and suffered very severe losses. The Eighth New York Heavy of Gibbon's division took 505 casualties, including 207 killed. The Seventh New York Heavy, leading Barlow's advance, suffered a total of 418 casualties, of whom 127 were killed. Confederate casualties numbered only about one-fifth to one-quarter of the aggregate Federal loss. In his memoirs Grant acknowledged that he "always regretted that the last assault at Cold Harbor was ever made. . . . [N]o advantage whatever was gained to compensate for the heavy loss we sustained." Brig. Gen. Evander Law would concur, having observed the slaughter of the Union men from his Confederate brigade's well-engineered works. Years later he lamented, "It was not war; it was murder."[48]

CHAPTER SEVEN

Across the James

There were no major changes in the positions of either army during the night of June 3. As Lt. Col. Theodore Lyman wrote to his wife after the battle, "there the two armies slept—almost within an easy stone's throw of each other; and the separating space ploughed by cannon-shot and dotted with the dead bodies that neither side dared to bury." The close proximity of the enemy gave him pause. "I think nothing can give a greater idea of the deathless tenacity of purpose, than the picture of those two hosts, after a bloody and nearly continuous struggle of thirty days, thus lying down to sleep with their hands almost on each other's throats!" The violence of the previous day remained fresh in everyone's minds.[1]

Fortunately for Warren and the men of the Fifth Corps, in one minor adjustment that occurred during the night, the enemy retired a short distance west on the Shady Grove Road, where they remained without taking the offensive the next day. Indeed, there was no major fighting on June 4. Nevertheless, with the opposing sides so close, considerable firing across the lines occurred, though nothing compared to the chaos and devastation of the previous day. A sergeant in Kitching's brigade, hunkered down in the works, remembered that although Federal batteries shelled the enemy from time to time, "the Johnnies kept their temper admirably." Major Roebling recalled that it began to rain that evening, but the "night passed quietly."[2]

On the morning of June 5, the Fifth Corps received orders to prepare to withdraw that night and move to the Leary farm, almost two miles in rear and to the northeast of Old Cold Harbor. From this position, near where the road to Parsley's Mill branched from the Old Cold Harbor–Old Church Road, the corps would hold as a reserve. Meanwhile, the men had little idea of what the day had in store for them. In camp that afternoon Kitching's heavies discussed a rumor of a ninety-day armistice. Later, their tents pitched, they began to settle in for the evening when orders arrived to strike the tents and prepare to move at a moment's notice. At sunset Ayres's brigade made a slight demonstration to hold the enemy in place so that the Fifth Corps could move. As Kitching's heavies struck their tents and packed their belongings, Confederates charged their picket line. "We were ordered into the works," recalled a sergeant in the brigade, but the firing soon ceased. Then "at 9 o'clock we moved off by the left flank as silently as possible and marched till well toward morning." On the long night march, Crawford's division, still including Kitching's heavies, led the way. Cutler's division and then Griffin's followed, with the artillery scattered throughout the column. "The night was very dark; in places the road was quite muddy causing the men to straggle along slowly," Roebling reported. Griffin's division did not leave Bethesda Church until almost dawn. Despite the slow movement, the enemy did not pursue. Later that day, June 6, the entire Fifth Corps arrived safely in camp around Leary's in the Federal rear.[3]

The men of the Fifth Corps took advantage of this respite. Despite warm weather and dusty conditions, they made themselves comfortable and received an issue of new clothing and shoes, greatly needed after the difficult campaigning. One of Kitching's officers welcomed the opportunity to finally "put up Shelter Tents for to stay two or three days." Many appreciated the small things. One heavy thankfully recorded how he "drew clothing and washed up," while another enjoyed "getting rid of the dirt and lice. I am lousy, but they can't skirmish on me much, the officers and all the boys were in the same fix."[4]

Those at higher levels in the Fifth Corps spent much of their time at the Leary farm implementing yet another restructuring of the corps, as directed by Warren in a June 5 order. Crawford reverted to command of the Third Division, now comprising Col. Peter Lyle's brigade, Col. James L. Bates's brigade, and the brigade of veteran Pennsylvania Reserves under Col. James Carle. Warren's reorganization also elevated Brig. Gen. Romeyn Beck Ayres to division command. His reconstituted Second Division would include his own former First Division brigade, now commanded by Col. Edgar M. Gregory; Col. Nathan Dushane's Second (Maryland) Brigade, and Kitching's Third Brigade. Other changes resulted from the high incidence of dysentery and other sicknesses brought on by the lengthy exposure to hardships during the campaign coupled with poor drinking water and generally unsanitary conditions. Around the time of the Fifteenth's movement to Leary's, Colonel Schirmer fell ill. Although he attempted to remain with his command by traveling in an ambulance for over a week afterward, declining health forced him to leave the regiment. Lt. Col. Michael Wiedrich then assumed command of the Fifteenth New York Heavy Artillery.[5]

Schirmer would eventually recover, but he would never rejoin the regiment. His trip to New York from Brandy Station that April "to settle up . . . matters connected with recruiting [his] regiment" that "imperil[ed] [his] honor" had not achieved its objective. Near the end of August, the colonel, still on medical leave, was arrested in New York and then imprisoned in Washington. Subsequently charged with several offenses, most relating to irregularities in connection with raising his regiment—among them, embezzlement of funds and misappropriation of soldiers' bounties—Schirmer would be tried by a general court-martial beginning in March 1865 and ultimately convicted. In addition to being cashiered from the service of the United States, his sentence would include a heavy fine and imprisonment for three years at hard labor.[6]

As Wiedrich settled in to his new role as commander of the Fifteenth and Federal troops continued to dig in around Cold Harbor, Grant pondered his next move. He mused to Halleck about how, "after more than thirty days of trial, that the enemy deems it of the first importance to run no risks with the armies they now have." Instead, Grant judged that the Confederates "act purely on the defensive, behind breastworks, or feebly on the offensive immediately in front of them, and where in case of repulse they can instantly retire behind them." Now, virtually at Richmond's gates, the general in chief realized that his plan to draw Lee into the open and defeat him in a decisive battle had misfired. To break the stalemate, he decided to take the Army of the Potomac across the James River to strangle Richmond by cutting off its supply lines from the south and west.[7]

Late on June 6 Meade ordered Warren to send two divisions at daylight the next morning to the left of the Second Corps to picket along the Chickahominy River. As directed, Griffin's and Cutler's divisions, the two least affected by the reorganization, at daylight moved out for the Chickahominy, some five miles to their south. Meanwhile, the Fifteenth New York Heavy and the balance of Ayres's division, along with Crawford's division, remained in the fields around Leary's as the army's strategic reserve. Warren maintained his headquarters near the house at a location Wainwright described as "a wretched spot, being right at the corner of two roads where trains are all the time passing covering them with dust."[8]

At midmorning on June 7, elements of Early's Corps tried to work around the Union right flank by pressing the Ninth Corps. Humphreys directed Warren to hold Ayres's and Crawford's outfits in readiness to move to Burnside's support. Warren complied, although he complained that "to be always ready is to be never ready, for men cannot stand with belts, knapsacks, &c, on all the time without being broken down." Stand they did, however. Ayres's and Crawford's divisions "were kept under arms all day to go to the assistance of Burnside who was very apprehensive for his right flank, not knowing that it was covered by Allen's Mill dam." In the end, however, the Ninth Corps held its line and did not require assistance.[9]

The Fifth Corps enjoyed a relatively quiet day on June 8. The following day, Ayres reviewed Kitching's brigade. Other than that, June 9 and the next day remained quiet for the heavies and for the army as a whole. Roebling visited the troops along the Chickahominy on the tenth, finding the "pickets at the R. R. bridge exchanging papers and trading tobacco. Our people taking up rails on the R. R." The period of quiet and rest would soon end, however. The next day the Army of the Potomac received orders to withdraw from Cold Harbor and move to the James River.[10]

The main body of the army would begin its withdrawal as soon after dark as practicable on June 12. Warren's Fifth Corps, after crossing the Chickahominy River at Long Bridge, would swing to the west, marching out the Long Bridge Road toward a critical intersection, near Riddell's blacksmith shop on the old Glendale battlefield, of three roads running to Richmond. Warren would remain there while the rest of the army passed to his rear. In addition to screening the movement of the army, Grant designed the corps's feint to the west to deceive the enemy. He wanted the Confederates to believe that the Army of the Potomac intended to either advance on Richmond north of the James or to cross the river near Malvern Hill. Col. George H. Chapman's brigade of cavalry would lead the corps in this strategic move toward Riddell's Shop.[11]

At daybreak on the eleventh, "as perfect a June day as is possible to get up," according to Wainwright, Kitching's heavies, with the rest of Ayres's and Crawford's outfits, broke camp and began their march. The Second Division took the lead, followed by the Third, the reserve artillery, and the pontoon trains. "The road," Wainwright remembered, "though sandy, and somewhat dusty, was good, not having been cut up by previous travel." As they marched, Roebling reported, "great care was taken that our movement should not become known to the enemy; pickets were placed all around to keep in the stragglers." The column halted around 11 A.M. and went into camp on the grounds of the Moody house—"a little house, as it were on skids, like a corn barn," with "several pleasant catalpas around it"—and nearby Providence Church. The camps were kept as compact as possible, and commanders forbad any unnecessary fires that might alert the enemy of their presence. The corps remained in camp for the night and rested throughout the twelfth, "a beautiful day; very enjoyable here off from the rest of the army," Wainwright thought.[12]

At 6 P.M. the Fifth Corps commenced its movement to the Chickahominy and the James. Ayres's division again took the lead, followed by Crawford's division and then Wainwright's artillery. Meanwhile, at dark Griffin's and Cutler's divisions slipped quietly out of their positions unobserved by the enemy and proceeded toward Long Bridge. "There was a great charm in moving on such a beautiful clear night through the quiet country, and over good roads," Wainwright remembered. He perhaps romanticized how "the air had something exhilarating in it so that everyone moved along cheerfully," but the move went smoothly in any case. Shortly after dark Ayres's men neared Long Bridge. Without the pontoon bridge in place and with the cavalry in the road before them, the general halted his outfit for a short rest while Crawford's division massed behind them. Although hindered by deep water and Confederate resistance, the cavalry succeeded in establishing a bridgehead on the other side of the river after about an hour. Laying the pontoon bridge now commenced in earnest; the engineers had it completed by 1 A.M. on June 13.[13]

As soon as Chapman's troopers crossed the bridge, Crawford's division followed, then Ayres's men. Kitching's heavies crossed the Chickahominy at around 3 A.M. A need to remove obstructions in the road slowed the cavalry, so the infantry behind them could not begin to move out the Long Bridge Road until dawn approached. By sunrise Warren reached a plateau nearly two miles west of Long Bridge. There Crawford halted and placed his division into line. By 5 A.M. Ayres's division joined them, while Griffin's and Cutler's divisions continued crossing the river. The cavalry skirmished ahead, eventually driving Confederate troopers north up a road intersecting the Long Bridge Road and then across the bridge over White Oak Swamp. Once relieved by a brigade of Crawford's infantry, Chapman's cavalry resumed its advance west toward Riddell's Shop and the New Market Road. They initially engaged only Confederate cavalry at the intersection, but in the afternoon enemy infantry began to arrive. Crawford advanced his remaining troops in support, and both the Riddell's Shop intersection and the White Oak Swamp Bridge were held throughout the day and into the evening.[14]

Meanwhile, as dawn broke, Confederate pickets at Cold Harbor discovered that the Army of the Potomac had vanished from their front. "Our skirmishers were advanced between one and two miles, but failing to discover the enemy[,] were withdrawn," Lee would report to Secretary of War Seddon that evening. As a result, "the army was moved to conform to the route taken by him." The only specifics about the Union troops' whereabouts focused on the Fifth Corps's thrust westward from Long Bridge toward Riddell's Shop. Consequently, Lee's orders to "conform to the route taken" by the Federals led to Anderson's and Hill's Corps slipping south across the Chickahominy to take up a line running south from White Oak Swamp to Malvern Hill. For several critical days, Lee would have no clear understanding of Grant's movements or his intentions.[15]

As Lee tried to discern his adversary's position, the Federals continued to make progress. After Hancock's Second Corps crossed the Chickahominy, by 3:15 P.M. the engineers had begun taking up the pontoon bridge. The plan now called for Warren to follow the Second Corps and then for the cavalry to withdraw and trail the Fifth as rear guard. The Fifth's mission now complete, in the early afternoon Cutler's division started out first, guarding the corps trains, the division marching out the road from Long Bridge to Charles City Court House directly behind the Second Corps. At 8 P.M. Ayres's division, followed by Griffin's, moved by a shortcut Roebling had scouted toward Samaria Church, some six to seven miles distant. At the same time, Crawford and the cavalry withdrew from their advanced positions and fell in line behind Griffin. Despite the rain that evening, the head of the main column reached Samaria Church around midnight; Kitching's brigade arrived about two hours later. The men trudged into the fields around the church and went into camp for the night. Their sparring with the enemy that day resulted in combined losses among Crawford's division and Chapman's cavalry of approximately 300 killed and wounded. Even with those casualties, the Fifth Corps's screening mission was a success. Furthermore, the Federals' effort to deceive

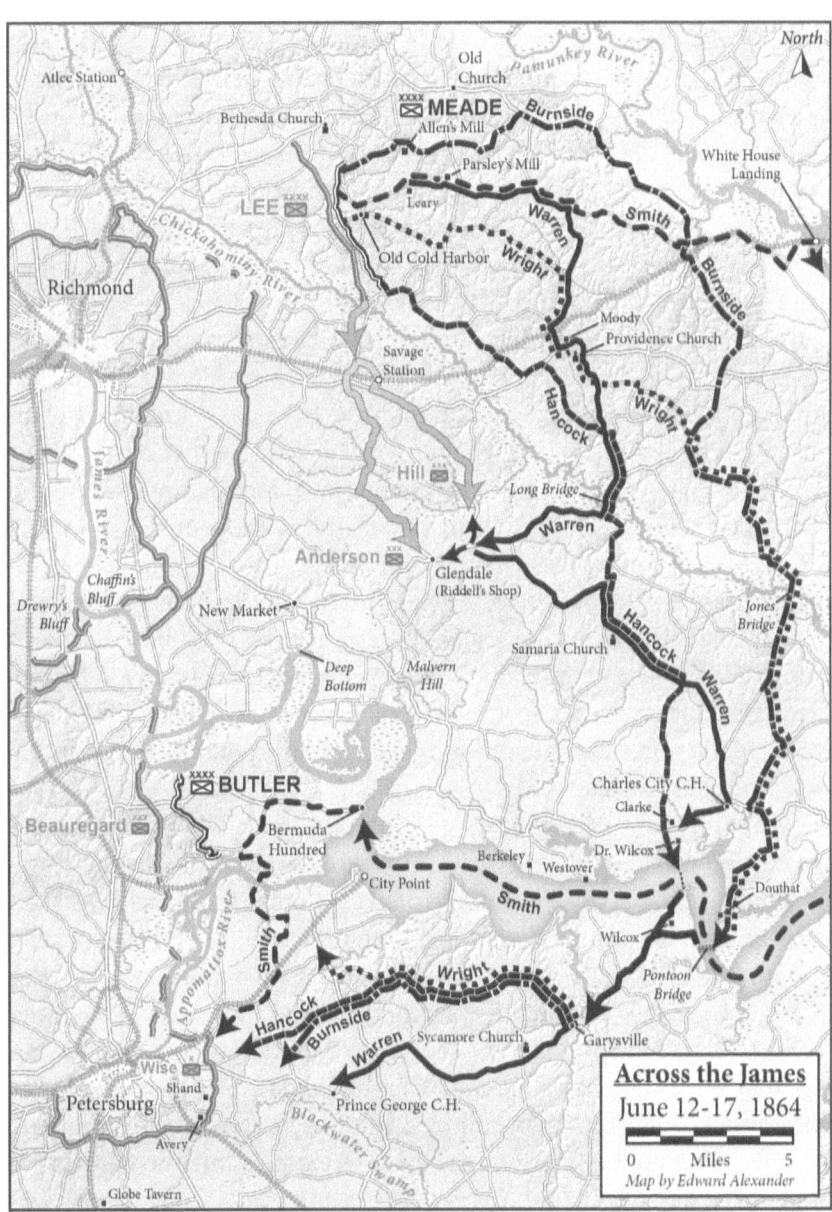

Lee as to their intentions by sending the corps out the Long Bridge Road had proven equally effective.[16]

Early the next morning the Fifth Corps resumed its move toward Charles City Court House. Arriving around noon after a march of about eight miles, the troops encamped a short distance west of the village. Kitching's brigade, one heavy recalled, set up camp "in sight of vessels on the James River." Riding across a wide field with Maj. James C. Duane, Meade's chief engineer, Lyman beheld what he first thought to be "a fog bank, or a grey ploughed field, or a great dust." Then Duane announced, "There's the river," and "the optical cheat cleared up" for Lyman as he "appreciated that [he] stood not far from the edge of a bluff overlooking a mighty river a mile wide. Six weeks in the Wilderness, and the James River at last!"[17]

By that evening (June 14), all four corps of the Army of the Potomac were encamped at the James. After their long and exhausting marches—between twenty-five and thirty-five miles or longer, depending on the route—the men awaited orders. The engineers immediately began constructing a pontoon bridge to span the river from below Douthat's place on the north bank to Windmill Point on the south, a distance of about 2,100 feet. The span required 101 pontoons. At midchannel, where the water was more than 80 feet deep, they anchored the pontoons to vessels moored for that purpose. Further complicating matters, the engineers had to construct the bridge with a readily removable section midchannel to allow the passage of river traffic. Even preparing the approaches provided a challenge, as they had to cut down huge cypress trees and heavily corduroy in boggy areas. In one of the monumental engineering achievements of the war, Grant's engineers completed the pontoon bridge in the predawn hours of June 15.[18]

While the army consolidated as it prepared to cross the James, the men also constructed defensive works in a broad arc to protect the crossing points, with the center near Charles City Court House and the flanks curving back toward the river. First to arrive late on the thirteenth, the Second Corps had constructed the works on the left of the line to the west of the town. Here the line ran essentially parallel to and about one mile from the river. When the Fifth Corps arrived around noon the following day, they relieved Hancock's men, who moved down to the James to begin crossing. Warren's men tumbled into the readymade fortifications for a well-deserved rest, although one of Kitching's men noted that the brigade remained behind the works "in line of battle" during the day and all the night of their arrival there. Upon reaching the Charles City Court House that day, the Sixth Corps dug in on the right of the Fifth Corps, with the Ninth Corps, the last to arrive, taking position to the Sixth's right and extending the line to the river.[19]

On the morning of June 15, Griffin's and Cutler's divisions shifted to the high ground in the vicinity of the Dr. Wilcox and Clark houses and nearer the James in order to cover the road leading from Westover. Wainwright found Dr. Wilcox's house, about a half mile from the river, "for Virginia . . . a good house, and in quite decent order outside and around"; he added, "the doctor's daughter, a married woman, is very agreeable." The colonel camped south of the house in a grove of mature locust trees, with "a fine grass field" to his front and a good view of the James. Clark's cherry trees proved an irresistible temptation to the bluecoats, as did everything edible in and around the beautiful house, including shad and bacon, which was soon confiscated by the hungry soldiers. Meanwhile, Crawford's and Ayres's divisions remained in the works to the west of Charles City Court House and enjoyed a most welcome day of relative rest and calm. "We lounged about our tents," one of Ayres's soldiers remembered, "enjoying the luxury of idleness that came only at rare intervals." As they relaxed the troops could not ignore the sound of intermittent firing from the direction of Petersburg. With the issuance that afternoon of four days' rations, Ayres's men knew they had more hard work ahead.[20]

Buoyed by the success of the army's rapid and apparently undetected march to the James, the day before a confident Grant had reported to Halleck: "Our forces will commence crossing the James today. The enemy show no signs yet of having brought troops to the south side of Richmond." He optimistically predicted, "I will have Petersburg secured, if possible, before they get there in much force."[21]

To that end, Grant decided Butler's Army of the James should immediately attempt to capture Petersburg before it could be reinforced. Less than two weeks after the start of the spring offensives, instead of operating against Richmond and Petersburg as ordered, Butler withdrew his forces into the Bermuda Hundred north of the Appomattox River. There, although in a very secure position, the army was, Grant observed, "as completely shut off from further operations directly against Richmond as if it had been in a bottle strongly corked." The general in chief now wanted the Army of the James back on the offensive. Crossing by steamer to Butler's headquarters at Bermuda Hundred, Grant personally ordered him to capture Petersburg. He directed Butler to send Smith's Eighteenth Corps, arriving by transports from White House throughout that day, forward that night and reinforce them with all the troops he could spare. Assuring him that Hancock's corps would support the assaulting force if needed, Grant then hurried back to press the Army of the Potomac's crossing.[22]

Petersburg's defenses consisted of an approximately ten-mile-long line of works surrounding the town—the "Dimmock Line"—with both flanks anchored on the Appomattox River. By about 1:30 P.M. on June 15, Smith approached the fortifications and halted his command to reconnoiter the position and prepare for the attack. The line appeared formidable, but in fact it was a hollow shell. Only Brig. Gen. Henry A. Wise's brigade, a handful of militia—the proverbial "old men and young boys" of the Home Guard—some artillery, and a brigade of cavalry manned it. This concentration of virtually all of Petersburg's defenders on the left of the Dimmock Line to meet the Federal advance left the remainder of the line virtually abandoned.[23]

His troops finally in position, Smith ordered the advance at approximately 7 P.M. Striking a salient in the Confederate line near where the City Point Railroad crossed the Dimmock Line, the attackers swept into Batteries 5 and 6 within twenty-five minutes. In domino-like fashion, additional enemy batteries also fell, two to the north nearer the river and five to the south. The Federals had cracked the Dimmock Line with amazing ease. They took a mile and a half of entrenchments and sixteen guns in less than two hours, and with very few losses. As dusk approached, rather than exploiting the opportunity to press ahead, Smith worked to consolidate his position and make troop dispositions to hold the ground gained. The Second Corps finally arrived but too late to resume offensive operations. Delays throughout the day, compounded by Smith's decision to wait until morning to press the Union army's advantage, resulted in the loss of a golden opportunity.[24]

Confederate general P. G. T. Beauregard, in command of Petersburg's defenses, had worried about the possibility that Grant might cross the James and strike the city. Throughout June 14, he communicated to Gen. Braxton Bragg, Pres. Jefferson Davis's chief of staff, his concern for the security of Petersburg. Still uncertain of the whereabouts of bulk of the Army of the Potomac, Lee remained unconvinced. Nevertheless, shortly after 9 P.M. Bragg informed Beauregard that Lee had dispatched Maj. Gen. Robert F. Hoke's division to Drewry's Bluff, where he could call upon it for support if the Federals threatened the city. Summoned early on June 15 when Wise's force initially made contact with Smith's advance, Hoke's lead brigade, Brig. Gen. Johnson Hagood's South Carolinians, arrived by rail in Petersburg about dark.[25]

When initial reports arrived at Beauregard's headquarters that Batteries 3 through 7 had been carried, Hagood immediately headed out the City Point Road in the dark and unfamiliar territory and managed to identify a position for a new line west of and roughly parallel to Harrison's Creek. He placed his brigade on the left near the Appomattox River behind Batteries 1 and 2 of the Dimmock Line. The new position, called the Hagood Line, ran south from that point to where it intersected the Dimmock Line near Battery 17 and lay roughly 800 yards west of that portion now in Federal hands. As the balance of Hoke's Division arrived throughout the night, they fell in behind Hagood's troops and began to entrench. At 10:20 P.M. on June 15, Beauregard ordered Maj. Gen. Bushrod R. Johnson to withdraw his division from the Howlett Line at Bermuda Hundred and proceed to Petersburg. Johnson would arrive at 10 A.M. the next day.[26]

While the fighting raged in Petersburg, north of the James at a little before 9 P.M. on June 15, Warren received orders to take his Fifth Corps across the river at daylight the following morning. Griffin's and Cutler's divisions, encamped near Clark's and Wilcox's, would move the short distance down to the river and ferry across from Wilcox's Wharf. Ayres's and Crawford's divisions would instead have a much longer march to board ferries at a point Meade described as "near the bridge." The crossing operation would begin at 4 A.M., and the movement order required division commanders to "use the utmost promptness" in shifting their troops to the ferries by the appointed hour. The corps trains and artillery would assemble near the pontoon bridge and would use it to cross the James. As the Fifth Corps crossed, the Sixth Corps would then pull out and follow as rear guard. Meanwhile, the Ninth Corps that afternoon had already begun crossing via the pontoon bridge and proceeding to Petersburg.[27]

As ordered, before daybreak on June 16, Crawford's and Ayres's divisions marched down Weyanoke Point to Douthat's Landing just upriver from the pontoon bridge, where they were to pick up the transports for the short trip across the James. Meanwhile, the remaining two divisions, Griffin's and Cutler's, began crossing from Wilcox's Wharf by about 6 A.M. After marching five or six miles, Kitching's heavies arrived at the river near noon. Boarding the transports *John Brooks* and *Monohassett,* the men soon found themselves on the south bank of the river on the fields of Flowerdew Hundred, a working plantation owned by yet another Wilcox and dating from colonial times. The prior day hungry troops of the Second Corps had harvested the owner's vegetables and cherries, enjoyed hoecakes eagerly sold to them by the owner's slaves, and consumed any other delicacies they could find. As planned, the corps trains and artillery crossed on the pontoon bridge. The marching men and rolling trains on the bridge, one of Ayres's men crossing by steamer observed, made it "appear like some gigantic serpent stretching from one bank of the river to the other."[28]

While waiting on the south side for the infantry to arrive and consolidate on a "very hot" day, "far [hotter] than any we have had before this season," Wainwright parked his artillery about a mile from the terminus of the bridge and made himself comfortable under the trees surrounding the Wilcox house. Despite the visit by the Second Corps the prior day, he found the residents, at least the women, sympathetic toward the Union soldiers suffering from the heat. "The ladies in the house, of whom there seemed a number, were very kind to these poor fellows;" he reported, "they could not have been more so had they been 'Yankees' themselves instead of Virginians."[29]

By 1 P.M. all of the Fifth Corps infantry had arrived. A soldier in Ayres's division noted, "Both banks of the river were swarming with activity as the boats plied back and forth carrying their loads of soldiers, and the pontoon bridge seemed alive with the moving trains and artillery wagons." Amid the hustle and bustle, he recalled, "The river flowed serenely between banks of green verdure, crowned here and there with large trees throwing their shade upon the grass and moving water." Apparently discounting the soldiers, artillery wagons, and pontoon bridge, the soldier concluded, "The setting of this scene was more appropriate for peace and harmony than war and strife." The later arrival of the army's main trains, including the artillery train guarded by Dieckmann's battalion, all of which would cross by the pontoon bridge later that day and into the night, certainly must have rendered the "scene's" appearance less pastoral. The following day, June 17, Brig. Gen. Edward Ferrero's Ninth Corps

Fourth Division, comprising US Colored Troops, escorted the trains nearer Petersburg to their park between Bailey's Creek and City Point.[30]

At about 2 P.M., after a short rest, the Fifth Corps moved off toward Petersburg. After leaving Flowerdew Hundred, the men passed through Garysville, following a direct route that would take them through Prince George Court House and into the Army of the Potomac's line near its left flank. They found the fourteen-mile march difficult in part because, as Roebling reported, "the day was very hot and dusty, no water along the road." Near Sycamore Church, about six miles into the march, a courier arrived with a dispatch Grant had sent earlier in the day directing Meade to "hurry Warren up by the nearest road to reach the Jerusalem Plank Road, about three miles out from Petersburg." Warren informed the army commander that he was "on the road and will make as good time as possible, and reach there before camping." But he clarified, "It, of course, could not be expected of me to be there before dark, but I certainly will be [there] before morning." As the hot, thirsty, dusty, and exhausted troops of the Fifth Corps plodded along, they heard heavy artillery and musket firing ahead.[31]

As Burnside's men had arrived on the fields east of Petersburg that morning, Grant ordered them to mass on the left of the Second Corps. At 9:30 P.M. Meade directed Warren to advance and take position on Burnside's left. The men of the Fifth Corps continued to trudge along in the darkness. "Everyone was very sleepy, the heat of the previous day seeming to have taken all the vigour out of the men," Wainwright recalled. So worn out were they that "after every little halt more or less of the infantry were left asleep on the side of the road." By midnight the Fifth Corps arrived within a few miles of the lines and camped along the Prince George Court House Road near a small run. Although Warren soon discovered they had several miles to go to reach Petersburg, he allowed the exhausted men to remain where they were for the night.[32]

Very early the next morning, June 17, Brig. Gen. Robert B. Potter's Ninth Corps division attacked and successfully captured a section of the enemy line in the vicinity of the Shand house. The Confederates fleeing Potter's pursuing men, however, regrouped on a new line to the west. When, at about 8 A.M., Roebling went forward to reconnoiter, he could clearly see the new Confederate position in the distance running nearly north–south along the eastern edge of a body of timber. By midmorning the Fifth Corps infantry began to arrive on the field. Cutler's division and the Maryland

Brigade moved into line east of the Avery house on the Ninth Corps's left, with Cutler's left reaching to the Norfolk and Petersburg Railroad. All day long Rebel sharpshooters occupying the house plied their trade on the nearby Federals.[33]

Meanwhile, Ayres's and Crawford's divisions filed to the rear of the Ninth Corps behind the old Dimmock Line, with Griffin's division massed behind them. At 11 A.M. Warren reported to Meade, "I am ready for whatever is to be done, and have been some time." During the afternoon and early evening, elements of the Ninth Corps launched two more attacks against the Hagood Line—Crawford supported the evening attack—and although some parts of the line were seized, the Federals were eventually driven back. Ayres's division, a short distance to the rear of this action, did not participate.[34]

Most of the day and throughout that night, Kitching's heavies lay in the old Dimmock Line works, now reversed to face the new Confederate position, to the east of the Avery house. During the afternoon, Company B, First Battalion, Fifteenth New York Heavy, the company that had remained at Brandy Station on provost-guard duty when the campaign began, arrived and reported for duty with the regiment. John Gedney of the Sixth New York Heavy remembered, "heavy firing and fighting going on. . . . [T]he enemy amused themselves . . . by shelling our position but they did not hurt anyone." But shell fragments did hit twenty-four-year-old Capt. William D. Dickey, commander of the Fifteenth's Company M, in the thigh as the regiment lay in reserve in the works. Refusing to leave the field, Dickey led his company in the attacks that would take place the following day. For this unselfish act, he was cited for "most distinguished gallantry in action" and would receive the Medal of Honor.[35]

At 11 P.M. that night, Meade directed that the whole of the Second, Fifth, and Ninth Corps, as well as one division from each of the Sixth and Eighteenth Corps, launch a "vigorous assault" at 4 A.M. the next day. As ordered, Crawford's and Cutler's divisions stepped out near daylight on Saturday, June 18. Roebling accompanied Cutler's vanguard as it moved forward. After cautiously advancing a short distance, they discovered the enemy had abandoned the Avery house and the entrenchments near it. "One old fellow was found asleep in the Avery house," Roebling remembered, but he offered no assistance as to the enemy's location. Instead, he told them that "there was a line of battle there when he fell asleep in the middle of the night." When Roebling returned to corps headquarters to convey the news, similar reports began to filter in from other parts of the field. The Rebels had clearly evacuated the line they had fought so tenaciously to hold the previous evening.[36]

Even as, on the morning of June 17, Lee had remained hesitant, uncertain of the location of Grant's forces, Beauregard recognized that he could not hold his overextended position and would have to withdraw to a shorter line. In anticipation of this eventuality, during the day he and Col. David B. Harris laid out the new "Harris Line." This ran from the Appomattox River on the north in a generally southerly direction until intersecting the old Dimmock Line, which at that point continued in a generally westerly direction. The Harris Line ran about 800 yards behind the Hagood Line in the sector near the river and slightly over a mile to the rear near its southern terminus at the Dimmock Line. The Norfolk and Petersburg Railroad crossed the abandoned section of the Dimmock Line just south of the Avery house, then swung sharply to the right so as to nearly parallel the new line until crossing it at an acute angle at about its midway point. By late afternoon Lee was finally convinced of the danger to Petersburg and began transferring a significant force south to bolster the city's defenders. Shortly after midnight, Beauregard carefully withdrew his men to the Harris Line, where they began to further strengthen the position. By 11:30 A.M. on June 18, Lee himself assumed overall command of Petersburg's defense.[37]

It was not long before the Federals confirmed, through information gleaned from Confederate prisoners, that the defending forces had retired during the night to a contracted line nearer Petersburg. Consequently, at 5:55 A.M. Meade ordered that "corps and other independent commanders will, at once, advance their respective commands, keeping up prompt communication with the troops on their right and left, and develop the enemy's new position." The Army of the Potomac cautiously resumed its advance. The Second Corps, led by Maj. Gen. David Birney that day, encountered the new Confederate line first. Birney launched a series of attacks attempting to overcome the Rebel position over the next several hours, but all ended in failure and with heavy losses.[38]

To the left of the Second Corps, Brig. Gen. Orlando B. Willcox's and Brig. Gen. Robert B. Potter's Ninth Corps divisions moved out beyond the abandoned Hagood Line and toward the Taylor house. From the open ground in front of the house, they could see the new, strongly entrenched Confederate line. The railroad cut and the ravine through which Poor Creek ran separated the Federals from the enemy line. As Willcox's bluecoats pressed ahead, they tumbled into the thirty-foot-deep railroad cut, with a nearly vertical wall on the side toward the Rebel position. The Union attack faltered as the men struggled to scale the western wall of the cut, even by trying to cut steps in it.[39]

Earlier, after the enemy's withdrawal had been confirmed, Roebling departed Fifth Corps headquarters and galloped back to Cutler with Warren's order to develop the new enemy position. As the division advanced beyond the Avery house, a rifled battery on the crest of a ridge to the west opened fire. Roebling could see an entrenched line along the ridge as well as men standing on the parapets. Cutler's bluecoats next encountered the railroad cut and a line of skirmishers. After some delay, but now with artillery support, they pressed the skirmishers back, Cutler re-forming his line on the western side of the railroad cut. But the hailstorm of artillery fire and musketry from the enemy's defenses rendered any further advance very hazardous. Moving in rear of Cutler's troops and then to the west, Ayres's men proceeded astride the vacated Confederate fortifications running toward the connection between the new Harris Line and the still-occupied sector of the Dimmock Line. A bulge in the line at this junction came to be known as Rives's Salient. Kitching's heavies moved on the division's right, remaining inside the old Dimmock Line. Taking position on Cutler's left, Ayres's outfit now occupied the army's extreme left flank.[40]

Meanwhile, Crawford had advanced his division as well, keeping station on the left of Willcox's outfit as it moved. As a separation opened between Crawford's and Cutler's advancing lines, Griffin's division moved up from its position behind a body of woods near the Shand house to fill the gap. His men advanced through the fields south of Baxter Road and eventually astride the road, Crawford's division to their right, until they reached the railroad cut. After discovering that the bridge carrying the road over it had been destroyed, the men piled into the cut. Its depth and sheer walls again posed a significant obstacle to the advance, or as Roebling reported, "after the men were got into it, it was hard to get them out again." Under heavy fire, Griffin's men eventually scaled the deep cut and established a lodgment just beyond it. When Crawford's men finally emerged from the cut as well, they reformed on its western brow.[41]

Throughout the morning, Meade had pressed his commanders to launch a coordinated assault along the whole of the enemy's new line. Warren replied by outlining the significant difficulties confronting him. First, the Fifth Corps had a greater distance to advance than any of the others. In addition to the problems presented by the deep railroad cut, the various ravines at the head of Poor Creek made for a difficult passage in most possible approaches. In front of Ayres's outfit—where the terrain was relatively level—the enemy artillery at Rives's Salient had such sweep that just forming a line of battle would be a costly proposition. But Meade ignored Warren's explanations. "The attack ordered will be made by your command promptly at 12 M." Roebling later characterized this peremptory order as implying they move "at all hazards, no matter whether we understood the ground or not, or were prepared anyhow." Warren persisted, "I cannot be ready to attack in line or column before 1 P.M." Meade, his patience at its limit, again asserted his authority. "Everyone else is ready. You will attack as soon as possible after the hour designated."[42]

Yet Warren did not complete his preparations for the assault until almost 3 P.M. The time required to transmit the attack order to the four division commanders, coupled with widely differing terrain facing each, necessarily resulted in a disjointed advance. Griffin's men achieved the

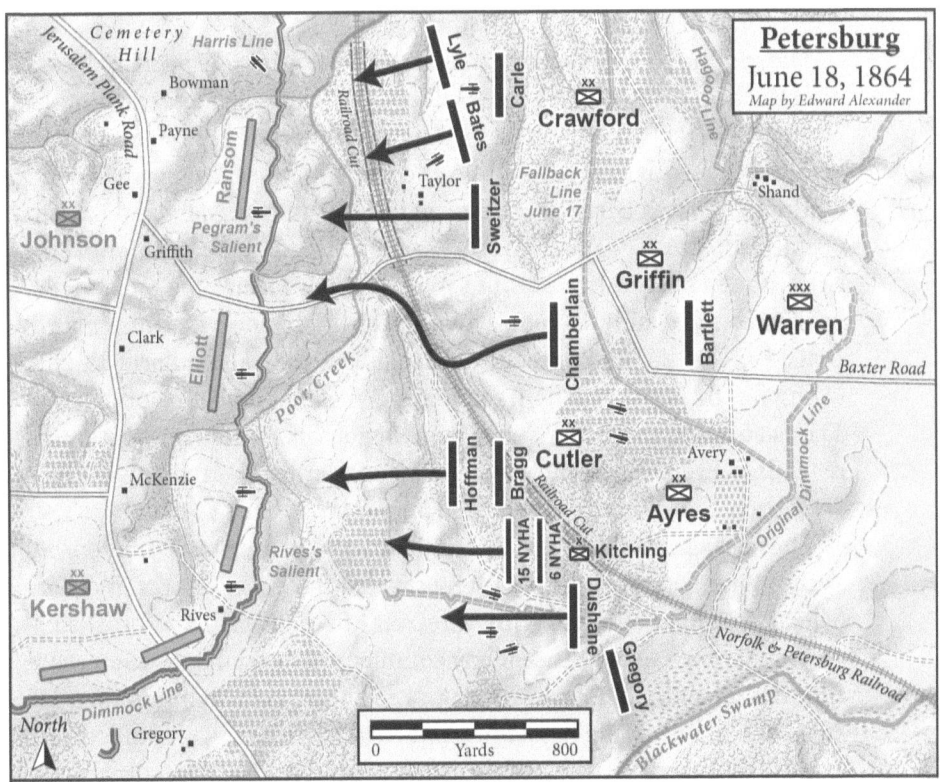

greatest success. Splashing across the boggy Poor Creek and up the ridge on the other side, all the time under a galling fire, some of his men made it to within yards of the Confederate works. In the end they held an advanced position west of Poor Creek, a mere 150 yards from the enemy entrenchments. Crawford also made additional gains to within about the same distance of the enemy's works.[43]

The Fifth Corps's left faced a different situation. The protection provided by the railroad cut and the reverse slopes of ridges beyond it, all quite close to the enemy position, afforded Griffin and Crawford certain advantages not enjoyed by the corps's other two divisions. Cutler and Ayres, attacking farther from the enemy line, did not have the benefit of protective ground. When Cutler advanced shortly after 3 P.M., his division faced sweeping enemy artillery fire, including a few guns within long canister range. Some of Cutler's veterans broke and fled to the rear, but a contingent of the outfit gained and held a ridge to the east of Poor Creek. A handful of his men at one point even advanced to within approximately seventy-five yards of the enemy works. In this attempt Cutler lost about one-third of his men killed and wounded.[44]

The ground to Ayres's front and Cutler's left was wide open and level, directly facing the Confederate artillery in Rives's Salient. Kitching arrayed his brigade of heavies in two lines on the right of the formation, with the Fifteenth as the front line and initially connecting with Colonel Hoffman's Fourth Division brigade on its right and the Maryland Brigade on the left. Col. Edgar M. Gregory's First Brigade took position to the left of the Maryland Brigade. But Ayres did not receive the attack order in time to move simultaneously with Cutler. This delay left the Fourth Division's left flank uncovered during its advance and subject to enfilading fire from the salient. In addition, Ayres had problems of his own. The flat ground to his front was, Roebling observed, "fairly swept by the rebel fire." Even so, upon receiving the attack order and making his final dispositions, Ayres took his division forward.[45]

The heavies moved out in "beautiful order," Kitching remembered, but as they entered a cornfield relatively close to the enemy works, the Confederates opened on them with "a fearful fire of artillery and musketry." Captain Gedney noted, "the enemy commenced to shell us as soon as we appeared in sight and kept it up." As a result, 159 of Kitching's men fell killed or wounded. The Fifteenth suffered 7 men killed, with 1 officer and 43 men wounded. A man in the veteran 146th New York Infantry on the division's left remembered that for a few minutes the position "was as uncomfortable as any in which the regiment had ever been placed." After advancing about 300 yards, the Second Division halted and its men began to dig in to protect themselves from the scathing fire. As they worked, Wiedrich reported, his heavies faced a "murderous fire of the enemy's sharpshooters." Gedney remembered "the enemy keeping an incessant fire so we did not dare to stand up." Ayres eventually refused his left so as to rest within the old Dimmock Line works. Kitching later described to his father the speed with which his men could now throw up sufficient earth to protect them in dangerous circumstances. "Bayonets, spoons, hands, sticks,—almost anything is used to 'scratch dirt,'" he explained, "and like magic a line of two or three thousand men who are one moment exposed to every shot will be pitching head foremost into the earth, like moles."[46]

The Federals fared no better on the army's right flank. Elements of the Sixth and Eighteenth Corps advanced and took the first line of enemy rifle pits before halting and digging in without gaining much more ground. A subsequent Second Corps attack around 4 P.M. also ended in failure and with considerable loss. By now even the battle-tested veterans of Hancock's renowned corps had had enough, and many refused to go forward. Some of the newer "green" troops, however, continued simply to do as they were told. For example, when Brig. Gen. Gershom Mott ordered his brigade forward about 4:30 P.M., only the First Maine Heavy Artillery stepped out. After a fight that did not last more than fifteen minutes, 632 of the approximately 900 men who went forward were counted as casualties, of whom 210 were killed. The First Maine suffered one of the highest aggregate losses by a single regiment in either army during the war.[47]

At 9:50 P.M. Meade summed up the day's efforts to Grant. He expressed confidence that "these assaults were all well made," and despite the failures he felt "satisfied that all that men could do under the circumstances was done." Meade also expressed "great regret that I am not able to report more success." Grant agreed with his assessment, however, assuring Meade, "I am perfectly satisfied that all has been done that could be done." In his journal Wainwright admitted that he saw matters slightly differently than did his army's commander. "I cannot say that our men went in well, or at all as if they meant to carry the works." After such a trying campaign, however, Grant planned to "rest the men and use the spade for their protection until a new vein can be struck." His campaign of maneuver had not produced a decisive victory in Virginia or destroyed Lee's army on open ground. He would have to revise his strategy, especially since the men now knew of its dangers. As Wainwright observed, "The attack this afternoon was a fiasco of the worst kind." He hoped that "it will be the last attempt at this most absurd way of attacking entrenchments. . . . Even the stupidest private now knows it cannot succeed. . . . [T]he men will not try it. The very sight of a bank of fresh earth now brings them to a dead halt." The war of maneuver was over. Both armies now prepared for a siege.[48]

CHAPTER EIGHT

In the Trenches before Petersburg

Nighttime did not bring an end to the firing. When Pvt. Carl Matteson of the Fifteenth New York Heavy received a letter from his sister on the night of June 18, 1864, he had to wait until things calmed down a bit the next day to respond. As he explained to her, "I lit a candle and read the greater part of it while the Johny Rebs blazed their humming birds around my head." Of the fight the prior day, he reported, "I took a new chum about a week ago to tent with me, he was shot in the head beside me yesterday afternoon." Still, Matteson tried to focus on mundane aspects of life, requesting that his sister send envelopes and stamps, which, along with paper, were increasingly scarce for men "out here in front." He had to close his short letter quickly, explaining, "Here comes the shell and bullets and we must soon send our compliments to the Johneys."[1]

The Army of the Potomac did not launch offensive operations on the nineteenth, but sharpshooters on both sides remained active. As Colonel Wainwright mused, "This has been a day of rest; that is, so far as remaining under a constant fire of musketry, and an occasional outpouring of artillery can be called rest." The Federals held the position they had gained the previous day, and Colonel Kitching informed his father, "so close are we to the 'Johnnies,' that both sides are living in holes in the ground." Although he and his staff initially attempted "to live without cover," they had to "go into garrison" after enemy fire hit two of his headquarters guards and three of the brigade staff's horses. They then built a small bombproof headquarters of pine logs covered with sand that protected them "so long as we can remain inside." From his position of safety, Kitching boasted: "Many of my men are becoming splendid marksmen. The men from western New York, that I got last winter, are almost all good shots, and have been inflicting severe punishment upon the enemy." He confided that he had to restrain these proficient marksmen in some instances. "I have stopped the firing of my pickets once or twice, for I think it nothing less than murder, but just so soon as my men stop, the rascals commence to crawl up towards us so that we are forced to open fire again."[2]

The two Federal armies before Petersburg now settled into what many anticipated as a siege, and Grant turned his attention to the investment of the city by cutting its remaining lines of supply and communication. Petersburg served as a main rail center through which supplies to Richmond continued to flow, so severing its rail links to the rest of the Confederacy would slash a vital lifeline to the Confederate capital. Three railroads still served the city. On the north the Richmond and Petersburg passed in rear of the Howlett Line and continued on to Richmond. Entering the Cockade City from the west, the South Side Railroad connected it with Lynchburg and points farther west. Finally, the Weldon and Petersburg Railroad ran south from the city to Weldon, North Carolina, where it joined with the Wilmington and Weldon Railroad, providing a crucial supply line from the port of Wilmington, North Carolina.[3]

Achieving this broad objective required extending the Federals' left to sever the Weldon and Petersburg Railroad, often referred to more simply as the "Weldon Railroad," and then ultimately the Southside Railroad. The Federals made their first attempt on June 22, when the Sixth Corps, supported by the Second, drove west from a point several miles south of the army's left flank to reach and cut the Weldon Railroad. They abandoned the effort after encountering stiff Confederate resistance and suffering significant casualties. As a result, by late in the evening on June 23, the Sixth Corps held a position to the left of the Second, thrown back facing the railroad and a little more than a mile from it. Hancock's corps, with its right resting near the Jerusalem Plank Road, maintained a connection with Griffin's division, then on the Fifth Corps's left.[4]

The days immediately following this unsuccessful attempt saw some shuffling of units on the Union line that ultimately affected the Fifth Corps. When it was completed, Warren's troops occupied about a mile and a half of the main line. Cutler's division on the corps's right connected with Willcox's Ninth Corps division at the Baxter Road. Ayres's division sat on Cutler's left, with Griffin next in line, his left resting on the Jerusalem Plank Road. Across the Plank Road, Crawford's division extended the line to the southwest.[5]

As other units shifted, Kitching's heavies had remained in the position they occupied since the stalled June 18 attack. The relative inactivity afforded the men an opportunity to write home. Private Matteson reflected on the Fifteenth's evolution as a fighting unit since its first taste of battle in the Wilderness. "The first fight our Regiment went into . . . there was some big skadaddling you bet, but that got played out." Now that the men had more experience, "our boys go in with yells and fight like very devils. There is no soger [soldier] what dreads to go into action but when once started our boys *fight*." Matteson had more time to write a couple of days later, so he described the regiment's new life in the trenches. "This day is opened with the heaviest cannonading I ever heard. The shells are bursting over our heads. The bullets zip and kill and wound some of our men, but our sharp shooters and pickets are not idle."[6]

The men of the Army of the Potomac had endured brutal fighting and marching between the Rapidan River and Petersburg; the days in the trenches now offered only marginal improvement. Relieved from the exhaustion of constant marching and relatively safe from enemy fire, they now dealt with oppressive heat and lack of water. With no rain since the beginning of June, springs, marshes, and ponds were dry. The constant passing of troops and their wagons through the area had pulverized the earth, resulting in a fine dust several inches thick on roads and plains that rose in large clouds to cover everything and everyone. Even without surface water, Chief of Staff Humphreys reported that below the porous top soil "at no great depth" lay a strata of clay on top of which "there was an abundance of water that did not prove unhealthy." Wells were dug, Major Roebling observed, providing water that "was of prime quality."[7]

Colonel Dushane's Second (Maryland) Brigade had been pulled out of the line on June 22 and sent south to support the Second Corps in its attack. This left the Fifteenth in the trenches next to the 146th New York Infantry, one of Colonel Gregory's First Brigade regiments. The days became blistering hot, and Frederick Ernst of the 146th resolved to go to the woods in the Union rear to refill his canteen with water. Although the men in the line usually supplied themselves with water at night or in the early morning, it rarely lasted through the day. Ernst encouraged some of his trenchmates to join him; all declined but asked him to fill their canteens, too. Ernst grabbed those of a few of his closest friends and then, he remembered, "took a long breath for the hundred yard dash across the open space." Hunching as close to the ground as possible, he drew Confederate fire upon emerging from the works. As he continued toward the water source, "men from my regiment and the one next to us (the Fifteenth New York Heavy Artillery) were watching me. . . . [T]hey shouted after me words of encouragement and sarcastic advice." Ernst successfully reached the woods without getting "clipped" and enjoyed a long drink of water before he filled the canteens. He worried about his return to the trenches, realizing he would "be very lucky" to get "back to the line safely." As he ran, "legging it as hard as I could," enemy sharpshooters, who had been waiting patiently, shot at him. "The bullets struck all around me, some of them so close that I could hear the whistle," but he dodged the missiles and tumbled safely back into the line, resolving it would be "the last time I tried the experiment."[8]

Others, however, did not resolve to avoid the danger. Ernst recalled that "the men of the [Fifteenth New York] Heavy Artillery regiment, nearly all of whom were Germans, had seen me, and one of them decided that he would try it." The thirsty heavy "made the trip to the woods . . . and filled his canteens and cooked some coffee." On the soldier's return, however, "within a few yards of the intrenchments he was struck by a bullet in the forehead and was killed instantly." Seeing the man fall, one of Ernst's trenchmates "immediately ran out and appropriated the canteens and coffee the unfortunate man had been carrying." This action infuriated the men of the Fifteenth. "The man's companions . . . threatened to come to our part of the line and whip us. They swore at us in German for some time, but before the matter came to blows some officers interfered and put an end to the trouble." Fortunately, the incident, which amounted simply to soldiers being soldiers, would have no lasting repercussions. The Fifteenth and 146th would go on to serve side by side collegially for the rest of the war.[9]

Under the oppressive sun and enemy fire, the bluecoats continued to improve their trenches and, under cover of night, placed abatis along their front. From the relative safety and comfort of corps headquarters near the Avery house, Wainwright recorded that "the weather has been waxing warmer the last two days, and today [Friday, June 24] has been a real piper." He also reflected on his privileged position: "Fortunately I have next to nothing to do, but try to keep cool and kill time," while "the men in the trenches . . . must suffer very much from this great heat." In addition to the almost debilitating heat, Federal troops continued to suffer from enemy action. For example, the Fifth Corps sustained thirty to seventy casualties per day during the first days in the trenches. Wiedrich reported that the Fifteenth lost one officer and three men killed and one officer and twenty-eight men wounded by sharpshooters through June 24, observing, "It was impossible to work in the day time, the sharpshooters keeping up a constant fire."[10]

The proximity of Confederate and Federal lines allowed the opposing forces not only to easily observe but also to target one another. As Jacob Van Vleck of the Fifteenth's Company M wrote to his wife on June 24, "we have lain here since Saturday last, sleeping and eating and watching the movements of the rebs who lay across a Cornfield from us right in view." Hunkered down in the line, Van Vleck and his company could "see the steeples [of Petersburg] from where we stand now." He tried to place the distance between the opposing forces in context for his wife: "we are just about as far from the Reb Line of Battle as from our house down to the graveyard so they are afraid to come out on us and we are not ready to go in yet to them." Others reported similar details. In a letter to his mother, Kitching observed: "Our lines are now so close to the enemy that if a man shows his head above the breastworks on either aside—bang! bang! a volley of musketry will warn him not to be guilty of such rashness again." Nighttime offered some freedom. "Immediately after dark . . . we all jump out of our holes and stretch ourselves; spades, shovels and picks are put in requisition to strengthen the line or to dig underground passages from one line to the other, and officers visit each other to talk over the little events of the day." As a result, "until midnight the entire line appears to be alive."[11]

On June 25 the Maryland Brigade relieved Kitching's brigade. Initially withdrawing into the second line of works, the heavies quietly slipped a half mile to the rear near the Norfolk and Petersburg Railroad. The colonel reported: "I have my men now encamped in a nice woods, not quite out of reach of shell, but where it is clean, and where both officers and men are enjoying themselves, washing and resting." They welcomed the reprieve from the broiling sun—a thermometer at Ayres's headquarters read 101 degrees in the shade—endured by those in the trenches. While there, the Fifteenth reconstituted as a full—or nearly so—regiment for the first time since the afternoon of May 11 near Spotsylvania Court House.

The conclusion of the campaign of maneuver and the establishment of a secure supply base at City Point obviated the need for a large guard for the ammunition train and artillery park. Consequently, Companies E, G, and H of Major Dieckmann's battalion rejoined the Fifteenth on the twenty-fifth; only Capt. Calvin Shaffer and his Company F remained at the army's artillery park at City Point. After the short but welcome break, the brigade returned to the trenches on the evening of June 28 to relieve the First Brigade. Kitching's heavies went into line on the left of Ayres's division, with the Maryland Brigade on their right and Griffin's division to their left. The Fifteenth remained essentially in this position until nearly the end of July.[12]

As June turned to July, the firing from pickets and sharpshooters began to diminish to some extent along much of the Fifth Corps's front. On June 30 Kitching wrote that the opposing men had arrived at a tacit arrangement "not to fire at each other unless to combat some movement." Despite this agreement, the colonel remained at risk because it "does not include officers. . . . The moment an officer shows himself he becomes a target for several rifles from the enemy." When Kitching rode along his line the previous day, "one of my staff officers remarked my large horse would probably draw fire, when 'zip!' a rifle bullet whistled past his head, making him rear and plunge." The colonel escaped unscathed.[13]

Notwithstanding the informal ceasefires, life in the trenches remained both difficult and dangerous. A man in Kitching's brigade, Samuel Pierce, described to his brother how enemy fire randomly killed a soldier in his company. The unsuspecting victim "was talking to his brother-in-law and two or three others when a shell struck him killing him instantly." Pierce lamented that the man "was 29 years of age and leaves a wife and four children to mourn his loss." Others died or were wounded in a similar fashion. Lieutenant Colonel Wiedrich reported that from late June to near the end of July, the Fifteenth suffered nine men wounded "by [a] premature explosion from our batteries in our rear" and one officer and two men wounded "by stray balls."[14]

On July 3 the Fifteenth's Company M fell in for what would be an unexpected, though exceedingly modest, treat. Private Matteson of Company M described the scene to a friend at home. As the orderly sergeant distributed surprise supplies to the men he said, "Well boys here is a few cans of canned meats that the officers give to you, [that] the Sanitary Commission sent . . . to the Officers." As he proceeded to hand them out, he had the men "count off from the right in squads of ten men." For each group there was "a sergeant or a Corporal that will open the cans and divide them [into ten portions]. A table spoon full to each man and what little remains the corporal gets." Matteson declined his spoonful, fearing that "such delicacies might make me sick."[15]

Such treats did not arrive frequently, and even when they did, life quickly returned to normal in the trenches. Lyman observed that the Confederates expected an attack on July 4, but "Grant does not deal in such theatricals." Throughout that day, bands on both sides played patriotic music. The Maryland Brigade's musicians struck up a rendition of "Hail Columbia," and "a N. Carolina regiment opposite rose and cheered!" Kitching remembered a similar exchange with the Tar Heels across from his brigade. "When we raised our 'stars and stripes' on our breastworks and the band played Star Spangled Banner," he wrote his father, "the rebs took in their secession rag and cheered lustily." Of the good-natured exchange, he opined, "I believe that were it not for our politicians these two armies would settle this matter and reconstruct the Union in twenty-four hours."[16]

Without an attack, the men spent the day celebrating America's independence. The Sanitary Commission provided fresh vegetables to help make the day's meal special for the troops. Wainwright complained that although the aggregate quantity of vegetables brought out "was doubtless large, so that it will figure well in the papers, the distribution was very much of the 'penny ice cream and two spoons' order—three onions or two tomatoes to a man." The colonel, on the other hand, dined with some fellow officers on canned green peas and salmon, both imported from France and that he had been hording since Christmas. The sutler provided some champagne, but Wainwright considered it "of the poorest Jersey brand. I could not drink a glass of it myself, and stuck to a bottle of common madeira I found in my box."[17]

The Independence Day luxuries and celebrations did not persist. On July 6 Ayres's division worked on "straightening" its sector of the line. One Fifth Corps senior officer considered the word "straightening" a mischaracterization, instead describing the activity as a process by which "the worst of the crooks had been taken out, for the line itself is a curve." Kitching wrote his father, "I am gradually crawling up to the 'Johnnies'' works." He offered more detail on both the operation and the attitudes of his heavies. "I moved forward last night more than one hundred yards without losing a man. My men are just in the spirit of it," they "advanced so cautiously and quietly that the 'Johnnies' were apparently exceedingly astonished this morning, to find a stout line of rifle pits a hundred yards nearer them than at 'tattoo.'" His troops would continue advancing the line that night. "To-morrow morning, if I am successful tonight, my line will be within about 400 yards of theirs."[18]

A man in Kitching's outfit similarly described the heavies' nighttime labors. "We worked all night throwing up a breastwork of logs and dirt about 12 feet wide and 4 ½ feet high—we had to do it very quietly or else we would have been shelled." He also reported on their success. "At daylight the next morning the Rebel batteries opened on us and kept it up for quite some time, most of the shells and shot went over us." But even those that struck had little effect. "Two solid shot struck the works in front of me each weighing twelve pounds but they did not penetrate the works." The strength of their new entrenchments, he bragged, "shows . . . what we can do in one night with the pick and shovel." Nevertheless, he recalled, "one shell burst before it reached us and a piece of it flew and struck one of our recruits by the name of Christian, who died in fifteen minutes after." Despite the improvements, life in the trenches remained dangerous.[19]

Work continued both day and night on new forts and their connecting lines. Warren reported "spending the whole day superintending the works on my left, where I find my rank and experience combined were very much needed." By July 12 the men of the Fifth Corps helped secure the army's left flank with three new forts in its sector. To further strengthen the left and rear, they also helped construct a secondary line that stretched back from Fort Prescott, crossed the Petersburg and Norfolk Railroad, and terminated at Blackwater Swamp. Wiedrich reported that, during this period, the Fifteenth "had to furnish strong details for fatigue work and to be ready to meet an attack at any time."[20]

The long period in the trenches allowed soldiers on both sides to drop some of their reserve. Although officially frowned upon, men on opposite sides of the picket line often fraternized. Drawn together by the common bonds of war and service and bored in the trenches, they carried on conversations and a considerable trade. A man in Ayres's division noted, "The 'Johnnies' were always glad to exchange tobacco for anything for personal use, as coffee, sugar, needles, thread, etc." In addition, "It has become no unusual sight to see the men of both armies sitting on top of their redoubts in the evening holding animated conversations and gaily bantering each other." An officer in the same division observed, "The other day two men of our regiment engaged with a couple of 'Johnnies' in a game of cards, the stakes being the fate of the country." He proudly asserted that as to the outcome, "of course, our side was victorious."[21]

Even with these makeshift amusements, the hot, dusty days dragged on. After forty-seven such days, the men on both sides rejoiced that finally, on July 19, it rained. Lyman thankfully noted, "It rained nearly all day and soaked the dust to the hard pan." Wainwright remembered it cooled down the weather and left "the nights really cold with their heavy dew." But the much-welcomed rain also caused problems. Warren reported that his Fifth Corps troops had to continually drain the water from their rifle pits and trenches and repair the damage to the works caused by the running water. But the respite and inconvenience would not last long. In a few days the surface dried out, the dust clouds rematerialized, and life returned to what had become routine for the soldiers.[22]

The Fifteenth had by now been largely immobilized in the trenches for over four weeks. Private Van Vleck reported to his wife on July 20, "we are just about as we were a month ago—we have no fighting to do now—but do not know how soon as the Rebs & us lay looking at each other day after day." He explained they continued to receive hungry and demoralized Rebel deserters into his section of the line, but "we keep ourselves ready day and night in case [the enemy] attack us." "I have no doubt you pity us all," he surmised, "but I think we are well off just now, & I hope we will never be worse—eating, sleeping and watching the Rebs is all we do as we have the most of the hard marching over for a while." Van Vleck knew that the situation would change at some point. "As for taking Petersburg we do not know when that will be—Keep up your spirits anyway, for I'll try and come home safe."[23]

Meanwhile, as the men of the Fifteenth toiled at improving their fortifications, other Yankees pursued a different type of labor. Since late June, as engineer Roebling characterized it, Burnside and his men had been "quietly boring away at his mine." Meade and Grant's initial skepticism about Burnside's idea lessened as they witnessed the work progress. The Ninth Corps commander intended the mine as a possible means to breach the Confederate fortifications to his front and end the ongoing siege. Others in the army, however, were doubtful. According to Wainwright, "the mine which General Burnside is making causes a good deal of talk and is generally much laughed at." He dismissed the project as "an affair of his own entirely, and has nothing to do with the regular siege operations, or the engineers with it."[24]

Burnside formulated the mine plan with the help of mining engineer Lt. Col. Henry Pleasants of 48th Pennsylvania Infantry of Brig. Gen. Robert B. Potter's division. The regiment contained a large number of coal miners from Schuylkill County in southeastern Pennsylvania. From their position barely 100 yards from a bulge in the Confederate works known as Elliott's or Pegram's Salient, Pleasants's men conceived of a plan to run a mine forward to terminate under the enemy works. Then, after being charged with explosives, they would explode the mine to breach the enemy's defenses. The lieutenant colonel took the plan to Potter, who took it to Burnside. Burnside embraced the proposal and requested Meade's approval. Although he did not harbor the same level of enthusiasm, Meade authorized the work—which had already begun on June 25—to continue. The miners constructed the horizontal shaft by burrowing into the bank of Poor Creek. By July 2 the unfinished shaft extended some 250 feet.[25]

Several weeks later, on July 25, as work on the mine continued, Grant ordered Meade to take the offensive north of the James by sending Hancock's corps across the river on bridges laid from the extremity of Jones's Point at Bermuda Hundred to Deep Bottom on the north bank. Two divisions of Sheridan's cavalry, augmented by Brig. Gen. August V. Kautz's troopers from the Army of the James, would accompany the Second Corps. Once across the James, the infantry would advance rapidly to Chaffin's Bluff and take up a line in order to prevent the cavalry from being cut off. Meanwhile, Sheridan's men would pursue the primary objective of the expedition by striking the still-functional Virginia Central Railroad as close to Richmond as possible and advancing along the railroad as far as the South Anna River, destroying the rails along the way.[26]

About a quarter mile in rear of the Rebel works under which Pleasants's miners were tunneling, the Jerusalem Plank Road ran south from the hamlet of Blandford along a ridge known as Cemetery Hill, referencing the cemetery of the Old Blandford Church on its crest. This ridge separated Petersburg, which lay immediately to its west, from the Army of the Potomac. The Federal high command knew they needed to take that ridge to launch a successful assault on the city. The discovery that the Confederates had detached works along Cemetery Hill but no connected line greatly improved the chances for a successful attack from Burnside's front. Moreover, the enemy's response to Hancock's and Sheridan's probes north of the James could also result in a weakening of the forces defending Petersburg. Consequently, Grant instructed Meade to have Burnside make preparations to charge the mine in the shortest possible time.[27]

At this point the mine consisted of a main gallery approximately 511 feet long with, at its termination, two lateral side galleries, each extending nearly 40 feet. Each gallery contained four magazines, into each of which was loaded about 1,000 pounds of powder in 25-pound kegs—an aggregate of approximately four tons of explosives. The 10 feet at the entrance of each lateral gallery and the adjoining first 34 feet of the main gallery was tamped with bags of sand to direct the force of the explosion upward.[28]

To set Grant's plan in motion, Hancock's and Sheridan's outfits began crossing the James River early on the morning of July 27. Sweeping aside a Confederate advance force, the infantry proceeded toward New Market, with the cavalry to the right. When they reached Bailey's Creek, the bluecoats found the enemy strongly posted in well-constructed works on the opposite bank. The opposing forces sparred, but neither could achieve a decisive advantage. On the afternoon of July 28, the Federals abandoned the expedition, with the last of their forces slipping back across the James the following night. Although unsuccessful in its primary objective, nevertheless and very significantly, the Union foray caused Lee to shift forces to counter it. This had reduced the Confederate infantry holding Petersburg to only three divisions and had drawn two of the three Rebel cavalry divisions north of the James.[29]

Meanwhile, as Hancock was setting out on his expedition, planning for the detonation of the mine continued. Cooperating in the postdetonation attack would be the Eighteenth Corps, since July 22 commanded by Maj. Gen. Edward O. C. Ord. Supporting on Burnside's left would be the Fifth Corps. Warren planned to keep Crawford in position from the Plank Road, to the army's left, and have Griffin extend to the right to relieve Ayres's division. He would hold Ayres's outfit, with a reported aggregate strength at that time of 4,979 men, in reserve and keep Cutler's depleted division in line on its narrow front on Burnside's immediate left. On July 27 Brig. Gen. Joseph Bartlett's First Division brigade relieved most of Ayres's line, including Kitching's brigade. The heavies and the other troops so relieved pulled out of the line, shifted to the rear, and went into camp.[30]

Meade's July 29 orders for the operation called for the Ninth Corps to explode the mine at 3:30 A.M. the following morning. Immediately after,

Burnside's assaulting columns were to "move rapidly upon the breach, seize the crest in the rear, and effect a lodgment there." The Eighteenth Corps, massed in rear of Burnside's attackers, and Warren's supporting force on the Ninth Corps's left-rear—Ayres's division—would each be "prepared" to join the assault. Warren ordered the general to mass his troops in the railroad cut before daylight on July 30 and be prepared to go in after Burnside's men. Ayres established his headquarters with Warren's at the five-gun battery in the corner of the woods west of the Avery house and in rear of the railroad cut. From this position they could observe the advance of the assaulting columns.[31]

The attackers, however, faced obstacles in merely moving within their own lines to reach the exit point for the assault. A Ninth Corps staff officer observed, "The approaches to the Union line at this particular point were so well covered by the fire of the enemy that they were cut up into a network of covered ways almost as puzzling to the uninitiated as the catacombs of Rome." In preparation for the Fifth Corps's part in the attack, Roebling also inspected the approaches to the lines near the mine. "One single narrow and very crooked covered way led to the ground near the mouth of the mine," he reported. Furthermore, "the space here was very limited and entirely inadequate for assembling a large body of men for making a rush." The approaches through which the attackers had to move concerned him. "Owing to the *place d'armes* being so small," he concluded, "the progress of the column coming down the covered way would necessarily be very slow, leaving them exposed to the enemy's fire so much longer."[32]

Kitching's brigade began maneuvering into position at 2 A.M., the heavies formed in the railroad cut by 3 A.M. They would lead the division in its supporting advance. Kitching had an ominous feeling, and before leaving camp he wrote to his wife asking her to carry on without him should the worst happen. The colonel closed his letter, however, with optimism: "I will write tomorrow night, God willing. I trust I may date my letter in Petersburg." The heavies did not share their commander's misgivings. While waiting for the order to advance, Kitching "never saw men so eager for a fight." He "could scarcely keep them quiet. Every man could see the enemy's weakness and just what was required to enable us to rout them completely."[33]

Men and officers along the Federal line had no idea what to expect when the mine was finally sprung. Roebling remembered, "As no one present had ever seen that much powder exploded at once, the most extravagant expectations were indulged in as to the effect." Then, the appointed hour came and went without an explosion. After waiting nearly an hour, a sergeant and an officer ventured into the mine and discovered that the fuse had gone out at a splice. Repairing and relighting the fuse, they scrambled out of the tunnel. When the charge at last detonated, it hurled men, guns, carriages, timbers, and a huge mass of earth into the air and opened a large crater about 130 feet long, 90 feet wide, and 25 feet deep where the Confederate battery had been. With the explosion, Federal artillery all along the line opened a severe fire.[34]

Kitching's heavies had been hunkered down in the railroad cut about a quarter mile east of the enemy works waiting for the detonation. When it finally occurred, recalled a captain in the brigade, "we was all started by a terrific explosion and convulsive heave of the earth and on looking over to the Enemys Position we beheld one of the enemy Forts blown into the air." He confessed: "The sight was horrid. . . . Men Cannon and sticks of timber shooting in the air in all directions and these descending again to the earth, the shock was so terrific that it rolled our men off of the bank of the Rail Road down on the Track." The artillery fire that immediately followed added to the chaos. "I never hear such a cannonade before," one heavy remembered.[35]

This chaos changed everything. Those leading the assault, men in Brig. Gen. James H. Ledlie's Ninth Corps division, hesitated when they thought that the mass heaved into the air by the blast was now falling directly within their line of advance. When they continued to the edge of the crater, they saw upended guns, broken gun carriages, timbers, and huge chunks of clay. Amid this debris they also saw men buried in all possible orientations—some up to their necks, others to their waists, and others with only their legs or feet showing. One Confederate officer, asleep when the mine exploded, described waking wriggling midair and then descending before lapsing into unconsciousness. As the bluecoats at the edge of the crater gazed in horror at the scene, others behind them began to press up—here the plan began to go drastically awry. Many of Ledlie's attackers piled into the crater rather than streaming around it. For his part, Ledlie remained in a protected angle within the Union line, exercising no direct control as his division advanced.[36]

This delay and confusion in the Union ranks allowed the Confederates time to recover and respond. Men who had initially fled their position in the works when the mine detonated returned and fired into the advancing

Federals and those in the crater. A Rebel battery nearby swept the crest of the crater with canister as others opened up from greater range.[37]

Additional Federal brigades did little to stem the slaughter. Confederate artillery and musketry fire forced many of the newly arrived men to seek cover either in the chaos within the crater or in the captured works adjacent to it, mainly to its north. Little effort was made to advance beyond this point. "Every organization melted away, as soon as it entered this hole in the ground." The attacking formations became, one observer reported, "a mass of human beings clinging by toes and heels to the almost perpendicular sides [of the crater]. If a man was shot on the crest he fell and rolled to the bottom of the pit." Although other men succeeded in achieving lodgments in the enemy works alongside the crater, increasing Confederate resistance prevented them from exploiting these footholds. Over two hours after the detonation of the mine, Burnside's last division became engaged. Ferrero's African American division advanced under the galling fire, and while some entered the crater, most of the troops joined the Federals already in the works to the north. Moving to their right along the outside of the line, they leapt over the works and engaged the enemy. In a sharp fight, much of it hand to hand, the Black troops captured as many as 200 Confederates as well as a stand of colors.[38]

Kitching's heavies prepared to lead Ayres's division into the maelstrom when, as Roebling reported, "a sudden stampede occurred among the colored troops at the crater; a black swarm of men was seen rushing for our lines, and presently everyone saw that it was over for the day." Mahone's Division had begun arriving in rear of the crater at around 9 A.M. Just as two and part of a third of Ferrero's regiments had reorganized their line and began to advance in an attempt to take the crest beyond, elements of Mahone's Confederates charged. They drove many of Ferrero's men into the crater, but most fled back to the Union entrenchments. Joining in their rapid retreat was a large number of the white troops in the crater and the works flanking it. Mahone's men reclaimed most of the captured Confederate lines north and south of the crater, but an estimated 1,000 Federals remained in the crater and in short sections of works on either side. Warren witnessed the precipitous flight, too, and realized, "All our advantages are lost." At 9:45 A.M. Meade informed him: "All offensive operations are suspended. You can resume your original position with your command."[39]

As the day wore on, the temperature rose to ninety-nine degrees, and the intense sun caused great suffering in the crater. Many men succumbed to sunstroke. "Wounded men died there begging piteously for water . . . and soldiers extended their tongues to dampen their parched lips until their tongues seemed to hang from their mouths." The misery increased throughout the day. "The sun was pouring its fiercest heat down upon us and our suffering wounded. No air was stirring within the crater. It was a sickening sight: men were dead and dying all around us; blood was streaming down the sides of the crater to the bottom, where it gathered in pools for a time before being absorbed into the hard red clay." At roughly 1 P.M. Mahone's final counterattack came. The Confederates advanced to the crater, and desperate hand-to-hand combat ensued. The exhausted Yankees soon realized that further resistance was futile, laid down their arms, and surrendered. Soon, Roebling remembered, "a slaughter commenced which pretty much lasted all day. Most of the white troops were captured and the niggers were pretty much all killed before night." He observed that "every little while some fellow would run the gauntlet and get back to our lines, but many were shot on the way back."[40]

The Battle of the Crater had been not only a disaster but also, owing to the failure to effectively exploit the breach in the Confederate line created with the mine's detonation, a lost opportunity. The Federals suffered nearly 3,800 casualties, including over 1,400 men captured or missing. Dead and dying Union soldiers lay in the no-man's-land between the lines on the morning of July 31. Warren reported: "Our helpless wounded are still lying close to the enemy's line and they give them no help. . . . They could help them if they would. The wounded seem to be mostly colored men who are writhing with their wounds in this almost insufferable sun, and I think the neglect of them must be intentional." The armies set a truce for August 1 to tend to the wounded and bury the dead, but by that point only about twenty wounded Federals remained alive. Lyman climbed upon the parapet, and the scene sickened him. "The heat and intense sun of 48 hours has so swollen and blackened [the bodies] that negroes were not to be told from whites, save by the hair!" Furthermore, "The faces and hands of many were actually white with a moving layer of maggots!" The fallen comrades in arms, white and black, would share the soldiers' common grave.[41]

The failed offensive humiliated all in the Army of the Potomac. Kitching reluctantly wrote to his mother on August 2 about "our recent disgraceful failure." He had tried to write the previous day but discovered he "was saying many things an officer commanding a brigade ought not to say, so I tore my letters up, said my prayers, and went to bed." Now, ignoring that Burnside's three white divisions had gone in before Ferrero's, the colonel employed a bigoted trope to place blame for the failure: "When the storming party did move, it was composed of blacks, instead of white soldiers, as it should have been, and in consequence the work was but half done." Despite what he interpreted as a failure unique to the African American troops, he asserted, "if our division had been ordered to support them, all would have gone well; but for some reason no order came to Warren to put us in." The events disheartened everyone. "The entire army is terribly chagrined at the 'fizzle;' a board of officers is investigating the matter now, and I trust the responsible party may suffer."[42]

Colonel Wainwright shared Kitching's views, describing the affair as "a fiasco, a most terrible fizzle." Writing in his journal in the wake of the failed attack, he confessed, "Never before have I felt that the Army of the Potomac was disgraced; failed it has frequently, and botches its commanding generals have made of more than one piece of work, but the army itself has always come out with honor." His biases came through as the colonel discussed the African American troops. He stated that the commander of one of the Black regiments told him that "his men behaved admirably in the excitement of the first onset, but soon lost heart; also that every man who was hit yelled and groaned most hideously, which tended to demoralize the others." Disregarding that soldiers of any color, especially those experiencing combat for the first time, may have reacted similarly, Wainwright claimed, "As both the traits are natural to the negro character, I have no doubt of his correctness."[43]

Common soldiers also regretted the outcome. In an August 6 letter to his wife, Private Van Vleck of the Fifteenth New York Heavy declared regret at not getting the opportunity to participate and help bring about a favorable result. "We had a fight here last Saturday—I could see it but I was not in it—we was all ready to go in but dident." He felt confident that "if we had all gone in we could took Petersburg easy so the Rebels say—but we cannot help it now." One of Ayres's men asserted that the general had requested "the privilege of leading his command forward in an attempt to secure the desired point," but Warren declined, deeming it by then too late. Learning of this exchange, another soldier recalled that the men in his regiment began to speculate, thinking that "the division might have achieved an undying fame and hastened the end of the war by several months" if they had gotten the opportunity to engage. Yet they also recognized that they "might have met the fate of the hundreds of brave men who were sent into the awful pit of death." After watching the fight and making ready to "pitch in," Private Matteson of the Fifteenth confessed to being "glad we were not ordered in."[44]

After the spectacular defeat and disaster, a court of inquiry convened in front of Petersburg on August 6 "to examine into and report upon the facts and circumstances attending the unsuccessful assault on the enemy's position on the 30th of July, 1864." After seventeen days the panel issued its findings concerning the parties responsible for the "want of success" of the assault. It deemed Burnside primarily accountable owing to both poor planning and faulty execution and Ledlie for "neglect of duty" in its execution. By August 14 Burnside had been granted a thirty-day leave of absence. He would never resume command of the Ninth Corps, replaced by Maj. Gen. John G. Parke, the corps's chief of staff. Ledlie, after an extended leave of absence for physical disability, resigned from the army.[45]

Meanwhile, immediately upon suspension of offensive operations on July 30, Ayres's division had returned to its camp in rear of the Fifth Corps and remained there in reserve. Large work details toiled away daily on the lines and forts, instigating, as Roebling reported, "much dissatisfaction" among the troops. The Fifteenth Heavy had fortunately suffered only one man wounded in the crater operation, and the rest of the men resumed camp life. Kitching complained on August 7: "This has been a terribly uncomfortable day. The heat intense, the dust suffocating, and the flies unbearable. . . . Not flies as we have at home, but great green chaps that bite like rattle-snakes, and stick like glue." Even in the relative calm, the weather and insects made life extremely difficult for the men. "We can scarcely eat except before daylight and after dark, and as to obtaining a wink of sleep, it is quite out of the question."[46]

By now Kitching was well aware that he and his regiment were soon to be detached from the Army of the Potomac. In response to Confederate lieutenant general Jubal Early's nearly successful advance from the Shenandoah Valley on Washington in mid-July, Grant planned to dispatch a heavy artillery regiment from the army to help garrison the fortifications surrounding the capital city. On the afternoon of July 21, Meade informed Grant that he had chosen the Sixth New York Heavy Artillery for the assignment. Many of Kitching's soldiers expressed excitement at the opportunity. "My regiment, officers and men, are delighted, and have been cutting such capers on their breastworks that the Johnnies wanted to know what was the matter." The colonel told his father that his regiment's selection resulted from Meade's belief that it "had done infantry duty so long and so well, and had suffered so heavily, it deserved the first chance for rest and recuperation." Kitching expressed his personal happiness at the new assignment. "I cannot help being pleased; for coming as the order does, unsolicited, and as a kind of reward of merit, it does us no harm as soldiers, and is very acceptable."[47]

Meade's selection upset Warren's plans to reorganize the Fifth Corps. He wanted Kitching to remain commanding a brigade, "in which capacity," he reported to Assistant Adjutant General Williams on July 26, "he has been officially commended by Meade and also recommended by me for promotion." Warren summoned Kitching to solicit the latter's view on sending the Fifteenth Heavy to Washington in place of the Sixth, but by then matters had progressed too far for any changes. The Fifteenth remained with the Army of the Potomac as the Sixth departed on August 13 under orders to "proceed forthwith to City Point, to embark thence for Washington."[48]

The Sixth New York Heavy left camp around 3 P.M., preceded by the Fifteenth's brass band, and marched out toward City Point, arriving at about midnight. Pvt. Samuel Pierce of the Sixth described the ten-mile trek as "not a very tiresome march, but . . . a dusty one. Clouds of dust would rise around us so thick that you could not recognize a man five feet from you, and as the weather was very warm we sweat considerable so you can imagine how pleasant it was, dust choking you at every step (almost) and sweat blinding you." At City Point the men had "a most delightful sleep," and the next morning "most . . . had a good bathe in the James River." Then around 9 A.M. on August 14, the Sixth embarked for Washington on two transports.[49]

After learning that Warren had recommended him for promotion to brigadier general, Kitching wondered in writing to his father. "I cannot understand why everybody is making such a fuss about me, for I have not done anything that I am aware of, which calls for it." He continued, "My men have indeed done nobly and I am proud of them; but it really makes me feel very sad when I think that I am in any manner being benefitted by the loss of so many brave men; and I almost feel ashamed that I have not been hit." Kitching soon was relieved of that cause for shame. In command of a provisional division in Sheridan's Army of the Shenandoah on October 19, 1864, the colonel and his men, encamped on the high ground above the banks of Cedar Creek just north of Strasburg, were rousted from sleep at early dawn and hastily formed into line. In the fog Ramseur's Division of Early's Second Corps—an old adversary—struck them and broke their line. As Kitching sat his horse and attempted to rally his men despite the confusion, a Minié ball crashed into his foot. Although he remained in the saddle until the Federals rallied, Kitching eventually left the field as a result of severe blood loss. Doctors in New York City amputated his foot in November. After a brief period of improvement, his condition worsened, and he succumbed at Dobbs Ferry, New York, on January 10, 1865. The army posthumously promoted John Howard Kitching to brigadier general, to date from August 1, 1864, for his meritorious and distinguished service in the 1864 campaigns before Richmond.[50]

With the departure of the Sixth Heavy, the Fifteenth Heavy remained in the trenches acting by itself as the Third Brigade, Second Division, Fifth Corps. Grant's three attempts since reaching Petersburg in mid-June to either capture the city or cut Richmond's rail lines of supply had each ended in failure. Even as the Sixth was marching to City Point on its way to Washington, Grant's next attempt to achieve one or both of those objectives had already begun.

CHAPTER NINE

Cutting the Weldon Railroad and the Battle of Globe Tavern

As the troops enjoyed a comparative lull after the Battle of the Crater, they continued to relay news and their opinions back to loved ones at home. On August 12, 1864, Carl Matteson of the Fifteenth's Company M wrote to a friend. "I hope that the North will turn out more men for Grant needs them" to replenish the Army of the Potomac. "Out of nearly 200 men that left Brandy Station only 45 remain that are able to carry a rifle including Seargeants & Corporals in Co. M." Disillusioned with infantry duty, Matteson complained, "About a dozen of us boys would like to leave this dutch regiment and enter the regulars light Artillery, but all the wires we have pulled has *failed.*" Despite his wishes, Matteson's infantry service in the Fifteenth would continue.[1]

From intelligence gathered in early August, Grant concluded that Lee had sent one cavalry and three infantry divisions from Petersburg to support Early's force then operating in the Valley. This convinced him to again take the offensive to prevent additional troops leaving to reinforce Early, and possibly even to compel the recall of those already dispatched. Grant planned to send a force across the James River at Deep Bottom to threaten Richmond from the east while cavalry swept around to destroy the Virginia Central north of the capital. The bluecoats would enter the city if the opportunity presented itself. In effect, the plan mirrored that of the earlier movement by Hancock and Sheridan.[2]

Grant again tasked the Second Corps, this time supported by two Tenth Corps divisions and a division of cavalry, with executing the operation north of the James. The Federals launched this undertaking on the night of August 13. It initiated several days of sparring with Confederate defenders, ultimately resulting in a draw with significant casualties. When offensive operations ceased, Hancock's command lingered north of the river, maintaining a threatening posture, and remained there until withdrawn after dark on the twentieth.[3]

Meanwhile, as that movement began, the Federal high command considered a strike toward the enemy's right flank as well. At 10:30 P.M. Meade's chief of staff, Brigadier General Humphreys, informed the commanders of the Fifth and Ninth Corps of the plan. "If Hancock's movement should lead to the almost entire abandonment of the enemy's entrenchments in our front," then "the commanding general will take advantage of it by withdrawing the greater part of the Fifth and Ninth Corps ... , and undertake such operations as may seem best." Grant was again eyeing the Weldon Railroad, but cutting it would not be easy. As Meade's aide-de-camp Lieutenant Colonel Lyman opined, "It is touching a tiger's cubs to get on that road!" Nevertheless, in anticipation of a thrust toward that objective, the Fifth Corps withdrew from the line under cover of darkness on August 14. By the next morning Warren's men were massed behind the main line, with Cutler's division on the right, Griffin's division near the Chieves house on the left, and Ayres's and Crawford's divisions between them.[4]

On August 17 it appeared that Hancock's operation had, indeed, weakened the enemy's forces at Petersburg. Although Grant determined that the army could not achieve a decisive result by moving a single corps to the Federal left, he nevertheless considered that such a movement could "get to the Weldon road and, with the aid of a little cavalry, cut and destroy a few miles of it." With this goal in mind, he instructed Meade to "start Warren in the morning." The general in chief urged caution, however. "I do not want him to fight any unequal battles nor to assault fortifications. His movements should be more a reconnaissance in force, with instructions to take advantage of any weakness of the enemy he may discover." As reports filtered in that day suggesting a shift of additional Confederate units north of the James, Grant's optimism grew. At 10 P.M. he mused to Meade, "Warren may find an opportunity to do more than I had expected." Indeed, only three Confederate infantry divisions now remained south of the river to protect the Cockade City.[5]

Warren's orders called for him to start the Fifth Corps at 4 A.M. on August 18 and "endeavor to make a lodgment upon the Weldon railroad, in

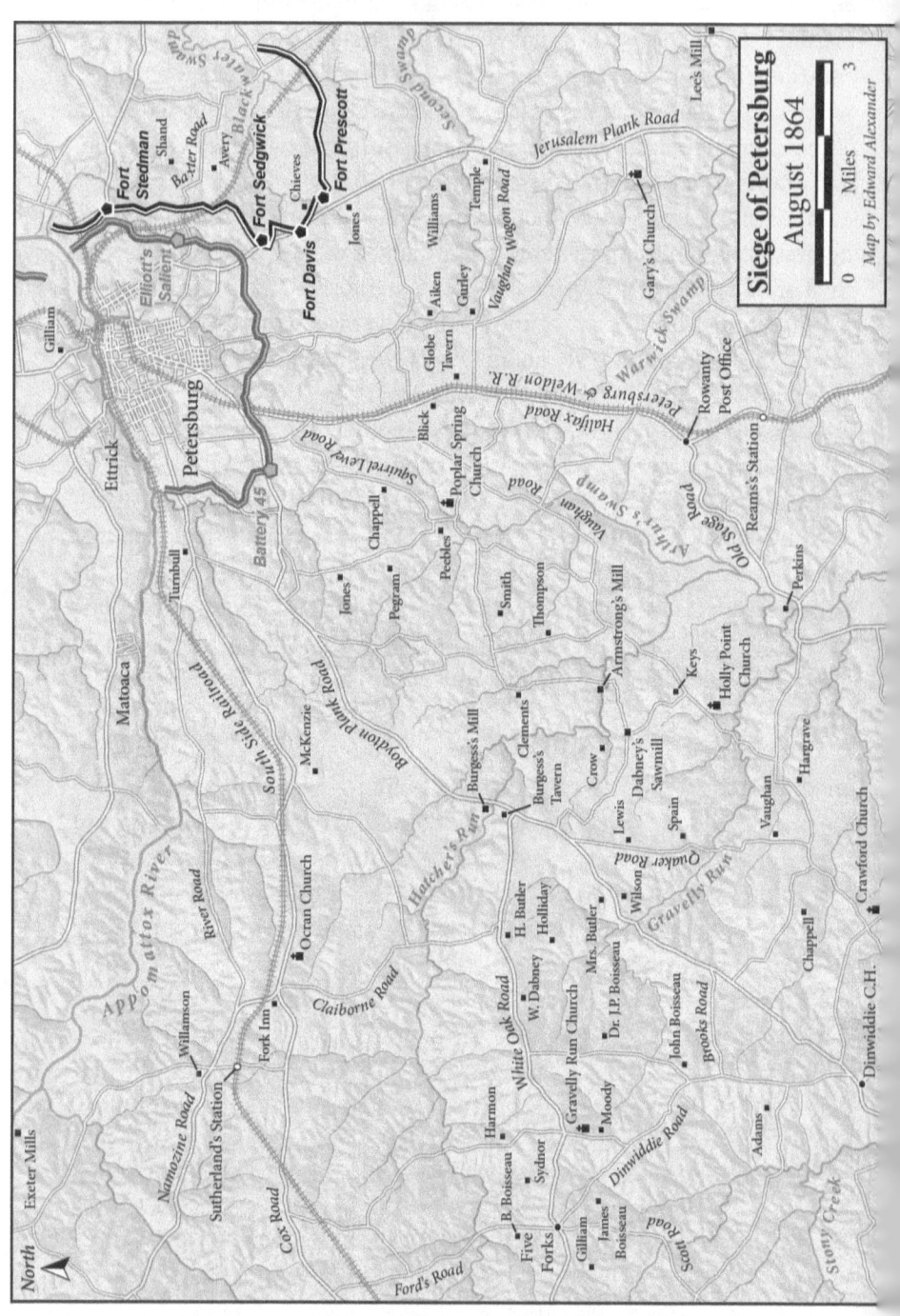

the vicinity of Dr. Gurley's house . . . , and destroy the road as far as you can, carrying out the destruction as far south as possible." Furthermore: "the movement should also be considered a reconnaissance in force. . . . [Y]ou will take advantage of any weakness of the enemy that you may perceive." Humphreys added that it appeared the Confederates had withdrawn nearly all of their cavalry from south of the James and that "considerably less than four" infantry divisions remained in the Petersburg defenses.[6]

Lieutenant Colonel Wiedrich prepared his one-regiment Third Brigade for the movement toward the Weldon Railroad without two of his three senior lieutenants. Major Dieckmann, who was admitted to the division hospital on July 22 and then transferred to the general hospital in Alexandria, where remained with acute rheumatism. In addition, Third Battalion commander Major Duysing had reported to the division hospital in early August for "dyspepsia," a condition that the Fifteenth's surgeon, Hermann Ideler, concluded led to inflammation of Duysing's liver. Senior captains William F. Papemeyer and William D. Dickey would command the Second and Third Battalions, respectively. Of the regular battalion commanders, only thirty-seven-year-old Maj. Louis Eiche, commanding the First Battalion, remained on duty. By this point a veteran, Eiche had served with the old Third Battalion since September 1861 and began the Overland Campaign as a captain commanding Company C. He earned promotion to major on July 1 to fill the billet left vacant upon Maj. Leander Schamberger's death from his wounding in the battle at the Harris farm.[7]

Despite the heavy rains that fell throughout the night and into the morning of August 18, the Fifth Corps broke camp at 4 A.M. and about an hour later began its march. Griffin's division, followed by Ayres's, Crawford's, and then Cutler's, trudged south on the Jerusalem Plank Road for nearly three miles. A fifteen-minute hiatus while men repaired the bridge over Second Swamp allowed the column to close up. Reaching the Temple house, Warren swung his corps to the right into a narrow road and headed west. Two miles beyond lay the home of a Dr. Gurley, and a mile farther, where the road struck the Weldon Railroad, lay the deserted Globe Tavern. The men now marched through heavily timbered areas punctuated with occasional clearings, all in extremely warm and oppressive weather. A tropical rain continued to fall, making the road very muddy and rendering it almost impassable for the wheeled vehicles.[8]

The lead elements of the Fifth Corps halted at the Gurley house around 7 A.M. By 8:20 A.M., as the column closed, Griffin formed his First and

Second Brigades into line of battle. Preceded by a strong skirmish line, he advanced rapidly, sweeping aside enemy pickets and striking the railroad at 9 A.M. An hour later Warren informed Humphreys that his two lead divisions were up as he pushed out in all directions to secure his position. He noted, "The marching is very slow, and there are a great many cases of sunstroke." His aide Major Roebling reported "short squalls, alternating with an hour or two of intense heat."[9]

Unlike the wooded area the Fifth Corps had traversed between the Plank Road and Dr. Gurley's, the ground beyond the home toward the railroad proved more or less open. The Halifax Road ran south from Petersburg parallel to and immediately alongside the Weldon Railroad at this point. Beyond it, a mile to the west, lay the Vaughan Road, angling to the northeast and intersecting the Halifax Road near the W. P. Davis house about a mile and a half north of Globe Tavern. A large, yellow brick building with four chimneys in a "ruinous" condition, the tavern was situated about 100 yards east of the Halifax Road. Warren established his headquarters there despite its ramshackle condition. According to Lyman, "a good part of the house [Globe Tavern] had no floors; and much of the plastering that was not peeled off was ornamented by rebel charcoal inscriptions." The roof afforded a good view of the very flat surrounding countryside, and Warren adapted the attic into a signal station. The open ground surrounding it extended from the Gurley house all the way west to the Vaughan Road and north of the tavern for slightly over a half mile, where a belt of timber some 500 yards wide ran from east to west bordering the clearing.[10]

Griffin's men began tearing up the track, taking measures to ensure neither the rails nor the ties could be reused. They would take hold of a section and lift it, ties and all, from the road bed. The ties first were separated from the rails by twisting the section, then the men would gather and place them in piles, set these on fire, and finally place the rails across the top. When the middle section of the rails became red hot, troops removed them and quickly bent them around a tree or telegraph pole. In many cases the rails were twisted into the shape of the Fifth Corps's *cross pattée*, or Maltese cross, insignia.[11]

When Ayres arrived on the field around 10 A.M., Warren ordered his division deployed to advance up the railroad toward Petersburg and the enemy fortifications south of the city, with Crawford's division to its right. Ayers established a line near the Blick house, which stood on the Halifax Road slightly less than a half mile north of Globe Tavern. Brig. Gen.

Joseph Hayes formed his First Brigade in two lines of battle, his right on the railroad and a strong skirmish line in front. To Hayes's left and slightly to the rear, Ayres placed Col. Nathan Dushane's Second (Maryland) Brigade, while holding Wiedrich's Third Brigade in reserve.[12]

A few minutes after 11 A.M., Ayres's division advanced. Not long after entering the belt of woods, the skirmishers engaged enemy pickets and drove them slowly back through a dense undergrowth of pine and oaks. While a torrential rainstorm further impeded their progress, the bluecoats nevertheless pressed forward. Emerging from the north side of the belt of woods, they encountered a large field with a thick growth of standing corn extending on both sides of the railroad. The skirmishers continued advancing and eventually pressed the Confederate pickets beyond the W. P. Davis house and the intersection of the Halifax and Vaughan Roads.[13]

The Fifth Corps's arrival in the cornfield did not come as a surprise to the Southerners. That morning Brig. Gen. James Dearing notified his superiors that his cavalry vedettes had encountered Warren's advance. In response, Maj. Gen. Henry Heth, with the Letcher Virginia Artillery as well as brigades commanded by Brig. Gen. Joseph R. Davis and Col. Robert M. Mayo, moved out to counter the Federal thrust. Aware of the seriousness of the situation and after Heth's scratch force had moved out from the Petersburg line, Beauregard ordered Brig. Gen. Alfred H. Colquitt's brigade of Georgians to also proceed toward the Weldon Railroad. Screened by the tall corn and Dearing's cavalry, Heth worked quickly to complete his troop dispositions north of the intersection of the Vaughan and Halifax roads. He placed Davis's brigade on the right, its left resting on the railroad, and Mayo's just across the tracks on the left.[14]

Just before 2 P.M., as Ayres's main line prepared to advance from the tree line into the Davis cornfield, Roebling rode out to examine the left of Dushane's brigade. He "noticed that the flankers on the left of the Md. Brig. were not far enough out in that direction, not far enough to give warning at any rate." This oversight would prove a costly miscalculation. Just as the Federals stepped out of the woods, a gray line of battle charged through the corn, driving the blue-clad skirmishers before them. The butternuts struck Hayes's brigade, as one of his officers reported, "in front and flank" with great violence. The Maryland Brigade, to the left and perhaps seventy yards behind Hayes, was, according to Roebling, "just in the act of getting over a large rail fence running at right angles with the [railroad]" when they were hit. At the onset of enemy fire, the

Yankees responded. "The order to fire was promptly and vigorously executed, and the enemy sought shelter," Col. Samuel Graham of the Maryland Brigade's Purnell Legion reported.[15]

The Confederates soon resumed the attack, exploiting the Second Brigade's open left flank as well as the gap between its right and the First Brigade. Hayes's men and the Marylanders found themselves in an untenable position and were compelled to fall back. Dushane's withdrawal, according to Graham, "was executed in considerable confusion, owing to the density of the woods and proximity of the enemy." Both brigades retired to the southern edge of the belt of woods. Farther to the right, the men of Lyle's Third Division brigade were not yet all up and had not established a firm connection with Hayes's line when the Confederates struck. As the outfits to their left were forced to retire, so too were they.[16]

Minutes before, south of the belt of woods, Wiedrich's heavies were moving forward in column. As they marched, the thunder of a violent engagement suddenly rolled from their front, interrupting a conversation between Captain Dickey and the lieutenant colonel. They knew little of the disposition of the friendly forces in the woods ahead of them. Nevertheless, they realized that, as Lt. John Richie, temporarily commanding Dickey's Company M, reported, "whatever there was of ours in there was being rapidly hustled to the rear and would be upon us in a very few seconds." The heavies lost no time swinging into action.[17]

The Fifteenth filed to the right on the run and formed into line of battle west of the railroad, facing the woods and about twenty-five yards from the edge of the underbrush. Dickey's Third Battalion took position on the left, with Company M on its extreme left, and its flank, according to Ritchie, "absolutely 'in the air.'" The heavies soon observed the wreck of the Maryland Brigade approaching from the edge of the woods, Rebels nipping at their heels while yelling, firing, and knocking men down with the butts of their muskets. To calm the jittery heavies, Dickey called out, "Steady, boys, steady now; here's where we get them." As Richie worked to get his men "into shape to receive the coming avalanche," he turned and saw the captain coolly surveying the whirling mass in front. "His example was the only thing needed," Ritchie remembered. When his men saw it, "the line became firm as a rock." The heavies held their fire. "Let this riffraff get out of the way, and then we'll sock it to them," shouted Dickey.[18]

Astride his horse to the heavies' rear, General Ayres did his best to survey the action. He shaded his eyes with one hand as he peered into the

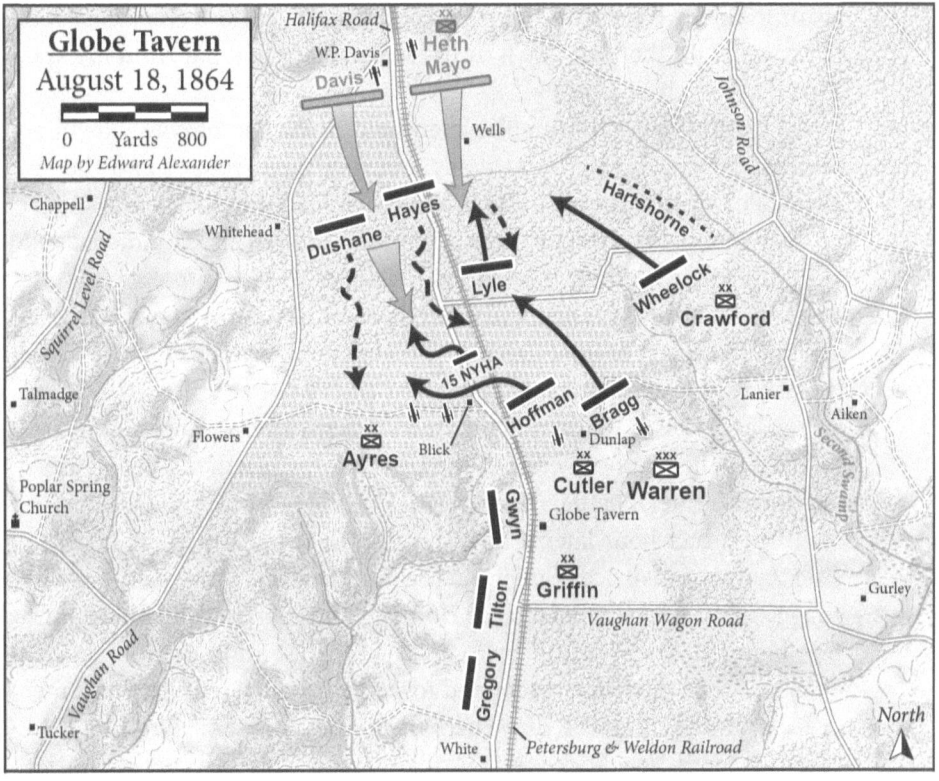

gloom and dimness of the woods. The Fifteenth opened ranks to allow the remnants of Dushane's brigade to pass to the rear. Then, Richie recalled, "a little ripple of musketry passed along our front, followed by an awful crash, as our fire smote the enemy fair in [the] face." This fusillade checked the wild rush, but the Rebels, concealed by the undergrowth, maintained their ground. In minutes butternuts infiltrated a spur of woods projecting into the open field no more than fifty feet from the Fifteenth's left. As the Confederates crept around to the left and rear of Company M, Dickey refused his left until fully two-thirds of Company M faced in the direction of the spur. Jacob Van Vleck described the fight as "dreadful." He narrowly escaped injury when, while avoiding a hail of bullets, "one Ball went in the ground at my nose when lying down—and came out again at my Belt Plate." As the fighting raged, Van Vleck and the heavies ran low on ammunition and redistributed among those still standing cartridges from the boxes of the dead and wounded. When the ammunition was nearly exhausted, Dickey had to make a quick decision. "Very well," he shouted, "we'll fix bayonets and fight it out hand to hand. This flank must be held."[19]

All along Wiedrich's line the men held firm. The heavies, Roebling recalled, "stood their ground nobly, pouring rapid volleys into the enemy checking them at once and driving them speedily back to the shelter of their cornfield." Despite having repulsed the Rebels, he noted, "only with difficulty was their martial ardor abated." By this time, the Second Brigade, according to Dushane, had "disentangled from the woods." Advancing to the left of the Fifteenth, the Marylanders assisted in checking the enemy in that quarter while Hayes's men rallied on the right. Then, at 3:30 P.M. Col. J. William Hoffmann's Fourth Division brigade moved forward to the southern edge of the belt of forest north of Globe Tavern and formed line of battle, its left resting on the railroad.[20]

About a half hour later, Cutler detached Hoffman's brigade and sent it to Ayres's assistance. Cutler's remaining brigade, Brig. Gen. Edward Bragg's, moved forward to replace Hoffman and support the tenuous junction between Ayres's and Crawford's divisions. Shifting to the west side of the railroad, Hoffmann reported to Ayres for duty, relieved Dushane's brigade, and opening fire, drove back the Confederates. As Ayres reported, "The Fifteenth New York Heavy Artillery was steady and cool . . . , [and] Colonel Hoffmann's brigade moved as on drill." When the firing finally petered out, Hayes's First Brigade remained on the right of Ayres's division east of the railroad, with Wiedrich's heavies across the railroad to its left, then Hoffmann's brigade, and the Maryland Brigade on the far left curving to the rear. The Fifteenth had successfully anchored the crumbling line during the battle but sustained many casualties. These losses included its commander, Wiedrich, who suffered a gunshot wound to his right shoulder. The senior officer present, Major Eiche, took temporary command of the regiment.[21]

At 4 P.M. the Fifth Corps commander informed Humphreys that "the falling back of Ayres's division has deranged my plans considerably," but he was "getting things in order again" to resume the advance. An hour and a half later, Warren reported that his skirmish line pressed forward and discovered the Confederates still in their original positions. Even so, he continued to advance the corps's right "through dense woods, which makes it slow and difficult, as it is almost impossible to command men there." He added that "the Fifteenth Heavy Artillery have behaved remarkably well." Their efforts that day led Warren to single them out again in his official report of the action: "The Fifteenth New York Heavy Artillery acted very handsomely." Meade's aide Lyman also took note, remarking "that the 13th [sic] N. Y. Heavy Artil. all behaved well and fired steadily" while adding gratuitously, "They are Germans."[22]

This must have been a difficult admission for Lyman, as he held immigrant German soldiers in utter contempt. In a letter to his wife written only a week earlier, he railed about those in government and the army "who would burden us with these poor, poor nigs, and these nerveless, stupid Germans. As soldiers *in the field* the Germans are nearly useless; our experience is that they have no native courage to compare with Americans." In the same vein he opined, "I wish these gentlemen who would overwhelm us with Germans, negroes, and the offscourings of the cities could only see . . . a Rebel regiment in all their rags and squalor," who are "like wolfhounds, and not to be beaten by turnspits." He then directed his bluster toward "our 'Dutch' heavy artillery: we think no more of trusting them than so many babies" while claiming "ill-disciplined, or cowardly, or demoralized troops may be useful behind walls . . . in open campaigning they literally are useless." He urged his wife to "impress" upon her brother, who "has influence in recruiting . . . , that every worthless recruit he sends to this army is one card in the hand of General Lee and is the cause, very likely, of the death of a good soldier." Seemingly spent by his diatribe on this "important" topic, he concluded by "suggest[ing] to the honorable City of Boston that, when the Germans arrive, they should be let out as gardeners."[23]

Although Warren began the operation expecting to depend entirely on his own resources, Meade and Grant now committed to assisting him in holding the Weldon Railroad by dispatching the Ninth Corps to his support. That night once relieved, Willcox's and Potter's divisions, as well as Ledlie's former division, now commanded by Brig. Gen. Julius White, pulled out of the main line and headed west. Willcox's outfit arrived near Globe Tavern first, at about 7:30 A.M. on August 19, and bivouacked in a field nearby.[24]

Not surprisingly, Lee and Beauregard wanted to break the Federals' grip on the Weldon Railroad. But the Confederates' increasing understanding of Yankee strength there made it apparent that to do so they would need more infantry than had been employed earlier that day. Throughout the night of August 18 and into the following morning, they assembled a force under Lieutenant General Hill's command. In addition to Davis's and Mayo's brigades under Heth's direction, Colquitt's brigade of Georgians and Brig. Gen. Thomas Clingman's Tar Heel brigade, both operating as a separate wing under Little Billy Mahone, would participate in the attack. To strengthen his force, Mahone added his former brigade of Virginians, now commanded by Col. David A. Weisiger.[25]

Considerable rain fell that night, leaving the ground, Roebling recalled, "very sloppy and slippery." A solider remembered that August 19 dawned "a nasty, rainy, drizzling day." Frequent rain showers, many of them heavy, restricted visibility and made movement difficult. Orders received before dawn directed Bragg's Iron Brigade of the Fourth Division to report to Crawford, who instructed the general to deploy on the far right flank and if possible establish a connection with the left of the main Federal line. Numbering only around 760 men that morning, the Iron Brigade would have to cover the gaping separation between the Fifth Corps's right and the main body of the Army of the Potomac.[26]

Meanwhile, the Rebels had devised a plan to regain the Weldon Railroad by employing Mahone's force to break the junction between Bragg's brigade and Mott's division, the later holding the left of the main Federal line. Mahone successfully maneuvered his three brigades undetected to Bragg's front, and soon after 4 P.M. his command knifed into the thin blue line, cutting it in two. Facing right, toward the west, the exuberant graycoats surged ahead and began to roll up the Federal line, striking it in flank and rear. The Iron Brigade made several stands in a stubborn delaying action but soon crumbled under the overwhelming force.[27]

Before long, the attackers reached Crawford's division. By this time Heth's two brigades were advancing from north of the Davis cornfield—Mayo's Brigade, commanded this day by Col. William S. Christian, east of the railroad, and Davis's Brigade to the west. Crawford's outfit was now pressed both in front and flank. The bluecoats faced chaos in the thick, gloomy, rain-soaked woods, and many of Crawford's men fell, were taken prisoner, or withdrew. Crawford himself narrowly avoided capture after enemy troops surrounded him. The gray tide continued to roll westward toward Ayres's division, even as its momentum began to ebb.[28]

The Confederates soon encountered the farthest right of Ayres's brigades, that of Joseph Hayes, which straddled the railroad. Although Hayes's men held their own against the frontal assault by Mayo's brigade, the sudden withdrawal of Lyle's Third Division brigade exposed their

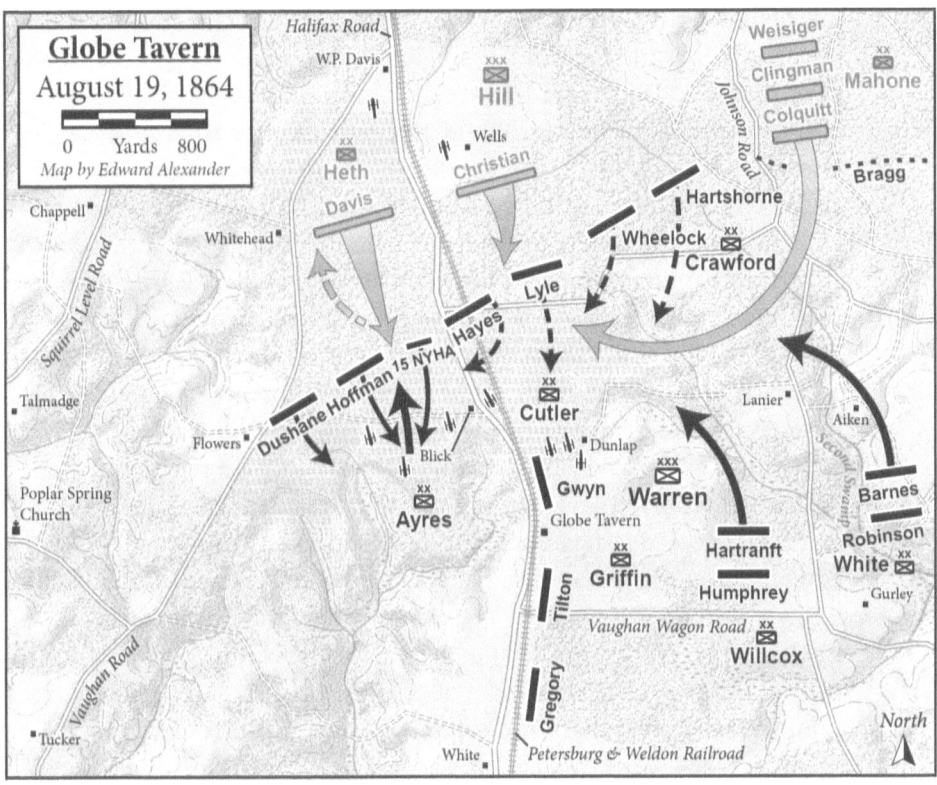

right flank to Mahone's surging attackers. A flood of Rebels soon enveloped the front line on the right of the brigade, comprising the regulars of the Tenth, Eleventh, Twelfth, Fourteenth, and Seventeenth US Infantry. Confederates captured many of the regulars and also surrounded Hayes, forcing him to surrender. Command of the brigade devolved upon Col. Frederic Winthrop of the Fifth New York Veteran Volunteers.[29]

With his division's right pressed back, Ayres ordered a portion of his command to execute a tactical withdrawal to arrest further progress by the flanking Rebels. Just across the Halifax Road and on Winthrop's left, Eiche's heavies faced Davis's Mississippians and Tar Heels attacking to their front, but on orders the Fifteenth New York fell back several hundred yards over the rising ground to a line occupied by Federal artillery. The maneuver, one heavy recalled, was conducted "under a severe cross fire and at a mighty lively gait."[30]

Ayres reformed his line under the artillery's protection, then ordered it forward to regain the position. The Fifteenth at first hesitated. "It was one of those critical moments" Lieutenant Richie of Company M remembered, "when an act, a word, a single man breaking to the rear would have caused a disgraceful flight." But Captain Dickey stepped in front of the wavering line and seized the regimental colors from their bearer. Waving them over his head in one hand, he pointed toward the enemy and shouted, "Come on, boys." At this appeal, "The line stiffened up as with an electric shock," and the "men sprang forward with a yell." With "irresistible momentum" the heavies swept the enemy before them as they retook their original line. To their right, Winthrop's brigade moved forward rapidly and, the colonel reported, "with great spirit." As Ayres's men regained their position, they captured a number of wounded Confederates and also freed some previously captured Federals.[31]

Meanwhile, to Ayres's right, many of Crawford's men regrouped, while Willcox's division advanced from its position east of Globe Tavern to join them. A confused struggle soon ensued. Both the Federals and their opponents launched and received attacks as the lines swayed to and fro in a melee among the tangled, wet, dense woods in which visibility was frequently only fifty yards. White's First Division, Ninth Corps arrived on the right of the combined forces of Crawford and Willcox, pushing the Confederates before them and capturing numerous prisoners.[32]

Hill's attack was now spent, and the graycoats streamed to the rear. The Federals captured at least two stands of colors and many soldiers. Nevertheless, the Rebels still attempted to dislodge the Federals from the regained ground. On the left, Eiche's heavies and the balance of Ayres division repulsed a determined enemy counterattack about ten minutes after regaining their works. Shortly after, at about dark, they repulsed another effort. Before midnight, reinforcements allowed several of Winthrop's regiments to retire into a second line of works for the cold, drizzly night. A man in the 140th New York, positioned just west of the railroad and to the right of the Fifteenth Heavy, recorded, "The mud is over our shoe tops, corn is plenty at present, all rations are wet in Haversacks." The soldiers spent a long, miserable night in their rain-filled earthworks.[33]

As darkness fell on August 19, the Federals essentially occupied the same position they had that morning. Warren had throughout the day provided army headquarters reports of first the Confederate breakthrough, then the withdrawal from and subsequent retaking of Crawford's and Ayres's position. In the end, Meade was "delighted to hear the good news you send, and most heartily commend you [and] your brave officers and men on your success. . . . It will serve greatly to inspirit the whole army, and proves that we only want a fair chance to show our capacity to defeat the enemy." The army commander even declared, "I hope [the enemy] will try it again."[34]

If the rank and file of the Army of the Potomac knew the details of the action Meade thought would "inspirit" them, they might have thought otherwise. The Federals maintained their grip on the Weldon Railroad, but it was at a very high cost. Warren reported more than 2,700 casualties for the Fifth Corps that day—46 killed, 218 wounded, and an astounding 2,457 missing. Roebling reported, "Our losses footed up very heavy for the day, at least 2500 prisoners; the whole of the [Pennsylvania] reserves, half of Bragg, and numbers from Lyle, Coulter [Wheelock] and Hays [sic]." The Ninth Corps sustained losses, too, but far fewer than those of the Fifth. Confederate casualties numbered fewer than 600 men, so comparatively light that a man in Colquitt's Brigade casually summed up the engagement in his diary: "we did not do but little fighting. we got very badly scattered. I do not think there were many killed on either side."[35]

On the morning of August 20, Ayres "temporarily" assigned the Fifteenth Heavy to his First Brigade, commanded by Colonel Winthrop. This temporary assignment would wind up lasting for the duration of the war. In addition to the Fifteenth, the First Brigade included the remnants of eight other battle-hardened regiments. Five of these were the "regulars"—the now tiny Tenth, Eleventh, Twelfth, Fourteenth, and Seventeenth US Infantry Regiments. Two years earlier these regiments had constituted fully half of a Fifth Corps division of regular army infantry. Altogether, the number of remaining regulars, who had suffered heavy losses again the previous day, now counted barely the strength of a single regiment.[36]

The 140th New York Infantry, raised in Rochester and its environs in Monroe County, also served in the First Brigade. Originally assigned in 1862 to the Fifth Corps brigade commanded by Warren, the regiment saw its first action at Fredericksburg that December and subsequently participated in all of the Army of the Potomac's major actions in 1863. Enemy fire killed the regiment's first commander, Col. Patrick H. O'Rourke—a name familiar to many in the Fifteenth—as he led his men in the defense of Little Round Top at Gettysburg on July 2, 1863. In March 1864 the 140th joined the First Brigade, Second Division, Ayres's command, at the beginning of the Overland Campaign.[37]

The First Brigade also included the 146th New York Infantry, recruited principally from Utica, Rome, and the surrounding area of Oneida County. The regiment mustered in for three years at Rome in October 1862. From that time on, its service in the Army of the Potomac closely paralleled that of the 140th. Brigaded with that unit from November 1862, the 146th also saw its first action at Fredericksburg. Then, in 1863 the regiment fought at Chancellorsville and participated in the defense of Little Round Top. Like the 140th, the 146th had suffered heavy losses throughout the 1864 campaign.[38]

The Fifth New York Veteran Volunteers completed the First Brigade. In late May 1863 Col. Cleveland Winslow, the last commander of the regiment, reorganized his remaining men into the Fifth New York Veteran Volunteers. The new outfit also incorporated men initially recruited for two other veteran New York regiments, the Thirty-First and the Thirty-Seventh, which were never completed. Even with these additions, Winslow's efforts only resulted in enough men to constitute a four-company battalion. This cadre left New York City in late October 1863 and served for nearly seven months in and around Washington before reporting to the Army of the Potomac on May 31, 1864. Once with Meade's army, two companies remaining in service from the old Twelfth New York and four companies remaining from the Eighty-Fourth New York (also known as the Fourteenth Brooklyn) joined Winslow's ranks to bring the regiment to its full complement of ten companies.[39]

Living up to the hard-earned reputation of its predecessor, the Fifth Veteran had fought well since joining Meade's army at Bethesda Church, sustaining heavy losses commensurate with those of other Fifth Corps regiments. There, it had suffered 108 casualties in its first action on June 2, mere hours after joining the army. One of these was Colonel Winslow, who would succumb to his wounds on July 7. Upon the recommendation of Warren, and with the hearty endorsement of the officers of the Fifth, the adjutant general of New York appointed Colonel Winthrop, a former captain in the Twelfth US Infantry, to command the Fifth, a post he assumed on August 6. Born into a prominent New York City family, Winthrop began his war service as a private in the Seventy-First New York Militia at twenty-five after working as a bank clerk. When the Seventy-First completed its brief term of service, he wrangled an appointment to captain in the regiment of regulars. Winthrop also served briefly on Ayres's staff.[40]

The Fifth Veteran's Zouave uniforms, modeled after those of the French army's elite North African troops, stood out on the field. While colors varied depending on the unit, Zouave uniforms typically featured a short, open coat buttoned near the top, with decorative accents of a contrasting color; pants of varying degrees of bagginess, with a sash worn around the waist; leggings; and a distinctive fez cap. Although when first organized the 140th and 146th wore regulation infantry garb, as a reward for their proficiency in drill and in combat, the 146th received Zouave uniforms in mid-1863 and the 140th early in January 1864. Thus, apart from the few regulars left in the brigade, the Fifteenth Heavy was now an island of standard-issue uniforms in sea of Zouaves.[41]

The continuing heavy rain soaked the ground and left many roads impassable on August 20. Nevertheless, the Confederates still refused to cede control of the Weldon without another, more forceful attempt to dislodge the Federals. The brigades that participated in the two prior assaults returned to the trenches, and fresh troops readied for another attack. But difficult marches to get to the front left these "fresh" troops exhausted. Some outfits trudged from north of the James River and spent the long night navigating dark, muddy roads. To break the Federals, Beauregard had stripped even man possible from the Petersburg defenses. He assured Lee that he would "try [an] attack in the morning with all the force I can spare." Eventually, he assembled nine brigades and part of a tenth, nearly twice the number of troops engaged in the August 19 fighting. Beauregard planned for Heth to assault from the north down the railroad with three brigades. Mahone, with the balance of the attackers, would swing to the west via the Vaughan Road and strike eastward, taking the left of the Federal line in flank and rear. The plan was flawed, however. Confederate scouts failed to detect Griffin's First Division, Fifth Corps in position stretching south along the railroad and assumed the Federal line was vulnerable, its flank hanging "in the air."[42]

As the Confederates prepared for this next try, the Federals strengthened and consolidated their grip on the Weldon. To avoid another fight in the wet, tangled woods, Warren withdrew from the thickets and, by midmorning on August 20, began constructing a new line in the middle of the large field nearer Globe Tavern. The heavily entrenched line would form a right angle, its apex near the Blick house, one leg extending south, parallel to the railroad, and the other leg running roughly eastward past the Dunlop house. This new position would give the Federal artillery and infantry the benefits of a full, open field of fire against any attackers. The shortening of the line also offered a further advantage, allowing Warren a sizeable infantry reserve that could be shifted wherever he needed it to respond to enemy movements.[43]

The Ninth Corps and Crawford's division withdrew to their new positions nearer Globe Tavern first, commencing in the late morning and early afternoon. That afternoon Bragg's brigade entrenched west of the railroad near the Blick house. The weather remained difficult. "The day was very cold and the rain came down in sheets and our fellows sat on their knapsacks and haunches with rubber blankets over their heads in vain efforts to keep dry," a man in the Iron Brigade remembered. At about 8 P.M. Hoffman's brigade settled in on Bragg's left and began to entrench. Griffin's division, which spent the day strengthening its works, sat in echelon several hundred yards to Hoffman's rear. Its line ran south parallel to the railroad for a distance of almost three-quarters of a mile. Colonel Wainwright, his Fifth Corps batteries nestled within and all along the new line on slightly higher ground, threw up protective works in front of all the guns.[44]

Meanwhile, Ayres's division remained in its forward position. From early in the morning, the Second Division's pickets maintained contact and occasionally exchanged fire with their Confederate counterparts. Winthrop's brigade sat astride the railroad, the Fifteenth on the left. Despite the rain and cold, the men continued to improve their defensive line and to slash timber in front. After dark they received word of the planned withdrawal and orders to level the works they had spent the day building. One of Winthrop's men complained that they "worked very hard at getting up a breastwork, at 9 P.M. ordered to tear it down. Rain. Rain. Rain." After they destroyed their hard day's work, the men remained "standing in the rain and darkness with the breastworks leveled down."[45]

At about 2 A.M. on August 21, Ayres finally withdrew to the new position. The division fell back about 700 yards to the crest of a gentle slope in the large field north of Globe Tavern. With Winthrop's brigade on the right still straddling the railroad and Dushane's Marylanders on the left connecting with Bragg's brigade, they held the apex of the new Federal line. The Second Division's exhausted men immediately began to construct yet another earthwork. The backbreaking job of wrestling the thick, heavy mud into a defensive fortification in the rain continued throughout the night. After the new line took shape, Roebling speculated that "enough work was done during the night to enable us to withstand any attack in the morning."[46]

As Ayres's outfit began falling back to its new line, the Confederates were beginning to stir. The continuing rain made progress slow as the graycoats slogged out the Squirrel Level Road through the mud and water. Swinging to the left, Mahone halted the long column near Poplar Spring Church, about a half mile west of the Vaughan Road. Leaving Brig. Gen. Johnson Hagood's brigade of South Carolinians in reserve at the church, Mahone deployed his remaining five brigades along the Vaughan Road, with the midpoint of the formation around the Flowers house. Meanwhile, twelve guns of Lt. Col. William J. Pegram's artillery battalion unlimbered near the house. Eight more of Pegram's guns had already rolled into position in the Davis cornfield near the junction of the Vaughan and Halifax Roads. As the day neared 8:30 A.M., the sun began to break through the morning fog, and as one bluecoat recalled, it "shone bright and warm and our chaps hung out their blankets and shirts to dry."[47]

All hell broke loose minutes later, when Pegram ordered his five batteries to open up. The artillery fire from the north and the west converged on the apex of the Federal line. To the men in Ayres's and Cutler's divisions hunkered down there, it seemed like the shot and shells came from all sides. One of Ayres's men remembered that the enemy "attacked on 3 sides for an Hour the shelling we got from the Rebs was most awful." Winthrop reported that his brigade "was here subjected to a most deadly cross-fire of artillery, but, as usual, fully sustained its old reputation for calmness and steadiness." Roebling, galloping west along the line toward the apex, observed that "the air seemed to be alive with cannon balls coming from the direction of the Flower house; it required the utmost agility to dodge them." Nearing the Blick house, the major found "it was very hot," and "the Blick was at one time subjected to a fire equal to if not surpassing any at Gettysburg."[48]

Before long, a gray battle line emerged from the woods north of Globe Tavern. Federal artillery immediately opened on enemy troops. "There was so much powder smoke," Roebling remembered, "that I doubt whether many of our infantry saw them in time." Once the Yankee infantry did see the enemy, every man loaded and fired into the advancing ranks. Under the scathing artillery and musketry fire, the Rebels pressed resolutely forward toward Winthrop's position. Eventually unable to withstand the withering fire, the butternuts fell back. The colonel reported,

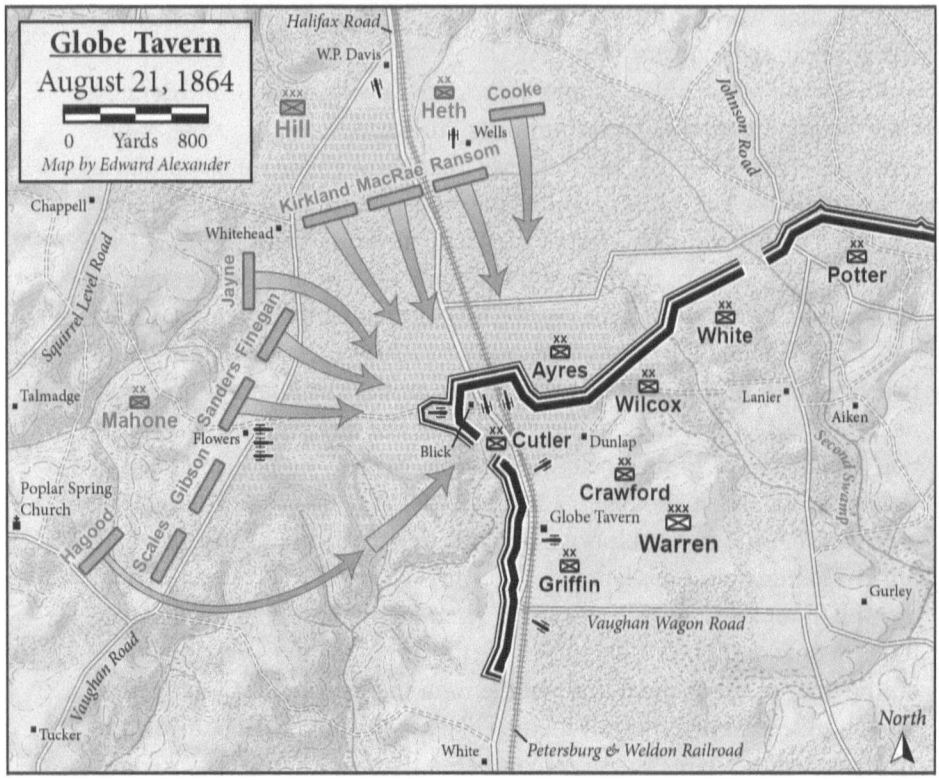

"The enemy's assault resulted in a severe repulse." As the Confederates fell back, he ordered his men to maintain a scattering fire on the enemy skirmishers and sharpshooters lingering in the edge of the woods to the brigade's front, who "were annoying our artillery by their fire."[49]

Along the west face of the Federal line, Mahone's brigades pressed ahead toward Cutler's position, which they mistakenly understood to be the vulnerable, extreme left of the Federal line. As the graycoats came within range, devastating fire from Hart's and Mink's Fifth Corps batteries raked their lines. Near the left of the Confederate line, Brig. Gen. John C. Sanders's Alabamians and Brig. Gen. Joseph Finegan's Floridians advanced. Finegan's outfit, as Brig. Gen. Nathanial H. Harris recalled, "was repulsed by the heavy and galling fire of artillery and musketry opened on them by the enemy; and fell back in confusion and disorder." Harris's Mississippians, commanded that day by Col. Joseph M. Jayne, moved forward to bolster the line. "This command charged right up to the face of the enemy's works; but the fire being so severe and the Brigade being unsupported, we were compelled to retire."⁵⁰

Roebling reported that the Confederate attack "was repulsed with ease" and that "they did not even come near enough to be very severely punished, running back under cover of the woods after standing the fire for a few moments." Similarly, Ayres, watching the action from his position on Cutler's right, saw the assault "easily and splendidly repulsed." Wainwright reported that some enemy soldiers penetrated to within 150 yards of Hart's battery only to be "driven back by heavy discharges of canister." Yet at least some Confederate units displayed their usual grit. Another Union observer saw the Rebels moving forward from the woods through the standing corn in four lines of battle. "Six times the flag of the first line of Confederates fell, and six times a color corporal picked it up and was killed. After that it laid on the ground until it was captured. The corn stalks were cut off by the bullets as if with a knife."⁵¹

As Mahone's attack faltered, Hagood's brigade came forward from its position in reserve. The South Carolinians swung to the south beyond the presumed flank of the Union position, crossed a swamp, and halted briefly to reform at the base of the low plateau upon which Griffin's line waited. Hagood did not realize his precarious position until his brigade resumed the advance and reached the crest of the plateau. As Roebling aptly described the moment, "the rebs. had got out of the frying pan into the fire, because here they were exposed to the full fire of Griffin's line, which they did not expect to find." One of Bragg's men relished this: "we waited patiently to get satisfaction for the chase they gave us, Friday, and we did." When Hagood's men came into view, the soldier continued, "Our batteries opened on them with double shotted canister and cut lanes through them, but they came on with their heads down and arms at a trail." He reported "doing my best to 'welcome them to hospitable graves.'" Wainwright, too, savored the Yankee success. "Their [rebel] yell . . . was stopped in their throats before it was well out. Never were they in so perfect a trap!" Mahone's attack had failed, and the survivors hastily withdrew.⁵²

In the four days of fighting near Globe Tavern, both sides suffered considerably. Union losses numbered nearly 4,300, including over 3,000 men taken prisoner. Of this number, the Fifteenth Heavy counted 27 killed or mortally wounded, 62 wounded, and 5 missing. Hayes's old brigade sustained 720 casualties. The Confederates lost fewer men, around 2,300 total, with about 800 of those prisoners—at this point of the war, they could scarce spare any losses. When Hagood's South Carolinians regrouped near Poplar Spring Church after the action on August 21, only 291 answered the roll of the approximately 740 officers and men going in to the attack. Of the human wreckage scattered before the Federal works on the afternoon of August 21, Ninth Corps division commander Willcox mourned that, "besides all of the wounded, over two hundred Confederates lay dead upon the field in front of our defenses." He described the scene as "a sad sight, for, enemies as they were, they were bone of our bone and flesh of our flesh."[53]

Despite the casualties, the outcome of the Battle of Globe Tavern gratified the Federals. Warren reported, "During these four days' operations men and officers performed their duties as well as any ever did under the circumstances." Wainwright gushed over the fine showing of his artillery. "We had a love of a fight today. For once it was all on our side, everything was well managed, and Lee got a lesson which I guess will keep him from attempting this place again."[54]

The heavies of the Fifteenth could also take pride in their performance in the battle, and this boosted their confidence. As he enjoyed a few days of hard-earned rest, one wrote to his sister, "I am all OK and never felt better in my life—we gave the Johnnies a good thrashing." Another man described to his wife how he survived "a Dreadful Battle or two." He mused about the future and described their conditions. "Where we will go next I know not—we have had some very wet weather lately." He reported, with a sense of satisfaction, "we have no trouble now with the Rebs as we licked them back every time they have tried to drive us from here."[55]

The men of the Army of the Potomac, and especially those of the Fifth Corps, were right to be satisfied with their accomplishments at Globe Tavern. The Weldon Railroad had finally been cut, and the Federal line was extended more than two miles west to cover that point. The noose around the Cockade City was beginning to tighten. But with the encirclement far from complete, supplies continued to trickle into the city to support its beleaguered defenders. More hard work and sacrifice would be required of the Fifteenth Heavy and their Army of the Potomac comrades before Grant's objective to strangle Petersburg—and by extension Richmond—could be achieved.

Col. Louis Schirmer (Roger D. Hunt Personal Collection)

Bvt. Col. Michael Wiedrich (Civil War Carte-de-Visite Collection, New York State Military Museum)

15. Regiment,
Schwere Artillerie,
Oberst Louis Schirmer,
stationirt in Fort Lyon, bei Washington.

Es werden für dieses Regiment noch 200 Mann verlangt, um es auf die Stärke von 1800 Mann zu bringen.

677 Dollars Bounty für neue Rekruten,   und   **852 Dollars Bounty** für Veteranen.

Veteranen bekommen Cash bevor sie abmarschiren 525 D. llars.
Rekruten „ „ „ „ „ 450 „
Prämie von 25 Dollars für Veteranen.
„ „ 15 „ „ Rekruten wird Denjenigen bezahlt, welche die Leute nach den verschiedenen Officen bringen.
Familien erhalten Unterstützung.

Hauptquartier: No. 91 Bowery, New-York.
CHARLES HERZOG,
Adjutant.

Card soliciting recruits for the Fifteenth New York Heavy Artillery (Louis Schirmer Court-Martial Records, National Archives)

Lt. Gen. Ulysses S. Grant (Civil War Glass Negatives and Related Prints, Library of Congress)

Maj. Gen. George G. Meade (Civil War Glass Negatives and Related Prints, Library of Congress)

Maj. Gen. Henry J. Hunt (Civil War Glass Negatives and Related Prints, Library of Congress)

Col. J. Howard Kitching (Roger D. Hunt Personal Collection)

Lt. Col. Theodore Lyman (Roger D. Hunt Personal Collection)

Maj. Gen. Gouverneur K. Warren (Civil War Glass Negatives and Related Prints, Library of Congress)

Todd's Tavern (MOLLUS-Mass Civil War Photographs Collection, vol. 67, US Army Heritage and Education Center)

Maj. Washington A. Roebling (Roebling Collection [MC 4], Institute Archives and Special Collections, Rensselaer Polytechnic Institute, Troy, NY)

Col. Charles S. Wainwright (RG98s—Civil War Photos, US Army Heritage and Education Center)

Confederate soldier killed in the battle at Harris Farm (Civil War Glass Negatives and Related Prints, Library of Congress)

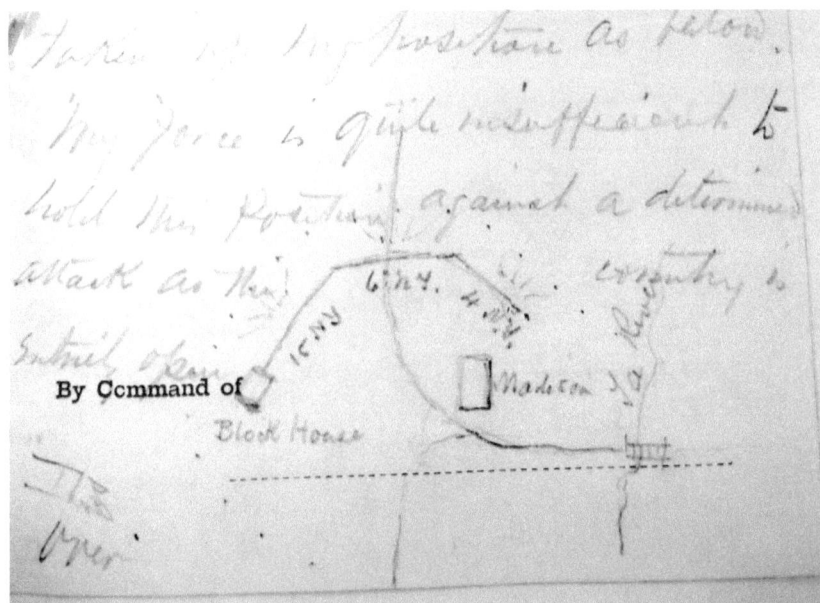

Kitching's sketch of position of the Heavy Artillery Brigade at Madison's Ordinary, night of May 21, 1864 (Gouverneur Kemble Warren Papers, New York State Library)

Jericho Mills, showing the pontoon bridge over which the Fifteenth New York Heavy Artillery crossed the North Anna River (Civil War Glass Negatives and Related Prints, Library of Congress)

Pontoon bridges at Hanovertown, over which the Fifth Corps crossed the Pamunkey River (Civil War Glass Negatives and Related Prints, Library of Congress)

Brig. Gen. Samuel W. Crawford (Civil War Glass Negatives and Related Prints, Library of Congress)

Maj. Gen. Romeyn B. Ayres (Civil War Glass Negatives and Related Prints, Library of Congress)

Maj. William D. Dickey (Civil War Carte-de-Visite Collection, New York State Military Museum)

Bvt. Brig. Gen. Frederic Winthrop (Roger D. Hunt Personal Collection)

General Warren and his staff pose before the Fifth Corps flag near Petersburg, late June 1864 (Civil War Glass Negatives and Related Prints, Library of Congress)

Typical section of Federal trench line on the Petersburg front (Civil War Glass Negatives and Related Prints, Library of Congress)

Globe Tavern (Civil War Glass Negatives and Related Prints, Library of Congress)

The bloodstained photograph of Jacob Van Vleck's daughter, removed from his body on the Hatcher's Run battlefield (Jacob Van Vleck Letters, New York State Library)

Maj. Gen. Philip Sheridan (Civil War Glass Negatives and Related Prints, Library of Congress)

Maj. Gen. Charles Griffin, last commander of the Fifth Corps (Civil War Glass Negatives and Related Prints, Library of Congress)

Brig. Gen. Joseph Hayes, last commander of the First Brigade, Second Division, Fifth Corps (MacDonald Collection, Maine State Archives, Augusta)

Maj. William D. Dickey and Third Battalion officers at Fort Woodbury, probably taken in late July 1865 (Civil War Carte-de-Visite Collection, New York State Military Museum)

CHAPTER TEN

The Battle of Peebles's Farm

In the immediate aftermath of the Battle of Globe Tavern, the heavies of the Fifteenth and their Fifth Corps comrades enjoyed several relatively peaceful days. Although they experienced some heavy rain showers, the weather generally ameliorated. The improved conditions facilitated work to strengthen their new position. The corps also underwent some leadership and reorganizational changes after the battle. On August 22 Colonel Winthrop reverted to command of the Fifth Veteran when Col. Charles P. Stone of the Fourteenth US Infantry reported for duty with the Fifth Corps and joined the Second Division. Stone's regular-army commission trumped Winthrop's volunteer rank, so Ayres assigned Stone to command the First Brigade. Two days later Warren elected to break up Cutler's small, two-brigade Fourth Division. He temporarily assigned Bragg's Iron Brigade to Crawford's Third Division. In Ayres's command, the departure of the Sixth New York Heavy and the transfer of the Fifteenth to the First Brigade had vacated the Third Brigade entirely. Thus, Warren dispatched, again temporarily, Colonel Hoffman's brigade to the Second Division, Ayres designating it as his Third Brigade.[1]

Warren's firm grip on the Weldon Railroad at Globe Tavern had severed rail service by that route into Petersburg. But the Confederates continued to use that road as a supply line by bringing provisions by rail to within one day's wagon haul of Petersburg, then into the city via the Boydton Plank Road. The Federal high command wanted to deprive the enemy of that option. On August 22 Grant informed Meade of his desire to hold the Weldon and to destroy it as far south as possible, ideally to its crossing over Rowanty Creek, about thirteen miles below Globe Tavern. This would compel the Confederates to haul their supplies by wagon at least thirty miles from the Stony Creek station to Petersburg. An operation several days later by two of Hancock's Second Corps divisions with supporting cavalry to achieve that objective, although successful in destroying about three additional miles of the railroad, failed to fully realize Grant's goal. It ended in a decisive Federal defeat at Reams's Station, about four miles south of Globe Tavern.[2]

Meanwhile, commanders and their troops at Globe Tavern remained apprehensive of a possible Confederate attack. A diarist in Stone's brigade recalled falling in about noon on August 25 to repel an anticipated Rebel assault that never materialized, then sleeping under arms throughout that showery night. Warren's continued concern about an attack from the south resulted in an order to both Griffin and Ayres to withdraw the bulk of their divisions at daylight, leaving a single rank in the breastworks. Those withdrawn were to begin construction of a south-facing line of light breastworks for use to defend against an attack from the rear.[3]

Desertion was not uncommon in either army, and on the Federal side, the problem was undoubtedly exacerbated by the recent influx of unwilling conscripts and substitutes. In an effort to discourage the practice within the Fifth Corps, on August 26 the entire corps assembled in open ground in front of five open graves, each with a coffin in front of it. There they witnessed five convicted deserters in blue trousers and white flannel shirts paraded before them, accompanied by clergy, an escort with arms reversed, and a firing detail. As the deserters marched onto the field, a band played the mournful notes of the dead march. Each deserter was blindfolded and then seated on the end of his coffin. Thirty paces away the firing detail—ten men for each prisoner—prepared to fire. When the order rang out, fifty muskets thundered. Four of the men immediately fell backward onto their coffins, but the fifth remained in a sitting position. A surgeon then stepped forward and, upon examination, pronounced all five men, including the upright one, dead. The grim spectacle certainly must have achieved its goal of giving pause to any soldier considering desertion.[4]

The low-lying, often swampy ground around Globe Tavern—Lt. George Breck of Battery L, First New York Light described it as "composed of clay and a sort of quick-sand"—began to pose sanitation problems. Toward the end of August, the Fifth Corps commander directed Ayres to have his men clean out all of the obstructions in the ditches in the area they now occupied to "make every effort to secure good drainage in order to prevent sickness." The army soon instituted additional methods to achieve this same end. As cases of malarial fever began to break out, Breck reported, "half a ration (half a gill) of whiskey containing quinine, is issued to the 5th corps—and will continue to be as long as they remain in this locality—every night and morning, at sunrise and sunset." He explained, "The malarious nature of the country about here requires that this issue be made to preserve the health of the men." The new ration, although somewhat bitter, was likely welcomed by some troops for more than medicinal reasons. One of Ayres's men noted, "There is an abundance of whiskey & quinine in camp."[5]

During this period, much-needed troop replacements continued bolstering the ranks of the Fifth Corps. Although many of the new men were conscripts, others were volunteers, some of them veterans with prior service. Colonel Wainwright attributed the influx of volunteers in part to the "enormous" bounties that recruits received. "This is all wrong. Not one cent should be offered, but the draft put straight through," he fumed. The corps artillery commander also mused, "Heavy artillery service, which swallowed so many recruits last winter, is now at a discount; Cold Harbour and Petersburg have brought it down to the level of common infantry in the eyes of those who look for comfort and safety on enlisting." Wainwright saw new recruits shying away from the heavy artillery for this reason while observing that consequently "there is quite a rush" to serve in his arm, the light artillery, which also needed an infusion of new blood to replace its losses.[6]

After nearly two weeks in the same position warily eyeing the same opponent, the inevitable fraternization of pickets across the lines resumed. These contacts frequently occurred as exchanges of rations, newspapers, or other articles the soldiers valued. Negotiations might begin, "Hallo, Yank! Have you'uns any coffee?" to which the reply would be, "Say, Johnny, got any tobacco?" One of Warren's clerks reported that as the soldiers exchanged these luxuries, "Pleasantries of one kind or another often pass between [the men], perhaps of some recent or long-past engagement, in which both took part, and, at times, the rejoinders are more forcible than polite, but they are always taken good-humoredly, so far as I have ever heard." A man in Stone's brigade similarly remembered that after a week or two, the close proximity of the picket lines led to "a spirit of good fellowship . . . among the outposts of the two armies." In these welcome, peaceful moments, the common bond between soldiers, and the realization of being an American whether wearing gray or blue, seemed to overcome the differences between these enemies in a war most of them must have wished could be ended.[7]

Although after the Globe Tavern battle, Warren had made certain temporary modifications to the Fifth Corps's organization, Meade had more sweeping changes in mind. In particular, in addition to permanently discontinuing the Fourth Division, he wanted all of the troops from the old First Corps grouped into one division. After Meade's approval of his proposal to achieve these objectives, on September 12 Warren assigned all of the old First Corps troops, with the exception of the Maryland Brigade, to Crawford's Third Division. Consequently, to better balance the strengths of the divisions, he transferred to Ayres's division the 190th and 191st Pennsylvania Regiments—the veteran Pennsylvania Reserves—or at least what remained of them after the Globe Tavern fight. Within the Second Division, the organization of the First Brigade and the Second (Maryland) Brigade remained unchanged. The veteran Pennsylvania Reserves, along with the Third and Fourth Delaware and the 157th Pennsylvania, constituted the new Third Brigade, commanded by Col. Arthur H. Grimshaw of the Fourth Delaware. As the corps's organization changed, so did the First Brigade's commander. While on leave, Col. Charles Stone resigned from the army on September 13. Col. Frederic Winthrop then reassumed command of the brigade.[8]

From late August through mid-September, large working parties from the infantry corps continued improving and constructing earthworks. On two occasions in early September, Warren reported that there were 2,400 men at work daily on the defenses in the Fifth Corps's sector. The "men . . . employed on the forts" built a large one, Fort Wadsworth, near the former site of the Blick house on the remains of the apex of the works thrown up during the Globe Tavern fight. They constructed a second large fort, Fort Dushane, about a mile south of Wadsworth and just west of the railroad and Halifax Road. Both strongholds were completed by the third week of September.[9]

Meanwhile, work parties from the Ninth and Second Corps extended the line east from Warren's right near Fort Wadsworth to Fort Davis on the Jerusalem Plank Road and also constructed a secondary line in rear facing south. This secondary line extended west from the Williams house near the Plank Road, past Dr. Gurley's, and connected with Warren's left near the Weldon Railroad. This work, too, was nearly completed by the third week of September. The monthlong effort resulted in a heavily fortified peninsula about a mile wide north–south and extending from the Jerusalem Plank Road west to the Weldon Railroad. Also completed by this time was a military railroad stretching fourteen miles back to City Point, which ran through the center of this occupied territory, allowing the army to supply the fortifications as well as all points along the way quickly and efficiently.[10]

On September 18 Warren directed that brigade drills be held every day until certain maneuvers "are fully comprehended." The order included a long list of necessary drills: "To face by the rear rank; to face by the front rank; to march to the front in line of battle; to march to the rear in line of battle; to change front to rear on the right or left battalion; to change front forward on the right or left battalion; to come by right or left by file into line." For the heavies of the Fifteenth, this order evoked memories of their earlier days at Brandy Station. On subsequent afternoons commanders put the First Brigade through its paces executing the required drills. About this time Winthrop fell ill and returned to New York to recuperate. In his absence, Lt. Col. Elwell S. Otis of the 140th New York commanded the brigade. When Ayres reviewed the brigade on September 22, "all went off fine," according to a man in the brigade. Although it rained heavily that night, the following day dawned "pleasant," and the men once again stood to inspection as Warren reviewed Ayres's entire division.[11]

As the Federals continued to stretch their line to the west, the Confederates recognized the vulnerability of their Boydton Plank Road and South Side Railroad supply lines. With this in mind, General Lee determined to curtail the enemy's westward movement by extending his own defenses across their path. On September 16 Confederates began work on a new fortified line running to the southwest from Battery 45 in the main line around Petersburg. This new line would extend slightly over two miles to beyond the Harmon Road, roughly paralleling the Boydton Plank Road and at a distance southeast from it varying between one-half to one mile.[12]

Four days later the Confederates began work on another line originating at the main Petersburg defenses. This one roughly paralleled the Squirrel Level Road and, at its northern end, ran primarily on the east side of it. The line then angled over to the west side near the W. W. Davis house, about a mile north of the intersection of the Squirrel Level Road with the Church Road. A small redoubt, Fort Cherry, covered the crossing at the Davis house. From that point the line continued along the west side of the road, where, about a half mile from Fort Cherry and after it crossed the Chappell farm, Fort Bratton, an enclosed earthwork, was situated. The works then extended southwest across the Church Road and over the farm of William Peebles. Beyond this, about a half mile after crossing a creek known as Arthur's Swamp, the line came to an end, with the terminus protected by another enclosed work, Fort MacRae. Where the new line crossed Church Road, an important avenue of approach to the Boydton Plank Road, a third enclosed work stood, Fort Archer. About three-eighths of a mile south of the Church Road intersection, the Poplar Spring Church Road ran east from the Squirrel Level Road to the Vaughan Road.[13]

As both sides continued to dig in, some men took time to reflect on their experiences and to write home about them. "That talk about Southerners whipping ten Yanks is played out," a private in the Fifteenth wrote his sister in early September. He spoke from personal experience. "I have been on the skirmish line often, and when the Johnnies were full as strong as we were, our Officers would only have to say, boys get ready, three cheers and Charge." He found the opposing sides evenly matched. "I never was on the line when we failed to drive them, and on a fair field they lost as many as we." Although he may have exaggerated in his letter, he revealed his confidence in his unit. After its inauspicious beginning in combat in the Wilderness, the Fifteenth had performed well whenever called upon to engage the enemy. As the war continued, they would have more opportunities to demonstrate their mettle.[14]

As the close of September neared, the two Federal armies confronting Richmond and Petersburg had for well over a month remained largely inactive as far as offensive operations were concerned. This respite was about to end. Grant now elected to launch another offensive on the Confederate capital and, if the opportunity presented itself, the important rail center and supply routes to its south in the vicinity of Petersburg. North of the James, on the morning of September 29, two infantry corps of Butler's army would strike toward Richmond, the primary objective, with cavalry support. Regardless of the enemy's reaction, Grant anticipated a successful operation. He assured Butler that if the enemy resisted this thrust with sufficient force to prevent success, "it is confidently expected that General Meade can gain a decisive advantage on his end of the line."[15]

Meade received orders outlining his army's role in the offensive. By 4 A.M. on September 29, the entire Army of the Potomac was to be up and under arms. Its early morning activities were intended to divert enemy attention from the main attack north of the James. Beyond that, Grant allowed Meade broad discretion as to his next actions. Should the enemy siphon off sufficient force to justify a movement toward the South Side Railroad or Petersburg, the general in chief authorized him "to do it without waiting for instructions and in your own way." In the two days prior to the beginning of the offensive, Meade formed a striking force of four divisions in case he needed it. He designated two divisions from the Ninth Corps, Willcox's and Potter's, and two divisions from the Fifth Corps, which Warren would select. Warren tapped Griffin's and Ayres's divisions, as well as Colonel Hoffman's Third Division brigade, as the Fifth Corps's contribution to the mobile force.[16]

The Fifteenth would have to take the field still without its commander Lieutenant Colonel Wiedrich, who remained on leave at his home in Buffalo since mid-September due to ill health. In his absence, and with Major Dieckmann and Major Duysing still in the hospital, Major Eiche remained in command of the heavies. Eiche was well known to the men of the Fifteenth, having begun his service in the old Third Battalion New York Heavy Artillery in late 1861. He had also been active in recruiting for the regiment in 1863. There can be little doubt that the heavies vested full confidence in this steadfast and experienced officer to lead them into action.[17]

As planned, Butler's force began moving toward Richmond early on September 29. After initial success, including capturing Fort Harrison, the advance faltered by afternoon as Confederate reinforcements poured in. During the course of the day, nine Confederate infantry brigades shuttled across the James to counter this Federal thrust. Sporadic action continued, but the stalled attack north of the river would not open the way to Richmond. During the night, the bluecoats began digging in to secure their modest gains.[18]

South of the James on September 29, on what one of Otis's men described as a "pleasant and cool" morning, the Army of the Potomac stood under arms and ready to move. Although reports filtered in throughout the day of the enemy shifting troops from below to above the James, Meade decided by midafternoon that it was too late in the day for a movement to the left. Indeed, by that night both he and Grant had second thoughts about the wisdom of an attempt to strike all the way to the South Side Railroad. They instead agreed on a more modest objective. The Army of the Potomac would merely extend its line to the left and, if commanders saw an opportunity, advance toward Petersburg or wherever circumstance may direct.[19]

At 8:15 A.M. the next day, a pleasant and warm Friday, Grant ordered the army into action. He notified Meade that Butler's command north of the James would stay put for the moment. Meade should "move out now and see if an advantage can be gained," Grant advised. "It seems to me the enemy must be weak enough at one or the other place to let us in." The army commander immediately launched his striking force. He directed Warren to move out via the Poplar Spring Church Road to gain its intersection with the Squirrel Level Road. Meade also ordered Parke to follow in support with the Ninth Corps and try to open a route across Arthur's Swamp south of Poplar Spring Church so as to come up on Warren's left.[20]

Meade's troops sprang into action. The column began moving south on the Halifax Road by 9 A.M. Griffin's First Division led the way, followed by one battery. Next came Ayres's Second Division and then Hoffman's Third Brigade of the Third Division, which was temporarily attached to Ayres. Wainwright's remaining five batteries brought up the rear of the Fifth Corps column. After clearing their fortifications and swinging to the right onto the Poplar Spring Church Road, Griffin's men pressed westward across the Vaughan Road. Just before the intersection, the open ground through which the Poplar Spring Church Road passed gave way to a thick growth of woods and scrubby pine well suited for concealing an enemy. The column slowed as the Federals cautiously picked their way ahead along the narrow but good road. Not until approximately two and a half hours after Warren's vanguard stepped off did the lead Ninth Corps division fall into line of march behind Wainwright's batteries.[21]

After tramping along for about two hours, the lead of Griffin's division approached Poplar Spring Church, which Lyman mockingly referred to as "a stately building, say 25 × 15, of wood, without bell or steeple, resembling in fact a chapel of easance." Griffin's advance struck graycoat skirmishers about 200 yards west of the church, where a north–south running branch of Arthur's Swamp crossed the road. After driving off the enemy, Griffin used the protection afforded by the ravine through which the branch ran to deploy his outfit into attack formation. Meanwhile, to clear the road and allow the Ninth Corps to move up to support Griffin, Warren directed

Ayres to shift his troops off the Poplar Spring Church Road and into the fields just north of it near the Vaughan Road intersection. Not only would this movement alleviate the traffic jam on the narrow road but it also would put Ayres's men in a position to guard against any Confederate attempt to cut off the strike force from its base near Globe Tavern. The Second Division took position in line of battle facing north astride the Vaughan Road, where it remained for the next two hours. Potters's and Willcox's Ninth Corps divisions moved past them, reaching Poplar Spring Church shortly after noon.[22]

Just after 1 P.M. Griffin's men debouched from their covered position and rushed toward the Confederate line stretching through William Peebles's fields. Successfully dashing across 500–600 yards of open ground and passing the abandoned plantation house, the blue tide crossed Fort Archer's fourteen-foot-wide, ten-foot-deep ditch and swarmed up the parapets. The attackers soon overwhelmed the defenders, principally cavalrymen, and captured the fort and its adjoining breastworks. By 1:30 P.M. Warren reported that Griffin had captured the works on Peebles's farm "in splendid style," later characterizing the charge as "one of the boldest I ever saw." In addition to taking a number of prisoners, the attack yielded the first artillery piece captured by the Fifth Corps since the campaign's start. Federal losses were relatively light. Griffin, and soon after Warren, rode forward to the captured fort to the cheers of joyful bluecoats.[23]

After securing Fort Archer, elements of Griffin's Third Brigade swept northeast up the Confederate line and the Squirrel Level Road. As the handful of graycoats defending Fort Bratton fled before them, the First Michigan and Eighteenth Massachusetts continued across Chappell's fields, reached the W. W. Davis farm, and occupied Fort Cherry by 2 P.M. The remaining three regiments of the Third Brigade came up to their support. In only about an hour, a large segment of the Squirrel Level Road line had been taken along with two if its three enclosed forts.[24]

To the east, Ayres pushed his picket line forward on the Vaughan Road. This allowed the Second Division picket line to connect with Griffin's men east of W. W. Davis's and Fort Cherry sometime before 3 P.M. Meanwhile, Ayres led the balance of his division, with Otis's brigade in the vanguard, along the Poplar Spring Church Road and up the Squirrel Level Road to Fort Bratton. Arriving around 3 P.M., Ayres's men relieved the Ninth Corps brigade that had been placed there to bolster Griffin's right. For the heavies of the Fifteenth and their Second Division comrades, the day's march to this point had been about four miles. So far, the Federal movement had gone smoothly and without significant opposition. This was about to change.[25]

As Griffin reorganized his division, Parke's two divisions prepared to move forward toward the Boydton Plank Road. Potter's division headed northwest along the axis of the Church Road, through the belt of woods between the Peebles and Pegram farms, past the Oscar Pegram house and its surrounding fields, and eventually through another belt of woods and onto the fields of the Robert Jones farm. Willcox's division followed to Potter's left-rear in support. Finally, at this time the Confederate high command took decisive action to repulse this strong enemy incursion. Maj. Gen. Cadmus Wilcox led Brig. Gen. James H. Lane's brigade of Tar Heels and Brig. Gen. Samuel McGowan's South Carolinians out the Boydton Plank Road and down the Church Road to oppose the Federal advance. Major General Heth, with Brig. Gen. William MacRae's Tar Heel outfit and Brig. Gen. James J. Archer's brigade, soon followed. The Confederates slammed into the advance of Potter's division late in the afternoon and forced the Federals to retreat. They next struck and pressed Willcox's bluecoats, who nevertheless began to blunt the Confederate onslaught. Griffin, who had not advanced as expected to cover Potter's right, eventually came up to occupy a ridge across the Church Road, which anchored a new defensive line. With the remnants of Potter's division and Willcox's men on his left, the line extended westward beyond the Pegram house, with its left flank refused and resting on Arthur's Swamp.[26]

Meanwhile, Ayres's men assumed responsibility for protecting the Squirrel Level Road sector. With Otis's First Brigade still facing north astride the road at Fort Bratton, Grimshaw's Third Brigade came up on its right, and the Second (Maryland) Brigade, commanded here by Col. Samuel Graham, extended the line even farther east toward the Vaughan Road. Ignoring the relatively small body of graycoats that had reclaimed the W. W. Davis house and Fort Cherry, the Federals began entrenching a new line through Fort Bratton. To cover that work, Ayres pushed a strong skirmish line out the Squirrel Level Road. Late in the evening Otis settled his men into the newly constructed works for the night. He positioned the Fourteenth US on the right of Fort Bratton, the Fifth Veteran and 146th New York in the fort, and the Fifteenth Heavy and Eleventh US to its left. He held the 140th New York and Seventeenth US in reserve to the rear. The regulars of the Tenth and Twelfth US relieved the heavy skirmish line thrown out earlier.[27]

That evening the skies opened with a torrential downpour. Hunkering in the mud and rain, the heavies of the Fifteenth and their brigade-mates continued improving their works. By morning they had constructed a formidable barrier to any enemy advance. As Otis's men toiled away that night, Meade directed Parke to pull his line back into the Confederate entrenchments captured earlier in the day and Warren to take position with his left "holding the redoubt in Peebles' field" and his right connecting with the works on the Weldon Railroad.[28]

After the fighting waned on September 30, the Confederate forces near Pegram's farm disengaged and withdrew toward the Boydton Plank Road. But A. P. Hill intended to renew the fight the next day and assembled a new strike force during the night. He brought MacRae's and Archer's wet and tired brigades from the Boydton Plank Road front to join two of Heth's fresh brigades—Brig. Gen. John R. Cooke's North Carolinians and Brig. Gen. Joseph R. Davis's brigade. Willie Pegram's artillery would support the infantry in the advance. Hill planned to send the infantry straight down the Squirrel Level Road to hit the enemy in what he supposed to be the weaker flank. Wilcox's two brigades, which remained on the Boydton Plank Road front, as well as a supporting battery would distract the main Federal force facing northwest in the old Confederate line with a coordinated diversionary thrust toward their advanced guard, Hoffman's brigade, dug in on Pegram's farm.[29]

October 1 dawned misty and dreary, and before long rain again began to fall. Heth's attacking force slipped out from the Petersburg defenses and moved down the Squirrel Level Road toward the Davis house. Arriving in the fields just south of it before 7 A.M., he deployed his brigades astride the road, with MacRae and Archer in front and Davis and Cooke in the second line. At daylight the 140th New York and Seventeenth US had headed out to relieve the Tenth and Twelfth US on Otis's picket line. The relief was completed when, about 8 A.M., a Confederate skirmish line rushed the newly arrived pickets; gray lines of battle followed. The thin blue line began firing briskly but could not hold in the face of the enemy's larger numbers. The Confederates forced the Union pickets back to the main line of works. But when Heth found his division facing a well-fortified and heavily manned line of works instead of a weak flank, he paused in a band of woods to

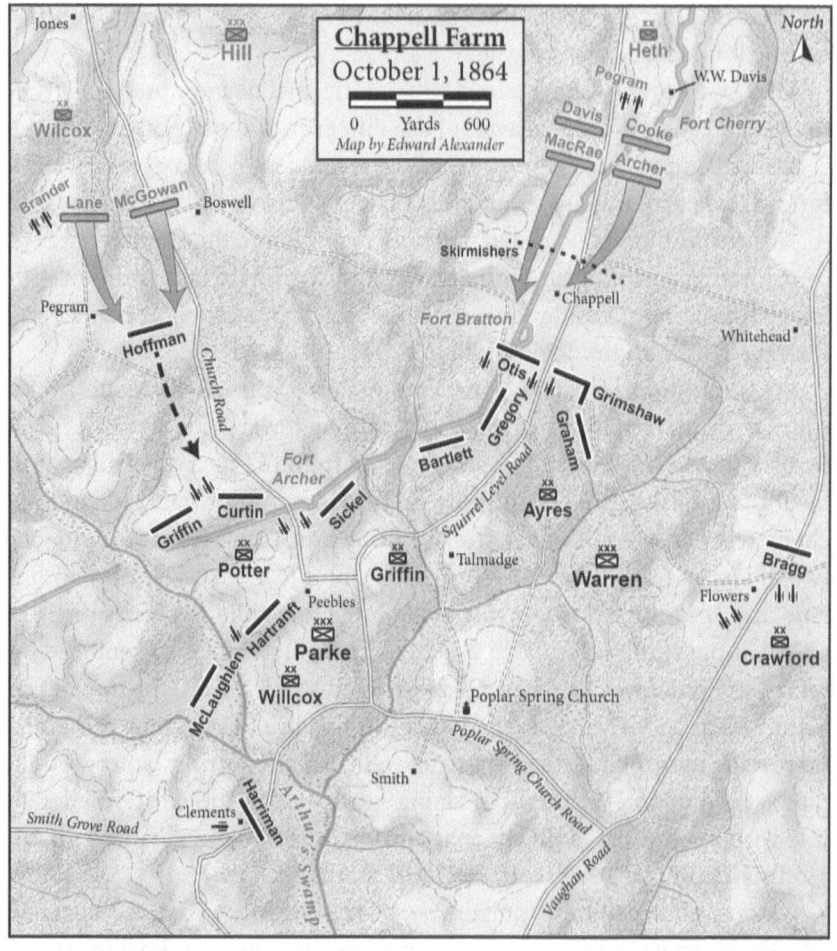

assess his options. Meanwhile, Wilcox launched his diversionary attack at the sound of the firing; he succeeded in capturing a number of prisoners and sending the Federals in the advanced positions scurrying back to their main defense line at Peebles's farm. At the first sound of firing, Warren notified Chief of Staff Humphreys that the enemy remained in their previous night's position near the Pegram house and were "making a pretty strong demonstration" on Ayres's line near the Chappell house. As a result, Warren "expect[ed] a hard time."[30]

Despite Warren's predictions, Heth would be the one to experience the "hard time" that day. Piecemeal attacks and the unfavorable weather doomed Heth's assault. As MacRae's Tar Heels shrieked a rebel yell and advanced at a run, a torrential rain drenched them, rendering the already muddy ground even more difficult to navigate. "The Rebs came up within speaking distance" of Otis's and Grimshaw's troops, who fought from behind their mud fortresses directly under the watchful eye of division commander Ayres. According to one of Otis's men, the enemy "rec'd such a shower of lead that they went back like sheep." With MacRae's attack thwarted, Archer and Davis moved forward. Yet Archer maneuvered his brigade to oblique to the right across Davis's line of march, and the ensuing confusion disorganized both outfits. This disruption halted parts of both brigades in their tracks, while most of their comrades plodded on through the mud and the hail of lead, soon repulsed with heavy loss. As men carried Otis, who had suffered a severe wound in the face, from the field, Maj. James Grindlay of the 146th took command of the First Brigade. "The enemy continued to advance and charged our line," Grindlay reported. In the end, however, the Confederates "were gallantly repulsed, and, owing to the well-directed fire from our line, fell back suffering great loss." Most of Cooke's Brigade never made contact with the bluecoats. Heth had no choice but to abandon the attack and his plan to cut through the Union line. Sharp picket firing continued for much of the day, but First Brigade skirmishers advanced and drove the butternut sharpshooters from the woods and houses in their front.[31]

When Warren reported the good news of Heth's repulse to Humphreys, he also informed him that he had pulled Hoffman's brigade from its position near Pegram's and transferred it to the right of Ayres's division. Warren had already shifted Bragg's brigade to the Vaughan Road near the Flowers house, so slipping Hoffman into line on the Maryland Brigade's right plugged the remaining gap in the line running to the east back to the Vaughan Road and to the Weldon Railroad beyond. Although he also reported that "Lieut. Col. E. S. Otis, commanding First Brigade of Ayres' division, is mortally wounded," Otis would eventually recover.[32]

The rain had subsided early on October 2, and as the morning progressed, rays of sunlight at long last broke through the clouds. As ordered, a push to gain a lodgment on the Boydton Plank Road began before 8 A.M. The bluecoats pressed forward, one outfit reportedly reaching "to within a few rods" of the enemy's line, but they did not establish a secure foothold. Meade, with Grant's consent, decided to throw in the towel. At 11:15 A.M. he informed Parke and Warren of the new plan "to take up the best line for connecting to the Weldon railroad, and making the left secure, and then to intrench." The Federals retired and established their new line across Pegram's farm, with their left resting along Arthur's Swamp and their right eventually stretching back to the fortifications at the Weldon Railroad.[33]

Meanwhile, on the Squirrel Level Road front, Ayres decided to eliminate the Confederates who were still lingering around the Davis house and had subjected his men to harassing fire all morning. To support Grimshaw's brigade, thrown forward toward the Davis's farm around midmorning, he ordered up the Fifth Veteran and 140th New York. Together these outfits took the house and Fort Cherry with ease. By midafternoon they recognized that no large enemy force remained nearby, and because this advanced position held little value in relation to the new line soon to be taken up, the bluecoats retired to Ayres's main position. As the Fifth and the 140th piled back into the works around Fort Bratton, the Fifteenth and the 146th pulled out and fell back about 250 yards. They commenced building a new line of breastworks, which would become the permanent line in this sector.[34]

The fighting that raged over the fields of Peebles's and Pegram's farms produced numerous casualties. One reliable estimate puts the Army of the Potomac's losses at over 2,900 men, with 189 killed, 905 wounded, and slightly over 1,800 missing; most of the missing were from Parke's corps. The Fifteenth suffered relatively few casualties, with 5 men killed or mortally wounded and another 2 wounded, demonstrating the benefit of fighting from behind entrenchments rather than attacking them. Confederate forces operating south of the James lost slightly over 1,300 men. Although unsuccessful in reaching the Boydton Plank Road, the Federals extended their line around Petersburg another two and a half miles, and the Boydton Plank Road now lay only a little over a mile to the west.[35]

Lyman described the three days' action at Peebles's farm to a friend at home. "We extended our line, and the enemy retired to their second—we looked at them—they looked at us—*voila tout*," he judged. But that was not all. There remained a great deal more work in the construction of the new line to stretch it from its westernmost point near Pegram's back to the existing line then terminating near the Weldon Railroad. As usual, the infantry would supply the vast majority of the manpower required for the task. Engineers began laying out the line even as the battle continued on October 2. The wraparound design of the new line would give Meade's troops protection from an attack not only from Petersburg or the Boydton

Plank Road but also from the south. The line extended west from Fort Wadsworth on the Weldon Railroad to near the Pegram house, swung south to the Squirrel Level Road, and then turned east, running back to Fort Dushane. Work progressed rapidly; a confident Meade reported on October 3, "I do not think the enemy will attempt to disturb us now."[36]

As part of a general realignment of the Fifth Corps's position on October 3, Grindlay moved his brigade to near the Flowers house on the Vaughan Road to relieve Bragg's outfit. Griffin's division extended to its right, and Ayres's division slid to its right to reach and cover the Vaughan Road. These changes freed Crawford's division for work on the south-facing line extending from Parke's left to Fort Dushane and the Weldon Railroad. Ayres also had to furnish the fatigue details necessary to complete construction on a new redoubt, Fort Keene, near Flowers on the west side of the Vaughan Road. After finishing the line, the First Brigade occupied the works they had built for the next several weeks. This relative inactivity afforded the troops more time for relaxation. A man in the Fifteenth writing to his sister during this period explained, "A soldiers life is gay, if he chooses to make it so, there is plenty of music here, and many gay sogers, and the principle amusements is, carding, ball, gymnastics and tricking."[37]

Even as the days grew shorter, Grant contemplated "a formidable movement" to the army's left to seize and hold the South Side Railroad. According to information available to the Federal high command, the Confederates had extended a section of their Petersburg entrenchments roughly paralleling the Boydton Plank Road to a point on Hatcher's Run about a mile above Armstrong's Mill. These entrenchments did not cross or extend up the run. Beyond that point, with the exception of some artillery emplacements and infantry parapets near where the Boydton Plank Road crossed Hatcher's Run, Federal commanders knew of no other entrenched enemy positions. Consequently, on October 24 Grant instructed Meade to "make your preparations to march out at an early hour on the 27th to gain possession of the South Side Railroad, and to hold it, and fortify back to your present left.[38]

Meade's concept of the operation called for a three-pronged movement using between 30,000 and 35,000 infantry supported by about 3,000 cavalry. He wanted two divisions of Hancock's Second Corps to head south and cross Hatcher's Run via the Vaughan Road, then swing northwest on a road passing Dabney's steam sawmill to strike the Boydton Plank Road near the White Oak Road intersection. Proceeding slightly less than two miles west out the White Oak Road, the column would turn right into the Claiborne Road, recross Hatcher's Run, and continue north until they struck the South Side Railroad about three miles east of Sutherland's Station. Brig. Gen. David McMurtrie Gregg's cavalry division would operate on Hancock's left, while Parke's Ninth Corps would slip out of the works and proceed west to surprise the enemy, believed to be relatively few in number, holding the incomplete works. If Parke could not break through the Confederate line, he would confront them while the Second and Fifth Corps operated to turn the Confederate right.[39]

The Fifth Corps would move simultaneously to the vicinity of Armstrong's Mill on Hatcher's Run to support Parke's left. If Parke successfully broke the line, Warren would move up on the left of the Ninth Corps. If Parke failed, Warren would cross Hatcher's Run, move northwest along its bank, and try to turn the Confederate right by recrossing the run above the Boydton Plank Road bridge, all while the Ninth Corps confronted the line to pin down the defenders. Warren's force also would cover Hancock's right.[40]

Meade set his plan in motion at 3:30 A.M. on October 27. Gregg's troopers swung into their saddles and galloped down the Halifax Road from the jumping-off point near Fort Dushane, while Hancock's infantry marched toward the Vaughan Road. Sweeping aside token Confederate resistance, by 12:30 P.M. both Hancock and Gregg had gained footholds on the Boydton Plank Road. Near 1 P.M. Hancock received orders to halt as Meade and Grant arrived on the field. The commanders worried about the vulnerability of the Second Corps's unprotected right flank and the gap between it and the Fifth Corps.[41]

Meanwhile, the Ninth Corps had pulled out of the line and marched west early on that dark, rainy morning. Upon encountering a strongly held line of breastworks, Parke halted and ordered his troops to entrench. At about 5:30 A.M., as it became light, the vanguard of the Fifth Corps's column exited the Federal works near Fort Cummings and, keeping to the left of the Ninth Corps's flankers, moved southwesterly along a cart road through the woods. Fearing he was moving too far to the south as he reached the vicinity of the R. Thompson house, Warren ordered a road cut to the west through the woods for a distance of about a half mile to meet the Duncan Road just south of the Clements house. Discovering a cart road leading west from there, Griffin's First Division advanced another quarter mile until, at about 9 A.M., it struck enemy skirmishers. Gregory's Second Brigade drove the graycoats before it and pushed through the woods until the troops encountered the same line of breastworks that had halted Parke's advance.[42]

As Griffin advanced, Ayres's division massed along the road cut through the woods, with Crawford's division halted behind it. Warren rode ahead to assess the practicability of breaking the Confederate line to his front, but like Parke, he considered such an attack unlikely to succeed. Warren met Meade and Grant upon his return. After hearing his descriptions of the situation to his front and flank, they directed Warren to send a division across Hatcher's Run. Guiding with its right flank on the run, the division would advance upstream to support Hancock's right. When it arrived at the right of the enemy's line opposite Griffin's outfit, the division would attack the Confederate line in flank and compel its defenders to retire. This maneuver would open the way for the rest of the Fifth Corps, as well as the Ninth, to advance.[43]

Warren thought the Third Division best positioned to take on the assignment. Consequently, Crawford's outfit marched to Armstrong's Mill, where the Duncan Road crossed Hatcher's Run, and began crossing the stream at 11:45 A.M. The general then pushed his command north along the run. The dense woods and tangled undergrowth, a sharp westward bend in the stream, and timber felled by the Confederates rendered the movement extremely slow and difficult. Once he drew abreast of Griffin's line on the opposite bank, Crawford recognized that the steep sides and felled timber would make recrossing Hatcher's at that point impracticable. It had taken his men over four hours to advance a mile and a half.[44]

The Confederates did not remain idle amid all of this Yankee activity. A. P. Hill responded to counter the enemy thrust toward the Boydton Plank Road and South Side Railroad. He placed Heth in command of a column of four brigades of infantry, about 4,500 men. Heth, in concert with Mahone, conceived a plan to cross Hatcher's Run and move through the heavily wooded terrain between the Second and the Fifth Corps to strike Hancock's right. Simultaneously, Maj. Gen. Wade Hampton's cavalry would assail the Second Corps's left and rear.[45]

Heth's men burst from the trees at approximately 4 P.M., slamming into the Second Corps's right-rear. They initially drove the bluecoats back, but the Federals regrouped and counterattacked, sweeping the Confederates from the field and driving them in confusion back into the woods. Reacting to the sound of Heth's attack, five brigades of Hampton's cavalry pressed Gregg's troopers from the south and the west until dark. The Federals held their ground, and the Rebel cavalry, as Gregg reported, accomplished nothing "other than its own punishment, which was severe."⁴⁶

Upon learning of the attack on the Second Corps, Meade directed Warren to hurry Crawford to Hancock's assistance. Aware of the difficult terrain, Warren informed him that Ayres's two brigades could more readily shift to that point. Around 5 P.M. Ayres advanced his First and Third Brigades from the newly cut road into the Duncan Road and south toward Armstrong's Mill. Yet by this time darkness was approaching. After crossing Hatcher's Run, the general halted his men at the mill, where the Fifteenth's heavies and the other men in the First and Third Brigades spent the night in a heavy rain.⁴⁷

Even though Hancock's and Gregg's men had held their ground, Grant and Meade ordered Hancock to maintain his position until morning and then withdraw by the road on which he had advanced. With the South Side Railroad still some six miles away and the element of surprise lost, the general in chief realized that the operation would not achieve its primary objective. With his ammunition nearly exhausted and the rain continuing to worsen the roads, Hancock decided to withdraw that night instead. Unable to bring ambulances up the narrow lane from Dabney's Sawmill while his withdrawing troops moved down it, he had to abandon a number of seriously wounded men, leaving them in the care of Federal surgeons.⁴⁸

As the Second Corps withdrew, the Fifth and Ninth Corps prepared to disengage from the enemy and withdraw to the Federal works around Peebles's farm the next morning. At 7:15 A.M. Humphreys instructed Warren to send Ayres's two brigades as soon as possible "to fill up the vacant space between Parke's right and the fort at the Clements house," Fort Cummings. Just before 9 A.M. he then directed Ayres to report to Parke and "mov[e] to his assistance at any point he may require and be withdrawn by him." The infantry, with an accompanying detachment of cavalry providing a rear guard, began pulling out after the wagons, wounded, and prisoners had cleared the roads. By afternoon the bluecoats were safely within their entrenched line and making their way back to the camps they had departed less than forty-eight hours earlier.⁴⁹

As supplies continued to flow into the Cockade City on the South Side Railroad, the return to the lines frustrated many soldiers. "Back at the old spot again, and nothing accomplished! Nothing save a few hundred more men laid under the sod and a hundred or two carried off with a ball in their body or minus a leg or arm," Wainwright reflected in his October 28 journal entry. "Two years ago such a failure would have raised a hornet's nest about the ears of the commanding general," he continued, "but now the country is accustomed to it, and the whole thing will be glossed over in some way." Lyman agreed with the colonel's sentiments, remarking, "As the mine was to be termed an *ill*-conducted fizzle, so this attempt may be called a *well*-conducted fizzle." Viewing the matter in a considerably narrower perspective, of the Fifteenth's involvement in the latest offensive, Pvt. Jacob Van Vleck of Company M wrote to his wife, "I went out to fight on Thursday, but got no Chance to do it—as the 2d Core done it all, so we came back to where we started."[50]

CHAPTER ELEVEN

The Raid on the Weldon Railroad and the Battle of Hatcher's Run

Upon their return from the failed expedition of late October 1864, the men of the First Brigade once again settled into their camps behind the line near the Vaughan Road. Their temporary home sat upon a thin layer of sandy soil underlaid with clay, which prevented rainwater from seeping into the subsoil; the flat and poorly drained surface made the area miserable and unhealthy. To ward off malaria, the men again began receiving quinine as part of their daily rations. "We began, in fact, to think that our commissary department considered that delectable article as taking the place of something more substantial," recalled a soldier in the brigade, "for our food at this time was of a grade even lower than that to which we were usually accustomed." In this setting the men worked on composite log-and-canvas huts in anticipation of the onset of winter. With log walls, canvas roofs, and chimneys made of wood, brick, or stone, the huts would provide some measure of warmth and protection from the elements.[1]

As the brigade prepared for winter camp, an October 31 order required the regiments of regulars in the First Brigade, judged by Warren as "mere skeletons" of the original units, to report immediately to Maj. Gen. John A. Dix in New York City to help keep peace during the upcoming presidential election. They would not return to the brigade. The regulars had fought long and hard in the Fifth Corps, but few of their losses had been replaced. Their departure left the First Brigade comprised entirely of regiments from the Excelsior State.[2]

Routine drills and fatigue duties resumed, and the days sometimes bled together for the soldiers. But on Tuesday, November 8, the army canceled regular activities so that the men could vote in the presidential election. The following day telegraph and newspaper reports confirmed President Lincoln's reelection. Soldiers' votes helped secure his second term. Within the Army of the Potomac alone, Lincoln won a large majority over his opponent, former army commander George McClellan. The men of the Fifth Corps supported Lincoln by a ratio of nearly two and a half to one. The incumbent's victory ensured a continuance of the current policies toward prosecution of the war.[3]

Camp life continued in its mostly predictable ways after the election—men drilled, wrote letters home, and entertained themselves as best they could. Staunch Democrat Fred Winthrop's promotion to brevet brigadier general, which came concurrent with Lincoln's reelection, overshadowed his dismay over the election results. Soon after his promotion, Winthrop issued orders aimed at improving the overall military bearing and appearance of his brigade. In compliance with Meade's earlier order forbidding the wearing of "long boots" in the army, Winthrop's November 10 order reiterated that prohibition as well as forbidding men from tucking their pant legs into their socks. These admonitions seemed directed at members of the Fifteenth Heavy since all other troops in the brigade wore leggings as part of their Zouave uniforms. To ensure immediate conformity, the general called a brigade drill the afternoon he issued the order.[4]

Despite Winthrop's unflagging insistence on discipline, Colonel Wainwright described him as "very pleasant, a thorough gentleman, a most capital officer, and universally liked." He recalled that the brigade's headquarters flew an "exquisite" new flag brought back by Winthrop from a recent leave to New York. The banner was "the gift of [Winthrop's] lady love," Wainwright quipped, which was "quite coming back to the times of chivalry, only that the flag was made at Tiffany instead of being the work of her own fair hands."[5]

The heavies of the Fifteenth and their Fifth Corps comrades whiled away the month of November working on their huts, restoring and improving the works, drilling, and pulling their tours on the picket line. Pvt. Jacob Van Vleck of the Fifteenth explained to his wife, "we drill and cook and pass the time as best we can." Some days were more exciting than others. In one letter he described how they "had a Target Shoot today—the first one," and that he "hit the post that held up the Target—the orderly Sergt. was the nearest to the Bullseye." Letters home also afforded an opportunity for the men to request care packages containing supplies and luxuries not available to them in the field. Van Vleck expressed hope that in his next box his wife would include "more Cake, Pies, Biscuts [sic] & Butter and such things and not tomato Catsup—Pickles." After reconsidering, he revised his request: "If you have any Catsup that is not so salt & spicy—you can send it, a bottle or so." Although his wife requested that he send any old clothes or blankets he could spare, he wrote, "I would rather take a Blanket than send one as they are much needed here and very scarce."[6]

Letters also described special occasions in camp. Van Vleck reported on a military version of a precooked Thanksgiving dinner. "There was some Thanksgiving stuff came last night (Friday) to the Regt. I got an apple & the leg of a chicken." Apparently, however, the food did not rival his usual holiday meal, as he admitted, "I could not eat it, so I threw it in the fire this morning." Fifth Corps headquarters clerk Robert Tilney agreed. On November 25 he noted: "So far as this army was concerned Thanksgiving Day was an utter failure. I do not know how other Corps fared, but ours has not yet received one particle of any of the 'dinner' that we were promised. All that has come so far is 138 barrels of apples, which have been distributed." The next day, however, saw an improvement. "We were agreeably surprised ... by the arrival of a large load of poultry, so we shall dine to-morrow on turkey and chicken. We have fared better than we expected to in our Thanksgiving dinner, on the installment plan."[7]

Meanwhile, significant changes took place in the Fifteenth Heavy while the men remained in camp. In early November a healthy Major Dieckmann resumed command of the Second Battalion as First Battalion commander Major Eiche took an approved fifteen-day leave—five days shorter than requested—to go to New York to assist his wife in settling her deceased father's estate. Upon his return in mid-December, officials arrested Eiche for overstaying his leave. In his absence, on December 1 Lieutenant Colonel Wiedrich ordered Dieckmann to take over the First Battalion, while Capt. George Roman of Company H assumed command of the Second. Capt. Edward Kaysing, who had been temporarily commanding the First, resumed command of Company C.[8]

On December 4 the Sixth Corps began to arrive at City Point after their service under Sheridan in the Shenandoah Valley. Each arriving division was dispatched to the front to relieve a division of the Fifth, which then moved to the rear between the Halifax and Jerusalem Plank Roads. News of the impending withdrawal reached some men in the corps even before their orders. One officer returning to his hut on that cold December morning discovered a couple of unknown officers complacently scanning the interior of his comfortable lodging and overheard them remark that "these would suit amazingly." The strangers explained to him that the Sixth Corps had been ordered to relieve the Fifth in the lines. Soon after this encounter the orders to turn over the line to the Sixth arrived, and a gracious transfer of the quarters ensued. In a similar account one Sixth Corps officer recorded: "The 5th Corps left some very good log huts. The one that I am living in has a good fire place and is quite comfortable." Warren's troops had all made it to the rear by the night of the sixth.[9]

Still determined to sever what one journalist aptly described as "a vein continually imparting life and strength" to the Confederacy, on December 3 Grant instructed Meade "to move with the Second and about two divisions of the Fifth Corps down the Weldon Railroad destroying it as far south as possible." A week earlier, Hancock had been reassigned, and Meade's chief of staff, Maj. Gen. Andrew Atkinson Humphreys, assumed command of the Second Corps. Warren being senior to Humphreys, Meade instead proposed to Grant that Warren command the operation, bringing with him the entire Fifth Corps and supported by a division of the Second—a force of about 25,000 men. The general in chief agreed, and on December 6 Meade sent Warren his "Confidential" orders. With his entire Fifth Corps, Maj. Gen. Gersham Mott's division of the Second Corps, and most of Brig. Gen. David McMurtrie Gregg's cavalry division, Warren would move at daylight the following morning and strike the Weldon Railroad "below Stony Creek and effectually destroying it from that point as far as Hicksford, if possible." He would then return "by moving to the eastward and crossing the Nottoway [River] as low down as practicable." Warren and his command prepared to execute a risky wintertime thrust deep into enemy territory.[10]

The operation began at 6 A.M. on December 7. The cavalry led the column, followed by Crawford's division, then Griffin's, Ayres's, and Mott's, with the battery assigned each division accompanying it and the combined wagon train at the rear. The soldiers trudged through rain, turning south into the Jerusalem Plank Road. By 11 A.M. most of three divisions, with the artillery and pontoon train, had crossed Warwick Swamp and were moving briskly down the Plank Road. A chaplain in Mott's division considered the rain "a decided benefit . . . , saving annoyance from dust, improving the roads, and preventing the enemy from learning our movements and strength."[11]

By midafternoon the column reached a crossroads near Hawkinsville, described by one soldier as "a series of old buildings, in a dilapidated condition, inhabited by a few 'poor white trash,' and surrounded by negro huts." Turning right from the Plank Road into the intersecting road, the Federals continued south for about a mile until, two hours before dark, their vanguard reached Freeman's Ford on the Nottoway River and discovered the bridge there destroyed. Work commenced on laying a 140-foot-long section of pontoon bridge spanning the rain-swollen river. By 4 P.M. Griffin's and Ayres's divisions arrived at the crossing. With the bridge-laying completed about an hour later, Warren's command began to cross the Nottoway.[12]

After completing the day's nearly sixteen-mile march, Griffin's and Ayres's men remained for the night north of the river. Gregg's troopers forded the Nottoway and continued south another four miles to the village of Sussex Court House. Crawford's division crossed the pontoon bridge and also proceeded to Sussex, where it bivouacked. Mott's division, passing Griffin's and Ayres's camps, crossed the bridge about 7:30 P.M. and, after advancing about a half mile, halted for the night. Wainwright later recalled the beautiful evening after the sky had cleared. "The soft night air; the tall, leafless trees under which we bivouacked . . . ; the wide, open plain on the opposite bank; the bridge, lighted up by many great pitch-pine fires" combined with "the noise of the men, horses and mules—all contributed to make a picture such as one dreams of."[13]

The beauty of the evening terminated abruptly around midnight, when the skies clouded over and rain fell in a deluge. Wiedrich's heavies hunkered down and tried to sleep before they and the rest of Ayres's men arose at about 2 A.M. on Thursday, December 8, to prepare to cross the Nottoway. Falling in behind Griffin's First Division, the Second Division crossed the river by 4:30 A.M. "It was raining heavily at this time, so that we were almost as wet as if we had swum the river instead of crossing over by way of the bridge," one of Winthrop's men recalled. The bridge was taken up by daylight, when the rain finally ceased. Gregg's troopers had, at 4 A.M., departed Sussex Court House—"a small village with a rather pretentious stucco Court House" and "a dilapidated jail and tavern"—for the Weldon Railroad. Crawford's Third Division followed.[14]

Two miles south of Sussex, the column swung to the west on a road passing through Coman's Well, a small hamlet, and continuing toward Jarret's Station on the Weldon Railroad. Marching now in warm, dry, and pleasant weather, many men discarded seemingly unnecessary equipment like blankets and overcoats. Warren's command now rolled like a juggernaut through country described by one of Winthrop's men as "entirely free of the ravages of war and present[ing] a pleasing appearance, when contrasted to the desolate, almost desert, in which we had been accustomed to operate." He recalled, "Fertile fields extended as far as the eye could see on every side, farmhouses bordered the road, and there were cattle and livestock of every description." Few male inhabitants were encountered. Most of the houses were either deserted or occupied only by women and children, though there were indications "men had been lurking in the woods." To the dismay of the remaining residents, occasionally bluecoats fell out of the column to take "hogs, sheep, turkeys, geese, chickens, or other bird or animal whose meat promised a welcome change from the fare provided by the commissary."[15]

In addition to access to the area's plentiful livestock, the Yankees also found homemade apple brandy—"apple jack"—tempting. It was found in abundance in the homes and farms along their route, and the soldiers did not hesitate to partake. Gregg told Wainwright that he had over fifty barrels of the beverage destroyed that day, although some men still become "beastly" drunk. The artillery chief witnessed one of Gregg's men "so drunk he could not stand; his joints were entirely powerless." A small squad of Confederates suddenly appeared, and one graycoat "shot him through the brain with a pistol while the others pulled off his boots and left the body. The whole thing was done in a minute and within sight of where Gregg was sitting at the time."[16]

About 9 A.M. the cavalry struck the Halifax Road, which paralleled the railroad, near the bridge over the Nottoway. Gregg immediately dispatched one brigade to destroy the 160-foot-long railroad trestle spanning the river. Warren massed the infantry at the Halifax Road until the entire force was up and the wagon train safely parked. The weary soldiers cooked dinner and relaxed in the warm afternoon sun after their fourteen-mile march. Around midafternoon Winthrop's brigade arrived

General Warren's raid—soldiers bending the heated rails of the Weldon Railroad. (Author's collection.)

at the railroad and settled in for a few hours of rest. Warren instructed the three Fifth Corps divisions to begin their work destroying the railroad at 6 P.M. Ayres's division would begin at the destroyed bridge over the Nottoway, Crawford's men working to his left, and Griffin's command to Crawford's left. As soon as one division worked down to a place finished by another, they would leapfrog the destroyed section, move down the line, and begin on a fresh section of track. The troops had orders to continue their destructive work until midnight.[17]

At the appointed hour, the men of the Fifth Corps went to work. Ayres instructed Winthrop's brigade to move to the division's right to tear up the track from just below the destroyed bridge. The work progressed rapidly in the moonlit night, despite the considerable labor necessary to separate the rails from the bolted coupling irons connecting them. The men piled the removed ties along the roadbed, laid the rails over them, and ignited the ties. When red hot in the center yet still cool at the ends, the men removed the rails and twined them around tree trunks, often in the shape of the Fifth Corps's Maltese-cross insignia. "No scene could be more grand," a newspaper correspondent accompanying the expedition reported. "Groups of swarthy, smoke-begrimed men moved through the leaping flames, or stood tall and grand and gloomy upon the bank, noiseless spectators." One of Mott's officers remembered: "Though the work was very laborious and fatiguing, officers and men labored with the greatest zest till a late hour at night. The sight presented by the burning road, bridges, piles of wood, and fences, was sad and grand in the extreme—a terrible comment on the waste and ravages of war." By shortly after midnight about eight miles of the Weldon Railroad, from the Nottoway to below Jarratt's Station, had been completely destroyed. The station—recently rebuilt after Federal cavalry burned it that May—was torched as well as the associated water tanks. Their evening work completed, Warren's exhausted command went into bivouac.[18]

The men who discarded blankets and coats along the march regretted it when December 9 dawned cold and windy. At daylight, while Griffin's division guarded the trains, Mott's outfit took position at the first portion of railroad not destroyed the previous night, with Ayres's division to its left, and Crawford's to Ayres's left. Destruction of the Weldon resumed, and Winthrop's brigade was hard at work by 7 A.M. Warren's clerk Robert Tilney observed, "The track disappeared fast."[19]

Meanwhile, Gregg's troopers galloped south along the railroad toward the twin towns of Belfield and Hicksford on the Meherrin River. Belfield, on the north bank, consisted only of a railroad depot, a tavern, and several farms. The much larger Hicksford, on the south bank, served as Greensville County's seat. The cavalry arrived at Belfield around 4 P.M. and encountered Confederate defenders. They drove the enemy across the river into three forts armed with artillery at Hicksford. Warren and Wainwright arrived on scene to assess the situation. The general judged that "it was impracticable to force a crossing at that point." Although they hesitated to leave the Confederates in place, both officers realized, as Wainwright summarized, " it would cost us at least one day's delay, and probably two or three hundred men; half our rations were gone, and the most dangerous part of our work, the getting back, [was] still to do." With supplies running low and bad weather threatening, they instead decided to return to the army at Petersburg.[20]

The infantry toiled throughout the day. At 7 P.M. Winthrop's brigade crossed Three Creek and destroyed about three-eighths of a mile of the railroad beyond, while Crawford's men razed the remaining bridges over the creek. By 8 P.M., with the Weldon now demolished all the way from the Nottoway to Belfield, the work ceased. Winthrop's brigade went into bivouac in a cornfield on the north bank of the Meherrin River. After the long, hard day, Tilney viewed a "grand sight!" from Warren's headquarters:

"Along the high embankment countless blazing fires stretched as far as the eye could trace, all one glowing mass of flame, while a high bridge in front of our headquarters was also in flames."[21]

That evening Warren informed his troops: "The object of the expedition having been accomplished, the command will commence to return

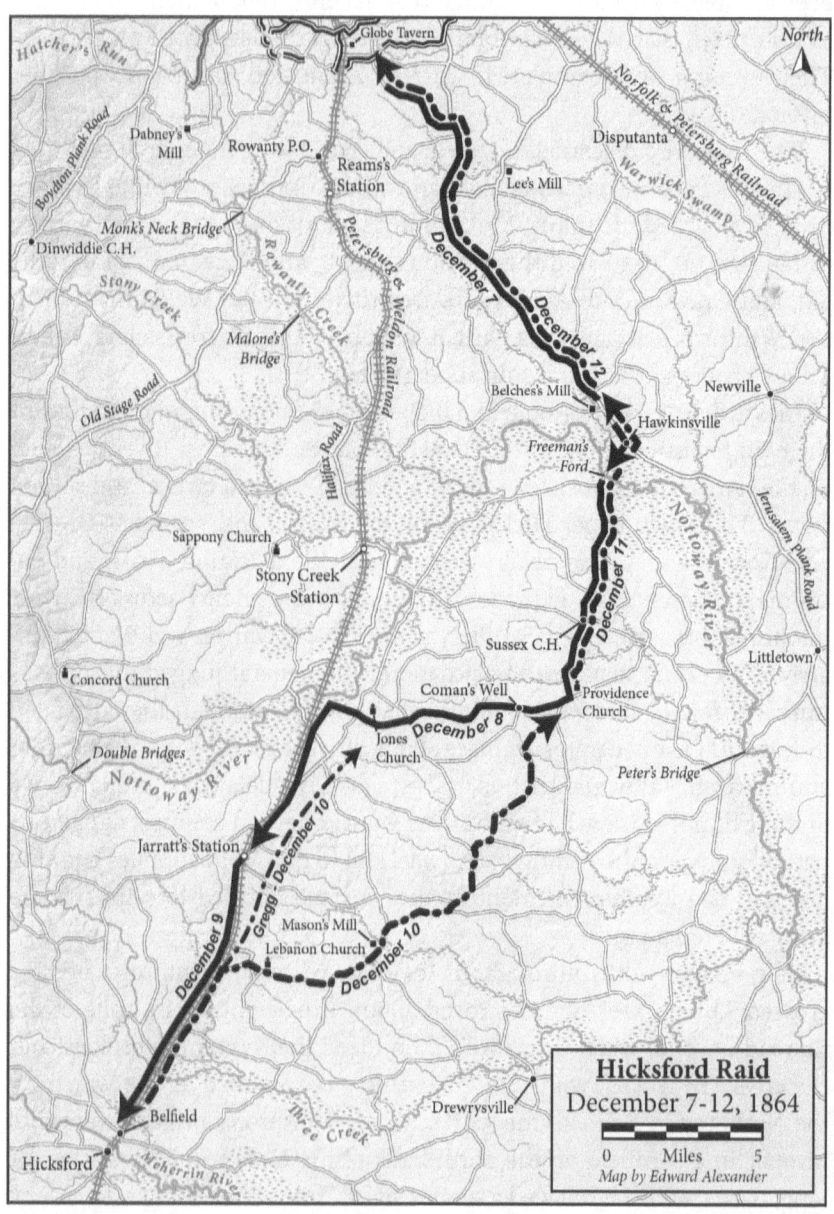

Hicksford Raid
December 7-12, 1864

0   Miles   5
Map by Edward Alexander

tomorrow." Griffin's division, guarding the wagon train, would take the lead, followed by Ayres's division, Mott's, and finally Crawford's. One brigade of cavalry would precede the infantry, with Gregg and his two other brigades acting as rear guard. Snow began to fall around 8 P.M. but soon turned into sleet and freezing rain. Warren stated that the storm "lasted through the night, causing the men and animals much suffering," and continued as day dawned. On the morning of December 10, a sheet of ice covered the waking men's blankets. Winthrop told Lyman: "It blew, snowed and sleeted all night, and when reveille beat in the morning, you could only see what seemed a field full of dead bodies, each covered with a rubber blanket and encased with ice. Some of the men had to kick and struggle, they were so hard frozen down." Wainwright noted that "everything was sheeted with ice; each spray of trees and blade of grass was completely coated, making the country a most beautiful sight when the sun came out, but the roads terrible for the footmen."[22]

The frozen column began its long return march at 7 A.M. by a more direct route to Sussex Court House than that traveled down the Weldon to Belfield. About six miles north of Belfield, the Federals veered right off the Halifax Road onto a road passing Lebanon Church and continuing in the direction of Sussex. Gregg and his two trailing brigades did not follow, keeping instead to the Halifax Road to protect the left flank of the column. After driving a significant force of Rebel cavalry toward the Nottoway, his horsemen entered the road through Coman's Well and continued east to rendezvous with the infantry near Sussex Court House.[23]

The poor roads, muddy from the melting ice, rendered the going difficult. Adding to the difficulty was the increasing number of slaves seeking the protection of the troops in hopes of finding safety and freedom in the Union lines. "Considerable numbers of colored people joined the column during the day, one company numbering nineteen and embracing every period of life, from infancy to old age," an officer recalled. The soldiers could do little to assist them, but some still did what they could. One man, noting the great number of women with young children among the group, recalled that "as soon as a wagon of the supply train was emptied of its contents, it was filled with negro mothers with their children." By nightfall the collection of soldiers and civilians was forced to stop. Unable to continue in the dark on roads blocked by wagons stuck in the mud, the bulk of the infantry column halted about three miles south of Sussex Court House and went into bivouac. The exhausted soldiers, the majority of whom had marched over twenty miles that day, simply fell to the ground where they stopped and tried to sleep. Yet, as Warren recalled, "the mist continued to fall and keep the men cold and wet all night, so that they got little sleep or rest."[24]

Despite the intrusion of the Yankees into this region previously untouched by the war and the destruction they inflicted on the local farms and infrastructure, one woman living near Sussex Court House, in a display of the better nature of the human spirit, fed Amherst Belcher of the Fifteenth and his battalion commander, Major Duysing. After not eating for almost two days, Belcher asserted: "I do not think I will ever forget that meal. I remember drinking seven full-sized tumblers of milk poured from a long tin pail made to hang in a well."[25]

At 7 A.M. on December 11, the wet and weary Federal column began moving again. Warren directed Griffin's division to take the lead with the pontoon train and to secure the crossing at Freeman's Ford on the Nottoway, the infantry protecting the engineers laying the bridge. The other infantry outfits would halt and mass before crossing. After Warren's force crossed the river and reached the Jerusalem Plank Road, the column swung northwest toward Petersburg as darkness approached. Near Belches's Mill, about a mile and a half up the Plank Road from its intersection with the road from Sussex, the command went into bivouac. During the night the weather cleared, and the temperature dropped. At 7 A.M. on Monday, December 12, Warren's exhausted men began the last leg of their long march, with Mott's division taking the lead, followed by Griffin's, Ayres's, and Crawford's. The wagons moved easily over the frozen mud, but, as Warren reported, "the men suffered very much from their feet, that were now quite sore and blistered, insomuch that numbers walked barefoot over the frozen ground."[26]

Sundown found the Fifth Corps once again bivouacked between the Halifax and Jerusalem Plank Roads, near where their grueling trek had begun. Winthrop's brigade camped between the Gurley house and Globe Tavern. Warren's command had covered over a hundred miles on the mission and destroyed approximately sixteen miles of track, about seven and a half miles of that by Ayres's division. Warren proudly reported, "The men marched and behaved most praiseworthily during this tiring expedition in most disagreeable weather—weather which almost precluded rest and sleep." They had suffered relatively few losses. The cavalry, which had frequent skirmishes with the enemy, sustained about

140 casualties, of which 56 were counted as missing. Casualties among the infantry were not more than 200 killed, wounded, and missing; the Fifteenth Heavy suffered only 5 enlisted men missing. Many of the missing were stragglers who, Warren observed, "became drunk to complete prostration on apple jack found on the way, which, to our surprise, was in almost every house in appreciable quantities."[27]

While Warren's raid on the Weldon Railroad was a military success, it also exhibited a dark side demonstrating just how uncivil the war had become. As the Federal column had neared Sussex Court House on the return march, African Americans reported that many Union stragglers had been murdered by Rebel guerrillas. Reaching the town, the bluecoats discovered the corpses of a number of the presumed stragglers. Some, stripped naked, appeared as if they had been shot while kneeling in a circle. Naked corpses hung from trees by the side of the road, their throats slashed. Several more murdered Union soldiers were in the road in front of the courthouse, while another was pinned to the courthouse grounds by a stake driven through his mouth. Other men's "heads were crushed in by blows of an axe, the breast pierced by a knife." These and similar atrocities provoked some of the Yankees to retaliate. Soon they had set nearly every building—houses, privies, barns, pigsties, among others—ablaze. Some also vented their anger by raping women, African American as well as white, and hanging civilians suspected of being complicit in the murders. Wainwright lamented such actions: "For this barbarism there was no real excuse, unless exasperation and the innate depravity of mankind is one. . . . So pitiable a sight as the women and children turned adrift at nightfall, and a most severe winter night too, I never saw before and never want to see again." Appalled by what he witnessed, he declared: "If this is a raid, deliver me from going on another."[28]

On December 14 Ayres commended his three brigade commanders, "and the officers and men under them, for the prompt and efficient manner in which all his commands were executed under the many trying circumstances in which they were placed" during the raid. With the arduous operation concluded, the heavies of the Fifteenth set to work again laying out their winter camp and constructing quarters. Their new camp was on higher and better ground than their previous location near the Vaughan Road. Their experience with constructing log-and-canvas winter huts now served them well, and they completed most of the construction by Christmas. The men settled into a period of relative inactivity at the beginning of an unusually severe winter. They did their best to shelter and enjoy themselves under the circumstances.[29]

On a cold but pleasant Christmas Day, the Fifth Corps troops had to settle for their usual rations of salt pork and hardtack instead of something more festive. But one of Winthrop's men wandered over to the nearby Fifth Corps headquarters and found the staff dining on "roast beef, roast potatoes, plum pudding, bread, butter, coffee"—treats in which he was fortunately invited to partake. The men and officers also celebrated the news that, after taking Atlanta at the beginning of September and marching toward the Atlantic coast, Maj. Gen. William T. Sherman's forces had now captured Savannah, Georgia. Of this success clerk Tilney declared, "We are moving on; it makes us veterans quite elated." To celebrate Savanah's occupation, Meade ordered a 100-gun salute fired at 7 A.M. the following morning.[30]

The Fifteenth's winter quarters remained works in progress. To reduce smoke swirling through the camp, the huts needed chimneys of sufficient height to ensure proper draft. On New Year's Day, 1865, Wiedrich directed the officer of the day "to see that the fires are put out in all tents whose chimneys are not built as high as directed by tomorrow evening." That did not solve all of the problems. On January 12 the lieutenant colonel ordered company commanders to ensure "their respective Streets are corduroyed, leaving a space of two feet on each side of the Street for the purpose of being formed into a drain." He also required wooden floors in the men's quarters to help ensure warmth and dryness.[31]

Meanwhile, as the men improved their new camp, on January 11 a general court-martial convened at Fifth Corps headquarters for the trial of Major Eiche on the charge of absence without leave. Eiche did not dispute the charge he faced. The court, therefore, found him guilty of the charge and its single specification and sentenced him "to be dismissed the service of the United States." Warren approved the proceedings and sentence and forwarded them to army headquarters for final action. Meade, likewise, on February 2 approved the proceedings and sentence of the tribunal, but, fortunately for Eiche, remitted the sentence. Eiche would be allowed to return to duty with the regiment, but he would be in command of the Second Battalion. Dieckmann retained command of Eiche's old battalion, the First.[32]

Camp life continued as usual, with a mix of preparations, entertainments, down time, letter writing, and soldiering. During the lull in active campaigning, the heavies continued to hone their military bearing and train. They sometimes had Sunday inspections, including one at 10 A.M. on January 15, when orders directed that they turn out "in heavy marching Order," fully equipped for field service with muskets, knapsacks, haversacks, cartridge boxes, and all other accoutrements. The inspection would not occupy all of their time that day. At 2 P.M. the Rev. John Buch would deliver a sermon in German, and "any officers and men desirous of hearing the same, will attend at that hour in rear of Co. M."[33]

As the heavies soldiered on at the front, their wives and families at home faced threats from con artists. Wiedrich received a report of "thieves and Sharpers" in New York City, sometimes dressed as officers, calling on families and friends of men in the regiment. Representing themselves as belonging to the Fifteenth, these imposters obtained money and other valuables from their victims. In late January Wiedrich warned his men of this scheme and suggested they advise their families and friends to reject such advances "unless they [any such callers] have a written order from themselves or are personally known to such friends or relations."[34]

Knowledge that their families faced threats from conmen and the ever-present desire to see loved ones prompted many soldiers to request leave that winter, but few in the ranks were so fortunate as to receive one. It became apparent that the likelihood of seeing home and family over the winter pause in action was slim at best. One of Wiedrich's men, Jacob Van Vleck, wrote to his wife, "I spoke to the Captain about a furlough today—he told me there was to [sic] many ahead of me, So I don't know when I will get one." His wife's constant questions about leave and her frustration with his absence combined to heighten Van Vleck's own frustration over the matter. "Don't Bother me any more about getting one until I get it for it is no use talking about all the time when I cannot get" one. He explained to her, "there is a very strict order out against giving furloughs only to very 'urgent cases'—So I must just wait like Plenty more." He did not lose hope, however, and instead focused on the larger picture. "I think we will all have furloughs for good as the War will be ended by the Spring—it looks like it now anyway."[35]

At the end of January, Wiedrich ordered company drills held daily from 10 A.M. until noon. On Tuesday, January 31, the entire regiment formed in heavy marching order at 10 A.M. for inspection by General Winthrop. The men of the Fifteenth apparently looked very sharp that day. Winthrop wrote Wiedrich: "I cannot but express to you my admiration at the appearance of your command on drill today, and I beg that you will communicate to the officers and men for me, the very high appreciation which I entertain for them as soldiers. I am truly proud of your regiment and my only regret is that I have not a few more such Battalions as the 15th N. Y. Arty." This commendation by their brigade commander, an accomplished infantry officer, undoubtedly buoyed the men's spirits. But more important than their performance on drill was their work on the battlefield. They had learned and accomplished much in the campaigns of 1864 as they successfully transitioned from the role of artillerymen to infantry. Very soon they would be called upon to again engage a stubborn, hard-fighting enemy on the battlefield.[36]

At the beginning of February, the severe winter weather moderated. The Federal high command knew that Petersburg was being supplied by wagon trains moving from Hicksford—now the northern terminus of the Weldon Railroad—up the Meherrin River valley to the Boydton Plank Road, then onward via the Plank Road through Dinwiddie Court House. Grant determined to disrupt this supply line. On February 4 he directed Meade "to take advantage of the present good weather to destroy or capture as much as possible of the enemy's wagon train." They tasked Gregg's cavalry division to spearhead the effort, with the Fifth Corps supporting the horsemen and two divisions of Humphreys's corps—Mott's and Brig. Gen. Thomas Smyth's—supporting the Fifth.[37]

At 3 A.M. on February 5, Gregg's bleary-eyed troopers swung into their saddles and headed south. About two miles below Reams's Station, the column left the Halifax Road and turned to the southwest on the Malone's Bridge Road. Gregg paused at the Rowanty Creek crossing to repair the bridge and drive away a contingent of enemy cavalry defending it. The blue column then rolled an additional nine miles to the west, striking the Boydton Plank Road at Dinwiddie Court House around noon. The Yankee horsemen thereafter ranged up and down the Plank Road. They had expected to snare a treasure trove of enemy wagons and supplies, but instead the cavalrymen netted only twenty-five wagons with 100 mules along with fifty prisoners. Gregg headed back to Malone's Bridge to bivouac for the night, and report back to Warren.[38]

Humphreys's two divisions moved at 7 A.M. to plug the gap between what would be Warren's right and the main Union line while covering the crossings of Hatcher's Run at the Vaughan Road and Armstrong's Mill. About three hours later Mott's lead brigade swept aside a small Confederate force at the Vaughan Road crossing of Hatcher's Run and continued across. Smyth diverted his division before the crossing, following a road paralleling Hatcher's and leading to the Armstrong house. He deployed his command in an arc, with his left covering Armstrong's Mill and his right extending beyond the house and anchored on Rocky Branch. Beyond the stream, Mott's remaining two brigades extended the line, which terminated in a swampy area. To their distant right, Brig. Gen. Nelson A. Miles's Second Corps division occupied the left of the main Petersburg line. Humphreys ordered one of Miles's brigades, Brig. Gen. John Ramsey's, to march south to bolster Mott's right. From their position Smyth's men could see a formidable line of Confederate works about 1,000 yards away, roughly parallel to the Boydton Plank Road, approximately a mile to its east, and extending to Hatcher's Run.[39]

As the Federals completed their final dispositions, around 5:15 P.M. the enemy struck. With a blood-curdling rebel yell, elements of Heth's and Brig. Gen. Clement Evans's divisions assailed the blue line. Heth's men concentrated on a seam in the Federal position to the east of Rocky Branch. The entrenched Yankees fired volley after volley into the attackers. Three times the Confederates advanced, and each time they were repulsed. To the left, Smyth's division defeated attacks by Evans's three brigades. Unable to either crack or turn the Federal position, the graycoats withdrew to their works as darkness fell. Now fully aware that the Union movement would not go uncontested, Meade brought in more reinforcements from the Petersburg line. Maj. Gen. Frank Wheaton's Sixth Corps and Brig. Gen. John Hartranft's Ninth Corps divisions slipped into line on Humphreys's right that evening, extending the Union position nearly to the abatis at Fort Cummings in the main line.[40]

The Fifteenth was on the march by 7 A.M. that Sunday morning. Three squadrons of cavalry took the advance, with Ayres's division leading the Fifth Corps infantry. Griffin's outfit came next, then Crawford's, the ambulances, fifty wagons with the infantry's reserve ammunition, and Gregg's train of fifty-six wagons heavily loaded with forage and ammunition. Entering the Halifax Road at Globe Tavern, the column continued south for just over three miles to Rowanty Post Office, where it turned onto a road heading southwest to the Monk's Neck Bridge crossing of Rowanty Creek near the W. Perkins house. They moved through fairly open country; what timber there was mostly skirted one side of the road at a time. The cavalry dashed ahead, intent on gaining the bridge a quarter mile below the point where the Rowanty was formed by the confluence of Hatcher's Run and the smaller Gravelly Run. The head of the column reached the Rowanty at about 10 A.M. only to discover the bridge razed and the stream, about sixty feet wide at that point, too deep for either horses or men to ford.⁴¹

Brig. Gen. James Gwyn's Third Brigade, leading Ayres's division that morning, crossed the stream by swimming, wading, or skating on the thin layer of ice in some places. They also drove about 100 enemy infantry defending the crossing from their works on the opposite bank. Winthrop's men reluctantly crossed next. "This order to plunge into the ice cold water in the middle of winter was promptly obeyed, but not particularly relished by any of us," recalled a man in the brigade. "Some of the taller men waded over but most of us had to strike out and swim although trees were cut down and thrown into the stream to assist those in crossing who could not swim." As the infantry splashed across in this manner, bridges were constructed for the cavalry, artillery, and trains. Once across the creek, the foot soldiers continued on the Monk's Neck Road to its intersection with the Vaughan Road, then out the Vaughan Road in the direction of Dinwiddie Court House to the vicinity of the J. Hargrave house, where they fanned out. Griffin's division covered the western approaches toward Dinwiddie as Ayres's covered the Quaker Road. Crawford's division eventually took up a position near the intersection of the Vaughan and Monk's Neck Roads. Winthrop's brigade halted and lay in line of battle at the intersection of the Vaughan and Quaker Roads.⁴²

Winthrop's men quickly built fires to dry their clothes and prepare a hasty meal. "The small comfort of hot coffee and dry clothes was indeed most heartily welcomed," one man recalled. Meanwhile, the attack on Humphreys's command led Meade to fret over the security of the Vaughan Road, which tenuously linked the two commands. To prevent a further attack on the Second Corps the next morning, at 9 P.M. Meade's new chief of staff, Maj. Gen. Alexander S. Webb, directed Warren to move the Fifth Corps four miles up the Vaughan Road to its crossing at Hatcher's Run and have one division cross to the other side as a reserve. The other two divisions would remain west of the run and hold a line between Humphreys's left at Armstrong's Mill and the Vaughan Road crossing.⁴³

In Norfolk when the movement began, Winthrop at this moment finally caught up with his brigade, galloping into camp to the cheers of his men. Just as the men prepared to bivouac for the night, they received an order to fall in. Griffin's division was to take the lead in the march up the Vaughan Road, but withdrawal of his pickets delayed his movement until nearly midnight. The trains followed the First Division, then came Ayres's Second Division, the artillery, and finally Crawford's Third Division. It was a very cold night, and the roads froze hard before morning. At 4 A.M. Gregg's cavalry joined Warren and brought up the rear, skirmishing with the enemy cavalry at their heels. Winthrop's brigade did not reach Hatcher's Run until daylight. The men were exhausted, having had little rest and no sleep. The brigade occupied a line of breastworks to the left of the Vaughan Road and about a mile west of the run.[44]

To protect against an attack from Vaughan Road, in the early morning of February 6, Gregg's three brigades moved out the road to a position near the Keys house. Later that morning Warren dispatched Winthrop's brigade to their support. Meanwhile, at 1:15 P.M., Warren ordered Crawford to march his division out the Vaughan Road and then swung to the right onto the road heading northwest toward Dabney's steam sawmill. As they moved the Third Division would drive the enemy back and ascertain the location of their entrenched line. The plan called for Ayres's division to follow on Crawford's left, as Gregg's troopers pushed any Confederates down the Vaughan Road as far as Gravelly Run. Assuming the cavalry could easily hold the Vaughan Road, Warren intended that Winthrop's brigade should rejoin the Second Division for the advance. But as Ayres prepared to direct him to withdraw, heavy firing could be heard from the direction of Winthrop's position on the Vaughan Road.[45]

Around 1 P.M., with the cavalry engaged in heavy skirmishing down the Vaughan Road, Winthrop ordered the 146th to relieve the vedettes. He then positioned the Fifth Veteran and 140th on the right side of the road, while the heavies of the Fifteenth formed line of battle in a large open field to its left. Just as these dispositions were completed, Gregg advanced to the attack, with Brig. Gen. Henry Davies's brigade moving on the right of the road, Col. J. Irvin Gregg's on its left, and Col. Oliver Knowles's in support. Pushing down the Vaughan Road, the Yankee horsemen unexpectedly encountered a large enemy force. There, not only Maj. Gen. William H. F. "Rooney" Lee's cavalry division awaited them but also the Tar Heel infantry brigades of Brig. Gen. Robert D. Johnston and Brig. Gen. William G. Lewis of Brig. Gen. John Pegram's division. The infantry had taken position north of the road, with Lee's troopers on the south side. A devastating volley from Johnston's outfit ripped into Irvin Gregg's mounted brigade, wounding the colonel, as Davies's and Knowles's men pressed forward dismounted. Despite the brisk return fire from their repeating

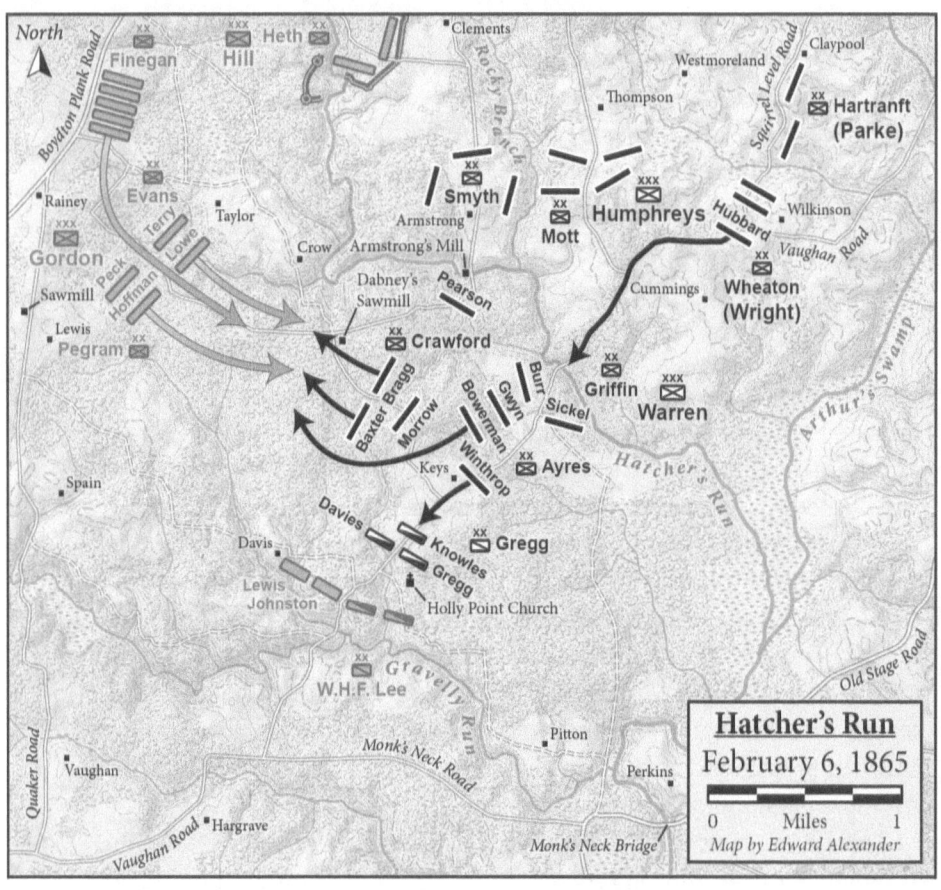

**Hatcher's Run
February 6, 1865**

0   Miles   1
Map by Edward Alexander

carbines, the Yankees realized they could not dislodge the enemy force confronting them. Men and horses bolted for the rear, while the Rebels followed in hot pursuit.[46]

As the Federal cavalry retired "in considerable confusion" into the field in front of him, General Winthrop ordered his three regiments to advance at the double-quick. Racing forward with a resounding cheer and delivering "some very fair volleys," the heavies of the Fifteenth and their Zouave comrades not only successfully checked the advancing Confederates but also drove them back. In the Fifteenth's front the enemy retired to the shelter of the woods at the far end of the open field. Considering it imprudent to pursue further, Winthrop halted his brigade. The enemy then attempted to advance twice more, but each time the First Brigade repulsed them.[47]

Amid the battle, Quartermaster Sgt. Robert Rae, normally a noncombatant, grabbed a musket and joined the fight. He opined that his fellow heavies "stood best. They wavered twice—when they saw the Zouaves flinch on our right but the Zouaves rallied and came up again. So our fellows Stuck to it." Some of the men of the Fifteenth sought cover behind the rails of a fence in the open field, but even that did not offer safety. As Rae knelt on one knee behind it, removing percussion caps from the box of a fallen heavy, "one ball hit me on the left side of the nose Scratching it a little, it knocked off my cap at the same time." Undaunted, he fired several times at a Rebel flag observed streaming over the gray line to his front. "I had the satisfaction of seeing it fall to the ground once," although "who hit it of course, I cannot say." The chaos and danger of the battle impressed him. He later mused, "I don't know what the Papers will say about [the battle]— but I call it Desperate." Rae relished the outcome and the persistence of his regiment and brigade. "I did think at one time we was licked—but the men did not know it—and kept Blazing away till the Rebels ran."[48]

Others more accustomed to a combatant role also struggled in the chaos of the back-and-forth battle and its deadly consequences. As the fighting raged, Amherst Belcher was firing rapidly, with two heavies reloading for him, when someone shoved his cap down over his eyes. Pushing it back up he discovered Lt. Adolf Riemann, formerly an enlisted man in his company, waving and smiling at him. Belcher returned the greeting and resumed firing. Only minutes later an officer let Belcher know that "Lieutenant Riemann wants you." He found his old friend on the ground twenty or thirty yards away with a mortal wound to his groin. "I loved him," Belcher later lamented, "and went back to my work crying." Riemann would die two days later in the hospital at City Point.[49]

Winthrop's men by now were running low on ammunition. At around 3 P.M. Griffin, at Warren's direction, ordered his First Brigade, commanded by Brig. Gen. Horatio G. Sickel, out the Vaughan Road. Gregg directed Sickel to move his unit down the road to support Winthrop, "whose line at the time," according to the cavalry commander, "was being pressed by a vigorous assault of superior numbers of the enemy." Sickel found Winthrop's men "fiercely engaging the enemy upon the open ground on the west side of the Vaughan Road," formed his brigade into line of battle, and charged into the fray. Winthrop's men, with little ammunition left, fell back some 75–100 yards to the just-arrived ordnance wagons. The sudden appearance of a fresh Federal brigade apparently drained the Confederates' remaining spirit. "The enemy broke at the first volley from our men and left the field in great disorder," Sickel reported, "leaving their killed and wounded in our hands, together with several prisoners." The New Yorkers, with replenished cartridge boxes, rejoined Sickel's outfit; the two brigades, along with the cavalry, took position across the Vaughan Road facing west. Near 5:30 P.M., the Vaughan Road sector fell silent, but the troops could hear considerable firing to the right and rear.[50]

Earlier, about 2 P.M., Crawford's division had recrossed Hatcher's Run and began its march northwest up the road toward the Dabney's steam sawmill about a mile away; the abandoned mill's ruins and large sawdust pile remained prominent landmarks. As resistance to the Third Division's advance stiffened, Ayres's division went forward to cover its left but immediately faced trouble. The leftmost brigade, Gwyn's, was broken by what its commander reported as "the stampede of a portion of General Gregg's cavalry" and became disoriented. Consequently, Ayres reached the mill site with relatively few men. Although Crawford's troops initially drove the enemy beyond the old mill, the graycoats soon pushed his left back. The battle lines swayed to and fro across the mill site amid continuously heavy fighting.[51]

By this point the Union advance had encountered only Evans's Division and that part of Pegram's division—a brigade commanded at the time by Lt. Col. John G. Kasey—not operating against Winthrop and Gregg on the Vaughan Road. Mahone's old division, under the command of Brig. Gen. Joseph Finegan, now slipped into line between Evans and Kasey as the entire gray line rolled forward with the shrill rebel yell. A trickle of blue soon turned into a flood as one Union outfit after another broke under the weight of the attack and streamed to the rear. The tide of fleeing men could not be stemmed, Warren's adjutant reporting, "their officers [had] no control over them whatever."[52]

At around 5:30 P.M. Col. James Hubbard's Sixth Corps brigade arrived on the field and formed line of battle, at last stabilizing the precarious situation. Various Fifth Corps regiments, whose commanders reestablished order, as well as most of Pearson's brigade from Griffin's division joined Hubbard. The firing subsided with the growing darkness, and the day's battle ended. The Confederates had driven the Fifth Corps elements at Dabney's Sawmill that afternoon nearly back to the works on the west side of Hatcher's Run.[53]

At dark Winthrop received orders to withdraw, leaving Sickel's brigade and a small contingent of cavalry to defend the Vaughan Road. His brigade moved up the Vaughan Road and, about 10 P.M., relieved Hubbard's skirmish line and Pearson's brigade covering the road to Dabney's Sawmill. Winthrop's right connected with the left of the Second Corps near Armstrong's Mill. The brigade remained in this advanced position throughout the bitterly cold night. Rain, sleet, and snow fell on the exhausted men, who huddled freezing on the cold ground.[54]

Cold rain and sleet continued to fall and shrouded the earth and trees in ice by the morning of February 7. Peering through the gloom, Winthrop's men detected movement near the advanced line of enemy rifle pits. They heard the distinctive sound of men felling trees, clearly indicating the enemy were hard at work fortifying their position. At 10 A.M. Warren ordered a First Division brigade to relieve Winthrop's weary outfit so they could retire within the breastworks in reserve. The heavies of the Fifteenth and the rest of Ayres's command, as well as Griffin's division, would see little action that day. The same, however, could not be said for the Third Division. Crawford's men, after a day of fighting—at times in a driving hailstorm—succeeded in driving the enemy out of their advanced rifle pits and into their new line near the sawmill, thus regaining part of the battlefield of the previous day and allowing burial of the Union fallen. But exhausted from fighting both the enemy and the weather, they could advance no farther. Thus, the Battle of Hatcher's Run ended in yet another stalemate.[55]

Grant and Meade decided to hold the Vaughan Road crossing over Hatcher's Run as a point from which to mount future operations against the Confederate right. Meade ordered a new section of line constructed from Fort Sampson, at the southwestern apex of the existing Petersburg line, to the Vaughan Road crossing of Hatcher's Run, with a new fortification erected on its west bank to secure the crossing. Like the existing line, the more than three-mile-long extension would feature batteries in selected positions connected by breastworks. The Federals would also extend the military railroad to supply the troops garrisoning the new position.[56]

Meade estimated Federal casualties in the battle at 1,539. The Fifth Corps lost the most men, with 131 killed, 970 wounded, and 159 missing. Confederate losses stood at only about 1,000. The Fifteenth suffered more casualties than any other regiment in the First Brigade—1 officer, Adolf Riemann, and 7 men killed or mortally wounded, with a further

22 men wounded. Private Van Vleck's denied request for a furlough two weeks before meant that he never saw his wife and children again. The grievously wounded soldier died en route to a field hospital. When he passed, "our Butcher happened to be there—he knew Jacob—and got his letters and papers out of his pockets before they buried him," Sergeant Rae explained. Rae sent the recovered treasures, including the bloodstained photographs of Van Vleck's wife and young daughter, to a mutual friend at home with a note: "This is Part of his Papers—this is Jacob's Blood on it—I could get no other to send—as we did not fetch all our things from our old Camp yet . . . there is hardly a dozen sheets of paper in the Regiment." Others also mourned Van Vleck. Prior to the Hatcher's Run expedition, he was helping Belcher build the latter's winter quarters. "My shack was nearly completed except for the chimney and Will Wood and Jake Van Vleck would finish that in another day." But neither man would complete the job. "We struck trouble at Hatchers Run," remembered Belcher, "and in a sharp fight about 4 P.M. both my chimney men were killed. So it goes."[57]

Regrettable as the losses in the Fifteenth were, the heavies and Zouaves of Winthrop's brigade had played a pivotal role in the battle. Their tenacious defense had checked the Confederate attack up the Vaughan Road and prevented the Rebels from taking the Fifth Corps in flank and rear during its advance toward Dabney's Sawmill. Ayres paid tribute to the First Brigade's role in the battle, noting, "General Winthrop handsomely repulsed the enemy's attack on the Vaughan Road." Winthrop had two horses shot from under him during the action but remained uninjured. For his part, Winthrop credited his men with the First Brigade's success that day. "It is but simple justice to say that I have rarely seen troops fight with more animation or maintain their ground so stubbornly against such superior numbers," he reported. "With such troops I shall always feel confident of success."[58]

CHAPTER TWELVE

To the White Oak Road and Five Forks

From the Fifteenth's new camp near Hatcher's Run, Sergeant Robert Rae complained in early February 1865, "The weather is Cold, wet, frosty, snowy—almost everything that is Disagreeable." Although "we Suffer much from the Cold," he quipped, "plenty of wood & Whiskey helps to relieve us of our Care and Trouble in that respect." Rea was confident they would hold the new line gained in the fight at Hatcher's Run several days before: "We mean to stay here now. . . . [T]he Waggons is gone for our tents & etc." Located near the Vaughan Road on a high, rolling field above Arthur's Swamp, the new camp offered good water and plenty of wood. Another soldier in General Winthrop's First Brigade recalled that for the third time that winter, "we erected log huts covered with canvass and made ourselves as comfortable as possible." Nevertheless, their toils were not without reward, as the "benefit of the improved site of our camp was immediately visible in the prompt disappearance of all sickness."[1]

The Fifth Corps settled in while it worked to complete the new line extension. General Warren described his corps's new camps as laid out in woods "in line of battle," running nearly east from Hatcher's Run to within about a half mile of the Halifax Road. General Ayres's Second Division occupied the center, with General Griffin's First Division west of it and General Crawford's Third Division to its east. Griffin's encampment sat relatively close to Hatcher's Run and the new line, while Ayres's and Crawford's camps were over a mile away. Although not fully completed, the Federals had occupied their new line by February 10. The Second

Corps held the sector from Fort Sampson to the Vaughan Road crossing, and the Fifth Corps the works at the crossing and along the run to the end of the line.²

As the Fifteenth built its new huts and took part in constructing the new line, the Federal high command on two occasions actively considered detaching the regiment from the Army of the Potomac. On February 10 Grant ordered Meade to send some of his "old, reliable and reduced regiments" to Baltimore to take charge of the camps of newly drafted men. Meade transmitted the request to Warren, and one of several brigades he suggested be sent was Winthrop's, which at the time fielded 53 officers and 950 men, "the major part of which is a heavy artillery regiment (the Fifteenth New York Heavy Artillery)." But Meade instead selected another veteran Fifth Corps brigade for the assignment. Ten days later Grant asked him to designate a heavy artillery regiment to garrison Fort McHenry in Baltimore harbor. "We think a good deal of our heavies; they are about as good fighters as we have," Meade bragged. Still, he agreed to send the "weakest" of his heavy artillery regiments. Based on current strengths provided for each regiment of heavies, Meade ordered the Seventh New York to Baltimore. The Seventh had been decimated since it joined the Army of the Potomac days before the fight at the Harris farm, and in February 1865 it numbered only 37 officers and 571 men.³

The troops spent most of their days immersed in the daily routines of camp life. But in an unexpected break from that routine, on the afternoon of March 16, the Fifth Corps formed near Humphreys's Station on the now extended military railroad for review by a party of dignitaries led by Secretary of War Edwin M. Stanton. Winthrop, sporting a brand new uniform with accoutrements made at Tiffany's in New York, found Stanton "very affable." He also reported that the secretary "complimented my Brigade in high terms. It looked magnificently and everyone agreed that it made the finest appearance of any Brigade in the Corps."⁴

As the Army of the Potomac tightened its grip on Petersburg, success had been achieved in another theater of the war. After taking part in the final defeat of Early's forces in the Shenandoah Valley, on March 19 "Little Phil" Sheridan and his cavalry arrived at White House on the Pamunkey River. Grant urged him to push on and join the armies investing Richmond and Petersburg as quickly as possible. The general in chief believed that with the support of a large infantry force, Sheridan's reequipped and reinforced command could move out to the left from the Union lines near the Boydton Plank Road to cut both the South Side and the Richmond and Danville Railroads. His prodding produced the desired result. Sheridan's troopers, looking somewhat worse for the wear, finally galloped into the Federal lines at Petersburg and on March 27 went into camp near Hancock's Station on the military railroad.[5]

With the elimination of any further threat from the Valley, Lee correctly anticipated that Sheridan and his cavalry would soon rejoin the Federals confronting Richmond and Petersburg. He was also concerned that victorious Union forces from the Carolinas might move north to augment those armies. Consequently, by early March the Confederate high command recognized the likely necessity of abandoning the Richmond and Petersburg lines to allow all, or at least part, of the Army of Northern Virginia to slip to the south toward Danville. There, Lee could link up with Gen. Joseph E. Johnston's army, which at the time was being driven northward through the Carolinas by Sherman. But the Confederates needed to hold the Federals in place at least until the winter weather ameliorated and the roads improved sufficiently to allow the withdrawal. To this end, on March 25 Lee launched an attack on Fort Stedman in the Ninth Corps's sector. Before dawn, the three divisions of Maj. Gen. John B. Gordon's Second Corps charged across the narrow space between the lines, capturing the fort and several smaller gun emplacements adjacent to it. But after a vigorous counterattack, by 8 A.M. the Federals reclaimed their positions. The Confederates suffered heavily in killed and wounded in this sharp engagement, and lost an additional 1,900 men as prisoners of war.[6]

The heavies of the Fifteenth and their Fifth Corps comrades awoke that morning to the sound of the heavy fighting several miles to the northeast. The corps was soon in motion toward the rattle of the guns. After about a two-mile march, the column halted, with Crawford's division at the Gurley house, Ayres's behind it, and Griffin's near the Wyatt house. Around 9:15 A.M. Crawford's and Ayres's divisions proceeded to the support of the Ninth Corps and, reaching the vicinity of Fort Stedman, were held in reserve. With the fighting all but over, they were soon released and trudged back to their camps without having fired a shot. Meanwhile, Chief of Staff Webb had directed Griffin to support the Second and Sixth Corps. With the enemy apparently massed more than five miles to their northeast for the attack on Fort Stedman, Humphreys and Wright suspected that the force left holding the line to their front had been weakened. With Meade's agreement, the two corps commanders seized the opportunity to assault the enemy's right. These attacks persisted throughout the day and, with Griffin's aid, met with ultimate success when the Federals reached and were able to hold the Rebels' fortified picket line. As night fell the full consequences of the attack on Fort Stedman became clear. The Confederates had not only sacrificed thousands of irreplaceable troops but also some four miles of their entrenched picket line paralleling their main line along the Boydton Plank Road.[7]

Two days later, with the dust from the failed Fort Stedman offensive barely settled, the Federals seized the initiative. At Grant's direction, Meade issued instructions to set his Army of the Potomac in motion around the Confederate right flank. Departing at 3 A.M. on March 29, Warren would march the Fifth Corps across Rowanty Creek and then out the Stage Road to its intersection with the Vaughan Road. There, he would establish communications with the Second Corps, which, leaving several hours later, would follow the Vaughan Road across Hatcher's Run and Gravelly Run. The Sixth and Ninth Corps along with elements of the Army of the James, now commanded by Major General Ord, would hold the works at Petersburg.[8]

Grant ordered Sheridan and his cavalry to strike out as early as possible on March 29, move in rear of and then around the left of the Fifth Corps, and pass "to or through Dinwiddie" into the Confederate right and rear. He did not intend the cavalry to attack the enemy in his works, but held that if the Confederates ventured out, Sheridan should "move in with [his] entire force in [his] own way, and with full reliance that the army will engage or follow the enemy as circumstances will dictate." If the Rebels did not challenge, Sheridan should "cut loose" for the Richmond and Danville Railroad to destroy as much of it as possible and at least a part of the South Side Railroad.[9]

When the Fifteenth took the field for the offensive, only ten of its companies would remain in Winthrop's brigade. In preparation for the movement, Capt. William D. Dickey's Company M was detached and assigned to Wainwright's Fifth Corps Artillery Brigade, serving with it throughout the coming operations. Capt. Calvin Shaffer's Company F also remained behind, still attached to the Army of the Potomac's artillery reserve near City Point.[10]

Warren remembered that "the excitement of moving and the necessary preparations kept almost every one from sleeping any of the preceding portion of the night." Regardless, Ayres's division stepped out at precisely 3 A.M. on Wednesday, March 29. Griffin's division moved out next, followed by Crawford's. Warren reported that his corps began the march in pleasant weather through country "of the forest kind common to Virginia, . . . well watered by swampy streams." Although "the surface is level and the soil clayey or sandy," movement could become difficult "where these mix together, like quicksand." Yet even in good weather, "the soil, after the frosts of winter leave it, is very light and soft, and hoofs and wheels find but little support."[11]

The vanguard reached the Monk's Neck crossing of Rowanty Creek at 4:45 A.M. Enemy lookouts fired a few shots but did little else to hinder the Fifth's crossing. As the engineers laid a canvas pontoon bridge, the infantry began to scramble across the creek on fallen trees and what remained of the bridge that had previously stood there. By shortly after 8 A.M. the head of the column passed the junction of the Vaughan and Old Dinwiddie Stage Roads. As Warren awaited news of Humphreys's progress, the Second Division advanced along the Vaughan Road to its intersection with the Quaker Road. Ayres positioned two brigades near the intersection and sent the third a short distance up the Quaker Road. Griffin's division continued on the Vaughan Road to the vicinity of the J. Hargrave and Chappell farms, about two miles from Dinwiddie Court House. At 10:20 A.M. Warren received a dispatch directing him to instead "move up the Quaker Road to Gravelly Run crossing" and establish contact with Humphreys "by throwing out parties" to his right.[12]

Warren immediately pulled Griffin's division back and sent it up the Quaker Road, Brig. Gen. Joshua Chamberlain's brigade in the lead. Crawford's outfit followed Griffin's. Chamberlain found the bridge over Gravelly Run in ruins, and Confederates on the high north bank disputing any advance. He forced a crossing anyway, pushing the enemy a mile up the Quaker Road to the buildings of the Lewis farm about three-quarters of a mile south of the Boydton Plank Road intersection. When Rebel resistance stiffened, Chamberlain halted to await reinforcements. Griffin's remaining two brigades, Col. Edgar Gregory's and Brig. Gen. Joseph Bartlett's, crossed the run on a hastily constructed bridge and pushed up the heavily obstructed Quaker Road, reaching Chamberlain around 4 P.M. Chamberlain, with Gregory and Bartlett supporting, advanced and engaged three brigades from Maj. Gen. Bushrod Johnson's division in a terrific struggle around the Lewis farm buildings and an old sawmill just north of them. Superior Yankee numbers coupled with the arrival of Federal artillery eventually turned the tide. After a two-hour fight, Johnson pulled his forces back across the Boydton Plank Road and into the line of works covering the White Oak Road.[13]

While the battle raged at the Lewis farm, Warren directed the Third Division to move out on a farm road running diagonally from the Quaker Road about a quarter mile south of the Lewis house northwest to the Boydton Plank Road to get to Griffin's left. Pushing enemy skirmishers before them, Crawford's men reached the Plank Road and halted. Meanwhile, Warren sent two of Ayres's brigades, one being Winthrop's, up the Quaker Road and across Gravelly Run to support Griffin and Crawford, but they arrived too late to participate in the fight. After the Rebel repulse, Griffin advanced beyond the junction of the Quaker and Plank Roads. As gathering darkness precluded further operations, the Federals had finally reached and held the Boydton Plank Road. The First Division camped in a north-facing arc covering the road junction near the J. Stroud house, while Crawford's division extended the line southwest down the Plank Road. Griffin's right connected with Humphreys's corps, which stretched southeastward to Hatcher's Run. Ayres's brigade bivouacked for the night along the Quaker Road just north of Gravelly Run near the R. Spain house.[14]

Marching about fifteen miles, the heavies of the Fifteenth had endured a long and difficult day. They settled in for the night as a fierce storm struck. Rain fell in sheets, the wind howled, and the drenched men occasionally heard the crash of splintering limbs and branches. Even with the racket, a man in Winthrop's brigade noted that they "were so fatigued by the day's marching that even this great 'war of the elements' did not prevent us from sleeping soundly despite the fact that we were exposed to its full force."[15]

Sheridan camped that night at Dinwiddie Court House. Earlier that morning Little Phil and his 9,000 troopers had set out from near Hancock's Station. They moved past Reams's Station and traversed Rowanty Creek at Malone's Crossing, about three and a half miles below Warren's crossing point. Sheridan left one division, Maj. Gen. George A. Custer's, at the crossing to protect the trains and occupied Dinwiddie Court House with two divisions by nightfall. Grant, buoyed by the success at the Lewis farm and the largely unopposed movement to Dinwiddie, drastically altered Sheridan's principle objective that night. "I now feel like ending the matter if it is possible to do so before going back." He told Sheridan, "I do not want you . . . to cut loose and go after the enemy's roads at present." Instead, "in the morning, push round the enemy if you can and get into his right rear."[16]

The heavy rain continued unabated through the morning of March 30, rendering the roads, according to Meade's aide-de-camp Lyman, "a hopeless, sandy pudding." Despite the difficult conditions, Griffin's division and Humphreys's corps early on began a cautious advance to feel for the enemy. After forcing the pickets back to their main line and upon attaining the intersection of the road from Dabney's Sawmill with the Boydton Plank Road, Griffin halted across the Plank Road. With this advance, Humphreys's corps, which connected to Griffin's right, extended generally eastward, striking Hatcher's Run near the Crow house. Warren considered a further advance inadvisable since at little more than a half mile beyond Griffin's position could be seen a heavily entrenched Confederate line running across the Plank Road at Burgess's Tavern and continuing west down the White Oak Road. The bluecoats began digging in.[17]

Meanwhile, Chief of Staff Webb informed Warren, "General Meade does not think you hold as much of the front line as the strength of your command would warrant." The commanding general wanted him to "make use" of both Ayres's and Crawford's outfits to "develop to the left." Webb also advised him of Grant's amended orders to Sheridan to attack or turn the enemy's right but that he should "act independently of Sheridan, and, protecting your flanks, extend to your left as far as possible." Warren believed that his corps already covered the maximum front it could and was concerned that extending to his left would jeopardize his entire positon. He fumed that he had already informed his commander: "I could not extend further with safety . . . , and yet this dispatch required me to extend farther; and did not define how far, nor for what object." Nevertheless, he committed to send Ayres's division "to develop the enemy's line" and "where he can co-operate with General Sheridan if he comes within reach."[18]

At 10:30 A.M. Warren ordered the Second Division on a reconnaissance "northwest from Mrs. Butler's, or as near that direction as may be practicable." This home sat about a quarter mile up a north-running forest road originating at the Boydton Plank Road just under a mile below its intersection with the Quaker Road. Beyond Mrs. Butler's, after crossing a tributary of Gravelly Run, the road passed by the Holliday cabin. Three-quarters of a mile north of Holliday's, at Halter Butler's farm, the road struck the White Oak Road just west of its junction with the Claiborne Road and near the western end of the Confederate line. From this point the Claiborne Road continued north across Hatcher's Run and on to Sutherland's Station on the South Side Railroad some three miles beyond. Warren directed Ayres to halt his main force not more than a mile from the Plank Road and then advance skirmishers to "develop the character of the country and the enemy's position." He assured Ayres that if his division were attacked, then he would rush Crawford's division to his assistance.[19]

After an early reveille, Winthrop's heavies and Zouaves wolfed down a meager breakfast of coffee and hardtack and prepared to move out. About noon Ayres led his division from their bivouac across the Plank Road and past Mrs. Butler's. Two brigades halted about a half mile off the Plank Road, while Winthrop's brigade deployed in skirmish line and plowed ahead across the Gravelly Run tributary. The heavy rain had swollen the rivulet into a difficult, nearly waist-deep swamp that prevented the movement of artillery. Winthrop's advance eventually pushed to within 400 yards of the White Oak Road, likely at a position about three-quarters of a mile west of the Claiborne Road intersection. Ayres reported no enemy fortifications to his immediate front at this point. This was certainly the case since, unknown to Ayres, at the intersection the Rebel entrenchments running west along the White Oak Road from the Boydton Plank Road turned north and continued along the west side of the Claiborne Road for about a mile to Hatcher's Run. Winthrop's picket line, manned by the 146th, stretched in an arc from the W. Dabney house south of the White Oak Road eastward to connect with Griffin's pickets on the main line. The Fifteenth and the balance of Winthrop's outfit bivouacked that night in the wet fields and woods near Holliday's, less than half a mile from the White Oak Road.[20]

Concerned with the division's isolated position, Meade at 9 P.M. directed Warren to "support General Ayres in his position and strengthen yourself at that point." Consequently, Warren directed Ayres to consolidate his division on Winthrop's brigade at daylight, while Crawford held his outfit ready to follow. Griffin's men, relieved that night by Brig. Gen. Nelson Miles's Second Corps division, would proceed down the Plank Road to near Mrs. Butler's to support both Ayres and Crawford. Acknowledging Warren's and Ayres's precarious positions, Grant instructed Sheridan to "be prepared to push up with all your force to [Warren's] assistance" if the enemy attacked his left flank in the morning. Yet in sanctioning the consolidation of the Fifth Corps, Grant was not merely concerned with Ayres's safety. He was entertaining a plan to send Warren's corps on the offensive the following day, and if he did, they likely would be under Sheridan's immediate command.[21]

When the Federals' sweeping movement to turn the Confederate right was first detected, Lee acted quickly to counter it. At the time R. H. Anderson, whose corps consisted only of Bushrod Johnson's division, manned the Confederate right along the White Oak Road. On the morning of March 29, Lee shifted Brig. Gen. Samuel McGowan's brigade of Wilcox's Division from east of Hatcher's Run to Anderson's sector. He also ordered Maj. Gen. George Pickett's division of Longstreet's Corps to bolster the position. Pickett's outfit arrived at Sutherland's Station by rail from Petersburg late on March 29. In the cold rain the men trudged down the dark, muddy Claiborne Road, across a swollen Hatcher's Run, and tumbled into the White Oak Road works. The next morning Pickett marched cautiously west out that road the four miles to Five Forks with three of his brigades, two brigades of Johnson's Division, and six of Col. William J. Pegram's guns. Arriving around 4:30 P.M., Pickett's infantry rendezvoused with Maj. Gen. Fitzhugh Lee's, Maj. Gen. "Rooney" Lee's, and Maj. Gen. Thomas L. Rosser's cavalry divisions. From Five Forks, this combined force, under overall command of Pickett, would head south toward Dinwiddie Court House the following morning to confront Sheridan.[22]

Winthrop's soggy men—it had commenced raining again at 3 A.M.—stirred early on the gloomy morning of Friday, March 31. Soon after 7:30 A.M. Ayres consolidated his division in fields northwest of Holliday's. He positioned the most forward brigade, Winthrop's, in Halter Butler's elevated open field south of the White Oak Road near the Claiborne Road intersection. From there, about a half mile from the White Oak Road, Winthrop's men could see Rebels sheltered in their works. Ayres posted General Dennison's Maryland Brigade nearby in a wooded ravine facing northwest toward the Dabney house and General Gwyn's brigade to Winthrop's right rear. After struggling across the rain-swollen tributary, Crawford's outfit halted near the Holliday cabin about 500 yards behind Ayres. By 10 A.M. Griffin had massed his division near Mrs. Butler's house on the southeast side of the swollen stream, about 1,000 yards in rear of Crawford but still in supporting distance. The rain had ceased, the sun even peeking through the clouds, as Griffin's men settled in and started to prepare breakfast.[23]

After being relieved by the 140th on the First Brigade's picket line, the men of the 146th built fires and spread their blankets in the sun to dry. Their moment of relative rest ended quickly. One of Warren's staff officers, Maj. Emmor B. Cope, brought an order directing Ayres to take the White Oak Road and entrench a brigade upon it, with Brig. Gen. Richard Coulter's Third Division brigade supporting the operation. At the order to fall in, Winthrop's heavies and Zouaves formed line of battle, with the Fifth Veteran on the left, the Fifteenth in the center, and the 146th on the right. The brigade stepped out at the double-quick around 10:30 A.M. and passed through the skirmishers of the 140th. Winthrop's brigade advanced first, but Gwyn's brigade soon moved ahead in echelon on its right-rear. The Maryland Brigade held its position, while Coulter's outfit filed into place where Winthrop's brigade had formed before its advance.[24]

Meanwhile, the enemy recognized that Warren's left flank was hanging in the air and thus extremely vulnerable. An attack here could not only roll up the Yankee line but also prevent the bluecoats from interposing between the fortified White Oak Road line and Pickett's command to the west near Five Forks. Bushrod Johnson assumed tactical control of four brigades to execute the attack. Two of these, Brig. Gen. Henry A. Wise's Virginians and Brig. Gen. Young Moody's Alabamians, commanded that day by Col. Martin L. Stansel, were from Johnson's own division. Brig. Gen. Eppa Hunton's Virginians and McGowan's South Carolinians joined from Pickett's Division and Wilcox's Division, respectively. Three of the brigades, McGowan on the right, Stansel in the center, and Hunton to his left, slipped from the protection of the works and, unobserved by the Yankees, took position in the woods across the White Oak Road from Halter Butler's field. Wise's brigade remained farther to the east. McGowan planned to slip around the Yankee left, hit the bluecoats in the flank, and drive them in front of the other brigades, which could then lay a devastating fire on them. McGowan began to work around the Yankee left flank, but before his brigade was in position to attack, Winthrop's advance precipitated battle.[25]

As Winthrop's men stepped out, Maj. William W. Swan of Ayres's staff watched them "go steadily forward in painful silence. Not an enemy was to be seen, not a musket was fired." When "the advancing troops were halfway across the field, . . . suddenly along the edge of the wood at the other end there appeared a long blue line of smoke." One of Winthrop's men recalled that when the Rebels "gave it to us hot and heavy," chaos ensued.

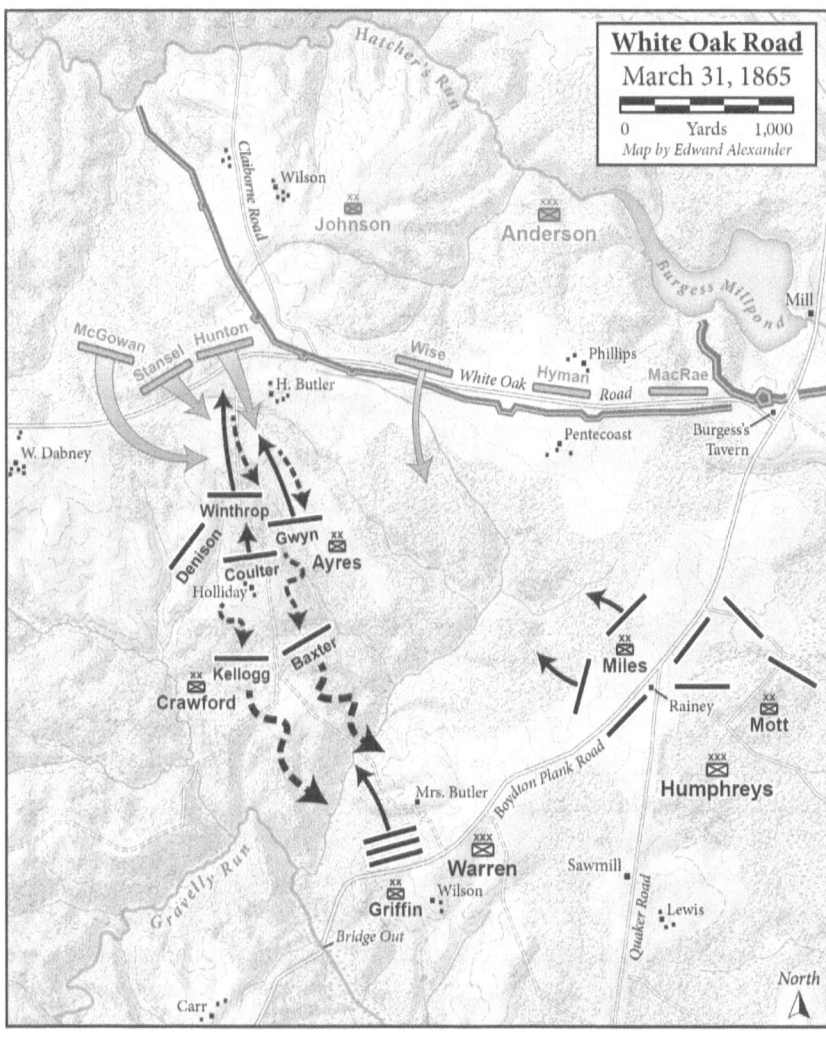

White Oak Road, March 31, 1865. Map by Edward Alexander

"The enemy's fire wrought havoc to our line; men were falling on every side, but still we pressed forward." As they plowed onward, heads down as if in a hailstorm of lead, Winthrop's men closed gaping holes in their line left by the fallen. When the Federals had approached to within twenty-five yards, Hunton's Virginians emerged from their concealed position in the woods, hurling themselves across the White Oak Road toward Winthrop's weakened brigade. Stansel's Alabamians followed on Hunton's right. McGowan's South Carolinians soon joined the melee by delivering a galling fire into the left flank of the New Yorkers, then advancing to sweep them before Hunton's and Stansel's surging masses. Ayres at once realized the enemy had "four or five to my one." A desperate contest ensued, but overwhelmed, Winthrop's outfit began to crumble from left to right; first the Fifth, then the Fifteenth, and finally the 146th gave way.[26]

Winthrop ordered an about face, and the brigade conducted a fighting withdrawal. When it reached Gwyn's battle line, the New Yorkers halted, and the two outfits made a brief stand. But Hunton and Stansel drove them back as McGowan's South Carolinians hit Dennison's Marylanders and also compelled them, along with Coulter's brigade, to retire. Ayres twice attempted unsuccessfully to rally his troops as they fell back. The fleeing men crashed through the ranks of Crawford's other two brigades while the Confederates assailed them in front and flank, and these outfits also broke. Now, both the Second and Third Divisions scurried back toward the Boydton Plank Road. Swan reported that Winthrop's men "returned slowly to the branch of Gravelly Run. There was no order. . . . Each man was looking for himself and all were making for the entrenched line . . . The men did not run." As the mob approached Griffin's position, the general warned, "For God's sake, let them through, or they will break our line." Chamberlain observed that the men seemed "reckless of everything but to get behind the lines on the Boydton Road, plunging through the swampy run, breaking through Griffin's right where he and Bartlett re-form them behind the Third Brigade."[27]

The Rebels, themselves now disorganized, pressed on toward the rain-swollen stream. They soon encountered the fire of the four 12-pounder Napoleons of Battery H, First New York Light. Bvt. Maj. Charles Mink had rolled the Napoleons into battery in an excellent position overlooking the swampy run as well as the small open field and woods beyond it. His gunners raked the ground with shell and canister as Griffin's infantry fired volley after volley into the butternuts. Confederate dead and wounded soon dotted the field. A stunned Warren approached Chamberlain: "Will you save the honor of the Fifth Corps? That's all there is about it." Chamberlain promised to "try it, General; only don't let anyone stop me but the enemy." At about 2:30 P.M. Chamberlain's men splashed across the swollen run and began driving the graycoats back. Gregory's brigade followed to his right, with Bartlett's to Chamberlain's left-rear. Ayres's reformed division also advanced in echelon by brigade to support the left-rear of Griffin's formation, while Crawford's looked to its right.[28]

Chamberlain's advance reached Holliday's with little difficulty and continued beyond into the southern edge of Butler's open field. The opposition then stiffened as the enemy opened a heavy fire from the rifle pits dug earlier by Ayres's men. Warren ordered Chamberlain to halt. Fearing he would suffer as many losses stopped as he would pitching into the enemy, Chamberlain entreated Griffin and Warren to let him attack. His request was granted. With Gregory's brigade on Chamberlain's right, the bluecoats surged forward, driving Hunton's and Stansel's men from the rifle pits and back into the works north of the White Oak Road. The blue-clad troops crossed the White Oak Road west of the Claiborne Road intersection and began digging in across from the Confederates' fortified line. Ayres's division took position near the W. Dabney house facing west toward Five Forks, while Crawford remained northwest of Holliday's. McGowan's South Carolinians, isolated to the west by the Federal advance, moved in a sweeping arc around the Yankees and into the fortifications along the Claiborne Road.[29]

The Fifth Corps not only regained the lost ground but also achieved an even more significant tactical success. It had cut the White Oak Road, isolating Pickett's force from the main body of Lee's army. But the cost was high. Warren reported 937 officers and men killed or wounded and 470 missing, for an aggregate loss of 1,407. Winthrop's brigade suffered severely, with the Fifth Veteran's total casualties at 63 and the 140th and 146th each sustaining about 50 casualties. The Fifteenth, larger in size, suffered the most casualties of any regiment in the brigade—13 men killed outright, 1 officer and another 8 men mortally wounded, as many as 13 officers and 75 men wounded, and up to another 131 missing. Third Battalion commander Major Duysing, the once lieutenant colonel of the old DeKalb Regiment whom Amherst Belcher praised as "a good friend to me always, and a good soldier," was the mortally wounded officer. He would die in Petersburg on April 21 from a gunshot wound to his right thigh.[30]

While the Fifth Corps fought furiously that afternoon, Sheridan and his cavalry, far from being in position to support Warren as Grant had intended, were being driven around the Virginia countryside by Pickett in a series of clashes known collectively as the Battle of Dinwiddie Court House. Nightfall found Little Phil more or less where he had started the day, with his command posted in and around Dinwiddie but now hemmed in by Pickett's infantry and cavalry. Sheridan pleaded for help, complaining, "This force is too strong for us." Yet with his characteristic flair for drama, he pledged to "hold on to Dinwiddie Court House until I am compelled to leave." At 10:45 P.M. Grant informed him that the Fifth Corps had orders to support him in his efforts "to destroy the force which your command has fought so gallantly today." As noted, Sheridan would be in operational control of Warren and the Fifth Corps.[31]

For Warren, the night's orders produced much confusion and were rife with contradictions. At about 10:50 P.M. he received Meade's instructions to send Griffin's division down the Boydton Plank Road to Sheridan's support and to move the balance of his corps south down a road intersecting the White Oak Road to strike the enemy threatening Sheridan in rear. Exasperated, Warren replied that, as directed by Webb an hour earlier, he had already begun to pull his divisions back from the White Oak Road to the Plank Road in the order in which they could most rapidly be moved—that is, Ayres's, followed by Crawford's, and then Griffin's. This placed the First Division farthest from the Plank Road, meaning it would have to pass the Third and Second Divisions on the dark, narrow forest road to reach the Plank Road. "I cannot change them to-night without producing confusion that will render all my operations nugatory," he explained. But to comply with the spirit of his orders, he would send Ayres's division down the Plank Road to Sheridan while taking Griffin's and Crawford's outfits back up to White Oak Road and then toward the enemy's rear by the route prescribed. Adding to the confusion—and unknown to army headquarters until about this hour—two days earlier the enemy had destroyed the bridge carrying the Boydton Plank Road over Gravelly Run. The span would have to be repaired before Ayres's men could cross the now rain-swollen waterway. Finally, if Meade's intentions and instructions were not already sufficiently confusing and contradictory, at 1 A.M. on April 1 Warren received an indecisive directive from the army commander: "Would not time be gained by sending the troops by the Quaker Road? . . . If necessary, send troops by both roads and give up the rear attack." This in effect placed the ultimate burden for making the final call on Warren's shoulders.[32]

After an exceedingly difficult day, the men of the Fifteenth now faced a difficult night. They got scant rest, if any. With Winthrop's brigade leading, the Second Division moved back along the muddy woods road and across the temporary bridge constructed over the Gravelly Run tributary toward the Boydton Plank Road. At 11 P.M. Ayres received the instructions countermanding his previous orders to remain at the Plank Road and directing him instead to proceed down it to Dinwiddie Court House and report to Sheridan. "Tired out as we were," one of Winthrop's men recalled, "we reluctantly fell in line and midnight found us making another difficult night march." The journey was rough. "If there ever was a dark night it was that night. . . . It seemed literally impossible to see one's hand before one's face and we stumbled along in the darkness in a manner by no means calculated to raise our spirits."[33]

With the bridge over Gravelly Run now repaired, Ayres's division crossed soon after 2 A.M. and headed southwest toward Dinwiddie Court House, some four miles distant. About a mile short of the town, one of Sheridan's staff officers intercepted the column and directed it to countermarch nearly a mile to the Brooks Road, which ran west toward the left and rear of the Confederates confronting Sheridan. As the column approached in the early morning light, the enemy, Ayres reported, "hastily decamped" and retired to the north. Approximately a mile and a quarter from the Plank Road, the Second Division halted at the junction of the Brooks Road and the road between Dinwiddie and Five Forks.[34]

Warren remained behind to supervise Griffin's and Crawford's withdrawals, first allowing the men to rest as long as possible. At 5 A.M. on April 1, the First Division began marching southwest cross-country from the White Oak Road in the direction of the John Boisseau residence. After a cautious withdrawal in the face of the enemy, the Third Division followed. Upon crossing Gravelly Run at the front of Griffin's column around 7 A.M., Chamberlain spotted Federal cavalry approaching, with Sheridan's "weird" battle flag in the van. As soon as Chamberlain reported to him, Little Phil immediately demanded to know: "Why did you not come before? Where is Warren?" His response that Warren remained at the rear of the column elicited a dismissive comment from Sheridan: "That is where I expected to find him." Griffin's and Crawford's exhausted men halted near John Boisseau's three-quarters of a mile north of Ayres's outfit and began to prepare breakfast.[35]

As Federal infantry began to arrive, Pickett's command retired to Five Forks, a strategically important intersection of three roads with the White Oak Road, which ran east and west from the intersection. To the north, Ford's Road crossed Hatcher's Run and continued onward to the South Side Railroad, approximately three miles from the junction. The Scott Road entered from the south and extended Ford's Road. Finally, the

Dinwiddie Road ran southeast to Dinwiddie Court House via the John Boisseau intersection, were the Fifth Corps was now massed. As a gateway to the all-important South Side Railroad, Lee had directed Pickett to hold the intersection "at all hazards."[36]

To hold Five Forks, Pickett's men threw up a defensive line that ran about a mile west of the intersection and three-quarters of a mile to its east along the White Oak Road. At the eastern end of the line, a short return or "angle" of about 150 yards was constructed perpendicular to the road. Pickett posted Brig. Gen. Matthew Ransom's Tar Heel brigade on the extreme left at the angle. To his right, in order, Brig. Gen. William Wallace's, Brig. Gen. George Steuart's, Brig. Gen. William Terry's (commanded that day by Col. Joseph Mayo), and Brig. Gen. Montgomery Course's brigades extended the line. Mayo's and Course's commands sat west of Five Forks. Pickett positioned three of Pegram's guns on Course's right and another three between Mayo and Steuart at the forks. The four guns of McGregor's battery of horse artillery covered the return in rear of Ransom's men. A regiment from Munford's cavalry division and Roberts's Brigade of Rooney Lee's Division picketed the ground on Wallace's left along the White Oak Road, while the remainder of Munford's troopers stretched along the Ford Road toward Hatcher's Run. The balance of Rooney Lee's cavalry covered the extreme right beyond Course. Rosser's Division of Virginia troopers guarded the trains on Ford's Road north of Hatcher's Run.[37]

At about 9:30 A.M. Warren received a message from Webb informing him that "in the movements following your junction with General Sheridan you will be under his orders and will report to him." Warren, however, failed to report to Sheridan in person until 11 A.M. After being roughly handled the day before and given the Fifth Corps's late arrival—at least in Sheridan's estimation—Little Phil was not in the best of humor. Warren's tardiness in reporting only made matters worse. After a caustic reply by Sheridan to Warren's off-the-cuff comment about the prior day's engagements, according to Warren, "we ceased conversation." Just before noon Col. Orville B. Babcock of Grant's staff arrived at Sheridan's headquarters. "General Grant directs me to say to you," he reported, "that if in your judgment the Fifth Corps would do better under one of the division commanders, you are authorized to relieve General Warren, and order him to report to General Grant, at headquarters." Sheridan likely harbored a disdain for him rooted in the tiff between the two along the

Brock Road on the way to Spotsylvania months before, perhaps also in Warren's complaint—with which Meade and his then chief of staff Humphreys tended to agree—that the cavalry had failed in its mission to protect the infantry's flanks near Bethesda Church. Sheridan was also still pouting because Grant had denied his request that his favorite corps, the Sixth, which had served under him in the Valley, be sent and instead had dispatched the Fifth Corps. Now his mentor, Grant, had extended the aggrieved and ill-tempered Sheridan carte blanche to settle his grudge with Warren, justly or not, should he be so inclined.[38]

At 1 P.M. Sheridan ordered Warren to bring up the Fifth Corps. Warren transmitted the order to his division commanders and galloped ahead to meet with Sheridan. Little Phil explained that while Custer's division executed a feint against Pickett's right, the Fifth Corps was to assail the Rebels' left at the return. The sound of this engagement would signal Brig. Gen. Thomas Devin's cavalry division, principally dismounted and supported by one of Custer's brigades, to launch a frontal attack on the Confederate entrenchments. During this assault, Brig. Gen. Ranald Mackenzie's Army of the James cavalry division, which had slipped onto the White Oak Road about three miles east of the forks, would move west to join the fray. Sheridan's plan, if successful, would isolate Pickett's force from Lee's army by driving it westward, where it could be destroyed. Sheridan informed Warren that the enemy's left rested close to the intersection of the Gravelly Run Road with the White Oak Road. He instructed him to form his line to strike the angle of the return with his right-center, while his left engaged the enemy's left-front. Once Warren's formation crossed the White Oak Road, it would wheel to the left perpendicular to the road.[39]

Warren retraced his steps toward John Boisseau's, but about a mile before reaching the house, he turned left onto the Gravelly Run Road and headed north about a half mile. The Fifth Corps would stage its attack here by forming in the fields of the J. Moody farm, some 700–800 yards south of the White Oak Road and screened from it by a belt of woods. From Moody's, the east side of the Gravelly Run Road had woods extending to the White Oak Road, but on the west the ground was open beyond the belt of woods. The simple Gravelly Run Church was situated in a small clearing on the east side of the road about a quarter mile from its intersection with the White Oak Road near the presumed extreme left of Pickett's line. Sheridan had instructed Warren to form his corps oblique to the White Oak Road, its right advanced, with two divisions in front and the other behind the right division. This would bring the heaviest force to bear directly on the angle.⁴⁰

Marching from near John Boisseau's, Crawford's division arrived first in the Moody field, with Griffin's close behind. Crawford's troops formed near the wood line to the east of the road, and Griffin's took position in echelon to Crawford's right-rear. Ayres's division, the smallest in the corps and last to arrive, deployed near the wood line to the west of the road. Warren estimated that his 12,000 effectives stretched the corps's front over 1,000 yards. Ayres arrayed his division with the Maryland Brigade on the left, Gwyn's brigade on the right, and Winthrop's brigade in the rear in support. Winthrop deployed the heavies of the Fifteenth on the right of his front line, with the Fifth Veteran to their left. The 140th took position in rear of the Fifteenth, with the 146th on its left. As Ayres's division formed, Winthrop asked Chamberlain for a bite to eat, explaining: "We moved so suddenly I had to leave everything. I have had scarcely a mouthful today." The general rounded up what he could but recalled, "The best was poor . . . and there was not much of it." While eating their meager meal, the two men sat on a log and talked. Finished in less than ten minutes, the brigadiers rose to assume their places to lead their men into battle and bade each other what would be a final farewell.⁴¹

Around 4:15 P.M. the command "Forward!" rang out. With bayonets fixed, the massive formation lumbered ahead. After Ayres's men struggled through the ravines and rough terrain north of Moody's fields, they emerged from the band of woods and into an open field stretching about 400 yards to the White Oak Road and continuing beyond it for another 300 yards. The enemy line supposed to be to their front was nowhere to be seen. A heavy musketry and artillery fire, emanating from the wood line and underbrush bordering the western edge of the open ground, hit Ayres's outfit in the left flank as it approached the White Oak Road. Indeed, the intelligence Sheridan provided Warren had been grossly inaccurate. The left flank of Pickett's line at the return actually sat nearly three-quarters of a mile west of the intersection of the Gravelly Run and White Oak Roads. Ayres adjusted by changing front to the left. He had the Maryland Brigade face to the left and then file to the left. Ayres next threw Winthrop's brigade forward at the double-quick into the front line to the left of the Marylanders. The complex maneuver completed, the division forged ahead westward, parallel to the White Oak Road. Winthrop's heavies and Zouaves, now guiding on the White Oak Road, marched directly toward the apex at the return.[42]

With a shout of "move in lively there men, move in lively," the general pushed his brigade forward down a slight hill and through a swampy area until they observed the enemy line through the dense underbrush. Winthrop, coolly puffing on a cigar, ordered the charge. Bayonets fixed, the heavies and Zouaves surged forward. They struggled not only through a hail of lead but also through the thick underbrush and the enemy's abatis and slashing. But the cheering men pressed on, Ayres riding along shouting encouragement and waving his sword. A Rebel volley staggered the advancing line, but, a staff officer witnessing the advance recalled, "such material could suffer but a momentary check." Despite the heavy fire, "Ayres, with drawn saber, rushed forward once more with the veterans, who now behaved as if they had fallen back to get a 'good ready.'" Out of nowhere, Sheridan appeared waving his crimson-and-white battle flag. "Bullets were humming like a swarm of bees" as he rode among the advancing men, "shaking his fist, encouraging, threatening, praying, swearing, the very incarnation of battle." From the center of his brigade, Winthrop ordered the double-quick.[43]

As the attackers reached the enemy line and Winthrop spurred his horse toward the works, he reeled in his saddle, a musket ball having passed through his left lung. Col. James Grindlay of the 146th took over the brigade from the stricken general. At the head of the Fifteenth, Lieutenant Colonel Wiedrich also went down, and Major Eiche assumed command. Not losing a step, the First Brigade pressed on, swarming over the works. A brief but brutal hand-to-hand struggle ensued. Amid this melee Cpl. Augustus Kauss of Company H seized the colors of one of Ransom's Tar Heel regiments. With resistance at the intersection of the works suppressed, the heavies and Zouaves wheeled to the left and poured a withering fire into the exposed flank of the Rebel defenders. As Grindlay struggled to reorganize the brigade, a counterattack developed on their flank, catching the New Yorkers by surprise. But Grindlay rallied his men, who then drove the graycoats from their position.[44]

Ayres's men had inflicted, according to one report, an "utter and complete rout" of the enemy. Even before the Yankees reached the return, a number of Ransom's men fled while McGregor's battery limbered up and pulled out; any graycoats who remained faced death or captivity. In addition to seizing the key to Pickett's position, the First Brigade took more

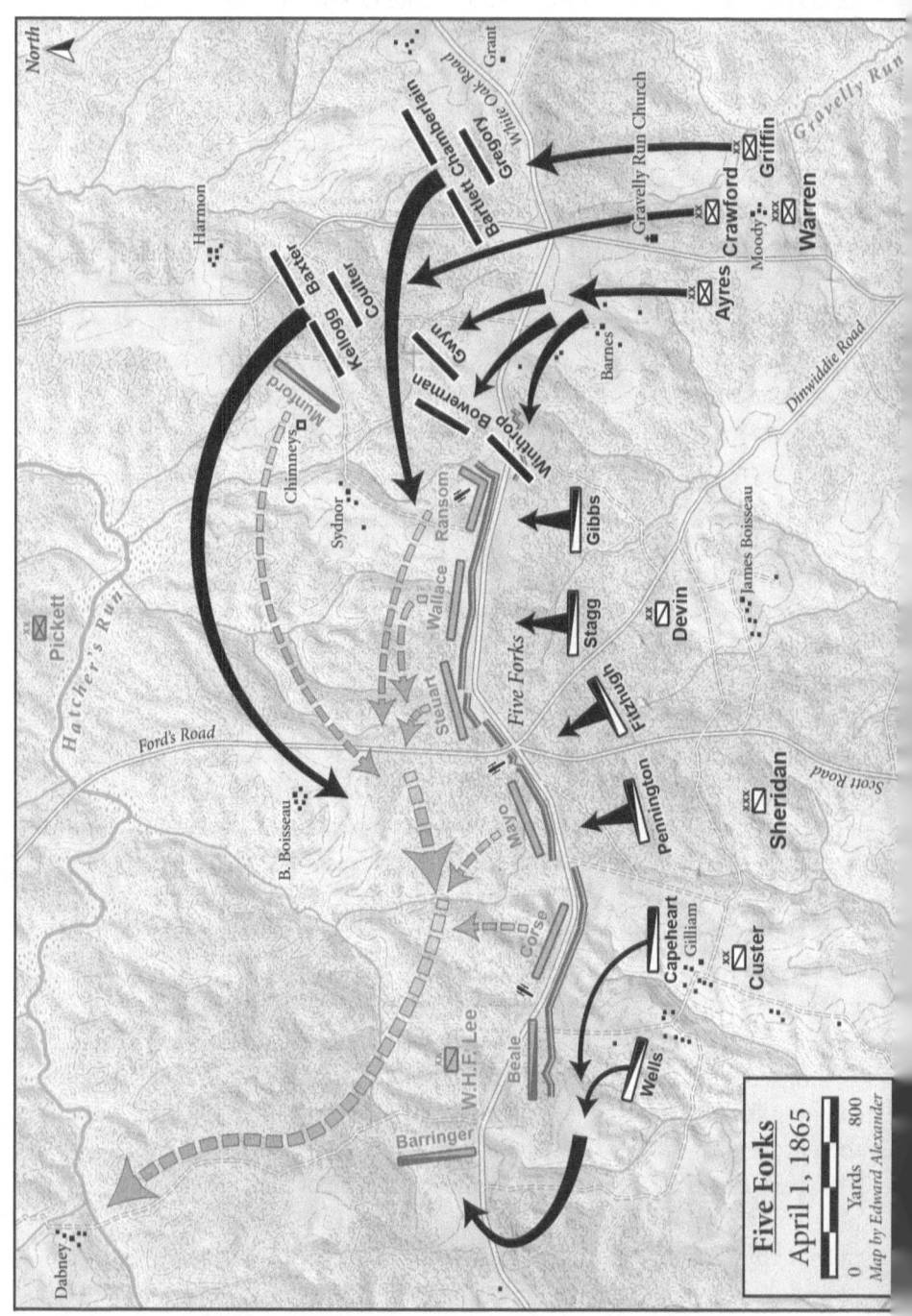

than 1,000 prisoners and four stand of colors in the struggle. Sheridan spurred his horse, Renzi, over the angle and into the midst of a line of prisoners huddling along the breastworks. Some asked, "Whar do you want us-all to go?" Sheridan pointed to the rear and began a running dialogue with the "Johnnies" as they filed out of the works: "Get right along now. Drop your guns; you'll never need them any more. You'll all be safe over there. Are they any more of you? We want every one of you fellows."[45]

Although the return had been taken, the battle was far from over. Assailed in front by Sheridan's troopers and in flank by Ayres's infantry, Pickett's defensive line began to crumble. After a brief halt to reorganize his men, Ayres began to "[push] rapidly forward" to the west down the enemy line, his men "marching steadily in line of battle, the First Brigade leading."[46]

Earlier, when the Second Division changed front, Crawford's and Griffin's divisions continued in their original line of march, mainly through woods north of the White Oak Road, opening a large gap on Ayres's right. Warren, working to resolve the problem, found the First Division near the ruins of the chimneys of an old structure in the eastern portion of the large open fields of the R. Sydnor farm. Griffin, on instructions from Warren's staffer Major Cope, had already changed direction to march his division southwest and come in on Ayres's right. Ahead, some of Steuart's Virginians, along with the remnants of Ransom's and Wallace's brigades, had hastily constructed a crude earthwork perpendicular to the original line. The Rebels offered a determined resistance, but Griffin's troops plowed ahead. Meanwhile, to Griffin's left, Ayres's outfit with the First Brigade still in the lead, continued to push west, rolling up the enemy's main line.[47]

Warren next set out to locate the wayward Third Division. After crossing the White Oak Road, Crawford had continued marching to the north for several hundred yards and then began to wheel his division toward the west. When Warren finally caught up, the division had just crossed Ford's Road north of B. Boisseau's and was north and well to the west of the other two divisions. Facing Crawford's troops to the south, Warren pushed them down Ford's Road toward Five Forks. Enemy outfits shifted to block their advance but were compelled to retire to the main line west of the forks. Warren then obliqued Crawford's division to the right, advancing southwest to cut the White Oak Road. Meanwhile, the dismounted troopers of Col. Alexander Pennington's brigade of Custer's division along with Devin's division pressed the Rebel line from below the White Oak Road. They took the intersection and Pegram's artillery minutes before Ayres's men arrived.[48]

At the White Oak Road, Crawford's division formed a line in woods at the eastern edge of the Gilliam field, with its right extending into the timber north of the road. Across the field to the west, Course's Virginians couched behind hastily constructed works. Crawford's men exchanged fire with the enemy but appeared reluctant to advance. Warren rode forward with the Fifth Corps flag and called to all within earshot to follow. With a mighty cheer, Crawford's men surged into the field and into a galling enemy fire, capturing the position as well as many of its defenders. A few yards in front of the Rebel line, Warren's white horse, Cap, was shot out from under him. As he struggled to his feet, Col. Hollon Richardson of the Seventh Wisconsin leapt between the general and the enemy, falling grievously wounded. With this final charge led by Warren, the Battle of Five Forks essentially concluded in a resounding Union victory.[49]

Unknown to Warren, as Ayres's and Griffin's men had neared Five Forks, Sheridan had ordered Griffin to assume command of the Fifth Corps. Warren received the news around 7 P.M. in a message delivered by a member of Sheridan's staff. It read: "Major-General Warren, commanding Fifth Army Corps, is relieved from duty, and will report at once for orders to Lieutenant-General Grant, commanding Armies of the United States." Warren galloped across the battlefield to appeal to Sheridan. Perhaps considering the recent victory achieved as his vindication, he beseeched him to "reconsider your determination." Sheridan would not budge. "Reconsider? Hell! I don't reconsider my determination." Without uttering a word and with bowed head, Warren rode off into the gathering darkness.[50]

The remainder of Pickett's command withdrew to the South Side Railroad and then moved east to Sutherland's Station early the next morning. There his troops united with Fitz Lee's cavalry and Bushrod Johnson's three infantry brigades from the Claiborne Road line. But the Yankees had achieved a complete and decisive victory at Five Forks, and the Confederates now could do little to prevent Sheridan from cutting the South Side Railroad. The Federals captured 4,500 of Pickett's men, thirteen stand of colors, and six guns. The Fifth Corps claimed 3,244 prisoners, eleven regimental colors, and a four-gun battery. Ayres's and Griffin's divisions took most of the prisoners. The Federals suffered losses, too, but far fewer than their enemy. The Fifth Corps's total casualties numbered 633, with 300 from Crawford's division, 208 from Ayres's, and 125 from

Griffin's. Even though Winthrop's brigade marched directly into the vortex during the opening phase of the battle, it emerged with only four killed and thirty-seven wounded. The Fifteenth left no accurate count of its wounded but suffered only one fatality from a mortal wound.[51]

During the battle, Fifth Corps artillery chief Wainwright remained near the corps hospital at Gravelly Run Church. A little over twenty minutes after the infantry advanced, he began to see squads of prisoners turning down the road toward the church. "Presently old Wiedrich comes along," he recalled, "wounded in the arm, but in charge of a good thousand rebels, as near as I could calculate." The prisoners moved along "without one particle of that sullenness which formerly characterized them under similar circumstances." The captured Johnnies joked with the Yankees: "We are coming back into the Union, boys, we are coming back into the Union." Wainwright thought "it . . . a joyful and exciting sight" that he hoped meant "that the war was about over, the great rebellion nearly quelled." After turning over his prisoners, doctors treated Wiedrich's wounded right arm. He would recover but not return to the Fifteenth, being honorably discharged with effect from June 2, 1865. The vacancy in the Fifteenth's command structure created by his discharge was never permanently filled. On August 22, 1865, Wiedrich would be breveted a colonel in the US Volunteers for gallant and meritorious service in the battles along the Weldon Railroad.[52]

As Wainwright waited by the church while the prisoners continued to file by, he soon witnessed a sight that was not so joyful. In the middle of the thousand prisoners captured by his own brigade "came poor Winthrop; dead or at least very nearly dead, quite insensible and borne on the shoulders of four of his men." Before being carried from the field, the dying general had inquired if the brigade had done well and carried the works. Informed that they had, he remarked, "Thank God for that, I am willing to die." After two painful hours at the corps hospital, Winthrop succumbed at 6:30 P.M. with his aide, Lt. James Campbell, by his side. Campbell revealed Winthrop's last moments to his family, assuring them that "he died easily and as a soldier dies." Wainwright proclaimed it "a glorious death to die, in the very moment of victory; a glorious funeral procession, the victor's body surrounded by the prisoners he had captured." He also acknowledged the tragedy, noting it "very sad to be shot down so young, so beloved, so promising, just before the fight appears to be closing, and after having gone through four years of it unscathed."[53]

Warren, too, survived the Battle of Five Forks unscathed—at least physically—but was perhaps the battle's most tragic casualty. Both officers and men bemoaned his fate. Wainwright thought that Warren's "removal at this time, and after the victory had been won, appears wrong and very cruel." Lyman agreed. "Poor Warren! A man of marked ability and valor, . . . and now cast down at the turning point of this great war. In his day he was wont (like many young men) to make severe criticisms on others, but this humiliation he did not deserve." Like many others in Winthrop's brigade, one soldier stressed, "As our corps commander, all his men learned to love and respect him, for, although his bravery and gallantry were beyond all question, he was never impetuous to the point of rashness nor was he ever guilty of needlessly sacrificing his men to gain glory for himself." Unfortunately, Gouverneur K. Warren would never recover—professionally or emotionally—from the cruel blow dealt him that day at the moment of his greatest victory. Nor would he ever know of his eventual vindication by an 1879 military court of inquiry, which rejected the four "imputations" on which Sheridan justified relieving him of command at Five Forks. Warren died three months before the findings were published. Some of his last words were reported to be, "I die a disgraced soldier."[54]

CHAPTER THIRTEEN

To Appomattox Court House

Long before dawn on April 2, 1865, the men of the Sixth Corps slipped quietly from their works and massed about midway between the opposing lines, with the forward-most outfits in the Confederate's entrenched picket line the corps had captured the day of the Fort Stedman attack. At daybreak, around 4:40 A.M., the bulk of the corps surged forward. The bluecoats braved heavy artillery and musketry fire to sweep aside the enemy pickets and swarm over the Rebel works. Several miles to the east, the Ninth Corps overcame similar obstacles to gain a lodgment for 400 yards on each side of the Jerusalem Plank Road in the enemy line opposite Fort Sedgwick. Lieutenant Colonel Lyman rejoiced that, with the achievement of these long-sought-after successes, "the fate of the Army of Northern Virginia was sealed." Although Parke's offensive bogged down in the captured enemy works, Wright exploited his breakthrough by throwing in more troops and sweeping up and down the Confederate lines.[1]

Meanwhile, Nelson Miles's Second Corps division proceeded north on the Claiborne Road toward Sutherland's Station on the South Side Railroad about ten miles west from Petersburg's center. To protect the railroad, Heth had ordered what remained of the Army of Northern Virginia's Third Corps to concentrate at the station. Brig. Gen. John R. Cooke led this defense with the remaining 1,200 men of Cooke's, MacRae's, Scales's, and McGowans's Brigades. The heavily outnumbered Confederates withstood two of Miles's attacks but not the third one, launched about 2:45 P.M. When the Confederates retreated north toward the Appomattox

River, they left 600 prisoners behind. With the South Side Railroad at last cut, south of the James River, only the Richmond and Danville Railroad remained serviceable to supply Lee's army.[2]

On the night of April 1, after a hard day of fighting, the Fifth Corps had bivouacked in the fields around Five Forks. The next morning Sheridan marched two of its divisions about two miles down the White Oak Road toward the Claiborne Road, intent on supporting Miles. Halting the column near the W. Dabney house at 11 A.M., Little Phil, ascertaining that Miles had matters there in hand, ordered the men to about-face and march back to Five Forks. Around noon the corps, still led by Griffin, headed north on Ford's Road. The First Division, now commanded by Maj. Gen. Joseph J. Bartlett, led, followed by Ayres's Second Division, and then Crawford's Third Division. After crossing Hatcher's Run the column advanced rapidly toward the South Side Railroad. Chamberlain's brigade, in the vanguard, reached the Ford's Road crossing of the South Side, where they captured a train—the last to attempt to run the gauntlet from the hard-pressed Cockade City—loaded with passengers. The refugees fleeing the city were of "a mixed company as to color, character, and capacity"; among them were Confederate officers and soldiers.[3]

At the Cox Road intersection a half mile beyond the railroad, Chamberlain's infantry faced off against 500 dismounted cavalry. His troops secured the position, while the rest of the Fifth Corps destroyed the railroad from the Ford's Road crossing east toward Sutherland's Station. They could hear Miles's assaults on the enemy at Sutherland's four miles to the east. At 3:30 P.M. Sheridan ordered Griffin to move out the Cox Road toward Sutherland's, but by the time the Fifth arrived there, the fighting had ended. The corps went into camp north of the railroad near the Williamson house at the intersection of the Namozine and River Roads. On the heels of the physical and mental demands of the preceding two days, the exhausted heavies of the Fifteenth New York had marched roughly twelve miles that day.[4]

Recognizing the gravity of the morning's rapidly evolving events, at midafternoon Lee ordered the abandonment of the Petersburg-Richmond lines beginning at 8 P.M. His objective now was to unite with Joe Johnston's forces in North Carolina to carry on the fight, employing the Richmond and Danville Railroad as the principal supply line as he moved south. Before heading to North Carolina, however, Lee's army would assemble at Amelia Court House, situated along the Richmond and Danville slightly over thirty-five miles northwest of Petersburg and about an equal distance southwest of Richmond. After issuing his withdrawal orders, Lee reluctantly telegraphed Pres. Jefferson Davis, "I think it is absolutely necessary that we should abandon our position to-night" or risk being cut off. By 11 P.M. Davis and his cabinet boarded a train headed for Danville in south-central Virginia, several miles from the North Carolina border. By the next morning, the Petersburg-Richmond lines had been evacuated.[5]

Grant correctly assumed that Lee's retiring army would march toward Danville on its way to unite with Johnston's forces via the Richmond and Danville Railroad. Instead of simply pursuing the Army of Northern Virginia, Grant wanted to intercept it at Burkeville Junction, where the South Side and the Richmond and Danville Railroads crossed, to cut its line of retreat. Grant ordered Meade to leave one division to hold Petersburg and join Sheridan and the Fifth Corps with the rest of his army to corral their old adversary once and for all. He also directed General Ord, with three divisions from his Army of the James, to join in this operation.[6]

Meanwhile, Sheridan's troopers and the Fifth Corps continued to pursue the remnants of Bushrod Johnson's infantry and Fitz Lee's cavalry westward down the Namozine Road. Elements of Rooney Lee's cavalry made a concerted stand near Namozine Church, but Custer's troopers, leading the pursuit, routed the Confederates and took many of them prisoner. Custer's vanguard next encountered several brigades of Johnson's infantry near the hamlet of Mannboro. In a running fight the bluecoats succeeded in pushing the Rebel infantry west beyond Sweathouse Creek. There, with darkness approaching, the pursuers halted for the night. The Confederates continued across Deep Creek and withdrew several miles to the northwest before bivouacking.[7]

Throughout the day the Fifth Corps troops struggled along muddy roads made worse by the passage before them of the seemingly countless horses of Sheridan's cavalry. They "saw many evidences of the haste with which the enemy were moving, in abandoned wagons and pieces of artillery . . . , scattered knapsacks, blankets, and even side arms which had been discarded in the flight." In addition they rounded up Confederate "stragglers . . . , in a pitiful condition from lack of food and the months of suffering and exposure they had endured . . . , only too willing to give themselves up for the sake of something substantial to eat." The corps crossed Sweathouse Creek and continued another three miles to Deep Creek, where the men spread out along the banks for the night. Brig.

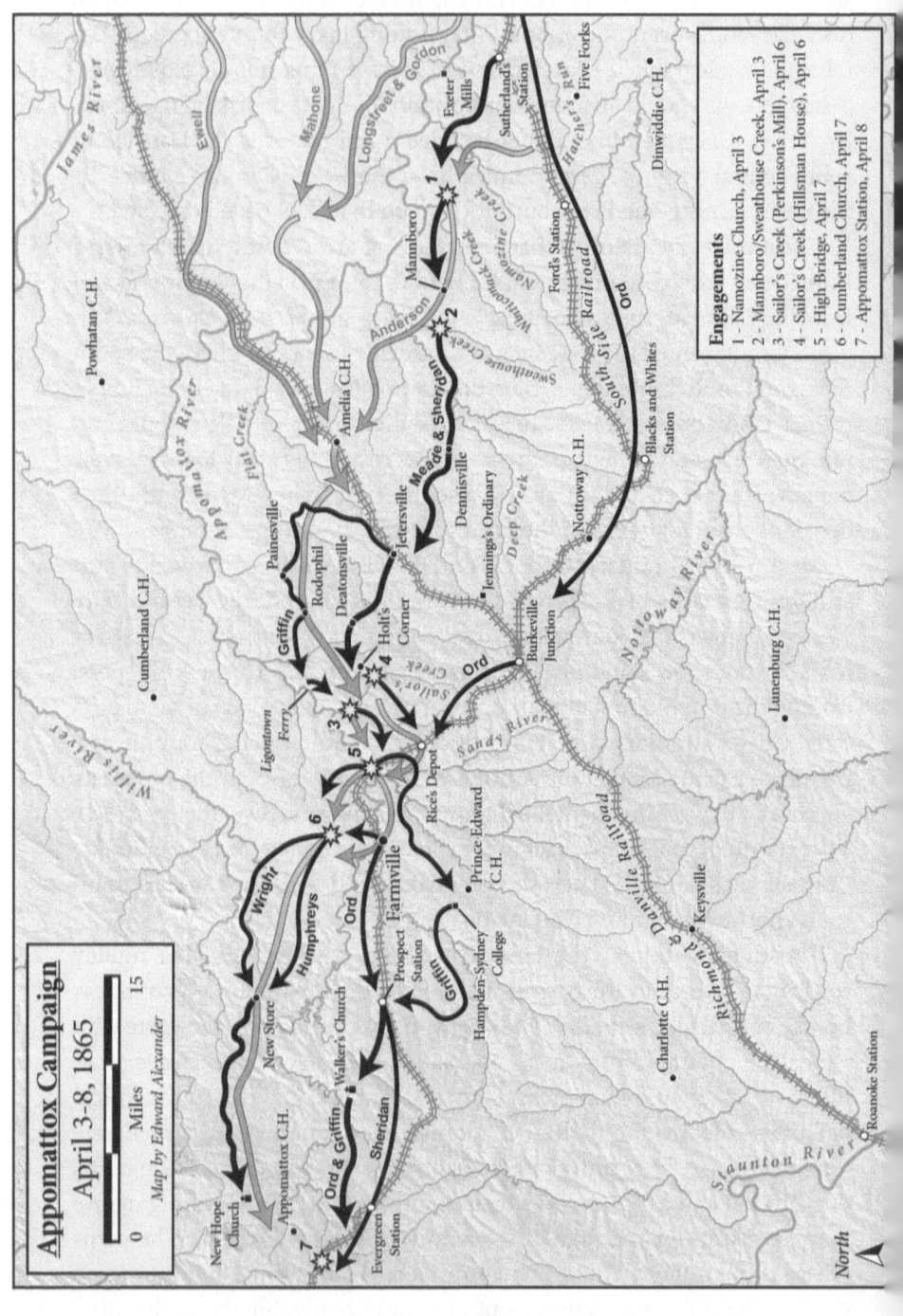

Gen. Joseph Hayes—who had been paroled in late 1864 and only this day arrived to resume command of Ayres's First Brigade—claimed his men had marched sixteen miles that day. "We were footsore and weary from our long day's march," one of his men recalled, "and while some took the opportunity to bathe in the creek the great majority were content to 'drop in their tracks' and sleep." Wainwright that evening vented his frustration at the Fifth Corps's racing throughout the day to keep pace with the cavalry. Sheridan's "Irish blood shone out today in the haphazard way he drove ahead, first on one road then on another, seeming to think that infantry and artillery could go wherever his own horse did, and a whole corps turn in an equally small space."[8]

Convinced of Lee's intent to consolidate his forces at Amelia Court House, Sheridan ordered Maj. Gen. George Crook's cavalry division to ride out at 3 A.M. the following morning, April 4, and strike the Richmond and Danville midway between Jetersville and Burkeville Junction. Crook was then to move northeast along the railroad to Jetersville, situated about midway between the junction and Amelia Court House. Sheridan also directed Griffin to march the Fifth Corps directly to Jetersville. The occupation of that town would deprive Lee of the use of the Richmond and Danville either as an avenue of supply or one of movement toward Danville. The weary soldiers of the Fifth Corps were on the road again by 5 A.M., with Crawford's division leading, followed by Bartlett's, and then Ayres's. The column marched west on the Namozine Road through Dennisville and swung to the right onto an intersecting road toward Jetersville. After a twelve-hour march, the men took a short break to eat before the entire corps set to work entrenching across the railroad about a half mile south of town. They continued their work late into the night, anxiously awaiting the arrival of the rest of the army.[9]

As the Fifth Corps approached Jetersville that afternoon, Lee's exhausted and famished legions converged on Amelia Court House, slightly more than seven miles to the northeast. The general expected to find over 300,000 rations waiting there, but the railcars contained only large quantities of ordnance supplies. To feed his troops, Lee sent wagons into the surrounding countryside to collect food from the locals, offering to pay for whatever supplies they could spare. The farmers had already been visited by Confederate commissaries and quartermasters, however, and their barns and storage sheds were nearly empty. The wagons returning to Amelia Court House the following gray and drizzly day contained little food or fodder. His army remained unfed, and Lee had lost a day to his pursuers—a loss he would later describe as "fatal."[10]

This pause provided Sheridan and the Fifth Corps much welcomed breathing room. After an anxious night huddled in their works, Griffin's troops continued to strengthen their position early in the morning of April 5. They completed the line by noon, creating what Wainwright described as "a capital [position] against an attack in front. . . . Our men built excellent works, . . . [with] guns in nicely advanced batteries . . . [to] cross a fire in front of our whole line." Delayed by Sheridan's cavalry blocking the way as well as by supply trains stuck in the muddy road, the Second Corps joined the Fifth in Jetersville about 2:30 P.M., with the Sixth Corps not far behind. The Second moved into position on the Fifth's left and the Sixth on its right, with cavalry covering the flanks. With three corps of the Army of the Potomac now grouped at Jetersville, that evening, Sheridan returned the Fifth Corps to Meade's command at his request, later reflecting, "I afterward regretted giving up the corps." As Wainwright settled in for the night, he puzzled over Lee's failure to attack earlier that day. "It seems to me queer for Lee must have known that there was only one corps of infantry here until quite late in the afternoon. I cannot understand it; for it was a grand chance for him if he has any large force with him." So confident in the strength of the Fifth Corps's work was the artillery chief that he "almost wished Lee would attack."[11]

Wainwright came closer to having his wish granted than he realized. After his unsuccessful foraging expedition, Lee had no real alternative but to move on. He started his army down the railway toward Burkeville Junction that afternoon, hoping to find one of the trains loaded with rations ordered up from Danville. When his cavalry reported the way ahead blocked, Lee decided to swing the army to the right around the Federal flank and move west toward Farmville, twenty-three miles from Jetersville, on the South Side Railroad. He hoped to resupply there, then resume the march to Danville, proceeding south to hit the Richmond and Danville Road near Keysville. Time was of the essence, and the hungry men trudged down the muddy roads throughout the night.[12]

As Lee was beginning his move, the Federals were planning to take the offensive. On the evening of the fifth, Grant endorsed Meade's idea that the Second, Fifth, and Sixth Corps advance on Amelia Court House at 6 A.M. the following morning to "attack [the enemy] vigorously if found in position." The movement began on time, with Ayres's division taking the lead in the center of the massive formation. At about 8:30 A.M., after advancing around four miles, Humphreys spotted Confederate infantry and trains moving west beyond Flat Creek. Similar reports from other sources left no doubt that Lee had evacuated Amelia Court House and was heading west. Meade ordered his army to pursue the fleeing Rebels. He instructed the Second Corps to swing left toward Deatonsville and take the center of the advance; the Fifth Corps, passing through Painesville, to move onto its right; and the Sixth Corps to peel off to its right, circle back through Jetersville, and strike westward to operate with the cavalry on the Second's left.[13]

The Fifth Corps's deployment through Painesville effectively took it out of action for the rest of that day. Heading north on the Pridesville Road from near Amelia Court House, the corps then swung west, passed through Painesville and Rodophil, and halted that night near Ligontown Ferry on the Appomattox River, having marched roughly twenty-five miles. Although meeting no significant opposition, Griffin's troops captured about 300 enemy soldiers and numerous wagons. Several miles to their south, the Second and Sixth Corps had caught up with and engaged the rear guard of the fleeing Confederates. "After three o'clock," Wainwright recounted, "we could not only hear them, but distinctly see the smoke of their guns; still we were unable to get far enough ahead to close in on them, though we pushed as hard as it was possible for the men to go."[14]

After turning west from Amelia Court House that morning, Humphreys's Second Corps, moving via Detonsville, had spent the day engaged in a sharp running fight with Gordon's Second Corps, the rear guard for the retreating Confederates. About three miles west of Deatonsville, the road forked near the Holt house. The right fork ran north, parallel to and about a mile east of Little Sailor's Creek, while the other continued across the creek toward Rice's Depot on the South Side Railroad. Anderson, with Johnson's and Pickett's Divisions, crossed the creek and deployed on high ground along the road to Rice's Depot facing south. Ewell's command—the remnants of Richmond's defensive forces—followed and formed facing northeast on a ridge along the creek across from the Hillsman farm. The wagon train headed up the right fork, with Gordon's troops protecting it. Ahead of Anderson, Longstreet's Corps had nearly reached Rice's Depot.[15]

When Humphreys arrived at the fork at Holt's about 4:30 P.M., he pursued Gordon and the train. The running contest continued for three miles, with the road "strewn with tents, baggage, cooking utensils, some ammunition, and materials of all kinds" as well as abandoned wagons, forges, and limbers. Gordon's last attempt to make a stand, just before dark near Perkinson's Mill on Sailor's Creek, met with disaster. The remnants of his corps slipped away to High Bridge during the night, leaving behind many dead and wounded, a large part of Lee's main wagon train, and approximately 1,700 men taken prisoner. As devastating as this was to the Southern cause, it was only a part of the damage inflicted by the Federals in the three distinct actions composing the Battle of Sailor's Creek.[16]

While Humphreys pursued Gordon to the north, the Sixth Corps arrived on the field, and two of Wright's divisions attacked down the gentle slopes of the Hillsman farm, across the creek, and into Ewell's command. At the same time, Crook's, Custer's, and Devin's cavalry divisions assailed Johnson's and Pickett's outfits from the south. These combined assaults shattered the Confederate line. The attack left almost all of Ewell's 3,400 men dead, wounded, or captured. Ewell and Lee's eldest son, Custis, were among the six generals captured. Losses from Johnson's and Pickett's Divisions numbered around 2,600. After nightfall, fugitive graycoats slipped west toward Rice's Depot. Upon sighting the fleeing Confederates, Lee uttered: "My God! Has the army been dissolved?"[17]

The prisoners from Sailor's Creek were transported to the sprawling Union base at City Point, where bluecoats witnessed their arrival and celebrated the success of the Federal armies in the field. At the City Point hospital, Pvt. Stephen F. Come of the Fifteenth would report sighting "7500 Rebel prisoners pass along in one squad the other day besides I have seen a good many other squads from 100 up to 3000 & more." Among them "was a good many Generals . . . , General Ewell was one of them. . . . He was the General in command of the Johnnies who fought us on the 19th of May. But he dident look mutch like fighting now for he had one leg off & was in an ambulance."[18]

While the remnants of Lee's army that had engaged at Sailor's Creek regrouped and began to make their way west, Longstreet's Corps departed Rice's Depot and marched through the night to Farmville, where, early on the morning of April 7, they discovered rations waiting. Resupplied, his men crossed a bridge to the north side of the Appomattox River. Gordon's command along with Johnson's division crossed the Appomattox at High Bridge—a 2,400-foot-long, 125-foot-high span east of Farmville that carried the South Side Railroad over the river—and reached the town later that morning. Unfortunately for his Second Corps troops, by this time the supply trains had been sent west for safety. Gordon then recrossed to the north side of the Appomattox at Farmville, and after marching north about three miles, the column halted near Cumberland Church, rendezvoused with Longstreet's First Corps and Mahone's Division, and began to entrench.[19]

Humphreys and Wright continued their pursuit of the enemy on the morning of April 7. The Second Corps crossed the Appomattox on a wagon bridge below the partially destroyed High Bridge, and two divisions headed west toward Cumberland Church. The Sixth Corps, meanwhile, arrived in Farmville at about 2 P.M. and found the bridges across the Appomattox burned and the river unfordable; the troops prepared temporary bridges but did not get across the river until dark. Humphreys reached the vicinity of Cumberland Church at about 1 P.M. and discovered the remainder of Lee's army. Unaware of the destruction of the bridges at Farmville but conscious of the opportunity presented to destroy the Rebel forces, Meade ordered the Sixth Corps to attack from the south while Humphreys hit the Southerners from the east. Assuming, incorrectly, that firing heard around 4:30 P.M. heralded Wright's anticipated push up from Farmville, Humphreys advanced and suffered considerable losses when the Confederates repulsed the attack. As night closed in, the Federals' opportunity to crush Lee at Cumberland Church slipped away.[20]

As the Second and Sixth Corps pursued Lee, the Fifth shifted from the extreme right flank of the army to its far left. Late on April 6 Meade directed Griffin to march at 5 A.M. to Farmville via Rice's Depot. Departing at the specified hour, the troops trudged south toward Sailor's Creek and crossed the prior day's battlefield near the location of Humphreys's fight with Gordon. When they reached the railroad near Rice's Depot, the men could hear brisk firing to the west. After resuming the march, the head of the column halted near High Bridge at around 9:30 A.M. There, Griffin received modified instructions from Meade to pass in rear of the Second and Sixth Corps and proceed with all dispatch to Prince Edward Court House, about five miles south of Farmville. From this point the corps could operate with Sheridan's cavalry and elements of Ord's command to dash ahead and block Lee's route toward Appomattox Station.[21]

On the way to Prince Edward Court House, the Fifth Corps marched through "country . . . [that] had seen nothing of the war . . . a fertile, productive region." The soldiers took advantage of "the well-stocked larders of what were yet thrifty plantations." The heavies of the Fifteenth already had spent most of the past two days marching but continued to trudge along until about 7:30 P.M. When the corps halted to bivouac near Hampden-Sydney College, about two miles north of Prince Edward Court House, most of the men had marched eighteen or more miles that day. Wainwright finally reached camp at 11 P.M., where he went to sleep "supperless" rather than lose a half hour's rest after "another awful hard march. . . . [N]ot so many miles passed over perhaps as yesterday, but many more hours on the road and very much more fatiguing to man and beast." Chamberlain thought the day's operation akin to "a cavalry-sweep around . . . Lee's rushing army."[22]

When the Fifth Corps resumed marching at 6 A.M. on April 8, Hayes's New Yorkers took the lead. Marching past Hampden-Sydney College on the clear, cold morning, frost sparkled in the sun. The column proceeded northwest on the road from Prince Edward Court House to Prospect Station on the South Side Railroad, where they fell in behind Ord's two remaining divisions—the third had returned to Petersburg. Elements of Sheridan's cavalry preceded Ord and pressed toward Appomattox Station. After following the road paralleling the tracks for several miles, the column veered northwest on a different road that, after passing Walker's Church, swung to the west and eventually rejoined the railroad a mile west of Evergreen Station. Their march took them through relatively flat and mostly wooded countryside, described by Wainwright as "about as sterile as any I have seen." The corps found the going slow and tedious—frequent long halts of Ord's column obstructed the road. After marching a total of approximately twenty-nine miles, the Fifth Corps halted at 2 A.M. and bivouacked near the South Side Road about three miles short of Appomattox Station.[23]

As Griffin's men engaged in their grueling march from Prince Edward Court House, Federal cavalry had swept into Appomattox Station ahead of them late in the afternoon. By 9 P.M., after several hours of jousting with enemy defenders, the troopers had captured between twenty-four and thirty guns, 150–200 supply wagons, nearly 1,000 prisoners, and three trains carrying tons of equipment and hundreds of thousands of rations for the desperate Confederate army. The captured artillery constituted the advance of Lee's forces that had pulled out from Cumberland Church during the night. Behind the artillery, Gordon's corps led the infantry and, after a long and difficult march, had gone into camp about a mile northeast of Appomattox Court House. The balance of Lee's army, strung out for ten miles along the Richmond–Lynchburg Stage Road, trudged wearily toward the village, Humphreys's corps pressing their rear guard and Wright not far behind. With Sheridan's cavalry now across Lee's intended route and the Second and Sixth Corps closing in from behind, the Federals hoped once and for all to close the vice on the Southerners. At 9:20 P.M. Sheridan predicted to Grant that if Ord and the Fifth Corps "can get up tonight we will perhaps finish the job in the morning."[24]

The night passed all too quickly for the exhausted soldiers of both sides. In the predawn hours of April 9, Gordon's infantry formed line of battle across the Lynchburg Stage Road on the western outskirts of Appomattox Court House, with Fitz Lee's cavalry on its right. About sunrise, with a shrill rebel yell piercing the morning calm, the formation began to execute a left wheel intended to sweep any Federal cavalry from the Stage Road and open that avenue of escape. The Confederates soon drove back the troopers of the lone Union cavalry brigade positioned across the road about a half mile to the west of the village. Sheridan rushed additional cavalry forward, successfully delaying the graycoats with a fighting withdrawal back toward Appomattox Station. Meanwhile, Gordon's infantry completed their maneuver and now faced south, with the Lynchburg Road to their rear; only one infantry brigade on the extreme right faced to the west. With apparently no Federal infantry yet on the field, Lee's route of escape appeared open.[25]

Bugles sounded reveille in the Fifth Corps camps long before dawn that Palm Sunday. Hungry and with only two hours' sleep, at 4 A.M. the bleary-eyed heavies of the Fifteenth fell in and, with their corps, moved rapidly toward Appomattox Court House. Ayres's division again led the column, with Hayes's brigade in the vanguard. As the day dawned bright and beautiful, around 6 A.M. Griffin's men began arriving near Sheridan's headquarters. While Ord's command advanced to support the cavalry pressed back along the Lynchburg Road, the Second Division moved at the double-quick on Ord's right. South of the village, Ayres deployed two regiments as skirmishers and formed the rest of his division in two lines of battle in a belt of woods on the ridge along which the LeGrand Road ran. With Hayes's brigade on Ayres's right, Bartlett's division took position in an open field to their right, similarly arrayed in two lines of battle and preceded by a skirmish line.[26]

With Ord's command now perpendicular to and across the Lynchburg Road, Griffin prepared to advance the Fifth Corps northeast toward the

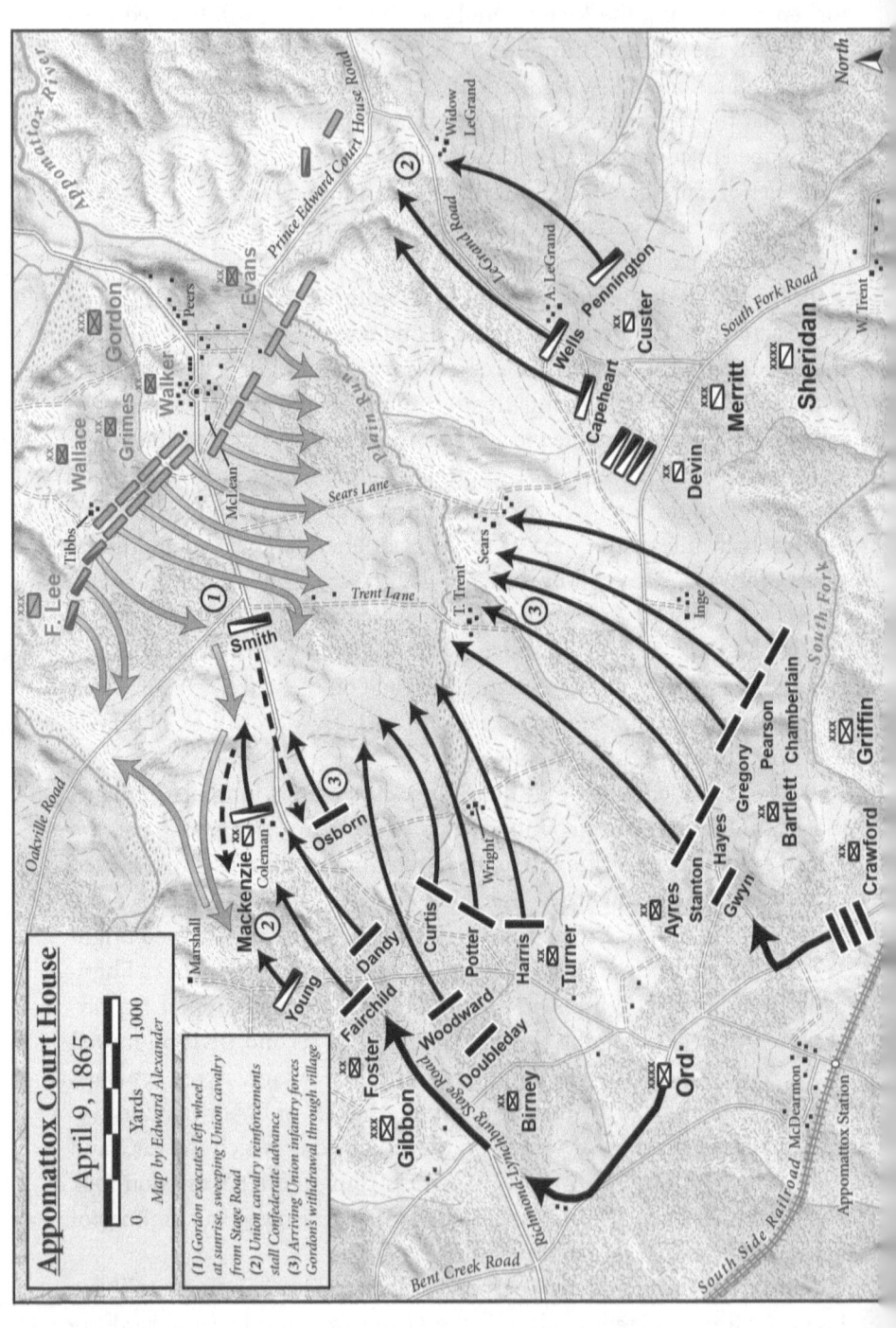

village. "While in the woods," one of Hayes's officers expected "nothing more, than, perhaps, an hours engagement between the 2d Division and the rear guard of the rebel army." He was not prepared for the grand spectacle he was about to behold. When the brigade emerged from the woods, he saw "the country was beautifully rolling. From the ridges one could see our battle formations, concentric to the right and left, for miles, four lines deep, at intervals of 150 to 200 yards, and bayonets fixed." There was little time to take in the sight as the First Brigade now began to move forward. "Our skirmish line goes out," he remembered, "slowly and surely they move up; 'forward!' comes to us, and how the bright bayonets dance and dazzle in the sunlight."[27]

Hayes's brigade charged down a slope and across a field south of Plain Run, where it was taken under fire by enemy artillery. The men pressed on. As the Federals advanced, the butternuts retreated through the village and into the valley of the Appomattox River and the high ground beyond it. A portion of the Fifth Corps's skirmish line entered the village, with the main battle lines not far behind. Now, by midmorning, the Federals virtually surrounded the Army of Northern Virginia. Ord's men blocked the Lynchburg Road to the west, the Fifth Corps and Sheridan's cavalry pressed in from the south, and the Second and Sixth Corps waited on the approach just over three miles northeast of Appomattox. The dearth of major roads to the north did not offer a favorable prospect of escape by that direction—of course, Lee's whole purpose had been to head south. Lee's army was compressed into the small bowl of the valley containing the headwaters of the Appomattox River. As Hayes's outfit prepared to attack enemy artillery positioned on a small knoll in George Peers's yard east of the courthouse, a Confederate officer with a white flag of truce appeared in the Fifth Corps's front.[28]

When orders came down for hostilities to be suspended, one of Hayes's officers remembered: "There was a moment's stillness, without breathing, and then—hurrah! hurrah!! hurrah!!!" The celebration began. "Hats and caps went up like leaves in the whirlwind, there was swinging of sabers, and cheering, and crying, and whistling, and shouting, and singing, interminably. It seemed as if the tumultuous joy should never end; and why should it?" Hayes's New Yorkers remained in line of battle for an hour, then they received the command to stack arms and "In place rest." The exhausted men stretched out on the ground, still in their line of battle, to relax. When they received news of the official surrender a little after

3 P.M., the soldiers renewed their celebration. Bugles sounded and drums rolled all along the lines. One of Hayes's Zouaves recalled: "Discipline for the moment was forgotten. A general jubilee took place." They broke their lines, and "some . . . gave expression to our feelings by running to an orchard near by and throwing our canteens, haversacks, and coats into the trees, grabbing each other and rolling over and over on the ground; some laughed, some cried, all were overjoyed." The rain that night did not dampen their spirits. With victory secured, the men of the First Brigade slept well, "lying where our battle line extended; most of us so tired we fell asleep without waiting for supper or even to make a cup of coffee."[29]

Lee and Grant each designated three commissioners "to carry into effect the stipulations" of the surrender. Grant chose Maj. Gen. John Gibbon of Ord's command, Bvt. Maj. Gen. Wesley Merritt, and Griffin, while Lee designated Longstreet, Gordon, and Brig. Gen. William N. Pendleton, his chief of artillery. The bulk of the Army of the Potomac departed the following morning, April 10. But Grant's choice of Griffin as one of his commissioners resulted in the Fifth Corps remaining at Appomattox Court House until the Confederates' surrender of their arms, artillery, and other public property, as well as the parole of Lee's soldiers, was completed. Still, the spirits of the men of the Corps remained high, despite the intermittent rain throughout the day. Clerk Tilney reveled: "What a glorious campaign this has been. . . . From the very first, success has been with us, and in twelve days from the time we moved the rebel army is no more." As the day lengthened, the men began to search for food to augment the rations issued. "The limited supply of subsistence continuing, the rations became microscopic in quantity," a man in the corps grumbled. To sate their hunger, and without official sanction, they decided that "there was nothing but the country to look to for food," although one man complained that "extensive slaughter of old cows yielded such garlicky meat that even hungry stomachs rebelled."[30]

Even with food in short supply, the bluecoats shared what they had with their former foes. Confederate soldiers began wandering into the Fifth Corps camps at daylight on April 10. "The sweet aroma of real coffee staggered the Confederates, condensed milk and sugar appalled them, and they stood aghast at just a little butter," wondering out loud, "do they give you rations like that?" When what food was available had been consumed, the men turned to trading all manner of items, including tobacco, pipes, knives, money, and even shoes. The exchanges, Chamberlain observed, flew "about as brisk as the bullets had done a few days ago." He judged that the Fifth Corps's camp looked "like a country fair, including the cattle-show." This extensive trade between the soldiers ultimately led to a ban on fraternization between the butternuts and bluecoats. Nevertheless, the Yankees continued rejoicing the end of hostilities, "celebrating the surrender with improvised fire works" that night. Wainwright took "some time before I could make out how they managed to obtain what appeared to be hundreds of roman candles." Eventually, he "discovered they were shooting rebel fuses from their muskets with small charges of powder. These exactly resembled the balls thrown out by Roman candles. The effect together with the camp fires was really beautiful."[31]

April 12, 1865, the day of the formal surrender of the arms and colors of the infantry of the Army of Northern Virginia, dawned chill and gray. The First Division, Fifth Corps formed at the sunrise hour along either side of the Lynchburg Stage Road from near its crossing over the Appomattox westward to beyond Appomattox Court House. As the Confederate column approached with Gordon at its head, the Federals in succession by regiments, from one end of the line to the other, snapped from "order arms" to "shoulder arms," saluting their former enemies. Gordon and his men returned the gesture in kind. Thus it continued throughout most of the day, as each Confederate outfit made the long, sad march to stack arms for the last time, hang their cartridge boxes on them, and fold and lay down their colors. Afterward, they were free to return to their homes.[32]

The heavies of the Fifteenth remained in Appomattox Court House for another two days. On April 14, with duties stemming from the surrender completed, the Fifth Corps received orders to march the next day for Burkeville. Ayres's division led, followed by Crawford's, and then Bartlett's. The corps artillery and the trains followed the infantry, with one regiment bringing up the rear and instructed to "drive up every straggler." The corps began its march at the relatively luxurious hour of noon, but, as one of Hayes's Zouaves remembered, "the roads were knee deep with mud and our bedraggled appearance must have resembled the retreat of a defeated army, rather than an army that had participated in a great victory." Another man judged that they "had often marched from fields of defeat with more martial display" than they did that day in the rain. Still hungry, the men trudged grimly along, hoping to come across a supply train bringing them provisions. They marched until shortly after dark. Where the corps halted for the night, "the ground was so thoroughly soaked with water it stood around our feet." The troops "had no means with which to build fires. We could only spread our blankets on the soggy ground and endeavor to sleep. The rain poured down on us all night."[33]

When they resumed marching at 6 A.M. on Sunday, April 16, the men endured a chilly rain and low clouds. Early in the afternoon the corps crossed the Appomattox and went into camp near Farmville. The skies had cleared, and the brilliant sunshine, coupled with the arrival of a supply train carrying rations, brightened their spirits. In camp they "stacked arms and laid around . . . and for the first time realized that the war was over." But a dispatch announcing Lincoln's death that arrived around 4 P.M. interrupted their sense of satisfaction and cast a gloom over the entire army. "It is impossible to describe the feeling that existed; we had all loved Lincoln so much," one soldier remembered. The entire camp went into mourning. "The color bearers of the various regiments, to drape their flags in mourning, resorted to the device of dyeing white handkerchiefs or other fabrics at command, from ink secured from the men." In addition, all officers wore a mourning badge on their left arm and their swords.[34]

At daylight on April 17, the Fifth Corps resumed its journey toward Burkeville but, nearing the town, erroneously hiked several miles up the line of the Richmond and Danville before halting near Little Sandy River after a fifteen-mile march. Griffin reported of their camp there, "The ground is good and water plenty." Recognizing the error, the next morning the corps retraced its steps and camped near Burkeville. It remained there on April 19, a day set aside to honor Lincoln as his funeral took place in Washington.[35]

The next day the Fifth Corps marched to Nottoway Court House, with instructions to relieve the Ninth Corps, which had been guarding the South Side Railroad between Burkeville and Petersburg. The First and Third Divisions then headed farther east to guard designated sections of the track, while Ayres's division covered the approximately eight-mile stretch between Burkeville and Nottoway Court House. It was immediately apparent to the men that the region had suffered greatly from the conflict. "All round about us the country gave every evidence of the ravages of war," one of Hayes's men recalled, "and it seemed as though everything edible, whether in the form of plant or animal, had been taken by the Confederates." Although this man placed the blame on the Confederates, to be sure the Federal armies moving through the area had also at times lived off this land. In addition to guarding the railroad, the Fifth

Corps, along with the Second and Sixth, was instructed by the Army of the Potomac's provost marshal to "issue rations to impoverished families living in the neighborhood of your corps upon their taking the oath of allegiance." In the vein of reconciliation, the men were also directed to assist defenseless citizens contending with the outbreak of lawlessness in the absence of local civil authority by providing such "protection as can be furnished them by division and brigade provost-marshals." While white men, possibly including a few Union and certainly some former Confederate soldiers, contributed to this problem, Chamberlain found "the negroes especially unruly.... The only notion of freedom apparently entertained by these bewildered people was to do as they pleased."[36]

Despite primary responsibility to guard the railroad as well as efforts to support local residents, other military activities resumed. During the First Brigade's dress parade on the morning of April 25, and as directed by Grant for all units in the army, Hayes read aloud an official statement regarding Lincoln's assassination. During the day, artillery salutes were fired in honor of the fallen leader. In the following days Hayes ordered routine daily drills and inspections, with each day's activities culminating in a 6 P.M. dress parade. He also required that the Fifteenth's band report to the parade ground at 8:45 A.M. each morning to lend pomp and pageantry to the ceremonial mounting of a brigade guard consisting of one sergeant and twenty men from each regiment.[37]

With the end of the war in the eastern theater, Ayres had the opportunity to reward his men for their service. On April 27 the general, responding to a request by Meade, submitted a list of men in his division who he believed deserved promotion by brevet for "meritorious services in the recent campaign." From the Fifteenth's Company C, Ayres recommended Capt. Edward Kaysing for promotion to major for distinguishing himself at Five Forks as well as Lt. George F. Schwartz for promotion to captain "for gallantry and coolness" during the same battle. He also resubmitted a list prepared the previous autumn of officers in the First Brigade worthy of promotion by brevet for distinguished service in the 1864 battles. This list included Lieutenant Colonel Wiedrich, recommended for promotion to colonel for distinguished service at the Weldon Railroad; Major Eiche, Capt. Edward Kaysing, and Capt. William D. Dickey for their service at the Weldon Railroad and Chappell house; 1st Lt. Gustav Schimmel for promotion to captain for service at the Weldon Railroad and Petersburg; and 2d Lt. John J. Diehl and 2d Lt. John Boker to first lieutenant, as well as

1st Lt. Oscar Macholz and 1st Lt. George F. Schwartz to captain, all for their service at Petersburg and Chappell house. Ayres considered failure to previously act on this earlier list an oversight, noting of the First Brigade, "These regiments are as distinguished as any regiments in the armies of the United States, or of any regiments in any armies in the world." Apparently, Meade agreed, as he approved all of Ayres's recommendations and conferred the brevets, most dated from March 1865.[38]

Ayres also worked to ensure that the Fifteenth received the credit it deserved for its role in all of the battles in which it had engaged and played a significant role. An Army of the Potomac directive issued on March 7 required each regiment to inscribe the names of the battles in which it had "borne a meritorious part" on their colors. The battles each was entitled to inscribe had been determined by boards considering the contribution of the various regiments in the battles of the army. When Meade circulated the boards' determinations in early March, the Battle of the Weldon Railroad, also known as Globe Tavern, did not appear on the Fifteenth's list. On April 28 Ayres drew army headquarters' attention to the omission: "I find that the Fifteenth New York Heavy Artillery Regiment are not credited with the battle of the Weldon Railroad in General Orders, No. 10, March 7, 1865 (the color order)." He assumed it "an oversight" because "that regiment was particularly distinguished in that battle." Therefore, the general asked for "authority to insert with a pen 'Weldon Railroad' in the list of battles of this regiment, and that it may be corrected in some order." Griffin agreed, adding, "It is well known in the corps that this regiment behaved most gallantly at the time referred to, and it is presumed the omission was accidental."[39]

With that notable addition, the official list of battles in which the Fifteenth played a "meritorious part" through March 7, 1865, reads: "Wilderness, Spotsylvania, North Anna, Totopotomoy, Bethesda Church, Weldon Railroad, Chappell House, Hatcher's Run." Moreover, in the Army of the Potomac's operations subsequent to March 7, 1865, the regiment had clearly sustained its record of meritorious service in the Battles of the White Oak Road and Five Forks as well as during the Appomattox Campaign and the final push at Appomattox Court House. The heavies of the Fifteenth could take satisfaction that in their adoptive role as infantry, they had served meritoriously in every battle of the Overland, Petersburg, and Appomattox Campaigns in which their corps at the time had participated. Derided as comprising "band box soldiers" when it joined the Army of the Potomac, and despite the nativist sentiments directed toward it by some in that army, the Fifteenth had clearly proven itself. The impressions of its senior commanders confirm that where it mattered most—conduct on the battlefield—the Fifteenth had earned a reputation as a reliable, combat-hardened infantry regiment.[40]

CHAPTER FOURTEEN

To the Defenses of Washington— and Home

The Fifteenth's duties guarding the South Side Railroad were to come to an end after only ten days, as would their just over a year of operating in the field. With the conclusion of hostilities in the East, on April 29 Grant directed the Army of the Potomac to proceed to Alexandria. The first segment of Fifth Corps's long trek north—a march to Manchester opposite Richmond on the James River—began on Monday, May 1. Ayres's Second Division, the westernmost of the corps, was on the road by 9 A.M. As his men, marching along the railroad, passed Blacks and Whites Station, Crawford's Third Division fell in behind them. After more than sixteen miles, the column halted at Wilson's Depot, the First Division's headquarters, for the night. The march resumed early the next morning, with Bartlett's First Division taking the lead. By 2 P.M., after a twenty-three-mile hike, the entire corps halted for the night west of Petersburg near Sutherland's Station. Corps clerk Robert Tilney rightly observed, "you may conclude that we marched pretty fast."[1]

The men of the Fifth Corps desired to salute Warren, their former commander and now military commander of Petersburg, as they marched through the city, and Griffin arranged a review. Flags flying and bands playing, at 11:30 A.M. on May 3, the corps marched through the Confederate works they had struggled so long to breech and into the city. Warren, his wife, and some of his staff assembled on the balcony of the Bolingbroke House to receive the honors. As each regiment passed, the men "gave cheer after cheer for our gallant former commander." Chamberlain described the moment: "Up turned the worn, bronzed faces; up went the poor old caps; out rang the cheers from manly hearts along the Fifth Corps column;—one half the numbers, old and new together, that on this very day a year ago mustered on the banks of the Rapidan, their youthful forms resplendent as the onlooking sun."[2]

The corps passed through the city, crossed the Appomattox, and then took the turnpike connecting Petersburg with Richmond. The road was both wide and in good condition, and after a relatively easy eighteen-mile march, the column halted below Drewry's Bluff for the night. Early the next morning a short trek brought the corps to the outskirts of Manchester, where it camped, the troops enjoying "a fine view of the city of Richmond." As the men rested through the following day, they were joined by the Second Corps.[3]

When the Fifth Corps resumed its march on May 6, its route took the blue-clad soldiers through Richmond. After a 6 A.M. start, the column crossed the James on the upper pontoon bridge. Proceeding through the city, the Fifth and Second Corps passed before the assembled Twenty-Fourth Corps, where Maj. Gen. Henry Halleck, now commanding the Department of Virginia, and Meade reviewed the troops. The outfits exchanged salutes, Chamberlain remembered, and the men of the Twenty-Fourth offered a "hearty greeting; quite transcending orders and regulations." One soldier recalled, "The streets and windows of houses were filled with spectators, whose sullen looks plainly told their feelings towards us." It was after noon by the time the Fifth Corps exited Richmond. A man in the First Division, near the head of the column, ruefully noted, "Soon it became evident that the time lost in Richmond was to be made up in the rapid manner in which we pushed along; it looked as if the desire of our corps commander was to reach Washington, if possible, by daybreak." The men at last went into bivouac about 10 P.M. near Hanover Court House after marching over twenty miles that day.[4]

The Fifth Corps spent the next several days on long, monotonous marches. On May 7 Ayres's division led as the column tramped through Hanover Court House, crossed the Pamunkey River on a pontoon bridge, and went into camp near Concord Church after marching approximately twelve miles. They logged sixteen miles the following day, crossing the Mattapony and bivouacking around 5 P.M. near Milford Station. May 9 saw the corps pass through Bowling Green and, after moving briskly along a turnpike much of the way, crossing the Rappahannock River below

Fredericksburg. At 4 P.M., having covered another twenty miles, the weary troops went into camp opposite the town. On the road at 5 A.M. on May 10, the Fifth crossed Potomac, Aquia, and Chopawamsic Creeks, finally settling wearily into camp near Dumfries after another twenty-mile trek.[5]

Despite having marched nearly ninety miles in five days, the Fifth Corps still had a long way to go. Although May 11 began much like the previous days, in this stretch the soldiers had to deal with poor roads and hilly terrain. Worse, that afternoon they encountered heavy rain and howling winds. As the storm struck, Chamberlain "chanced to be for that moment on the summit of a very high hill, from which I could see the whole corps winding its caravan with dromedary patience." Through the downpour he "could see the whole black column struggling on and Ayres a mile behind urging and cheering his men . . . while this ever-recurrent pulse of flame leaped along the withering column like a river of fire." The lightning made it look "as if the men had bayonets fixed, the points of light flew so sharp from the muzzles sloping above their shoulders." Lightning strikes would kill at least one man and several horses that day. Even so, the column struggled across a rain-swollen Occoquan Creek and eventually camped about 8 P.M. on soggy ground about a mile from Fairfax Station, having survived a difficult eighteen-mile march.[6]

Storms resumed as the men prepared their evening meal, putting an abrupt end to thoughts of supper. "We were flooded, blankets and everything soaked, and so we lay all night, the rain beating through the canvass in torrents; . . . the wind blew furiously, and we were drowned and frozen all night long." Tilney labeled the troops' last night in the field as "decidedly the roughest night we ever put in." Another man in the corps agreed: "It proved to be about the worst night during our term of service. Rain, mud and cold combined, causing repeated efforts in the morning to drive the stiffness from our limbs."[7]

Although the rain ceased during the night, conditions remained difficult. By 4 A.M. the wet, freezing, and exhausted men began to stir and eat breakfast before commencing the last leg of their long march. At the crest of every hill, they peered anxiously ahead in an effort to spot Washington City, with its crowning Capitol dome. When those to the rear heard cheers coming from the troops leading the column, they knew they were near. "Gaining the point from which the cheers had come," one soldier remembered, "there, in full view, it stood, its white dome reflecting the rays from the sun, backed by the blue sky in the distance, presenting a beautiful sight to our view; with hearts full of gratitude, we thanked god for the privilege of again beholding with our eyes what our arms had helped to preserve for coming ages, 'A free and united country.'" Not only had the men of the Fifth Corps who crested this final hill that bright, sunny morning contributed significantly to the preservation of the Union, unlike many thousands of others who had served alongside them, they had survived the long and bloody ordeal.[8]

After sighting the dome, the troops marched east on the Columbia Pike, crossed Four Mile Run, and encamped on its left bank on either side of the pike about five miles west of Washington. After days of continuous marching, they were delighted when informed it was "probable the corps will remain in its present camp for some days." For this extended stay, commanders strove to ensure the men established "well arranged" camps with "sinks built, and every attention paid to the police of their camps and vicinity." Settling in to their new "homes," they enjoyed full rations and regular mail delivery.[9]

While the Army of the Potomac awaited the arrival of Sherman's triumphant western armies, its troops prepared for a grand review through the streets of the capital. The Potomac Army would pass in review on Tuesday, May 23, with Sherman's forces doing the same the following day. Wainwright estimated that the eastern army would field near 80,000 men in the review. The planning and execution of the event proved almost as complex as that of a major wartime offensive. The men in Hayes's brigade polished brass and blackened leather in preparation. While most of the troops welcomed the ceremony as an opportunity for well-deserved public recognition, others would rather observe than participate. Clerk Tilney had planned to ride with the Fifth Corps headquarters staff but then realized that "they start at 4:00 A.M.,—too early for me,—and they will have to wait five hours in the city before our column moves." Instead, he decided "to start about 9:00 o'clock and go on foot." One of Hayes's men lamented "all . . . the poor boys who will fall dead in the streets, from the heat of the sun, as some of them did in Richmond the day we came through." Although it had rained and thundered incessantly for three days prior to the review, a few hours before the Fifth Corps moved out, Wainwright remembered, "the clouds broke away with a gentle northerly wind which cooled the air and dried the mud, without rendering it dusty."[10]

The men of the Fifth Corps departed their camps at 4 A.M. and were greeted by the sun as they approached the Long Bridge over the Potomac.

They marched down Maryland Avenue south of the Capitol and by 6 A.M. took their assigned position on Pennsylvania Avenue east of it. The review would take place along Pennsylvania Avenue to the west, with the reviewing stand near the White House. The participating units staged in assigned order, with the Ninth Corps leading the infantry, followed by Brig. Gen. William Dwight's division of the Nineteenth Corps. Next came the Fifth Corps, with its divisions arranged in numerical order, followed by the artillery and the Second Corps. The infantry marched in company front, twenty men abreast. At 9 A.M. the review stepped off, with Meade and his staff leading the lengthy procession along Pennsylvania Avenue. As the rear of Dwight's division began moving, General Griffin mounted his steed, and his corps began its triumphant march down the avenue. Leading the Fifteenth, Bvt. Lt. Col. Louis Eiche ordered his heavies to shoulder arms and "Forward, march!"[11]

Crowds thronged the sides of Pennsylvania Avenue, and young girls robed in white threw flowers and wreaths to the victors as they passed. A man in the corps remembered, "With steady tread we marched over the broad avenue, receiving one continued ovation." When Ayres's division approached the viewing stand, one journalist remembered that it originally had been "all regulars. Now the command is reduced to a handful and scattered almost to the winds," but "in its place are good and sturdy men." At Pres. Andrew Johnson's invitation, General Chamberlain fell out of the column to witness the pageant from the reviewing stand. Upon assuming his place, he soon spotted "a form before which the tumult of applause swells in mightier volume. It is Ayres, born soldier, self-commanding, nerve of iron, heart of gold—a man to build on." Immediately following the general and his staff came "the First Brigade: this of New York,—the superb 5th, 140th, and 146th, and the 15th Artillery, their equal in honor." Chamberlain mourned the loss of his friend, the brigade's former commander, as well as other fallen comrades: "At the head of this, on the fire-swept angle at Five Forks the high-hearted Winthrop fell. . . . It was a hard place for brigade commanders—the Fifth Corps in those 'all summer' battles—and for colonels too." Proclaiming, "so they pass, those that had come to take the place of the regulars; they pass into immortal history," Chamberlain reflected on the many brave men who had fought and died under the banner of the Second Division. He wondered if any in the exuberant crowd lining the street harbored similar feelings, musing, "Good people smiling, applauding, tossing flowers, waving handkerchiefs from your lips with vicarious suggestion—what forms do you see under that white cross, now also going its long way?"[12]

Soldiers similarly recognized a certain somber quality to the celebration. Amid the thunderous applause and accolades, they reflected on their lost comrades. One of Hayes's New Yorkers expressed what must have been in the minds of many: "In that moment of our supreme triumph those who had been with us when we marched to the front but who have been lost to us forever during the rigors of the long war were not forgotten." With mixed emotions he acknowledged this: "Mingled with the great joy which the occasion inspired was the great sorrow and regret that they could not be with us to share it. That we had survived while they had perished we had come to regard as one of those great mysteries which it was never given for man to understand." After passing the crowds and crossing Seventeenth Street, where the review ended, the men of the Fifth Corps marched west to Georgetown, crossed the Potomac on Aqueduct Bridge, and returned to their quiet camps. It was a stark contrast to the cheering crowds that had welcomed them along Pennsylvania Avenue, and while the men could not know it, this was the last time the venerable Fifth Corps would ever again assemble. It had been a long day of hard marching—a bittersweet experience for many—but the exhausted men could at least turn their thoughts to a long-awaited return to their homes.[13]

On the second evening following the review, a spontaneous candlelight display took place within the Army of the Potomac's camps. The Second Corps began the show, and, not to be outdone, the Fifth and others soon joined them. "The commissaries were soon cleared of their stocks of candles," remembered Tilney, "and soon every man had a piece stuck in the socket of his bayonet. Then they formed lines, went through the 'manual of arms' and several movements which looked very beautiful." One large party even formed a Catherine's wheel. Soon the men in the Fifth Corps began a procession, including their bands and drums corps. They visited each brigade, division, and corps commanders' headquarters. "What a splendid sight it was!" Tilney recalled. "Ten thousand men, with at least one candle each. . . . I would go a long way to see such a sight again." The celebration continued late into the night. Even without the celebratory display, at night the camps nestled among the rolling hills offered memorable sights and sounds. One Fifth Corps soldier reported, "The illuminations of camps after dark presented a picturesque appearance, the hillsides dotted with white, lit up with rays from thousands of candles, the loud cheering, shrill notes from bugle and soul-stirring fife and drum left impressions time cannot obliterate."[14]

With the war over and the Grand Review complete, the character of the First Brigade changed dramatically. Even before returning to Washington, while at Nottoway Court House, two veteran regiments, the 61st Massachusetts and the 114th Pennsylvania, had joined the brigade. Now began efforts to discharge regiments close to the end of their terms of service, including the 140th and 146th New York. On June 3 the 140th New York mustered out and began returning home. About 200 men with more lengthy terms of service remaining were transferred to the Fifth Veteran. The same day Meade directed the Fifth Veteran to report to New York City, where its men would eventually serve as prison guards on Hart's Island in Long Island Sound. With their 200 recent transfers, the Fifth departed for New York that night by train. The soldiers of the 146th and the heavies of the Fifteenth, however, remained with the First Brigade.[15]

Although their time in the service was growing short, like it or not, the men of the First Brigade were still soldiers and were still expected to perform the military evolutions soldiers typically performed. Echoing the order at Nottoway Court House two months earlier, on June 17 Hayes ordered the First Brigade to begin a daily mounting of a brigade guard with twenty privates, three corporals, one sergeant, and one officer for duty from each regiment. He ordered the brigade guard, in light marching order, to assemble at 9 A.M. on the parade ground. As in the Nottoway order, the Fifteenth's band was to report there at 8:45 A.M. to lend a martial air to the ceremony. But the Fifteenth's participation in the daily mounting of the guard would be short lived.[16]

On June 23 the commander of the Twenty-Second Corps, within the Department of Washington, directed the dismantling of most of the forts in the wartime defenses of Washington and the return of the restored land to its owner. Timber, tools, and any other salvageable materials were to be sold at public auction, the proceeds deposited in the US Treasury. But the order also directed that certain forts remain operational, including, south of the Potomac, Forts Lyon, Weed, Farnsworth, O'Rourke, and Ellsworth. The next day the Fifteenth Heavy transferred to Brig. Gen. Gustavus De Russy's division of the Twenty-Second Corps, in which it had served prior to departing for Brandy Station. De Russy directed the Fifteenth to relieve the First Wisconsin Heavy Artillery, whose term of service would soon expire, garrisoning Forts Lyon, Weed, Farnsworth, O'Rourke, Willard, and Ellsworth. Having garrisoned most of these forts for many months prior to joining the Army of the Potomac, the regiment's return would, in a sense, be a homecoming. Yet the heavies would also experience a parting. After many nights on far-flung fields, this would be the Fifteenth's last with the Fifth Corps. Indeed, at this juncture the days of the Fifth Corps were numbered. In less than a week, a directive from the army's adjutant general stated that effective immediately, the Army of the Potomac and the Fifth Corps, among others, "cease[d] to exist" as organizations.[17]

The men of the Fifteenth rose early on June 25. Departing at 4:30 A.M., after an easy four-mile march, the regiment, now commanded by Maj. Julius Dieckmann, relieved the garrisons of their assigned forts. The First Battalion under Eiche, comprising Companies B, C, D, G, and H, garrisoned Fort Lyon's four redoubts, with B at Fort Farnsworth, C at O'Rourke, D at Weed, and Companies G and H at Willard. Capt. Calvin Shaffer's Second Battalion, comprising Companies A, E, and F, manned Fort Lyon. Finally, Companies I, K, L, and M, composing Bvt. Maj. William Dickey's Third Battalion, occupied Fort Ellsworth. The Third Battalion also garrisoned Blockhouses 1 and 2, constructed in the summer of 1864. Blockhouse 1 sat at the southern end of the bridge over Hunting Creek, with Blockhouse 2 on Duke Street, about a half mile west of Fort Ellsworth.[18]

In a June 30 letter to his wife, Pvt. Stephen Come reported his changed situation. "We are in Fort Ellsworth & we don't see any signs of our getting paid or getting discharged." He observed that "Fort Ellsworth is pleasantly situated on a hill on the west side of Alexandria, & only about 100 rods from the city." Come apparently received good news about his back pay while in the process of writing, since near the end of his letter he announced, "we are to muster today for six months pay." He promised to send the money "as quick as I could get it."[19]

The Fifteenth remained in the familiar forts on the western and southern outskirts of Alexandria for approximately three weeks. On July 16 the regiment relocated to garrison five forts situated in an arc running from just south to west of Robert E. Lee's Arlington House on the heights overlooking Washington. Regimental headquarters was established at Fort Craig, with the regiment also occupying, moving clockwise around the arc from the southernmost, Forts Albany, Tillinghast, Cass, and Woodbury; Fort Craig sat between Albany and Tillinghast. Come, writing to his wife from Fort Albany, welcomed the move because it allowed a part-time return to his civilian occupation. "I was over to Washington on the 20th & got me some *Shoemakers* tools & some Leather so now I am a Shoe Making once more." He relished the opportunity: "I don't have any other duty to do and I get pay for my work besides." He also felt secure in that: "The officers say they will furnish me transportation for my Kit of tools if we move so I am all right on that score." It seems the paymaster did not visit the Fifteenth when Come was at Fort Ellsworth after all, but the men finally received their back pay on the day they moved to their new forts. Come immediately sent his wife $100 by express and enclosed the express receipt with his letter. As for when he might see his wife again, he could only offer, "I do not know when we will get Home but it is the general talk that all Vollunteers shall be discharged as soon as practicable."[20]

The combination of money, free time, temptations of the nearby city, and easy availability of alcohol resulted in the inevitable lapses in discipline. Near the end of July, the Fifteenth's brigade commander, Bvt. Brig. Gen. Joseph N. G. Whistler, ordered post commanders to arrest "all persons found within or near the limits of the Post engaged in selling liquors, Ale, or Lager Beer—whether from shops, wagons or on foot." Consequently, Dieckmann directed his fort commanders to prohibit "the sale of ale and cider on the Columbia Pike and on the road heading from Long Bridge to Columbia Pike," ordering daily patrols from each fort to arrest "all parties selling liquor." Not only were the purveyors of alcohol taken to task, so too were the mischievous soldiers who partook of their beverages—or for other reasons violated rules and regulations.[21]

At the direction of brigade headquarters, the Fifteenth convened a regimental court-martial in early August, with Eiche as trial officer, to try twenty-six privates and noncommissioned officers, mainly for absence without leave, although the only sergeant in the group faced a charge of disobedience to orders. Eiche found all of the men guilty, and most were sentenced to forfeiture of either five or eight dollars in pay. In a novel sentence he required a bugler to sound all of the bugle calls at his fort for the next eight days in addition to forfeiting his pay. The harshest sentence fell upon the sergeant, probably because Eiche considered disobedience a more egregious offense than unauthorized absence, especially when committed by a senior noncommissioned officer. He fined the sergeant fifteen dollars, restricted him to his barracks for a month, and (despite being restricted to quarters) required him to turn out with his company for duty.[22]

With their days in the army winding down, some heavies began to take a lackadaisical approach to their duties and soldiering in general. In an August 2 circular, Whistler drew attention to "a laxity of zeal in the furtherance of discipline and the very great neglect in the exaction of a proper performance of guard duty." He expressed his frustration that guards had been allowed to absent themselves from their posts, "to sit down while on their beats, bear themselves in unmilitary style, and dress without rebuke." To deal with "the evil [that] has become . . . serious," the general ordered the "prompt and effectfull stoppage" of such transgressions as well as a brigade inspection for Sunday, August 6. The Fifteenth's officers took steps to address the problems cited by Whistler. Eiche ordered his company commanders "to be careful to observe that the offenses . . . complained of are not committed in their Commands" and, in preparation for the inspection, directed that arms and accoutrements be placed in "the best of order." To prevent men from deserting in order to avoid punishment for a crime with which they had been charged, Dieckmann informed company commanders he held them "strictly responsible for the safe keeping of all men in their [commands] who may be under arrest and against whom charges had been made." To keep his men occupied, the major held a regimental dress parade at 6 P.M. on August 10 in front of his Fort Craig headquarters.[23]

At the end of the July, the Fifteenth's company commanders had already begun preparing lists of the men lost from each company, including the circumstances of the man's loss—that is, whether by discharge, transfer, death, or desertion. Dieckmann instructed that "the utmost particularity will be observed in the remarks concerning them, and Date & place in every case will be given." Company commanders were to submit the lists, along with all company books and papers, to regimental headquarters by August 21. From Fort Woodbury on August 12, Private Come happily announced "some good news" to his wife. "Our Regt is ordered to be mustered out immediately and they are at work now a making out the muster out rolls." Even as the men prepared to head home, Dieckmann, in an effort "to prevent any over display of feeling or unsoldierlike conduct," reminded company commanders that "until final payment and discharge [their men] are subject to the Regulations of the Army, and the Articles of War, and that their Officers are responsible for their proper behaviour."[24]

News of the regiment's mustering out traveled quickly. On August 21 the *New York Times* reported, "The Fifteenth Regiment of Heavy Artillery,

New York Volunteers, has its muster rolls completed and will be mustered out to-day or to-morrow, and immediately leave for home." Enumerating the campaigns and battles in which it had participated, and noting that less than half of its original 2,100 soldiers would be returning from the war, the article lionized the regiment, whose "torn and tattered flags and shattered flag-staffs bear ample testimony to the desperate and bloody struggles through which it has passed" and "its gallantry in action." The next day, Tuesday, August 22, 1865, the Fifteenth New York Heavy Artillery Regiment was honorably discharged and mustered out of Federal service at its camps in Washington. Two days later the men departed for New York.[25]

Of course, many of the thousand or so men who were not returning with the regiment had previously left because their enlistments had expired and they elected not to reenlist. This was particularly the case with men from the old Third Battalion, who had signed up for three years in 1861 and whose terms expired in middle to late 1864. Furthermore, a few officers had resigned and left the regiment. And regrettably—but not unlike most other infantry regiments—some men had deserted. Nevertheless, many who so proudly marched off to Brandy Station with the Fifteenth had become casualties of war. The regiment lost two officers and 81 enlisted men killed in action, with an additional six officers and 67 men dying from wounds received in battle. Another five officers and 183 enlisted men were counted as missing in action, 63 of whom died in the hands of the enemy. Disease and other causes, including the explosion at Fort Lyon, claimed another three officers and 225 enlisted men. Finally, twenty-five officers and 464 men were wounded in action and recovered; they would carry with them for the rest of their lives scars testifying to their service and sacrifice in the Fifteenth. The aggregate of men and officers killed, wounded, and missing in action in the battles of 1864 and 1865 stood at 833, a casualty rate of over 40 percent.[26]

After months in battle and on the road, the Fifteenth Heavy arrived in New York City the evening of Friday, August 25, and quartered that night at the Battery Barracks. The next morning a delegation of veterans of the regiment, including some from the old Third Battalion, greeted the returning men, and at 9:15 A.M. the large party departed for a formal reception in their honor hosted by the German community at Liberty Gardens. The men walked to the reception, with the veterans leading the parade. Bvt. Col. Michael Wiedrich rode triumphantly behind them in a carriage, followed by the band, which throughout its service had provided martial music for ceremonial occasions as well as entertainment on many a lonely and dreary evening. Major Dieckmann and the roughly fifty officers and 980 men of the Fifteenth followed the band. The procession moved from The Battery up Broadway to Canal Street, continued several blocks east on Canal, then turned north on Bowery to Liberty Gardens. At the celebratory reception the men received "a bountiful repast." After eating quickly, they thanked their hosts and marched back to The Battery. From there they were ferried to Hart's Island, where they remained for several days for final processing, pay, and mustering out. The days of the Fifteenth had come to an end. The heavies bade each other a soldiers' farewell and departed for their homes, carrying with them memories— of times good and hard, of sights magnificent and horrific, of comrades living and dead—that would endure for the rest of their lives.[27]

CONCLUSION

The Fifteenth New York Heavy Considered

The Fifteenth's odyssey during the last two years of the Civil War had taken the regiment from the relative safety of the Washington defenses, through many of the most terrible battles of the war to be witness to the surrender of Gen. Robert E. Lee's vaunted Army of Northern Virginia, and back again. Although beginning this long journey serving as heavy artillery for which they had enlisted, for significantly more than half of this period, the men had performed service for which they did not volunteer—infantry. Upon entering into this duty at Brandy Station in March 1864, the heavies were scoffed at by many veterans in the field as "band box soldiers" and even before that, as predominantly German immigrants, were judged by many as being inept and "cowardly" soldiers. It is fitting to consider whether these preconceived notions were borne out during the slugfests in which the Army of the Potomac engaged, beginning in the Wilderness in May 1864 and ending, finally, at Appomattox Court House in April 1865.

The Fifteenth's first performance in the chaotic Battle of the Wilderness was unimpressive. Importantly, however, with experience came rapid improvement. Slightly over two weeks later, the regiment, along with other heavy artillery units, confronted some of the best outfits in the Confederate army near the Harris farm and not only held its ground but also contributed to a critical victory by preventing the Federal army's right flank from being turned. At Bethesda Church Col. J. Howard Kitching's heavies stood shoulder to shoulder with the veteran Pennsylvania

Reserves and routed Maj. Gen. Stephen Ramseur's attacking division. During the opening actions at Globe Tavern in mid-August 1864, the Fifteenth arguably saved the day by plugging the gap when the Maryland Brigade was overwhelmed by the unanticipated enemy attack; the heavies continued to perform soundly throughout that four-day battle. Their solid performance continued after being brigaded with the veteran and battle-hardened Fifth, 140th, and 146th Veteran New York infantry regiments, from the action at Globe Tavern until the end of hostilities in the theater at Appomattox Court House. The Fifteenth's heavies and their Zouave comrades not only consistently fought hard and well but also made vital contributions to Federal success on several occasions, such as at the Battles of Hatcher's Run and Five Forks.

The record demonstrates that, far from being "band box soldiers," the officers and men of the predominantly German Fifteenth New York Heavy Artillery Regiment adapted to their new role as infantry and fought courageously and effectively. The heavies earned their stripes in the crucible of combat as infantrymen and successfully responded to the requirements the service demanded of them. A similar conclusion may be drawn with respect to the other heavy artillery regiments that fought as infantry in the Army of the Potomac beginning with the Overland Campaign. Indeed, army commander Maj. Gen. George G. Meade, who had personally experienced more than his share of combat, came to regard "our heavies," as he once referred to them, including the Fifteenth, not only as reliable, hard-fighting soldiers but also among the best fighters in his army.[1]

Moreover, the Fifteenth's solid record in combat defies the nativists' very broad assertion that, as a group, Germans were poor soldiers lacking in courage. The story of the regiment speaks for itself in refuting these narrow-minded, politically oriented criticisms. The officers and men of the Fifteenth clearly did not fit the "flying Dutchmen" moniker wrongly attributed to all German regiments. In a broader context, as noted by historian Joseph Reinhart, roughly 200,000 German Americans fought for the Union during the war, with about 36,000 serving in "uniquely"—perhaps more accurately described, "predominantly"—ethnic German regiments. There is no rational basis to conclude that on the whole the performance of these German troops were any different from that of the German officers and men of the Fifteenth Heavy.[2]

Of course, such disrespect was never about truth, objectivity, or fairness. The prejudice displayed toward German American soldiers was initially driven by nativists' fears of immigrants who seemed strange and different from them. After Chancellorsville in May 1863, this was heightened by a need to assign blame for that major Union defeat to someone or something other than the failed army leadership that placed the Eleventh Corps in a positon with its flank "in the air" or the Anglo-American units that also fought there. Although this anti-German bias was clearly unfounded with regard to the quality of German American soldiers generally, this is not to imply that there did not exist a broad spectrum in terms of the personal courage and commitment of individual soldiers—men or officers—and in the combat effectiveness of their outfits. Rather, it seems far more plausible—and also more consistent with human nature—that, as suggested by historians Walter Kamphoefner and Wolfgang Helbich, "some German (and Irish and American) regiments fought well, and others did not, and that there were excellent, mediocre, and incompetent officers of all ethnic backgrounds."[3]

When the Fifteenth New York Heavy Artillery Regiment marched down Pennsylvania Avenue in the Grand Review that bright, sunny morning in May 1865, the officers and men—the vast majority of whom were recent immigrants to the United States—could rightly take pride in their service and sacrifices in the recently concluded conflict. Marching with the army's infantry, a recognition of their successful metamorphosis from heavy artillerymen, they had proven themselves in their adoptive combat role in every respect as worthy as their infantry peers to receive the accolades of the spectators lining the sidewalks or gazing from the windows or rooftops of the buildings along Pennsylvania Avenue. Whether Anglo-American or born in Germany, Ireland, or some other European country, the crowd celebrated and cheered not only the infantry but also the whole army—Sherman's armies the following day—simply as American soldiers, each of whom had made his contribution to suppressing the rebellion, preserving the Union, and ultimately putting an end to the curse of slavery.

As the Army of the Potomac and the other Civil War armies were disbanding in 1865 and the regiments preparing to return home, New York governor Reuben E. Fenton issued a declaration that was to be read to all New York troops, expressing the gratitude of the people of their state for the service of these volunteers. In it he thanked the veterans and welcomed them home: "The people will regard with jealous pride your welfare and honor, not forgetting the widow, the fatherless, and those who were dependent on the fallen hero." Fenton closed the missive with these words, which ring true today as they did then: "The fame and glory you have won for the State and the Nation shall be transmitted to our children as a most precious legacy lovingly to be cherished and reverently to be preserved."[4]

More than a century and a half after the end of the great American conflict, the Fifteenth New York Heavy Artillery Regiment, and the men who marched, fought, and died beneath its colors, endure only in memory. As Fenton urged, today it remains for us, as it did for our forbearers, to keep their memory—and the memory of their service and sacrifice—alive and to transmit those remembrances to our children and to future generations to be cherished and preserved.

Acknowledgments

As a first-time author trained as an engineer who claims no formal education as a historian, I have completed a steep learning curve in writing this book. Nearly fifteen years ago I concluded that the story of the Fifteenth New York Heavy Artillery Regiment was worthy of being told and that I needed tell it. Despite my lack of experience, many individuals willingly pitched in to educate and support me throughout this long journey, thereby enabling this project to be brought to fruition. While it is impossible to name all who assisted, it is fitting to recognize those to whom I am particularly indebted for sharing their time, talents, resources, and knowledge.

Noted historian the late Dr. Richard Sommers of Carlisle, Pennsylvania, inspired me to write this book and offered invaluable guidance in initiating my research. His colleague at the US Army War College, Dr. Christian Keller, reviewed an early draft of the manuscript and, in addition to more substantive comments, lent much welcomed encouragement to continue the project. Walton H. "Wally" Owen, former assistant director and curator of the Fort Ward Museum and Historic Site in Alexandria, Virginia, examined my chapters on the Washington defenses and not only made the resources of the museum available to advance my research but also volumes from his personal collection of rare Civil War books. Author and educator Dr. Douglas E. Clark of Alexandria expanded my minimal understanding of presses, proposals, and publishing practices. Fellow retired Coast Guard commander and a former colleague at the US Department of Transportation the late Edward H. Bonekemper III—in his own right the author of several books on Civil War subjects—reviewed my earliest efforts, providing insightful comments and suggestions on both subject matter and style.

Current or former National Park Service historians John J. Hennessy of the Fredericksburg and Spotsylvania National Military Park, Robert E. L. "Bobby" Krick of the Richmond National Battlefield Park, Jimmy Blankenship and Tracy Chernault of the Petersburg National Battlefield, and Patrick A. Schroeder of the Appomattox Court House National Historical Park introduced me to letters, articles, diaries, and similar materials in their respective collections and graciously shared their intimate knowledge of those battlefields. Bobby Krick and Patrick Schroeder intrepidly forged through my very rough early drafts of the chapters covering events that occurred in their respective locations, offering valuable suggestions for improvement. Patrick also shared over a dozen photos of soldiers in the Fifteenth from his personal collection. Retired Park Service ranger J. Michael Greenfield, currently with the staff of the Central Virginia Battlefields Trust, helped me untangle the complex action at the Harris farm. A. Wilson Greene, former president of Pamplin Historical Park and the National Museum of the Civil War Soldier in Petersburg—preeminent authority on the Petersburg Campaign—compared notes with me on some of the Fifteenth's actions in the battles around Petersburg, giving valuable feedback on the chapters relating to that nearly ten-month-long campaign.

Numerous dedicated archivists and librarians at many institutions, including but not limited to the National Archives, the New York State Library in Albany, the Library of Congress, the US Army Heritage and Education Center in Carlisle, the Buffalo and Erie County Historical Society, the Folsom Library at Rensselaer Polytechnic Institute, and the Westchester County Historical Society, courteously and professionally responded to my many requests for information, documents, or images. Special acknowledgement is due to Jim Gandy at the New York State Military Museum and Veterans Research Center in Saratoga Springs. Jim not only steered me to sources relating to the Fifteenth in their collection but also facilitated the use of several of the museum's images of officers in the regiment. I am also indebted to Roger D. Hunt for granting permission to use several images from his vast personal collection.

Author and historian Dr. Lisa Tendrich Frank reviewed the entire manuscript and proffered literally hundreds of ideas to enhance content as well as to transform my oft-times overly detailed script into a smoother, far more readable product. Similarly, Kevin Brock pored over the manuscript, applying his knowledge of the Civil War and his writing skills to considerably improve not only the text but the notes and bibliography as well. Special acknowledgement is also owed historian and cartographer Edward Alexander. Edward's personal knowledge of the campaigns and battles examined in this volume, combined with his skill as a cartographer, produced the excellent maps that bring the narrative of the odyssey of the Fifteenth to life.

Will Underwood, former director of the Kent State University Press, saw merit in this project and initiated the long process leading to the publication of this book. His successor and current director of the press, Susan Wadsworth-Booth, and Civil War Soldiers and Strategies series editor, Dr. Brian Steel Wills, continued that process, reviewing several manuscript revisions and offering valuable insights and suggestions for improvement. To them I am indebted. To Susan's colleagues at the Kent State University Press, who applied their knowledge and skills to produce this book—in particular Assistant Editor Kat Saunders, Managing Editor Mary Young, Design and Production Manager Chris Brooks, and Marketing and Sales Manager Julia Wiesenberg—I am profoundly grateful.

Finally, this book would not have seen the light of day were it not for the support of my family and friends, who graciously endured endless lectures on the Fifteenth and my progress on "the book." To those whose support and contributions I may have inadvertently failed to recognize, I extend my sincere apologies. As to any errors that may remain in this book, I assume full responsibility.

APPENDIX I

The Court-Martial of Louis Schirmer

On July 26, 1864, seven weeks after an ailing Col. Louis Schirmer departed his regiment, the War Department issued a brief but rather unusual directive to Army of the Potomac commander Maj. Gen. George Meade. It stated that "if Colonel Schirmer, 15th New York Artillery, tenders his resignation, it be not accepted, without authority from this Department." Special Commissioner of the War Department Col. Henry Steel Olcott, who specialized in investigating fraud relating to the mustering and disbursement offices in New York, had only days before informed Assistant Secretary of War Charles Dana that he was investigating allegations of a "serious nature" made against Schirmer. To guarantee that he remained subject to army jurisdiction in the interim, Olcott had recommended regarding the colonel's resignation, "if tendered, [let it] be not received."[1]

The investigation into Schirmer began with an accusation by twenty-nine-year-old Henry Lautermann. The German-born Lautermann had enlisted as a private in the Third Battalion New York Heavy Artillery in August 1862 in New York City and eventually rose to the rank of first lieutenant. Citing ill health, he resigned and was discharged at Brandy Station on April 20, 1864. A week later Lautermann wrote to Secretary of War Edwin Stanton alleging that the government "will discover a big swindle and humbug made by Colonel L. Schirmer" if they interviewed an officer from the Fifteenth, 1st Lt. John Veith, then in the army's hospital in Georgetown.[2]

Veith, also a native of Germany, enlisted in the Fifteenth in New York City on July 3, 1863, at the age of forty and mustered in as a second lieutenant in Company K. He subsequently earned promotion to first lieutenant that December. Then on April 18, 1864, while in camp at Brandy Station, Veith tendered his resignation, citing "gradually declining" health. Although Schirmer forwarded it, recommending its acceptance, the brigade surgeon had reservations. On April 26 Veith received orders to report to the army's medical director in Washington, who admitted him to the army's Seminary Hospital in Georgetown several days later.[3]

Veith did not remain in the hospital long. By the time he returned to New York City in early June—without obtaining leave from his regiment—he had met with Olcott and executed an affidavit outlining several allegations against Schirmer, most of which related to misappropriation of bounty monies through preparation of fraudulent musters. He also accused him of accepting bribes and selling government property. At the end of July, Veith found himself detained by the War Department as a witness.[4]

Olcott pursued his investigation of Schirmer throughout July, obtaining affidavits from other parties, including the Fifteenth's current adjutant, 1st Lt. Ewald Engels. On July 30 Olcott transmitted the evidence so far compiled to Assistant Secretary of War Dana, noting, "I have long had the impression that Schirmer has been guilty of dishonorable conduct, and that he is unworthy of the position he now holds in the service." Dana referred the evidence to the army's judge advocate general, Brig. Gen. Joseph Holt, to "prepare charges and specifications and bring Col. Schirmer to trial." On August 3 Olcott wrote to Holt, "I have reason to believe this man [Schirmer] is a scoundrel of the most unmitigated nature and that a mass of evidence can be collected with a little care." He suggested: "You had better recommend that the case be referred back to me. I will treat you to a spread of the D'Utassy order."[5]

Holt returned Olcott's evidence to the War Department on August 6, accompanied by two draft charges. He tentatively charged Schirmer with conduct unbecoming an officer and a gentleman and with misappropriating property of the United States. Holt acknowledged Olcott's ongoing investigation: "If the frauds now suggested are established by further proof, a still graver charge than those now presented may be preferred against [Schirmer]."[6]

As the investigations into his conduct proceeded, Schirmer remained in New York on medical leave through August. On the twenty-fourth Dana directed Maj. Gen. John Dix, commanding the Department of the East in New York, to arrest Schirmer, who, reports suggested, was "about to sail for Europe in order to avoid trial for his frauds." After his arrest two days later, the colonel was transported to Washington and confined in Carroll Prison. Schirmer complained to the army's inspector general, Col. James Hardie, "On the way to my regiment, being absent on a sick leave, I was arrested . . . two days before the expiration of my leave of absence, and since that date confined [at Carroll Prison]." Although more than a month had passed since his arrest, Schirmer noted that he was "to this day without the charges for my arrest. I have made several requests for them, also, for release from confinement on parole, from all of which I am without an answer."[7]

Receiving no response from the authorities, Schirmer hired the Washington firm of A. G. Riddle and S. Wolf as legal counsel, with prominent Republican Albert Gallatin Riddle serving as his attorney. On November 7 Riddle wrote to the secretary of war requesting parole for Schirmer, now incarcerated at the Old Capitol Prison. He argued that authorities had yet to charge the colonel and had not allowed him to meet with counsel. Riddle asserted that confinement negatively contributed to Schirmer's failing health.[8]

Schirmer, too, blamed prison conditions in part for his continually worsening health. On November 25 he wrote to the superintendent of the Old Capitol Prison: "I demand to know by what right I am held in duress. . . . It will not be pretended that I have not up to this date borne my humiliation with commendable submission, but I begin to feel that there is a point beyond which endurance ceases to be a virtue." He further complained, "My health is failing fast and I have been compelled to have recourse to medical treatment for over a month, the consequence of wounds received and diseases contracted in the service of my adopted country." He wanted to know if "this [was] the kind of treatment and . . . gratitude . . . due to one who has given 3½ years of faithful service to the country of his adoption?" Again the colonel received no answer.[9]

With Schirmer in custody, Olcott worked to promote his "spread of the D'Utassy order." The government had assigned Maj. Horace B. Burnham to prepare the charges against Schirmer and prosecute the case. To support the prosecution, Olcott gathered additional evidence from Sgt. Maj. Thomas Henry Percy Grey, who, after reporting to Fort Lyon in August 1863, had served for a time as Schirmer's clerk. A native of London, England, Grey had risen rapidly through the enlisted ranks, by May 1864 serving as regimental sergeant major of the Fifteenth Heavy. On September 24 the War Department ordered him to report to Washington, where they detained him as a witness and put him to work as a clerk in Olcott's office—a peculiar arrangement for a trial witness.[10]

Schirmer remained confined without being charged until, finally, on February 13, 1865, the Adjutant General's Office directed that he be tried by general court-martial and enumerated the charges he faced. The six charges ultimately leveled against him were "conduct to the prejudice of good order and military discipline," "conduct unbecoming an officer and a gentleman," "embezzlement . . . of money . . . belonging to enlisted men," "drunkenness on duty," "willfully causing to be destroyed arms belonging to the United States," and "knowingly making false musters of men, and willfully signing muster rolls wherein such false musters were contained." To shore up its case, the government had confiscated Schirmer's personal papers and denied him access to them. Immediately prior to the March 20 trial, the colonel at last was paroled; he remained free throughout his trial.[11]

Most of the charges against Schirmer related to the receipt and disbursement of bounties and premiums intended for men recruited into the Fifteenth. An unwritten arrangement between the colonel and officials of the City of Troy and Rensselaer County, a county that offered significant bounties to fill the state's recruiting quota, became central to the issue. This arrangement gave Rensselaer credit for all enlistees regardless of their origins. In return, each man would receive the county's $300 bounty and the regiment $100 as a premium for procuring him. Each new recruit also would receive a New York State bounty of $75, and many reenlisting veterans who previously served in New York regiments were entitled to $150 from the state. The government's investigation concluded that Schirmer credited 401 men of the Fifteenth to Rensselaer County, resulting in a county payout of approximately $151,000. Of this money, officials allegedly paid out over $26,000 to Schirmer as "premiums."[12]

Unfortunately, the two officials perhaps most essential in establishing the truth surrounding these payments were by now deceased, their deaths occurring under unusual circumstances. The first, R. A. Flood, the City of Troy's treasurer, had met with Schirmer at Fort Lyon on several occasions in early 1864 to "settle up" the payments. On the morning of March 2, reportedly while carrying a large sum of money that may have been for Schirmer, a carriage struck and killed Flood near the Alexandria railroad depot. After Flood's death, Schirmer attempted to collect money owed him by dispatching 1st Lt. Max Von Bosch to Troy. When Von Bosch reported his lack of success, Schirmer responded, "Men here apply for it every hour." He directed the lieutenant to wait in Troy for the money, declaring, "I am ruined if they do not pay without delay."[13]

In his position as the Fifteenth's regimental adjutant at the time of the alleged infractions, the second potential witness, twenty-two-year-old 1st Lt. William Bundy, played a key role in recruiting. While Schirmer had remained mainly at Fort Lyon commanding the growing regiment, Bundy managed the Fifteenth's recruiting offices in New York. In this capacity he handled large sums of money for rent, payment of the recruiting officers, and bounties. Bundy knew how the Fifteenth handled recruiting monies as well as which men were and were not actually with the regiment.[14]

Schirmer, however, became suspicious of Bundy's handling of regimental funds. In an early December 1863 letter reproduced in his "Private Letter Book"—a document the prosecution believed Schirmer fabricated in its entirety after the fact—the colonel demanded Bundy transmit "full detailed reports every day" lest "necessary changes" be made at the recruiting stations. The following day Schirmer wrote to his uncle in New York, Dr. William Schirmer, that he had heard the lieutenant was spending great sums of money. On December 15 Schirmer appointed 1st Lt. Charles Herzog as adjutant to replace Bundy. Nevertheless, in April 1864, when the colonel applied for a leave of absence from Brandy Station to proceed to New York City "to settle up and arrange old matters connected with recruiting my Regiment," it was Bundy who accompanied him. On April 26, while still on this leave of absence, Bundy died of a fall from a window of a Washington City hotel.[15]

The general court-martial of Colonel Schirmer, presided over by Brig. Gen. Henry Shaw Briggs, convened in Washington at 10 A.M. on Monday, March 20, 1865. Each charge and its supporting specifications were read aloud, with the accused pleading "not guilty" to each. The court then turned its attention to the first charge, conduct prejudicial to good order and military discipline. The majority of the forty-four supporting specifications alleged that Schirmer was responsible for the forgery of soldiers' signatures, thereby improperly receiving and appropriating either the man's state bounty, county bounty, or both. The prosecution maintained that the state or county paid bounties for eighteen men who Schirmer knew to have deserted prior to applying for payment as well as three others he knew had died. In addition, the court called nine soldiers mentioned in these specifications to testify about their signatures on documents and their receipt of bounty money.[16]

In cross-examination Riddle generally argued the fallacy of assuming that Schirmer personally signed or directed someone else to forge those names that witnesses denied signing. Two witnesses who indicated they signed the documents testified they never asked for their bounty, did not suppose Schirmer had it, and wanted no bounties. One man swore he did not sign a receipt or authorize anyone to sign it for him but that he still received his bounty. The defense suggested this man's testimony "destroys the idea of forgeries, in all the specifications" since it showed it made no difference whether a man signed a receipt or not. After all, "he got his money all the same."[17]

The testimony of another witness, Ernest Wannfried, who deserted in New York shortly after enlisting, contradicted that logic. After six weeks, Wannfried returned to the regiment and learned that the state had issued his $150 bounty check during his absence. He testified that he never signed a receipt for the bounty or authorized anyone else to do so. In fact, at Brandy Station when the soldier requested his money, Schirmer told him, "I will see what I can do, but it is better that you keep quiet and that I keep quiet." Wannfried testified that he never received the money.[18]

In the case of deceased soldiers, or when deserters could not be located, the prosecution produced various documents, including bounty checks or receipts endorsed by the man in question. They then called Sergeant Major Grey and others to help establish if the signature was that of the man in question, and if it was not, who had signed. The prosecution implied that the accused, Schirmer, signed them or had them signed by others. In response to these allegations, the defense called men from the regiment, often officers, who testified that the man concerned made the signature or mark prior to his desertion or death. The defense also argued that Adjutant Bundy had paid the men in New York prior to their death or desertion. Bundy's own death made this assertion difficult to disprove.[19]

Lt. Col. Michael Wiedrich took the stand on Saturday, March 25, to testify in connection with an accusation under the broad first charge that Schirmer had assessed officers a fee for their commissions. Wiedrich testified that as the ailing Schirmer left the field in an ambulance, the colonel gave him a list of names of officers from whom he should collect monies. Schirmer also instructed him to send it all to him in New

York. The prosecution alleged that these monies were charges levied by Schirmer for commissions, which he then "pretended" was reimbursement for his own expenses in procuring the commissions. The defense's witnesses testified that because of the delay in processing paperwork for new commissions, Schirmer, indeed, advanced money to officers traveling to Albany to expedite the process.[20]

Wiedrich was called to the stand again that afternoon to testify in connection with the charge that Schirmer was drunk on duty. The prosecution alleged that the colonel appeared "grossly drunk" during the May 19, 1864, fight at the Harris farm. A private, formerly of the Fifteenth, testified that Schirmer "appeared to be excited through the influence of liquor" that day. When the judge advocate inquired if he appeared drunk, the witness replied "between and betwixt—neither." Asked if Schirmer appeared to be able to properly discharge his duties, the man opined that the colonel "acted rashly, it made him too rash." Questioned by the prosecution if he thought Schirmer sufficiently sober to properly perform his duties that day, the witness finally answered "no."[21]

Wiedrich countered he had been with Schirmer that afternoon and did not see him drink, nor did he believe Schirmer was drunk that day. Burnham then touched upon an alleged drunken rant that afternoon. "Was he not then cursing and swearing at the damned Yankees because they would not go over and take those breastworks and saying there was not a Yankee officer in the whole Army that knew anything?" Wiedrich coolly replied, "The conversation was that those breastworks should be taken." The prosecutor continued to press about Schirmer's alleged "cursing and going on at a terrible rate, either mad or crazy, or drunk," but Wiedrich maintained his commander's sobriety. Riddle pursued this point, asking if the lieutenant colonel had heard "Schirmer on the 19th of May 1864, or any other day, impugn the character or courage of any American officer or any other class of officers or damn them." Wiedrich had not. Less than two weeks after this testimony, the government dismissed the charge of drunkenness on duty as well as—without calling a single witness to testify on the matter—the charge of willful destruction of arms belonging to the United States.[22]

Returning to the specifications enumerated under the charge of conduct prejudicial to good order and discipline, the court tackled the allegation that Schirmer appropriated premiums in the amount of $26,812.50 disbursed by Rensselaer County instead of paying them to the recruits. Schirmer and his attorney maintained that the county paid the premiums for enlisted men credited to it and were intended as a fund to defray regimental expenses. Indeed, Jeremiah Green and another Troy official testified that Rensselaer County's informal agreement with Schirmer held that the premiums be employed for the "benefit of the regiment."[23]

Larger war news then interrupted the trial. When word reached the courtroom on the morning of April 10 of "the capture of the rebel General Lee and his whole army," they adjourned for the remainder of the day to celebrate. The trial resumed for the next three days, but the court also adjourned early on April 14 for Good Friday and a day set aside for the raising of the "Old Flag over Fort Sumter." When court convened the following day, Judge Advocate Burnham announced President Lincoln's death. Out of respect, the court adjourned until Monday morning, when it immediately adjourned again until Thursday, April 20, the day following the president's funeral. These necessary delays made an already long process for Schirmer even more excruciating.[24]

When the court reconvened, it turned to the charges of conduct unbecoming an officer and a gentleman and embezzlement of money belonging to enlisted men. The first of these stemmed from Schirmer's alleged role in causing enlisted men's names to be falsely signed to bounty rolls or receipts and then drawing the bounties and appropriating them for his own use, obtaining state bounties for three deceased men and seventeen men who deserted, and causing five deserters' names to be forged on state bounty receipts and appropriating those payments for his own use. The embezzlement charge alleged Schirmer embezzled and misappropriated ten men's bounties. The evidence offered and the testimony of witnesses in support of these charges essentially mirrored that of those used for the first charge of conduct prejudicial to good order and discipline. Likewise, the defense employed arguments similar to those it used to contradict the first charge.[25]

The court then addressed the charge that Schirmer certified three false muster lists for Company K that included men allegedly known by him as not present at the time and who in fact were deserters. Following standard protocols, Schirmer had signed the certification statement on each document: "I have carefully examined this muster roll and ... have mustered and minutely inspected the company, the condition of which is found to be as expressed in my remarks hereunto annexed." The prosecution relied on testimony from Company K's Lieutenant Veith that he had no knowledge of the presence of the men in question at Fort Lyon at the time of the muster rolls' completion or any time afterward.[26]

Defense attorney Riddle countered that the documents presented were not muster rolls at all, but rather names of men purporting to be assigned to Company K entered on a standard muster sheet without any of the other columns completed. No evidence existed to show that Schirmer had ever submitted these lists to authorities in the War Department or New York. Rather, they were removed from his personal regimental papers. Further, Veith, as company officer, had signed the most recent of the documents on December 1, 1863. Consequently, Riddle claimed that Schirmer signed the commander's certification statement without question because he assumed Veith took an accurate muster.[27]

The defense called several quite notable character witnesses to testify regarding Schirmer's reputation in the army, including Maj. Gen. Franz Sigel. Sigel knew Schirmer "in his official capacity" and "was generally satisfied with his services." He considered the colonel an "energetic" officer who performed his duties "pretty well" and "had no complaints about him." When asked by Riddle if Schirmer's reputation among the officer corps was as a "man of honor," Sigel responded that "no complaints were made to me." He elaborated, "I suppose he was on good terms with them" but that fellow officers "thought he was a little harsh" in "his manner of conversation and also in regard to discipline." Riddle argued that Sigel's "'pretty well,' and 'pretty good,' to those who know General S[igel], are his superlatives of commendation when applied to his own countrymen." Burnham countered that "to my plain sense they are the cautious expressions of one who could not more explicitly commend."[28]

Other witnesses offered more glowing reviews of the accused. For example, Brig. Gen. Gustavus A. De Russy, commander of the Washington defenses south of the Potomac, testified that Schirmer's service while under his command was "very satisfactory indeed" and that his reputation was good among the officer corps. In addition, De Russy "consider[ed] him a man of honor and integrity."[29]

Maj. Gen. Henry Hunt testified that "Colonel Schirmer was a very active, intelligent officer in the different positions he filled." On Schirmer's status as a man of "honor, of honesty and of integrity," Hunt responded that he had "met him . . . at different times in the last four years, during the whole length of his service nearly and never heard it called into question."

On cross-examination Hunt recalled that some officers from the Fifteenth visited him at Christmas 1864 and alerted him to the colonel's arrest. He remembered that either Wiedrich or Maj. Julius Dieckmann called the charges against Schirmer false, noting "that some trifling fellow formerly a Lieutenant in the regiment had trumped up some charges against him to make mischief."[30]

On the morning of Friday, May 19, the prosecution rested its case. After testimony from two more witnesses, the defense also rested. Riddle requested, and the court granted, a delay until May 31 to prepare his closing arguments. When court reconvened, Riddle opened his arguments for the defense by asserting, "The accused is either a giant criminal or the Government has been gravely misled." He criticized the inordinate delay in formally charging Schirmer, which made it so that "the accused could throw no arguments in the way of the government." Such mishandling of the case left Schirmer "shut away from every body and thing." Riddle continued: "His papers were in the hands of Government officers. His clerks had become their secretaries, and the tongues of his enemies, unsilenced by his absence, were busy discoloring, distorting, and misrepresenting the accidents, and, perhaps, the misjudgments and mismanagements, incident to the sudden recruiting and organization of two thousand men." All of these issues impeded Schirmer's access to a fair trial.[31]

Riddle pointed out that it had never been suggested that the government was the "victim" of the alleged crimes and frauds. Further, if the officers and men of the regiment were the "victims" of these crimes, then after Schirmer's arrest "these injured, insulted, and betrayed men would have hailed it with a shout of deliverance, and would have overwhelmed him with their given evidence." That had not happened. Instead, none of them "ever preferred a complaint against the accused. They were not the prosecutors, nor did they stimulate a prosecution." This, instead, fell to John Veith, "a poor creature who shrunk from sharing the fortunes of his regiment, . . . slunk away to a hospital, and . . . to avoid a return to duty, stripped his craven carcass of the uniform he disgraced, and stole off a deserter to New York." Riddle charged that the lieutenant's "only hope of impunity and safety was in getting up a prosecution against his superior officer." Consequently, Veith "entered upon it promptly; and with discolorings, misrepresentations, and flagitious lies, he pursued it diligently and successfully."[32]

After systematically addressing each charge and specification, Riddle closed with a vigorous defense of his client. "We have shown in every specified offense the undoubted innocence of the accused . . . or have so clearly pointed out the gaps and wanting links in the proofs of the government, that it can in no case claim, that the accused is proven guilty." Although "all has been done that could be done, every witness and paper produced that could in any way inculpate the accused," Riddle "exult[ed] in that knowledge that the Government failed, in innumerable instances, to produce important proof; it failed to supply connecting evidence, because that evidence and those connecting links had no existence . . . because the defendant was never a criminal." He concluded: "We leave him where the law found him, clothed with its presumption of innocence, . . . that must abide upon him, until cut away shred by shred, with inexorable evidence—evidence that we now know never had an existence."[33]

The court adjourned again until June 12 to allow the prosecution to prepare its reply. When it reconvened, Judge Advocate Burnham began by acknowledging Riddle's claim that the government had not been directly defrauded, but he maintained that "the rights of the officers and soldiers for whose protection it was pledged were violated; and to redress those wrongs and punish the offender, of whatever rank or station, was the solemn duty of the government." Burnham harshly dismissed the arguments that Schirmer faithfully served the country, claiming "his body does not bear very strong evidence of his reckless daring or of his invaluable service." He further asserted that "the arm of the service upon which he entered [heavy artillery] . . . is not fraught with such an imminent danger as would have so frightened so brave a man as the 'native of Germany,' a soldier from early youth."[34]

As the defense had done, Burnham reviewed each specification of each charge, citing the testimony and evidence presented to support the accusation. He acknowledged that although he may not have proven a handful of the specifications, testimony and evidence clearly proved the government's case. "The accused and his transactions as commanding officer of the 15th N. Y. artillery are so completely covered with conduct unworthy of an officer and a gentleman, and so prejudicial to the service in the introduction of corruption and corrupting influences in the enforcement of unlawful or unjust commands, that the military law demands its vindication at [the court's] hands."[35]

The court then recessed to conduct its deliberations. Officers and men of the Fifteenth, now returned from the field and camped at Arlington Heights, had closely followed Schirmer's trial. To make their views on Schirmer known to the court, on June 13 thirty-four officers of the Fifteenth signed and submitted a testimonial expressing utmost confidence in the colonel. They attributed the success of the regiment to his "untiring energy, zeal, and self-sacrifice" as well as their colonel's concern for the welfare of both its officers and men. They argued that "not only the best interest of the Regiment would be promoted by [Schirmer's] restoration to its command but also the interest of our common country. We trust that he will without delay be restored to the command of his and our Regiment, the regiment which has ever been proud to own him as its leader" that has been "deprived of seeing his noble form at its head."[36]

At 9:00 A.M. on Monday, June 19, the court reconvened to render its verdict. It found Schirmer guilty of conduct prejudicial to good order and military discipline and of conduct unbecoming an officer. The court found him not guilty on the charges of embezzlement and misapplication of money belonging to enlisted men and held in trust, of the withdrawn charges of drunkenness on duty and destruction of government property, and of making and signing false muster rolls.[37]

Although the court acquitted Schirmer on four of the six charges leveled against him, they convicted him on two and handed down a severe sentence. In addition to being "cashiered and dishonorably dismissed" from the army, he also forfeited all pay and allowances due him, faced a $10,000 fine, and was directed to be confined at "hard labor at such place as the proper authority may direct" for three years. In addition, Schirmer was "forever disqualified from holding any office of honor, trust or profit under the Government of the United States." Olcott had indeed "treated" the prosecution "to a spread of the D'Utassy order"—and more.[38]

As he awaited the president's final action on the court's decision and sentence, Schirmer remained free on parole. After discovering that Schirmer had violated his parole and gone to New York without authority, Assistant Adjutant General E. D. Townsend instructed General Dix to arrest him and await further orders. But on July 5, before the authorities could act on the order, Olcott arrested Schirmer and confined him at Fort Lafayette in New York harbor. On August 3, 1865, the War Department published notification of the president's approval of the court's sentence and designated Fort

Warren in Boston harbor for his imprisonment. With this order, Schirmer "ceas[ed] to be an officer in the United States service."[39]

Those who considered Schirmer wronged by the harsh punishment continued to advocate on his behalf. Just over a week after notification of the president's approval was published, approximately forty officers of the Fifteenth petitioned Johnson to pardon Schirmer, citing his monumental effort in bringing a regiment of "2000 effective men" into the field as well as his loyal service to his adopted United States. An accompanying certificate by Dr. Hermann Ideler stressed Schirmer's ill health as justification for a pardon. The regimental surgeon asserted that his "health and constitution was so delicate that it requires the utmost precaution to restore him, and to prevent danger to his life."[40]

In support of this petition, Riddle and his law partner, S. Wolf, filed a seven-page brief offering "a glance at the merits of the case" to further press for a presidential pardon. They argued that the government had failed to provide proof that "Col. S. ever converted, in any legal sense of that term, a single dollar of any of these monies to his own use." They also stressed the importance of the petition by the officers of the Fifteenth, because its authors, having "thoroughly tried [Schirmer] in the crucible of war, in battle, on the march, by the camp fire, and the idleness of camp, cannot be deceived in him, nor can they now have any motive to deceive the President." Consequently, they urged Johnson to consider "the unanimous devotion of this body of brave men," which "in itself is entitled to the kind consideration of the President." They suggested that a "great misapprehension must have existed in reference to Col. Schirmer's supposed means" since he "cannot pay any part of the fine assessed upon him" or his "Counsel for his long and labored defense, and has a wife and children dependent upon him."[41]

Three prominent Republicans, active supporters of the administration from New York's German community—Andreas Willman, George F. Steinbrenner, and presidential elector A. Outenhoefer—also petitioned Johnson on Schirmer's behalf. Assuring the president that they had known Schirmer for a number of years and citing the convicted man's honorable service, they believed that because the court acquitted him of the principal charges, the sentence handed down was "very severe, especially in view of his previous good character and able services." They urged the president to take into account Schirmer's nearly yearlong pretrial imprisonment as well as the suffering these events had brought upon his family. They thereby requested that Johnson grant Schirmer "a free and unconditional pardon."[42]

Mary Jane Schirmer, "the unhappy wife of the unfortunate Col. Schirmer, recently convicted before a Court Martial," also wrote to Johnson in late August. She did not believe him guilty or "understand how, or why, he was convicted," stressing to Johnson that "to me he is a true and devoted husband, and to our children, a loving father," as well as "a gallant and able leader in battle, and ever a brave heroic soldier." She urged the president to consider that, in prison, her husband was "suffering from disease, and heart broken, in disgrace and hopeless." Finally, she pleaded with him to "restore us all to each other, and make continued life possible to him, and tolerable to me."[43]

Officials released Schirmer from Fort Lafayette on September 9, 1865, but only for transfer to Fort Warren. He arrived there the next day and began serving his long sentence. Yet Schirmer's time at Fort Warren would be unexpectedly brief. Whether the petitions for pardon bore fruit, owing to his declining health, or perhaps both, he was released on December 7. What became of Schirmer afterward is unknown. No further definitive record of him residing—or even dying—in the United States has been uncovered. With his career and reputation in ruins, it is likely that Louis Schirmer and his family returned to his native Germany.[44]

APPENDIX 2

Faces of the Fifteenth

All photos are courtesy of the Patrick A. Schroeder Collection.

Lt. John J. Diehl

Sgt. Henry S. France

1st Sgt. Alexander Hunt

Sgt. Samuel Biggin and Robert Deppa

Cpl. George W. Williams

Robert S. Beecroft

Lt. Joseph M. Dickey

Joseph H. Bush

George V. Rediker

John St. Laird

Henry E. Wright and Sylvannus Cherry

Unidentified 2nd Lt.

Unidentified

Unidentified

Unidentified

Notes

ABBREVIATIONS

In citing works in the notes, short titles have generally been used. Works frequently cited have been identified by the following abbreviations:

15NYHA	Fifteenth New York Heavy Artillery Regiment
ACHNHP	Appomattox Court House National Historic Park, Appomattox, VA
B&L	Robert U. Johnson and Clarence C. Buel, eds., *Battles and Leaders of the Civil War*, 4 vols. (New York: Century, 1887–88)
BECHS	Buffalo and Erie County Historical Society, Buffalo, NY
CSR	Compiled Military Service Records
FSNMP	Fredericksburg and Spotsylvania National Military Park, Fredericksburg, VA
LC	Library of Congress, Washington, DC
NA	National Archives and Records Administration, Washington, DC
NYSL	New York State Library, Albany
OR	US War Department, *The War of the Rebellion: A Compilation of Official Records of the Union and Confederate Armies*, 130 vols. (Washington, DC: Government Printing Office, 1880–1901). Unless otherwise stated, all references are to ser. 1.
PNB	Petersburg National Battlefield Archives, Petersburg, VA
RG 94	Record Group 94, Records of the Office of the Adjutant General
RG 153	Record Group 153, Records of the Office of the Judge Advocate General (Army)
USAHEC	US Army Heritage and Education Center, Carlisle, PA
WCHS	Westchester County Historical Society, Elmsford, NY

PROLOGUE

1. Krick, *Civil War Weather in Virginia*, 101; Special Order 2, June 5, 1863, Regimental Order Book, 15NYHA Regimental Books, RG 94, NA; *OR*, 27(2):871; *New York Times*, June 11, 1863; Wills, *Inglorious Passages*, 236; Olcott, *Civil War Letters of Lewis Bissell*, 126. The five companies of the Third Battalion later merged with seven newly raised companies to form the Fifteenth New York Heavy Artillery Regiment. First Lt. Leo Kuhne of Company E was in charge of the detail processing the ammunition.

2. Krick, *Civil War Weather in Virginia*, 101; *OR*, 27(2):871; *New York Times*, June 11, 1863; Wills, *Inglorious Passages*, 236; Olcott, *Civil War Letters of Lewis Bissell*, 126;Companies A–E Descriptive Books, 15NYHA Regimental Books, RG 94, NA.

3. Olcott, *Civil War Letters of Lewis Bissell*, 127.

4. *OR*, 27(2):871; Wills, *Inglorious Passages*, 237.

5. Olcott, *Civil War Letters of Lewis Bissell*, 127.

6. Olcott, *Civil War Letters of Lewis Bissell*, 128. Company records confirm that twenty-one men died on the day of the explosion and that two men injured in the blast subsequently died in the hospital—one on June 15 and the other on June 18. Companies A–E Descriptive Books, 15NYHA Regimental Books, RG 94, NA. The victims of the accident still rest in what is now the Alexandria National Cemetery, located at the western foot of Wilkes Street in Old Town Alexandria, Virginia.

7. *OR*, 42(3):639, 642. The magazine contained 17,500 pounds of powder in barrels as well as 900 cartridges for 22-pounders, 750 cartridges for 24-pounders, 500 cartridges for 30-pounder Parrott guns, and about 200 rounds for field pieces. The logs comprising the ceiling of the magazine measured fifteen inches square and eighteen feet long and were covered by eight feet of earth.

8. Cooling and Owen, *Mr. Lincoln's Forts*, 4, 5, 7, 47, 48; Fry, "McDowell's Advance to Bull Run," in *B&L*, 1:168; Lossing, *Pictorial Field Book of the Civil War*, 1:483.

9. *OR*, 5:611, 628, 680; Cooling and Owen, *Mr. Lincoln's Forts*, 68, 69. Fort Lyon mounted ten 32-pounder guns, ten 24-pounder guns, seven 6-pounder guns, two 10-inch mortars, and four 24-pounder Coehorn mortars.

10. *OR*, 5:611, 628, 681; Cooling and Owen, *Mr. Lincoln's Forts*, 123, 129.

11. *OR*, 19(2):391, 392, 25(2):179, 27(3):596.

12. *OR*, 21:905; Cooling and Owen, *Mr. Lincoln's Forts*, 58–66.

13. *OR*, 29(2):154; Cooling and Owen, *Mr. Lincoln's Forts*, 64, 65. Fort Weed was armed with three 24-pounder guns, two 12-pounder howitzers, and six 30-pounder Parrotts. Fort Farnsworth mounted four 24-pounder guns, two 12-pounder howitzers, and four 4.5-inch Ordnance Rifles.

14. *OR*, 29(2):154; Cooling and Owen, *Mr. Lincoln's Forts*, 59, 60, 63. Fort O'Rourke's armament consisted of two 8-inch seacoast howitzers, one

24-pounder gun, two 12-pounder howitzers, and six 20-pounder Parrotts. Fort Willard mounted two 24-pounder siege guns, two 12-pounder howitzers, four 4.5-inch Ordnance Rifles, four 6-pounder guns, two 10-inch siege mortars, and two 24-pounder Coehorn mortars.

15. *OR*, 2:768–69; Kamphoefner and Helbich, *Germans in the Civil War*, 20; Reinhart, *German Hurrah!*, 1; Keller, *Chancellorsville and the Germans*, 11, 12; "Dedication of Monument, 41st Regiment Infantry, 'De Kalb Regiment,' July 3, 1893: Historical Sketch," in New York Monuments Commission, *Final Report on the Battlefield of Gettysburg*, 304.

16. Phisterer, *New York in the War of the Rebellion*, 2:1498; CSR, Adam Senges, RG 94, NA; *New York Times*, Nov. 29, 1861; Records Showing Service of Military Units, RG 94, NA, M594. Companies A, B, C, and E garrisoned Fort Ethan Allen, with Company D stationed at Fort Marcy.

17. Orders and circulars issued from late 1861 to mid-1863, Companies A–E Descriptive Books and Companies A–E Order Books, 15NYHA Regimental Books, RG 94, NA; Olcott, *Civil War Letters of Lewis Bissell*, 118.

18. *OR*, 12(3):602, 710, 711; Records Showing Service of Military Units, RG 94, NA, M594.

19. Records Showing Service of Military Units, RG 94, NA, M594; *OR*, 12(3):711, 712. On September 14 General Barnard noted that Fort Lyon was a very large work requiring a garrison of 1,400 men for its defense, but at the time it was held by only "three companies" of the "Third New York Artillery Battalion, numbering between 300 and 400 men." In order to bolster that force, he wanted "to take the fourth company of this battalion from [Fort Ellsworth] and send it to Fort Lyon." *OR*, 19(2):291. Barnard never accounted for the fifth company, but the number of men he reported to be in Fort Lyon appears to coincide approximately with the aggregate strength of the battalion at that time—estimated only a few days earlier to be "about 300 strong"—less the contingent at Fort Ellsworth. *OR*, 12(2):711. Benjamin Cooling and Walton Owen report that the part of Company E garrisoning Ellsworth departed there on September 15. *Mr. Lincoln's Forts*, 51.

20. Olcott, *Civil War Letters of Louis Bissell*, 122, 133, 134.

21. Olcott, *Civil War Letters of Louis Bissell*, 125.

22. Olcott, *Civil War Letters of Louis Bissell*, 118, 138, 161.

23. CSR, Adam Senges, 15NYHA, RG 94, NA; CSR, Louis Schirmer, 15NYHA, RG 94, NA; Phisterer, *New York in the War of the Rebellion*, 2:1519; Lewis Schirmer, family 425, dwelling 393, free inhabitants in Ward 1, Memphis, Shelby County, TN, 1860 U. S. Census, digital image, Ancestry.com, http://www.ancestry.com (subscription required); Riddle, *Argument for the Defense*, 6.

24. Olcott, *Civil War Letters of Lewis Bissell*, 160, 167.

INTRODUCTION

1. As many as twelve other heavy artillery regiments served as infantry in the Army of the Potomac from the Overland Campaign to the end of the war. For an informative essay on immigrant soldiers in the Union army, why and from where they came, the reasons they fought, and their assimilation into American society after the war, see Keating, "Immigrants in the Union Army," https://www.essentialcivilwarcurriculum.com/immigrants-in-the-union-army.html. For a more in-depth treatment of the immigrant experience during the Civil War as soldier or civilian, see Keller, *Chancellorsville and the Germans*; Reinhart, *German Hurrah!*; Alison Clark Efford, *German Immigrants, Race, and Citizenship in the Civil War Era* (New York: Cambridge Univ. Press, 2013); Kamphoefner and Helbich, *Germans in the Civil War*; Stephen Engle, *Yankee Dutchman: The Life of Franz Sigel* (Fayetteville: Univ. of Arkansas Press, 1993); and Susannah J. Ural, ed., *Civil War Citizens: Race, Ethnicity, and Identity in America's Bloodiest Conflict* (New York: New York Univ. Press, 2010).

2. Companies A–M Descriptive Books, 15NYHA Regimental Books, RG 94, NA; Phisterer, *New York in the War of the Rebellion*, 2:1499; Reinhart, *German Hurrah!*, 12, 14; Kamphoefner and Helbich, *Germans in the Civil War*, 21, 22.

3. Keller, *Chancellorsville and the Germans*, 10, 24, 25; Kamphoefner and Helbich, *Germans in the Civil War*, 7, 13, 20; Reinhart, *German Hurrah!*, 1, 10, 11; "Dedication of Monument, 41st Regiment Infantry, 'De Kalb Regiment,' July 3, 1893: Historical Sketch," in New York Monuments Commission, *Final Report on the Battlefield of Gettysburg*, 304. It would not be until the close of the Franco-Prussian War in early 1871 that these German states would be unified into the German Empire.

4. Keller, *Chancellorsville and the Germans*, 56, 78, 80, 87, 88, 92; Reinhart, *German Hurrah!*, 15, 17; Kamphoefner and Helbich, *Germans in the Civil War*, 23–25.

5. Agassiz, *Meade's Headquarters*, 130, 131. At least one other predominantly German regiment, the 98th Pennsylvania Infantry, also served in the Army of the Potomac at the time.

6. Keller, *Chancellorsville and the Germans*, 10–12, 14, 15, 163, 164; Kamphoefner and Helbich, *Germans in the Civil War*, 7, 8; Reinhart, *German Hurrah!*, 15, 16, 299–301. The Know Nothings had fertile ground in which to plant their seeds of nativism and divisiveness. Keller writes: "Americans looked with apprehension at their cities, now bulging with the foreign-born, replete with entire sections where English was not the predominant tongue, if spoken at all, and storefronts boasted signs in a foreign language. It did not take long for paranoia, fear, and, eventually, a political backlash to develop." Keller, *Chancellorsville and the Germans*, 12. He estimates that it took several decades following the war for German Americans to put the legacy of Chancellorsville behind them and to more fully embrace American society outside of their ethnic communities.

7. Nevins, *Diary of Battle*, 459.
8. *OR*, 33:721, 729. Although his action could undoubtedly be viewed as a significant breach of trust, if not of a moral contract, with the heavies, Grant clearly considered the exigencies of the service paramount.
9. The Enrollment Act of 1863, codified at 12 Stat. 731, Ch. LXXV, was enacted by the Thirty-Seventh Congress on March 3, 1863. Kamphoefner and Helbich, *Germans in the Civil War*, 21, 22.
10. Of the twelve New York heavy artillery regiments that completed organization and entered duty, four—the Sixth, Seventh, Eighth, and Ninth—were initially organized and designated as infantry. Yet within as few as two weeks and at most three months, each was redesignated as heavy artillery.
11. Reinhart, *German Hurrah!*, 302; Keller, *Chancellorsville and the Germans*, 9; Kamphoefner and Helbich, *Germans in the Civil War*, xxi.

1. THE FIFTEENTH NEW YORK HEAVY

1. *OR*, 2:768,769; CSR, Louis Schirmer, 29th New York Infantry, RG 94, NA; Phisterer, *New York in the War of the Rebellion*, 3:2066, 2074. Indeed, an article appearing in the *New York Times* on June 22, 1861, the day after Colonel von Steinwehr's command departed for Washington, reported that the regiment "numbers upwards of 800 men, fully two-thirds of whom have seen service on other fields." It added; "In one company alone there were no fewer than fifty who had served in the German and Crimean wars." Of the officers the reporter declared, "without exception, [they] are experienced and well educated soldiers."
2. *OR*, 2:315, 424, 427, 769; Phisterer, *New York in the War of the Rebellion*, 2:1562, 3:2062.
3. Phisterer, *New York in the War of the Rebellion*, 2:1562–64.
4. *OR*, 12(3):583; "The Opposing Forces in the Valley Campaigns," in *B&L*, 2:300; "The Opposing Forces at the Second Bull Run," in *B&L*, 2:497; "The Opposing Forces in the Chancellorsville Campaign," in *B&L*, 3:236; Phisterer, *New York in the War of the Rebellion*, 2:1498, 1562–64; CSR, Louis Schirmer, 15NYHA, RG 94, NA; Louis Schirmer Court-Martial Records, Case MM-2297, RG 153, NA.
5. Schirmer Court-Martial Records, RG 153, NA.
6. Schirmer Court-Martial Records, RG 153, NA; CSR, Julius Dieckmann, 15NYHA, RG 94, NA; Phisterer, *New York in the War of the Rebellion*, 2:1507.
7. CSR, Julius Dieckmann, 29th New York Infantry, RG 94, NA; CSR, Julius Dieckmann, 13th New York Independent Battery, RG 94, NA; Phisterer, *New York in the War of the Rebellion*, 2:1564, 1590, 1591, 1593, 3:2068.
8. *OR*, 12(2):304; "The Opposing Forces at the Second Bull Run," in *B&L*, 2:497; Hennessy; *Return to Bull Run*, 351; Phisterer, *New York in the War of the Rebellion*, 2:1591.

9. *OR*, 25(1):167, 635, 25(2):418; Howard, "Eleventh Corps at Chancellorsville," in *B&L*, 3:198; Sears, *Chancellorsville*, 238, 272, 275, 462.

10. CSR, Julius Dieckmann, 13th New York Independent Battery, RG 94, NA; CSR, Julius Dieckmann, 15NYHA, RG 94, NA; Phisterer, *New York in the War of the Rebellion*, 2:1500, 1509. By the time Dieckmann tendered his resignation from the Thirteenth, the newly promoted Lieutenant Colonel Schirmer had left the Eleventh Corps. The acting chief of artillery for the Eleventh Corps, Capt. Michael Wiedrich, approved and forwarded Dieckmann's resignation to the corps commander.

11. Schirmer Court-Martial Records, RG 153, NA; Companies F–M Descriptive Books, 15NYHA Regimental Books, RG 94, NA; Phisterer, *New York in the War of the Rebellion*, 2:1498, 1563.

12. Phisterer, *New York in the War of the Rebellion*, 2:1498, 1499; Company F Descriptive Book, 15NYHA Regimental Books, RG 94, NA.

13. Phisterer, *New York in the War of the Rebellion*, 2:1498, 1499; Companies G, H, and I Descriptive Books, 15NYHA Regimental Books, RG 94, NA.

14. Phisterer, *New York in the War of the Rebellion*, 2:1498–1500, 1519; Company K Descriptive Book, 15NYHA Regimental Books, RG 94, NA; CSR, Leander Schamberger, 15NYHA, RG 94, NA.

15. Phisterer, *New York in the War of the Rebellion*, 2:1498, 1519; CSR, Louis Schirmer, 15NYHA, RG 94, NA.

16. Phisterer, *New York in the War of the Rebellion*, 2:1498, 1499; Company L Descriptive Book, 15NYHA Regimental Books, RG 94, NA. Company L mustered in to Federal service on December 11, 1863.

17. Phisterer, *New York in the War of the Rebellion*, 2:1498, 1499; Company M Descriptive Book, 15NYHA Regimental Books, RG 94, NA. Company M mustered in to Federal service on January 30, 1864.

18. Belcher, "Reminiscences of the Civil War," 383.

19. Belcher, "Reminiscences of the Civil War," 383, 384.

20. "Dedication of Monument, 41st Regiment Infantry, 'De Kalb Regiment,' July 3, 1893: Historical Sketch," in New York Monuments Commission, *Final Report on the Battlefield of Gettysburg*, 304; Phisterer, *New York in the War of the Rebellion*, 2:1510; CSR, Emil Duysing, 41st New York Infantry, RG 94, NA; CSR, Emil Duysing, 15NYHA, RG 94, NA.

21. Schirmer Court-Martial Records, RG 153, NA; CSR, Michael Wiedrich, 15NYHA, RG 94, NA; *Geschicte der Deutschen im Buffalo*, 192; Phisterer, *New York in the War of the Rebellion*, 2:1210, 1522.

22. *Gesichcte der Deutschen im Buffalo*, 192; Phisterer, *New York in the War of the Rebellion*, 2:1210; CSR, Michael Wiedrich, Battery I, 1st New York Light Artillery, RG 94, NA.

23. *OR*, 12(1):664, 671, 12(2):304, 305, 25(1):646, 647; Krick, *Conquering the Valley*, 197; Hennessy, *Return to Bull Run*, 384, 386, 387, 551, 552; *Geschicte der Deutschen im Buffalo*, 192; Sears, *Chancellorsville*, 273, 277, 462, 463.

24. *OR*, 27(1):703, 749, 751, 752; Pfanz, *Gettysburg: The First Day*, 322, 323; Pfanz, *Gettysburg: Culp's Hill and Cemetery Hill*, 266–69. A monument to Battery I stands at this position on Cemetery Hill.

25. *OR*, 31(2):384–87; CSR, Michael Wiedrich, Battery I, 1st New York Light Artillery, RG 94, NA. Battery I remained in the western theater for the duration of the war.

26. *OR*, 36(1):607, 608.

27. Special Orders No. 1, June 5, 1863, Regimental Order Book, 15NYHA Regimental Books, RG 94, NA; Special Orders No. 4, June 13, 1863, Regimental Order Book, 15NYHA Regimental Books, RG 94, NA.

28. Order, Sept. 13, 1863, Regimental Order Book, 15NYHA Regimental Books, RG 94, NA; Records Showing Service of Military Units, RG 94, NA, M594; Cooling and Owen, *Mr. Lincoln's Forts*, 65–71.

29. Olcott, *Civil War Letters of Louis Bissell*, 160, 164.

30. Phisterer, *New York in the War of the Rebellion*, 1502; Orders, Oct. 9, Nov. 12, 1863, Regimental Order Book, 15NYHA Regimental Books, RG 94, NA; Order, Mar. 12, 1864, Company A Order Book, 15NYHA Regimental Books, RG 94, NA; Order, Feb. 21, 1864, Company F Order Book, 15NYHA Regimental Books, RG 94, NA.

31. For example, orders, Aug. 4, Sept. 29, 1863, Regimental Order Book, 15NYHA Regimental Books, RG 94, NA.

32. For example, orders, June 13, Oct. 3, 17, Nov. 27, 1863, Jan. 8, Feb. 15, 1864, Regimental Order Book, 15NYHA Regimental Books, RG 94, NA; and order, Dec. 29, 1863, Company M Order Book, 15NYHA Regimental Books, RG 94, NA.

33. Orders, Aug. 1, 15, 1863, Regimental Order Book, 15NYHA Regimental Books, RG 94, NA.

34. Orders, Nov. 13, 16, 17, 1863, Regimental Order Book, 15NYHA Regimental Books, RG 94, NA.

35. Orders, Dec. 14, 1863, Regimental Books, Regimental Order Book, 15NYHA Regimental Books, RG 94, NA.

36. Olcott, *Civil War Letters of Louis Bissell*, 122, 131, 132, 137, 142.

37. Orders, Oct. 8, Nov. 8, 26, 1863, Regimental Order Book, 15NYHA Regimental Books, RG 94, NA. No record is known to exist of the number of barracks built at Fort Lyon, nor if barracks were even built for Forts Weed, Farnsworth, or O'Rourke. But Fort Willard, with its three-company garrison, had three barracks buildings of these approximate dimensions. Cooling and Owen, *Mr. Lincoln's Forts*, 60. Quartermaster plats and other engineering drawings from the period provide numerous examples of barracks of these approximate dimensions and standard design. See, for example, *Mr. Lincoln's Forts*, 154, 155, 160, 161, 168.

38. Orders, Nov. 18, 1863, Regimental Order Book, 15NYHA Regimental Books, RG 94, NA.

39. Order, Dec. 12, 1863, Regimental Order Book, 15NYHA Regimental Books, RG 94, NA.

40. Order, Mar. 15, 1864, Regimental Order Book, 15NYHA Regimental Books, RG 94, NA.

41. Order, Feb. 22, 1864, Company F Order Book, 15NYHA Regimental Books, RG 94, NA; Davis, Perry, and Kirkley, *Atlas to Accompany the Official Records*, Plate 89, Map 1; Krick, *Civil War Weather in Virginia*, 118.

42. Regimental circular, Jan. 3, 1864, Company M Order Book, 15NYHA Regimental Books, RG 94, NA; order, Mar. 20, 1864, Company D Order Book, 15NYHA Regimental Books, RG 94, NA. Although Duysing's Third Battalion order appears in what the National Archives identifies as the Company D Order Book, the content of some of the orders therein and the process of elimination suggest that this may in fact be the Company L Order Book. Indeed, Company D was not at this time in the Third Battalion. Nevertheless, this book is hereafter cited as the Company D Order Book.

43. Schirmer Court-Martial Records, RG 153, NA.

44. Schirmer Court-Martial Records, RG 153, NA.

45. Martin Cole to "Dar Wife," Mar. 15, 1864, New York State Military Museum and Veterans Research Center, Saratoga Springs. Cole would himself die of disease on August 16, 1864, in the Confederate prison at Andersonville, Georgia.

46. Order, Mar. 3, 1864, Company F Order Book, 15NYHA Regimental Books, RG 94, NA.

47. Orders, Mar. 14, 15, 1864, Regimental Order Book, 15NYHA Regimental Books, RG 94, NA; Regimental Special Orders No. 58, Mar. 24, 1864, Company D Order Book, 15NYHA Regimental Books, RG 94, NA.

48. Order, Mar. 21, 1864, Regimental and Company B Order Books, 15NYHA Regimental Books, RG 94, NA.

49. Order, Mar. 9, 1864, Company D Order Book, 15NYHA Regimental Books, RG 94, NA.

50. Rhea, *Battle of the Wilderness*, 8, 11, 15, 22, 23, 29, 30; Humphreys, *Virginia Campaign*, 1–3.

51. Humphries, *Virginia Campaign*, 1–3; *OR*, 33:390, 391; Rhea, *Battle of the Wilderness*, 8, 11, 12, 25; Powell, *Fifth Army Corps*, 587.

52. *OR*, 33:669; Grant, *Personal Memoirs*, 357–59; Powell, *Fifth Army Corps*, 588, 589.

53. *OR*, 33:721, 729, 730.

54. Department of Washington order, Mar. 25, 1864, Company D Order Book, 15NYHA Regimental Books, RG 94, NA.

55. Order, Mar. 25, 1864, Company D Order Book, 15NYHA Regimental Books, RG 94, NA; Special Orders 62, Mar. 26, 1864, Company D Order Book, 15NYHA Regimental Books, RG 94, NA.

56. Krick, *Civil War Weather in Virginia*, 120; Belcher, "Reminiscences of the Civil War," 384.

2. INTO THE WILDERNESS

1. Belcher, "Reminiscences of the Civil War," 384.
2. Orders, Mar. 28, 29, 30, 1864, Regimental Order Book, 15NYHA Regimental Books, RG 94, NA; Lowe, *Meade's Army*, 117–19.
3. *OR*, 33:760, 761.
4. Regimental Special Orders No. 66, Mar. 31, 1864, Company A Order Book, 15NYHA Regimental Books, RG 94, NA. The reorganization of the battalions is based on analysis of regimental and battalion orders issued during the period from March 28 until the end of April 1864.
5. CSR, Louis Schirmer, 15NYHA, RG 94, NA; orders, Apr. 2–9, 1864, Regimental Order Book, 15NYHA Regimental Books, 15NYHA, RG 94, NA. The dates of departure and return of Schirmer and the duration of his absence are based upon the identity of the officer issuing the daily regimental orders during this period.
6. CSR, Louis Schirmer, 15NYHA, RG 94, NA; orders, Apr. 21–27, 1864, Regimental Order Book, 15NYHA Regimental Books, 15NYHA, RG 94, NA. Again, the dates of Schirmer's absence are based on the name of the officer issuing the daily regimental orders.
7. *OR*, 33:907, 908; orders, Apr. 13, 20, 1864, Regimental Order Book, 15NYHA Regimental Books, RG 94, NA; Hess, *Rifle Musket in Civil War Combat*, 68, 90; Pritchard, *Civil War Weapons and Equipment*, 48, 49; Lowe, *Meade's Army*, 125. Meade's observation regarding weapons discovered with multiple rounds in the muzzle may have been based on findings at the close of the Battle of Gettysburg the summer before. Both Earl Hess and Russ Pritchard report that of around 24,000 loaded muskets recovered on the field after the battle, about half of them had two loads each, with 6,000 of those containing anywhere from three to ten loads in the barrel. One musket had twenty-three rounds jammed into the tube. This may not in all cases, or even most, be attributed to men not knowing how to fire their weapons. For example, another cause could be the relatively high occurrence of a misfire, which might go unnoticed by a soldier in the smoke, noise, and general chaos of battle, who would then reload his weapon.
8. Agassiz, *Meade's Headquarters*, 81.
9. *OR*, 33:816, 817; order, Apr. 14, 1864, Companies B and D Order Books, 15NYHA Regimental Books, RG 94, NA.
10. Order, Apr. 14, 1864, Companies B and D Order Books, 15NYHA Regimental Books, RG 94, NA.
11. *OR*, 33:584, 829, 1044; Phisterer, *New York in the War of the Rebellion*, 2:1349; First Brigade Artillery Reserve General Orders No. 1, Apr. 15, 1864, Companies B and D Order Books, 15NYHA Regimental Books, RG 94, NA; Capt. John Gedney Diary, Apr. 15, 1864, WCHS.
12. Irving, *"More Than Conqueror,"* 4–14, 22, 50, 75; *OR*, 11(1):621.

13. Irving, "More Than Conqueror," 82–84; Phisterer, *New York in the War of the Rebellion*, 2:1348, 1349, 1366, 1367. With date of rank as colonel from April 1, 1863, Kitching was over six months senior to Schirmer, leading to the former's assignment to command the new brigade.

14. Irving, "More Than Conqueror," 119, 120.

15. Order, Apr. 18, 1864, Company D Order Book, 15NYHA Regimental Books, RG 94, NA; Irving, "More Than Conqueror," 119, 120; Lowe, *Meade's Army*, 124.

16. Regimental circular, Apr. 10, 1864, Companies B and D Order Books, 15NYHA Regimental Books, RG 94, NA.

17. Regimental circular, Apr. 21, 1864, Companies B and D Order Books, 15NYHA Regimental Books, RG 94, NA; order, Apr. 20, 1864, Company I Order Book, 15NYHA Regimental Books, RG 94, NA.

18. *OR*, 33:935, 36(1):286, 287, 608; Naiswald, *Grape and Canister*, 477, 478; Irving, "More Than Conqueror," 120. The "24-pounder" designation is based on the approximate weight of a solid shot with a diameter corresponding to the caliber of the weapon, not the actual weight of the Coehorn's shell. The Coehorn's 5.7-inch diameter shell actually weighed about seventeen pounds.

19. Circular, Apr. 26, 1864, Regimental and Companies B and I Order Books, 15NYHA Regimental Books, RG 94, NA.

20. *OR*, 36(1):12–14; Grant, *Personal Memoirs*, 364, 365; Bonekemper, *Victor, Not a Butcher*, 149, 150, 153, 154; Simpson, *Ulysses S. Grant*, 268, 269, 272, 273. Although advocating a strategy of relentless war, as Simpson notes, Grant did not desire "to trade casualties in accordance with a harsh calculus of war" and had in his prior roles "been frugal with human life during his offensive operations."

21. *OR*, 36(1):16, 17; Grant, *Personal Memoirs*, 366, 367.

22. *OR*, 33:808, 828, 36(1):15; Grant, *Personal Memoirs*, 369; Humphreys, *Virginia Campaign*, 14; Rhea, *Battle of the Wilderness*, 48; Simpson, *Ulysses S. Grant*, 269, 272; Gallagher, *Lee & His Army in Confederate History*, x, xi, 33.

23. Humphreys, *Virginia Campaign*, 10–12.

24. *OR*, 36(1):17, 36(2):331–34; Grant, *Personal Memoirs*, 371; Humphreys, *Virginia Campaign*, 12, 13, App. D. A division of cavalry tasked with securing and holding the river crossings and assisting in laying the pontoon bridges would precede both columns. In addition, troopers would be stationed at all occupied houses along the way to prevent local inhabitants from sounding an alarm of the Yankee approach.

25. *OR*, 36(1):1070; Law, "From the Wilderness to Cold Harbor," in *B&L*, 4:118, 119; Davis, Perry, and Kirkley, *Atlas to Accompany the Official Records*, Plate 81, Map 1; Longstreet, *From Manassas to Appomattox*, 556; Humphreys, *Virginia Campaign*, 15; Rhea, *Battle of the Wilderness*, 25, 26.

26. Belcher, "Reminiscences of the Civil War," 384.

27. *OR*, 36(1):189, 287, 318, 607, 608; Henry J. Hunt Journal, May 4, 1864, Papers of Henry Jackson Hunt, LC; Lowe, *Meade's Army*, 131; William J. Dailey Diary, May 4, 1864, Civil War Times Illustrated Collection, USAHEC; Calvin C.

Shaffer letter, *National Tribune* (Washington, DC), July 30, [?], FSNMP; Humphreys, *Virginia Campaign*, 19.

28. *OR*, 36(1):18, 539, 659, 905; Powell, *Fifth Army Corps*, 599; Humphreys, *Virginia Campaign*, 19, 20.

29. *OR*, 36(1):1070; Humphreys, *Virginia Campaign*, 22; Longstreet, *From Manassas to Appomattox*, 556, 557; Rhea, *Battle of the Wilderness*, 79, 80.

30. *OR*, 36(1):189, 318, 539; Humphreys, *Virginia Campaign*, 23–25.

31. *OR*, 36(1):189, 539, 540; Law, "From the Wilderness to Cold Harbor," in *B&L*, 4:121; Longstreet, *From Manassas to Appomattox*, 558.

32. *OR*, 36(1):189, 190, 318–20; Humphreys, *Virginia Campaign*, 28–33.

33. *OR*, 36(1):190, 540; Law, "From the Wilderness to Cold Harbor," in *B&L*, 4:122, 123; Longstreet, *From Manassas to Appomattox*, 558, 559; Humphreys, *Virginia Campaign*, 32–34; Washington A. Roebling, "Report of the Operations of the Fifth Corps, Army of the Potomac in General Grant's Campaign from Culpepper to Petersburg as Seen by W. A. Roebling, Major and A.D.C., 1864," Gouverneur Kimble Warren Papers, NYSL, 9, 10.

34. *OR*, 36(1):190, 320, 321, 540; Grant, *Personal Memoirs*, 404; Humphreys, *Virginia Campaign*, 36. General Getty had been wounded on May 5, and the division was now commanded by Brig. Gen. Frank Wheaton.

35. *OR*, 36(2):406, 415.

36. *OR*, 36(1):287, 608; Hunt Journal, May 5, 1864, LC; History of Company B, May 5, 1864, Company B Order Book, 6th New York Heavy Artillery Regimental and Company Order Books, RG 94, NA.

37. Rhea, *Battle of the Wilderness*, 77, 78; Belcher, "Reminiscences of the Civil War," 384. Adolf Riemann was promoted to second lieutenant on January 1, 1865. He died at City Point, Virginia, on February 7, 1865, of wounds received at the Battle of Hatcher's Run.

38. Irving, *"More Than Conqueror,"* 125, 126.

39. *OR*, 36(1):287, 540, 608; Dailey Diary, May 6, 1864, USAHEC.

40. *OR*, 36(1):320, 540, 611; Lowe, *Meade's Army*, 136, 137; Humphreys, *Virginia Campaign*, 36, 38; Powell, *Fifth Army Corps*, 620, 621.

41. Law, "From the Wilderness to Cold Harbor," in *B&L*, 4:123, 124; Longstreet, *From Manassas to Appomattox*, 559; Humphreys, *Virginia Campaign*, 38; Powell, *Fifth Army Corps*, 618; Oates, *War between the Union and the Confederacy*, 343.

42. Law, "From the Wilderness to Cold Harbor," in *B&L*, 4:124; Longstreet, *From Manassas to Appomattox*, 560; Humphreys, *Virginia Campaign*, 38, 39.

43. Law, "From the Wilderness to Cold Harbor," in *B&L*, 4:125.

44. Law, "From the Wilderness to Cold Harbor," in *B&L*, 4:125; Oates, *War between the Union and the Confederacy*, 345; Perry, "Reminiscences of the Campaign of 1864," 51, 52; Rhea, *Battle of the Wilderness*, 303–5.

45. *OR*, 36(1):287, 540, 608, 36(2):449; Roebling, "Report of the Operations of the Fifth Corps," 3, 4, Warren Papers, NYSL.

46. Brown, *Diary of a Line Officer*, 34, 35.

47. *OR*, 36(1):608, 611; Irving, "More Than Conqueror," 132; Dailey Diary, May 6, 1864, USAHEC.

48. Oates, *War between the Union and the Confederacy*, 345; Perry, "Reminiscences of the Campaign of 1864," 51, 52; Gedney Diary, May 6, 1864, WCHS; Rhea, *Battle of the Wilderness*, 303–5.

49. *OR*, 36(1):608; Oates, *War between the Union and the Confederacy*, 345, 346; Perry, "Reminiscences of the Campaign of 1864," 51, 52; Irving, "More Than Conqueror," 132. In a letter to his father dated May 29, 1864, Kitching stated that after reforming his brigade, his men "went in and 'flaxed' the rebs out," but there is no evidence that the brigade renewed its advance. The identity of the "higher authority" that would not allow the brigade to advance, according to Wiedrich, is not known.

50. *OR*, 36(1):608; Oates, *War between the Union and the Confederacy*, 346; Perry, "Reminiscences of the Campaign of 1864," 51, 52.

51. *OR*, 36(1):608; Gedney Diary, May 6, 1864, WCHS; Phisterer, *New York in the War of the Rebellion*, 2:1349, 1499; Companies E and L Descriptive Books, 15NYHA Regimental Books, RG 94, NA.

52. *OR*, 36(1):190, 323, 324; Humphreys, *Virginia Campaign*, 43–45; Law, "From the Wilderness to Cold Harbor," in *B&L*, 4:125, 126; Longstreet, *From Manassas to Appomattox*, 562–64; Rhea, *Battle of the Wilderness*, 499.

53. *OR*, 36(1):190, 906, 907; Humphreys, *Virginia Campaign*, 46, 47; Rhea, *Battle of the Wilderness*, 380, 385, 399, 400, 401.

54. *OR*, 36(1):190, 540; Law, "From the Wilderness to Cold Harbor," in *B&L*, 4:126, 127; Humphreys, *Virginia Campaign*, 49, 50; Rhea, *Battle of the Wilderness*, 424, 435, 440.

55. *OR*, 36(1):608, 657, 36(2):495, 496; Nevins, *Diary of Battle*, 354; Stephen D. Burger Diary, May 6, 1864, FSNMP; Roebling, "Report of the Operations of the Fifth Corps," 17, Warren Papers, NYSL.

3. TO SPOTSYLVANIA COURT HOUSE

1. Capt. John Gedney Diary, May 6, 1864, WCHS; Stephen D. Burger Diary, May 7, 1864, FSNMP; Calvin C. Shaffer letter, *National Tribune* (Washington, DC), July 30, [?], FSNMP; William J. Dailey Diary, May 7, 1864, Civil War Times Illustrated Collection, USAHEC.

2. *OR*, 36(1):114, 287, 555, 560, 608, 36(2):495, 496, 498, 499, 500; Gedney Diary, May 7, 1864, WCHS.

3. *OR*, 36(1):18, 19, 36(2):481; Humphreys, *Virginia Campaign*, 57; Simpson, *Ulysses S. Grant*, 300.

4. *OR*, 36(1):291, 608, 36(2):502; Humphreys, *Virginia Campaign*, 58; Henry J. Hunt Journal, May 7, 1864, Papers of Henry Jackson Hunt, LC; Burger Diary, May 7, 1864, FSNMP; Gedney Diary, May 7, 1864, WCHS.

5. OR, 36(1):287, 608; Burger Diary, May 7, 1864, FSNMP. Although the modern spelling of the name of the river crossed by the brigade is "Ni," the wartime spelling, "Ny," is used throughout this book.

6. OR, 36(1):540; Grant, *Personal Memoirs*, 411; Humphreys, *Virginia Campaign*, 58; Simpson, *Ulysses S. Grant*, 300, 301.

7. OR, 36(1):1041, 1056; Law, "From the Wilderness to Cold Harbor," in *B&L*, 4:128; Grant, *Personal Memoirs*, 412; Humphreys, *Virginia Campaign*, 63.

8. Rhea, *Battles for Spotsylvania Court House*, 40; Agassiz, *Meade's Headquarters*, 103.

9. OR, 36(2):551, 552; Humphreys, *Virginia Campaign*, 58, 59; Rhea, *Battles for Spotsylvania Court House*, 40.

10. OR, 36(1):540, 541, 36(2):538, 539; Humphreys, *Virginia Campaign*, 59, 60; Rhea, *Battles for Spotsylvania Court House*, 33, 45–47.

11. OR, 36(1):540, 541, 36(2):539, 540; Humphreys, *Virginia Campaign*, 60, 61; Agassiz, *Meade's Headquarters*, 104. Federal cavalry had briefly held the town prior to the arrival of Confederate infantry.

12. OR, 36(1):1042, 1056; Powell, *Fifth Army Corps*, 633–36; Rhea, *Battles for Spotsylvania Court House*, 60–65.

13. Lowe, *Meade's Army*, 144.

14. OR, 36(1):329, 36(2):534, 535; Humphreys, *Virginia Campaign*, 62–65.

15. OR, 36(1):287, 329, 330, 36(2):534, 535; Hunt Journal, May 8, 1864, LC; Gedney Diary, May 8, 1864, WCHS.

16. OR, 36(1):287, 330, 514, 608, 36(2):565; Hunt Journal, May 9, 1864, LC; Dailey Diary, May 9, 1864, USAHEC; Burger Diary, May 9, 1864, FSNMP; Gedney Diary, May 9, 1864, WCHS.

17. OR, 36(2):566; Hancock had initially ordered the heavy artillery brigade to move out from Todd's with his corps and to remain in reserve near General Birney's division. OR, 36(2):568.

18. OR, 36(1):287; Hunt Journal, May 9, 1864, LC.

19. Belcher, "Reminiscences of the Civil War," 384; Carl Matteson to "Dear Cyrus," May 16, 1864, Carl Matteson Letters, Civil War Collection, BECHS.

20. OR, 36(1):330, 490, 494, 499, 502, 504, 36(2):568, 573; Humphreys, *Virginia Campaign*, 76, 77. General Hancock reported that Mott's division was withdrawn from Todd's Tavern "during the afternoon." OR, 36(1):330. Andrew Humphreys repeats this in his memoirs. Yet a preponderance of evidence suggests the withdrawal was actually effected in the morning of May 10. Not only was Mott ordered to depart at 3 A.M. on May 10, but also, very late in the evening of May 9, he continued to issue orders from Todd's indicating the intent to depart the next day at 3 A.M. Moreover, all brigade and regimental reports in the OR by units in Mott's division confirm departing from Todd's early on May 10.

21. Shaffer letter, *National Tribune* (Washington, DC), July 30, [?], FSNMP.

22. Shaffer letter, *National Tribune* (Washington, DC), July 30, [?], FSNMP; Burger Diary, May 10, 1864, FSNMP; Gedney Diary, May 10, 1864, WCHS.

23. Humphreys, *Virginia Campaign*, 73–75; Stanley, *Battle of Spotsylvania Court House* (series of twenty-four battle maps), Map 7 (May 10, 2:30 P.M. to 5 P.M.). The Stanley maps are available at FSNMP's bookstore.

24. *OR*, 39(1):333, 334, 541; Humphreys, *Virginia Campaign*, 81, 82.

25. *OR*, 36(1):608, 755; Hunt Journal, May 10, 1864, LC; Dailey Diary, May 10, 1864, USAHEC; Burger Diary, May 10, 1864, FSNMP; Gedney Diary, May 10, 1864, WCHS.

26. *OR*, 36(1):608; Hunt Journal, May 10, 1864, LC; Gedney Diary, May 10, 1864, WCHS.

27. *OR*, 36(1):334; Hunt Journal, May 10, 1864, LC; Lowe, *Meade's Army*, 150.

28. *OR*, 36(2):630, 631; Washington A. Roebling, "Report of the Operations of the Fifth Corps, Army of the Potomac in General Grant's Campaign from Culpepper to Petersburg as Seen by W. A. Roebling, Major and A.D.C., 1864," 32, Gouverneur Kemble Warren Papers, NYSL; Kirk, *Heavy Guns and Light*, 203.

29. *OR*, 36(1):608; Hunt Journal, May 11, 1864, LC; Roebling, "Report of the Operations of the Fifth Corps," 32, 33, Warren Papers, NYSL.

30. *OR*, 36(1):334, 335, 36(2):629, 635; Grant, *Personal Memoirs*, 420, 421; Humphreys, *Virginia Campaign*, 90.

31. *OR*, 36(1):334, 657; Roebling, "Report of the Operations of the Fifth Corps," 34, 35, Warren Papers, NYSL; Humphreys, *Virginia Campaign*, 92; Dailey Diary, May 12, 1864, USAHEC; Burger Diary, May 12, 1864, FSNMP. Kitching's picket line consisted of Companies A and C, Sixth New York Heavy Artillery, possibly augmented by other companies from the brigade.

32. *OR*, 36(1):334, 335; Humphreys, *Virginia Campaign*, 92; Kirk, *Heavy Guns and Light*, 205; Rhea, *Battles for Spotsylvania Court House*, 230.

33. *OR*, 36(1):334; Humphreys, *Virginia Campaign*, 92.

34. *OR*, 36(1):335; Lowe, *Meade's Army*, 153; Rhea, *Battles for Spotsylvania Court House*, 259. The figures for prisoners, artillery pieces, and colors captured are as provided by General Hancock in his official report of the action. On the day after the attack, lower numbers were reported to General Meade by Hancock, including a total of twenty artillery pieces and twenty-one stand of colors. *OR* 36(2):708.

35. *OR*, 36(1):336, 661; Humphreys, *Virginia Campaign*, 97, 99; Rhea, *Battles for Spotsylvania Court House*, 259; Galloway, "Hand-to-Hand Fighting at Spotsylvania," in *B&L*, 4:170–72; Kirk, *Heavy Guns and Light*, 206–9.

36. Burger Diary, May 12, 1864, FSNMP; Roebling, "Report of the Operations of the Fifth Corps," 35, Warren Papers, NYSL.

37. *OR*, 36(2):661, 662; Roebling, "Report of the Operations of the Fifth Corps," 36, Warren Papers, NYSL; Humphreys, *Virginia Campaign*, 100, 101; Rhea, *Battles for Spotsylvania Court House*, 283.

38. *OR*, 36(2):663, 664, 668, 669, 671; Humphreys, *Virginia Campaign*, 101.

39. *OR*, 36(2):662, 663; Gedney Diary, May 12, 1864, WCHS; Belcher, "Reminiscences of the Civil War," 385; Burger Diary, May 12, 1864, FSNMP; Rhea, *Battles for Spotsylvania Court House*, 283.

40. OR, 36(2):673; Burger Diary, May 12, 1864, FSNMP; Lt. George W. P. Bouton Diary, May 12, 1864, FSNMP; Dailey Diary, May 12, 1864, USAHEC; Lowe, Meade's Army, 155.

41. OR, 36(1):539, 669; Lowe, Meade's Army, 155; Galloway, "Hand-to-Hand Fighting at Spotsylvania," in B&L, 4:171,172; Rhea, Battles for Spotsylvania Court House, 290, 291.

42. Lowe, Meade's Army, 155; Burger Diary, May 12, 1864, FSNMP; Rhea, Battles for Spotsylvania Court House, 290, 291.

43. Baquet, First Brigade, New Jersey Volunteers, 125; Bicknell, Fifth Regiment Maine Volunteers, 321.

44. Baquet, First Brigade, New Jersey Volunteers, 125; Bicknell, Fifth Regiment Maine Volunteers, 321; Galloway, "Hand-to-Hand Fighting at Spotsylvania," in B&L, 4:173.

45. Cockerell and Ballard, Mississippi Rebel, 255, 260.

46. OR, 36(1):192, 541, 611, 612, 36(2):668, 670, 672; Humphreys, Virginia Campaign, 101, 102, 104.

47. Cockerell and Ballard, Mississippi Rebel, 261, 262.

48. Baquet, First Brigade, New Jersey Volunteers, 125, 126; Galloway, "Hand-to-Hand Fighting at Spotsylvania," in B&L, 4:173; Bouton Diary, May 12, 1864, FSNMP; Bicknell, Fifth Regiment Maine Volunteers, 321.

49. Belcher, "Reminiscences of the Civil War," 385.

4. TO THE HARRIS FARM

1. Irving, "More Than Conqueror," 126, 127.

2. OR, 36(1):143, 541, 36(2):716, 724, 725. Indeed, by order of Hunt, three days earlier the Second Battalion had already been detached from Kitching's brigade for service with the Artillery Reserve.

3. Stephen D. Burger Diary, May 13, 1864, FSNMP; Capt. John Gedney Diary, May 13, 1864, WCHS; William J. Dailey Diary, May 13, 1864, Civil War Times Illustrated Collection, USAHEC; Washington A. Roebling, "Report of the Operations of the Fifth Corps, Army of the Potomac in General Grant's Campaign from Culpepper to Petersburg as Seen by W. A. Roebling, Major and A.D.C., 1864," 39, Gouverneur Kimble Warren Papers, NYSL.

4. OR, 36(2):700, 716, 720, 721; Humphreys, Virginia Campaign, 106, 107; Roebling, "Report of the Operations of the Fifth Corps," 39, Warren Papers, NYSL; Rhea, To the North Anna River, 33, 67, 68.

5. OR, 36(2):721, 722; Roebling, "Report of the Operations of the Fifth Corps," 39, 40, Warren Papers, NYSL.

6. Humphreys, Virginia Campaign, 107, 108; Roebling, "Report of the Operations of the Fifth Corps," 40, Warren Papers, NYSL; Grant, Personal Memoirs, 424.

7. Roebling, "Report of the Operations of the Fifth Corps," 40, Warren Papers, NYSL; Burger Diary, May 13, 1864, FSNMP; Gedney Diary, May 13, 1864, WCHS; Dailey Diary, May 13, 1864, USAHEC.

8. OR, 36(1):542, 36(2):755, 756; Powell, *Fifth Army Corps*, 651.

9. OR, 36(2):756, 757; Humphreys, *Virginia Campaign*, 107; Rhea, *To the North Anna River*, 73.

10. OR, 36(1):542, 555, 556; Rhea, *To the North Anna River*, 77, 78; Roebling, "Report of the Operations of the Fifth Corps," 41, 42, Warren Papers, NYSL.

11. OR, 36(1):542, 556, 670, 36(2):758–60, 762, 763; Burger Diary, May 14, 1864, FSNMP; Humphreys, *Virginia Campaign*, 107, 108; Roebling, "Report of the Operations of the Fifth Corps," 42, Warren Papers, NYSL; Rhea, *To the North Anna River*, 78–80, 84–87, 89. Capt. John Gedney of the Sixth New York Heavy also reported in his diary, "the Rebs commenced to shell us with Rail Road Iron." Gedney Diary, May 13, 1864, WCHS.

12. OR, 36(2):784; S. Williams, "Head Quarters Army of the Potomac Special Orders," May 15, 1864, Military Papers, Papers of Henry Jackson Hunt, LC.

13. OR, 36(1):287, 36(2):813, 843; Grant, *Personal Memoirs*, 427; Naiswald, *Grape and Canister*, 489, 490; Henry J. Hunt Journal, May 16, 1864, Papers of Henry Jackson Hunt, LC; Humphreys, *Virginia Campaign*, 110. The ammunition-train guard would eventually be reduced to a single company, Capt. Calvin Shaffer's Company F.

14. J. Howard Kitching to Brig. Gen. S. Williams, May 15, 1864, Military Papers, Papers of Henry Jackson Hunt, LC.

15. Kitching to Williams, May 15, 1864, Military Papers, Papers of Henry Jackson Hunt, LC. See also S. Williams, May 16, 1864, handwritten endorsement on Kitching's letter. Military Papers, Papers of Henry Jackson Hunt, LC. No order or other record has been uncovered formally transferring Kitching's brigade to the Fifth Corps other than the May 13 message from Williams to Maj. Gen. Horatio Wright directing the Sixth Corps commander to order Kitching, after sending one battalion to the Reserve Artillery at Tabernacle Church, to report to Warren with his remaining two battalions. See OR, 36(2):725. But the formal "Organization of the Army of the Potomac" in effect on May 31, 1864, shows Kitching's command within the Fifth Corps as the "Independent Brigade." See OR, 36(1):203.

16. OR, 36(2):788, 789; Burger Diary, May 15, 16, 1864, FSNMP; Dailey Diary, May 16, 1864, USAHEC.

17. Carl Matteson to "Dear Cyrus," May 16, 1864, Carl Matteson Letters, Civil War Collection, BECHS. In referring to Mine Run, Matteson undoubtedly was describing events from the Battle of the Wilderness.

18. OR, 36(1):337, 361, 36(2):695, 696, 844; Humphreys, *Virginia Campaign*, 109. According to Hancock, Tyler's division and the Corcoran Legion, which also joined the Second Corps at that time, together numbered approximately 8,000 men—by far the bulk being heavy artillery.

19. OR, 36(1):337, 609, 661; Humphreys, Virginia Campaign, 110; Nevins, Diary of Battle, 376, 377; Kirk, Heavy Guns and Light, 217; Brown, Diary of a Line Officer, 47, 48; Burger Diary, May 18, 1864, FSNMP; Dailey Diary, May 18, 1864, USAHEC; Phisterer, New York in the War of the Rebellion, 2:1519. Also on picket along the Ny River was Company E, Sixth New York Heavy. According to Warren's aide Roebling, at 9 A.M. "part" of Kitching's brigade was sent to the Myers house, the balance of the command remaining at Anderson's. See Roebling, "Report of the Operations of the Fifth Corps," 47, Warren Papers, NYSL.
20. OR, 36(2):873, 875, 878.
21. OR, 36(1):337, 338, 361, 362, 661, 36(2):866–70; Humphreys, Virginia Campaign, 110, 111.
22. OR, 36(1):338, 362, 609; Roebling, "Report of the Operations of the Fifth Corps," 47, Warren Papers, NYSL; Humphreys, Virginia Campaign, 111.
23. OR, 36(2):864, 865; Humphreys, Virginia Campaign, 119; Rhea, To the North Anna River, 156, 157.
24. OR, 36(2):866, 869, 871, 879, 881; Humphreys, Virginia Campaign, 119; Rhea, To the North Anna River, 157.
25. OR, 36(2):876.
26. OR, 36(2):878.
27. OR, 36(1):338, 609, 612, 36(2):913, 915, 922, 923; Kirk, Heavy Guns and Light, 218, 219; Brown, Diary of a Line Officer, 48; Matter, If It Takes All Summer, 317–20; Rhea To the North Anna River, 72, 180; Irving, "More Than Conqueror," 133. Estimates of the strength of the cavalry detachment vary between 300 men and the 500 reported by Humphreys.
28. Kirk, Heavy Guns and Light, 218.
29. OR, 36(1):1073; Freeman, Lee's Lieutenants, 3:439; Rhea, To the North Anna River, 167.
30. OR, 36(1):1073, 1088; Freeman, Lee's Lieutenants, 3:439; Matter, If It Takes All Summer, 317, 320; Rhea, To the North Anna River, 110, 168, 170.
31. OR, 36(2):923, 924, 931, 932.
32. OR, 36(1):542; Roe and Nutt, First Regiment of Heavy Artillery, Massachusetts Volunteers, 152; Massachusetts Artillery, Souvenir, 23; Matter, If It Takes All Summer, 321; Rhea, To the North Anna River, 170, 171.
33. OR, 36(1):1082; Matter, If It Takes All Summer, 321.
34. OR, 36(1):1082, 1083, 36(2):924; Matter, If It Takes All Summer, 321; Brown, Diary of a Line Officer, 48, 49, 50; Kirk, Heavy Guns and Light, 220.
35. Roe and Nutt, First Regiment of Heavy Artillery, Massachusetts Volunteers, 153, 154; Massachusetts Artillery, Souvenir, 24, 25.
36. OR, 36(1):1073, 1082, 1083; Roe and Nutt, First Regiment of Heavy Artillery, Massachusetts Volunteers, 154; Massachusetts Artillery, Souvenir, 25, 26, 28.
37. OR, 36(1):609; Gedney Diary, May 19, 1864, WCHS; Irving, "More Than Conqueror," 129; Dailey Diary, May 19, 1864, USAHEC; Philemon C. Heath to

"Dear Sister," May 20, 1864, Philemon C. Heath Letters, Civil War Miscellaneous Collection, USAHEC.

38. Roebling, "Report of the Operations of the Fifth Corps," 49, Warren Papers, NYSL; Matter, *If It Takes All Summer*, 322, 323.

39. *OR*, 36(1):602; Matter, *If It Tales All Summer*, 322, 323.

40. *OR*, 36(1):600, 602, 605, 1073, 1083; Matter, *If It Tales All Summer*, 323, 324, 326; Rhea, *To the North Anna River*, 183; Roe and Nutt, *First Regiment of Heavy Artillery, Massachusetts Volunteers*, 155; Massachusetts Artillery, *Souvenir*, 26.

41. *OR*, 36(1):1073, 1083, 36(2):911, 912, 915–21, 36(3):8, 12; Matter, *If It Takes All Summer*, 325.

42. Roe and Nutt, *First Regiment of Heavy Artillery, Massachusetts Volunteers*, 156; Lowe, *Meade's Army*, 164; Roebling, "Report of the Operations of the Fifth Corps," 51, Warren Papers, NYSL.

43. Nevins, *Diary of Battle*, 379.

44. *OR*, 36(1):609, 36(3):12.

45. Roe and Nutt, *First Regiment of Heavy Artillery, Massachusetts Volunteers*, 165; Brown, *Diary of a Line Officer*, 52, 53; Rhea, *To the North Anna River*, 189.

46. Mrs. David Mills to "Dear Sir," May 19, 1864, U. S. Army, 15th New York Artillery, Co. M Records, NYSL; CSR, David Mills, 15NYHA, RG 94, NA.

47. *OR*, 36(1):1073, 36(3):3; Brown, *Diary of a Line Officer*, 52. Confederate dead left on the field were estimated to equal the Union soldiers killed—a figure not including any dead Confederates buried or removed by their comrades.

48. *OR*, 36(1):609; Phisterer, *New York in the War of the Rebellion*, 2:1349, 1499, 1519; CSR, Leander Schamberger, 15NYHA, RG 94, NA. For example, Gordon Rhea's *To the North Anna River* and William Matter's *If It Takes All Summer* focus principally on the action on the right of the Federal line and the casualties suffered by the heavy artillery and other units fighting there, with little or no mention of the fighting on the left or the casualties incurred by the Sixth and Fifteenth New York Heavies.

49. Roebling, "Report of the Operations of the Fifth Corps," 50, 51, Warren Papers, NYSL.

50. *OR*, 36(3):6.

51. Philemon C. Heath to "Dear Sister," May 20, 1864, Heath Letters, USAHEC.

5. TO THE NORTH ANNA

1. *OR*, 36(3):8; Humphreys, *Virginia Campaign*, 119, 120; Rhea, *To the North Anna River*, 192; Miller, *North Anna Campaign*, 13.

2. *OR*, 36(3):13, 14, 16, 17; Humphreys, *Virginia Campaign*, 120.

3. *OR*, 36(3):7; Henry J. Hunt Journal, May 20, 1864, Papers of Henry Jackson Hunt, LC.

4. *OR*, 36(3):801, 812; Humphreys, *Virginia Campaign*, 120, 121; Miller, *North Anna Campaign*, 23.

5. *OR*, 36(3):53–55, 62, 64; Washington A. Roebling, "Report of the Operations of the Fifth Corps, Army of the Potomac in General Grant's Campaign from Culpepper to Petersburg as Seen by W. A. Roebling, Major and A.D.C., 1864," 52, 53, Gouverneur Kimble Warren Papers, NYSL; Humphreys, *Virginia Campaign*, 120, 121.

6. *OR*, 36(1):542, 612, 36(3):55; Roebling, "Report of the Operations of the Fifth Corps," 53, Warren Papers, NYSL; William J. Dailey Diary, May 21, 1864, Civil War Times Illustrated Collection, USAHEC.

7. *OR*, 36(1):542, 662, 911, 912; Lowe, *Meade's Army*, 167, 168; Miller, *North Anna Campaign*, 28–32; Roebling, "Report of the Operations of the Fifth Corps," 53, 54, Warren Papers, NYSL; Humphreys, *Virginia Campaign*, 121, 122. Burnside had initially gone south on the Telegraph Road as far as Stanard's Mill on the Po River. But believing, incorrectly, that Confederates in strong force held the opposite bank, he decided to countermarch his corps back up the Telegraph Road and then follow the Fifth Corps route to Guinea Station.

8. *OR*, 36(1):1058, 1074, 36(3):95, 814, 815; Humphreys, *Virginia Campaign*, 123; Miller, *North Anna Campaign*, 27, 31, 32.

9. *OR*, 36(3):56, 57; Roebling, "Report of the Operations of the Fifth Corps," 54, 55, Warren Papers, NYSL; Rhea, *To the North Anna River*, 235. The orders and reports from the period consistently refer to the Ta River as the one crossed by the road leading from Catlett's to Madison's Ordinary. It is actually the Matta River. This discrepancy probably is attributable to errors in the maps available to the Federal forces.

10. *OR*, 36(3):57, 58; Roebling, "Report of the Operations of the Fifth Corps," 55, Warren Papers, NYSL; Rhea, *To the North Anna River*, 247.

11. Agassiz, *Meade's Headquarters*, 119, 120.

12. *OR*, 36(3):60; Roebling, "Report of the Operations of the Fifth Corps," 55, Warren Papers, NYSL.

13. *OR*, 36(3):60; Roebling, "Report of the Operations of the Fifth Corps," 55, Warren Papers, NYSL; Rhea, *To the North Anna River*, 247; Brown, *Diary of a Line Officer*, 54; Lowe, *Meade's Army*, 173. While the march that day may have seemed like twenty-five miles to Brown, the distance covered by Kitching's brigade was closer to fifteen miles.

14. *OR*, 36(1):542, 36(3):58, 59, 87, 88; Roebling, "Report of the Operations of the Fifth Corps," 55, 56, Warren Papers, NYSL; Rhea, *To the North Anna River*, 247, 248.

15. *OR*, 36(3):823; Roebling, "Report of the Operations of the Fifth Corps," 55, 56, Warren Papers, NYSL; Humphreys, *Virginia Campaign*, 125; Rhea, *To the North Anna River*, 257, 258.

16. *OR*, 36(3):94; Miller, *North Anna Campaign*, 35; Roebling, "Report of the

Operations of the Fifth Corps," 56, Warren Papers, NYSL; Stephen D. Burger Diary, May 22, 1864, FSNMP; Dailey Diary, May 22, 1864, USAHEC; Capt. John Gedney Diary, May 22, 1864, WCHS; Brown, *Diary of a Line Officer*, 54.

17. Roebling, "Report of the Operations of the Fifth Corps," 56, Warren Papers, NYSL.

18. Roebling, "Report of the Operations of the Fifth Corps," 56, 57; *OR*, 36(1):191, 36(2):552, 36(3):88; Lowe, *Meade's Army*, 144; Nevins, *Diary of Battle*, 383.

19. *OR*, 36(1):542, 36(3):80; Humphreys, *Virginia Campaign*, 125, 126.

20. *OR*, 36(3):85; Roebling, "Report of the Operations of the Fifth Corps," 58, Warren Papers, NYSL; Nevins, *Diary of Battle*, 383.

21. *OR*, 36(3):91, 95, 96; Burger Diary, May 22, 1864, FSNMP; Dailey Diary, May 22, 1864, USAHEC; Gedney Diary, May 22, 1864, WCHS; Brown, *Diary of a Line Officer*, 54, 55.

22. *OR*, 36(3):130. Cutler's division had not moved with the rest of the Fifth Corps, instead following a road running south from Lebanon Church about a mile and a half east of the Telegraph Road.

23. *OR*, 36(1):543, 36(3):116, 117, 130, 131; Roebling, "Report of the Operations of the Fifth Corps," 59, 60, Warren Papers, NYSL; Humphreys, *Virginia Campaign*, 128.

24. *OR*, 36(1):238, 36(3):125; Humphreys, *Virginia Campaign*, 128; Roebling, "Report of the Operations of the Fifth Corps," 60, 61, Warren Papers, NYSL; Rhea, *To the North Anna River*, 290, 291.

25. *OR*, 36(1):543, 563, 36(3):125–27; Roebling, "Report of the Operations of the Fifth Corps," 61, Warren Papers, NYSL; Humphreys, *Virginia Campaign*, 128, 129.

26. *OR*, 36(1):563, 582; Humphreys, *Virginia Campaign*, 129; Nevins, *Diary of Battle*, 384, 385; Roebling, "Report of the Operations of the Fifth Corps," 61, 62, Warren Papers, NYSL; Rhea, *To the North Anna River*, 293, 294, 304; Miller, *North Anna Campaign*, 62, 63, 69.

27. *OR*, 36(3):127; Burger Diary, May 23, 1864, FSNMP; Dailey Diary, May 23, 1864, USAHEC; Gedney Diary, May 23, 1864, WCHS; Brown, *Diary of a Line Officer*, 55.

28. *OR*, 36(1):563, 612; Roebling, "Report of the Operations of the Fifth Corps," 62, Warren Papers, NYSL; Miller, *North Anna Campaign*, 72–74; Rhea, *To the North Anna River*, 304.

29. *OR*, 36(1):612, 638, 645, 655; Nevins, *Diary of Battle*, 385; Roebling, "Report of the Operations of the Fifth Corps," 62, Warren Papers, NYSL; Miller, *North Anna Campaign*, 72, 73.

30. *OR*, 36(1):609; Burger Diary, May 23, 1864, FSNMP; Dailey Diary, May 23, 1864, USAHEC; Gedney Diary, May 23, 1864, WCHS; Roebling, "Report of the Operations of the Fifth Corps," 62, Warren Papers, NYSL.

31. *OR*, 36(1):612, 621, 622, 626, 655, 656; Nevins, *Diary of Battle*, 386; Roebling, "Report of the Operations of the Fifth Corps," 62, Warren Papers, NYSL; Miller, *North Anna Campaign*, 79, 81, 82; Rhea, *To the North Anna River*, 314, 315.

32. Irving, "More Than Conqueror," 133, 134.
33. Nevins, Diary of Battle, 386.
34. OR, 36(3):129, 130; Nevins, Diary of Battle, 383, 384, 387.
35. Freeman, Lee's Lieutenants, 3:496, 497; Roebling, "Report of the Operations of the Fifth Corps," 62, 63, Warren Papers, NYSL.
36. Rhea, To the North Anna River, 320, 321; Miller, North Anna Campaign, 88, 89.
37. Humphreys, Virginia Campaign, 132; Rhea, To the North Anna River, 322, 323; Miller, North Anna Campaign, 89.
38. Gedney Diary, May 23, 1864, WCHS; Belcher, "Reminiscences of the Civil War," 385.
39. Lowe, Meade's Army, 172; Agassiz, Meade's Headquarters, 123; Meade, Life and Letters, 2:198.
40. OR, 36(3):80; Hunt Journal, May 20, 24, 1864, LC; Rhea, To the North Anna River, 275.
41. OR, 36(1):912, 929, 36(3):165, 166.
42. OR, 36(3):162, 163.
43. OR, 36(3):151, 159, 163; Roebling, "Report of the Operations of the Fifth Corps," 63, 64, Warren Papers, NYSL Roebling.
44. OR, 36(1):918, 36(3):167, 199; Roebling, "Report of the Operations of the Fifth Corps," 64, Warren Papers, NYSL; Miller, North Anna Campaign, 100–103, 105, 106, 119; Rhea, To the North Anna River, 337–39, 341, 342.
45. OR, 36(1):609; Brown, Diary of a Line Officer, 55, 56; Burger Diary, May 24, 1864, FSNMP; Dailey Diary, May 24, 1864, USAHEC; Gedney Diary, May 24, 1864, WCHS.
46. Freeman, Lee's Lieutenants, 3:497, 498; Rhea, To the North Anna River, 345, 346; Miller, North Anna Campaign, 119, 120.
47. OR, 36(3):160, 161, 168, 169, 171; Roebling, "Report of the Operations of the Fifth Corps," 64, 65, Warren Papers, NYSL.
48. Kirk, Heavy Guns and Light, 246.
49. OR, 36(1):609, 36(3):193; Burger Diary, May 25, 1864, FSNMP; Dailey Diary, May 25, 1864, USAHEC; Gedney Diary, May 25, 1864, WCHS; Brown, Diary of a Line Officer, 56; Roebling, "Report of the Operations of the Fifth Corps," 65, 66, Warren Papers, NYSL.
50. OR, 36(3):206, 207; Rhea, Cold Harbor, 20–23; Roebling, "Report of the Operations of the Fifth Corps," 66, Warren Papers, NYSL; Nevins, Diary of Battle, 388.
51. Nevins, Diary of Battle, 388.
52. OR, 36(3):183.
53. Mrs. Phebe Hamilton to "Mr Dickey," May 27, 1864, 15th New York Artillery, Co. M Records, NYSL; CSR, John Hamilton, 15NYHA, RG 94, NA.

6. TO THE TOTOPOTOMOY AND BETHESDA CHURCH

1. *OR*, 36(3):211; Humphreys, *Virginia Campaign*, 160, 161; Brown, *Diary of a Line Officer*, 56. Although the modern spelling of the name of the river that the supply trains paralleled is "Mattaponi," the wartime spelling, "Mattapony," is used throughout this book.

2. *OR*, 36(1):609; Humphreys, *Virginia Campaign*, 160; Washington A. Roebling, "Report of the Operations of the Fifth Corps, Army of the Potomac in General Grant's Campaign from Culpepper to Petersburg as Seen by W. A. Roebling, Major and A.D.C., 1864," 66, 67, Gouverneur Kimble Warren Papers, NYSL; Kirk, *Heavy Guns and Light*, 246; Brown, *Diary of a Line Officer*, 57; Stephen D. Burger Diary, May 26, 1864, FSNMP; William J. Dailey Diary, May 26, 1864, Civil War Times Illustrated Collection, USAHEC; Capt. John Gedney Diary, May 26, 1864, WCHS.

3. *OR*, 36(1):543, 609, 36(3):252; Roebling, "Report of the Operations of the Fifth Corps," 67, Warren Papers, NYSL; Nevins, *Diary of Battle*, 388; Humphreys, *Virginia Campaign*, 160, 161; Brown, *Diary of a Line Officer*, 57; Burger Diary, May 27, 1864, FSNMP; Dailey Diary, May 27, 1864, USAHEC.

4. *OR*, 36(1):609, 36(3):253; Roebling, "Report of the Operations of the Fifth Corps," 67, Warren Papers, NYSL; Nevins, *Diary of Battle*, 389; Brown, *Diary of a Line Officer*, 57; Burger Diary, May 27, 1864, FSNMP; Dailey Diary, May 27, 1864, USAHEC. While Captain Brown's estimate of the length of the march was reasonably accurate, the actual distance from Mount Carmel Church to Dowell's Creek by the route taken is probably nearer twenty miles.

5. *OR*, 36(1):609, 36(3):270; Nevins, *Diary of Battle*, 389; Lowe, *Meade's Army*, 178; Roebling, "Report of the Operations of the Fifth Corps," 68, Warren Papers, NYSL; Brown, *Diary of a Line Officer*, 57; Burger Diary, May 28, 1864, FSNMP; Dailey Diary, May 28, 1864, USAHEC; Gedney Diary, May 28, 1864, WCHS.

6. *OR*, 36(1):543, 36(3):258, 259, 269, 271, 272; Roebling, "Report of the Operations of the Fifth Corps," 68, Warren Papers, NYSL; Rhea, *Cold Harbor*, 43, 76; Brown, *Diary of a Line Officer*, 57; Burger Diary, May 28, 1864, FSNMP; Dailey Diary, May 28, 1864, USAHEC; Gedney Diary, May 28, 1864, WCHS.

7. *OR*, 36(1):793, 36(3):273; Humphreys, *Virginia Campaign*, 164, 165. Haw's Shop is now the town of Studley.

8. *OR*, 36(3):836–40; Humphreys, *Virginia Campaign*, 165, 166; Rhea, *Cold Harbor*, 44, 45, 59.

9. *OR*, 36(1):1074, 1083, 36(3):846; Freeman, *Lee's Lieutenants*, 3:498, 499; Rhea, *Cold Harbor*, 60.

10. *OR*, 36(1):543, 564, 36(3):294, 300–302, 304, 305; Roebling, "Report of the Operations of the Fifth Corps," 69, 70, Warren Papers, NYSL; Humphreys, *Virginia Campaign*, 167; Rhea, *Cold Harbor*, 99, 100, 104.

11. *OR*, 36(3):209, 210, 291, 298, 302, 304, 305; Brown, *Diary of a Line Officer*, 58; Kirk, *Heavy Guns and Light*, 249, 250. The original Second Division had been temporarily disbanded at Spotsylvania Court House on May 9 owing to General Robinson's wounding and the heavy losses it sustained there and at the Wilderness.

12. *OR*, 36(1):343, 365, 511, 512, 36(3):300, 331, 332; Brown, *Diary of a Line Officer*, 58; Kirk, *Heavy Guns and Light*, 255; Rhea, *Cold Harbor*, 102, 103.

13. *OR*, 36(1):527; Brown, *Diary of a Line Officer*, 58, 59; Kirk, *Heavy Guns and Light*, 252, 256; Jno. M. Craig, assistant adjutant general, Artillery Head Quarters, Army of the Potomac, to Capt. Robert K. Stanton, May 31, 1864, author's collection; John C. Tidball to Brig. Gen. H. J. Hunt, June 6, 1864, Military Papers, Papers of Henry Jackson Hunt, LC.

14. *OR*, 36(1):287; Henry J. Hunt Journal, June 6, 1864, Papers of Henry Jackson Hunt, LC. The Coehorns were once again employed with good effect on the afternoon of May 30, but whether at the time still served by Company E, Fifteenth New York or by Company D, Fourth New York is unclear. Rhea, *Cold Harbor*, 125, 126.

15. *OR*, 11(2):32, 387–89, 36(1):202, 36(3):305, 336, 347; Hardin, *Twelfth Regiment, Pennsylvania Reserve*, 191.

16. *OR*, 36(3):337, 338; Roebling, "Report of the Operations of the Fifth Corps," 70, Warren Papers, NYSL; Rhea, *Cold Harbor*, 139.

17. *OR*, 36(3):850, 851.

18. *OR*, 36(3):854.

19. *OR*, 36(3):350; Humphreys, *Virginia Campaign*, 168; Roebling, "Report of the Operations of the Fifth Corps," 71, Warren Papers, NYSL; Rhea, *Cold Harbor*, 130; Hardin, *Twelfth Regiment, Pennsylvania Reserve*, 188, 189; McBride, *In the Ranks*, 66, 67; James B. Thompson, "Reminiscences of Prison Life in the South," Civil War Miscellaneous Collection, USAHEC; Charles Henry Minnemeyer Diary, May 30, 1864, Civil War Soldiers Collection, Special Collections and Univ. Archives, Indiana Univ. of Pennsylvania, Indiana; Nevins, *Diary of Battle*, 393; Rhea, *Cold Harbor*, 130.

20. *OR*, 51(1):244; Roebling, "Report of the Operations of the Fifth Corps," 71, Warren Papers, NYSL; Hardin, *Twelfth Regiment, Pennsylvania Reserve*, 189; McBride, *In the Ranks*, 67; Woodward, *Our Campaigns*, 317; Nevins, *Diary of Battle*, 393.

21. Burger Diary, May 30, 1864, FSNMP; Irving, *"More Than Conqueror,"* 134, 135; Modified Journal of Company C, May 30, 1864, 6th New York Heavy Artillery Regimental Papers, Civil War Miscellaneous Collection, USAHEC.

22. Nevins, *Diary of Battle*, 393. In addition to Kitching's brigade, Fisher's brigade of Pennsylvania Reserves had moved in support of Hardin.

23. *OR*, 36(1):609; Hardin, *Twelfth Regiment, Pennsylvania Reserve*, 190; Burger Diary, May 30, 1864, FSNMP.

24. OR, 36(1):609; Gedney Diary, May 30, 1864, WCHS; Hardin, *Twelfth Regiment, Pennsylvania Reserve*, 190; Burger Diary, May 30, 1864, FSNMP; Woodward, *Our Campaigns*, 317; Nevins, *Diary of Battle*, 393, 394.

25. OR, 36(1):646, 652, 653, 656; Nevins, *Diary of Battle*, 393; Roebling, "Report of the Operations of the Fifth Corps," 72, Warren Papers, NYSL; Rhea, *Cold Harbor*, 142.

26. OR, 36(1):646, 656, 658; Nevins, *Diary of Battle*, 393; Woodward, *Our Campaigns*, 317, 318; Hardin, *Twelfth Regiment, Pennsylvania Reserve*, 190; Roebling, "Report of the Operations of the Fifth Corps," 72, Warren Papers, NYSL; Rhea, *Cold Harbor*, 143.

27. Christian, "Battle at Bethesda Church," 57–59; William Allan Reminiscences, Southern Historical Collection, Univ. of North Carolina, Chapel Hill; Rhea, *Cold Harbor*, 144; Furgurson, *Not War but Murder*, 68.

28. Christian, "Battle at Bethesda Church," 59.

29. McBride, *In the Ranks*, 68, 69; Woodward, *Our Campaigns*, 318; Burger Diary, May 30, 1864, FSNMP.

30. Christian, "Battle at Bethesda Church," 59, 60.

31. Christian, "Battle at Bethesda Church," 60, 61.

32. OR, 36(1):610, 36(3):344, 351, 389, 390, 397; Irving, "More Than Conqueror," 134, 138; Dailey Diary, May 30, 1864, USAHEC. Frederick Phisterer gives a slightly higher number of fatalities within the Fifteenth—six men killed and one officer and six men mortally wounded—but this is for the period of May 27–31. *New York in the War of the Rebellion*, 2:1499.

33. OR, 51(1):244, 245, 51(2):975; Allan Reminiscences, Southern Historical Collection, Univ. of North Carolina, Chapel Hill.

34. Burger Diary, May 31, 1864, FSNMP; McBride, *In the Ranks*, 69; Woodward, *Our Campaigns*, 319.

35. OR, 36(1):610, 613, 36(3):376, 381, 382, 388, 395, 404, 406; Humphreys, *Virginia Campaign*, 170, 171.

36. OR, 36(3):434, 447, 448, 454.

37. OR, 36(1):662, 680, 999, 1000; Humphreys, *Virginia Campaign*, 170, 171, 175, 176; Rhea, *Cold Harbor*, 154, 185, 187, 243, 255, 265. In the attacks on June 1, the Sixth Corps suffered approximately 1,200 men killed and wounded and the Eighteenth Corps about 1,000.

38. OR, 36(3):486; Roebling, "Report of the Operations of the Fifth Corps," 74–77, Warren Papers, NYSL.

39. OR, 36(3):433, 439–52, 494, 495. Lockwood disputed Warren's interpretation of events. On June 10 he wrote to General Williams to offer him "and my friends near you" the facts as he saw them. In the letter Lockwood quoted an order received from Warren directing him to advance his "entire command" to his left "along" the Old Cold Harbor Road to support the Sixth Corps—which, he declared, was precisely what he was doing when he encountered Roebling. OR, 36(3):726–28.

40. *OR*, 36(3):440, 441, 486–89, 499, 500; Humphreys, *Virginia Campaign*, 176–78.

41. Roebling, "Report of the Operations of the Fifth Corps," 77, 78, Warren Papers, NYSL; Humphreys, *Virginia Campaign*, 178; Nevins, *Diary of Battle*, 399.

42. *OR*, 36(1):610, 914, 36(3):491, 493; Humphreys, *Virginia Campaign*, 179, 180; Roebling, "Report of the Operations of the Fifth Corps," 79, 80, Warren Papers, NYSL; Gedney Diary, June 1, 1864, WCHS; Powell, *Fifth Army Corps*, 673, 674; Rhea, *Cold Harbor*, 296, 297, 301–5.

43. *OR*, 36(1):344, 36(3):492, 493; Humphreys, *Virginia Campaign*, 178, 180; Roebling, "Report of the Operations of the Fifth Corps," 82, 83, Warren Papers, NYSL.

44. *OR*, 36(1):565, 914, 930, 36(3):536–38, 546–48; Roebling, "Report of the Operations of the Fifth Corps," 83, 84, Warren Papers, NYSL; Humphreys, *Virginia Campaign*, 188; Nevins, *Diary of Battle*, 402, 404. In his report of the battle, Burnside stated that the Ninth Corps had "never fought more bravely than on this occasion."

45. *OR*, 36(1):603, 613, 36(3):553; Humphreys, *Virginia Campaign*, 181; Burger Diary, June 3, 1864, FSNMP.

46. *OR*, 36(1):345, 1006; Humphreys, *Virginia Campaign*, 182–86.

47. *OR*, 36(3):526, 528, 529, 544, 545, 530, 531, 553.

48. Bonekemper, *Victor, Not a Butcher*, 310, 311; Humphreys, *Virginia Campaign*, 191; Rhea, *Cold Harbor*, 385; Furgurson, *Not War but Murder*, 279; Grant, *Personal Memoirs*, 444, 445; Law, "From the Wilderness to Cold Harbor," in *B&L*, 4:141.

7. ACROSS THE JAMES

1. Lowe, *Meade's Army*, 190.

2. *OR*, 36(3):576, 577; Washington A. Roebling, "Report of the Operations of the Fifth Corps, Army of the Potomac in General Grant's Campaign from Culpepper to Petersburg as Seen by W. A. Roebling, Major and A.D.C., 1864," 85, 86, Gouverneur Kimble Warren Papers, NYSL; Stephen D. Burger Diary, June 4, 1864, FSNMP; Rhea, *On to Petersburg*, 46, 47.

3. *OR*, 36(1):544, 610, 914, 915, 36(3):603, 610–12, 614–16, 619, 649; Roebling, "Report of the Operations of the Fifth Corps," 87, 88, Warren Papers, NYSL; Burger Diary, June 5, 1864, FSNMP.

4. *OR*, 36(3):649–51; Roebling, "Report of the Operations of the Fifth Corps," 88, Warren Papers, NYSL; Capt. John Gedney Diary, June 6, 1864, WCHS; Burger Diary, June 7, 1864, FSNMP; Carl Matteson to "My Dear Sister," June 10, 1864, Carl Matteson Letters, Civil War Collection, BECHS.

5. *OR*, 36(1):610, 36(3):613, 614, 652; Humphreys, *Virginia Campaign*, 190, 191; Rhea, *On to Petersburg*, 85, Louis Schirmer Court-Martial Records, Case MM-2297, RG 153, NA.

6. CSR, Louis Schirmer, 15NYHA, RG 94, NA; Schirmer Court-Martial Records, RG 153, NA. For a full accounting of the circumstances leading up to Schirmer's arrest, his pretrial incarceration, and his three-month-long trial and its aftermath, see the appendix, "The Court-Martial of Louis Schirmer."

7. OR, 36(1):22, 36(3):598; Humphreys, *Virginia Campaign*, 194.

8. OR, 36(3):650, 651, 676, 677; Roebling, "Report of the Operations of the Fifth Corps," 89, Warren Papers, NYSL; Nevins, *Diary of Battle*, 409.

9. OR, 36(3):674, 675, 681; Roebling, "Report of the Operations of the Fifth Corps," 89, Warren Papers, NYSL; Humphreys, *Virginia Campaign*, 193; Rhea, *On to Petersburg*, 106, 107, 109, 110.

10. OR, 36(3):747; Burger Diary, June 9, 1864, FSNMP; Gedney Diary, June 9, 1864, WCHS; Roebling, "Report of the Operations of the Fifth Corps," 90, 91, Warren Papers, NYSL.

11. OR, 36(3):747–49; Humphreys, *Virginia Campaign*, 200–202.

12. OR, 36(3):731; Roebling, "Report of the Operations of the Fifth Corps," 91, Warren Papers, NYSL; Nevins, *Diary of Battle*, 413; Rhea, *On to Petersburg*, 176; Lowe, *Meade's Army*, 201; Modified Journal of Company C, June 11, 1864, 6th New York Heavy Artillery Regimental Papers, Civil War Miscellaneous Collection, USAHEC; Burger Diary, June 11, 1864, FSNMP; Gedney Diary, June 11, 1864, WCHS.

13. OR, 36(1):544, 36(3):762, 763, 767; Roebling, "Report of the Operations of the Fifth Corps," 92, 93, Warren Papers, NYSL; Nevins, *Diary of Battle*, 414, 415; Burger Diary, June 12, 1864, FSNMP.

14. OR, 40(1):453, 40(2):6, 34, 35; Roebling, "Report of the Operations of the Fifth Corps," 93, 94, Warren Papers, NYSL; Burger Diary, June 13, 1864, FSNMP; Rhea, *On to Petersburg*, 197–200, 210–14.

15. OR, 40(2):645, 647; Humphreys, *Virginia Campaign*, 204; Freeman, *Lee's Lieutenants*, 3:528; Hess, *In the Trenches at Petersburg*, 15, 18; Lowe, *Meade's Army*, 203.

16. OR, 40(1):453, 455, 473, 40(2):8; Roebling, "Report of the Operations of the Fifth Corps," 94, 95, Warren Papers, NYSL; Humphreys, *Virginia Campaign*, 202; Burger Diary, June 14, 1864, FSNMP; Gedney Diary, June 14, 1864, WCHS; Wittenberg, *Glory Enough for All*, 293n9. Samaria Church was known to the Federals as Saint Mary's Church, perhaps because "Samaria" sounded to the Yankee ear as "Saint Mary's" when spoken in the local Virginia dialect.

17. OR, 40(1):453, 471; Roebling, "Report of the Operations of the Fifth Corps," 95, 96, Warren Papers, NYSL; Lowe, *Meade's Army*, 202, 204.

18. OR, 40(2):23, 24, 49, 51; Humphreys, *Virginia Campaign*, 202, 203; Roebling, "Report of the Operations of the Fifth Corps," 96, 97, Warren Papers, NYSL; Hess, *In the Trenches at Petersburg*, 17; Lowe, *Meade's Army*, 205.

19. OR, 40(1):471, 496, 522; Roebling, "Report of the Operations of the Fifth Corps," 95, 96, Warren Papers, NYSL; Burger Diary, June 15, 1864, FSNMP; Hess, *In the Trenches at Petersburg*, 13, 15, 16; Rhea, *On to Petersburg*, 225, 227, 229.

20. *OR*, 40(2):63; Roebling, "Report of the Operations of the Fifth Corps," 96, Warren Papers, NYSL; Nevins, *Diary of Battle*, 418; Rhea, *On to Petersburg*, 226; Brainard, *Campaigns of the One Hundred and Forty-Sixth Regiment*, 224.

21. *OR*, 40(2):18.

22. *OR*, 36(1):16, 20; Grant, *Personal Memoirs*, 454, 455; Humphreys, *Virginia Campaign*, 206; Hess, *In the Trenches at Petersburg*, 16; Rhea, *On to Petersburg*, 241, 242.

23. *OR*, 40(1):705; Humphreys, *Virginia Campaign*, 207, 208; Beauregard, "Four Days of Battle at Petersburg," in *B&L*, 4:540; Freeman, *Lee's Lieutenants*, 3:529; Hess, *In the Trenches at Petersburg*, 18; Rhea, *On to Petersburg*, 247, 248. The Dimmock Line derived its name from the engineer who supervised its construction.

24. *OR*, 40(1):306, 705, 40(2):60, 61, 75; Humphreys, *Virginia Campaign*, 208, 212, 213; Hess, *In the Trenches at Petersburg*, 18, 19.

25. *OR*, 40(1):801, 40(2):652, 653, 656–58; Beauregard, "Four Days of Battle at Petersburg," in *B&L*, 4:541; Freeman, *Lee's Lieutenants*, 3:529, 530.

26. *OR*, 40(1):801; Beauregard, "Four Days of Battle at Petersburg," in *B&L*, 4:541; Freeman, *Lee's Lieutenants*, 3:529, 530; Hess, *In the Trenches at Petersburg*, 19, 20.

27. *OR*, 40(1):522, 40(2):50, 51, 63, 64, 95, 96; Hess, *In the Trenches at Petersburg*, 17.

28. *OR*, 40(1):453; Roebling, "Report of the Operations of the Fifth Corps," 97, Warren Papers, NYSL; Rhea, *On to Petersburg*, 232, 233; Burger Diary, June 16, 1864, FSNMP; Belcher, "Reminiscences of the Civil War," 385; History of Company B, June 16, 1864, Company B Order Book, 6th New York Heavy Artillery Regimental and Company Order Books, RG 94, NA; Nevins, *Diary of Battle*, 420; Brainard, *Campaigns of the One Hundred and Forty-Sixth Regiment*, 224. Diarists in Kitching's brigade made specific mention of crossing in the steamers *John Brooks* and *Monohassett*, although the spelling used for the latter vessel varies. Other vessels may also have been employed in transporting the brigade—Capt. John Gedney of the Sixth mentions the steamer *Thomas Powell*. Gedney Diary, June 16, 1864, WCHS. References suggest that the *John Brooks*, formerly a New York City ferry, could itself transport up to 1,500 troops. *OR*, 40(2):102, 144.

29. Nevins, *Diary of Battle*, 420.

30. *OR*, 40(1):23, 192, 193, 199, 453, 40(2):95, 96, 139; Roebling, "Report of the Operations of the Fifth Corps," 97, Warren Papers, NYSL; Brainard, *Campaigns of the One Hundred and Forty-Sixth Regiment*, 225; Humphreys, *Virginia Campaign*, 203.

31. *OR*, 40(2):86, 94; Roebling, "Report of the Operations of the Fifth Corps," 97, Warren Papers, NYSL.

32. *OR*, 40(1):453, 40(2):94, 95, 97; Roebling, "Report of the Operations of the Fifth Corps," 98, Warren Papers, NYSL; Nevins, *Diary of Battle*, 422.

33. *OR*, 40(1):473, 522, 545, 40(2):125, 128, 129, 134, 135; Humphreys, *Virginia*

Campaign, 217–19; Roebling, "Report of the Operations of the Fifth Corps," 98–100, Warren Papers, NYSL; Hess, *In the Trenches at Petersburg*, 25, 26, 28.

34. OR, 40(1):472, 522, 523, 40(2):125, 129; Humphreys, *Virginia Campaign*, 218, 219; Roebling, "Report of the Operations of the Fifth Corps," 99, 100, Warren Papers, NYSL; Greene, *Campaign of Giants*, 164–67.

35. OR, 36(1):608, 40(1):471; CSR, William D. Dickey, 15NYHA, RG 94, NA; Gedney Diary, June 17, 1864, WCHS; Mulholland, *Military Order*, 438. A fellow officer of the Fifteenth later opined in a letter to the secretary of war that Dickey was by far more entitled to that honor for his even more heroic action in a desperate struggle on yet another field of battle. But the unfolding of those dramatic events, unforeseen by the men of the regiment as they hunkered down in their breastworks on the night of June 18, 1864, lay two months in the future.

36. OR, 40(1):473, 40(2):120, 172, 173, 203; Humphreys, *Virginia Campaign*, 221; Roebling, "Report of the Operations of the Fifth Corps," 103, Warren Papers, NYSL.

37. OR, 40(1):761, 40(2):662, 664, 665, 668; Beauregard, "Four Days of Battle at Petersburg," in B&L, 4:542, 543; Freeman, *Lee's Lieutenants*, 3:532–35; Humphreys, *Virginia Campaign*, 219–21; Davis, Perry, and Kirkley, *Atlas to Accompany the Official Records*, Plate 64, Map 1. On June 15 the Confederate secretary of war had ordered all officers exercising separate command in Virginia and North Carolina to report to and receive orders from General Lee. OR, 40(2):654.

38. OR, 40(1):318, 40(2):161, 162, 166, 170; Humphreys, *Virginia Campaign*, 222, 223; Hess, *In the Trenches at Petersburg*, 30. Hancock was unable to command the corps that day because the wound he received at Gettysburg had reopened.

39. OR, 40(1):523, 545, 572, 40(2):192, 193; Nevins, *Diary of Battle*, 424; Hess, *In the Trenches at Petersburg*, 31; Greene, *Campaign of Giants*, 180, 181.

40. OR, 40(1):470, 471, 473, 474, 476, 40(2):187; Roebling, "Report of the Operations of the Fifth Corps," 103–5, Warren Papers, NYSL; Bearss and Suderow, *Petersburg Campaign, Volume 1*, 126.

41. OR, 40(1):188–90, 455–57, 572, 40(2):174, 175; Lowe, *Meade's Army*, 213; Roebling, "Report of the Operations of the Fifth Corps," 104, Warren Papers, NYSL; Bearss and Suderow, *Petersburg Campaign, Volume 1*, 105, 106; Greene, *Campaign of Giants*, 182, 183.

42. OR, 40(2):175–77; Roebling, "Report of the Operations of the Fifth Corps," 105, Warren Papers, NYSL.

43. OR, 40(1):455, 456, 459, 40(2):216, 217; Roebling, "Report of the Operations of the Fifth Corps," 106, 107, Warren Papers, NYSL; Trulock, *In the Hands of Providence*, 209.

44. OR, 40(1):473, 474, 476; Roebling, "Report of the Operations of the Fifth Corps," 106, 107, Warren Papers, NYSL; Nevins, *Diary of Battle*, 424, 425.

45. OR, 40(1):471, 474, 40(2):184; Roebling, "Report of the Operations of the Fifth Corps," 107, Warren Papers, NYSL; Greene, *Campaign of Giants*, 198, 199.

46. OR, 40(1):471; Roebling, "Report of the Operations of the Fifth Corps," 107, Warren Papers, NYSL; Irving, "More Than Conqueror," 151; Gedney Diary, June 18, 1864, WCHS; Brainard, Campaigns of the One Hundred and Forty-Sixth Regiment, 227; Greene, Campaign of Giants, 199.

47. OR, 40(1):318, 40(2):170, 204, 205; Humphreys, Virginia Campaign, 223; Mulholland, Military Order, 438; Hess, In the Trenches at Petersburg, 33, 34.

48. OR, 40(2):156, 157; Nevins, Diary of Battle, 425.

8. IN THE TRENCHES BEFORE PETERSBURG

1. Carl Matteson to "My Dear Sister," June 18, 1864, Carl Matteson Letters, Civil War Collection, BECHS.

2. OR, 40(2):215; Washington A. Roebling, "Report of the Operations of the Fifth Corps, Army of the Potomac in General Grant's Campaign from Culpepper to Petersburg as Seen by W. A. Roebling, Major and A.D.C., 1864," 108, Gouverneur Kimble Warren Papers, NYSL; Nevins, Diary of Battle, 426; Irving, "More Than Conqueror," 151, 152.

3. Humphreys, Virginia Campaign, 226–28; Hess, In the Trenches at Petersburg, 38.

4. OR, 40(1):325–30; Humphreys, Virginia Campaign, 228, 229; Roebling, "Report of the Operations of the Fifth Corps," 109–12, Warren Papers, NYSL; Hess, In the Trenches at Petersburg, 38, 39.

5. OR, 40(2):344, 345, 348, 360, 362, 366, 380, 381, 385, 389, 397; Roebling, "Report of the Operations of the Fifth Corps," 112, Warren Papers, NYSL. Crawford relieved Gibbon's battered division on the Second Corps's right.

6. Carl Matteson to "My Dear Sister," June 22, 1864, Matteson Letters, BECHS; Carl Matteson to "Dear Cyrus," June 24, 1864, Matteson Letters, BECHS.

7. Humphreys, Virginia Campaign, 243; Roebling, "Report of the Operations of the Fifth Corps," 113, Warren Papers, NYSL.

8. Brainard, Campaigns of the One Hundred and Forty-Sixth Regiment, 229, 230; Greene, Campaign of Giants, 243, 244.

9. Brainard, Campaigns of the One Hundred and Forty-Sixth Regiment, 229, 230.

10. OR, 40(1):471, 40(2):569, 588; Nevins, Diary of Battle, 428, 429; Roebling, "Report of the Operations of the Fifth Corps," 112, Warren Papers, NYSL.

11. Jacob Van Vleck to "My Dear Wife & Children," June 24, 1864, Jacob Van Vleck Letters, NYSL; Irving, "More Than Conqueror," 154.

12. OR, 40(1):471, 472, 40(2):346; Stephen D. Burger Diary, June 25, 1864, FSNMP; Capt. John Gedney Diary, June 25, 1864, WCHS; Irving, "More Than Conqueror," 154; Nevins, Diary of Battle, 429.

13. Roebling, "Report of the Operations of the Fifth Corps," 113, Warren Papers, NYSL; Irving, *"More Than Conqueror,"* 156.

14. OR, 40(1):472; Samuel B. Pierce to "Dear Brother & Friends," July 10, 1864, Samuel B. Pierce Letters, NYSL; Gedney Diary, June 25, 1864, WCHS.

15. Carl Matteson to "Dear Cyrus," July 4, 1864, Matteson Letters, BECHS.

16. Lowe, *Meade's Army*, 229; Irving, *"More Than Conqueror,"* 158.

17. Nevins, *Diary of Battle*, 433.

18. OR, 40(3):43; Nevins, *Diary of Battle*, 433; Irving, *"More Than Conqueror,"* 157.

19. Samuel B. Pierce to "Dear Brother & Friends," July 10, 1864, Pierce Letters, NYSL.

20. OR, 40(1):472, and pt. 3, 65, 100, 161–63, 166, 214, 240, 241; Roebling, "Report of the Operations of the Fifth Corps," 115–17, Warren Papers, NYSL; Hess, *In the Trenches at Petersburg*, 58. By this time the Sixth Corps had been withdrawn from the left and sent to Washington. On July 13 the Second Corps would pull out and move to a position behind the Union center. This would leave the Fifth Corps on the extreme left of Grant's line.

21. Brainard, *Campaigns of the One Hundred and Forty-Sixth Regiment*, 230, 231.

22. OR, 40(3):336; Lowe, *Meade's Army*, 235.

23. Jacob Van Vleck to "My Dear Wife & Children," July 20, 1864, Van Vleck Letters, NYSL.

24. Roebling, "Report of the Operations of the Fifth Corps," 119, Warren Papers, NYSL; Nevins, *Diary of Battle*, 439.

25. OR, 40(1):523, 524, 546, 556, 557, pt. 2, 590, and pt. 3, 266; Humphreys, *Virginia Campaign*, 250; Hess, *In the Trenches at Petersburg*, 45.

26. OR, 40(3):437, 438, 443, 448; Greene, *Campaign of Giants*, 393.

27. OR, 40(3):428, 438, 458; Humphreys, *Virginia Campaign*, 251.

28. OR, 40(1):557, 40(3):475, 477; Powell, "Battle of the Petersburg Crater," in B&L, 4:546, 548.

29. OR, 40(1):309–11, 40(3):551–53, 602, 603, 795, 796, 807–9; Humphreys, *Virginia Campaign*, 248, 249; Greene, *Campaign of Giants*, 406, 407, 415, 417.

30. OR, 40(2):301, 40(3):407, 408, 518, 524, 607; Roebling, "Report of the Operations of the Fifth Corps," 119, Warren Papers, NYSL; Humphreys, *Virginia Campaign*, 253; Burger Diary, July 27, 1864, FSNMP; Gedney Diary, July 27, 1864, WCHS; Greene, *Campaign of Giants*, 419, 420. Maj. Gen. William F. "Baldy" Smith had requested—and was granted—relief from command of the Eighteenth Corps.

31. OR, 40(1):77, 40(3):596, 597, 607; Roebling, "Report of the Operations of the Fifth Corps," 120, Warren Papers, NYSL.

32. Powell, "Battle of the Petersburg Crater," in B&L, 4:549; Roebling, "Report of the Operations of the Fifth Corps," 120, 121, Warren Papers, NYSL.

33. Irving, *"More Than Conqueror,"* 165, 167, 168, 170; Gedney Diary, July 30, 1864, WCHS; Carl Matteson to "Dear Cyrus," Aug. 6, 1864, Matteson Letters, BECHS.

34. OR, 40(1):527, 557; Roebling, "Report of the Operations of the Fifth Corps," 121, Warren Papers, NYSL; Powell, "Battle of the Petersburg Crater," in B&L, 4:550, 551; Greene, Campaign of Giants, 436.
35. Gedney Diary, July 30, 1864, WCHS; Burger Diary, July 30, 1864, FSNMP; Carl Matteson to "Dear Cyrus," Aug. 6, 1864, Matteson Letters, BECHS.
36. Powell, "Battle of the Petersburg Crater," in B&L, 4:551–53; Greene, Campaign of Giants, 441, 442.
37. OR 40(1):527, 528; Powell, "Battle of the Petersburg Crater," in B&L, 4:553; Humphreys, Virginia Campaign, 256, 257; Roebling, "Report of the Operations of the Fifth Corps," 123, Warren Papers, NYSL; Greene, Campaign of Giants, 449–51.
38. OR, 40(1):527, 528; Powell, "Battle of the Petersburg Crater," in B&L, 4:553–55; Humphreys, Virginia Campaign, 257, 260; Hess, In the Trenches at Petersburg, 92, 93, 95, 96; Greene, Campaign of Giants, 460–62.
39. OR, 40(3):654; Powell, "Battle of the Petersburg Crater," in B&L, 4:558; Humphreys, Virginia Campaign, 259, 260, 262; Roebling, "Report of the Operations of the Fifth Corps," 125, Warren Papers, NYSL; Hess, In the Trenches at Petersburg, 98–100; Greene, Campaign of Giants, 470, 471, 481–84.
40. Powell, "Battle of the Petersburg Crater," in B&L, 4:558; Humphreys, Virginia Campaign, 259, 261–63; Houghton, "In the Crater," in B&L, 4:562; Hess, In the Trenches at Petersburg, 101, 102; Roebling, Report of the Operations of the Fifth Corps, NYSL, 125, 126; Greene, Campaign of Giants, 490, 496, 498–500.
41. OR, 40(3):699, 821, 42(2):10; Humphreys, Virginia Campaign, 263; Lowe, Meade's Army, 244; Hess, In the Trenches at Petersburg, 104, 105.
42. OR, 40(1):17; Irving, "More Than Conqueror," 167–70.
43. Nevins, Diary of Battle, 443, 447.
44. Jacob Van Vleck to "My Dear Wife & Family," Aug. 6, 1864, Van Vleck Letters, NYSL; Brainard, Campaigns of the One Hundred and Forty-Sixth Regiment, 234; Carl Matteson to "Dear Cyrus," Aug. 6, 1864, Matteson Letters, BECHS.
45. OR, 40(1):42, 43, 128, 129, 42(2):44, 168, 177, 178; Humphreys, Virginia Campaign, 264, 265, 430, 431; Hess, In the Trenches at Petersburg, 106.
46. OR, 40(1):472; Irving, "More Than Conqueror," 171; Roebling, "Report of the Operations of the Fifth Corps," 126, 127, 129, 130, Warren Papers, NYSL.
47. OR, 40(3):313, 314, 345; Irving, "More Than Conqueror," 163, 164.
48. OR, 40(3):349, 469, 42(2):151.
49. Samuel B. Pierce to "Dear Brother," Aug. 21, 1864, Pierce Letters, NYSL; Gedney Diary, Aug. 13, 14, 1864, WCHS; Burger Diary, Aug. 13, 14, 1864, FSNMP.
50. OR, 43(1):33, 55, 128, 403; Merritt, "Sheridan in the Shenandoah Valley," in B&L, 4:516, 520; Irving, "More Than Conqueror," 152, 201, 209, 213, 214, 224–27, 231–33. Confederate major general Stephen Dodson Ramseur also fell severely wounded in the action at Cedar Creek. He died the following day in Federal hands.

9. CUTTING THE WELDON RAILROAD AND THE BATTLE OF GLOBE TAVERN

1. Carl Matteson to "Dear Cyrus," Aug. 12, 1864, Carl Matteson Letters, Civil War Collection, BECHS.

2. *OR*, 42(1):216, 42(2):112, 114, 115, 132, 133; Humphreys, *Virginia Campaign*, 267–69; Horn, *Destruction of the Weldon Railroad*, 5. Early and his corps had been dispatched to operate in the Shenandoah Valley in mid-June. In fact, only one Confederate infantry division, Kershaw's, had been sent at the beginning of August to reinforce Early. Also early in August, Sheridan assumed command of the Federal forces the Valley, taking with him two of the Army of the Potomac's cavalry divisions.

3. *OR*, 42(1):216–21, 677, 678; Humphreys, *Virginia Campaign*, 268–72.

4. *OR*, 42(2):153, 201; Bearss and Suderow, *Petersburg Campaign, Volume 1*, 240n2; Agassiz, *Meade's Headquarters*, 217; Washington A. Roebling, "Report of the Operations of the Fifth Corps, Army of the Potomac in General Grant's Campaign from Culpepper to Petersburg as Seen by W. A. Roebling, Major and A.D.C., 1864," 131, Gouverneur Kimble Warren Papers, NYSL.

5. *OR*, 42(2):244, 245, 251; Humphreys, *Virginia Campaign*, 273; Willcox, "Actions on the Weldon Railroad," in *B&L*, 4:568; Bearss and Suderow, *Petersburg Campaign, Volume 1*, 240.

6. *OR*, 42(2):251; Humphreys, *Virginia Campaign*, 273; Roebling, "Report of the Operations of the Fifth Corps," 132, 133, Warren Papers, NYSL.

7. CSR, Julius Dieckmann, 15NYHA, RG 94, NA; CSR, Emil Duysing, 15NYHA, RG 94, NA; CSR, Louis Eiche, 15NYHA, RG 94, NA; Phisterer, *New York in the War of the Rebellion*, 2:1500, 1510; order, Aug. 15, 1864, Regimental Order Book, 15NYHA Regimental Books, RG 94, NA. Major Duysing would not return to duty until early October, while Dieckmann would not until the end of that month.

8. *OR*, 42(1):428, 458, 42(2):252; Powell, *Fifth Army Corps*, 710, 711; Brainard, *Campaigns of the One Hundred and Forth-Sixth Regiment*, 237; Roebling, "Report of the Operations of the Fifth Corps," 132, 133, Warren Papers, NYSL; Edwin C. Bearss, "Battle of the Weldon Railroad," n.d., PNB, 5; Hess, *In the Trenches at Petersburg*, 129.

9. *OR*, 1:458, 42(2):272; Roebling, "Report of the Operations of the Fifth Corps," 133, 134, Warren Papers, NYSL; Powell, *Fifth Army Corps*, 711; Survivors' Association, *Corn Exchange Regiment*, 498.

10. Powell, *Fifth Army Corps*, 711; Brainard, *Campaigns of the One Hundred and Forth-Sixth Regiment*, 237, 238; Roebling, "Report of the Operations of the Fifth Corps," 135, Warren Papers, NYSL; Bearss, "Battle of the Weldon Railroad," PNB, 6, 7; Lowe, *Meade's Army*, 251; Nevins, *Diary of Battle*, 452; George Breck to *Rochester Union and Advertiser*, Sept. 4, 1864, Lt. George Breck Letters to *Rochester Union and Advertiser*, PNB.

11. *OR*, 42(1):429, 458; Bearss, "Battle of the Weldon Railroad," PNB, 6; Horn, *Destruction of the Weldon Railroad*, 58, 59. This method of destroying railroads was commonplace. When practiced by Sherman's western forces, the rails left bent around trees or telegraph poles were often referred to as "Sherman's neckties."

12. *OR*, 42(1):471, 474, 480, 42(2):273; Powell, *Fifth Corps*, 712; Roebling, "Report of the Operations of the Fifth Corps," 134, Warren Papers, NYSL; Hess, *In the Trenches at Petersburg*, 130; Bearss and Suderow, *Petersburg Campaign*, Volume 1, 247–49.

13. *OR*, 42(1):471, 474, 491, 540; Roebling, "Report of the Operations of the Fifth Corps," 136, Warren Papers, NYSL; Brainard, *Campaigns of the One Hundred and Forty-Sixth Regiment*, 238; Nevins, *Diary of Battle*, 452.

14. *OR*, 42(2):1186; Horn, *Destruction of the Weldon Railroad*, 61, 62; Bearss, "Battle of the Weldon Railroad," PNB, 9–11; Bearss and Suderow, *Petersburg Campaign*, Volume 1, 251, 252; Washington L. Dunn Diary, Aug. 18, 1864, United Daughters of the Confederacy Transcripts, Georgia Department of Archives and History, Morrow.

15. *OR*, 42(1):471, 474, 480, 503, 42(2):273; Roebling, "Report of the Operations of the Fifth Corps," 136, 137, Warren Papers, NYSL; Horn, *Destruction of the Weldon Railroad*, 62, 63; Bearss, "Battle of the Weldon Railroad," PNB, 11.

16. *OR*, 42(1):429, 471, 474, 480, 491, 540, 42(2):273; Roebling, "Report of the Operations of the Fifth Corps," 136, 137, Warren Papers, NYSL; Horn, *Destruction of the Weldon Railroad*, 60, 62, 63; Bearss, "Battle of the Weldon Railroad," PNB, 8, 9, 11.

17. *OR*, 42(1):471; Mulholland, *Military Order*, 439.

18. Mulholland, *Military Order*, 439.

19. Mulholland, *Military Order*, 439; Jacob Van Vleck to "My Dear Wife & Family," Aug. 20, 1864, Jacob Van Vleck Letters, NYSL.

20. *OR*, 42(1):480, 483; Roebling, "Report of the Operations of the Fifth Corps," 137, 138, Warren Papers, NYSL; Horn, *Destruction of the Weldon Railroad*, 63, 64; Bearss, "Battle of the Weldon Railroad," PNB, 12.

21. *OR*, 42(1):471, 483, 484, 534; Horn, *Destruction of the Weldon Railroad*, 64; Bearss, "Battle of the Weldon Railroad," PNB, 12, 13. Wiedrich would return to duty within weeks.

22. *OR*, 42(1):429, 42(2):274, 275; Lowe, *Meade's Army*, 251.

23. Agassiz, *Meade's Headquarters*, 207–9.

24. *OR*, 42(1):544, 545, 550, 589, 42(2):265, 266, 268–71, 281–83, 288–90, 293, 305, 316; Bearss, "Battle of the Weldon Railroad," PNB, 19, 20; Horn, *Destruction of the Weldon Railroad*, 66, 67, 70.

25. *OR*, 42(2):1190; Horn, *Destruction of the Weldon Railroad*, 74, 76, 77; Bearss, "Battle of the Weldon Railroad," PNB, 28.

26. *OR*, 42(1):429, 492, 493, 535, 539, 42(2):305; Roebling, "Report of the Operations of the Fifth Corps," 140, Warren Papers, NYSL; Bearss, "Battle of the

Weldon Railroad," 22; Mickey of Co. K [James P. Sullivan], "The Fight for the Weldon Railroad," *Milwaukee Sunday Telegraph*, June 28, 1885, PNB.

27. OR, 42(1):429, 493, 535, 536; Powell, *Fifth Army Corps*, 713–15; Willcox, "Actions on the Weldon Railroad," in B&L, 4:569; Horn, *Destruction of the Weldon Railroad*, 78; Bearss, "Battle of the Weldon Railroad," PNB, 30, 31.

28. OR, 42(1):429, 430, 493, 494, 510; Powell, *Fifth Army Corps*, 713, 714; Willcox, "Actions on the Weldon Railroad," in B&L, 4:569; Horn, *Destruction of the Weldon Railroad*, 79–81; Bearss, "Battle of the Weldon Railroad," PNB, 31, 33, 34.

29. OR, 42(1):471, 472, 474, 475, 479.

30. OR, 42(1):472, 474; Mulholland, *Military Order*, 439; Horn, *Destruction of the Weldon Railroad*, 82.

31. OR, 42(1):430, 472, 474, 475; Mulholland, *Military Order*, 440.

32. OR, 42(1):430, 494, 510, 550, 589, 590; Willcox, "Actions on the Weldon Railroad," in B&L, 4:569, 570; Roebling, "Report of the Operations of the Fifth Corps," 144–46, Warren Papers, NYSL; Powell, *Fifth Army Corps*, 715; Horn, *Destruction of the Weldon Railroad*, 82, 84–86.

33. OR, 42(1):430, 458, 472, 475, 550; Roebling, "Report of the Operations of the Fifth Corps," 146, 147, Warren Papers, NYSL; Powell, *Fifth Army Corps*, 715; Horn, *Destruction of the Weldon Railroad*, 87; Bearss, "Battle of the Weldon Railroad," PNB, 343; S. J. Jackson Diary, Aug. 19, 1864, ACHNHP.

34. OR, 42(2):308, 309; Horn, *Destruction of the Weldon Railroad*, 87; Humphreys, *Virginia Campaign*, 275, 276.

35. OR, 42(1):430, 595, 596; Roebling, "Report of the Operations of the Fifth Corps," 146, 149, Warren Papers, NYSL; Horn, *Destruction of the Weldon Railroad*, 88; Dunn Diary, Aug. 19, 1864, Georgia Department of Archives and History.

36. OR, 12(3):587, 42(1):475, 42(2):345; Phisterer, *New York in the War of the Rebellion*, 2:1499; Horn, *Destruction of the Weldon Railroad*, 81, 82.

37. OR, 27(1):651; Phisterer, *New York in the War of the Rebellion*, 4:3615, 3616; Powell, *Fifth Army Corps*, 608, 609. Coincidentally, many of the heavies of the Fifteenth had earlier served in the fort in the Washington defenses named for O'Rourke.

38. OR, 27(1):651; Phisterer, *New York in the War of the Rebellion*, 5:3687, 3688; Powell, *Fifth Army Corps*, 608, 609.

39. Phisterer, *New York in the War of the Rebellion*, 2:1769, 1770; Schroeder, *We Came to Fight*, 119, 121.

40. OR, 40(3):320, 321; Phisterer, *New York in the War of the Rebellion*, 2:1779; Schroeder, *We Came to Fight*, 139, 155, 157, 168, 169, 180; Hunt and Brown, *Brevet Brigadier Generals in Blue*, 684.

41. Smith, *American Civil War Zouaves*, 30; Schroeder, *We Came to Fight*, 121, 157; Bennett, *Sons of Old Monroe*, 349–51, 368.

42. OR, 42(2):1192; Horn, *Destruction of the Weldon Railroad*, 91, 92; Bearss, "Battle of the Weldon Railroad," PNB, 54, 55.

43. *OR*, 42(1):430; Roebling, "Report of the Operations of the Fifth Corps," 148, Warren Papers, NYSL; Horn, *Destruction of the Weldon Railroad*, 93.

44. *OR*, 42(1):458, 505, 515, 518, 521, 534, 536, 540, 541, 551, 552, 590, 594, 596; Roebling, "Report of the Operations of the Fifth Corps," 148–50, Warren Papers, NYSL; Horn, *Destruction of the Weldon Railroad*, 93, 94; Bearss, "Battle of the Weldon Railroad," PNB, 51–53; Mickey of Co. K, "Fight for the Weldon Railroad," July 5, 1885, PNB.

45. *OR*, 42(1):472, 475, 481, 42(2):344; Jackson Diary, Aug. 20, 1864, ACHNHP; Roebling, "Report of the Operations of the Fifth Corps," 149, 150, Warren Papers, NYSL; Brainard, *Campaigns of the One Hundred and Forty-Sixth Regiment*, 240; Horn, *Destruction of the Weldon Railroad*, 94, 95.

46. *OR*, 42(1):472, 475; Roebling, "Report of the Operations of the Fifth Corps," 150, Warren Papers, NYSL; Brainard, *Campaigns of the One Hundred and Forty-Sixth Regiment*, 240; Horn, *Destruction of the Weldon Railroad*, 95.

47. Bearss, "Battle of the Weldon Railroad," PNB, 56; Horn, *Destruction of the Weldon Railroad*, 96; Mickey of Co. K, "Fight for the Weldon Railroad," July 5, 1885, PNB.

48. *OR*, 42(1):430, 472, 475; Roebling, "Report of the Operations of the Fifth Corps," 150, 151, Warren Papers, NYSL; Jackson Diary, Aug. 21, 1864, ACHNHP; Bearss, "Battle of the Weldon Railroad," PNB, 55, 56, 58; Horn, *Destruction of the Weldon Railroad*, 96, 97.

49. *OR*, 42(1):430, 472, 475; Brainard, *Campaigns of the One Hundred and Forty-Sixth Regiment*, 241; Schroeder, *We Came to Fight*, 187.

50. *OR*, 42(1):430, 431, 472, 541, 542; Roebling, "Report of the Operations of the Fifth Corps," 151, Warren Papers, NYSL; Nevins, *Diary of Battle*, 454; Nathaniel Harris to William Mahone, Aug. 2, 1866, Mahone Family Papers, Virginia State Library Archives, Richmond; Bearss, "Battle of the Weldon Railroad," PNB, 59, 64; Horn, *Destruction of the Weldon Railroad*, 96, 97.

51. *OR*, 42(1):542, 472; Roebling, "Report of the Operations of the Fifth Corps," 152, Warren Papers, NYSL; Survivors' Association, *Corn Exchange Regiment*, 502.

52. Roebling, "Report of the Operations of the Fifth Corps," 152, 153, Warren Papers, NYSL; Powell, *Fifth Army Corps*, 718; Mickey of Co. K, "Fight for the Weldon Railroad," July 5, 1885, PNB; Nevins, *Diary of Battle*, 455; Horn, *Destruction of the Weldon Railroad*, 103; Bearss, "Battle of the Weldon Railroad," PNB, 65, 66.

53. *OR*, 42(1):123, 124, 128; Phisterer, *New York in the War of the Rebellion*, 2:1499, 1515, 1516; Horn, *Destruction of the Weldon Railroad*, 107, 111; Bearss, "Battle of the Weldon Railroad," PNB, 69; Willcox, "Actions on the Weldon Railroad," in *B&L*, 4:571.

54. *OR*, 42(1):476; Nevins, *Diary of Battle*, 453.

55. Carl Matteson to "My Dear Sister," Aug. 26, 1864, Carl Matteson Letters, Civil War Collection, BECHS; Jacob Van Vleck to "My Dear Wife & Family," Aug. 30, 1864, Van Vleck Letters, NYSL.

10. THE BATTLE OF PEEBLES'S FARM

1. OR, 42(2):370, 372, 453, 547, 615, 616; S. J. Jackson Diary, Aug. 22, 1864, ACHNHP; Schroeder, *We Came to Fight*, 189. Cutler had received serious wounds to his face during the August 21 fight.
2. OR, 42(1):222–28; Humphreys, *Virginia Campaign*, 278–82.
3. OR, 42(2):491, 492; Jackson Diary, Aug. 25, 1864, ACHNHP.
4. Tilney, *My Life in the Army*, 130.
5. Nevins, *Diary of Battle*, 460; George Breck to *Rochester Union and Advertiser*, Sept. 10, 1864, Lt. George Breck Letters to *Rochester Union and Advertiser*, PNB; Jackson Diary, Aug. 29, Sept. 4, 1864, ACHNHP.
6. Nevins, *Diary of Battle*, 459.
7. Tilney, *My Life in the Army*, 137, 138; Brainard, *Campaigns of the One Hundred and Forty-Sixth Regiment*, 242, 243.
8. OR, 42(2):631, 750–54, 789, 800, 801; Schroeder, *We Came to Fight*, 197.
9. OR, 42(1):164, 42(2):636, 705, 955; Hess, *In the Trenches at Petersburg*, 143, 144.
10. OR, 42(1):163–65, 42(2):682, 684–86, 689, 690; Hess, *In the Trenches at Petersburg*, 144–46.
11. OR, 42(2):903; Jackson Diary, Sept. 22, 1864, ACHNHP; Schroeder, *We Came to Fight*, 198, 199, 201, 203.
12. Sommers, *Richmond Redeemed*, 180; Hess, *In the Trenches at Petersburg*, 151.
13. Sommers, *Richmond Redeemed*, 180, 245, 246; Hess, *In the Trenches at Petersburg*, 151, 152.
14. Carl Matteson to "My Dear Sister," Sept. 4, 1864, Carl Matteson Letters, Civil War Collection, BECHS.
15. OR, 42(2):1046, 1047, 1058, 1059, 1084–86; Humphreys, *Virginia Campaign*, 284, 285; Sommers, *Richmond Redeemed*, 21, 22.
16. OR, 42(2):1046–48, 1069, 1075; Humphreys, *Virginia Campaign*, 290; Powell, *Fifth Army Corps*, 730; Bearss and Suderow, *Petersburg Campaign, Volume 2*, 4, 6, 7, 10.
17. CSR, Michael Wiedrich, 15NYHA, RG 94, NA; CSR, Julius Dieckmann, 15NYHA, RG 94, NA; CSR, Emil Duysing, 15NYHA, RG 94, NA; CSR, Louis Eiche, 15NYHA, RG 94, NA.
18. OR, 42(2):1090–92, 1109–11; Humphreys, *Virginia Campaign*, 285–89; Hess, *In the Trenches at Petersburg*, 160, 161, 163, 164; Bearss and Suderow, *Petersburg Campaign, Volume 2*, 15, 16.
19. OR, 42(2):1092–94; Jackson Diary, Sept. 29, 1864, ACHNHP; Humphreys, *Virginia Campaign*, 290, 291.
20. OR, 42(2):1118, 1131, 1137; Jackson Diary, Sept. 30, 1864, ACHNHP; Bearss and Suderow, *Petersburg Campaign, Volume 2*, 18, 19.
21. Powell, *Fifth Army Corps*, 730; Nevins, *Diary of Battle*, 466; Sommers, *Richmond Redeemed*, 240, 241, 247, 248.

22. OR, 42(1):477, 545, 578, 42(2):1131; Theodore Lyman to Francis Palfrey, Nov. 11, 1864, Lyman Papers, Massachusetts Military History Society Collection, Boston Univ., Boston, MA; Nevins, *Diary of Battle*, 467; Brainard, *Campaigns of the One Hundred and Forty-Sixth Regiment*, 245; Sommers, *Richmond Redeemed*, 248, 249.

23. OR, 42(1):546, 578, 42(2):1131, 1132; Powell, *Fifth Army Corps*, 730, 731; Nevins, *Diary of Battle*, 467; Sommers, *Richmond Redeemed*, 252–55; Hess, *In the Trenches at Petersburg*, 152.

24. OR, 42(2):1132; Sommers, *Richmond Redeemed*, 254, 255, 257.

25. OR, 42(1):477, 478, 578, 42(2):1132, 1135; Brainard, *Campaigns of the One Hundred and Forty-Sixth Regiment*, 245; Sommers, *Richmond Redeemed*, 258, 259.

26. OR, 42(1):546, 553, 579, 42(2):1121; Humphreys, *Virginia Campaign*, 291, 292; Powell, *Fifth Army Corps*, 731, 732; Sommers, *Richmond Redeemed*, 273, 274, 294, 295; Nevins, *Diary of Battle*, 467, 468; Bearss and Suderow, *Petersburg Campaign, Volume 2*, 42.

27. OR, 42(1):478; Brainard, *Campaigns of the One Hundred and Forty-Sixth Regiment*, 245; Sommers, *Richmond Redeemed*, 293, 294, 315, 316.

28. OR, 42(2):1132, 1133, 1137, 1138; Tilney, *My Life in the Army*, 140; Sommers, *Richmond Redeemed*, 316; Bearss and Suderow, *Petersburg Campaign, Volume 2*, 46.

29. Sommers, *Richmond Redeemed*, 307–9, 314; Bearss and Suderow, *Petersburg Campaign, Volume 2*, 55, 56.

30. OR, 42(1):478, 42(3):18; Jackson Diary, Oct. 1, 1864, ACHNHP; Sommers, *Richmond Redeemed*, 326, 328, 329.

31. OR, 42(1):478; Brainard, *Campaigns of the One Hundred and Forty-Sixth Regiment*, 245, 246; Sommers, *Richmond Redeemed*, 333–36; Jackson Diary, Oct. 1, 1864, ACHNHP.

32. OR, 42(2):1135, 42(3):18; Sommers, *Richmond Redeemed*, 316, 330, 331; Bennett, *Sons of Old Monroe*, 639, 641. Otis not only recovered from his wound but also was brevetted a brigadier general for his service that day. He rejoined the army after the war and enjoyed a long, distinguished career, eventually rising to the rank of major general before his retirement in 1902. Otis died in 1909 and is buried in Arlington National Cemetery.

33. OR, 42(1):344, 345, 546, 547, 580, 42(3):36, 41, 44, 45, 50, 51; Sommers, *Richmond Redeemed*, 378, 380, 383, 384, 408, 409; Hess, *In the Trenches at Petersburg*, 166.

34. OR, 42(1):478, 42(3):41–43, 50, 51; Brainard, *Campaigns of the One Hundred and Forty-Sixth Regiment*, 246; Sommers, *Richmond Redeemed*, 384, 385, 390, 391, 398, 399.

35. OR, 42(1):547; Humphreys, *Virginia Campaign*, 292; Sommers, *Richmond Redeemed*, App. B, 480, 499; Phisterer, *New York in the War of the Rebellion*, 2:1499; Nevins, *Diary of Battle*, 469; Hess, *In the Trenches at Petersburg*, 166; Bearss and Suderow, *Petersburg Campaign, Volume 2*, 80.

36. OR, 42(3):51, 80; Theodore Lyman to Francis Palfrey, Nov. 11, 1864, Lyman Papers, Boston Univ.; Hess, *In the Trenches at Petersburg*, 166–68.

37. OR, 42(1):478 42(2):86, 207; Brainard, *Campaigns of the One Hundred and Forty-Sixth Regiment*, 246; Nevins, *Diary of Battle*, 469, 470; Hess, *In the Trenches at Petersburg*, 167; Carl Matteson to "My Dear Sister," Oct. 9, 1864, Matteson Letters, BECHS. Fort Keene was named in honor of Capt. Weston H. Keene of the Twentieth Maine, who had fallen in the fighting around the Peebles's farm.

38. OR, 42(3):294, 317, 318; Humphreys, *Virginia Campaign*, 294; Hess, *In the Trenches at Petersburg*, 190, 191; Bearss and Suderow, *Petersburg Campaign, Volume 2*, 84, 85; Newsome, *Richmond Must Fall*, 119, 120, 129.

39. OR, 42(3):230, 340, 341; Humphreys, *Virginia Campaign*, 294, 295; Newsome, *Richmond Must Fall*, 133, 134.

40. OR, 42(3):340, 341; Humphreys, *Virginia Campaign*, 295; Bearss and Suderow, *Petersburg Campaign, Volume 2*, 89; Newsome, *Richmond Must Fall*, 133.

41. OR, 42(1):231, 232, 295–97, 42(3):379, 380; Humphreys, *Virginia Campaign*, 298, 299; Edwin C. Bearss, "The Battle of the Boydton Plank Road, October 27–28, 1864," [1966], PNB, 18–22, 26, 29, 30; Newsome, *Richmond Must Fall*, 197, 198, 201, 220, 221.

42. OR, 42(1):437, 459, 548, 549, 42(3):379, 385; Humphreys, *Virginia Campaign*, 296; Powell, *Fifth Army Corps*, 739, 740; Bearss and Suderow, *Petersburg Campaign, Volume 2*, 110; Newsome, *Richmond Must Fall*, 143, 178, 183–86.

43. OR, 42(1):437, 440, 42(3):379, 380; Humphreys, *Virginia Campaign*, 296, 297; Powell, *Fifth Army Corps*, 740; Bearss and Suderow, *Petersburg Campaign, Volume 2*, 111; Newsome, *Richmond Must Fall*, 192, 195, 229.

44. OR, 42(1):437, 438, 495–97, 42(3):386; Humphreys, *Virginia Campaign*, 297, 298; Bearss, "Battle of the Boydton Plank Road," PNB, 41, 42; Bearss and Suderow, *Petersburg Campaign, Volume 2*, 112; Newsome, *Richmond Must Fall*, 229–32. The Second (Maryland) Brigade had been detached from Ayres's division to operate with Crawford in the advance along Hatcher's Run.

45. Humphreys, *Virginia Campaign*, 300, 301; Hess, *In the Trenches at Petersburg*, 193; Bearss and Suderow, *Petersburg Campaign, Volume 2*, 118–21; Newsome, *Richmond Must Fall*, 212–14, 239, 244.

46. OR, 42(1):232–35, 297, 298, 359, 360, 411–13, 609; Humphreys, *Virginia Campaign*, 301, 302; Newsome, *Richmond Must Fall*, 247, 248, 254, 256, 258, 267, 268.

47. OR, 42(1):438, 439, 42(3):381, 403; Humphreys, *Virginia Campaign*, 302, 303; Powell, *Fifth Army Corps*, 743, 744; Newsome, *Richmond Must Fall*, 276, 277; Bearss and Suderow, *Petersburg Campaign, Volume 2*, 150.

48. OR, 42(1):235, 236, 42(3):380, 381; Humphreys, *Virginia Campaign*, 299, 300; Bearss and Suderow, *Petersburg Campaign, Volume 2*, 150, 152; Newsome, *Richmond Must Fall*, 277, 278.

49. OR, 42(1):439, 42(3):412, 413, 415; Bearss and Suderow, *Petersburg Campaign, Volume 2*, 157, 158, 160; Newsome, *Richmond Must Fall*, 287, 288.

50. Nevins, *Diary of Battle*, 477; Agassiz, *Meade's Headquarters*, 251; Jacob Van Vleck to "My Dear Wife & Family," Oct. 29, 1864, Jacob Van Vleck Letters, NYSL.

11. THE RAID ON THE WELDON RAILROAD AND THE BATTLE OF HATCHER'S RUN

1. Brainard, *Campaigns of the One Hundred and Forty-Sixth Regiment*, 248, 249; Tilney, *My Life in the Army*, 150.
2. *OR*, 42(3):444, 471, 479; Brainard, *Campaigns of the One Hundred and Forty-Sixth Regiment*, 249; Schroeder, *We Came to Fight*, 208.
3. *OR*, 42(3):549; Tilney, *My Life in the Army*, 151, 152; Nevins, *Diary of Battle*, 480, 481; Schroeder, *We Came to Fight*, 211.
4. *OR*, 42(3):483; Schroeder, *We Came to Fight*, 201, 211.
5. Nevins, *Diary of Battle*, 481, 482.
6. Jacob Van Vleck to "My Dear Wife and Daughter," Nov. 17, 1864, Jacob Van Vleck Letters, NYSL.
7. Jacob Van Vleck to "My Dear Wife Daughter & Friends," Nov. 16, 1864, Van Vleck Letters, NYSL; Tilney, *My Life in the Army*, 155, 156; Nevins, *Diary of Battle*, 482, 483; Agassiz, *Meade's Headquarters*, 278.
8. CSR, Julius Dieckmann, 15NYHA, RG 94, NA; CSR, Louis Eiche, 15NYHA, RG 94, NA; Regimental Special Orders No. 27, Dec. 1, 1864, Company G Order Book, 15NYHA Regimental Books, RG 94, NA.
9. *OR*, 42(3):794, 795, 798, 799, 829, 830; Survivors' Association, *Corn Exchange Regiment*, 532; Rhodes, *All for the Union*, 200.
10. *OR*, 42(3):705, 713, 714, 784, 785, 804, 805, 823, 824, 828, 829; R. H. McBride in *Chronicle Newspaper*, Dec. 12, 1864 (dateline), Warren Papers, NYSL. Hicksford is the site of present-day Emporia, Virginia.
11. *OR*, 42(1):350, 355, 443, 42(3):831, 855; Tilney, *My Life in the Army*, 161.
12. *OR*, 42(1):355, 443, 624; Nevins, *Diary of Battle*, 487; Calkins, "Apple Jack Raid," 19.
13. *OR*, 42(1):350, 355, 443, 482, 611, 624, 42(3):856; Nevins, *Diary of Battle*, 487.
14. *OR*, 42(1):443, 459, 473; Tilney, *My Life in the Army*, 162; Brainard, *Campaigns of the One Hundred and Forty-Sixth Regiment*, 250; Nevins, *Diary of Battle*, 488; Calkins, "Apple Jack Raid," 19.
15. *OR*, 42(1):369, 443, 498; Brainard, *Campaigns of the One Hundred and Forty-Sixth Regiment*, 250–53; Trudeau, *Last Citadel*, 269; Survivors' Association, *Corn Exchange Regiment*, 540; Calkins, "Apple Jack Raid," 19.
16. Nevins, *Diary of Battle*, 488, 489; R. H. McBride in *Chronicle Newspaper*, Dec. 12, 1864 (dateline), Warren Papers, NYSL; Calkins, "Apple Jack Raid," 20.
17. *OR*, 42(1):444, 498, 611, 612, 42(3):882; Brainard, *Campaigns of the One Hundred and Forty-Sixth Regiment*, 251.
18. *OR*, 42(1):355, 356, 444, 473, 477; R. H. McBride in *Chronicle Newspaper*, Dec. 12, 1864 (dateline), Warren Papers, NYSL; Brainard, *Campaigns of the One Hundred and Forty-Sixth Regiment*, 251; Survivors' Association, *Corn Exchange Regiment*, 534; Calkins, "Apple Jack Raid," 20.
19. *OR*, 42(1):444, 459, 460, 473, 477, 498, 42(2):914; S. J. Jackson Diary, Dec. 9, 1864, ACHNHP; Tilney, *My Life in the Army*, 163.

20. OR, 42(1):444, 612; Nevins, Diary of Battle, 489; Calkins, "Apple Jack Raid," 21, 22. The forces confronting Warren at Belfield/Hicksford were, in part, elements of Maj. Gen. Wade Hampton's cavalry. The Confederates had arrived there earlier in the day after being dispatched from Petersburg on December 7 shortly after the Federal movement was detected. Hampton was to be supported by Lt. Gen. A. P. Hill's corps, which was by now advancing from its position in the Petersburg defenses. But Hill would not arrive in time to prevent Warren's escape.

21. OR, 42(1):444, 473, 477, 496; Brainard, Campaigns of the One Hundred and Forty-Sixth Regiment, 252; Tilney, My Life in the Army, 163; Schroeder, We Came to Fight, 219.

22. OR, 42(1):350, 445, 498, 612, 42(3):915; Brainard, Campaigns of the One Hundred and Forty-Sixth Regiment, 252; Survivors' Association, Corn Exchange Regiment, 538; Agassiz, Meade's Headquarters, 300; Nevins, Diary of Battle, 489, 490; Schroeder, We Came to Fight, 219; Trudeau, Last Citadel, 278.

23. OR, 42(1):350, 356; 445, 460, 498, 612, 613; Brainard, Campaigns of the One Hundred and Forty-Sixth Regiment, 252; Survivors' Association, Corn Exchange Regiment, 538; Schroeder, We Came to Fight, 220; Calkins, "Apple Jack Raid," 22.

24. OR, 42(1):350, 356; 445, 460; Brainard, Campaigns of the One Hundred and Forty-Sixth Regiment, 253; Nevins, Diary of Battle, 491; Schroeder, We Came to Fight, 221; Survivors' Association, Corn Exchange Regiment, 538, Trudeau, Last Citadel, 279, 280.

25. Belcher, "Reminiscences of the Civil War," 386.

26. OR, 42(1):353, 445, 460, 482, 498, 42(3):932, 964; Schroeder, We Came to Fight, 221; Trudeau, Last Citadel, 284.

27. OR, 42(1):445, 473, 477, 613, 42(3):978; Phisterer, New York in the War of the Rebellion, 2:1499; Schroeder, We Came to Fight, 221; Belcher, "Reminiscences of the Civil War," 386.

28. OR, 42(1):445, 446, 482; Nevins, Diary of Battle, 490; Calkins, "Apple Jack Raid," 22, 23, Trudeau, Last Citadel, 280, 282, 283.

29. OR, 42(3):1001; Powell, Fifth Army Corps, 752, 753; Bennett, Sons of Old Monroe, 536, 537.

30. OR, 42(3):1073; Jackson Diary, Dec. 25, 1864, ACHNHP; Tilney, My Life in the Army, 170, 171.

31. Orders, Jan. 1, 12, 1865, Company I Order Book, 15NYHA Regimental Books, RG 94, NA.

32. OR, 46(2):353; CSR, Louis Eiche, 15NYHA, RG 94, NA.

33. Order, Jan. 14, 1865, Company G Order Book, 15NYHA Regimental Books, RG 94, NA.

34. Circular, Jan. 21, 1865, Company I Order Book, 15NYHA Regimental Books, RG 94, NA.

35. Jacob Van Vleck to "My Dear Wife & Family," Jan. 22, 1865, Van Vleck Letters, NYSL.

36. Orders, Jan. 30, 31, 1865, Company G Order Book, 15NYHA Regimental Books, RG 94, NA; Headquarters, First Brigade letter, Jan. 31, 1865, Company G Order Book, 15NYHA Regimental Books, RG 94, NA.

37. OR, 46(2):367, 368, 372, 373; Humphreys, Virginia Campaign, 312. Bearss and Suderow, Petersburg Campaign, Volume 2, 167, 168. Smyth's division was formerly commanded by Gibbon, who by now had assumed command of the Twenty-Fourth Corps.

38. OR, 46(1):151, 367–69, 46(2):409, 410; Humphreys, Virginia Campaign, 314.

39. OR, 46(1):191, 192, 212, 222, 225–27, 238; Humphreys, Virginia Campaign, 312, 313; Bearss and Suderow, Petersburg Campaign, Volume 2, 178–81; Trudeau, Last Citadel, 314, 315; Calkins, "Battle of Hatcher's Run," 12, 14.

40. OR, 46(1):192, 193, 212, 222, 298, 344; Humphreys, Virginia Campaign, 313, 314; Bearss and Suderow, Petersburg Campaign, Volume 2, 186–88, 190, 191, 197–99; Trudeau, Last Citadel, 315, 316; Calkins, "Battle of Hatcher's Run," 14, 16. Evans now commanded Maj. Gen. John B. Gordon's former division.

41. OR 46(1):253; Powell, Fifth Army Corps, 755, 756; Bearss and Suderow, Petersburg Campaign, Volume 2, 192, 193.

42. OR, 46(1):253, 258, 262, 277, 280, 284, 46(2):400, 402; Powell, Fifth Army Corps, 756; Brainard, Campaigns of the One Hundred and Forty-Sixth Regiment, 280, 281; Bearss and Suderow, Petersburg Campaign, Volume 2, 193, 194. Winthrop states in his report that the brigade halted at "the intersection of the military pike with the Vaughn Road." Probably this "military pike" was actually the extension of the Quaker Road south of the Vaughn Road.

43. OR, 46(1):150, 151, 254, 258, 280, 46(2):402–4; Powell, Fifth Army Corps, 757; Brainard, Campaigns of the One Hundred and Forty-Sixth Regiment, 280, 281; Bearss and Suderow, Petersburg Campaign, Volume 2, 196.

44. OR, 46(1):254, 258, 280, 46(2):430; Powell, Fifth Army Corps, 757, 758; Brainard, Campaigns of the One Hundred and Forty-Sixth Regiment, 281; Bearss and Suderow, Petersburg Campaign, Volume 2, 196, 197; Schroeder, We Came to Fight, 232, 233.

45. OR, 46(1):254, 277, 280, 366, 368, 46(2):432, 434; Powell, Fifth Army Corps, 758; Bearss and Suderow, Petersburg Campaign, Volume 2, 202, 204.

46. OR, 46(1):280, 366, 368–71; Brainard, Campaigns of the One Hundred and Forty-Sixth Regiment, 281; Bearss and Suderow, Petersburg Campaign, Volume 2, 209, 210; Schroeder, We Came to Fight, 234, 235.

47. OR, 46(1):254, 255, 258, 280; Brainard, Campaigns of the One Hundred and Forty-Sixth Regiment, 281, 282; Bearss and Suderow, Petersburg Campaign, Volume 2, 210, 211.

48. Robert Rae to J. E. Whipple, Feb. 9, 1865, Van Vleck Letters, NYSL. Rae describes the flag at which he fired as "a Blue flag with a white Diamond on it."

49. Belcher, "Reminiscences of the Civil War," 386; Phisterer, *New York in the War of the Rebellion*, 2:1518; CSR, Adolf Riemann, 15NYHA, RG 94, NA.

50. OR, 46(1):255, 258, 266, 280, 281; Brainard, *Campaigns of the One Hundred and Forty-Sixth Regiment*, 281, 282; Bearss and Suderow, *Petersburg Campaign, Volume 2*, 211; Robert Rae to J. E. Whipple, Feb. 9, 1865, Van Vleck Letters, NYSL. When later requested by Warren to state whether it was a fact that the First Brigade had entirely exhausted its ammunition at the time it was relieved by Sickel's brigade, Winthrop responded, "It is a fact that the brigade had certainly exhausted their ammunition." He further observed, "Out of ammunition, is an old story, and with me has always been received with a certain amount of suspicion, but in this instance there was some merit in it." OR, 46(1):281, 282.

51. OR, 46(1):255, 271, 277–79, 282, 283–85, 287, 51(1):286, 287; Powell, *Fifth Army Corps*, 759–61; Bearss and Suderow, *Petersburg Campaign, Volume 2*, 205, 208, 212–14.

52. OR, 46(1):255, 258, 259, 271; Powell, *Fifth Army Corps*, 760, 761; Nathaniel Harris to William Mahone, Aug. 2, 1866, Mahone Family Papers, Virginia State Library Archives, Richmond; Bearss and Suderow, *Petersburg Campaign, Volume 2*, 215, 216.

53. OR, 46(1):255, 259, 271, 272, 298, 299; Powell, *Fifth Army Corps*, 761; Nathaniel Harris to William Mahone, Aug. 2, 1866, Mahone Family Papers, Virginia State Library Archives; Bearss and Suderow, *Petersburg Campaign, Volume 2*, 217, 218.

54. OR, 46(1):259, 266, 272, 280, 299; Brainard, *Campaigns of the One Hundred and Forty-Sixth Regiment*, 282; Bearss and Suderow, *Petersburg Campaign, Volume 2*, 218, 219; Trudeau, *Last Citadel*, 320, 321.

55. OR, 46(1):256, 290. 291, 46(2):454, 458–61, 476, 487; Trudeau, *Last Citadel*, 321, 322; Bearss and Suderow, *Petersburg Campaign Volume 2*, 222, 224, 225; Calkins, "Battle of Hatcher's Run," 22.

56. OR, 46(2):447, 450, 480, 488; Powell, *Fifth Army Corps*, 763; Hess, *In the Trenches at Petersburg*, 232, 233.

57. OR, 46(1):67, 69; Bearss, "Battle of Hatcher's Run," PNB, 90; Greene, *Final Battles of the Petersburg Campaign*, 105; Trudeau, *Last Citadel*, 322; Phisterer, *New York in the War of the Rebellion*, 2:1499, 1518; Robert Rae to J. E. Whipple, Feb. 9, 1865, Van Vleck Letters, NYSL; Belcher, "Reminiscences of the Civil War," 386.

58. OR, 46(1):277, 278, 280; Schroeder, *We Came to Fight*, 239.

12. TO THE WHITE OAK ROAD AND FIVE FORKS

1. Robert Rae to J. E. Whipple, Feb. 9, 1865, Jacob Van Vleck Letters, NYSL; Brainard, *Campaigns of the One Hundred and Forty-Sixth Regiment*, 283.

2. OR, 46(2):515, 517–19, 528, 550.

3. OR, 46(2):513, 515, 519, 534, 609, 610.
4. OR, 46(3):6, 8; Schroeder, We Came to Fight, 247.
5. OR, 46(1):475, 476, 480, 46(2):993, 994, 46(3):27, 46, 67; Humphreys, Virginia Campaign, 316; Nevins, Diary of Battle, 504, 505.
6. OR, 46(1):51, 46(2):1295, 46(3):109, 110, 115; Humphreys, Virginia Campaign, 316–19; Hess, In the Trenches at Petersburg, 246; Greene, Final Battles of the Petersburg Campaign, 106–8, 112, 114, 115; Freeman, Lee's Lieutenants, 644, 645, 647–51.
7. OR, 46(1):51, 46(3):112–15; Freeman, Lee's Lieutenants, 651; Humphreys, Virginia Campaign, 320–21; Tilney, My Life in the Army, 194; Brainard, Campaigns of the One Hundred and Forty-Sixth Regiment, 287; Greene, Final Battles of the Petersburg Campaign, 116, 117, 133, 135, 139.
8. OR, 46(1):1160, 46(3):195, 196, 198, 199, 231; Humphreys, Virginia Campaign, 323–25; Greene, Final Battles of the Petersburg Campaign, 152, 153; Bearss and Calkins, Battle of Five Forks, 2–4.
9. OR, 46(1):52, 46(3):234. Still serving as commander of the Army of the Shenandoah and not part of the Army of the Potomac, Sheridan's instructions for the offensive came directly from Grant.
10. OR, 46(1):570, 898, 46(3):1027, 1031. Although some sources, including Phisterer, state that Company F returned to the regiment at the beginning of January 1865, orders in the company's order book issued during the first week in April, a letter written by Steven Come of Company F, and "Organization of the Army of the Potomac," April 30, 1865, all indicate the unit remained in City Point guarding the Army of the Potomac's artillery park. Company F Order Book, 15NYHA Regimental Books, RG 94, NA; Steven F. Come to "My Dear Wife," Apr. 9, 1865, Steven F. Come Letters, NYSL; OR, 46(3):1026.
11. OR, 46(1):53, 797–99, 46(3):229; Survivors' Association, Corn Exchange Regiment, 562; Powell, Fifth Army Corps, 778; Tilney, My Life in the Army, 198.
12. OR, 46(1):799, 46(3):254, 255; Bearss and Calkins, Battle of Five Forks, 17, 18; Bearss and Suderow, Petersburg Campaign, Volume 2, 331, 332; Brainard, Campaigns of the One Hundred and Forty-Sixth Regiment, 288.
13. OR, 46(1):800, 801, 46(3):255; Bearss and Suderow, Petersburg Campaign, Volume 2, 339–42, 344; Greene, Final Battles of the Petersburg Campaign, 158; Chamberlain, Passing of the Armies, 42, 43; Nevins, Diary of Battle, 507, 508.
14. OR, 46(1):676, 800–802, 870, 882, 886, 46(3):245, 255, 256, 266; Brainard, Campaigns of the One Hundred and Forty-Sixth Regiment, 289; Bearss and Suderow, Petersburg Campaign, Volume 2, 344–47; Schroeder, We Came to Fight, 252.
15. OR, 46(1):870, 871; Brainard, Campaigns of the One Hundred and Forty-Sixth Regiment, 289.
16. OR, 46(1):1101, 1102, 46(3):266; Humphreys, Virginia Campaign, 325; Greene, Final Battles of the Petersburg Campaign, 155, 162; Bearss and Suderow, Petersburg Campaign, Volume 2, 329, 330.

17. *OR*, 46(1):803, 804, 807, 808, 46(3):244, 257, 288–90, 292, 293; Humphreys, *Virginia Campaign*, 327; Powell, *Fifth Army Corps*, 778, 779; Lowe, *Meade's Army*, 353; Greene, *Final Battles of the Petersburg Campaign*, 165.

18. *OR*, 46(1):804, 805, 46(3):283, 298–300.

19. *OR*, 46(1):806, 46(3):309, 310; Powell, *Fifth Army Corps*, 779; Bearss and Suderow, *Petersburg Campaign, Volume 2*, 362, 363. Some maps and dispatches label the Holliday cabin simply as "Negroes" or the house "occupied by negroes."

20. *OR*, 46(1):809, 810, 849, 868, 871, 46(3):304; Brainard, *Campaigns of the One Hundred Forty-Sixth Regiment*, 289, 290; Bearss and Suderow, *Petersburg Campaign, Volume 2*, 367; Schroeder, *We Came to Fight*, 252, 253. Several sources, including Brainard, state the brigade camped in the vicinity of an S. Dabney's residence, yet no such house apparently existed. Warren's map of the positions of the Fifth Corps that night, which erroneously indicates the presence of this structure, suggests the brigade camped near the Holliday cabin, which was in the center-rear of the picket line. See *OR*, 46(1):810.

21. *OR*, 46(1):810, 811, 46(3):284–86, 294, 304–6, 325; Greene, *Final Battles of the Petersburg Campaign*, 167, 168; Bearss and Suderow, *Petersburg Campaign, Volume 2*, 374–76.

22. Humphreys, *Virginia Campaign*, 326, 328; Freeman, *Lee's Lieutenants*, 656–58; Bearss and Suderow, *Petersburg Campaign, Volume 2*, 324, 336, 337, 351; Greene, *Final Battles of the Petersburg Campaign*, 157, 158. Pickett's Division of Longstreet's Corps had transferred to Petersburg prior to the Fort Stedman attack.

23. *OR*, 46(1):811, 812, 814, 868, 46(3):361, 370; Humphreys, *Virginia Campaign*, 330; Brainard, *Campaigns of the One Hundred and Forty-Sixth Regiment*, 291; Powell, *Fifth Army Corps*, 781; Lowe, *Meade's Army*, 353; Survivors' Association, *Corn Exchange Regiment*, 568; Bearss and Suderow, *Petersburg Campaign, Volume 2*, 413, 414.

24. *OR*, 46(1):868, 871, 873, 896; Brainard, *Campaigns of the One Hundred and Forty-Sixth Regiment*, 291; Bearss and Suderow, *Petersburg Campaign, Volume 2*, 415, 56; Schroeder, *We Came to Fight*, 253; Bennett, *Sons of Old Monroe*, 588. The First Brigade's after-action report, submitted by Brig. Gen. Joseph B. Hayes, who was not on the field at the time, states that the Fifteenth was on the left and the Fifth Veteran in the center of the line of battle.

25. *OR*, 46(1):1287; Humphreys, *Virginia Campaign*, 330, 331; Bearss and Suderow, *Petersburg Campaign, Volume 2*, 411, 412, 415, 416; Greene, *Final Battles of the Petersburg Campaign*, 169, 170, 172.

26. *OR*, 46(1):868, 871, 873, 1287, 1288; Bearss and Suderow, *Petersburg Campaign, Volume 2*, 415 (Swan quote), 416; Brainard, *Campaigns of the One Hundred and Forty-Sixth Regiment*, 291.

27. *OR*, 46(1):814, 815, 846, 849, 868, 869, 873, 875, 876, 884; Bearss and Suderow, *Petersburg Campaign, Volume 2*, 416 (Swan quote), 418–23; Powell, *Fifth Army Corps*, 782, 783; Chamberlain, *Passing of the Armies*, 71, 72; Greene, *Final Battles of the Petersburg Campaign*, 172.

28. OR, 46(1):815, 846, 849, 869, 899; Survivors' Association, *Corn Exchange Regiment*, 569; Powell, *Fifth Army Corps*, 783; Chamberlain, *Passing of the Armies*, 72, 73; Bearss and Suderow, *Petersburg Campaign, Volume 2*, 423, 424, 431, 432; Greene, *Final Battles of the Petersburg Campaign*, 173, 174.

29. OR, 46(1):815, 816, 846, 849, 869, 876; Powell, *Fifth Army Corps*, 784, 784; Humphreys, *Virginia Campaign*, 332, 333; Chamberlain, *Passing of the Armies*, 74–77; Bearss and Suderow, *Petersburg Campaign, Volume 2*, 432–34; Greene, *Final Battles of the Petersburg Campaign*, 174. Chamberlain's and Gregory's advance was assisted by an attack by Miles's Second Corps division to their right, which drove Wise's Brigade back into the White Oak Road defenses.

30. Greene, *Final Battles of the Petersburg Campaign*, 174; Phisterer, *New York in the War of the Rebellion*, 2:1499, 1510; CSR, Emil Duysing, 15NYHA, RG 94, NA; Schroeder, *We Came to Fight*, 256; Belcher, "Reminiscences of the Civil War," 387. Casualty reports for the Fifteenth list the wounded and missing only as an aggregate for the period of March 29–April 9. While some officers and men were undoubtedly wounded on April 1, given the nature of the fighting on March 31 and April 1 and the relative numbers of killed and mortally wounded reported for these two days, the preponderance of the 13 officers and 75 men reported wounded and the 131 men reported missing for the period probably were casualties in the March 31 battle at the White Oak Road. One counted among the missing on March 31 was the writer's great-grandfather, Pvt. Jacob Altemos of Company C. He was paroled at Aiken's Landing, Virginia, on April 2. CSR, Jacob Altemos, 15NYHA, RG 94, NA.

31. OR, 46(3):380, 381; Humphreys, *Virginia Campaign*, 334–36; Greene, *Final Battles of the Petersburg Campaign*, 175–78.

32. OR, 46(1):821–23, 46(3):341, 342, 366, 367; Humphreys, *Virginia Campaign*, 338–40; Greene, *Final Battles of the Petersburg Campaign*, 180, 181.

33. OR, 46(1):821, 822, 869, 872, 46(3):369, 370; Brainard, *Campaigns of the One Hundred and Forty-Sixth Regiment*, 292.

34. OR, 46(1):820, 821, 824, 869, 872, 46(3):418; Humphreys, *Virginia Campaign*, 340; Chamberlain, *Passing of the Armies*, 102, 104; Powell, *Fifth Army Corps*, 790, 794; Bearss and Suderow, *Petersburg Campaign, Volume 2*, 452, 453.

35. OR, 46(1):824, 825, 838, 879, 880; Humphreys, *Virginia Campaign*, 343; Powell, *Fifth Army Corps*, 796; Chamberlain, *Passing of the Armies*, 103, 104; Bearss and Suderow, *Petersburg Campaign, Volume 2*, 454–56.

36. Bearss and Suderow, *Petersburg Campaign, Volume 2*, 462–64; Greene, *Final Battles of the Petersburg Campaign*, 182.

37. Humphreys, *Virginia Campaign*, 344; Greene, *Final Battles of the Petersburg Campaign*, 183; Freeman, *Lee's Lieutenants*, 3:663, 664; Bearss and Suderow, *Petersburg Campaign, Volume 2*, 465, 466.

38. OR, 36(3):609, 610, 627, 628, 46(1):826, 829, 1104, 46(3):380, 418; Porter, "Five Forks and the Pursuit of Lee," in *B&L*, 4:711; Sears, *Controversies & Commanders*, 274. Warren for his part later reported of the order to serve under

Sheridan, they "gave me much satisfaction at the time of its receipt." *OR*, 46(1):829.

39. *OR*, 46(1):829, 830, 1104, 1105; Humphreys, *Virginia Campaign*, 344, 345, 347; Powell, *Fifth Army Corps*, 800; Bearss and Suderow, *Petersburg Campaign, Volume 2*, 476, 477, 482; Greene, *Final Battles of the Petersburg Campaign*, 184.

40. *OR*, 46(1):829, 830; Porter, "Five Forks and the Pursuit of Lee," in *B&L*, 4:712; Schroeder, *We Came to Fight*, 263; Bearss and Suderow, *Petersburg Campaign, Volume 2*, 480, 483.

41. *OR*, 46(1):829, 830, 869, 1105; Schroeder, *We Came to Fight*, 265; Porter, "Five Forks and the Pursuit of Lee," in *B&L*, 4:712; Bearss and Suderow, *Petersburg Campaign, Volume 2*, 478, 479; Chamberlain, *Passing of the Armies*, 123; Schroeder, *We Came to Fight*, 263.

42. *OR*, 46(1):869, 872; Humphreys, *Virginia Campaign*, 347, 348; Schroeder, *We Came to Fight*, 265; Bearss and Suderow, *Petersburg Campaign, Volume 2*, 485, 486.

43. *OR*, 46(1):869, 870, 872; Porter, "Five Forks and the Pursuit of Lee," in *B&L*, 4:713; Schroeder, *We Came to Fight*, 265, 267; Bearss and Suderow, *Petersburg Campaign, Volume 2*, 488, 489.

44. *OR*, 46(1):569, 872, 1259; Brainard, *Campaigns of the One Hundred and Forty-Sixth Regiment*, 294, 295; Schroeder, *We Came to Fight*, 267, 269; Bearss and Suderow, *Petersburg Campaign, Volume 2*, 489, 490; CSR, Michael Wiedrich, 15NYHA, RG 94, NA. Kauss received the Medal of Honor for capturing the colors of the North Carolina regiment.

45. *OR*, 46(1):872; Porter, "Five Forks and the Pursuit of Lee," in *B&L*, 4:713; Bearss and Suderow, *Petersburg Campaign, Volume 2*, 489, 490.

46. *OR*, 46(1):870; Bearss and Suderow, *Petersburg Campaign, Volume 2*, 490, 490.

47. *OR*, 46(1):832, 833, 838, 861; Humphreys, *Virginia Campaign*, 348, 349; Bearss and Suderow, *Petersburg Campaign, Volume 2*, 491, 494, 496, 497.

48. *OR*, 46(1):834, 835, 880, 881, 885, 886, 1105; Humphreys, *Virginia Campaign*, 348–51, 353; Bearss and Suderow, *Petersburg Campaign, Volume 2*, 498, 500, 501, 504, 506, 507.

49. *OR*, 46(1):835, 881; Humphreys, *Virginia Campaign*, 351, 352; Powell, *Fifth Army Corps*, 808; Bearss and Suderow, *Petersburg Campaign, Volume 2*, 502, 510; Schroeder, *We Came to Fight*, 271, 273.

50. *OR*, 46(1):835, 836, 839, 886, 46(3):420; Powell, *Fifth Army Corps*, 809; Chamberlain, *Passing of the Armies*, 142, 151; Bearss and Suderow, *Petersburg Campaign, Volume 2*, 511, 512; Greene, *Final Battles of the Petersburg Campaign*, 186, 187.

51. *OR*, 46(1):836; Humphreys, *Virginia Campaign*, 353–55; Bearss and Calkins, *Battle of Five Forks*, 111, 113; Schroeder, *We Came to Fight*, 273; Phisterer, *New York in the War of the Rebellion*, 2:1499.

52. Nevins, *Diary of Battle*, 512; CSR, Michael Wiedrich, 15NYHA, RG 94, NA; Hunt, *Colonels in Blue*, 303. Wiedrich returned to Buffalo, New York, where he worked as a fire-insurance agent and collector of internal revenue. He died in 1899 at the age of sixty-eight.

53. Nevins, *Diary of Battle*, 512; Schroeder, *We Came to Fight*, 269.

54. Nevins, *Diary of Battle*, 514; Lowe, *Meade's Army*, 356; Brainard, *Campaigns of the One Hundred and Forty-Sixth Regiment*, 296; Sears, *Controversies & Commanders*, 283, 284; Greene, *Final Battles of the Petersburg Campaign*, 187. Upon his removal from command, Warren applied to Grant for a court of inquiry into Sheridan's actions. Grant insisted that under the circumstances at the time no inquiry could be conducted. Higher authority rebuffed Warren's subsequent requests for a probe. In 1879 Grant's successor as president, Rutherford B. Hayes, ordered the inquiry at a time when neither Grant nor Sheridan wielded significant political power. Over almost two years, many prominent Federal officers, including Grant, Sheridan, and Warren, as well as some former Confederate officers, presented testimony in the proceedings. The court absolved Warren of each of the four "imputations" cited by Sheridan as his basis for relieving the general at Five Forks. When the court transmitted its results to Secretary of War Robert T. Lincoln in early November 1881, he took no immediate action. Only a year later did he release the findings to the public, by which time Warren had died and been buried without military honors. See Powell, *Fifth Army Corps*, 821–28; Humphreys, *Virginia Campaign*, 357–61; Sears, *Controversies & Commanders*, 282–84; and Calkins, *Appomattox Campaign*, 41.

13. TO APPOMATTOX COURT HOUSE

1. *OR*, 46(1):902–4, 1016, 1017, 1174, 1179, 1215; Humphreys, *Virginia Campaign*, 364–66, 369, 370; Hess, *In the Trenches at Petersburg*, 268–70, 272–76; Calkins, *Appomattox Campaign*, 43–45; Lowe, *Meade's Army*, 357.

2. *OR*, 46(1):679, 680, 711, 712, 1106; Humphreys, *Virginia Campaign*, 367, 368; Hess, *In the Trenches at Petersburg*, 277, 278; Calkins, *Appomattox Campaign*, 47, 48; Greene, *Final Battles of the Petersburg Campaign*, 321, 324. A. P. Hill's death in action that morning led to Heth's assuming command of the Third Corps.

3. *OR*, 46(1):839, 851, 871, 888, 893, 1106; Humphreys, *Virginia Campaign*, 370; Chamberlain, *Passing of the Armies*, 184, 185, 192, 193; Brainard, *Campaigns of the One Hundred and Forty-Sixth Regiment*, 296; Survivors' Association, *Corn Exchange Regiment*, 583; Calkins, *Appomattox Campaign*, 53. Miles had reported to Sheridan that morning, but Little Phil sent him back down the White Oak Road toward the Claiborne Road, from where he moved north to attack the enemy at Sutherland's Station. It remains unclear which two divisions

of the Fifth Corps engaged in Sheridan's march of four or more miles up and down the White Oak Road.

4. OR, 46(1):839, 851, 882, 1106, 46(3):489; Humphreys, *Virginia Campaign*, 370; Powell, *Fifth Army Corps*, 832, 882; Chamberlain, *Passing of the Armies*, 193, 194; Schroeder, *We Came to Fight*, 278, 279. The twelve-mile length of the day's march reported by Hayes suggests the First Brigade took part in the early morning move up and down the White Oak Road.

5. OR, 46(3):1378–82; Freeman, *Lee's Lieutenants*, 3:680, 681; Humphreys, *Virginia Campaign*, 371, 372; Calkins, *Appomattox Campaign*, 59; Greene, *Final Battles of the Petersburg Campaign*, 278, 279, 342.

6. OR, 46(3):510, 512, 514, 532; Humphreys, *Virginia Campaign*, 373; Calkins, *Appomattox Campaign*, 66, 67; Greene, *Final Battles of the Petersburg Campaign*, 359, 360. One division of the Ninth Corps remained behind to guard Petersburg. Ord's command consisted of two divisions from Maj. Gen. John Gibbon's Twenty-Fourth Corps and Brig. Gen. William Birney's African American division of the Twenty-Fifth Corps.

7. OR, 46(1):1106, 1119, 1131, 1132; Humphreys, *Virginia Campaign*, 374; Calkins, *Appomattox Campaign*, 69–71, 73.

8. OR, 46(1):839, 871, 1106; Brainard, *Campaigns of the One Hundred and Forty-Sixth Regiment*, 297; Nevins, *Diary of Battle*, 517. In an arrangement between Grant and the Confederate commissioner, Col. Robert Ould, Hayes was paroled in January 1865. Under the agreement Hayes remained in Richmond where, through the assistance of Ould, he was responsible for distributing materials and supplies to Federal prisoners of war held throughout the South. These articles included clothing, blankets, commissary stores, and certain other items issued by the Federal government as well as a wide variety of other food, clothing, and personal-care items contributed by "friends" of the prisoners or other sources. When Richmond fell early in the day on April 3, 1865, Hayes was free to rejoin his brigade. OR, ser. 2, 7:1198, 1199, 8:45, 46, 220, 221.

9. OR, 46(1):871, 1106, 1107, 46(3):517, 519, 531, 532; Humphreys, *Virginia Campaign*, 374; Calkins, *Appomattox Campaign*, 78; Brainard, *Campaigns of the One Hundred and Forty-Sixth Regiment*, 297, 298.

10. Powell, *Fifth Army Corps*, 838; Freeman, *Lee's Lieutenants*, 3:689–91; Calkins, *Appomattox Campaign*, 75–77, 85; Bearss and Suderow, *Petersburg Campaign, Volume 2*, 550.

11. OR, 46(1):681, 840, 905, 1107, 46(3):550, 557; Humphreys, *Virginia Campaign*, 374, 375; Calkins, *Appomattox Campaign*, 89; Brainard, *Campaigns of the One Hundred and Forty-Sixth Regiment*, 298; Nevins, *Diary of Battle*, 518, 519.

12. Humphreys, *Virginia Campaign*, 376; Freeman, *Lee's Lieutenants*, 3:691–94; Calkins, *Appomattox Campaign*, 76, 90, 91; Bearss and Suderow, *Petersburg Campaign, Volume 2*, 550.

13. OR, 46(1):681, 682, 840, 905, 906, 46(3):577–80, 596, 597; Humphreys, *Virginia Campaign*, 377–79; Calkins, *Appomattox Campaign*, 93, 99, 100.

14. *OR* 46(1):840, 841; Calkins, *Appomattox Campaign*, 100; Brainard, *Campaigns of the One Hundred and Forty-Sixth Regiment*, 298, 299; Nevins, *Diary of Battle*, 519, 520. Griffin estimated the march at about thirty-two miles. If so, this would be the longest single day's march by the Fifth Corps in all of its campaigns. But his estimate seems somewhat high. Hayes estimated the day's march at only twelve miles, but that is considered far too low. A study of maps from the period suggests the march was more in the neighborhood of twenty-five miles—in any event, not an inconsequential distance under the circumstances.

15. *OR*, 46(1):682; Humphreys, *Virginia Campaign*, 379, 380; Powell, *Fifth Army Corps*, 841; Calkins, *Appomattox Campaign*, 105, 107, 112, 113.

16. *OR*, 46(1):682, 46(3):600; Humphreys, *Virginia Campaign*, 380, 381; Calkins, *Appomattox Campaign*, 114.

17. *OR*, 46(1):906, 907, 1108, 1120; Humphreys, *Virginia Campaign*, 382–85; Calkins, *Appomattox Campaign*, 108–11, 114, 115; Bearss and Suderow, *Petersburg Campaign, Volume 2*, 552, 553.

18. Steven F. Come to "My Dear Wife," Apr. 14, 1865, Steven F. Come Letters, NYSL. Come had been hospitalized for several months with a vision disorder he referred to as "moon blindness." Ewell, of course, had lost his leg as a result of a wound received at Second Manassas, well before encountering the Fifteenth at Harris farm on May 19, 1864.

19. Humphreys, *Virginia Campaign*, 385, 386, 388; Calkins, *Appomattox Campaign*, 101, 116, 117, 124, 128, 129; Bearss and Suderow, *Petersburg Campaign, Volume 2*, 553. Mahone's Division had marched directly from High Bridge to Cumberland Church, bypassing Farmville.

20. *OR*, 46(1):683, 684, 907, 908, 46(3):622–25, 629–31; Humphreys, *Virginia Campaign*, 387–90; Calkins, *Appomattox Campaign*, 126, 127, 130, 131, 133; Powell, *Fifth Army Corps*, 845, 846; Bearss and Suderow, *Petersburg Campaign, Volume 2*, 533. After having crossed, the Confederates destroyed several spans of High Bridge, rendering it impassable. But Humphreys's advancing men were able to extinguish the flames and save the wagon bridge. The firing Humphreys had heard came from elements of Crook's cavalry skirmishing with the enemy.

21. *OR*, 46(1):841, 852, 1109, 46(3):603, 604, 628; Humphreys, *Virginia Campaign*, 391; Calkins, *Appomattox Campaign*, 137; Bearss and Suderow, *Petersburg Campaign, Volume 2*, 554; Chamberlain, *Passing of the Armies*, 220, 221.

22. *OR*, 46(1):841, 871; Survivors' Association, *Corn Exchange Regiment*, 586, 587; Nevins, *Diary of Battle*, 520; Calkins, *Appomattox Campaign*, 138; Chamberlain, *Passing of the Armies*, 221.

23. *OR*, 46(1):841, 871, 1181, 1243; Brainard, *Campaigns of the One Hundred and Forty-Sixth Regiment*, 299; Nevins, *Diary of Battle*, 520; Chamberlain, *Passing of the Armies*, 227; Bennett, *Sons of Old Monroe*, 607, 608; Schroeder, *We Came to Fight*, 284; Calkins, *Appomattox Campaign*, 151, 152.

24. *OR*, 46(1):684, 908, 1109, 1132, 46(3):653, 654; Humphreys, *Virginia*

Campaign, 392, 395, 396; Calkins, *Appomattox Campaign*, 147–49, 152–55; Bearss and Suderow, *Petersburg Campaign, Volume 2*, 554.

25. *OR*, 46(1):1109; Humphreys, *Virginia Campaign*, 396, 397; Calkins, *Appomattox Campaign*, 159–62.

26. *OR*, 46(1):841, 1162, 1163; Powell, *Fifth Army Corps*, 849, 850; Bennett, *Sons of Old Monroe*, 608, 609; Brainard, *Campaigns of the One Hundred and Forty-Sixth Regiment*, 299; Survivors' Association, *Corn Exchange Regiment*, 588; Calkins, *Appomattox Campaign*, 162–64.

27. *OR*, 46(1):841, 1109, 1162, 1163, 1175; Humphreys, *Virginia Campaign*, 397; unknown lieutenant, Co. D, 140th New York, "private letter," *Rochester Daily Democrat and American*, Apr. 28, 1865, quoted in Marsh, "Rochester's Part in the Civil War," 71, 72.

28. *OR*, 46(1):841, 1110, 1163, 46(3):619, 641, 664–66, 670, 688; Humphreys, *Virginia Campaign*, 397, 398; Brainard, *Campaigns of the One Hundred and Forty-Sixth Regiment*, 299, 300; Schroeder, *We Came to Fight*, 285; Calkins, *Appomattox Campaign*, 164, 165; Bearss and Suderow, *Petersburg Campaign, Volume 2*, 555.

29. *OR*, 46(1):665, 666; "private letter," *Rochester Daily Democrat and American*, Apr. 28, 1865, quoted in Marsh, "Rochester's Part in the Civil War," 72; Brainard, *Campaigns of the One Hundred and Forty-Sixth Regiment*, 300; Schroeder, *We Came to Fight*, 287; Calkins, *Appomattox Campaign*, 173, 174.

30. *OR*, 46(3):665, 668, 685, 688, 1175; Lowe, *Meade's Army*, 370; Tilney, *My Life in the Army*, 199; Survivors' Association, *Corn Exchange Regiment*, 593; Calkins, *Appomattox Campaign*, 176. Also remaining at Appomattox was Gibbon's Twenty-Fourth Corps.

31. *OR*, 46(3):691; Survivors' Association, *Corn Exchange Regiment*, 593; Chamberlain, *Passing of the Armies*, 250; Chamberlain, *Appomattox*, 13; Nevins, *Diary of Battle*, 523.

32. Chamberlain, *Passing of the Armies*, 258, 260–62; Schroeder, *We Came to Fight*, 288, 289.

33. *OR*, 46(1):87, 46(3):731, 746; Bennett, *Sons of Old Monroe*, 614; Brainard, *Campaigns of the One Hundred and Forty-Sixth Regiment*, 301; Survivors' Association, *Corn Exchange Regiment*, 597, 598.

34. *OR* 46(3):758, 788, 789; Survivors' Association, *Corn Exchange Regiment*, 598; Chamberlain, *Passing of the Armies*, 276; Brainard, *Campaigns of the One Hundred and Forty-Sixth Regiment*, 301, 302; Powell, *Fifth Army Corps*, 870.

35. *OR*, 46(3):790, 811; Chamberlain, *Passing of the Armies*, 282; Survivors' Association, *Corn Exchange Regiment*, 599; Tilney, *My Life in the Army*, 218; Schroeder, *We Came to Fight*, 292.

36. *OR*, 46(3):833, 854, 863, 922, 1086, 1115; Brainard, *Campaigns of the One Hundred and Forty-Sixth Regiment*, 302; Chamberlain, *Passing of the Armies*, 287–89. Subsequently, the sector of the road the Fifth Corps would guard was terminated to the east at Sutherland's Station. *OR*, 46(3):922, 923.

37. *OR*, 46(1):788, 921, 923; Schroeder, *We Came to Fight*, 293, 294.

38. OR, 46(3):823, 972–76; Phisterer, New York in the War of the Rebellion, 2:1507, 1509, 1510, 1514, 1515, 1519, 1520, 1522; CSR, John Boker, 15NYHA, RG 94, NA. Ironically, Boker was breveted notwithstanding having been dismissed from the regiment on January 18, 1865, for being absent without leave in November 1864. Diehl ultimately was breveted major.

39. OR, 46(2):865, 869, 46(3):995, 996.

40. OR, 46(2):869. Whether the requested corrective order to add Weldon Railroad/Globe Tavern was ever issued is unknown.

14. TO THE DEFENSES OF WASHINGTON—AND HOME

1. OR, 46(1):87, 46(3):1005, 1016–18, 1021, 1058; Tilney, My Life in the Army, 228; Schroeder, We Came to Fight, 295. The Sixth Corps would remain in the Danville vicinity until mid-May.

2. Brainard, Campaigns of the One Hundred and Forty-Sixth Regiment, 302; Chamberlain, Passing of the Armies, 302, 303; Schroeder, We Came to Fight, 295.

3. OR, 46(1):88; Survivors' Association, Corn Exchange Regiment, 601; Chamberlain, Passing of the Armies, 304; Schroeder, We Came to Fight, 295.

4. OR, 46(1):88, 46(3):891, 1084, 1086, 1092, 1094; Survivors' Association, Corn Exchange Regiment, 602; Chamberlain, Passing of the Armies, 305, 307; Schroeder, We Came to Fight, 295.

5. OR, 46(1):88, 46(3):1102, 1107, 1115, 1119, 1120, 1128; Survivors' Association, Corn Exchange Regiment, 603; Chamberlain, Passing of the Armies, 310–12; Schroeder, We Came to Fight, 296, 297.

6. OR 46(1):88, 46(3):1128; Survivors' Association, Corn Exchange Regiment, 603, 604; Chamberlain, Passing of the Armies, 312–14.

7. Tilney, My Life in the Army, 234, 235; Survivors' Association, Corn Exchange Regiment, 604.

8. OR, 46(3):1135, 1140; Chamberlain, Passing of the Armies, 315; Survivors' Association, Corn Exchange Regiment, 604.

9. OR, 46(3):1140; Tilney, My Life in the Army, 234; Survivors' Association, Corn Exchange Regiment, 604.

10. OR, 46(3):1181; Tilney, My Life in the Army, 236, 237; Nevins, Diary of Battle, 526; Schroeder, We Came to Fight, 301.

11. OR, 46(3):1181, 1182, 1186–88; Nevins, Diary of Battle, 527; Chamberlain, Passing of the Armies, 338; Schroeder, We Came to Fight, 302.

12. Survivors' Association, Corn Exchange Regiment, 605; New York Times, May 24, 1865; Chamberlain, Passing of the Armies, 345–47. The "white cross" Chamberlain mentions is the flag of the Second Division, Fifth Corps, consisting of a white Maltese cross on a blue field.

13. OR, 46(3):1182; Brainard, Campaigns of the One Hundred and Forty-Sixth Regiment, 303.

14. Tilney, *My Life in the Army*, 240, 241; Brainard, *Campaigns of the One Hundred and Forty-Sixth Regiment*, 304; Bennett, *Sons of Old Monroe*, 621; Survivors' Association, *Corn Exchange Regiment*, 604.

15. *OR*, 46(3):923, 1164, 1165, 1250, 1252; Phisterer, *New York in the War of the Rebellion*, 4:3615; Bennett, *Sons of Old Monroe*, 621; Schroeder, *We Came to Fight*, 293, 309, 310, 328, 329. The 146th would not be mustered out of Federal service until July 16. Three days later the men were on a train bound for Syracuse. Brainard, *Campaigns of the One Hundred and Forty-Sixth Regiment*, 304, 305; Phisterer, *New York in the War of the Rebellion*, 5:3687. The Fifth Veteran would eventually be mustered out on August 21. Phisterer, *New York in the War of the Rebellion*, 2:1769.

16. First Brigade General Orders, June 17, 1865, Company I Order Book, 15NYHA Regimental Books, RG 94, NA.

17. *OR*, 46(3):1286, 1293, 1294, 1302, 1315; order, June 24, 1865, Company I Order Book, 15NYHA Regimental Books, RG 94, NA; Cooling and Owen, *Mr. Lincoln's Forts*, 22, 23, 52, 61, 65, 68, 71.

18. Record of Events, May and June 1865, Records Showing Service of Military Units, RG 94, NA, M594, roll 112; order, June 24, 1865, Company I Order Book, 15NYHA Regimental Books, RG 94, NA; order, June 28, 1865, Company K Order Book, 15NYHA Regimental Books, RG 94, NA; Hewett, *Supplement to the Official Records . . .*, Part II, 113–23; Cooling and Owen, *Mr. Lincoln's Forts*, 33, 34, 71, 72. The Fifteenth garrisoned Fort Willard, even though it was not on the list of forts to be retained as presented in the Twenty-Second Corps order dated June 23. *OR*, 46(3):1293.

19. Stephen F. Come to "My Dear Wife," June 30, 1865, Stephen F. Come Letters, NYSL.

20. Stephen F. Come to "My Dear Wife," July 22, 1865, Come Letters, NYSL; order, July 22, 1865, Regimental Order Book, 15NYHA Regimental Books, RG 94, NA.

21. Orders, July 22, 30, 1865, Regimental Order Book, 15NYHA Regimental Books, RG 94, NA.

22. Order, Aug. 4, 1865, Regimental Order Book, 15NYHA Regimental Books, RG 94, NA.

23. Headquarters First Brigade, De Russy's Division circular, Aug. 2, 1865, Regimental Order Book, 15NYHA Regimental Books, RG 94, NA; First Battalion order, Aug. 5, 1865, Regimental Order Book, 15NYHA Regimental Books, RG 94, NA.

24. Circular, July 31, 1865, Regimental Order Book, 15NYHA Regimental Books, RG 94, NA; order, Aug. 13, 1865, Regimental Order Book, 15NYHA Regimental Books, RG 94, NA; Stephen F. Come to "My Dear Wife," Aug. 12, 1865, Come Letters, NYSL.

25. Phisterer, *New York in the War of the Rebellion*, 2:1499; *New York Times*, Aug. 21, 1865; Stephen F. Come to "My Dear Wife," Aug. 29, 1865, Come Letters, NYSL.

26. Phisterer, *New York in the War of the Rebellion*, 2:1499.

27. *New York Times*, Aug. 27, 1865; Stephen F. Come to "My Dear Wife," Aug. 29, 1865, Come Letters, NYSL.

CONCLUSION

1. *OR*, 46(2):610.

2. Reinhart, *German Hurrah!*, 1; Kamphoefner and Helbich, *Germans in the Civil War*, 20. It should be noted that, as was the case with the Fifteenth, even the "uniquely" German regiments typically included men from various European countries, sometimes even from England, Ireland, or the United States. Thus, it is perhaps more appropriate to view such regiments as "predominantly" German.

3. Kamphoefner and Helbich, *Germans in the Civil War*, 25.

4. General Headquarters, State of New York Adjutant General's Office, General Orders No. 16, June 9, 1865, Company K Order Book, 15NYHA Regimental Books, RG 94, NA.

APPENDIX I

1. Thomas M. Vincent to George G. Meade, July 26, 1864, CSR, Louis Schirmer, 15NYHA, RG 94, NA; H. S. Olcott to Chas. A. Dana, July 20, 1864, CSR, Louis Schirmer, 15NYHA, RG 94, NA; *OR*, ser. 3, 4:886; *OR*, General Index and Additions and Corrections, 1240; "Colonel Henry Steel Olcott," *New World Encyclopedia*, https://www.newworldencyclopedia.org/entry/Henry_Steel_Olcott.

2. H. Lautermann to E. M. Stanton, Apr. 29, 1864, CSR, Louis Schirmer, 15NYHA, RG 94, NA; CSR, Henry Lautermann, 15NYHA, RG 94, NA; Phisterer, *New York in the War of the Rebellion*, 2:1500, 1515.

3. CSR, John Veith, 15NYHA, RG 94, NA; Louis Schirmer Court-Martial Records, Case MM-2297, RG 153, NA; Phisterer, *New York in the War of the Rebellion*, 2:1504, 1521.

4. CSR, John Veith, RG 94, NA; Schirmer Court-Martial Records, RG 153, NA.

5. H. S. Olcott to C. A. Dana, July 30, 1864, Schirmer Court-Martial Records, RG 153, NA; H. L. Olcott to "General" [Joseph Holt], Aug. 3, 1864, RG 153, NA; War Department General Orders No. 159, May 29, 1863, RG 153, NA. Olcott refers to the case against Frederick George D'Utassy, former commander of the 39th New York, also known as the Garibaldi Guard. D'Utassy was tried by court-martial in 1863 and found guilty of offenses in many respects not unlike those of which Schirmer was accused. He was sentenced to be cashiered and imprisoned for one year at hard labor.

6. Schirmer Court-Martial Records, RG 153, NA.

7. Telegram, C. A. Dana to Major General Dix, Aug. 24, 1864, CSR, Louis Schirmer, 15NYHA, RG 94, NA; Louis Schirmer to "Colonel" [James Hardie], Sept. 30, 1864, CSR, Louis Schirmer, 15NYHA, RG 94, NA.

8. A. G. Riddle to "Sir," Nov. 7, 1864, CSR, Louis Schirmer, 15NYHA, RG 94, NA; Riddle, *Recollections of War Times*, 2, 3. Riddle was a former member of the House of Representatives from Ohio.

9. Louis Schirmer to William P. Wood, Nov. 25, 1864, Schirmer Court-Martial Records, RG 153, NA; Riddle, *Argument for the Defense*, 4.

10. Schirmer Court-Martial Records, RG 153, NA; CSR, Thomas Grey, 15NYHA, RG 94, NA.

11. War Department General Court-Martial Orders No. 397, Aug. 3, 1865, CSR, Louis Schirmer, 15NYHA, RG 94, NA; Riddle, *Argument for the Defense*, 4.

12. Riddle, *Argument for the Defense*, 7–9; Burnham, *Reply . . . to the Defense*, 2. A copy of Burnham's *Reply* is in Schirmer Court-Martial Records, RG 153, NA.

13. Schirmer Court-Martial Records, RG 153, NA; Riddle, *Argument for the Defense*, 25, 26; Louis Schirmer, CLS Private Letters, 1863 [hereafter cited as "Private Letter Book"], Schirmer Court-Martial Records. Jeremiah D. Green and Titus E. Eddy, also officials of Troy, New York, sometimes accompanied Flood on his meetings with Schirmer.

14. CSR, William Bundy, 15NYHA, RG 94, NA; Riddle, *Argument for the Defense*, 7, 8, 32.

15. Schirmer, Private Letter Book; Schirmer Court-Martial Records, RG 153, NA; Riddle, *Argument for the Defense*, 32; CSR, Louis Schirmer, 15NYHA, RG 94, NA; CSR, William Bundy, 15NYHA, RG 94, NA.

16. Schirmer Court-Martial Records, RG 153, NA; Burnham, *Reply . . . to the Defense*, 16. Briggs, from Massachusetts, was also a lawyer. Rounding out the court were Col. Frederick H. Collier of the 139th Pennsylvania; Col. Theodore G. Ellis of the Fourteenth Connecticut; Lt. Col. Charles S. Emerson of the Twenty-Ninth Maine; Maj. Thomas T. Taylor of the Forty-Seventh Ohio; Capt. George P. Corts, assistant adjutant general of volunteers; and Lt. Col. Thomas S. Trumbull of the First Connecticut Heavy Artillery. Two days later Col. John M. Hedrick of the Fifteenth Iowa joined the court. Trumball would die of pneumonia on March 30 without having participated in any of the sessions.

17. Schirmer Court-Martial Records, RG 153, NA; Riddle, *Argument for the Defense*, 13, 14, 16, 18, 55.

18. Schirmer Court-Martial Records, RG 153, NA; Burnham, *Reply . . . to the Defense*, 27, 28; Riddle, *Argument for the Defense*, 49, 50. Despite having deserted for some time, Wannfried was apparently a brave soldier. He was wounded near Petersburg in June 1864 and, a little over a week after testifying at the Schirmer trial, would be killed in action at the White Oak Road on March 31, 1865.

19. Schirmer Court-Martial Records, RG 153, NA; Riddle, *Argument for the Defense*, 8, 32, 34, 37, 39, 40, 45, 49.

20. Schirmer Court-Martial Records, RG 153, NA; Burnham, *Reply . . . to the Defense*, 11, 44, 45; Riddle, *Argument for the Defense*, 65, 66. Schirmer was also alleged to have received a silver plate in return for obtaining a commission. The officer concerned testified that he had been unable to contribute to the regimental officers' purchase of a horse, which was presented to Schirmer as a new year's gift. So, being at the time in New York, he purchased a secondhand plated pitcher and goblet and sent them to Schirmer, also as a new year's present.

21. Schirmer Court-Martial Records, RG 153, NA; Burnham, *Reply . . . to the Defense*, 14; Riddle, *Argument for the Defense*, 66.

22. Schirmer Court-Martial Records, RG 153, NA; Burnham, *Reply . . . to the Defense*, 17; Riddle, *Argument for the Defense*, 66, 67. The approximately 200 muskets alleged destroyed were the arms of dead Confederates that soldiers of the Fifteenth had picked up on May 9, 1864, near Spotsylvania Court House. These were buried for want of transportation.

23. Schirmer Court-Martial Records, RG 153, NA; Burnham, *Reply . . . to the Defense*, 4–6, 11, 39, 40, 41; Riddle, *Argument for the Defense*, 58–62.

24. Schirmer Court-Martial Records, RG 153, NA.

25. Schirmer Court-Martial Records, RG 153, NA; Burnham, *Reply . . . to the Defense*, 12–14; Riddle, *Argument for the Defense*, 57, 58, 64, 65.

26. Schirmer Court-Martial Records, RG 153, NA; Burnham, *Reply . . . to the Defense*, 14, 15, 45, 46.

27. Riddle, *Argument for the Defense*, 67, 68.

28. Schirmer Court-Martial Records, RG 153, NA; Riddle, *Argument for the Defense*, 6; Burnham, *Reply . . . to the Defense*, 2.

29. Schirmer Court-Martial Records, RG 153, NA; Riddle, *Argument for the Defense*, 7.

30. Schirmer Court-Martial Records, RG 153, NA.

31. Schirmer Court-Martial Records, RG 153, NA; Riddle, *Argument for the Defense*, 4.

32. Riddle, *Argument for the Defense*, 5, 6.

33. Riddle, *Argument for the Defense*, 68–71.

34. Schirmer Court-Martial Records, RG 153, NA; Burnham, *Reply . . . to the Defense*, 1–3.

35. Burnham, *Reply . . . to the Defense*, 31, 33, 34, 46, 50.

36. "We the undersigned," June 13, 1865, Schirmer Court-Martial Records, RG 153, NA. Since the testimonial from the Fifteenth's officers was made a part of the record of Schirmer's court-martial, it probably was delivered to and viewed by the court.

37. Schirmer Court-Martial Records, RG 153, NA; War Department General Court-Martial Orders No. 397, Aug. 3, 1865, CSR, Louis Schirmer, 15NYHA, RG 94, NA. The court rendered its decisions on each specification and then on each charge overall, amending a specification as first written by removing

any part that was not considered fully proven; thus, Schirmer could be found guilty under an amended specification. Of the forty-four specifications supporting Charge I—conduct prejudicial to good order and discipline—Schirmer was found guilty of only two specifications as written. He was, however, found guilty either in whole or in part of twenty-two other specifications as amended by the court. On the charge as a whole, the panel found Schirmer guilty. On Charge II—conduct unbecoming an officer and a gentleman—the court found Schirmer not guilty of the first specification, guilty of another as written, guilty of two amended specifications, and guilty of the charge overall.

38. Schirmer Court-Martial Records, RG 153, NA; War Department General Court-Martial Orders No. 397, Aug. 3, 1865, CSR, Louis Schirmer, 15NYHA, RG 94, NA.

39. CSR, Louis Schirmer, 15NYHA, RG 94, NA; War Department General Court-Martial Orders No. 397, Aug. 3, 1865, 15NYHA, RG 94, NA. The Brooklyn Tower of the Verrazano Narrows Bridge now rises from the island on which Fort Lafayette stood.

40. Officers of the Fifteenth New York Heavy Artillery to Andrew Johnson, Aug. 11, 1865, Schirmer Court-Martial Records, RG 153, NA. Maj. Julius Dieckmann, then commander of the Fifteenth; Maj. and Bvt. Lt. Col. Louis Eiche; Bvt. Maj. William Dickey, a Medal of Honor recipient; the Fifteenth's surgeon, Hermann Ideler; and thirty-five other officers of the regiment all signed the petition.

41. A. G. Riddle and S. Wolf to the President of the United States, n.d., Schirmer Court-Martial Records, RG 153, NA.

42. Andreas Willman, George F. Steinbrenner, and A. Outenhoefer to "His Excellency Andrew Johnson," n.d., Schirmer Court-Martial Records, RG 153, NA.

43. Mary Jane Schirmer to "His Excellency Andrew Johnson," Aug. 30, 1865, Schirmer Court-Martial Records, RG 153, NA.

44. Selected Records of the War Department Relating to Confederate Prisoners of War, 1861–65, Records Relating to Prisoners, Oaths and Paroles, Record Group 109, NA, M598, rolls 85, 137.

Bibliography

ARCHIVAL MATERIALS

Appomattox Court House National Historical Park, Appomattox, VA
    S. J. Jackson Diary
Buffalo and Erie County Historical Society, Buffalo, NY
    Carl Matteson Letters, Civil War Collection
Fredericksburg and Spotsylvania National Military Park Archive, Fredericksburg, VA
    Lt. George W. P. Bouton Diary
    Stephen D. Burger Diary
    Calvin C. Shaffer letter, *National Tribune* (Washington, DC)
Georgia Department of Archives and History, Morrow
    Washington L. Dunn Diary, United Daughters of the Confederacy Transcripts
        Indiana University of Pennsylvania, Indiana
    Charles Henry Minnemeyer Diary, Civil War Soldiers Collection, Special Collections and University Archives
Library of Congress Manuscripts Division, Washington, DC
    Papers of Henry Jackson Hunt
        General Correspondence, 1846–1910
        Journals, 1857–65
        Military Papers, 1841–85
National Archives and Records Administration, Washington, DC
    Record Group 15, Pension Office Files
    Record Group 94, Records of the Office of the Adjutant General
        6th New York Heavy Artillery Regimental Books
        15th New York Heavy Artillery Regimental Books

Compiled Service Records
  2nd New York Independent Battery
  13th New York Independent Battery
  15th New York Heavy Artillery Regiment
  29th New York Infantry Regiment
  41st New York Infantry Regiment
Records Showing Service of Military Units. M594.
Record Group 109, Selected Records of the War Department Relating to Confederate Prisoners of War, 1861–65, Records Relating to Prisoners, Oaths, and Paroles
Record Group 153, Records of the Office of the Judge Advocate General (Army)
  Louis Schirmer Court-Martial Records, Case MM-2297
New York State Library, Albany
  15th New York Artillery, Company M Records
  Stephen F. Come Letters
  William Eakins Journal
  Wheeler Grant Letters
  Samuel B. Pierce Letters
  Jacob Van Vleck Letters
  Gouverneur Kemble Warren Papers
    Letterbooks, vols. 7–25
    Washington A. Roebling, "Report of the Operations of the Fifth Corps, Army of the Potomac in General Grant's Campaign from Culpepper to Petersburg as Seen by W. A. Roebling, Major and A.D.C., 1864"
New York State Military Museum and Veterans Research Center, Saratoga Springs
  Martin Cole Letter
  Calvin Shaffer Collection
Petersburg National Battlefield Archives, Petersburg, VA
  Edwin C. Bearss, "The Battle of Hatcher's Run, February 5–7, 1865," 1966
  ———, "The Battle of the Boydton Plank Road, October 27–28, 1864," [1966]
  ———, "Battle of the Weldon Railroad," n.d.
  Lt. George Breck Letters to *Rochester Union and Advertiser*
  Mickey of Co. K [James P. Sullivan], "The Fight for the Weldon Railroad," *Milwaukee Sunday Telegraph*, June 28, July 5, 1885.
  "Painting Number Two: Petersburg National Battlefield, Background to Event Depicted—General Hagood Meets Captain Daily"
US Army Heritage and Education Center, Carlisle, PA
  Civil War Miscellaneous Collection
    James R. Avery Collection
    Philemon C. Heath Letters
    Paul Lounsbury Letters
    Modified Journal of Company C, 6th New York Heavy Artillery Regimental Papers

Samuel B. Pierce Letters
James B. Thompson, "Reminiscences of Prison Life in the South"
William J. Daily Diary, Civil War Times Illustrated Collection
University of North Carolina, Chapel Hill
William Allen Reminiscences, Southern Historical Collection
Virginia State Library Archives, Richmond
Mahone Family Papers
Westchester County Historical Society, Elmsford, NY
Capt. John Gedney Diary

NEWSPAPERS

Harpers Weekly
New York Herald
New-Yorker Staadtszeitung
New York Times
New York Tribune

BOOKS, ARTICLES, AND OTHER PUBLICATIONS

Agassiz, George R., ed. *Meade's Headquarters, 1863–1865: Letters of Colonel Theodore Lyman from the Wilderness to Appomattox.* Boston: Atlantic Monthly Press, 1922.
Armstrong, Nelson. *Nuggets of Experience: Narratives of [the] Sixties and Other Days, with Graphic Description of Thrilling Personal Adventures.* Los Angeles: Times-Mirror P. and B. House, 1906.
Atkins, Thomas A., and John W. Oliver. *Yonkers in the Rebellion of 1861–1865.* Yonkers, NY: Yonkers Soldiers' and Sailors' Association, 1892.
Baquet, Camile. *History of the First Brigade, New Jersey Volunteers.* Trenton, NJ: MacCrellish & Quigley, 1910.
Bearss, Edwin C., and Chris Calkins. *Battle of Five Forks.* 2nd ed. Lynchburg, VA: H. E. Howard, 1985.
Bearss, Edwin C., with Bryce A. Suderow. *The Petersburg Campaign, Volume 1: The Eastern Front Battles, June–August 1864.* 2 vols. El Dorado Hills, CA: Savas Beatie, 2012–14.
———. *The Petersburg Campaign, Volume 2: The Western Front Battles, September 1864–April 1865.* El Dorado Hills, CA: Savas Beatie, 2014.
Beattie, Dan. *Brandy Station 1863: First Step towards Gettysburg.* Oxford: Osprey, 2008.
Belcher, Amherst Wisner. "Reminiscences of the Civil War." Book 10, chapter 1 of *The Belcher Family in England and America Comprehending a Period of Seven Hundred and Sixty-Five Years, with Particular Reference to the Descendants of Adam Belcher of Southfields, Orange County, New York,* by William Henry Belcher and Joseph Warren Belcher. Detroit: Privately published, 1941.

Bennett, Brian A. *Sons of Old Monroe: A Regimental History of Patrick O'Rourke's 140th New York Volunteer Infantry.* 2nd ed. Dayton, OH: Morningside House, 1999.

Beauregard, P. G. T. "Four Days of Battle at Petersburg." In Johnson and Buel, *Battles and Leaders of the Civil War,* 4:540–44.

Bicknell, George W. *History of the Fifth Regiment Maine Volunteers, Comprising Brief Descriptions of Its Marches, Engagements, and General Services from the Date of Its Muster In, June 24, 1861, to the Time of Its Muster Out, July 27, 1864.* Portland, ME: Hall L. Davis, 1871.

Bonekemper, Edward H., III. *Grant and Lee—Victorious American and Vanquished Virginian.* Westport, CT: Praeger, 2008.

———. *A Victor, Not a Butcher.* Washington, DC: Regnery, 2004.

Bradley, Susan H., ed. *Leverett Bradley: A Soldier-Boy's Letters, 1861–1865.* 1905. Reprint, Suffolk, VA: Robert Hardy, 1986.

Brainard, Mary Genevie Green, comp. *Campaigns of the One Hundred and Forty-Sixth Regiment New York State Volunteers also Known as Halleck's Infantry, the Fifth Oneida, and Garrard's Tigers.* New York: G. P. Putnam's Sons, 1915.

Brown, Augustus C. *The Diary of a Line Officer.* New York, 1906.

Burnham, Horace B. *Reply of Major H. B. Burnham, Judge Adv., U.S.A., to the Defense of the Accused, Col. Louis Schirmer.* Washington, DC, 1865.

Calkins, Chris M. "The Apple Jack Raid." *Blue and Gray Magazine* 22, no. 3 (Summer 2005): 18–25.

———. *The Appomattox Campaign: March 29–April 9, 1865.* 1997. Reprint, Lynchburg, VA: Schroeder, 2015.

———. "The Battle of Hatcher's Run." In *History and Tour Guide of Five Forks, Hatcher's Run, and Namozine Church.* Columbus, OH: Blue and Gray Magazine, 2003.

———. "The Battle of Weldon Railroad (or Globe Tavern), August 18, 19, & 21, 1864." *Blue and Gray Magazine* 23, no. 3 (Winter 2007): 7–25.

Carter, Robert G. *Four Brothers in Blue; or, Sunshine and Shadows of the War of the Rebellion: A Story of the Great Civil War from Bull Run to Appomattox.* Austin: Univ. of Texas Press, 1978.

Chamberlain, Joshua L. *Appomattox: Paper Read before the New York Commandery, Loyal Legion of the United States, October Seventh, 1903.* N.p., [1903].

———. *The Passing of the Armies.* New York: G. P. Putnam's Sons, 1915.

Christian, Charles B. "The Battle at Bethesda Church." *Southern Historical Society Papers* 33 (1905): 57–62.

Cockerell, Thomas D., and Michael B. Ballard, eds. *A Mississippi Rebel in the Army of Northern Virginia: The Civil War Private Memoirs of Private David Holt.* Baton Rouge: Louisiana State Univ. Press, 1995.

Cooling, Benjamin Franklin, III, and Walton H. Owen II. *Mr. Lincoln's Forts: A Guide to the Civil War Defenses of Washington.* Lanham, MD: Scarecrow, 2010.

Dornbusch, C. E., comp. *Regimental Publications & Personal Narratives of the Civil War: A Checklist*. New York: New York Public Library, 1961.
Duane, Capt. James C. *Manual for Engineer Troops*. 3rd ed. New York: D. Van Nostrand, 1864.
Dunn, Wilbur R. *Full Measure of Devotion: The Eighth New York Volunteer Heavy Artillery*. Kearney: Morris, 1997.
Dyer, Frederick H. *A Compendium of the War of the Rebellion*. 3 vols. 1908. Reprint, Dayton, OH: Morningside, 1979.
Early, Jubal A. "Early's March to Washington in 1864." In Johnson and Buel, *Battles and Leaders of the Civil War*, 4:492–99.
———. *A Memoir of the Last Year of the War for Independence in the Confederate States of America*. 1866. Reprint, edited by Gary W. Gallagher, Columbia: Univ. of South Carolina Press, 2001.
Freeman, Douglass Southall. *Lee's Lieutenants: A Study in Command*. 3 vols. New York: Charles Scribner's Sons, 1944.
Fry, James B. "McDowell's Advance to Bull Run." In Johnson and Buel, *Battles and Leaders of the Civil War*, 1:167–93.
Furgurson, Earnest B. *Chancellorsville 1863: The Souls of the Brave*. New York: Vintage Books, 1993.
———. *Not War but Murder: Cold Harbor 1864*. New York: Alfred A. Knopf, 2000.
Gallagher, Gary W. *Lee & His Army in Confederate History*. Chapel Hill: Univ. of North Carolina, 2001.
Galloway, G. Norton. "Hand-to-Hand Fighting at Spotsylvania." In Johnson and Buel, *Battles and Leaders of the Civil War*, 4:170–74.
Geschicte der Deutschen im Buffalo und Erie County, N. Y. Buffalo: Reinecke & Zesch, 1898.
Grant, Ulysses S. *Personal Memoirs of U. S. Grant*. 1885. Reprint, with introduction by William S. McFeely, New York: Da Capo, 1982.
Greene, A. Wilson. *A Campaign of Giants: The Battle for Petersburg*. Vol. 1,— *From the Crossing of the James to the Crater*. Chapel Hill: Univ. of North Carolina Press, 2018.
———. "April 2, 1865: Day of Decision at Petersburg." *Blue and Gray Magazine* 18, no. 3 (Winter 2001): 6–24, 42–53.
———. *The Final Battles of the Petersburg Campaign: Breaking the Backbone of the Rebellion*. 2nd ed. Knoxville: Univ. of Tennessee Press, 2008.
Hankey, John P. "The Railroad War: How the Iron Road Changed the American Civil War." *Trains Magazine* 71, no. 3 (Mar. 2011): 24–35.
Hanover County Historical Commission. *A Survey of Civil War Sites in Hanover County, Virginia*. N.p., 2002.
Hardin, M. D. *History of the Twelfth Regiment, Pennsylvania Reserve Volunteer Corps*. New York: Self-published, 1890.
Henderson, G. F. R.. *Stonewall Jackson and the American Civil War*. 2 vols. London: Longmans, Green, 1898.

Hennessy, John J. *Return to Bull Run: The Campaign and Battle of Second Manassas*. New York: Simon & Schuster, 1993.

Hess, Earl J. *In the Trenches at Petersburg: Field Fortifications and Confederate Defeat*. Chapel Hill: Univ. of North Carolina Press, 2009.

———. *The Rifle Musket in Civil War Combat: Reality and Myth*. Lawrence: Univ. Press of Kansas, 2008.

Hewett, Janet B., ed. *Supplement to the Official Records of the Union and Confederate Armies, Part II—Record of Events*. Vol. 42. Wilmington, NC: Broadfoot, 1997.

Hewett, Janet B., Noah Andre Trudeau, and Bryce A. Suderow, eds. *Supplement to the Official Records of the Union and Confederate Armies, Part 1—Reports*. Vol. 36. Wilmington, NC: Broadfoot, 1996.

Horn, John. *The Destruction of the Weldon Railroad: Deep Bottom, Globe Tavern and Reams Station*. Lynchburg: H. E. Howard, 1991.

Houghton, Charles H. "In the Crater." In Johnson and Buel, *Battles and Leaders of the Civil War*, 4:561–62.

Howard, Oliver O. "The Eleventh Corps at Chancellorsville." In Johnson and Buel, *Battles and Leaders of the Civil War*, 3:189–203.

Humphreys, Andrew A. *The Virginia Campaign of '64 and '65: The Army of the Potomac and the Army of the James*. New York: Charles Scribner's Sons, 1890.

Hunt, Roger D. *Colonels in Blue: Union Army Colonels of the Civil War*. Vol. 2, *New York*. Atglen, PA: Schiffer Military History, 2003.

Hunt, Roger D., and Jack R. Brown. *Brevet Brigadier Generals in Blue*. Gaithersburg, MD: Olde Soldiers Books, 1990.

Irving, Theodore. *"More Than Conqueror"; or, Memorials of Col. J. Howard Kitching*. New York: Hurd and Houghton, 1873.

Johnson, Robert U., and Clarence C. Buel, eds. *Battles and Leaders of the Civil War*. 4 vols. New York: Century, 1887–88.

Kamphoefner, Walter D., and Wolfgang Helbich, eds. *Germans in the Civil War: The Letters They Wrote Home*. Chapel Hill: Univ. of North Carolina Press, 2006.

Keating, Robert. *Carnival of Blood: The Civil War Ordeal of the Seventh New York Heavy Artillery*. Baltimore: Butternut & Blue, 1998.

Keller, Christian B. *Chancellorsville and the Germans: Nativism, Ethnicity, and Civil War Memory*. New York: Fordham Univ. Press, 2007.

Kirk, Hyland C. *Heavy Guns and Light: A History of the 4th New York Heavy Artillery*. New York: C. T. Dillingham, 1890.

Krick, Robert K. *Civil War Weather in Virginia*. Tuscaloosa: Univ. of Alabama Press, 2007.

———. *Conquering the Valley: Stonewall Jackson at Port Republic*. New York: William Morrow, 1996.

Law, Evander M. "From the Wilderness to Cold Harbor." In Johnson and Buel, *Battles and Leaders of the Civil War*, 4:118–44.

Longstreet, James. *From Manassas to Appomattox: Memoirs of the Civil War in America*. Philadelphia: J. B. Lippincott, 1895.
Lossing, Benson J. *Pictorial Field Book of the Civil War*. 3 vols. New York: T. Belknap, 1876.
Lowe, David W., ed. *Meade's Army: The Private Notebooks of Lt. Col. Theodore Lyman*. Kent, OH: Kent State Univ. Press, 2007.
Mackowski, Chris, and Kristopher D. White. "The Battle of the Bloody Angle or 'Mule Shoe'—Spotsylvania Court House, May 12, 1864." *Blue and Gray Magazine* 26, no. 1 (2009): 6–28, 43–50.
Marsh, Ruth. "A History of Rochester's Part in the Civil War." In *Rochester in the Civil War*, edited by Blake McKelvey. Rochester, NY: Rochester Historical Society, 1944.
Marvel, William. "Retreat to Appomattox." *Blue and Gray Magazine* 18, no. 4 (Spring 2001): 6–23, 46, 49–54.
Massachusetts Artillery, 1st Regiment. *Souvenir: First Regiment of Heavy Artillery Massachusetts Volunteers. Dedication of Monument, May 19, 1901*. N.p., [1901?].
Matter, William D. *If It Takes All Summer*. Chapel Hill: Univ. of North Carolina Press, 1988.
McBride, Robert E. *In the Ranks from the Wilderness to Appomattox Court-House*. Cincinnati: Self-published, 1881.
McMahon, Martin T. "The Death of General John Sedgwick." In Johnson and Buel, *Battles and Leaders of the Civil War*, 4:175.
Meade, George. *The Life and Letters of George Gordon Meade*. 2 vols. New York: Charles Scribner's Sons, 1913.
Merritt, Wesley. "Sheridan in the Shenandoah Valley." In Johnson and Buel, *Battles and Leaders of the Civil War*, 4:500–521.
Mertz, Gregory A. "General Gouverneur K. Warren and the Fighting at Laurel Hill during the Battle of Spotsylvania Court House, May 1864." *Blue and Gray Magazine* 21, no. 4 (Summer 2004): 6–23, 48–52.
Miller, Delavan S. *Drum Taps in Dixie: Memories of a Drummer Boy, 1861–1865*. Watertown, NY: Hunger-Holbrook, 1905.
Miller, J. Michael. *The North Anna Campaign, "Even to Hell Itself," May 21–26 1864*. Lynchburg, VA: H. E. Howard, 1989.
Mulholland, St. Clair A. *Military Order, Congress Medal of Honor Legion of the United States*. Philadelphia: Town Printing, 1905.
Naiswald, L. VanLoan. *Grape and Canister: The Story of the Field Artillery of the Army of the Potomac, 1861–1865*. New York: Oxford Univ. Press, 1960.
Newsome, Hampton. *Richmond Must Fall: The Richmond-Petersburg Campaign, October 1864*. Kent, OH: Kent State Univ. Press, 2013.
Nevins, Allan, ed. *A Diary of Battle: The Personal Journals of Colonel Charles S. Wainwright, 1861–1865*. New York: Harcourt, Brace, & World, 1962.
———. *The War for the Union*. Vol. 4, *The Organized War to Victory 1864–1865*. New York: Charles Scribner's Sons, 1971.

New York Monuments Commission for the Battlefields of Gettysburg and Chattanooga. *Final Report on the Battlefield of Gettysburg.* Vol. 1. Albany, NY: J. B. Lyon, printers, 1900.

New York State Adjutant General's Office. *Annual Report of the Adjutant-General of the State of New York for the Year 1897.* Albany, NY: Wynkoop, Hallenbeck, Crawford, 1898.

Oates, William C. *The War between the Union and the Confederacy and Its Lost Opportunities, with a History of the 15th Alabama Regiment and the Forty-Eight Battles in Which It Was Engaged.* 1905. Reprint, with introduction by Robert K. Krick. Dayton, OH: Morningside Bookshop, 1985.

Olcott, Mark. *The Civil War Letters of Lewis Bissell: A Curriculum.* Washington, DC: Field School Educational Foundation Press, 1981.

Perry, William F. "Reminiscences of the Campaign of 1864 in Virginia." *Southern Historical Society Papers* 7 (1879): 49—63.

Pfanz, Harry W. *Gettysburg: Culp's Hill and Cemetery Hill.* Chapel Hill: Univ. of North Carolina Press, 1993.

———. *Gettysburg: The First Day.* Chapel Hill: Univ. of North Carolina Press, 2001.

Phisterer, Frederick, comp. *New York in the War of the Rebellion.* 5 vols. 3rd ed. Albany, NY: Weed and Parsons, 1890.

Porter, Horace. "Five Forks and the Pursuit of Lee." In Johnson and Buel, *Battles and Leaders of the Civil War,* 4:708–22.

Powell, William H. "The Battle of the Petersburg Crater." In Johnson and Buel, *Battles and Leaders of the Civil War,* 4:545–60.

———. *The Fifth Army Corps.* New York: G. P. Putnam's Sons, 1896.

Priest, John Michael. *"Stand to It and Give Them Hell": Gettysburg as the Soldiers Experienced It from Cemetery Ridge to Little Round Top, July 2, 1863.* El Dorado Hills, CA: Savas Beatie, 2014.

Pritchard, Russ A., Jr. *Civil War Weapons and Equipment.* Guilford, CT: Lyons, 2003.

Reinhart, Joseph R., ed. *A German Hurrah!: Civil War Letters of Friedrich Bertsch and Wilhelm Stängel, 9th Ohio Infantry.* Kent, OH: Kent State Univ. Press, 2010.

Rhea, Gordon C. *The Battle of the Wilderness: May 5–6, 1864.* Baton Rouge: Louisiana State Univ. Press, 1994.

———. *The Battles for Spotsylvania Court House and the Road to Yellow Tavern: May 7–12, 1864.* Baton Rouge: Louisiana State Univ. Press, 1997.

———. *Cold Harbor: Grant and Lee, May 26–June 3, 1864.* Baton Rouge: Louisiana State Univ. Press, 2002.

———. *On to Petersburg: Grant and Lee, June 4–15, 1864.* Baton Rouge: Louisiana State Univ. Press, 2017.

———. *To the North Anna River: Grant and Lee, May 13–25 1864.* Baton Rouge: Louisiana State Univ. Press, 2000.

Rhodes, Robert Hunt, ed. *All for the Union: The Civil War Diary and Letters of Elisha Hunt Rhodes.* New York: Orion Books, 1991.

Riddle, Albert Gallatin. *Argument for the Defense in the Case of the United States vs. Colonel Louis Schirmer.* Washington, DC: A. G. Riddle and S. Wolf, 1865.

———. *Recollections of War Times: Reminiscences of Men and Events in Washington, 1860–1865.* New York: G. P. Putnam's Sons, 1895.

Rodenbough, Theodore F. "Sheridan's Richmond Raid." In Johnson and Buel, *Battles and Leaders of the Civil War,* 4:188–93.

Roe, Alfred Seelve, and Charles Nutt. *History of the First Regiment of Heavy Artillery, Massachusetts Volunteers, Formerly the Fourteenth Regiment of Infantry, 1861–1865.* Boston: Regimental Association, 1917.

Schroeder, Patrick A. *We Came to Fight: The History of the 5th New York Veteran Volunteer Infantry, Duryée's Zouaves (1863–1865).* Brookneal, VA: Schroeder Publications, 1995.

Sears, Steven W. *Chancellorsville.* New York: Houghton Mifflin, 1996.

———. *Controversies & Commanders: Dispatches from the Army of the Potomac.* New York: Houghton Mifflin, 1999.

Shaw, Horace H., and Charles J. House. *The First Maine Heavy Artillery, 1862–1865: A History of Its Part and Place in the War for the Union.* Portland, ME, 1903.

Simpson, Brooks D. *Ulysses S. Grant: Triumph over Adversity, 1822–1865.* New York: Houghton Mifflin, 2000.

Smith, Robin. *American Civil War Zouaves.* Oxford: Osprey, 1996.

Sommers, Richard J. *Richmond Redeemed: The Siege at Petersburg.* Garden City, NY: Doubleday, 1981.

Survivors' Association, comp. *History of the Corn Exchange Regiment, 118th Pennsylvania Volunteers.* Philadelphia: J. L. Smith, 1888.

Thomas, Henry Goddard. "The Colored Troops at Petersburg." In Johnson and Buel, *Battles and Leaders of the Civil War,* 4:563–67.

Tilney, Robert. *My Life in the Army: Three Years and a Half with the Fifth Army Corps, Army of the Potomac, 1862–1865.* Philadelphia: Ferris & Leach, 1912.

Trudeau, Noah Andre. "The Battle of Harris Farm—Woe to the Heavy Artillery." *Civil War Times Illustrated* 27, no. 1 (Mar. 1988): 16–23, 44.

———. *The Last Citadel: Petersburg, Virginia, June 1864–April 1865.* Boston: Little, Brown, 1991.

Trulock, Alice Rains. *In the Hands of Providence: Joshua L. Chamberlain & the American Civil War.* Chapel Hill: Univ. of North Carolina Press, 1992.

US War Department. *The War of the Rebellion: A Compilation of the Official Records of the Union and Confederate Armies.* 130 vols. Washington, DC: Government Printing Office, 1880–1901.

Whiteaker, Larry H., and W. Calvin Dickerson, eds. *Civil War Letters of the Tenure Family: Rockland County, New York, 1862–1856.* New City, NY: Historical Society of Rockland County, 1990.

Wittenberg, Eric J. *Glory Enough for All: Sheridan's Second Raid and the Battle of Trevilian Station.* Washington, DC: Brassey's, 2001.

Willcox, Orlando B. "Actions on the Weldon Railroad." In Johnson and Buel, *Battles and Leaders of the Civil War*, 4:568–73.

Williams, George F. *Bullet and Shell: War as the Soldier Saw It; Camp, March, and Picket; Battlefield and Bivouac; Prison and Hospital*. New York: Fords, Howard, & Hulbert, 1884.

Wills, Brian Steel. *Inglorious Passages: Noncombat Deaths in the Civil War*. Lawrence: Univ. Press of Kansas, 2017.

Woodbury, Augustus. *The Second Rhode Island Regiment: A Narrative of Military Operations in Which the Regiment Was Engaged from the Beginning to the End of the War for the Union*. Providence, RI: Valpey, Angell, 1875.

Woodward, Evan Morrison. *Our Campaigns*. Philadelphia: John E. Potter, 1865.

Young, Alfred C., III. *Lee's Army during the Overland Campaign: A Numerical Study*. Baton Rouge: Louisiana State Univ. Press, 2013.

MAPS

Appomattox Battlefield Map Series (twelve maps). Appomattox Court House National Historical Park, Appomattox, VA.

Davis, George B., Leslie J. Perry, and Joseph W. Kirkley, eds. *Atlas to Accompany the Official Records of the Union and Confederate Armies*. Washington, DC: Government Printing Office, 1891–95.

Gottfried, Bradley M. *The Maps of the Wilderness: An Atlas of the Wilderness Campaign, including All Cavalry Operations, May 2–6, 1864*. El Dorado Hills, CA: Savas Beatie 2016.

McCullough, Ginger, and Richard Easterbrook. *Battle of Five Forks: April 1, 1865*. Petersburg National Battlefield, n.d.

Michler, Nathaniel, and P. S. Michie. *Cold Harbor* (battlefield map). 1867. Copy at Richmond National Battlefield Park.

O'Reilly, Frank. *Battle of the Wilderness* (series of six battle maps). Conshohocken, PA: Eastern National, 2003.

Stanley, Steve. *Battle of Spotsylvania Court House* (series of twenty-four battle maps). N.p., 2000.

US Department of the Interior. *Troop Movement Map: Cold Harbor*. Master Plan, Richmond National Battlefield Park, 1960.

Woodhead, Henry, ed. *Echoes of Glory: Illustrated Atlas of the Civil War*. Alexandria, VA: Time-Life Books, 1991.

WORLD WIDE WEB

"Colonel Henry Steel Olcott." *New World Encyclopedia*. https://www.newworldencyclopedia.org/entry/Henry_Steel_Olcott.

Keating, Ryan W. "Immigrants in the Union Army." Essential Civil War Curriculum. Virginia Center for Civil War Studies at Virginia Tech. https://www.essentialcivilwarcurriculum.com/immigrants-in-the-union-army.html.

Index

Page numbers in *italics* refer to illustrations.

Accotink Turnpike, xx
A. G. Riddle and S. Wolf, 283, 289–90, 293
Alabama Brigade: Battle of White Oak Road, 228–29; Battle of the Wilderness, 33, 35, 37–38; Fifteenth Infantry, 33, 35–36, 38; Forty-Eighth Infantry, 33; Forty-Fourth Infantry, 33; Forty-Seventh Infantry, 33; Fourth Infantry, 33
Aldrich's, 40, 47, 48, 49
Alexandria, xvi–xviii, xxiii–xxiv, 6, 9–10, 12, 19, 262
Allan, William, 107, 110
Allen's Mill, 120
Alsop, Susan, 66
Alsop's farm, 42, 68, 70
Amelia Court House, 244, 247–49
Anderson, Richard Heron, 41, 78, 82, 122, 227; Appomattox Campaign, 249; Battle of Bethesda Church, 103, 110
Anderson house, 60, 63
Andersonville prison, 37
apple jack, 201, 207
Appomattox Campaign, 243–61, 246, 274; casualties, 250–51; Confederate line, 250; Confederate surrender, 255–57
Appomattox Court House, 252–54, 256–57, 274–75
Appomattox River, 125–27, 131, 243–44, 249–51, 255, 257–58, 263
Appomattox Station, 251–53
Aqueduct Bridge, 267
Aquia Creek, 264
Archer, James J., 186–87, 189
Arlington Heights, 292
Arlington House, 269

Armstrong house, 67, 106, 211
Armstrong's Mill, 191–94, 210–12, 217
Army of the James, 25, 125, 222, 245; Battle of Cold Harbor, 111; Battle of Five Forks, 235; First Battle of Deep Bottom, 146
Army of Northern Virginia, 17, 25–26, 58, 77–78, 82–83, 100, 221, 243, 245; Appomattox Campaign, 255; Battle of Five Forks, 239–40; Battle of Harris Farm, 64; Battle of Jericho Mills, 85–87, 89; Battle of North Anna, 94; Battle of White Oak Road, 228–29; surrender, 255–57, 274; Third Corps, 243
Army of the Potomac, 17–18, 22–23, 25–26, 29, 57, 61, 75, 95–96, 101–2, 119–20, 122, 124, 126, 154, 156, 169–70, 220, 222, 256, 260–61, 265, 267, 274–76, 281; Appomattox Campaign, 248; Battle of Cold Harbor, 116; Battle of the Crater, 151–53, 197; Battle of Globe Tavern, 166, 169, 176; Battle of Harris Farm, 65, 76; Battle of North Anna, 91, 93; Battle of Peebles's Farm, 183, 184, 190; battles at Spotsylvania Court House, 40, 42, 44–45, 48, 55; Battle of the Wilderness, 30–31; first assault at Petersburg, 126, 129, 131; provost, 259; rations, 48, 259; Reserve Artillery, 2–3, 8, 20, 23, 27, 29, 40, 57–58, 61; Siege of Petersburg, 137, 139, 146, 151–53; spring campaign, 27
Army of the Shenandoah, 154
Army of Virginia, 8; armament, 24
Arthur's Swamp, 182, 184, 186, 189, 219
Ashland, 100
Atlee's Station, 100
Auger, Christopher C., 11
Avery house, 130, 140

· 363 ·

Ayres, Romeyn B., 118, 120–22, 125, 157, 169, 170, 177–81, 219, 221–27, 244, 247, 257–60, 262–64, 266; Appomattox Campaign, 247–49, 253; Battle of Cold Harbor, 114; Battle of the Crater, 150, 152–53; Battle of Dinwiddie Court House, 232–33; Battle of Five Forks, 233, 236–40; Battle of Globe Tavern, 159–64, 166–69, 172–73, 175; Battle of Harris Farm, 60; Battle of Hatcher's Run, 211–13, 216–18; Battle of Jericho Mills, 84; Battle of Peebles's Farm, 183–87, 189–91, 193–94; Battle of White Oak Road, 227–28, 230–31; first assault at Petersburg, 127–28, 130, 132–35; headquarters, 141; raid on the Weldon Railroad, 199–200, 202–3, 205–7; Siege of Petersburg, 141–45, 147–48, 150, 152–53

Babcock, Orville, 234
Bailey's Creek, 129, 147
Barlow, Francis C.: Battle of Harris Farm, 63; Battle of Totopotomoy Creek, 116
Barnard, John G., xviii, xxiii
Bartlett, Joseph J., 223, 244, 257, 262; Appomattox Campaign, 247, 253; Battle of Cold Harbor, 114; Battle of Jericho Mills, 84, 87; Siege of Petersburg, 147
Bates, James, 118
Battery B, Fourth US, Battle of Jericho Mills, 85
Battery D, First New York, 106
Battery D, Second US Artillery, 22
Battery E, First New York, 86
Battery 45, in Confederate line at Petersburg, 181
Battery H, First New York: Battle of Bethesda Church, 106; Battle of Jericho Mills, 85; Battle of White Oak Road, 230; Light, 106, 230
Battery I, First New York, 7; Battle of Gettysburg, 8; battles for Chattanooga, 8; Valley Campaign, 7–8
Battery L, First New York, 178
Battle, Cullen, 69
Battle above the Clouds, 8
Battle of Brandy Station, xv–xvii; casualties, xvi–xviii
Battle of Chancellorsville, 3, 8, 27, 31
Battle of the Crater, 149–56; temperature, 150–51, 153; Union line, 149–50
Battle of Dinwiddie Court House, 231–33
Battle of Five Forks, 233–42, 259, 275; casualties, 240–42; Confederate line, 234; Union breastworks, 239
Battle of Gettysburg, 8, 22
Battle of Globe Tavern, 159–77, 163, 167, 174, 180, 260, 275; casualties, 169, 175–76; Confederate line, 174; Union line, 166, 171–74
Battle of Harris Farm, 57–75, 71, 220, 274, 287; casualties at, 62–64, 72–74; Confederate line, 63–65, 67–69; friendly fire, 72; Union line, 63, 65, 67, 70, 74

Battle of Hatcher's Run, 210–18, 275; casualties, 217–18; Confederate works, 211; Union breastworks, 213; Union line, 210; weather conditions during, 217
Battle of Jericho Mills, 84–89, 87; casualties, 89; Confederate line, 87; Union line, 84
Battle of North Anna, 89–95; casualties, 91, 94; Confederate inverted-V line, 89, 92–93; Union breastworks, 89; Union line, 92
Battle of Peebles's Farm, 177–95; casualties, 190, 194; Confederate line, 185, 192–93; Union line, 180–81, 189–91, 194
Battle of Sailor's Creek, 250
Battle of Totopotomoy Creek, 113
Battle of Weldon Railroad. *See* Battle of Globe Tavern
Battle of White Oak Road, 227–31; casualties, 231
Battle of the Wilderness, 19–38, 28, 139, 182, 274; casualties, 37–38; Confederate line, 38–39; Union breastworks, 39–40; Union line, 38–40
Baxter Road, 132, 139
Beauregard, P. G. T.: Battle of Globe Tavern, 161, 165–66, 171; first assault at Petersburg, 126–27, 131
Becker, Adolphus, 14–15
Belcher, Amherst, 6, 19, 231; Battle of Hatcher's Run, 215, 218; Battle of North Anna, 89; battles at Spotsylvania Court House, 44–45, 56; Battle of the Wilderness, 31; raid on the Weldon Railroad, 206
Belches's Mill, 206
Belfield, 203, 205
Belle Plain, 48
Benning, Henry G. "Rock," 33
Bermuda Hundred, 125, 127, 146
Bethesda Church, 103–8, 110–13, 118, 170, 235, 274
Beverly house, 59–60, 63
Bigelow, John, 106
Birney, David: Battle of Harris Farm, 71–72; first assault at Petersburg, 130
Bissell, Lewis, xv–xvii, xxiv–xxv, 9
Blacks and Whites Station, 262
Blackwater Swamp, 144
Blandford, 146
Blenker, Louis, xxii, 1–2, 7
Blick house, 160, 171–73, 180
Blockhouse 1, 269
Blockhouse 2, 269
Bloody Angle, 53–55
Boisseau, B., 239
Boisseau, John, 233–36
Boisseau house, 233
Boker, John, 259
Bolingbroke House, 262
Bookwood, Charles, 2
Bowerman, Richard, 59, 70
Bowles farm, 103–4, 106

Bowling Green, 65, 76–77, 90, 96, 263
Boydton Plank Road, 177, 181–82, 186–87, 189–93, 210–11, 222–26, 230, 232–33; Union lines near, 221
Bragg, Braxton, 126
Bragg, Edward S., 177; Battle of Globe Tavern, 164, 166, 169, 172, 175; Battle of Jericho Mills, 85–87; Battle of Peebles's Farm, 189, 191; first assault at Petersburg, 126–27
Brandy Station, 17–21, 25, 27, 29, 44, 49, 62, 119, 130, 156, 181, 268, 272, 274, 281–82, 285
Breck, George, 178–79; Battle of Bethesda Church, 106
Briggs, Henry Shaw, 285
Brock Road, 30, 37, 40–42, 46, 48, 67, 235
Brock's Bridge, 29
Brooks Road, 233
Brown, Augustus C.: Battle of Harris Farm, 68, 73; Battle of the Wilderness, 33
Brown, Henry W., 52–53
Brown, Joseph N., 85
Brown house, 49, 50
Buch, John, 209
Bull Run: First Campaign, 1–2; Second Campaign, 2–3, 8
Bundy, William, 3, 20, 285
Burger, Stephen: Battle of Harris Farm, 60; Battle of Jericho Mills, 86; battles at Spotsylvania Court House, 52–53; Battle of the Wilderness, 39
Burgess's Tavern, 225
burials, 73, 110–11
Burkeville, 258
Burkeville Junction, 245, 247–48
Burnham, Horace B., 283, 288, 291
Burnside, Ambrose E., 26, 58, 82, 120; Battle of Cold Harbor, 112–14; Battle of the Crater, 150, 152–53; Battle of Harris Farm, 65; Battle of North Anna, 90–92; battles at Spotsylvania Court House, 45, 49–51; Battle of the Wilderness, 31–34, 37; first assault at Petersburg, 129, 145–46; mine construction, 145–47; mine explosion, 148–50; Siege of Petersburg, 145–48, 150, 152–53
Burton, Henry S., 24, 40; battles at Spotsylvania Court House, 44, 47; Battle of the Wilderness, 20
Butler, Benjamin, 25, 125–26, 182; Battle of Cold Harbor, 111; Battle of Peebles's Farm, 183–84
Butler, Halter, 226–28
Butler house, 225–27, 231
Butterfield (general), 8, 110

Cahawha, 6
Campbell, James, 241
camp life, xxiv–xxv, 208–9
Cap, 240
Capitol, 264–66

Carle, James, 118
Carroll Prison, 283
Casey's Tactics, 24
Catharpin Road, 29–30, 40–41, 43
Catherine Furnace, 44
Catlett, Hugh, 78
Catlett's farm, 78–79, 81
Cedar Creek, 155
Cemetery Hill: Gettysburg, 8; Petersburg, 146
Chaffin's Bluff, 146
Chain Bridge, xviii
Chamberlain, Joshua, 223, 244, 256–57, 259, 262–64, 266–67; Appomattox Campaign, 252; Battle of Five Forks, 233, 236; Battle of White Oak Road, 230–31
Chancellor house, 29
Chancellorsville, 2, 29, 31, 40, 44, 170, 276
Chapman, George H., 120, 122–23
Chappell farm, 182, 185, 188, 223, 259–60
Charles City Court House, 122, 124–25
Chattanooga, 8
Chewning farm, 34
Chickahominy River, 119–22
Chieves house, 157
Chilesburg, 78
Chopawamsic Creek, 264
Christian, Charles B., 107–9
Christian, William S., 166
Christl, Otto, 12–13
Christmas Day, 208
Church Road, 182, 186
City Point, 142, 154–55, 181, 198, 215, 222, 250
City Point Railroad, 126–27, 129
City of Troy, 284–85, 288
Claiborne Road, 192, 226–27, 231, 240, 243–44
Clark house, 125
Clark's Mountain, 27–28
Clements house, 192, 194
Clingman, Thomas, 166
Cockade City, 138, 176, 194, 244
Coehorn mortars, 24, 47, 49, 54, 77, 92–93, 101–2; wagons carrying, 47–48
Cold Harbor, 112–14, 115, 119–20, 122, 179
Cole, Martin, 15
Colquitt, Alfred H., 161, 166, 169
Columbia Pike, 265, 270
Coman's Well, 201, 205
Come, Stephen F.: Appomattox Campaign, 250; letter to wife, 269–71
Company A, Fifteenth New York Heavy Artillery, 5, 9, 16; in the First Battalion, 20; in the Second Battalion, 269
Company B, Fifteenth New York Heavy Artillery, 5, 9, 12, 14, 16, 29, 49; in the First Battalion, 20, 130, 269
Company C, Fifteenth New York Heavy Artillery, 5, 9, 16, 198, 259; Battle of Globe Tavern, 159; in the First Battalion, 20, 269

Company D, Fifteenth New York Heavy Artillery, 5, 7, 9, 16; Battle of Harris Farm, 63, 68; in the First Battalion, 20, 269
Company D, Fourth New York Heavy Artillery, 68, 102
Company E, Fifteenth New York Heavy Artillery, 5, 9, 24, 53–54, 77, 92, 101, 102; Battle of North Anna, 92; battles at Spotsylvania Court House, 48–49; in the Second Battalion, 20, 48–49, 269; Siege of Petersburg, 142
Company F, Fifteenth New York Heavy Artillery, 4, 9, 39, 222; battles at Spotsylvania Court House, 45; in the Second Battalion, 20, 48, 269; Siege of Petersburg, 142
Company G, Fifteenth New York Heavy Artillery, 4–5, 9; battles at Spotsylvania Court House, 48; in the First Battalion, 269; in the Second Battalion, 20, 48; Siege of Petersburg, 142
Company H, Fifteenth New York Heavy Artillery, 1–5, 9, 198; Battle of Five Forks, 237; Battle of Harris Farm, 63, 68; battles at Spotsylvania Court House, 48; in the First Battalion, 269; in the Second Battalion, 20, 48; Siege of Petersburg, 142
Company H, Fourth New York Heavy Artillery, 68
Company I, Fifteenth New York Heavy Artillery, 4–5, 9; Battle of Harris Farm, 63; in the Third Battalion, 20, 269
Company K, Fifteenth New York Heavy Artillery, 5, 9–10, 282; Battle of Harris Farm, 63, 68; false muster lists for, 288–89; in the Third Battalion, 20, 269
Company K, Fourth New York Heavy Artillery, 68
Company L, Fifteenth New York Heavy Artillery, 5, 7, 9; in the Third Battalion, 20, 269
Company M, Fifteenth New York Heavy Artillery, 5–6, 15, 73–74, 130, 141–43, 156, 163, 168, 222; Battle of Globe Tavern, 162–63, 168; Battle of Harris Farm, 62–63; Battle of North Anna, 94; Battle of Peebles's Farm, 195; Battle of the Wilderness, 31; in the Fifth Corps Artillery Brigade, 222; Siege of Petersburg, 138, 141–43; in the Third Battalion, 20, 269
con artists, 209
Concord Church, 263
Confederate surrender, 255–56
conscription law (1863), 16
Cooke, John R., 243, 187, 189, 243
Cope, Emmor B.: Battle of Five Forks, 239; Battle of White Oak Road, 228
Corbin's Bridge, 41, 43
Coulter, Richard: Battle of Globe Tavern, 169; Battle of White Oak Road, 228, 230
Course, Montgomery, 234, 240
Cox Road, 244
Crawford, Samuel W., 59, 78, 83–84, 100–102, 118, 120–23, 125, 157, 177, 180, 219, 221, 223–26, 244, 257, 262; Appomattox Campaign, 247; Battle of Dinwiddie Court House, 232;
Battle of Five Forks, 233, 236, 239–40; Battle of Globe Tavern, 159–60, 164, 166, 168, 172; Battle of Harris Farm, 71–73; Battle of Hatcher's Run, 211–13, 216–17; Battle of Jericho Mills, 84–85, 87; Battle of North Anna, 90–91; Battle of Peebles's Farm, 191, 193–94; Battles of Bethesda Church and Cold Harbor, 103, 106, 108–10, 112–13; battles at Spotsylvania Court House, 55; Battle of White Oak Road, 227, 230–31; first assault at Petersburg, 127, 130, 132, 134; raid on the Weldon Railroad, 199, 200–201, 203, 205–6; Siege of Petersburg, 139, 147
Crittenden, Thomas L., 91
Crook, George, 247, 250
Crow house, 225
Culpepper Court House, 17
Cumberland Church, 251–52
Custer, George A., 224, 245; Appomattox Campaign, 250; Battle of Five Forks, 235, 239
Cutler, Lysander, 57, 59, 77, 79, 83–84, 100, 118–22, 125, 157, 177; Battle of Globe Tavern, 159, 164, 173–75; Battle of Harris Farm, 65–66; Battle of Jericho Mills, 85–86; battles at Spotsylvania Court House, 55; Battle of Totopotomoy Creek, 111, 113; first assault at Petersburg, 127–30, 132, 134; Siege of Petersburg, 138–39

Dabney, W., 226, 231, 244
Dabney Ferry, 98
Dabney house, 226–27, 231, 244
Dabney's Sawmill, 191, 194, 213, 216–18, 225
Daily, William, 62; Battle of Jericho Mills, 85; Battle of Totopotomoy Creek, 110; Battle of the Wilderness, 33
Dana, Charles, 281–82
Danville, 221, 245, 247–48
Davies, Henry, 213
Davis, Jefferson, 126, 245
Davis, Joseph R.: Battle of Globe Tavern, 161, 166–67; Battle of Peebles's Farm, 187, 189
Dearing, James, 161
Deatonsville, 249
Deep Bottom, 146, 156
Deep Creek, 245
DeKalb Regiment, 6, 231
Delafield, Richard, xvii
Delaware: Fourth, 180; Third, 180
Dennison, 227, 230
Dennisville, 247
Department of the East, 283
Department of Virginia, 263
De Russy, Gustavus, xvi, 11, 14–15, 268, 289
deserters, 10, 92, 178, 271–72
Devin, Thomas: Appomattox Campaign, 250; Battle of Five Forks, 235, 239
Dickey, William D., 73, 222, 259, 269; Battle of Globe Tavern, 159, 162, 164, 168; Battle of

North Anna, 94; first assault at Petersburg, 130; Medal of Honor, 130
Dieckmann, Julius, 3, 10, 20, 61, 76–77, 96, 102, 198, 208, 269–71, 273; Battle of Chancellorsville, 3, 8; Battle of North Anna, 90; Battle of Peebles's Farm, 183; battles at Spotsylvania Court House, 48; Battle of the Wilderness, 31; first assault at Petersburg, 128; health issues, 159; Siege of Petersburg, 142; Valley Campaign, 7
Diehl, John J., 259
Dimmock Line, 126–27, 130–32, 135
Dinwiddie, 222, 224, 231
Dinwiddie Court House, 210, 212, 223–24, 227, 231–32, 234
Dinwiddie Road, 234
disciplinary actions, 10, 270–71
Dix, John A., 196, 283, 292
Dobb's Ferry, 155
Douthat's Landing, 127
Douthat's place, 124
Dow, Edwin B., 43
Dowell's Creek, 97
Drewry's Bluff, 127, 263
Duane, James C., 124
Duke Street, 269
Dumfries, 264
Duncan Road, 192–94
Dunkirk, 96
Dunlop house, 172
Dushane, Nathan T., 119; Battle of Cold Harbor, 112; Battle of Globe Tavern, 161–64, 172; Battle of Harris Farm, 70; Siege of Petersburg, 139
D'Utassy, Frederick George, 282–83, 292
Duysing, Emil, 6–7, 14; Battle of Peebles's Farm, 183; Battle of White Oak Road, 231; Battle of the Wilderness, 20; death, 231; health issues, 159; promotion to major, 10; raid on the Weldon Railroad, 206
Dwight, William, 266

Early, Jubal A., 100, 107, 153, 155, 220; Battle of Bethesda Church, 103, 108, 110; Battle of Harris Farm, 68
Eastern Theater, 26
East Tennessee and Virginia Railroad, 25
Eiche, Louis, 259, 266, 269–71; arrest, 198; Battle of Five Forks, 237; Battle of Globe Tavern, 159, 164, 167–68; Battle of Peebles's Farm, 183; court martial, 208; leave of absence, 198, 208
Eighteenth Corps, 126; Battle of Cold Harbor, 111–12, 116; first assault at Petersburg, 130, 135; Siege of Petersburg, 147–48
Eighteenth Massachusetts Infantry, 185
Eighth New York Cavalry, 77
Eighth New York Heavy Artillery: Battle of Cold Harbor, 116; Battle of Harris Farm, 63, 71
Eighth New York Infantry, 1

Eighty-Fourth New York Infantry ("Fourteenth Brooklyn"), 170
Eleventh Corps, 3, 8, 276; Battle of Chancellorsville, 3, 8; Battle of the Wilderness, 31; Reserve Artillery, 2
Eleventh New York "Fire" Zouave Regiment, xviii
Eleventh US Infantry: Battle of Globe Tavern, 167, 169; Battle of Peebles's Farm, 186
Elliott's Salient, 146
Ellsworth, Elmer Ephraim, xviii
Ely's Ford, 27, 29
Enfield, 98
Engels, Ewald, 282
Enon Church, 100
Ernst, Frederick, 139–40
Evans, Clement, 211, 216
Evergreen Station, 252
Ewell, Richard S., 27, 29, 77–78, 100; Appomattox Campaign, 249–50; Battle of Harris Farm, 66–68, 70, 73, 76; Battle of the Wilderness, 30, 38–39; horse, 70–71

Fairfax Station, 264
Farmville, 248, 250–51, 258
Farnsworth, Elon J., xx
Fenton, Reuben E., 276–77
Ferrero, Edward: Battle of the Crater, 150, 152; first assault at Petersburg, 128–29; Siege of Petersburg, 150, 152
Field, Charles W., 33
Fifteenth New York Heavy Artillery, xxv, 1–21, 28, 61, 79, 97, 119–20, 155–56, 159, 171, 177, 197–98, 209, 219–22, 224, 226, 244, 257, 260, 262, 266, 268–69, 271–72, 281, 284–85, 287, 290–93; Appomattox Campaign, 250–53, 274; artillery target practice, 13; back pay, 270; "band box soldiers," 11, 75, 260–61, 274–75; Battle of Bethesda Church, 105, 110; Battle of the Crater, 152–53; Battle of Dinwiddie Court House, 232; Battle of Five Forks, 236–37, 241, 275; Battle of Globe Tavern, 162–65, 167–69, 172, 175–76, 260, 275; Battle of Harris Farm, 61, 65–67, 69, 72–74, 274; Battle of Hatcher's Run, 211, 213–15, 217–18, 275; Battle of North Anna, 89, 92–93; Battle of Peebles's Farm, 183, 185–87, 190–91, 194–95; battles at Spotsylvania Court House, 45, 47, 49, 53–54, 56; Battle of White Oak Road, 228–31; Battle of the Wilderness, 31–32, 34–40, 139, 182, 274; brass band, 154, 259, 268; commendations, 260–61; court martial, 270; discharge, 269–70, 272; dress parades, 11, 19, 259, 271; drilling, 14–17, 21, 24, 181, 209–10; drinking, 14, 270; education, 16; ethnic makeup, 1, 7, 23, 46, 165, 272–76, 282; first assault at Petersburg, 134, 142; headquarters, 18, 270; legacy of, 274–77; musical training, 13; passes issued to, 16; professional training, 13; raid on the Weldon Railroad, 206–7; rations, 11–12; recreational

368 · INDEX

Fifteenth New York Heavy Artillery (*cont.*) activities, 13–14; recruiting offices, 285; return to New York, 272–73; Siege of Petersburg, 137, 139–45, 152–53; uniforms, 11, 197; winter quarters, 208

Fifteenth New York Independent Battery: Battle of Harris Farm, 69; Battle of Jericho Mills, 85

Fifth Corps, 29, 40–42, 57–59, 61, 76–78, 82–84, 96–103, 117–18, 120–25, 154, 157, 169, 177–80, 196–97, 199, 210, 220–23, 227, 244–45, 247, 256–60, 262–67, 269; Appomattox Campaign, 247–49, 251–53, 255; Artillery Brigade, 34, 82, 97, 222; Battle of the Crater, 153; Battle of Dinwiddie Court House, 232; Battle of Five Forks, 234–35, 240–41; Battle of Globe Tavern, 159–61, 164, 166, 169, 172, 174, 176; Battle of Harris Farm, 60–61, 63–65, 72, 75; Battle of Hatcher's Run, 211–12, 216–18; Battle of Jericho Mills, 84–86, 88; Battle of North Anna, 89–90, 93–94; Battle of Peebles's Farm, 183–85, 192–94; Battles of Bethesda Church and Cold Harbor, 103, 106, 111–14; battles at Spotsylvania Court House, 42–46, 48–49, 51–52, 55; Battle of White Oak Road, 230–31; Battle of the Wilderness, 30, 32–34, 36–40; camp, 256–57; Christmas Day, 208; *cross pattée* insignia, 160, 202; deserters, 178; discharge, 269; first assault at Petersburg, 127–30, 132–34; flag, 240; headquarters, 32–33, 132, 198, 265; Heavy Artillery Brigade, 62; malaria outbreak, 179; raid on the Weldon Railroad, 202, 208; Siege of Petersburg, 138, 141, 143–45, 147–48, 153; train, 85

Fifth Maine Infantry, 56

Fifth New York Veteran Volunteer Infantry, 170, 177, 226, 268, 275; Battle of Five Forks, 237; Battle of Globe Tavern, 167, 275; Battle of Hatcher's Run, 213–15, 218; Battle of Peebles's Farm, 186, 190; Battle of White Oak Road, 228, 230–31; Zouave uniforms, 171, 197

Fifth US Artillery, battles at Spotsylvania Court House, 52

Fifty-Second Virginia Infantry, 107

Finegan, Joseph: Battle of Globe Tavern, 174; Battle of Hatcher's Run, 216

first assault at Petersburg, 126–36; casualties, 134–35; Confederate line, 131, 132

First Battalion, Fifteenth New York Heavy, 10, 20, 198, 208, 269; Battle of Bethesda Church, 105; Battle of Globe Tavern, 159; Battle of Harris Farm, 66, 69, 74; Battle of the Wilderness, 35

First Brigade, Reserve Artillery, 22; battles at Spotsylvania Court House, 42, 44, 48–49; inspection, 24

First Brigade, Second Division, Fifth Corps, 169–70, 177, 196, 219, 247, 259–60, 266, 268; Appomattox Campaign, 255–56; Battle of Five Forks, 237, 239; Battle of Globe Tavern, 159–62, 169; Battle of Hatcher's Run, 214–15, 217–18; Battle of Jericho Mills, 85–86, 88; Battle of Peebles's Farm, 186, 189, 191, 194; Battles of Bethesda Church and Cold Harbor, 103–4, 113; Battle of White Oak Road, 228; dress parade, 259; drills, 181; first assault at Petersburg, 134, 139, 142

First Connecticut Artillery, xvii

First Corps of the Army of Virginia, 2–3, 8, 41, 78, 81, 110

First Division, Fifth Corps, 118–19, 219, 224, 244, 257, 258, 262–63; Appomattox Campaign, 250; Battle of Dinwiddie Court House, 232; Battle of Five Forks, 233, 239; Battle of Globe Tavern, 168, 171; Battle of Harris Farm, 60; Battle of Hatcher's Run, 217; Battle of Jericho Mills, 87; Battle of Peebles's Farm, 183, 192; headquarters, 262; raid on the Weldon Railroad, 199; Siege of Petersburg, 147

First Maine Heavy Artillery, 63, 70; first assault at Petersburg, 135

First Maryland Infantry, 70

First Maryland Veteran Volunteer Regiment, 70

First Massachusetts Heavy Artillery: Battle of Harris Farm, 63, 67–68; Company D, 72

First Michigan Infantry, 185

First New York Artillery, Battle of Bethesda Church, 106

First Wisconsin Heavy Artillery, 268–69

Fisher, Joseph W., 102; Battle of Bethesda Church, 103–4, 106, 110

Five Forks, 227, 231, 233–42, 238, 244, 259, 266

Flat Creek, 249

Flood, R. A., 284–85

Florida Brigade: Battle of Globe Tavern, 174; Battle of the Wilderness, 37

Flowerdew Hundred, 128–29

Flowers house, 173, 189, 191

Ford's Road, 233–34, 239, 244

Forsyth, George A., 67

Fort Albany, 269–70

Fort Archer, 185

Fort Barnard, xxiii

Fort Blenker, xxiii

Fort Bratton, 182, 185–86, 190

Fort Cass, 269

Fort Cherry, 182, 185–86, 190

Fort Craig, 269, 271

Fort Cummings, 192, 194, 211

Fort Davis, 180

Fort Dushane, 180, 191, 192

Fort Ellsworth, xviii, xxiii, 268, 269–70

Fort Ethan Allen, xviii, xxii–xxiii

Fort Farnsworth, xx, 10, 13, 268–69

Fort Harrison, 183

Fort Keene, 191

Fort Lafayette, 292, 294

Fort Lyon, xv–xxv, xviii, xxiii, 1, 3–5, 8–9, 18, 20, 268–69, 285; dogs at camp, xxiv–xxv, engineer

INDEX · 369

drawing, *xvix;* food at, 11–12, 15; living conditions, 12; Redoubt A, xx, xxv; Redoubt B, xx; Redoubt C, xx, xxv; Redoubt D, xx, xxv; theoretical instruction, 12–13
Fort MacRae, 182
Fort Marcy, xviii, xxii–xxiii
Fort McHenry, 220
Fort O'Rourke, xx, 9, 10, 13, 268–69
Fort Prescott, 144
Fortress Monroe, 6, 25
Fort Richardson, xxiii
Fort Sampson, 217, 220
Fort Schuyler, 6
Fort Scott, xxiii
Fort Sedgwick, 243
Fort Stedman, 221–22, 243
Fort Sumter, xxii
Fort Tillinghast, 269
Fort Wadsworth, 180, 191
Fort Ward, xxiii
Fort Warren, 293–94
Fort Weed, xx, 9–11, 268, 269
Fort Willard, xx, xxii, 9, 269
Fort Woodbury, 269, 271
Fort Worth, xxiii
Forty-Eighth Pennsylvania Infantry, 146
Forty-Eighth Virginia Infantry, 107
Forty-First New York Infantry, 6
Forty-Ninth Virginia Infantry, 107–9
Four Mile Run, 265
Fourteenth US Infantry, 177; Battle of Globe Tavern, 167, 169; Battle of Peebles's Farm, 186
Fourth Division, Fifth Corps, 79, 100, 177, 180; Battle of Globe Tavern, 164, 166, 172
Fourth New York Heavy Artillery, xxiii, 18, 81, 101; Battle of Harris Farm, 63, 66–68, 73; battles at Spotsylvania Court House, 48; Battle of the Wilderness, 20, 22; Second Battalion, 63
Fourth Virginia Cavalry, 98
fraternization between troops, 179–80, 256–57
Fredericksburg, 40–41, 48, 61, 70, 170, 264
Fredericksburg Road, 45–46, 58, 60–61, 63–68, 70, 76–77
Freeman's Ford, 200, 206
Frémont, John C., 2, 7

Garysville, 129
Gedney, John: Battle of the Wilderness, 36; first assault at Petersburg, 130, 134–35
General Orders, No. 10, Army of the Potomac, 260
Georgetown, xviii, 267, 281–82
Georgia brigades: Battle of Globe Tavern, 161, 166; Battle of Jericho Mills, 86; Battle of the Wilderness, 33
Gerhardt (corporal), 110
Germanna Ford, 27, 29
Germanna Plank Road, 29, 32
German recruits, xv, xxii–xxiii, 1, 7, 46, 165, 272–73; dogs at camp, xxiv–xxv; native born, 5; nativist sentiments against, 261, 275–76; recruiting cards for, 4
Getty, George W., 30–32
Gettysburg, 169
Gibbon, John, 256; Battle of Cold Harbor, 116; Battle of Harris Farm, 63
Gilliam field, 240
Glendale battlefield, 120
Globe Tavern, 159–76, 178, 185, 206, 211
Gordon, John B., 221, 256–57; Appomattox Campaign, 249–53; Battle of Cold Harbor, 113–14; Battle of Harris Farm, 68–70
Gordon Road, 67
Gordonsville, 28
Goshen, New York, 5
Graham, Samuel: Battle of Globe Tavern, 162; Battle of Peebles's Farm, 186
Grand Review, 265–68, 276
Grant, Ulysses S., 17–18, 23, 25, 29, 40–41, 58–59, 75, 77, 82, 100, 119–20, 122, 124–26, 153, 155–56, 176–78, 182, 199, 210, 220, 222, 224–27, 245, 259, 262; Appomattox Campaign, 248, 253; Battle of Dinwiddie Court House, 232; Battle of Five Forks, 234–35; Battle of Globe Tavern, 165; Battle of Harris Farm, 60, 63–66, 72; Battle of Hatcher's Run, 217; Battle of North Anna, 93–95; Battle of Peebles's Farm, 183–84, 189, 191–94; battles at Spotsylvania Court House, 42, 48–51, 56; Battle of Totopotomoy Creek, 112, 116; Battle of White Oak Road, 231; Battle of the Wilderness, 40; Confederate surrender to, 256; first assault at Petersburg, 131, 135–36; Siege of Petersburg, 138, 145–47
Gravelly Run, 212, 222–526, 230, 232–33, 235
Gravelly Run Church, 235, 241
Gravel Road, xx
Green, Jeremiah, 288
Greensville County, 203
Gregg, David McMurtrie, 41, 199, 210; Battle of Peebles's Farm, 192, 194; Battle of Hatcher's Run, 213, 216; raid on the Weldon Railroad, 200–201, 203, 205
Gregg, J. Irving, 213
Gregg, John, Battle of the Wilderness, 33
Gregory, Edgar M., 119, 223; Battle of Peebles's Farm, 192–93; Battle of White Oak Road, 230–31; first assault at Petersburg, 134; Siege of Petersburg, 139
Grey, Thomas Henry Percy, 283–84
Griffin, Charles, 42, 57, 59, 77–78, 83–84, 100–101, 103, 118, 119–22, 125, 157, 178, 219, 221–26, 244, 256, 258, 260, 262, 266; Appomattox Campaign, 247–49, 251, 253, 255; Battle of Dinwiddie Court House, 232; Battle of Five Forks, 233, 236, 239–41; Battle of Globe Tavern, 159–60, 171–72, 175; Battle of Hatcher's Run, 211–13, 215–17; Battle of Jericho Mills, 84–85, 87; Battle of Peebles's Farm, 183–86,

Griffin, Charles (*cont.*)
    191–93; Battles of Bethesda Church and Cold Harbor, 106, 111, 113–14; battles at Spotsylvania Court House, 55; Battle of White Oak Road, 227, 230–32; first assault at Petersburg, 127–28, 130, 132–34; raid on the Weldon Railroad, 199, 200, 202, 205–6; Siege of Petersburg, 138–39, 142, 147
Grimes, Bryan: Battle of Bethesda Church, 104; Battle of Harris Farm, 69; first assault at Petersburg, 127
Grimshaw, Arthur H., 180; Battle of Peebles's Farm, 186, 189–90
Grindlay, James: Battle of Five Forks, 237; Battle of Peebles's Farm, 189, 191
Guinea Station, 77, 78, 81–83
Gurley house, 159–60, 181, 206, 221
Gwyn, James: Battle of Five Forks, 236; Battle of Hatcher's Run, 212, 216; Battle of White Oak Road, 227, 228, 230

Hagood, Johnson: Battle of Globe Tavern, 173, 175–76; first assault at Petersburg, 127
Hagood Line, 127, 130–31
Halifax Road, 160–61, 167, 173, 180, 184, 192, 199, 201, 205–6, 210–11, 219
Halleck, Henry W., 17–18, 119, 125, 263; Battle of Harris Farm, 63; Battle of North Anna, 93
Hamilton, John H., 94
Hamilton, Phebe, 94
Hamilton's place, 27
Hampton, Wade, 193–94
Hampton-Sydney College, 252
Hancock, Winfield Scott, 29–30, 40–41, 58, 76, 78, 82–83, 100–101, 122, 124, 126, 156–57, 178, 199; Battle of Harris Farm, 63–65; Battle of North Anna, 91–92; Battle of Peebles's Farm, 191–94; battles at Spotsylvania Court House, 42–45, 48–50, 52; Battle of the Wilderness, 30–32, 37; first assault at Petersburg, 135; movement to Cold Harbor, 112; Siege of Petersburg, 138, 146–47
Hancock's Station, 221, 224
Hanover Court House, 263
Hanover Junction, 78, 89
Hanovertown, 93–94, 96–98
Hardie, James, 283
Hardin, Martin D., 102; Battle of Bethesda Church, 103–6, 109–11
Hargrave, J., 212, 223
Hargrave house, 212, 223
Harmon Road, 181
Harpers Ferry, 23
Harris, Clement, 64
Harris, David B., 130
Harris, Nathanial: Battle of Globe Tavern, 174–75; battles at Spotsylvania Court House, 54
Harris farm, 57–75

Harris Line, 131–32
Harrison's Creek, 127
Harrison's Landing, xxiii
Harris's store, 82–83
Hart, Patrick "Paddy": Battle of Cold Harbor, 114; Battle of Globe Tavern, 174–75; Battle of Harris Farm, 69; Battle of Jericho Mills, 85
Hartranft, John, 211
Hart's Island, 273
Hatcher's Run, 191–94, 210–19, 214, 222, 224–27, 233–34, 244
Hawkinsville, 200
Haw's Shop, 98, 100
Hayes, Joseph, 247, 257–59, 265, 267; Appomattox Campaign, 252–53, 255–56; Battle of Globe Tavern, 160–62, 164, 166–67, 169, 175
Heath, Philomen, 75
Heavy Artillery Brigade, 77, 81, 97, 101; Battle of Cold Harbor, 113; Battle of Harris Farm, 63–65; Battle of North Anna, 91
Helbich, Wolfgang, 276
Henagan, John W., 42
Henry, Patrick, 101
Herzog, Charles, 285
Heth, Henry: Appomattox Campaign, 243; Battle of Cold Harbor, 113; Battle of Globe Tavern, 161, 166, 171; Battle of Hatcher's Run, 211; Battle of Jericho Mills, 87; Battle of Peebles's Farm, 186–89, 193
Hicksford, 199, 203, 210; raid, 204
High Bridge, 250–51
Hill, Ambrose P., 28–29, 122; Battle of Globe Tavern, 166, 168; Battle of Jericho Mills, 84, 88–89; Battle of Peebles's Farm, 187, 193; Battle of the Wilderness, 30
Hillsman Farm, 250
Hoffman, John, Battle of Harris Farm, 69–70
Hoffmann, J. William: Battle of Globe Tavern, 164, 172; Battle of Jericho Mills, 85, 87; Battle of Peebles's Farm, 177, 183–84, 187, 189; first assault at Petersburg, 134
Hoke, Robert F., 127
Holliday cabin, 225–27, 231
Holt, David, 54–55
Holt, Joseph, 282
Holt house, 249
Home Guard, 126
Hooker (general), 8
Howard, Oliver O., 3, 8; Battle of Chancellorsville, 31
Howlett Line, 127, 138
Hubbard, James, 216–17
Humphreys, Andrew A., 27, 57, 59, 76, 77, 82, 97, 103, 120, 157, 199, 210, 221–25; Appomattox Campaign, 249–51, 253; Battle of Cold Harbor, 114; Battle of Five Forks, 235; Battle of Globe Tavern, 160, 164; Battle of Harris Farm, 60, 66; Battle of Hatcher's Run, 210–12; Battle of

Peebles's Farm, 188–89, 194; battles at Spotsylvania Court House, 42, 44, 52, 55; Battle of the Wilderness, 39; Siege of Petersburg, 139
Humphreys's Station, 220
Hundley's Corner, 110
Hunt, Henry, 1, 19–20, 22, 24, 61, 76, 102, 289–90; Battle of Harris Farm, 72; Battle of North Anna, 90, 93; battles at Spotsylvania Court House, 42, 44, 47–49; Battle of the Wilderness, 31
Hunting Creek, xviii, 9, 269; Bridge, xvi, 18
Hunton, Eppa, 228–31

Ideler, Hermann, 159, 293
Independence Day, 143
"Iron Brigade," 81–82, 102, 166, 172, 177

Jackson, Thomas J. "Stonewall," 3
James River, xxiii, 25, 119–21, 123–25, 127–28, 146–47, 154, 156–57, 159, 171, 182–84, 244, 262–63
Jarratt's Station, 201, 203
Jayne, Joseph M, 174–75
Jersey Brigade, Sixth Corps, 54–55
Jericho Bridge, 84
Jericho Ford, 90, 91
Jericho Mills, 84–95, 87; Union line, 84
Jerusalem Plank Road, 129, 138–39, 146–47, 159–60, 180–81, 199–200, 206, 243
Jetersville, 247–49
John Brooks, 128
Johnson, Andrew, 266, 293–94
Johnson, Bushrod R., 223–24, 227, 245; Appomattox Campaign, 249–50; Battle of Five Forks, 240; Battle of White Oak Road, 228; first assault at Petersburg, 127
Johnston, Joseph E., 221, 244
Johnston, Robert D., 213
Jones, Robert, 186
Jones farm, 186
Jones's Point, 146
Jungk, Gottlieb, 14–15

Kamphoefner, Walter, 276
Kasey, John G., 216
Kauss, Augustus, 237
Kautz, August V., 146
Kaysing, Edward, 198, 259
Kelly's Ford, 98
Kershaw, Joseph B., 33
Keys house, 213
Keysville, 248
Kitching, J. Howard, 22, 24–25, 28–29, 40, 57–59, 61–62, 77–81, 83, 95–102, 117–22, 124, 274; Battle of the Crater, 149–50, 151–53; Battle of Harris Farm, 60, 62–70, 72, 74–75; Battle of Jericho Mills, 85–87; Battle of North Anna, 89–93; Battles of Bethesda Church

and Cold Harbor, 104–6, 108, 110–15; battles at Spotsylvania Court House, 42–49, 51–53, 55–56; Battle of the Wilderness, 31–32, 34–39; birth, 22; death, 155; first assault at Petersburg, 128, 130, 132, 134–35, 141; headquarters, 52; letters to father, 87–88, 137–38, 143–44, 153–54; letters to mother, 151–52; letters to wife, 57, 148; parents, 22–23; Siege of Petersburg, 137, 139, 142–44, 147–51, 153
Knowles, Oliver, 213

Lacy house, 31–32, 34, 38, 40
Landrum farm, 50, 58, 64
Lane, James H.: Battle of Jericho Mills, 85; Battle of Peebles's Farm, 184
Laurel Hill, 42, 46, 51
Lautermann, Henry, 281
Law, Evander: Battle of Cold Harbor, 116; Battle of the Wilderness, 33
Leary farm, 117–20
Lebanon Church, 78, 81–82, 205
Ledlie, James H.: Battle of the Crater, 149, 153; Battle of North Anna, 91; Siege of Petersburg, 149, 153
Lee, Custis, 250
Lee, Fitzhugh, 41, 227, 245; Appomattox Campaign, 253; Battle of Five Forks, 240
Lee, Robert E., 10, 17, 25–27, 41, 61, 76–78, 100, 119, 122, 165, 181, 221, 227, 244–45, 269, 288; Appomattox Campaign, 247–53, 255; Battle of Five Forks, 234–35; Battle of Globe Tavern, 165–66, 171, 176; Battle of Harris Farm, 60, 64–67, 72; Battle of Jericho Mills, 88–89; Battle of North Anna, 89, 92–95; Battles of Bethesda Church and Cold Harbor, 103, 110, 116; battles at Spotsylvania Court House, 48, 54–55; Battle of White Oak Road, 230; Battle of the Wilderness, 30, 33, 40; first assault at Petersburg, 126, 131, 135–36, 141; illness, 92; Siege of Petersburg, 147; surrender, 255–56, 274; wagon train, 250
Lee, William H. F. "Rooney," 227, 245; Battle of Five Forks, 234; Battle of Hatcher's Run, 213
LeGrand Road, 253
Letcher Virginia Artillery, 161
Lewis, William G., 213
Lewis farm, 223, 224
Liberty Gardens, 272–73
Ligontown Ferry, 249
Lincoln, Abraham, xvii, xxii, 17, 63, 197; death, 258–59, 288; funeral, 258
Little River, 89, 91, 93
Little Round Top, 169–70
Little Sailor's Creek, 249
Little Sandy River, 258
Lockwood, Henry H., 101; Battles of Bethesda Church and Cold Harbor, 106, 112
Long Bridge, 120–22, 265, 270

Long Bridge Road, 120, 122
Long Island Sound, 268
Longstreet, James, 8, 28–29, 100, 227, 256; Appomattox Campaign, 249–51; Battle of the Wilderness, 30, 32–33, 37
Lookout Mountain, 8
Lookout Valley, 8
Lowrance, William L., 86–87
Lyle, Peter, 118; Battle of Cold Harbor, 113; Battle of Globe Tavern, 162, 166–67, 169; Battle of Jericho Mills, 85
Lyman, Theodore, 19, 21, 23, 78, 80–81, 98, 124, 157, 225; Appomattox Campaign, 243; Battle of the Crater, 151; Battle of Five Forks, 242; Battle of Globe Tavern, 160, 165; Battle of Harris Farm, 72; Battle of North Anna, 89–90; Battle of Peebles's Farm, 184, 190, 195; battles at Spotsylvania Court House, 42; Battle of the Wilderness, 31; letter to wife, 21, 79, 117, 165; raid on the Weldon Railroad, 205; Siege of Petersburg, 143, 151
Lynchburg, 138
Lynchburg Stage Road, 253, 257
Lyon, Nathaniel, xviii

Macholz, Oscar, 260
Mackenzie, Ranald, 235
MacRae, William, 243; Battle of Peebles's Farm, 186–89
Madden's Tavern, 27, 29
Madison's Ordinary, 78–79, 81–82
Mahone, William "Little Billy," 216; Appomattox Campaign, 250; Battle of the Crater, 150–51; Battle of Globe Tavern, 166–67, 171, 173–75; Battle of Peebles's Farm, 193; battles at Spotsylvania Court House, 42; Siege of Petersburg, 150–51
malaria, 179, 196
Malone's Bridge, 210
Malone's Bridge Road, 210
Malone's Crossing, 224
Malvern Hill, 120
Manchester, 262–63
Mangohick Church, 97–98
Mannboro, 245
Marcy, Randolph Barnes, xviii
Maryland Avenue, 266
Maryland Brigade, 59, 83, 119, 180; Battle of Cold Harbor, 112–13; Battle of Five Forks, 236; Battle of Globe Tavern, 161–62, 164, 172; Battle of Harris Farm, 70; Battle of Peebles's Farm, 189; Battle of White Oak Road, 186, 227–28, 230; first assault at Petersburg, 129–30, 134; musicians, 143; Purnell Legion, 162; Siege of Petersburg, 139, 141–43
Mason's farm, 13–14
Massaponax Church Road, 58, 77
Matadequin Creek, 113

Mattapony River, 96
Matta River, 78–79, 81
Matteson, Carl, 156; Battle of the Crater, 153; Battle of Harris Farm, 62–63; battles at Spotsylvania Court House, 44; letter to sister, 137; Siege of Petersburg, 137, 139, 142–43, 153
Matthewson, Angell, 86
Mayo, Robert M.: Battle of Five Forks, 234; Battle of Globe Tavern, 161, 166–67
McClellan, George, xviii, xxiii, 7, 197
McCoull house, 54
McGilvery, Freeman, 61–62, 76; Battle of North Anna, 90
McGowan, Samuel, 227, 243; Battle of Jericho Mills, 85; Battle of Peebles's Farm, 186; Battle of White Oak Road, 228–31
McGregor, William M., 234, 237
Meade, George G., 9, 17–18, 21, 23, 25–27, 29, 40–41, 57–58, 76–78, 82, 96–98, 100–102, 119, 124, 153–54, 157, 170, 177–78, 180, 182–83, 197, 199, 208, 210, 220–22, 225–26, 245, 259–60, 263, 268, 275, 281; Appomattox Campaign, 248–49, 251; Battle of Cold Harbor, 112–14, 116; Battle of the Crater, 150; Battle of Dinwiddie Court House, 232; Battle of Five Forks, 235; Battle of Globe Tavern, 165, 168–69; Battle of Harris Farm, 60, 63, 65, 67, 72, 75; Battle of Hatcher's Run, 211–12, 217; Battle of Jericho Mills, 84, 88, 92; Battle of North Anna, 89–90, 94; Battle of Peebles's Farm, 183–84, 187, 189–94; battles at Spotsylvania Court House, 42–45, 48–51, 55; Battle of the Wilderness, 30–31, 34, 37; first assault at Petersburg, 127, 129–33, 135; headquarters at the Lacy house, 31–32; headquarters at Mount Carmel Church, 89–90; letters to wife, 90; Siege of Petersburg, 145–47, 150
Mechanicsville, 28, 103
Meherrin River, 203, 210
Merritt, Wesley, 41, 256
Metcalf, Richard, 52
Miles, Dixon, 2
Miles, Nelson A., 226; Appomattox Campaign, 243–44; Battle of Hatcher's Run, 211; battles at Spotsylvania Court House, 42–43
Milford Station, 76, 82, 263
Mill Creek, 100
Mills, David, 73–74
Mink, Charles E.: Battle of Bethesda Church, 106; Battle of Globe Tavern, 174; Battle of Jericho Mills, 85–88; Battle of White Oak Road, 230
Mississippi Brigade, battles at Spotsylvania Court House, 54–55
Monk's Neck Bridge, 211, 223
Monk's Neck Road, 212
Monohassett, 128
Moody, J., 235
Moody, Young, 228

Moody house, 121, 235–36
Mott, Gersham, 199, 210; Battle of Globe Tavern, 166; Battle of Hatcher's Run, 210–11; battles at Spotsylvania Court House, 44–45, 49; first assault at Petersburg, 135; raid on the Weldon Railroad, 199, 200, 202–3, 205–6
Mountain Run, 27, 29
Mount Carmel Church, 83–85, 90, 96–97
Mount Vernon Road, xx
Mud Tavern, 78
"Mule Shoe," 46, 50–51, 55, 58, 63–64, 67
Munford, Thomas T., 234
Myer's Hill, 60–61
Myer's house, 60

Namozine Church, 245
Namozine Road, 244–45, 247
Nancy Wright's Corner, 78–79, 81–82
New Bethel Church, 82
New Found River, 93
New Market, 147
New Market Road, 122
Newton, William, 98
Newton house, 98, 100
New Year's Day, 208
New York State Adjutant General's Office, 2
New York Thirteenth Independent Battery, 3; Reserve Artillery, 8
New York Times, 271–72
Nineteenth Connecticut Infantry, xvi, xxiv, 9
Nineteenth Corps, 266
Ninety-First Pennsylvania, 60
Ninth Corps, 26, 58–59, 78, 96, 120, 125, 157, 180, 221–22, 258, 266; Appomattox Campaign, 243; Battle of Cold Harbor, 111–14; Battle of the Crater, 149, 153; Battle of Globe Tavern, 165, 169, 172, 176; Battle of Harris Farm, 65; Battle of Hatcher's Run, 211; Battle of North Anna, 91–92, 94; Battle of Peebles's Farm, 183–84, 192–94; battles at Spotsylvania Court House, 45, 50, 55; Battle of the Wilderness, 30, 34, 37; first assault at Petersburg, 127–30; First Division, 91, 168; Fourth Division, 128–29; Second Division, 50; Siege of Petersburg, 139, 145, 147–49, 153
Norfolk, 212
Norfolk and Petersburg Railroad, 130–31, 141, 144
North Anna River, 76–97, 80, 100, 103
North Carolina brigades: Battle of Bethesda Church, 103, 107; Battle of Harris Farm, 69; Battle of Jericho Mills, 86; Battle of Peebles's Farm, 187
Nottoway Court House, 258, 268
Nottoway River, 199–203, 205–6
Ny River, 40–41, 58, 60, 63–67, 73–74

Oates, William C., 35–37
Occoquan Creek, 9, 264

Olcott, Henry Steel, 281–83, 292
Old Blandford Church, 146
Old Capitol Prison, 283
Old Chesterfield, 97
Old Church, 103
Old Church Road, 103–5, 108, 111, 114, 118
Old Cold Harbor, 111–12, 116, 118
Old Courthouse Road, 42, 46
Old Dinwiddie Stage Road, 223
157th Pennsylvania Infantry, 180
114th Pennsylvania Infantry, 268
140th New York Infantry, xx, 169–70, 181, 266; Battle of Five Forks, 236; Battle of Globe Tavern, 168, 275; Battle of Harris Farm, 60; Battle of Hatcher's Run, 213; Battle of Peebles's Farm, 186–87, 190; Battle of White Oak Road, 228, 231; discharge, 268; uniforms, 171
146th New York Infantry, 170, 226, 266, 275; Battle of Five Forks, 237; Battle of Hatcher's Run, 213–15, 218; Battle of Peebles's Farm, 186, 189–90; Battle of White Oak Road, 228, 230–31; discharge, 268; first assault at Petersburg, 134–35; Siege of Petersburg, 139–40; Zouave uniforms, 171, 197
135th New York Infantry, 22–23
Orange and Alexandria Railroad, xviii, 17
Orange Court House, 28
Orange Plank Road, 29–34, 37, 40–41
Orange Turnpike, 3, 29–32, 38
Ord, Edward O. C., 222, 245, 256; Appomattox Campaign, 251–53, 255; Siege of Petersburg, 147
Ordnance, 20
Orendorf, John W., 108–9
O'Rourke, Patrick H., xx, 169
Osterhaus (general), 8
Otis, Elwell S., 181; attack on Myer's Hill, Spotsylvania, 60; Battle of Peebles's Farm, 183, 186–87, 189
Outenhoefer, A., 293
Overland Campaign, 169, 275
Ox Ford, 89, 91–92

Painesville, 249
Palm Sunday, 253
Pamunkey River, 93–94, 96–99, 100–111, 220, 263
Papemeyer, William F., 159
Parke, John G.: Battle of the Crater, 153; Battle of Peebles's Farm, 183, 186–87, 189–94; Siege of Petersburg, 153
Parker's Store, 30, 34, 38–39
Parsley's Mill, 118
Pearson, Alfred L., 216–17
Peebles, William, 182, 185
Peebles's Farm, 182, 185–88, 190, 194
Peers, George, 255
Pegram, Oscar, 186

Pegram, William J., 227; Battle of Bethesda Church, 103, 107, 110; Battle of Five Forks, 234, 240; Battle of Globe Tavern, 173; Battle of Harris Farm, 69; Battle of Hatcher's Run, 213, 216; Battle of Peebles's Farm, 187
Pegram farm, 186–91
Pegram's Salient, 146
Pendleton, William N., 256
Peninsular Campaign, 103
Pennington, Alexander, 239
Pennsylvania Avenue, 266–67, 276
Pennsylvania Brigade, 85–86
Pennsylvania Campaign, 22
Pennsylvania Reserves, 102–3, 118, 274–75; Battle of Bethesda Church, 105, 112; Battle of Globe Tavern, 168; Eleventh, 108; First Brigade, 102, 104, 110; 190th, 180; 191st, 180; Third Brigade, 102, 180; Thirteenth ("the Bucktails"), 102
Perkins, W., 211
Perkins house, 211
Perkinson's Mill, 250
Perry, Edward A., 37
Perry, William F.: battles at Spotsylvania Court House, 42; Battle of the Wilderness, 33, 35–37
Petersburg, 125–36, 133, 160, 176–79, 182–84, 206, 217, 220–22, 227, 231, 243, 245, 252, 258–60, 262–63; court of inquiry at, 153; defenses, 126, 131, 147, 159, 161, 171, 181–82, 187, 190–91, 245; Siege of, 137–55; supply lines, 210–11
Peyton house, 66–68, 70
Pickett, George, 227; Appomattox Campaign, 249–50; Battle of Five Forks, 233–37, 239–40; Battle of White Oak Road, 228, 231
Pierce, Samuel, 154; Siege of Petersburg, 142
Piney Branch Church, 40–41, 43–47
Plain Run, 255
Pleasants, Henry, 146
Poague, William T., 32
Pole Green Church, 103
Poor Creek, 131, 133–34, 146
Pope, Edmund M., 77, 79, 81–82
Pope, John, 8
Poplar Spring Church, 173, 176, 184–85
Poplar Spring Church Road, 182, 184–85
Po River, 41, 43, 46, 48–49, 51–52
Potomac Creek, 264
Potomac River, xvi, xviii, xxiii–xxiv, 265, 267
Potter, Robert B.: Battle of Globe Tavern, 165; Battle of Peebles's Farm, 183, 185–86; battles at Spotsylvania Court House, 50; first assault at Petersburg, 129, 131; Siege of Petersburg, 146
Pridesville Road, 249
Prince Edward Court House, 251–52
Prince George Court House, 129
Prospect Station, 252
Providence Church, 121

Q. M. Stores, 20
Quaker Road, 212, 223, 224, 225, 232
Quarles's Ford, 91
Quarles's Mill, 90, 96
Quartermaster's Department, 18

Rae, Robert, 219; Battle of Hatcher's Run, 215, 218
Ramseur, Stephen D., 100, 155, 275; Battle of Bethesda Church, 103, 107–8; Battle of Cedar Creek, 155; Battle of Harris Farm, 68–70, 72
Ramsey, John, 211
Ransom, Matthew, 234, 237, 239
Rapidan River, 17, 27–29, 44, 48, 57, 139, 263
Rappahannock River, 17, 19, 263
Reams's Station, 178, 210, 224
Reinhart, Joseph, 275
Relief Committee of New York, 17
Rensselaer County, 284, 288
Renzi, 239
Rice's Depot, 249, 250–51
Richardson, Hollon, 240
Richardson, Lester I., 106, 108
Richardsville, 27
Richmond, 25, 65, 82, 88, 95, 100, 119, 120, 125, 146, 156, 182–83, 245, 249, 262–63, 265; supply lines, 119, 138, 155, 176
Richmond, Fredericksburg, and Potomac Railroad, 65, 89, 97
Richmond and Danville Railroad, 221–22, 244–45, 247, 248, 258
Richmond–Lynchburg Stage Road, 253
Richmond and Petersburg Railroad, 138
Riddell's Shop, 120, 122
Riddle, Albert Gallantin, 283, 289–90, 293
Riemann, Adolf, 31; Battle of Hatcher's Run, 215, 217; death, 215, 217
Ritchie/Richie, John, 162–63, 168
Rittenhouse, Benjamin F., 106, 114
River Road, 244
Rives's Salient, 132–34
Roberts, William P., 234
Robinson, John C., 42
Robinson, William W., 81–82; Battle of Jericho Mills, 85, 87
Rocky Branch, 211
Rodes, Robert E., 100; Battle of Harris Farm, 68, 70; Battles of Bethesda Church and Cold Harbor, 103–5, 113
Rodophil, 249
Roebling, Washington A., 58–59, 79, 81–84, 96, 117–18, 121; Battle of Cold Harbor, 112, 114; Battle of the Crater, 150–51, 153; Battle of Globe Tavern, 160–61, 164, 166, 169, 172–75; Battle of Harris Farm, 72, 74; Battle of Jericho Mills, 84, 86; battles at Spotsylvania Court House, 48; Battle of the Wilderness, 38; first assault at Petersburg, 129, 130–34; Siege of Petersburg, 139, 145, 148–51, 153

Rolfe, Frank A., 68–69
Roman, George, 198
Rosser, Thomas L., 227; Battle of Five Forks, 234
Rowanty Creek, 178, 210–12, 222–24
Rowanty Post Office, 211
Rural Plains, 101
Russell, David A., 96, 98; battles at Spotsylvania Court House, 54

Sailor's Creek, 250–51
Saint Margaret's Church, 83
Saint Paul's Church, 97
Samaria Church, 122
Sanders, John C., 174
Sanitary Commission, 143
Savannah, Georgia, 208
Scales, Alfred M., 243; Battle of Jericho Mills, 86
Schamberger, Leander, 5, 10; Battle of Harris Farm, 74, 159; Battle of the Wilderness, 20; death, 159
Schimmel, Gustave, 259; Battle of Harris Farm, 63
Schirmer, Louis, xxv, 1, 2, 7–12, 16, 19–20, 23, 119; accusations against, 16–17; alcohol prohibition, 14–15; Battle of the Wilderness, 31; birth, xxv; charges filed against, 284; court martial, 119, 281–94; headquarters in New York, 4; health issues, 282–83, 287, 293; leaves of absence, 20–21, 119, 282–83, 285; "Private Letter Book," 285; promotion to captain, 2; Valley Campaign, 7
Schirmer, Mary Jane, 294
Schirmer, William, 285
Schwartz, George F., 259–60
Second Battalion, Fifteenth New York Heavy, 10, 48, 61, 198, 208, 269; Battle of Globe Tavern, 159; Battle of North Anna, 92; Battle of Peebles's Farm, 193; battles at Spotsylvania Court House, 48; Battle of the Wilderness, 33, 35
Second Battalion, Fourth New York Heavy, 34, 93
Second Brigade, Second Division, Fifth Corps: Battle of Cold Harbor, 113; Battle of Globe Tavern, 160, 162, 164
Second Corps, xx, xxii, 22, 27, 29, 63, 76–77, 83, 96, 100–101, 119, 122, 124, 155–56, 178, 180, 199, 219–22, 226, 259, 263, 266–67; Appomattox Campaign, 243, 248–49, 251, 253, 255; Artillery Brigade, 92, 96; Battle of Cold Harbor, 103, 107, 110–11, 116; Battle of Harris Farm, 64–65, 67, 72, 75; Battle of Hatcher's Run, 211–12, 217; Battle of Jericho Mills, 85; Battle of North Anna, 90, 92; Battle of Peebles's Farm, 191–94; battles at Spotsylvania Court House, 42, 44, 46, 48–50; Battle of the Wilderness, 30–31, 37; first assault at Petersburg, 126, 128–31, 135; headquarters, 40; Siege of Petersburg, 138–39, 146
Second Division, Fifth Corps, 101, 112, 118, 121,
177, 219, 223, 225, 244, 262, 266; Appomattox Campaign, 253, 255; Battle of Dinwiddie Court House, 232; Battle of Five Forks, 239; Battle of Globe Tavern, 172; Battle of Hatcher's Run, 213; Battle of Peebles's Farm, 184–86; Battles of Bethesda Church and Cold Harbor, 106, 112; Battle of White Oak Road, 230; first assault at Petersburg, 135; raid on the Weldon Railroad, 199
Second New York Artillery, 22
Second New York Heavy Artillery, Battle of Harris Farm, 63, 67–69, 72
Second New York Independent Battery, 2, 3–4, 8; Valley Campaign, 7
Second Pennsylvania Heavy Artillery, 18
Second Swamp, 159
Seddon, James A., 122
Sedgwick, John, 29; Battle of the Wilderness, 38; death, 47, 50
Seminary Hospital, 282
Senges, Adam, xxii, xxv, 7
Seventeenth Street, 267
Seventeenth US Infantry: Battle of Globe Tavern, 167, 169; Battle of Peebles's Farm, 186–87
Seventh New York Heavy Artillery, 220; Battle of Cold Harbor, 116; Battle of Harris Farm, 63, 71
Seventh Wisconsin Infantry, Battle of Five Forks, 240
Seventy-First New York Militia, 170
Seymour, Horatio, 7
Shady Grove, 100
Shady Grove Church Road, 46
Shady Grove Road, 101, 103–6, 108, 113–14, 117
Shaffer, Calvin, 222, 269; battles at Spotsylvania Court House, 45–46; Battle of the Wilderness, 39; Siege of Petersburg, 142
Shand house, 129, 132
Shelton, Sarah, 101
Shelton house, 58, 101–2
Shenandoah Valley, 2
Sheridan, Philip "Little Phil," 41, 82, 99–100, 154, 156, 198, 220–22, 224–27, 244–45, 247; Appomattox Campaign, 247–48, 251–53, 255; Battle of Cold Harbor, 111; Battle of Dinwiddie Court House, 231–33; Battle of Five Forks, 233–37, 239–40, 242; Battle of North Anna, 91; battles at Spotsylvania Court House, 42–43; Battle of White Oak Road, 231; headquarters, 253; Siege of Petersburg, 146–47
Sherman, William T., 7, 208, 221, 265, 276
Sickel, Horatio G., 215–17
Siege of Petersburg, 137–55, 158; casualties, 141–42; Confederate line, 141; temperature, 150–51, 153; Union breastworks, 141; Union line, 148; Union mine/earthworks, 145–49
Sigel, Franz, 2, 25, 289

Sixth Corps, 22, 27, 29, 57–58, 61, 78–79, 82–83, 96–98, 125, 198–99, 221–22, 259; Appomattox Campaign, 243, 248–51, 253, 255; Battle of Cold Harbor, 105, 110–12, 116; Battle of Five Forks, 235; Battle of Harris Farm, 62, 64–66, 69, 74; Battle of Hatcher's Run, 211, 216; Battle of North Anna, 90, 93–94; battles at Spotsylvania Court House, 45–47, 49–50, 54–55; Battle of the Wilderness, 30, 36–38; casualties, 37; first assault at Petersburg, 127, 130, 135; Siege of Petersburg, 138
Sixth Maine Battery, 43–44
Sixth New York Heavy Artillery, 22–23, 57–58, 153, 155, 177; Battle of Bethesda Church, 105, 110; Battle of Harris Farm, 66, 74; battles at Spotsylvania Court House, 45, 52; Battle of the Wilderness, 34–36, 39; first assault at Petersburg, 130
Sixty-First Massachusetts, 268
Slough, John, xvi
Smith, William F. "Baldy," 126; Battle of Cold Harbor, 111–12, 114; first assault at Petersburg, 126–27
Smyth, Thomas, 210; Battle of Hatcher's Run, 211
Soldier's Cemetery, xvii
South Anna River, 93, 146
South Carolina brigades: Battle of Globe Tavern, 173, 175–76; Battle of Jericho Mills, 85; Battle of Peebles's Farm, 186; battles at Spotsylvania Court House, 42; Battle of White Oak Road, 228–30; first assault at Petersburg, 127
South Side Railroad, 138, 181, 183–84, 191–94, 221–22, 226, 234, 240, 243–45, 248, 249–50, 252, 258, 262
Spain, R., 224
Spain house, 224
Special Orders No. 62, 18
Spindle farm, 42
Spotsylvania, 78, 235
Spotsylvania Court House, 39–56, 47, 58, 61, 64, 77, 95, 141; casualties, 46, 49, 52, 54–56; Confederate line, 46, 49–51; Union breastworks, 44–45; Union line, 49, 55
Spotsylvania Road, 90
Squirrel Level Road, 173, 181–82, 184–87, 190–91
Stage Road, 222
Stansel, Martin L., 228–31
Stanton, Edwin M., 17, 220, 281
Stein (band leader), 13
Steinbrenner, George F., 293
Steuart, George, 234, 239
Stevensburg, 27, 29
Stevensburg-Richardsville Road, 27
Stevens house, 67–68
Stewart, James, 85
Stone, Charles P., 177–80
Stony Creek, 199

Stony Creek station, 178
Strasburg, 155
Stroud, J., 224
Stroud house, 224
Sussex, 201, 206
Sussex Court House, 200–201, 205–7
Sutherland's Station, 192, 226, 227, 243–44
Swan, William W., 228
Sweathouse Creek, 245
Sweitzer, Jacob B.: Battle of Cold Harbor, 114; Battle of Jericho Mills, 84, 85–87
Sycamore Church, 129
Sydnor, R., 239
Sydnor farm, 239

Tabernacle Church, 58, 61
Tapp farm, 32–37
Tar Heels: Battle of Bethesda Church, 104; Battle of Five Forks, 234, 237; Battle of Globe Tavern, 166–67; Battle of Harris Farm, 68; Battle of Hatcher's Run, 213; Battle of Jericho Mills, 85; Battle of Peebles's Farm, 186, 188–89; Siege of Petersburg, 143
Taylor House, 131
Telegraph Road, 61, 76–79, 81–83, 85, 90
Temple house, 159
Tenth Corps, 156
Tenth New York Heavy Artillery, 18
Tenth US Infantry: Battle of Globe Tavern, 167, 169; Battle of Peebles's Farm, 187
Terrill, James B., 109
Terry, William, 234
Texas Brigade, 33
Third Battalion, Fifteenth New York Heavy Artillery, 1, 2, 4–5, 8–10, 14, 159, 183, 272, 281; Battle of Bethesda Church, 105; Battle of Globe Tavern, 159; battles at Spotsylvania Court House, 48; Battle of White Oak Road, 230; Battle of the Wilderness, 35; Company D, 7; drinking, 14; drills, 9; ethnic makeup of, xxii–xxiii; fatigue duty, 9
Third Brigade, 119, 177, 180; Battle of Globe Tavern, 159, 161; Battle of Hatcher's Run, 212; Battle of Peebles's Farm, 184, 186, 194; Battle of Totopotomoy Creek, 103, 106, 112; Second Division, 112, 155
Third Corps, Army of Northern Virginia, 28, 78; Battle of Cold Harbor, 113; Battle of Jericho Mills, 84
Third Division, 101, 112, 118, 121, 177, 180, 219, 224, 244, 258, 262; Battle of Bethesda Church, 103; Battle of Dinwiddie Court House, 232; Battle of Five Forks, 233, 239; Battle of Globe Tavern, 162, 166–67; Battle of Hatcher's Run, 213, 216–17; Battle of Peebles's Farm, 183–84, 193; Battle of White Oak Road, 228, 230; raid on the Weldon Railroad, 201

INDEX · 377

Third Massachusetts Battery, 86
Thirteenth New York Independent Battery, 3–4, 8; Battle of Chancellorsville, 3, 8; Valley Campaign, 7
Thirteenth Virginia Infantry, 107, 109
Thirty-First New York Infantry, 170
Thirty-First Virginia Infantry, 107
Thirty-Fourth New York Independent Battery, 4
Thirty-Seventh New York Infantry, 170
Thomas, Edward L., 86–87
Thomas P. Way, 6
Thompson, R., 192
Thompson house, 192
Three Creek, 203
Tidball, John C., 18, 96, 101–2; Battle of North Anna, 92–93
Tilney, Robert, 198, 208, 256, 262, 265, 267; raid on the Weldon Railroad, 203–4
Tinsley house, 104
Todd's Tavern, 30–31, 41, 43–45
Toon, Thomas F., 107
Torbert, Alfred T. A., 76
Totopotomoy Creek, 100–101, 103
Townsend, E. D., 292
Tuck's house, 97–98
Twelfth New York Heavy Artillery, 4
Twelfth New York Infantry, 170
Twelfth US Infantry, 170; Battle of Globe Tavern, 167, 169; Battle of Peebles's Farm, 187
Twenty-Fourth Corps, 263
Twenty-Ninth New York Infantry, 1; Company H, 3
Twenty-Second Corps, Department of Washington, 11, 268
Tyler, Robert O., 101; Battle of Harris Farm, 63–64, 66–67, 72, 75

Upton, Emory, 22; battles at Spotsylvania Court House, 52, 54
US Colored Troops: Battle of the Crater, 150–52; movement to Petersburg, 128–29; Siege of Petersburg, 150–52
US Treasury, 268

Valley Campaign, 7–8
Van Vleck, Jacob: Battle of the Crater, 152; Battle of Globe Tavern, 163; Battle of Hatcher's Run, 218; Battle of Peebles's Farm, 195; death, 218; letters to wife, 197–98, 209; photographs of family, 218; Siege of Petersburg, 141, 145, 152
Varian, Joshua M., 1
Varian's Battery, 1
Vaughan Road, 160–61, 171, 173, 182, 184–86, 189, 191–92, 196, 207, 210, 212–13, 215–20, 222–23
Veith, John, 281–82, 288–90
Via house, 101, 113
Virginia Central Railroad, 84, 89, 91, 146, 156
Virginia Military Institute, 107

Von Bosch, Max, 285
von Gilsa, Leopold, 6–7
von Steinwehr, Adolf, 1, 7

Wadsworth, James S., 30–32, 34, 44
Wainwright, Charles S., 82, 97, 120–21, 125, 179, 197, 222, 247, 257, 265; Appomattox Campaign, 248, 252; Battle of the Crater, 152; Battle of Five Forks, 241–42; Battle of Globe Tavern, 172, 175–76; Battle of Harris Farm, 63, 72; Battle of Jericho Mills, 84–86; Battle of North Anna, 93, 94; Battle of Peebles's Farm, 184, 195; Battles of Bethesda Church and Cold Harbor, 105–6, 113–14; first assault at Petersburg, 128–29, 135–36; raid on the Weldon Railroad, 201, 203, 205, 207; Siege of Petersburg, 137, 140, 143, 145–46, 152
Walcott, Aaron: Battle of Bethesda Church, 106; Battle of Jericho Mills, 86
Walker's Church, 252
Wallace, William, 234, 239
War Department, 281–82, 284, 289, 292
Warren, Gouverneur Kemble, 29, 41–42, 58–59, 61–62, 76–77, 79, 81, 83–84, 97–99, 103, 117–21, 124, 154, 157, 169–70, 177–81, 196, 199, 208, 210, 219, 222–26, 262; Battle of the Crater, 150; Battle of Dinwiddie Court House, 232; Battle of Five Forks, 233–36, 239–40, 242; Battle of Globe Tavern, 159–60, 164–65, 168–69, 171–72; Battle of Harris Farm, 60, 64–67, 70, 72; Battle of Hatcher's Run, 212–13, 215–16; Battle of Jericho Mills, 84, 86, 88; Battle of North Anna, 90; Battle of Peebles's Farm, 183–85, 187, 189, 192–94; Battles of Bethesda Church and Cold Harbor, 103, 111–15; battles at Spotsylvania Court House, 42–44, 49, 51–52, 55; Battle of White Oak Road, 228, 231–32; Battle of the Wilderness, 30–32, 34, 38–39; Beverly house headquarters, 59–60; Catlett house headquarters, 78; death, 242; first assault at Petersburg, 127, 129–30, 132; Globe Tavern headquarters, 160; headquarters, Weldon raid, 203; inquiry into relief by Sheridan, 242; Newton house headquarters, 98; raid on the Weldon Railroad, 199, 201–7; relief from command of Fifth Corps, 234–35, 240; Siege of Petersburg, 138, 144–45, 147–48, 150; Tuck house headquarters, 97–98
Warwick Swamp, 199
Washington City, xv–xxv, 2, 7, 11–12, 17–18, 20–22, 36–38, 74, 94, 119, 153–55, 170, 258, 263–72, 283
Webb, Alexander S., 221, 225; Battle of Dinwiddie Court House, 232; Battle of Five Forks, 234; Battle of Hatcher's Run, 212
Weed, Stephen H., xx
Weisiger, David A., 166

Weldon, 138
Weldon and Petersburg Railroad, 138, 157, 159–61, 165–67, 169, 171–72, 176–78, 181, 187, 189–91, 241, 259; bending rails of, 202; raid on, 196–210
Westover, 125
West Point, 22, 107
Weyanoke Point, 127
Wheaton, Frank, 211
Whig Hill, 60
Whipple, A. W., xxiii
Whistler, Joseph N. G., 270–71
White, Julius, 165, 168
White House, 111, 126, 220, 266
White Oak Road, 191–92, 224–34, 229, 244
White Oak Swamp, 122
White Oak Swamp Bridge, 122
Wiedrich, Michael, 7–8, 119, 198, 208–10, 272–73, 286–87; arrest, 7; Battle of Five Forks, 241; Battle of Globe Tavern, 159, 161–62, 164; Battle of Harris Farm, 69; Battles of Bethesda Church and Cold Harbor, 105, 110–11, 113; Battle of the Wilderness, 31, 36–37; first assault at Petersburg, 135; honorable discharge, 241; illness, 183; promotion to colonel, 259; promotion to lieutenant colonel, 8; raid on the Weldon Railroad, 199; Siege of Petersburg, 141–42, 144
Wilcox, Cadmus, 227; Battle of Jericho Mills, 84, 87–89; Battle of Peebles's Farm, 187–88; Battle of White Oak Road, 228
Wilcox house, 125, 128
Wilcox's Wharf, 127–28
Wilderness Church, 31, 40, 44
Wilderness Run, 34, 39–40
Wilderness Tavern, 29–30
Willard, George L., xx, xxii
Williams house, 180–81

Williamson house, 244
Willcox, Orlando: Battle of Globe Tavern, 165, 168, 176; Battle of North Anna, 91; Battle of Peebles's Farm, 183, 185–86; first assault at Petersburg, 130–31; Siege of Petersburg, 139
Williams, Seth, 57, 61, 154; Battle of Harris Farm, 61; battles at Spotsylvania Court House, 50
Willis, Edward, 107; Battle of Bethesda Church, 108–9; death, 109–10
Willman, Andreas, 293
Wilmington, 138
Wilmington and Weldon Railroad, 138
Wilson's Creek, xviii
Wilson's Depot, 262
Windmill Point, 124
Winslow, Cleveland, 170
Winthrop, Frederic, 177, 180, 197, 209–10, 219–20, 222, 224, 226; Battle of Dinwiddie Court House, 232–33; Battle of Five Forks, 236–37, 241, 266; Battle of Globe Tavern, 167–69, 172–73; Battle of Hatcher's Run, 212–18; Battle of White Oak Road, 227–31; death, 241, 266; illness, 181; raid on the Weldon Railroad, 200–203, 205–6
Wise, Henry A.: Battle of White Oak Road, 228; first assault at Petersburg, 126
Wolf, Casper, 77, 102
Wolf, S., 293
Wood, Will, 218
Woody, David, 113
W. P. Davis house, 160–61
Wright, Horatio G., 57–58, 83, 221–22; Appomattox Campaign, 243, 250–51, 253; Battle of Cold Harbor, 111–12; Battle of Harris Farm, 63–64; battles at Spotsylvania Court House, 50–52, 55
W. W. Davis house, 166, 173, 181–82, 185–86, 190
Wyatt house, 221

www.ingramcontent.com/pod-product-compliance
Lightning Source LLC
Chambersburg PA
CBHW022007300426
44117CB00005B/67